*by Virginius Dabney*

# RICHMOND
The Story of a City

# Virginius Dabney

# RICHMOND
## The Story of a City

Doubleday & Company, Inc.
Garden City, New York
1976

PHOTO CREDITS

The Virginia Historical Society—No. 1, 8, 18, 38

Courtesy of Mrs. V. Lee Kirby—No. 2

The Papers of Benjamin Henry Latrobe, Maryland Historical Society—No. 3

Private Collection—No. 4

Richmond Newspapers—No. 5, 59, 61, 62, 63, 64, 65, 66, 67, 68, 69

Valentine Museum, Richmond, Virginia—No. 6, 7, 9, 10, 13, 15, 16, 20, 23, 24, 25, 26, 27, 28, 29, 30, 31, 32, 33, 34, 35, 36, 37, 39, 41, 42, 43, 44, 46, 48, 51, 52, 53, 54, 55, 57

Virginia State Library—No. 11, 12, 19, 47

Reynolds Metal Company—No. 17

Courtesy of Mrs. Charles Baird, Jr. Photo by Jeffrey M. O'Dell.—No. 21, 22

Courtesy of Mr. Langhorne Gibson—No. 40

University of Virginia, Department of Graphics—No. 45

Richmond Academy, 1911 Yearbook—No. 49

American Academy of Arts and Letters—No. 50

Newsweek Magazine—No. 64

Scott L. Henderson—No. 56

Courtesy of Edgar Allan Poe Museum—No. 58

Chase, Ltd.—No. 60

Library of Congress Cataloging in Publication Data

Dabney, Virginius, 1901–
Richmond: the story of a city.

Bibliography: p. 378
Includes index.
1. Richmond—History.    I. Title.
F234.R5D17        975.5'451
ISBN 0-385-02046-5
Library of Congress Catalog Card Number 73-9150

*To*
*Doug, Lucy and Heath*
*Richmonders All*
*This book is proudly*
*and affectionately dedicated*

# CONTENTS

# ILLUSTRATIONS

## MAPS

# FOREWORD

VICTORY and heartbreak, tragedy and triumph—each of these has had its role in Richmond's ongoing saga of more than three and a half centuries. The city has endured many trials since the first Englishmen journeyed upstream to the falls of the James in 1607, and it has survived them all.

In the pages that follow I have sought to portray Richmond "in the round"—to examine Virginia's capital in its economic, social, racial and cultural aspects, from the earliest times down to the present.

The contribution of women to Richmond's story has been presented with particular emphasis. Similarly the role of the blacks has been given special attention, and there is an entire chapter on the slave Gabriel's attempt to organize widespread insurrection and massacre.

An effort has been made to rescue unsung heroes and heroines from oblivion. Little-known events have been exhumed, as for example the circumstances surrounding William Byrd II's much-misunderstood founding of Richmond. There are unfamiliar facts concerning John Marshall, Edgar Allan Poe, Robert E. Lee, Dr. Robert Ryland; Dr. Hunter McGuire and his supposed feud with Dr. George Ben Johnston; James Branch Cabell, Ellen Glasgow, Henry W. Anderson and Dr. Douglas S. Freeman; and also concerning such notable blacks as James Lafayette, Gilbert Hunt, the Reverend John Jasper, Giles B. Jackson and John Mitchell, Jr.

I am fortunate in having had access to several sources of inestimable value. Dr. Wirt Armistead Cate allowed me to use his exceptionally thorough unpublished manuscript, A History of Richmond, 1607–1861, complete with footnotes and index. Bernard J. Henley permitted me to examine the thirteen important scrapbooks that he has compiled from Williamsburg and Richmond newspapers, beginning with the year 1736 and continuing, as of this writing, down to 1892. There is also a recently discovered scrapbook of Dr. William P. Palmer, erudite Richmond physi-

cian of the nineteenth century, containing more than a hundred historical
articles on Richmond, contributed by him to the Richmond *Times* in the
late 1880s and early 1890s. Evan R. Chesterman, Jr., has shown me the
numerous scrapbooks containing his father's valuable and informative
writings for the Richmond press. I have profited greatly from notes on
Richmond in the late nineteenth and early twentieth centuries kindly lent
me by Miss Frances Leigh Williams.

I am enormously indebted to John M. Jennings, director of the Virginia
Historical Society, and William M. E. Rachal, editor of the society's publications, who have given my manuscript a critical reading from beginning
to end. I am deeply obligated to Judge and Mrs. Ralph T. Catterall, who
also read the entire work. Others who have read portions are Clifford
Dowdey, Robert B. Mayo, Mrs. Stuart B. Gibson, Overton Jones and J.
Harvie Wilkinson, Jr. My thanks to each and all. They are not responsible
for any errors of mine.

Several libraries have accorded me exceptional cooperation. At the Richmond Public Library, Librarian Howard M. Smith, Miss Gertrude Dyson,
William M. Simpson, Jr., Mrs. Betty Burchill, Frank Bridge and the other
courteous members of the staff were never too busy to be of help. At the
Virginia State Library, Milton C. Russell, John W. Dudley, Mrs.
Katherine M. Smith, Mrs. Jewell T. Clark and their obliging colleagues
have left me greatly in their debt. The same should be said of the Valen-
tine Museum, with special thanks to former director Robert B. Mayo,
Mrs. Stuart B. Gibson, Mrs. Robert V. Anderson and Mrs. Elizabeth H.
Court. Constant cooperation was afforded at the Virginia Historical Soci-
ety, not only by Messrs. Jennings and Rachal but also by Howson W.
Cole, James A. Fleming, Waverly K. Winfree and Mrs. Kenneth W.
Southall, Jr. At Richmond Newspapers, I owe a special debt of gratitude
to Miss Mary Morris Watt, chief librarian, and also to John E. Leard,
James K. Sanford, John Goode, Mrs. Gwendolyn C. Wells and Miss
Brenda Lindsey. The University of Virginia library staff, including Librarian Ray W. Frantz, Jr., Edmund Berkeley, Jr., Gregory Johnson, Miss
Vesta Gordon, Ms. Charlotte G. Walker and Ms. Susan R. Murphy, was
uniformly helpful. The staffs of the libraries of the University of Richmond and Virginia State College were most cooperative, as were those at
the University of North Carolina, Duke University, Howard University
and the Library of Congress.

I owe a special debt to Dr. Maurice Duke for furnishing me with impor-
tant material, and to Dr. Ernest T. Thompson for a similar favor. Miss
Betty Winston was extremely helpful, as were General Edwin Cox, Mrs.
William R. Trigg, Jr., Dr. George M. Modlin, William R. Gaines, U. S.
Supreme Court Justice Lewis F. Powell, Jr., Dr. Fred R. Stair, Judge W.
Moscoe Huntley, Mr. and Mrs. Henry R. Miller, Jr., Henry M. Cowardin,
Mrs. Bessie McGahey, Mrs. B. D. Aycock and Dr. John Newton Thomas.

Thanks also should go to Saul M. Viener, Dr. Stanley F. Chyet, Dr. Bertram W. Korn, Dr. Jacob R. Marcus, the late J. Ambler Johnston, Booker T. Bradshaw, Richard W. Foster, William N. Paxton, Jr., J. D. Brown, Miss Mary Wingfield Scott, Mrs. Edward S. McCarthy, Mayor Thomas J. Bliley, Jr., Dr. Joseph C. Robert, Dr. Thomas S. Berry, General John A. Cutchins, the late Harry M. Meacham, William J. Ernst III, Parke Rouse, Jr., Dr. Reuben Alley, Davis T. Ratcliffe, W. W. Archer, Jr., former City Clerk William T. Wells and City Clerk E. A. Duffy.

I am also grateful to Rabbi Myron Berman, Adrian L. Bendheim, T. Leigh Williams, Ross R. Millhiser, Dr. Edgar E. MacDonald, Mrs. O. O. Ashworth, R. McLean Whittet, Eppa Hunton IV, Miss Virginia Richardson, F. D. Cossitt, Willis Shell, Richard A. Velz, Virginius C. Hall, Mrs. Charles Baird, Jr., Langhorne Gibson, Sr. and Jr., Robert Haskins, Clifton McClesky, Samuel A. Anderson III, Jeff M. O'Dell, Jan Laverge, Fred Minton, Charles MacDowell, James C. Park, Fred W. Windmueller, Mrs. Cassius M. Chichester and Ronald R. Belton.

Those who have typed my slovenly manuscript include the late Mrs. N. B. Neil Shriner, Mrs. Felicia T. Prendergast and my daughter, Mrs. James S. Watkinson.

My editor at Doubleday, Miss Sally Arteseros, has been constantly helpful, altogether understanding and constructively critical.

And last but far from least, my wife of more than half a century has not only read the entire manuscript and made numerous helpful suggestions, but from long experience has known how to deal with my not inconsiderable foibles and frustrations.

VIRGINIUS DABNEY

*Richmond, Virginia*

# RICHMOND

The Story of a City

# ONE

# The Cross at the Falls

OVER THE seething rapids of the James River and into the silent forest echoed "a great shout," followed by a prayer "for our King and our own prosperous success in this his action." One-armed Captain Christopher Newport had led a small band of intrepid English explorers upriver from Jamestown—following their epoch-making landing there ten days before— and had planted a wooden cross at The Falls, near the heart of today's downtown Richmond. It was May 24, 1607.

The men had sailed upstream in a shallop from Jamestown, a distance of some 60 miles, hoping to find the South Seas—that long-sought El Dorado with its fabulous treasures, reputed to be somewhere in the West.

Indians from a neighboring settlement watched sullenly as the "pale faces" went through their strange rites. Perceiving the red men's displeasure, Newport explained that "the two arms of the cross signified King Powhatah [Powhatan] and himself, the fastening of it in the midst was their united league, the shout the reverence he did to Powhatah."

This ingenious, and decidedly inaccurate, explanation seems to have been at least partially successful. Powhatan, who was not the great Powhatan—of whom the Englishmen had heard—but his son, "stalked off in a huff." Nauiraus, a friendly Indian guide, was able to calm the irate brave. Little Powhatan then became indignant because the English were talking of exploring more deeply into the interior. However, Newport decided, over the objections of the more aggressive Captain John Smith, that this would be inexpedient for the present. The placing of the cross, bearing the legend "Jacobus Rex, 1607," with Newport's name below, apparently signified that the men from beyond the sea were laying claim to the region in the name of King James.

Three centuries later, a cross was erected on Gamble's Hill at the foot of Richmond's Fourth Street, to commemorate the event.

The islet at The Falls on which the explorers set up the cross was probably "the almost circular little island indicated on early maps of Richmond as Lot No. 321, at the north end of Mayo Bridge," according to Wirt Armistead Cate, who made an intensive study of the matter. The island was subsequently incorporated into the mainland and included territory as far inland as the present Canal Street. In modern times, the freight depot of the Southern Railway occupied this site.

En route upstream, the Englishmen with their beards, curling hair and wide-brimmed hats, their doublets and hose, had been received in altogether friendly fashion by the natives. At Powhatan Village, consisting of twelve houses, "pleasantly seated on a hill," they were greeted hospitably by Little Powhatan. The village was on the site of today's grass-covered Powhatan Park on Fulton Hill in Richmond's extreme eastern end. Gabriel Archer, chief chronicler of the expedition, speaks of "a playne" between the hill and the river, "whereon he soes his wheate, beane, peaze, tobacco, pompions, gourdes, Hempe, flaxe, &c." This plain must have been the site of today's Fulton, which like Fulton Hill is named for Irish-born James Alexander Fulton, who married Eliza Mayo about 1800 and built for his bride beautiful "Mount Erin," where Powhatan Village once stood.

The Indian village was further described as facing "three fertile iles," near the opposite shore of the river. They have since disappeared in floods or been incorporated into the south bank.

The day after the explorers arrived from Jamestown, "Powhatan and some of his people satt with us" and ate "very freshly of our meat, Dranck of our beere, Aquavite and Sack."

The Englishmen then set up the cross at The Falls, after which they returned to Powhatan Village. Little Powhatan "tolde us he was very sick" and that he believed the "hott Drynckes . . . caused his greefe." In view of the calamitous combination of beer, brandy and Canary wine in which this lover of "fire-water" had overindulged, the consequences are hardly surprising.

The English assured Powhatan that his roaring headache and other disabilities would be improved on the morrow. This turned out to be the case. Whereupon the English were suddenly elevated to the status of medicine men, and ailing braves crowded round "upon every belliach to him [Newport] to know when they should be well."

The English returned to Jamestown, and more than a year passed before any of them went back to The Falls. Captain Newport, still ardent in his search for gold, decided in September 1608 on another journey to the future site of Richmond. He traveled in the pinnace and smaller boats with 120 men. Upon arrival the band marched forty miles westward along the south side of the James into the country of the Monacan Indians. But they found no gold, nor would the redskins provide them with corn. They

to Monacan town
(13 mi.)

Richmond

The Falls

FALLING CR.

Powhatan

CHICKAHOMINY RIVER

N

Kind
Woman's
Care

Arrohattoc

Mulberry
Shade

Poor
Cottage

Turkey Ile

Queen Appomattoc's Bower

Pamunkey Palace

Careless Point

APPOMATTOX

Appomattoc

Petersburg

Point
Weanoc

CHIPPOKES CR.

Paspahegh

• unnamed village

Quiyoughcohannock

Jamestown

Archer's Hope

WARWICK

PAGAN R.

Smithfield

JAMES RIVER

Kecoughtan

0   5   10   15   20
miles

to Cape Henry
(13 mi.)

(1) Map of James River showing the sixty-mile stretch over which a party of Jamestown settlers journeyed to The Falls in 1607, only slightly more than a week after their initial landing. At The Falls, the future site of Richmond, they planted a cross, with a "great shout."

returned to Jamestown, many of them hungry and ailing, with nothing to show for their pains.

The next year, when Smith was president of the Jamestown colony, he decided to make an attempt to establish a settlement at The Falls. Captain Francis West, brother of Lord De La Warr, was dispatched upriver with 120 men and "sixe months victtewells." Some months later Smith paid them a visit to see how the settlement was prospering. He was surprised, en route, to meet West returning to Jamestown, but proceeded upstream without requesting an explanation. Upon reaching the limits of Tidewater, he found that West had settled near the riverbank, where there was constant danger of floods, instead of higher up on Powhatan Hill.

Smith persuaded Little Powhatan to sell him the village on the hilltop for some copper. He wished, among other things, to help protect the werowance, or chief, against the incursions of the Monacans. Little Powhatan had told him two years before that these redskins "came Downe at the fall of the leafe and invaded his Countrye." But Smith's plan did not appeal to Captain West's Englishmen, who for some reason resented his intervention. It was apparently part of the eternal bickering and squabbling that went on among the Jamestown settlers.

West's contingent at The Falls, which greatly outnumbered Smith's, attacked the latter. Smith and his men left for Jamestown, whereupon the Indians assailed the English who remained, killing a number. It happened that Smith, whose boat had run aground a short distance downstream, heard reverberations from the fighting. He rushed back, and somehow managed to arrest several of the English ringleaders and to reassert his authority. Overruling West's stupid decision to settle near the river, he compelled the English to move to the high ground atop Powhatan Hill, or as he put it, "The rest he seated gallantlie at Powhatan, in their Salvage fort which they [the Indians] had built and pretilie fortified with poles and barkes of trees sufficient to have defended them from all the Salvages in Virginia." Smith called it "Nonsuch."

But West, once more defying Smith, moved the colony back to the riverside and named the place West's Fort. At this point Smith gave up. It was not like him, but tired, disgusted or frustrated—perhaps all three—he set sail for Jamestown. As the boat glided down the river, he went to sleep, with his powder bag on his lap. It somehow became ignited and burned him so badly that "to quench the tormenting fire, frying him in his cloathes, he leaped overboard in the deepe river where . . . he was neere drowned." Smith was so badly injured that he sailed for England in October 1609 and never returned to Virginia.

Later, West brought his entire force back to Jamestown, thus terminating, for the time being, all efforts to settle at The Falls.

Jamestown itself nearly went under during the winter of 1609–10, when the terrible "starving time" almost wiped out the colony. But the haggard and famished settlers who survived managed to hang on, and in 1611 Marshal Thomas Dale arrived from England.

Dale, a stern disciplinarian, even for that era when Draconian punishments were commonplace, did not hesitate to torture or put to death those who disobeyed his edicts. He was determined to have a reasonable degree of order and industry, and he also recognized the importance of building a settlement on high ground upriver, away from the swamps and mosquitoes of Jamestown. He did not go quite so far as The Falls, but chose a site some fourteen miles downstream on Farrar's Island at a sharp bend near Dutch Gap. He named it Henrico for Henry, Prince of Wales. The widespread impression that the name was Henricopolis is without foundation.

The buildings erected on the island and others subsequently added in the area were destroyed or damaged in the great Indian massacre of 1622, and many of the settlers were slain. The first ironworks in America, which had been established at Falling Creek, six miles below the head of Tidewater, were wrecked, and nearly everybody attached to them was killed.

These dire events did not disturb the quiet of The Falls, where year after year the murmuring waters splashed over the rocks, with none but the Indians, the wild birds, the deer, the leaping bass and the slithering water moccasins to keep them company.

Finally, in 1645, the year following another great Indian massacre, the Virginia Assembly directed that Fort Charles be constructed on the north side of the James where Virginia's capital city stands today. This was intended as a permanent stronghold for protection against the Indians. However, it was decided in 1646 to dismantle the fort and build another on the south side of the stream where the land was more suitable for cultivation.

All was relatively serene at The Falls for about a decade, when some six or seven hundred Indians suddenly appeared. Variously described as Iroquois from New York—known as Ricaherians in Virginia—or members of the Siouan tribe from the upper Rappahannock, they began taking possession of extensive tracts of land. Colonel Edward Hill of Shirley, Speaker of the House of Burgesses, was put in command of English warriors and several groups of friendly Indians, including Pamunkeys under famous Chief Totopotomoi. When efforts at peaceful persuasion failed to dislodge the intruders, Colonel Hill moved to the attack near Richmond's present Chimborazo Park.

The fight took place in 1656 in the vicinity of a small stream which rose at the juncture of what is now Marshall and Thirty-first streets, in the city's East End, and ran southeasterly around the base of Chimborazo into Gillies Creek. In modern times, it has been enclosed in a culvert. The sanguinary encounter caused the little stream to be named "Bloody Run."

Chief Totopotomoi was killed with many of his braves, and numerous white settlers were slain.

The defeat was so total that the colonists had to sue for peace. Colonel Hill, found guilty of "crimes and deficiencies," was suspended from "all offices military and civil" by unanimous vote of the Assembly, and was required to pay the costs of making peace. This extraordinary punishment apparently was subsequently felt to have been too drastic, since Hill was reelected Speaker three years later.

In that same year, 1659, Thomas Stegg, Jr.—son of a wealthy merchant and burgess who had been trading in lower Tidewater for about a quarter of a century—contracted for one thousand acres of land at The Falls. The tract was south of the river. Not long afterward, Stegg's friend, Governor William Berkeley, enabled him to acquire five hundred adjacent acres. Then, in 1661, Stegg bought three hundred more, for an over-all total of eighteen hundred. This "Falls Plantation," as it came to be known, extended from Goode's on Stony Creek almost to the present Mayo's Island.

Stegg prospered as a result of his own ability and a substantial inheritance from his father. He built a stone house on his property at The Falls, about a mile from the river on the south side, shown on William Byrd's title book. It had a chimney squarely in the middle, but otherwise resembled the Old Stone House which still stands on East Main Street. Stegg served on the powerful Colonial Council and as auditor-general.

His sister had married a London goldsmith, John Byrd. They had a son, William, who came to Virginia. When Stegg died childless in 1671, he left the greater part of his property, including the Falls Plantation, to this eighteen-year-old nephew. The latter lost no time in taking over.

Young William apparently moved into his uncle's stone house in the early 1670s. In 1673 he married twenty-one-year-old Mary Horsmanden Filmer, daughter of a well-connected Royalist officer, Colonel Warham Horsmanden, and widow of Samuel Filmer, third son of Sir Robert Filmer. Horsmanden was affiliated with the Cavalier faction and had left Cromwellian England. He served in the Virginia House of Burgesses, and returned to his native land after the restoration of Charles II to the throne. Young Byrd's marriage into this highly placed family got him off to an excellent start in Virginia. His ingenuity, intelligence and drive, combined with the inheritance from his uncle, did the rest.

The first child of Byrd and his young bride, William Byrd II, was born in 1674 in the lonely stone house. It was an isolated and dangerous spot for the daughter of a Royalist officer, reared among the gentry in England. The unpredictable and often murderous Indians were constantly on the prowl, and while the fort at The Falls afforded some protection, the precarious situation of a young woman living virtually alone under such conditions was obvious.

Byrd had moved quickly to establish a trading post at The Falls, whence he sent expeditions into the wild and unexplored back country, with commodities desired by the redskins. Indian trails, infested with wolves, panthers and bears, were the routes, and Byrd often had to leave his young wife and child and go on these perilous excursions. A number of his agents were killed by the Indians.

He was barely getting himself well established in this trade when serious trouble erupted with the redskins. A leader in urging retaliation was Nathaniel Bacon, a young Englishman of gentle birth who had come to Virginia in 1674 and who had also opened a trading post on the James at the head of Tidewater. It was located in what was known later as Bacon's Quarter, on today's West Broad Street, on the approximate site of the Richmond, Fredericksburg and Potomac freight depot. The small stream Bacon's Quarter Branch, which takes its name from this same tract, rises west of Brook Avenue and runs northward into Shockoe Creek. It is now enclosed in a culvert. Bacon's property in this section adjoined lands acquired by Byrd, who had been enlarging his holdings aggressively since his arrival in the colony.

The bloody struggle with the Indians broke out in 1675 when a Stafford County man and his son were murdered. Then treachery by white leaders, who slew several Indian chiefs contrary to a solemn agreement, caused the redskins to go on a wild orgy of killing in the frontier settlements. The slaughter lasted for months, and some five hundred men, women and children were slain, often after the most dreadful tortures. Among the victims were three of Byrd's servants and one of Bacon's favorite overseers.

When Governor Berkeley appeared reluctant to authorize an expedition against the Indians, planters in the vicinity of The Falls, including Byrd, looked to Bacon for leadership in defense of their homes and families. Byrd, fearing that it was too dangerous to leave his wife and little son exposed in such a place, sent them to England in care of "Father Horsmanden." Journeys across the ocean in that day were themselves long and hazardous.

Byrd led a company of English against the Indians, realizing that he was risking his future, if not his neck, in doing so without Governor Berkeley's permission. This risk he was willing to take. He later made his peace with the governor.

The Falls figured to only a minor degree in the upheaval, which lasted from the spring until well into the autumn of 1676. Bacon's and Berkeley's forces gathered there briefly several times, as the fighting ebbed and flowed.

Bacon's rebellion was crushed after Bacon's death, and a treaty was signed with the Queen of the Pamunkeys and subordinate tribes in the area. The queen was presented with a red velvet cap and handsome silver frontlet. The treaty did not prevent northern tribes from attacking at or near The Falls in 1678. Both commanding officers of the Henrico militia,

Colonel Francis Eppes and Major William Harris, were killed, Eppes by "an arrow in the throat." The redskins were driven off.

William Byrd remained in the good graces of Governor Berkeley, as is evidenced by his election to the General Assembly at Jamestown. The trading post he had established at The Falls was expanded, and his acreage in the vicinity was steadily increased. He brought Mary and little Will back from England.

The Byrds had four more children, three girls—Susan, Ursula and Mary —and a boy, Warham, who died in infancy. The conditions under which Mary Byrd reared her family on the desolate frontier in seventeenth-century Virginia are difficult for us of this generation to envision. After giving birth to five children in the bleak stone house, she made the tremendous sacrifice of sending the four survivors to England for their education. They were gone for years at a time. In fact, William Byrd II, who was to become so famous, was abroad throughout nearly his entire youth. When William I sent him to "Father Horsmanden" in 1681 for schooling in England, the boy was seven years old. His parents saw him for only two more relatively brief periods during the remainder of their lives.

The favorite among the girls appears to have been Ursula, affectionately known as "Little Nutty." She seems to have been the subject of more correspondence than her two sisters. Susan, who never returned to Virginia, married John Brayne of London. Mary came back to the Old Dominion and married James Duke, sheriff of James City County. "Little Nutty" returned to Virginia when about thirteen years of age, and some two years later, just before her fifteenth birthday, married Robert Beverley, Jr., the son of her father's friend Major Robert Beverley. Young Beverley was very much an "insider," since he was clerk of the General Court, of the Council of State and of the General Assembly. His bride gave birth to a son, William, before her sixteenth birthday, and died a year later, in 1698.

While several young Byrds were growing up in England, a devastating flood in 1685 nearly drove their parents from the stone dwelling at The Falls. Byrd wrote that he and his family "almost drowned" and that the water surged into the lower floor of his house. Various historians have made the erroneous statement that Byrd thereupon built handsome Belvidere across the river on what is now Oregon Hill to get away from future floods. There is no evidence to support this theory. Belvidere was built more than half a century later by Byrd's grandson, William Byrd III.[1]

Mary Horsmanden Byrd and her husband were cramped for space in the modest stone house. Their family was expanding rapidly. Byrd's governmental responsibilities also were increasing, as was his trade with the settlers and the Indians.

Byrd's caravans were traveling hundreds of miles from his trading post at The Falls into today's North and South Carolina, the country of the

Cherokees and the Catawbas. Cloth, kettles, hatchets, beads, rum, guns and ammunition were among the commodities that his traders bartered with the Indians for such things as beaver skins, deerskins, furs, herbs and minerals. Byrd was described in a letter to the Royal Society of London as knowing "more of Indian affairs than any man in the country."

But he did not confine himself to Indian trade; he also dealt extensively in African slaves. In 1684, for example, he referred in a letter to Perry & Lane, his London agents, to a voyage of the *Pinke*, saying, "if you sent" the ship "on our account, I would have by her 546 Negroes." He traded in rum by the thousands of gallons and molasses by the ton. A large tobacco warehouse at The Falls, where planters stored their crops and had them inspected—another of his profitable enterprises—was maintained by Byrd. He dealt extensively with English merchants, getting from them for sale in Virginia a great variety of articles, such as hats, cloth, wine, brandy, horse collars, tables, chairs and shoes. At the same time, he imported from England the articles that were useful in trade with the red men. Commodities that Byrd sent to England in exchange included tobacco, furs and Indian corn.

All the while, Byrd was greatly enlarging his landholdings by bringing over indentured servants from England, for each of whom he received fifty acres. By this and various other means he acquired vast tracts at or near the site of today's Richmond. Some of these grants were confirmed by the General Assembly as early as 1679, on condition that Byrd "seat and have in readiness . . . on beate of drumm, fifty able men, well armed, with sufficient ammunition and provisions for . . . defense against the enemy Indian." He was captain of the Henrico militia. Later he was chosen Receiver-General of the King's Revenue and auditor of Virginia, and finally president of the Council of State.

The loneliness of Mary Byrd at The Falls for almost a decade and a half, and the dangers that continued to surround her in that exposed position on the very edge of civilization, were important factors in persuading her husband, in 1688, to acquire the Westover plantation. It was 1,200 acres in extent and some twenty miles downstream. It adjoined Berkeley plantation, and was in an area where various other planters had residences and large tracts of land. Hence it was not only safer, but it afforded many more opportunities for social contacts.

Byrd began building a comfortable frame dwelling there in about the year 1689. He moved in with Mary as soon as it was completed. There they lived for the years that remained to them. Byrd's most conspicuous humanitarian service during that period was the assistance he gave to the hundreds of Huguenot refugees who arrived from France at the turn of the century and settled at Manakintown, twenty miles above The Falls in the present Powhatan County, across the James River from today's

Manakin. Byrd was extremely generous in assisting these almost destitute victims of religious persecution in all possible ways. The historian Beverley believed, in fact, that they could not have survived without his aid.

Byrd's health began to fail, and he died at Westover in 1704, aged fifty-two. His heroic wife, Mary, had preceded him to the grave five years before, aged forty-seven.

Their son, William Byrd II, had spent most of his youth in London, where he received a remarkably thorough education, including courses at the Middle Temple that led to his admission to the bar. He returned to Westover plantation in 1696, after completing his studies, but went back to London early in 1697. There he remained for several years, and he was not in Virginia when either of his parents died. After his father's death, Byrd returned in the spring of 1705 to Westover, which he inherited, along with lands totaling more than 26,000 acres. Most of this acreage was at or near the present site of Richmond, of which he is the recognized founder.

Few American cities can claim so distinguished a parentage. At age thirty-one, when Byrd came back to the Old Dominion, he was a sophisticated man of the world, welcome in the drawing rooms of London's elite, accustomed to mingle with earls and dukes, a member of the Royal Society at age twenty-two, the possessor of one of the most delightful literary styles of his time, a discriminating bibliophile and book collector, well versed in several languages, both ancient and modern, and without question one of the most brilliant men of his day. Byrd had his frailties, notably in his pursuit of women of high and low degree. This last must be viewed in the context of the moral standards prevailing in that age. Certainly the catholicity of his intellect and the breadth of his interests were amazing. Louis B. Wright, a foremost authority, has written that "all in all, he was as versatile in his learning as that later genius of Virginia, Thomas Jefferson."

Such was the polished, urbane and erudite young man who took over the house, the slaves and the land that he had inherited from his able and energetic father. He set about at once putting his affairs in order and preparing to take his place as a leader in early eighteenth-century Virginia.

An almost immediate objective was to marry and found a family. In the spring of 1706 he was wed to the beautiful Lucy Parke, daughter of Daniel Parke, a man of high social standing but described as a "rakish and violent gentleman." Colonel Parke was noted for having served with Marlborough, and for having brought the news of the British victory at Blenheim to Queen Anne. He was appointed soon afterward as governor of the Leeward Islands in the Caribbean, and was killed there by a mob. Parke's penchant for furious tantrums seems to have been transmitted to his daughter Lucy. She and her husband had many stormy altercations, as Byrd records in his diary.

Byrd lost no time in traveling to The Falls to inspect the extensive properties left him there by his father. His movements to and fro are not as definitely known as they later became, since the earliest diary that has come to light covers the period 1709–12. But there is no question that he took over his lands everywhere as soon as possible. At the same time, he sought the seat held by his father on the Council and the latter's posts as auditor and receiver-general. He was made receiver-general promptly, but the position of auditor went to someone else. He also had to wait until 1709 to obtain a place on the Council.

At first, Byrd spent two or three days every two or three months inspecting his six plantations at or near The Falls. Later, when he had a general overseer, he visited them once a year. His rich and extensive lands on the site of what would become the city of Richmond were the most valuable. They were on both sides of the James and extended almost without a break on the south side of the stream all the way to Falling Creek. There he had another plantation, on which were a sawmill, a tannery and a coal mine. Byrd's overseer discovered another coal field near The Falls.

Byrd was in England again before long, on some sort of governmental mission or missions. His sojourn lasted five years (1715–20), during which time Westover and his other plantations were left in the care of overseers. Lucy Byrd died in London of smallpox in 1716, leaving her husband with two daughters, Evelyn and Wilhelmina. It was during the years which followed Lucy's death that Byrd was particularly promiscuous in keeping mistresses and visiting London brothels, all of which he recorded in his London diary. He returned to Westover at the end of five years, but was soon back in England for another five-year period (1721–26).

Byrd was married there in 1724 to Maria Taylor, daughter of Thomas Taylor of Kensington. She bore him four children, including a son, William. This was William Byrd III, who was a talented and brave colonel in the French and Indian War, succeeding George Washington as commander of the Virginia forces. Unfortunately, he became an irresponsible wastrel and killed himself in 1777.

William and Maria Byrd sailed back to Virginia with several children in 1726, to remain for the rest of their lives. During the eighteen years left to Byrd he would not only see Richmond laid out and formally incorporated by the General Assembly, but he would build the great mansion at Westover that became one of Virginia's historic landmarks. He died there in 1744, aged seventy, and was buried in the garden. One may see today his handsome tomb with its elaborate and highly complimentary epitaph, supposedly written by Byrd himself.

# Byrd—The Reluctant Father

THE OFT-QUOTED reference in William Byrd II's writings to his projected founding of Richmond occurs in his *A Journey to the Land of Eden*, and concerns a visit in 1733 to large tracts of land that he had acquired along the Roanoke River on both sides of the present Virginia-North Carolina line. This entry, for September 19, reads, in part, as follows:

"When we got home we laid the foundations of two large Citys. One at Shacco's, to be called Richmond, and the other at the point of Appamattux River to be named Petersburgh. These Major Mayo offered to lay out into Lots without Fee or Reward. The Truth of it is, these two places being the uppermost landing of James and Appamattux Rivers, are naturally intended for Marts, where the Traffick of the Outer Inhabitants must Center. Thus we did not build Castles only, but also Citys in the Air."

Despite the foregoing entry in his diary, and contrary to prevailing views today, William Byrd II, long known as the "father" of Richmond, tried for years to prevent the establishment of a town at the falls of the James. By 1733, when he made the entry concerning "Citys in the Air," he had become reconciled to the idea of founding what he termed a "mart" at the head of Tidewater. But in 1727 he was doing everything in his power to obstruct this scheme, and to retain possession of his lands on both sides of the river and his profitable store and tobacco warehouses at The Falls.

He wrote Micajah Perry, his London agent, in May 1727, fervently protesting that the Virginia House of Burgesses had no right to compel him to dispose of fifty acres of his most valuable property for the purpose of establishing a town.[1] A bill to achieve this object, already in preparation for introduction at the upcoming legislative session, was the cause of Byrd's concern. He suspected that someone was trying to secure its passage with a view to setting up tobacco inspection facilities in competition with his own. While he realized that he would be compensated for the fifty acres in question, he believed the compensation would be wholly inadequate. Byrd even sneered at the Virginia legislature as "a little Assembly, the very shadow of a Parliament" which had no right to take his property. He hoped that Perry would communicate these sentiments at once to the Board of Trade in England, and that the Privy Council, of which the board was a committee, would interpose objections.

The measure which Byrd opposed so strongly did not then pass the Assembly, but its passage soon became foregone. The area around The Falls was becoming more and more thickly settled, and was developing as a center not only of the tobacco trade for planters over a wide region but also of extensive commerce with the back-country Indians. Byrd finally had to bow to the inevitable.

Four years elapsed, following the entry in Byrd's diary, before Major Mayo laid off the town. By 1737, when he did so, taverns had been opened at what are now Twenty-third and Main and Twenty-third and Cary streets, and Byrd had established a ferry. These, with his store and warehouses, combined to form the nucleus for the lively settlement that soon came into being.

Much of the area laid out by Mayo was along the river, at the foot of what is now Church Hill, but it extended to the crest of that elevation. Lots No. 97 and 98 were donated by Byrd for "The Church," soon to be erected and later to be named St. John's. It superseded "The Falls Chapel," which had been in existence since 1717, and whose location is not known.

Byrd named the new town Richmond because its situation and surroundings reminded him of Richmond on the Thames. As delineated by Mayo, it extended from what is now Seventeenth Street, First Street in his plan, to today's Twenty-fifth Street, then known as Ninth. The cross streets were designated by letters. The one nearest the river, now Cary, was D Street; Main was E; Franklin, F; Grace, G; and Broad, H.

Mayo divided the town into thirty-two squares (see map), with each square containing four lots. Byrd advertised in Williamsburg's *Virginia Gazette* that Richmond had been laid off with streets sixty-five feet wide, and that lots would be sold on condition that the purchaser build a house within three years, twenty-four by sixteen feet, and fronting within five feet of the street. The lots were to cost "seven pounds in Virginia currency."

In addition to these thirty-two numbered lots, there were sixteen others immediately west of the town limits, designated by letters, while to the north and east were larger tracts, from eight to seventeen acres in extent, to serve as sites for suburban villas. The latter bore such names as Kingston, Carlton, Guilford and Farrington.

Construction of a house of worship was one of the first concerns of

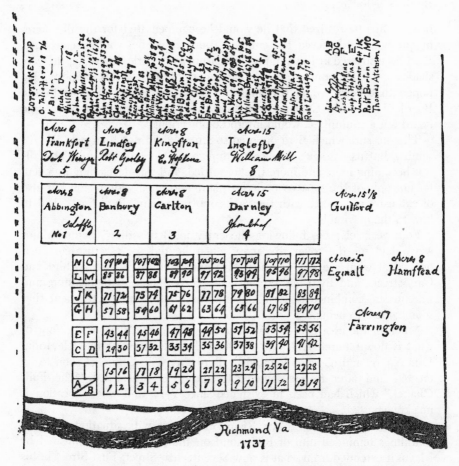

(2) Facsimile of the first map of Richmond from *Richmond: Her Past and Present* by W. Asbury Christian. The original was made by Colonel William Byrd II in 1737. Between Lot B and the James River, at the bottom of the map, was D Street, now Cary Street. Just west of Lot A, and at right angles to the river, was First Street, now Seventeenth. Then came Second, Third, Fourth, Fifth, Sixth, Seventh, Eighth and Ninth streets. Lots 97 and 98 were given to the city by Byrd for the Henrico parish church, later named St. John's.

those living in and near Richmond. The vestry of Curl's Church, in Henrico County some miles below Richmond, of which the Reverend William Stith, the historian, was rector, considered this matter in 1737. At that time, a site on or near the property of Thomas Williamson near Brook Road was preferred. The vestry voted in 1739 to build the church there, on land owned by William Byrd II. However, Byrd advised that "there are so many roads already thro that land that the damage to me would be too great to have another of a mile cut thro it." He urged that they accept from him two lots in what is now the Church Hill section of Richmond. The vestry agreed, and arranged for Richard Randolph to construct the building. This house of worship was completed in 1741. Much smaller than it was in subsequent years, and with the pulpit in the eastern end, it was known until about 1828 as "the Church," "the Upper Church," "the Richmond Hill Church" and "the Old Church." The structure was enlarged in 1772 by adding forty feet to its length and forty more feet on the north side, with galleries on both sides. The tower was built about 1830.

In an effort to attract German immigrants to the new town, Byrd sent Dr. Samuel Tschiffeli, Virginia agent of the Helvetian Society, to Philadelphia in 1738. Several Germans bought lots soon thereafter. Among them was Daniel Weisiger, a "high German" who purchased four lots near the river, and also eight acres in the suburban area to the north, which he named Frankfort. Dr. Tschiffeli acquired five lots and set up shop as "Chimist and Practitioner of Physick." He also advertised that he would test "any sort of Metals or Oars." Other Germans who were among the first to buy Byrd's land in the city were Adam Eigst, John Krantzmann, John Enders and General Nicholas Scherer.

Of special interest was the coming in 1738 of twenty-five-year-old Jacob Ege, a Württemberger, who purchased land on lower Main Street. About 1739 he is believed to have built the small stone dwelling between Nineteenth and Twentieth streets on Main, known today as the Old Stone House. Rocks from the river were apparently used in the construction of this, the oldest building still standing in Richmond. The letters "J.R." over the entrance were supposed for many years to have signified "Jacobus Rex," or "King James," and if so, the structure would have been built in or before 1688, the year when James II of England was dethroned. But there are strong reasons for believing that the Old Stone House does not date from the seventeenth century, so the initials must have some entirely different meaning. Reports that Washington, Jefferson and Madison visited or lodged in the house are apparently without foundation.

Jacob Ege, a cooper or tailor by trade, and presumed builder of the house, married Maria Dorothea Scherer in 1740, and it was the young couple's first home. Dorothea was the daughter of General Nicholas Scherer and his wife, who had been lady in waiting to the Queen of Hesse-Cassel. The Scherers came to Richmond at about the same time as Jacob Ege. Their son, Samuel, was a member of the Constitutional Convention of 1788. Many Richmond families are related in one way or another to the descendants of Jacob Ege and Dorothea Scherer, including Ruffins, Palmers, Robinsons, Adamses, McCabes, Harrisons, Gatewoods, Randolphs and Woolfolks.[2]

The Ege house was well below the falls of the river, but the sound of the cascading water may have been audible there. Early travelers often noted what they called the "roar of the falls." Witty William Byrd II was one of the first commentators on this phenomenon, albeit in slightly different terms. "The Falls," he wrote in his diary, "murmur loud enough to drown a scolding wife." Thomas Anburey, a paroled British officer, wrote in 1779 of the river "dashing from rock to rock with a most tremendous noise which may be heard for many miles." Just why the rapids of the James sent off such thunderous reverberations in that era when today there is, in normal times, merely a gentle splashing is difficult to explain.

With Richmond formally laid out, it remained for the General Assembly to pass an act of incorporation. This was done in 1742. The town had only 250 inhabitants and covered only one fifth of a square mile, but its situation at the head of navigation augured well for steady growth and development.

The act of assembly noted that William Byrd II had agreed to donate land for a common, running the length of the town along the river, and up the eastern bank of Shockoe Creek. The act also provided that Richmond should hold fairs lasting two days each May and November, for the sale of "all manner of cattle, provisions, victuals, goods, wares and merchandises whatever."

Early Richmonders were wont to build houses with wooden chimneys, and these led to frequent fires. The Assembly accordingly passed an act in 1744 requiring that in future all chimneys be of brick, and providing that existing wooden ones be pulled down within three years.

When William Byrd II died at Westover in 1744, his son, William III, succeeded to his large estate. The younger Byrd was appointed, along with Peter, Richard and William Randolph, Thomas Atchison, Samuel Gleadowe, Bowler Cocke the younger, Samuel DuVal and John Pleasants, "gentlemen," as Richmond's trustees to lay off and regulate the streets, settle disputes concerning boundaries, and so on.

The James River channel at Richmond was not deep enough to accommodate the large ships of that day, and they had to dock at Warwick, in what is now Chesterfield County, just above Falling Creek, where the channel approached the south shore. Today's Deepwater Terminal is on part of the site. Warwick had been an important shipping point as early as 1656. Mills were established there and tobacco inspection was begun at the Warwick warehouse in 1730. Warwick, which some contend was at one time larger than Richmond, was burned in Benedict Arnold's second revolutionary raid of 1781, and never rebuilt. It had been a supply point for the Virginia State Navy, and rope, shoes, leather and clothing for the Continental Army had been manufactured there.

The prominent Cary family owned much land in the area, and Henry Cary II apparently was instrumental in obtaining a charter for Warwick in 1748. The Cary mansion Ampthill had been built some two decades before. In modern times, the huge Du Pont plant was erected on a portion of the land where Warwick once stood, and Ampthill had either to be moved or demolished. Hunsdon Cary moved it in 1929–30 to the north side of the river in Richmond's far West End, and it later became the residence of D. Tennant Bryan, publisher of Richmond's newspapers, president of the American Newspaper Publishers Association and leader in many civic movements.

Another handsome colonial mansion, Wilton, built by William Randolph III in 1753 across the James from Ampthill, was removed in 1933 to Richmond's West End by the National Society of the Colonial Dames of America in the Commonwealth of Virginia and became the society's headquarters.

A third imposing mansion of the period, located only two miles east of the Capitol, was Powhatan Seat, built near the James between 1726 and 1732 by Joseph Mayo, brother of William Mayo. The Mayo family was one of the most conspicuous and influential in Richmond's early history. Powhatan Seat, a T-shaped dwelling, was situated originally on a plantation of some 2,000 acres. It remained in the Mayo family until 1866, and was finally torn down early in the twentieth century.

Eight miles below Warwick but across the river in today's Henrico another busy colonial port was developing in the late 1600s. It was known then as Jefferson's Landing. Thomas Jefferson's grandfather, also named Thomas, and officially designated a "gentleman,"[3] a significant distinction in that era, served in 1718–19 as sheriff of Henrico. He and Peter Jefferson, his son, were born at Osborne's. Peter moved later to Albemarle County, where he built a modest frame house, Shadwell. There the famous Thomas Jefferson was born in 1743 to Peter and his wife, the former Jane Randolph.

Henrico County, of which the early Jeffersons were citizens, was originally of vast extent, and stretched in the seventeenth century from the junction of the James and Appomattox rivers to the Blue Ridge. Nine other counties were subsequently carved from this territory. Goochland was lopped off in 1728 and Chesterfield in 1749. Henrico's county seat was Varina, below Richmond on the James, and it seemed desirable, after the formation of Goochland and Chesterfield, to move the courthouse to a point nearer the center of things. A new location in the recently established town of Richmond was accordingly chosen. The site was squarely in the middle of what later became Twenty-second Street, and just south of E Street (now Main). The new structure was completed in 1752, and the court was formally transferred from Varina to Richmond. In the 1840s, the building was taken out of the middle of Twenty-second Street and shifted to the corner of Twenty-second and Main. In 1974 the courthouse was moved back to Henrico, at the intersection of Parham and Hungary Spring roads west of the city.

After the founding of Richmond, the burial place of early citizens was

St. John's churchyard. One of the first, if not the first, of the 1,300 persons to be buried there was the Reverend Robert Rose, a native of Scotland who served Episcopal parishes in Essex and Albemarle, and died in Richmond in 1751. Described as "a sort of universal genius," he is said to have been consulted by Major William Mayo concerning the laying out of the city. Rose was not only known and admired by leading citizens of the colony, but he was a clergyman with extraordinary ingenuity and imagination in practical affairs. He handled various business transactions for Governor Spotswood and was executor for his estate. A pioneer in the navigation of the James River far above Richmond, he devised the system whereby two canoes, lashed together, could carry eight or nine heavy hogsheads of tobacco to market. An amateur practitioner of both law and medicine, he also operated a large plantation and traveled widely throughout Virginia. Despite these varied activities, he preached regularly, even several times a week. His death at age forty-six removed one of the most remarkable men of his generation. His tomb is among the best-preserved in the venerable churchyard of old St. John's.[4]

Rose had been one of the first to urge that the General Assembly take action to improve the navigability of the James. The Falls—actually rapids —extending for a distance of seven miles, were a serious obstacle. The channel above and below them also was in need of dredging to accommodate larger vessels. Due in part to Rose's agitation of these matters, the legislature passed a law in 1745 "for the more effectual clearing of the James and Appomattox Rivers." Nothing came of it for twenty years. Then, in 1765, when the need for better facilities for tobacco and coal shipments to and through Richmond was obvious, the Assembly approved legislation providing for a canal around the rapids, with adequate locks. Further legislation was passed in 1772. Yet progress was extremely slow, and the approach of the American Revolution brought work to a complete halt.

The town of Manchester, across the river from Richmond, and previously known as Rocky Ridge, was incorporated in 1769. This was a major shipping outlet for coal from the mines in the Midlothian area. Rocky Ridge included a number of cultivated and substantial citizens, and its potential for growth seemed good.

Much of the property there and on the opposite side of the James at Shockoes, the area west of Shockoe Creek, was owned by William Byrd III. But Byrd's lack of business ability and inveterate gambling habits had got him into deep financial trouble. Byrd owed the colony nearly £15,000—money lent him illegally from the treasury by Colonial Treasurer John Robinson in the wide-ranging John Robinson scandal. He also had contracted various other debts. Byrd decided that he would have to liquidate his large estate at The Falls, inherited from his father, to satisfy some of his creditors.

He advertised these properties for sale in the *Pennsylvania Gazette* of

April 23, 1767. Not only Belvidere but "a valuable tract of land, containing near 30,000 acres, lying on both sides of James River, at the falls thereof," was put on the block. Little or nothing seems to have come of this. Four months later Byrd decided to offer his holdings in a huge lottery, with advertisements in the *Virginia Gazette.*

The ads ran from August 1767 to October 1768, and drawings in the lottery were to take place in November 1768, at Williamsburg. There were 10,000 tickets at £5 each, and the prizes included seventeen improved town lots, 10,000 acres laid off in hundred-acre lots, ten islands, plus twenty-year leases on mills, fisheries, tobacco warehouses and Patrick Coutts' ferry, all valued at a total of £56,796. The lottery took place, as scheduled, and George Washington is said to have held one of the lucky tickets, but he seems not to have collected his prize.

One of Byrd's arguments for the high value of his lots and other holdings was that the obstructions at The Falls and above them would be removed, and the James made navigable westward for two hundred miles. Thus, he contended, the vast produce of the West would be brought downstream to this market, with the worth of the area at and near Richmond greatly enhanced.

Many of Byrd's holdings were disposed of through the lottery, but his problems were not solved. He continued to live at Belvidere until 1776, and then on New Year's Day, 1777, at Westover he shot himself. There are indications that Belvidere was offered in the lottery eight years before, and that Daniel L. Hylton, a Richmond merchant, held the winning ticket. For some reason, Hylton delayed until 1776 in taking over the mansion and grounds.

Byrd had built Belvidere sometime between 1755 and 1759 on what is now Oregon Hill. It was a mansion of wood on a brick foundation, with a frontage of 128 feet, including the wings. The Reverend Andrew Burnaby of England termed it in 1759 or 1760 "as romantic and elegant as anything I have ever seen." During the Revolution, British Lieutenant Anburey described it as "an elegant villa." It was surrounded by seventeen acres, on which were various dependencies, including kitchen, smokehouse, garden, paddock and slave quarters. The house was situated on ground bounded today by Laurel, China, Holly and Belvidere streets. A unique feature was a serpentine brick wall, variously reported to have girdled the entire seventeen acres or merely to have embraced part of the property. At all events, it seems likely that Thomas Jefferson copied Belvidere's serpentine walls when he built the University of Virginia. Where Byrd got the plans for them is unknown.

Belvidere was occupied for eighteen years by Daniel Hylton, after which it was acquired by "Light-Horse Harry" Lee for less than a year. He sold it to Bushrod Washington, who relinquished it in 1798 on being appointed to the United States Supreme Court. The next purchaser was Colonel John Harvie. Among the subsequent owners were Benjamin J.

Harris, William Anderson and his son, James M. Anderson, who inherited it about 1833. Belvidere was by this time distinctly on the downgrade. It was used for a schoolhouse and then as a rooming house for workers in the Tredegar and other nearby factories. The deteriorating mansion was destroyed by fire in 1854.[5]

The coal fields of Chesterfield County were important to the immediate area in the mid-eighteenth century and to a much wider region as production increased. This Midlothian coal field was the first to be mined in North America. William Byrd II, as we have seen, owned some of these mines in the early 1700s, but the first commercial production did not occur until 1748, when fifty tons were produced. Production rose to around 400 or 500 tons in the next three years, and to 14,000 by 1763. After the mines were modernized in 1798, the output of the Richmond basin mounted to 22,000 tons annually, and in the next thirty years to nearly 100,000. Exports of this coal went to New York, Philadelphia, Baltimore and New England, as well as to the West Indies and Europe. These eastern Virginia mines were the principal source of American coal until the 1830s. At that time, canals linked the Pennsylvania anthracite mines with the eastern seaboard, and Chesterfield coal began losing its more distant markets.[6]

During the colonial era, news of coal shipments and other matters of public interest appeared in the weekly *Virginia Gazette*. It was published at Williamsburg from its founding in 1737 until 1780, when Richmond became the capital and the paper was moved there.

Runaway wives, horses, dogs and slaves were advertised in the *Gazette*, which also contained much miscellaneous news, from notices of cockfights to the latest tidings from overseas, brought by ships taking several weeks, or more, for the crossing.

Richmond's population was growing steadily, although it was still an extremely small town. By 1769, the total number of inhabitants had increased to 574 from the 250 who were counted at the time of the incorporation in 1742. Annexation of an additional .54 of a square mile was accordingly decided upon, and was approved by the General Assembly. This gave Richmond an over-all area of .74 of a square mile, and brought within the corporate limits what is now Capitol Square and the territory westward as far as the present Foushee Street.

Houses in the Richmond of that day were not large or impressive. Eliza Ambler, whose sister would marry John Marshall a few years later, moved with her parents and sisters from Yorktown to Richmond when the capital was shifted to the latter place. She declared that although Richmond occupied "a beautiful situation" and "may at some future period be a great city," it afforded at that time "scarce one comfort of life." And she continued:

"With the exception of two or three families, this little town is made up of Scotch factors, who inhabit small tenements here and there from the river to the hill, some of which looking—as Colonel [Thomas] Marshall observes—as if the poor Caledonians had brought them over on their backs, the weaker of whom were glad to stop at the bottom of the hill, others a little stronger proceeded higher, while a few of the stoutest and boldest reached the summit." Eliza went on to say that "one of these hardy Scots has seen fit to vacate his little dwelling on the hill, and though our whole family can scarce stand up all together in it, my father has determined to rent it."

In addition to the Scottish merchants, there were craftsmen of various sorts, including cobblers, coopers, tailors, tinsmiths and cabinetmakers. They often had shops adjacent to their homes, and with the assistance of servants could operate what was tantamount to a small factory and retail store.

Horse races and cockfights were favorite diversions of Richmonders and other Virginians. There was much betting on these events. Wrestling matches and street brawls also provoked avid interest.

The tavern was the place of relaxation for males of high and low degree. Here gambling was frequent, and masculine society found an outlet for its energies. A clergyman wrote the *Virginia Gazette* in 1751 that taverns had "become the common Receptacle and Rendezvous of the People; even of the most lazy and dissolute." He deplored the "Cards, Dice, Horse-racing and Cock-fighting, together with Vices and Enormities of every other Kind."

Andrew Burnaby, the British visitor, found Virginians, including Richmonders, to be "indolent, inactive and unenterprising." He declared that the climate was responsible, and that it "operates very powerfully upon them."

As for Virginia ladies, Burnaby expressed the view that "they have but few advantages and consequently are seldom accomplished." He added that "they are immoderately fond of dancing, and indeed it is almost the only amusement they partake of."

This view is borne out to some extent by Edmund S. Morgan, who writes in his *Virginians at Home:* "It almost goes without saying that [Virginia] women [in the eighteenth century] did not read or write extensively. Their literary education generally ceased before they could become seriously interested in literature."

The foregoing would seem to be too sweeping. Virginia women of the upper classes were often taught to read and write good English. While they did not write books, highly literate letters are extant which show their familiarity with leading contemporary authors as well as those of earlier times.

Richmond and the James River Valley were visited in 1771 by one of the most terrible floods in their history. Exactly how it compared with such earlier disasters as those of 1667 and 1685, or such later ones as those of 1773, 1870, 1877, 1923, and 1969 is difficult to say, but it left death and catastrophe in its wake.

The huge wall of water that engulfed everything in its path hit Richmond with stunning force. Rain had been falling in torrents in the central Blue Ridge area for ten or twelve days in May 1771, but hardly a drop had dampened the capital city. Colonel Richard Adams, a highly responsible citizen, related that from the porch of his home on Church Hill he was astounded to see a flood "forty feet perpendicular" suddenly coming downstream. He added that anyone who had not viewed this amazing phenomenon with his own eyes would not have believed it possible. When the deluge reached full volume, dwellings came scudding on the surface of the raging river, along with warehouses, wine casks, hogsheads, trees, lumber and cattle. From the roofs of some of the fast-moving houses terrified persons called for help.

Richmond and its environs were struck a tremendous blow. The riverfront area was almost wrecked, the tobacco warehouses severely damaged and their contents largely ruined. The warehouses at Westham were washed downstream and out to sea, with three hundred hogsheads of tobacco. Ships also were swept from their moorings and lost. About a hundred and fifty persons, up and down the valley, are said to have died.

"In some places," according to an article in the *Virginia Gazette* of June 6, about a week after the flood, "trees, carcasses . . . are matted together from twelve to twenty feet in height and from the horrid stench there is no coming near enough to separate them."

So dire was the devastation that the General Assembly was called into special session. A total of £30,000 was provided for relief of those who had lost tobacco in warehouses.

The Randolph family of Turkey Island erected a monument to commemorate the disaster. The shaft, some eighteen feet high, was standing in 1976, surrounded by an iron fence, in woods on a farm at Turkey Bend in southeastern Henrico. The inscription reads:

The Foundation
of this PILLAR was laid
in the calamitous year
1771
When all the great Rivers
of this Country
were swept by Inundations
Never before experienced
Which changed the face of Nature
And left traces of their Violence
that will remain
For Ages.

# THREE

# Richmond in the Revolution

OMINOUS SIGNS of a clash with Great Britain loomed on the horizon in the early 1770s, and Richmonders, like other colonials, were aware that relations with the mother country were growing increasingly strained. Patrick Henry's defiant Stamp Act speech at Williamsburg in 1765 shocked the British, and the Stamp Act was repealed the following year. But the Boston Tea Party of 1773, when a mob threw hundreds of cases of British tea into Boston harbor, caused additional tension. There was a virtual blockade of Boston, and Richmonders joined with other colonists in sending food and money to the embattled citizens of that town.

The first Continental Congress at Philadelphia the following year adopted a Declaration of Rights and stated that the British Parliament had violated some of those rights. Intercolonial committees of correspondence were set up, and the government of Great Britain was greatly disturbed.

A Virginia convention, called without Governor Dunmore's permission, was summoned to meet in Richmond, since Williamsburg, the capital, was vulnerable to British attack. Richmond was hardly more than a village and smaller than either Norfolk or Fredericksburg. The largest meeting place available was the church atop the hill, later known as St. John's. Its dimensions were considerably less than those of today.

The possibility of armed hostilities with Great Britain, then the most powerful nation on the globe, was on the minds of many, as the delegates from throughout Virginia met in the little church on March 20, 1775. Patrick Henry had said the previous November that he regarded war as inevitable, but other leaders did not share that view, and hoped somehow for reconciliation with the far-flung empire of George III.

Virtually every great Virginian of the era was a member of the convention. George Washington, Thomas Jefferson, Richard Henry Lee, Richard

Bland, Archibald Cary, Edmund Pendleton, George Mason, Patrick Henry and dozens of others were delegates. They rode or drove to Richmond from lower Tidewater or beyond the mountains, some traveling as much as a week over abysmally bad roads and covering hundreds of miles. After tying their horses in or near the churchyard, and greeting one another, they entered the house of worship.

Peyton Randolph was elected chairman. Routine matters were disposed of on Monday, the opening day. Tuesday and Wednesday were largely concerned with proceedings of the recent Continental Congress. Then came Thursday. The atmosphere was electric as Patrick Henry rose in pew 47 to offer a resolution.

Henry was regarded as a firebrand and as the colony's foremost orator. Both Thomas Jefferson and John Randolph of Roanoke were to pronounce him, in later years, the greatest orator who ever lived. Jefferson, not his admirer in all respects, also declared him to have been "far above all in maintaining the spirit of the Revolution."

Henry was laboring, on that twenty-third day of March, 1775, under the spell of a great grief, for his wife, the former Sarah Shelton, had died shortly before at their Hanover County home, Scotchtown, after a long and distressing illness. Yet he threw himself into the debate with every ounce of his ardent nature.

His resolution provided that—

"A well-regulated militia . . . is the natural strength and only security of a free government. . . .

"Resolved, therefore, that this colony be immediately put into a posture of defense. . . ."

As he began to speak, with that indefinable quality in his voice noted by all observers, Henry was calm. Well aware that such men as Bland and Pendleton regarded his motion as premature, he was not dismayed. As he warmed to his subject his clear, resonant tones, with their strangely hypnotic effect, carried through the open windows to listeners outside.

Pulses in his audience were pounding as he proclaimed with mounting intensity, "We must fight! I repeat it, sir, we must fight!" And then, in words that were a bugle call to his countrymen, Patrick Henry uttered the phrases that were to make his name immortal:

"Why stand we here idle? . . . Is life so dear and peace so sweet as to be purchased at the price of chains and slavery? Forbid it, almighty God! I know not what course others may take; but as for me, give me liberty or give me death!"

Men sat stunned as the great orator concluded, so tremendous was the impact of his blazing eloquence. When his auditors had gathered their wits, two of them, Richard Henry Lee and Thomas Jefferson, supported his motion. But there was opposition, and when the debate was over, so much doubt remained as to the imminence of war that Henry's resolution carried by the narrow margin of 65 to 60. However, a strong committee, headed by Henry himself, was named to arm and train the militia. He had achieved his objective.

The "shot heard round the world" at Concord, Massachusetts, on April 19, 1775, and Governor Dunmore's seizure of the powder at Williamsburg on the following day were evidence that Patrick Henry's prophecy of war was being rapidly fulfilled.

Another convention was held at St. John's on July 17 for the purpose of organizing a provisional form of government. Defense of the colony was a prime objective. Plans were made for raising two regiments as well as various smaller units of minutemen and other fighting organizations. A Committee of Safety was appointed. It was decided to use tobacco in warehouses as money. A further brief convention took place at St. John's on December 1.

Years would pass before Richmond was again the scene of such momentous events. Meanwhile its young men were enlisting and drilling, in preparation for full-scale war. The cannon foundry at Westham, six miles above the town, was turning out guns. The Chatham Rope Yard was making rigging for ships, and the Rubsamen works across the river in Chesterfield was manufacturing powder.

Tory sentiment in Richmond was by no means so strong as in cosmopolitan Norfolk, with its six thousand inhabitants and substantial commerce with Great Britain. In Richmond, the relatively few Scottish merchants were the principal loyalists.

Great enthusiasm was manifested in the city at the end of June 1776 when news came from Williamsburg that a convention there had adopted a constitution for Virginia as an independent state, and had elected Patrick Henry governor.

Then, on August 5, the Declaration of Independence, adopted at Philadelphia on July 4, was "publicly proclaimed" in Richmond. It was a "court day," and the *Virginia Gazette* recorded that the ceremonies were attended by "a large concourse of respectable freeholders . . . and upwards of two hundred of the militia." There were "universal shouts of joy . . . reechoed by three vollies of small arms." The town was illuminated in the evening and "many patriotic toasts were drank." The "utmost decorum" prevailed.

Agitation for removal of the seat of government from Williamsburg to a more central location had been heard for decades, especially after the Capitol there was destroyed by fire in 1747. Finally, in 1779 the General Assembly decided to move, but Richmond was chosen by only a slight margin over the competing locality of Hanovertown, a small port on the Pamunkey River of which today not a trace remains.

The act of 1779 selecting Richmond as the capital provided that six squares of ground be set aside for the erection of public buildings. Public records had been taken to that city two years before for safekeeping from seizure by the British. Actual transfer of the capital occurred early in 1780.

An amazing event is said to have occurred in Richmond in May 1779. It furnished conversation for weeks, and diverted the minds of the citizenry from the war with Britain then raging far to the north and south.

Martin Hawkins, a great huntsman and fisherman, was dipping his net into the James for shad about half a mile above the site of the present Mayo's Bridge, when a huge sturgeon—a species plentiful in the river in earlier times—sidled up to the rock on which Hawkins was standing. The latter approached the fish stealthily from the direction of its tail and grabbed it suddenly and firmly in both gills. The sturgeon lurched violently, yanking Hawkins from his rock, but not breaking his grip. He rode the fish downstream. It went under, but Hawkins went too. Fish and rider emerged, with Hawkins' hold unbroken, as onlookers cheered. The giant sturgeon plunged again, but Hawkins held on. Fish and rider passed downstream, heading for Chesapeake Bay. By this time the sturgeon was becoming exhausted, as was Hawkins, but the latter managed to steer it to a sand bar on the Chesterfield side and wrestle it ashore. It measured ten feet long and weighed three hundred pounds. This "fish story" was vouched for by Dr. J. Russell Hawkins, clerk of the Kentucky Senate for twenty-five years, and was published in the *Religious Herald* for February 20, 1896. Dr. Hawkins, a nephew of the intrepid and powerful Martin, said his uncle was known thereafter as "the Sturgeon Rider."

The last year of the war, 1781, opened with the Benedict Arnold raid on Richmond. It was a humiliation to the city, which was caught completely by surprise.

Governor Thomas Jefferson was in residence, having succeeded Patrick Henry in 1779. He moved to Richmond the following year when the town became the capital. Exactly where the temporary, and modest, gubernatorial "mansion" was is not known. It was described as "on the hill," presumably Council Chamber Hill, a large mound southeast of today's Governor Street and long since leveled.

Jefferson was caught off guard by Arnold partly because, for reasons of economy, he had discontinued the couriers operating between Richmond and Hampton. He conceded later that if he had called out the militia two days earlier, Arnold probably would not have been able to reach Richmond with his force of some nine hundred men. Richmond and Virginia had relatively few defenders, since the best troops had been sent to those colonies where the active fighting was taking place.

The traitor Arnold, using the vastly superior British naval forces in the Hampton Roads area, was able to brush past the almost nonexistent patriot navy and proceed up the James at will. After pausing at Westover, he moved on to Four Mile Creek, twelve miles below Richmond. Arnold ordered Colonel J. G. Simcoe to march on the town in close formation, making as impressive an appearance as possible. The raw militia opposing the intruders numbered not more than three hundred and offered virtually no resistance. Arnold took Richmond practically without firing a shot. His forces remained in the town for almost twenty-four hours and did not lose a man.

When Governor Jefferson saw that his small force of militia could not cope with the British regulars, he ordered arms, military stores and important records taken to Westham for safekeeping. He was not then fully advised as to Arnold's objective, and thought it might be Williamsburg. But when he found that the renegade general was within a few miles of Richmond, he rode to Westham and supervised the sending of stores and records across the river. Jefferson remained at Westham until almost midnight and then went to Tuckahoe, the residence of his Randolph kinsmen. Next day he returned to Manchester and, looking across the river, saw the British entering unopposed. It was 1 P.M., January 5, 1781.

Mrs. Samuel Ege, whose husband was off serving the army as a commissary, watched from her Old Stone House as the British cavalry galloped down Richmond Hill, now Church Hill. Eliza Ambler wrote concerning the reaction of Richmond: "Such terror and confusion you have no idea of."

Arnold dispatched Simcoe and his Queen's Rangers to Westham, with orders to destroy the foundry, powder magazine and stores. He did a thorough job. Simcoe recorded in his *Military Journal* that "the trunions of many pieces of iron cannon were struck off," and a quantity of small arms and military stores were seized and demolished. Instead of blowing up the powder magazine the powder was carried "down the cliffs" and poured into the water. The warehouses and mills were set on fire, and "the foundry . . . a very complete one, was totally destroyed." Some of the important records taken to Westham by Jefferson also fell into British hands, as a result of misunderstood instructions. Simcoe brought his men back to Richmond that night, where, he conceded, "some of them got into private homes and there obtained rum." Other British soldiers captured additional stocks of liquor and a considerable debauch ensued. Headquarters of Arnold and Simcoe are understood to have been at the City Tavern, Nineteenth and Main streets, later Galt's Tavern.

Next day, the invaders burned a number of public and private buildings and destroyed large stores of tobacco, as well as valuable records in the Henrico County Courthouse. Arnold had offered not to burn the entire town if he were permitted to remove the tobacco from the warehouses and place it on board British ships. His offer had been immediately rejected by Governor Jefferson, so the British general proceeded to carry out his threat, at least in part. Fortunately, he did not put the whole town to the torch, and he apparently overlooked the crude three-story frame structure being used as a temporary capitol. This building at the northwest corner of what is today Fourteenth and Cary streets—the site is marked by a bronze tablet—was not touched. Neither was "Ye Olde Senet House," a one-story frame building adjoining it on the west side of Fourteenth.

A surprising incident was Arnold's effort to contribute twenty guineas for the relief of Richmond's poor. The money was given to James Buchanan, a local merchant, who, like Arnold, was a Mason. When Jefferson heard of it, he directed General von Steuben to see that the money was returned. Von Steuben complied.[1]

Arnold withdrew his troops from Richmond at noon on January 6. Jefferson was criticized for the raid, and some of the criticism was just. Much of it was not. He should have been more alert to the looming incursion, but once he realized that Arnold was about to attack Richmond, he was zealous in carrying out his duties. Jefferson was on horseback for many hours, much of it in snow and rain. In fact, his horse became exhausted and he had to get another to complete his journeyings.

Arnold was on the prowl again a few months later. In April, he and Major General William Phillips, who was in command, moved their forces up the James in eleven square-rigged vessels. Fortunately, Lafayette had been detached by Washington shortly before with a small contingent to aid in Virginia's defense. By forced marches, he arrived just in time to thwart the plans of Arnold and Phillips for taking Richmond once more. They got as far as Manchester, but finding themselves confronted on the opposite side of the stream by Lafayette, they deemed a river crossing too risky and contented themselves with burning the Manchester tobacco warehouses. They also destroyed similar warehouses in Petersburg, and permanently wrecked the thriving port of Warwick, below Richmond on the Chesterfield side.

Shortly thereafter, the General Assembly fled from Richmond to Charlottesville, on the approach of cavalry raiders under Colonel Banastre Tarleton, "the Hunting Leopard." Most of the assemblymen, along with Governor Jefferson and Patrick Henry, were saved from capture there by the heroic forty-mile ride of Captain Jack Jouett from Cuckoo Tavern. After driving the legislature out of Charlottesville and forcing it to move on to Staunton, Tarleton joined Cornwallis west of Richmond.

The Britons saw that the town was largely undefended, and took it easily. They remained there several days for rest and forage. Stores assembled since the Arnold raid in January were pillaged.

Lafayette learned that the British were in Richmond. Having been strongly reinforced by "Mad Anthony" Wayne, he prepared to attack them. The Americans arrived June 22, just after the enemy marched off to Williamsburg. Lafayette and Wayne continued in hot pursuit.

A marker designating the movements of Cornwallis and Tarleton was erected in 1916 near the former entrance to the Country Club of Virginia. It says:

"This Boulder Marks the Beginning of Three Chopt Road.

"The British Legion under command of Lt. Col. Tarleton passed over this road in June, 1781, when returning from the raid upon Charlottesville. Along the intersecting River Road, Earl Cornwallis led his force from the Point of Fork. The two forces united in the vicinity of this site and entered Richmond. On June 21, 1781, Cornwallis evacuated Richmond and marched toward Williamsburg."

It was during this period that James, a slave from a New Kent County plantation near Richmond, rendered valuable service to the patriot cause. Early in 1781 he obtained permission from his master, William Armistead, to enlist, and was attached to the entourage of General Lafayette. The latter placed so high a value on his services that he entrusted him with important espionage within the enemy lines. James was especially useful on dangerous missions to Portsmouth, then held by the British. He obtained valuable information concerning their plans and movements. Out of affection for his commander, James took the name of James Lafayette.

James Lafayette was in General Lafayette's service when the latter took part in the bottling up of Cornwallis at Yorktown in the autumn of 1781. The Briton surrendered his army to Washington on October 19, and for all practical purposes the war was over.

When General Lafayette was in Richmond after the Revolution, in 1784, he wrote a testimonial acknowledging James's "essential services to me" in obtaining "intelligence from the enemy" which was "industriously collected and more faithfully delivered." This resulted in James's emancipation by the General Assembly. The former slave bought forty acres in New Kent County, acquired a few slaves of his own, married and raised a family. Much later, in 1818, when he was seventy years of age, he petitioned the General Assembly for a pension, pointing to his service in the revolution and saying that in his old age he had suffered "a natural decline of his bodily powers." The Assembly promptly granted him $60 in cash and an annual pension of $40. James Lafayette died in 1830.

He had been something of a celebrity in his later years. John B. Martin, a leading portrait painter of the time, did his likeness in oil. When the elderly Marquis de Lafayette returned to Richmond on his famous visit in 1824, he greeted his former spy with great warmth.

James Lafayette was a leading character in James E. Heath's novel of the revolution, *Edge-Hill*, published in 1828 and praised by Edgar Allan Poe. Heath was Auditor of the State, and in that capacity paid Lafayette his pension. He was termed by Poe in 1841 "almost the only person of any literary distinction in Richmond."[2]

The surrender at Yorktown doubtless was celebrated in Richmond with loud cannonading, volleys of small arms, toasts in old Madeira and a day and night of wassail. The *Virginia Gazette* had temporarily suspended publication, so no account of the observance is available from that source. Yet one can easily imagine the fervor of the celebrations and the brilliance of the "illuminations"—from Richmond Hill to Shockoe Hill and everything in between.

The conflict heralded at Richmond six and a half years before in the fiery eloquence of Patrick Henry had ended at last in victory.

# FOUR

# Statesmen, Merchants, Fashions, Taverns and Hangings

HOSTILITIES with Britain had ended, but Richmond was licking its wounds from the Benedict Arnold raid. Tories were still extremely unpopular, and in 1782 Governor Benjamin Harrison ordered all British merchants to wind up their affairs and leave the state. Tempers cooled by the following year, however, and the General Assembly repealed the law forbidding Tories to return to Virginia, the only exceptions being those who had been on active service with the British forces. The merchants who had been ordered out came back and maintained their important role in Richmond's business community for many years.

Removal of the seat of government from Williamsburg to Richmond in 1780 brought an influx of prominent citizens, especially lawyers, to the new capital. These attorneys were soon to be recognized as spectacularly talented—so much so, that Edward S. Corwin has termed the Richmond bar the most brilliant in America at the period.

Among the first to arrive was Edmund Randolph, later governor of Virginia, U. S. Attorney General and Secretary of State. John Marshall took up his residence in Richmond in 1783, after being mustered out of the Continental Army and walking from Fauquier County to Philadelphia and back, averaging thirty-five miles a day, to get a smallpox inoculation. Marshall would be Richmond's foremost citizen for decades.

The town's leaders were anxious that Virginia's capital have formal recognition as a city. They obtained a charter of incorporation from the General Assembly in 1782.

Four years later, annexation of territory on Shockoe Hill and Church Hill increased Richmond's area to 1.08 square miles. This gave the city 280 houses, by actual count, and a population of about 1800, half of whom were slaves. There were 290 houses in Petersburg, 300 in Alexandria and 230 in Williamsburg.[1]

The city charter provided for the election by the property holders of a mayor and council, called the Common Hall. A meeting was therefore held at the Henrico County Courthouse on July 2, 1782, and the voters chose "twelve fit and able men." Again following directions, the twelve elected from among themselves a mayor, namely Dr. William Foushee; a recorder, William Hay; and four aldermen: Jaquelin Ambler, John Beckley, Robert Mitchell and James Hunter. The remaining six automatically became members of the Common Council. They were Richard Adams, Isaac Younghusband, James Buchanan, Samuel Scherer, Robert Boyd and John McKeand. There was not a tavern keeper on the list, since keepers of public houses were ineligible, under the charter, to hold any of these offices.

Richmond's physical contours were undergoing steady changes. The river front, for example, was hardly the same from one year to the next, for there was much filling in to create sites for buildings and streets, and the floods or "freshes" altered the terrain still further.

After the Revolution there was a popular river-front promenade from about Nineteenth to Twenty-third Street, "a grassy walk, shaded by elm and other trees." At the eastern end of this verdant footpath skirting the James was a high cliff, the base of which could be reached at low tide by strollers across the sands.

Shockoe Creek, which entered the river just west of Seventeenth Street, was a by no means negligible stream in those days. Main Street pedestrians crossed it by a narrow footbridge, while horse-drawn wagons forded it. In times of freshet, ferries had to be improvised.

There was, of course, nothing remotely resembling paving throughout the length of Main Street, the city's chief thoroughfare, except for occasional rough patches of sidewalk. The street terminated on the west at about the present Eleventh Street, and beyond that point there were gullies and swamps. During dry weather, Main Street was deep in choking dust, and in rainy seasons the mud was well nigh fathomless. Higher on the slopes of Shockoe Hill the contours of the land were in many respects different from those of today. The area known as the "public square," soon to become Capitol Square, was slashed by deep gulches. Its mounds would have to be leveled and its ravines filled in. What later became Governor Street, just east of the square, was a country road, winding down a steep and dangerous hill, near the edge of a high cliff.

Miniature canyons were ominous features of the landscape beyond the square to the north. Clay and Leigh streets were separated by one of these from Sixth to Sixteenth, while beyond Leigh a second declivity stretched from Fourth to Fourteenth. Marshall Street was blocked at Twelfth by still another.

Shockoe Hill, the present site of the Capitol, had been chosen by the General Assembly in 1780 as the location for that structure, and Governor Jefferson and the Directors of Public Buildings were empowered to acquire the land on which the Capitol and adjacent public buildings were to be placed. Colonel Richard Adams believed that Jefferson had promised to put the Capitol and the other public structures on Church Hill. Adams had agreed to donate the necessary site or sites. When the Assembly, with Jefferson's concurrence, selected Shockoe Hill, Adams considered that Jefferson had broken his promise, and their long friendship is said to have been permanently ruptured. Years before, Adams had purchased nearly all of Church Hill, most of it from William Byrd III and the rest from Isaac Coles.[2]

The site for the Capitol was acquired through condemnation proceedings. Once the location was definitely chosen, land values rose sharply in the area west of Shockoe Creek. Many persons who, a decade and a half earlier, had won tracts of land as prizes in William Byrd III's lottery, but had not claimed them, now became interested in acquiring these lots. Charles Carter, sole surviving trustee for Byrd's property, was accordingly empowered by the legislature to execute the deeds of conveyance for the tracts.

The barnlike structure erected in 1780 at the northwest corner of Fourteenth and Cary streets, which had been serving as a temporary capitol, would be used by the General Assembly until the new statehouse was ready for occupancy in 1788.

Governor Jefferson had completed his term, and was serving as Minister to France. He was requested by the Directors of Public Buildings to provide a suitable design for the headquarters of Virginia's government. Setting to work at once, he selected as his model the Maison Carrée, an ancient Roman temple at Nîmes, France, which he termed "one of the most beautiful, if not the most beautiful and precious morsels of architecture left to us by antiquity." He wrote that he had spent hours gazing at this temple, "like a lover at his mistress."

Jefferson requested C. L. Clérisseau, a well-known French architect, to make detailed drawings and have a model constructed of the projected building in Richmond. He directed Clérisseau to change the capitals on the columns from Corinthian to Ionic because of the difficulty in carrying out the more ornate Corinthian design. Adapting the Roman temple to the requirements of Virginia's government, Jefferson submitted to the architect a plan for the interior, with rooms for the discharge of legislative, executive and judicial functions. These were put into execution, Jefferson wrote subsequently, "with some variations, not for the better."

The cornerstone of the Capitol was laid August 18, 1785, with Masonic ceremonies. A large percentage of the citizenry was present, including Governor Patrick Henry.

By 1788, the Capitol was sufficiently near completion for the General Assembly to meet there in October of that year. However, various details had not been attended to, including a leaky roof. This was taken care of, but it was not until 1798 that stucco was applied to the brick exterior, in accordance with the specifications. Construction of the steps to the portico was delayed for well over a century—until 1906, when the two wings, not in the original plans, were added. Those plans also had called for the placing of a market and jail in Capitol Square, but the concept was abandoned.

In its partially completed state, the Capitol evoked various opinions from foreign visitors. Isaac Weld, Jr., of Dublin, wrote that "from the opposite side of the river this building appears extremely well, but on close inspection it proves to be a clumsy, ill-shapen pile." The French Duke de la Rochefoucauld-Liancourt, on the other hand, pronounced it "beyond comparison, the finest, the most noble and the greatest in all America." The duke's tribute may have been a bit extravagant, but Jefferson's genius had once more produced a masterpiece. The Capitol at Richmond influenced architectural trends profoundly, both in this country and abroad.

Robert Hunter, Jr., a young Englishman, found Richmond "one of the dirtiest holes of a place I ever was in." Cities in that era were hardly notable for cleanliness. John Page of Rosewell, writing from New York, pronounced Gotham's streets "very dirty and narrow, as well as crooked . . . full of hogs and mud."

The need to protect Richmond from destructive fires caused a group of prominent citizens to form the Fellowship Fire Company. It proved effective, in a small way, but on January 8, 1787, between 3 and 4 A.M., a devastating conflagration broke out. Fanned by a high wind, the flames spread rapidly and destroyed almost all of the buildings on the south side of Main Street from Tenth to Fifteenth and many north of Main, including Byrd's warehouse with quantities of tobacco. In all about fifty houses, with their contents, valued at more than $500,000, were wiped out—a grievous shock to the little town. It was only by the demolition of nearby buildings that the temporary capitol was saved. The Treasury Building, on the west side of Locust Alley below Franklin, had a narrow escape. The money and papers that it contained were hastily removed.

Sympathy for Richmond was expressed throughout Virginia, and committees for the collection of funds were appointed in all the principal towns. Steady progress in rebuilding was made, despite the statement of the French Marquis de Chastellux that "indolence and cupidity go hand in hand in Virginia."

The marquis and various other visitors were shocked by the gambling and brawling in the taverns, and the frequent street fights. Gouging out of eyes with long fingernails, hardened in a candle to make them diabolically lethal, was often a part of these savage physical encounters. So was biting the nose or the ears.

Isaac Weld, Jr., gives the most vivid picture of these violent affrays, which were almost always between members of what were called "the lower orders."

"Whenever these people come to blows, they fight just like wild beasts, biting, kicking, and endeavoring to tear each other's eyes out with their nails. . . . This is called *gouging*—the combatant twists his forefingers in the side locks of his adversary's hair and then applies his thumbs to the bottom of the eye, to force it out of the socket . . . their faces are generally cut in a shocking manner with the thumb nails. . . . But what is worse than all, these wretches . . . endeavor to their utmost to tear out each other's testicles. Four or five instances came within my own observation."

Dr. William Foushee—later Richmond's beloved first mayor, for whom Foushee Street is named—almost lost an eye when he was viciously attacked during the Revolution by someone who became enraged because he thought the doctor was too friendly with paroled British officers. Thomas Anburey, one of the officers, said that Foushee's assailant "flew at him, and in an instant had turned his eye out of the socket, and while it hung upon his cheek, the fellow was barbarous enough to endeavor to pluck it entirely out, but was prevented."

Anburey was high in praise of the "first class" of Virginians, "gentlemen of the best families and fortunes, which are more respectable and numerous here than in any other province." He was also one of many who praised the hospitality experienced by visitors to Richmond and other parts of the Old Dominion.

William Ellery Channing, who had just been graduated from Harvard, and who would become an eminent Unitarian divine, spent eighteen months in Richmond, as tutor in the family of David Meade Randolph. Young Channing was eloquent in his reference to the openhanded manner in which he was received everywhere. And he went on to say:

"I blush for my own people when I compare the selfish prudence of the Yankee with the generous confidence of a Virginian. Here I find great vices, but greater virtues than I left behind me. There is one single trait which attaches me to the people I live with more than all the virtues of New England. They *love money less* than we do. They are more disinterested. Their patriotism is not tied to their purse-strings. Could I only take from the Virginians their *sensuality* and their *slaves*, I should think them the greatest people in the world."

Bullfrogs, lightning bugs and thunderstorms impressed another visitor, J. F. D. Smyth of England. The frogs he described as "emitting a most tremendous roar, louder than the bellowing of a bull." He was also astonished by another "roar"—that of The Falls—which, he said, was "heard for many miles."

A youthful Bavarian surgeon, Johann D. Schoepf, was astonished by the lack of attention to business shown by members of the legislature. "This estimable assembly," he wrote, was not quite "five minutes together. Some are leaving, others coming in, most of them talking of insignificant or irrelevant matters . . . horse races, runaway Negroes, yesterday's play." Schoepf also criticized the informal and undignified attire of the lawmakers. Members, he said, "wore the same clothes in which one goes hunting or tends his tobacco fields." Another German traveler found conditions in the British House of Commons to be almost identical.

Schoepf went on to state that word of the final signing of the peace treaty with Great Britain in 1783 was the occasion in Richmond for "illuminations, fireworks, banquetings, and finally a ball at which the honor of the first dance fell by lot to the very honorable daughter of a very honorable shoemaker." This last was received "with great displeasure" by the "ladies of the Governor's family and his relatives."

Schoepf was lodged at Formicola's tavern, on the south side of Main between Fifteenth and Seventeeth streets. It was operated by a Neapolitan who had been maître d'hôtel to Lord Dunmore, governor of Virginia at the time of the Revolution. The Bavarian noted that here, as elsewhere in America, "it is expected that taverns are to be used only as places for sleeping, eating and drinking." He added that Formicola's had two large rooms on the ground floor and two on the upper. The upstairs bedrooms were occupied by numerous persons, with beds close together, and the doors open at all times—"an indelicate custom," he thought. The Assembly was meeting, the taverns were crowded, and Formicola's was no exception. There, "generals, colonels, captains, senators, assemblymen, judges, doctors, clerks and crowds of gentlemen of every weight and calibre . . . sat all together about the fire, drinking, smoking, singing and talking ribaldry."

Various other taverns were operating in the city, but no "hotels." Among the better-known establishments were the Bird in the Hand, on the northwest corner of Main and Twenty-fifth streets; Hogg's, southwest corner, Fifteenth and Main; Galt's, northwest corner, Nineteenth and Main; Cowley's, southwest corner, Twenty-third and Main; Bowler's, later the Bell, northeast corner, Fifteenth and Main; and the Swan, between Eighth and Ninth on the north side of Broad. Three other inns were situated in more out-of-the-way locations; Rocketts Landing Tavern, facing the river in the area of the docks, was one of these, and Baker's Tavern (later Goddin's), on Brook Avenue, and Richards' Tavern, on the north side of Broad between today's Fifth and Sixth streets, were the others.

Rocketts Landing catered to the crews of the many ships that tied up at Richmond's wharves, while Baker's and Richards' did business primarily with the drivers of fleets of wagons that came from the Piedmont or from beyond the Blue Ridge. These wagons, covered with dust or spattered with mud, were pulled by from four to six powerful horses, with bells jingling from their harness and bearskins over their withers. The lurching vehicles, with white canvas tops, often traveled in groups of six or eight, and were driven by weather-beaten, hairy men. They were loaded with furs, lead, tallow, maple sugar, salt, wax, ginseng, butter, flour, deer and bear skins, dried rattlesnakes for making "viper broth for consumptive patients" and other commodities. On arrival somewhere in the area of what is now First and Broad streets they headed for the nearest camping ground and bivouacked. At night, their campfires lit up the sky.

When they had rested, and perhaps had a round of drinks and a meal at Baker's or Richards' Tavern, they continued on to the city's business district, often crossing Capitol Square by a rough road leading diagonally from Ninth Street, at about where St. Paul's Church stands, to Eleventh and on down to Main.

The creaking wagons from the upcountry were in contrast to the elegant and brightly painted "coaches" and "chariots" in which the Richmond gentry traveled over the city streets and the suburban roads. These latter conveyances were usually imported from England and were customarily drawn by four horses.

The preferred color for the body of the "coach" was yellow, the wheels were red and the top black. Four passengers could be accommodated, in addition to the driver, and there were one or two footmen in the rear. The interior was usually lined with red morocco, and large lamps on either side lighted the way across the ruts and mudholes.

The "chariot" was less imposing and more utilitarian. It carried two passengers plus the driver, with no footman. Dark green and olive were often the colors for the superstructure, with the wheels a brighter hue. The chariot was regarded as better suited than the coach for long journeys.

In addition, there was the two-wheeled "chair," holding only one person and pulled by one horse. This vehicle was used by citizens in all stations of life, and was the predecessor of the "gig," which, in turn, was the forerunner of the "buggy." The gig was much like the chair, except that it could carry two persons.

Private carriages were unusually numerous for a town the size of Richmond. Walking on the unpaved streets and roads was difficult, even in the daytime, and while the town itself was small, a number of the wealthier families lived well outside the corporate limits. There were no hacks for hire in that era, so that without a carriage such a family was almost immobilized.

Richmonders in the late eighteenth century were great horse lovers. In addition to keeping the high-stepping animals that pulled their carriages, they were avid devotees of the race track and the hunting field. The quality of the Virginia horses used for these purposes was exceptional. Johann Schoepf, the surgeon with German mercenaries who fought beside the British in the Revolution, declared that "Virginia supplied the best and finest horses to the American cavalry." So fond of horses were the Virginians, he said, that "a horse must be mounted if only to fetch a prise of snuff from across the way." On the other hand, Schoepf asserted that the Virginians had "no good draught and work horses, and their teams, in the low country, at least, are extremely sorry."

Medicine in Richmond at the period was in a primitive state, by modern standards. Yet it had come a long way in a few decades, for during the middle years of the century the place had been infested with quacks, offering cures for cancer and other maladies. The General Assembly was frequently importuned by these characters for substantial sums, as a reward for supposed cures. The legislators apparently did not fall for their blandishments.

Somewhat earlier, William Byrd II had been an amateur medical practitioner of considerable merit. He was an ingenious user of herbs and other simple remedies—as, for example, ginseng, which, he said, "frisks the spirits beyond any other cordial."

After the Revolution, there were several prominent medical men in Richmond, notably Dr. William Foushee and Dr. James McClurg. Both had studied at the University of Edinburgh, and both served as president of the Medical Society of Virginia. Dr. Foushee was not only Richmond's first mayor, but he was also, at one time or another, a member of the General Assembly and the Council of State, postmaster of the city and president of the James River Company. He pioneered in the newly discovered inoculation for smallpox, and announced in 1788 that the magistrates of Henrico County had given him permission to do inoculations in a house outside the city. Dr. McClurg had studied elsewhere in Europe after finishing at Edinburgh. He served with the Continental Army in the Revolution, and then occupied the chair of medicine at the College of William and Mary. He was a Virginia delegate to the Constitutional Convention at Philadelphia in 1787 and was mayor of Richmond for three terms.

There were no dentists in Richmond in the late eighteenth century and only one "tooth-drawer," a Negro named Peter Hawkins, who lived on Brook Avenue. He rode around town on horseback, for, as Samuel Mordecai says in his charming book *Richmond in By-Gone Days*, "his practice was too extensive to be managed on foot, and he carried all his instruments, consisting of two or three pullikins, in his pocket." Mordecai goes on to declare that "his strength of wrist was such that he would almost infallibly extract, or break a tooth, whether the right or the wrong one . . . he extracted two for me, a sound and an aching one, with one wrench of his instrument."

"Tooth-drawing," or medical services, for planters with estates outside the city must have been difficult, in view of communication problems. However, many of these planters left their country places in the hands of overseers and spent the greater part of the year in their town houses. When these men were added to the better class of merchants and the state officials in the city, the level of intelligence among Richmond's upper crust would seem to have been relatively high. Yet Dr. John P. Little says in his history of Richmond that the city in the final years of the century was "more famous for its amusements in racing, drinking and frolicking . . . than for those of a higher intellectual character."

Such *divertissements* comported with Richmond's reputation for hospitality. Young Albert Gallatin, a native of Switzerland and later U. S. Secretary of the Treasury, was one of those who expressed gratitude for the manner in which he was received. Coming to the city in 1783, to remain during much of the next six years, Gallatin said he was accorded "that old Virginia hospitality, to which I know no parallel anywhere within the circle of my travels . . . everyone with whom I became acquainted appeared to take an interest in the young stranger." Among those who took a special interest were John Marshall and Patrick Henry.

Gallatin was received with open arms by Richmond's elite, but for persons having no special entree, prominent citizens of the town organized what was called the Amicable Society. Its purpose was to "relieve strangers and wayfarers in distress" and to promote various charitable causes. The society continued to function effectively until well into the nineteenth century, with social and business leaders forming its membership.

Ladies and gentlemen were wont in the 1780s to garb themselves in decidedly fancy raiment. An excellent insight into the kind of apparel that was being worn may be had from the advertisements in the *Virginia Gazette.* "Leghorn hats" were available to the ladies, and gentlemen could buy "rich flortenites for waist-coats and breeches"—a textile fabric of silk or wool. Both sexes could obtain paste shoe buckles at one emporium, while another announced that it had lately imported from France "bell hoops and ladies' Italian stays, muslins, plain, striped, sprigged and checked, drab coats, ladies' riding hats trimmed with feathers, satin and calimanco shoes, elegant lute strings [a glossy silk fabric for dresses and ribbons], satins, silk handkerchiefs, silk stockings, ribands, feathers, and artificial flowers, garlands, white and colored kid gloves for ladies and gentlemen, paste necklaces, puffs and hair powder, pomatum and perfumes."

Fashions began changing in the 1790s, under the impact of the French Revolution and with the arrival in Virginia of the French who had fled from Santo Domingo, following the massacres there. Richmond's cocked hats, breeches and stockings with top boots were on the way out, thanks to the French influence, and pantaloons and shoes were coming in. Coun-

try delegates to the General Assembly were agitated to discover "the fashion of narrow garments and the sect of naked ladies." French wines
replaced English beer and ale in many households and taverns.

The French influx was of considerable magnitude, and included a large
number of French language teachers or instructors in dancing. Earlier arrivals had been the Chevalier Quesnay de Beaurepaire and Jean Auguste
Marie Chevallié, of whom more anon.

Among the Germans in Richmond was Samuel Scherer, a veteran of the
Revolution, a member of the first Common Council and of the Virginia
Convention of 1788. Frederick William Ast, who pioneered in the field of
mutual fire insurance, was another important arrival from Germany. He
spent years promoting his ideas on how best to protect against destruction by fire, and in 1794 obtained a charter from the legislature for the Mutual Assurance Society Against Fire in Buildings. This organization, later
the vigorous and successful Mutual Assurance Society of Virginia, is the
oldest fire insurance company in the South. It wrote the first policies on
George Washington's Mount Vernon and Thomas Jefferson's Monticello,
as well as on the home of John Marshall in Richmond.

German Jews were a significant element in early Richmond. They had
much to do with founding Beth Shalome synagogue in 1789. The congregation also included Dutch, Spanish and Portuguese Jews, and in the early
years the services were conducted in Spanish and Portuguese. When
George Washington was inaugurated as President in 1790, Beth Shalome
was one of the six original Jewish congregations in the United States
which sent him congratulations.

Beth Shalome dedicated the first Jewish cemetery in Virginia in 1791. A
plot on the south side of Franklin Street between Twentieth and Twenty-
first streets was donated for the purpose by Isaiah Isaacs. When it was
abandoned in 1817 for the larger cemetery at the head of Fourth Street,
several bodies were removed to the new burying ground. As the years
passed, the old cemetery was almost forgotten. It came to be used as a coal
and wood yard and a dumping ground for junk. Not until the early years
of the twentieth century was there sufficient interest in this historic spot
for it to be cleared of rubbish and protected by a concrete wall. It was
taken over by the Cemetery Board of the city in 1909, and reconsecrated
with appropriate religious services.

Reference has been made to the Chevalier Quesnay de Beaurepaire, the
most eminent of the French émigrés to Richmond in the late eighteenth
century. Quesnay had been among the first of the French to volunteer in
1776 for service in the American Revolution. He fought as a member of
naval forces in the Chesapeake Bay area, and narrowly escaped death on
several occasions.

Quesnay was introduced to John Page, president of the Virginia Council of State, who suggested that, after the war, he should establish in this

country a French academy with a European staff of instructors. The cultured Frenchman was impressed with the proposal, and sought to carry it out, with a curriculum revolving around what he termed "the polite arts" —modern languages, the fine arts, music and the drama. He tried to launch the idea in New York City in 1784, but found the New Yorkers to be more interested in trivial diversions than in serious study. So the following year he decided to promote Page's idea in Richmond. After testing the waters, he was discouraged to find that Richmond, like New York, seemed largely indifferent. The people of the town, he declared, "are inclined to encourage none of the branches [of the polite arts] except dancing." He said he would give them one year to demonstrate that they wanted a fine arts academy.

Quesnay thereupon began an intensive campaign of promotion and money raising, which extended to Petersburg and Norfolk. He enlisted the cooperation of many leading citizens, including Governor Edmund Randolph and Mayor John Harvie. Sufficient funds were obtained to construct the central portion of the Academy Building, on Academy Square, bounded by the present Broad, Twelfth and Marshall streets, and extending slightly beyond College Street. Quesnay impounded a small nearby stream—there were numerous streams and springs in early Richmond—with a view to irrigating botanical gardens to be laid out behind the Academy Building.

Pending the collection of more adequate funds, and in the hope of strengthening his financial position, Quesnay rented out the Academy Building temporarily for theatrical purposes. The financial results were disappointing, and he resorted to accepting "country produce" at the box office from those unable to pay cash—thus antedating Robert Porterfield and his famous Barter Theatre at Abingdon by nearly a century and a half.

Discouraged by his lack of progress, Quesnay slipped quietly out of Richmond in 1787, confident that in Paris he could obtain the necessary backing for his project and the desired teaching staff. In France, he was well received in the highest circles, and he talked of expanding the Academy's curriculum and of establishing branches in New York, Philadelphia and Baltimore. His principal discouragement came from Thomas Jefferson, then Minister to France, who pronounced the project much too ambitious and expensive, and impossible of realization. Quesnay was proceeding, nevertheless, with his plans, when the fall of the Bastille on July 14, 1789, launched the French Revolution. Quesnay became deeply involved in this cataclysm on the side of the revolutionaries while most of those to whom he had looked for aid were aligned with the monarchy. The shattering effect of the Revolution was such that Quesnay's plans were totally disrupted. He did not return to Virginia. The Academy Building, then being used mainly for theatrical productions, was destroyed by fire in 1798, thus putting an end to the whole Academy scheme.

By far the most important event that had taken place in the Academy auditorium during its brief existence was the meeting of the Virginia Convention of 1788, called to decide whether the Old Dominion would ratify the Federal Constitution adopted at Philadelphia the year before. Much depended on the attitude of Virginia, the largest and most populous of the thirteen states.

Delegates to the convention moved on Richmond by stagecoach and private vehicle in late May and early June. Stage lines linking the town with Alexandria and Petersburg had been chartered a few years before. The conveyances and their passengers were caked with dust, for a severe drought had seared the countryside. Deliberations were to open on Monday, June 2, and on Sunday the taverns were crowded with both delegates and would-be spectators. Patrick Henry arrived at the Swan from his Southside plantation in "a plain topless stick gig," while Edmund Pendleton came from Caroline County in "an elegant vehicle then known as a phaeton." The two noted political antagonists met and exchanged greetings on the steps of the tavern near Ninth and Broad, where both had reserved rooms. The Swan was within strolling distance of the Academy, and a number of the leading participants in the conclave had lodgings there.

The sessions opened next day in the temporary capitol at Fourteenth and Cary streets, which was barely able to accommodate the delegates. After organizing, and electing Pendleton chairman, the convention adjourned to meet the following morning in the Academy, which had the largest auditorium in town.

Yet the number of spectators throughout the convention was such that it, too, was taxed beyond its capacity. Some of the most famous Virginians of the era were delegates, and the people of Richmond crowded the hot, humid galleries to see and hear them in action. Among these notables, in addition to Pendleton and Henry, were George Wythe, Edmund Randolph, "Light-Horse Harry" Lee, John Marshall, James Madison, George Mason and James Monroe.

The proponents of ratification were led by Madison, Wythe, Lee, Randolph, Marshall and Pendleton, while the arguments of the opposition were presented by Mason, Monroe and others, above all by Patrick Henry. The latter's thunderous denunciations fill more than one fifth of the convention's published proceedings.

Sentiment in the state is believed to have been opposed to ratification, and the outcome was in doubt until the final vote. George Washington, who had declined to be a delegate, made it plain in letters to Richmond friends that he was strongly in favor of the new Constitution. His support counted for much in determining the final result.

The debates were among the ablest ever heard in this country, and they lasted for more than three weeks. They were occasionally acrimonious, and at one point a duel was narrowly averted. A violent thunderstorm toward the end of the convention shook the foundations of the building and rattled the windows when Patrick Henry was delivering one of his reverberating orations. The roars and flashes outside the hall were an obbligato to the eloquence within.

Advocates of ratification realized that they probably could not win unless they urged that a Declaration of Rights be added to the Constitution at the earliest possible moment. Assurances were given that these representations would be made to Congress.

When the crucial vote was taken on June 25, ratification won, 89 to 79. It was a narrow victory, for the shift of half a dozen delegates would have meant defeat. Failure of Virginia to ratify might well have been catastrophic to the future of the Union, in view of the Old Dominion's size and importance. The state at that time included today's Kentucky and West Virginia, and hence bisected the country from the Atlantic to the Mississippi. But the advocates of ratification triumphed, albeit by a perilously thin margin. Richmonders who had watched the proceedings eagerly could go back to their horse races and cockfights, their card games of faro and loo.[3]

John Marshall had played a significant role in the convention, although he was hardly in the top echelon of leadership. As a lawyer he was recognized already as equal to any at the brilliant Richmond bar. Yet he was only thirty-two years old, and his formal legal training consisted of three months' study at the College of William and Mary, under the celebrated George Wythe. William Wirt, afterward U. S. Attorney General, said that Marshall had achieved such a reputation that when he appeared before the United States Supreme Court at Philadelphia in the early 1790s, he was "justly pronounced one of the greatest men of the country . . . followed by crowds, looked upon and courted with every evidence of admiration and respect for the powers of his mind."

Marshall was perhaps the worst-dressed man who ever rose to national prominence in America. His slovenly attire, his complete indifference to the sartorial amenities were marked characteristics throughout his long life. In addition, his movements were awkward and gangling, his voice hard and dry, and when he spoke publicly his gestures were stiff and inept.

All the more remarkable, then, is the fact that John Marshall was not only Richmond's first citizen for many years, but also the greatest Chief Justice in America's history. The tremendous force of his intellect and character was widely recognized, while his keen sense of humor and utter lack of pretense endeared him to his friends. His dress was atrocious, except when he wore his judicial robes, but his handsome face and fine dark eyes were exceptionally winning. Marshall's "lawyer dinners" in his Richmond home, where the Madeira flowed freely and the jests and quips crackled around the board, exemplified his hospitable disposition and his warm personality.

An event of the early 1800s serves to illustrate his informality and love of fun. He was Chief Justice at the time, but his dress was, of course, uncouth as he loitered on the fringes of Richmond's market. Taking him for a yokel, a stranger approached him with a newly bought turkey and asked him to carry it. Marshall took the bird and sauntered along behind the man. When they arrived at the latter's destination, the stranger tendered a coin. There are conflicting versions as to whether the Chief Justice accepted the gratuity or declined it. At all events, Richmond nearly split its sides over the episode.

Marshall was an active and prominent Mason, and as city recorder he took the lead in arranging for a lottery which made possible the construction of a Masonic Hall on the south side of Franklin Street between Eighteenth and Nineteenth. The cornerstone was laid in 1785 and the building was completed two years later. Today it is recognized as the oldest building in America used continuously for Masonic purposes. The mother of Edgar Allan Poe gave two concerts there not long before her death in 1811; the hall was used as a hospital in the War of 1812; and in 1824 it was the scene of a dinner for the Marquis de Lafayette, with Chief Justice Marshall presiding.

Marshall and his adored wife, "Polly," the former Mary Willis Ambler, moved in 1790 into their spacious new Richmond home at what was later known as Ninth and Marshall streets, to remain for the rest of their lives. It was in the city's fashionable "Court End," where many lawyers and judges lived. Marshall, as Chief Justice from 1801 to 1835, had to be in Washington and elsewhere on numerous occasions, but he spent much of his time in Richmond. Some of his most important opinions were written under the trees which shaded his home. He owned the entire block. Incredibly, the City School Board tried to tear down the Marshall house in the early 1900s with a view to enlarging an adjacent school playground, but this shocking scheme was thwarted. The city entrusted the care of the house to the Association for the Preservation of Virginia Antiquities.

The problem of getting across James River occupied Richmonders and citizens of Manchester to a major degree during the late eighteenth century. Patrick Coutts's ferry had been the sole connecting link for many years. Various petitioners sought to operate a rival ferry but were turned down by the General Assembly. Finally John Mayo, son of William Mayo who had laid off Richmond almost half a century before, was granted permission to build a toll bridge. The idea of bridging the James at Richmond was regarded by many as hopelessly visionary, and one legislator compared it to building "a ladder to the moon." Mayo was proceeding with plans, despite these discouragements, when he became ill and died.

In his will, he disinherited his daughter, Marianna, for joining the Methodists.

Mayo's son, John Jr., had committed no such indiscretion. He took over the bulk of his father's estate and his plans for the bridge, and was authorized by the General Assembly to proceed. The span was completed in 1788, after many financial vicissitudes, which reportedly included Mayo's going to jail for debt. From the Richmond side of the river as far as the island on which the tollhouse stood, the bridge was made of planks, fixed on rocks, while pontoon construction was used the rest of the way.

But the bridge was short-lived. Within a few months of its opening the river froze from bank to bank. Then a thaw set in, and blocks of ice were sent hurtling against the span. When it was all over, most of the superstructure had vanished downstream. Mayo began rebuilding at once. This was only the first of many instances in which Mayo's Bridge was wrecked, either by masses of ice or by floods. In addition, it was burned by the retreating Confederates in the evacuation of Richmond at the end of the Civil War.

Tolls from the bridge brought John Mayo, Jr., a sizable income. In the early years, his New Jersey-born wife would travel in her coach-and-four, with liveried driver, to the tollhouse and gather up the receipts for the day. Later Colonel Mayo himself would be driven there, armed with a sword as protection against robbers. The revenue from the bridge made Mayo a wealthy man, as evidenced by his handsome suburban estates— The Hermitage, on the site of what many years afterward was Broad Street Station, and Bellville, in the area that later became 1100 to 1600 West Grace Street and extended southward to today's Monument Avenue. Both residences burned in the mid-nineteenth century.

Mayo's Bridge was the center in 1794 of what almost became a shooting war between Richmond and Manchester. Smallpox had broken out in Richmond, and Manchester was determined to prevent its spread across the river. The authorities there accordingly announced that nobody would be allowed to cross Mayo's Bridge in a southerly direction. An armed guard of six men was posted at the span's Manchester end, and vedettes were stationed along the riverbank to prevent infiltration by boat. James Hayes of Richmond, former publisher of the *Virginia Gazette or the American Advertiser*, was one of those who objected strenuously to these restrictions. He sent two servants across the bridge and they were beaten by guards. He himself made two attempts to cross, and was arrested both times. A mob of Richmonders then gathered at the north end of the bridge, whereupon there were reinforcements at the other end. Before a general fracas could break out, Governor "Light-Horse Harry" Lee intervened with the Chesterfield militia. An agreement was reached whereby those having business in Manchester could cross, under limited conditions, and travelers from the north could pass through, provided they used the back street. The militia remained on duty until the smallpox scare was over.

Manchester was prospering during these years, thanks mainly to the large shipments of Midlothian coal. However, roving hogs were a problem. Some of the citizenry objected to these perambulating animals, and petitioned the General Assembly for legislation restricting their movements. Owners of the hogs contended, on the other hand, that they were beneficial to the town, since they "contributed to cleaning off the filth, whereby the health of the inhabitants is preserved." This novel argument failed to convince the lawmakers, and the hogs were ordered penned.

George Washington visited Richmond in 1784 for the first time since before the Revolution, and his coming was greeted with "the discharge of thirteen cannon, when every countenance showed the most heartfelt gladness in seeing our illustrious and beloved General in the Capital of the State and in the bosom of peace." In the evening, the city was illuminated, and the merchants of Richmond gave General Washington "an elegant dinner" at the Bell Tavern, with the Marquis de Lafayette as a guest. Both men addressed the General Assembly. Then the city government tendered "an elegant ball" in honor of the general. He was so greatly revered in Richmond that, beginning in 1788, eleven years before his death, his birthday was observed annually with a holiday celebration. His last visit to Richmond was made in 1791, in the course of his Southern tour. The principal event was a dinner for him at the newly constructed Eagle Tavern, on the south side of Main Street between Twelfth and Thirteenth, the town's leading hostelry.

Washington was greatly concerned for the "clearing and improving" of the James River, and on his visit to Richmond in 1784 he had appeared before the General Assembly in behalf of legislation to that end. He suggested that "the inland navigation of the Eastern waters" be extended, and that they be connected "with those that run to the westward." A major part of this plan was to improve the James as far upstream as feasible, and then to link it by road or canal with the Great Kanawha, which flows into the Ohio. By such means the trade of the West would be drawn to the Eastern ports instead of traveling down the Mississippi to New Orleans.

The bill advocated by Washington was promptly passed, and the James River Company was created to carry out the plan he proposed. A seven-mile canal around The Falls at Richmond was got under way, and was opened in 1800. The river was also cleared of obstructions from the upper terminus of the canal at Westham all the way to Crow's Ferry in Botetourt County, a distance of 220 miles.

George Washington's services to his country in the Revolution were so universally recognized that the General Assembly deemed it fitting that a marble statue be executed in his honor. Thomas Jefferson's advice was sought as to the best sculptor in Europe, and he recommended Jean Antoine Houdon, the noted French artist. Houdon spent more than two weeks at Mount Vernon in 1785, and then returned to Paris to finish the work. The statue was placed in the Capitol when the building was completed in 1796. There was a controversy over the inscription, prepared by James Madison. Houdon regarded it as too long, but it was carved on the base nevertheless.

Houdon's Washington is the only marble likeness of the Father of His Country done from life, and the resemblance to the subject is regarded as exceptional. "That is the man!" Rembrandt Peale, the noted painter, who knew Washington well, is said to have exclaimed on seeing Houdon's work. It portrays magnificently the serene strength and indomitable character of the commander in chief of the Continental Army. The statue is generally regarded as the most priceless piece of marble in the United States, and Virginia's greatest treasure.

A bust of Lafayette also was done by Houdon in Paris and placed in the Capitol.

Richmonders were astonished at about this time to see a mysterious monster ascend into the air from Capitol Square. It was a balloon. The first such ascension had taken place in Paris, France, and now this almost incredible marvel was witnessed by the people of the city. They stood openmouthed, as the strange contraption mounted into the sky, and actually traveled ten miles. It came down, without mishap, on the farm of Captain John Austin.

The captain was apparently no relation to Moses Austin, who had arrived in Richmond in 1784 from New England, and whose son, Stephen A. Austin, would become the founder of Texas. Moses Austin opened a dry goods importing business in Richmond, and remained about five years. Meanwhile Moses Austin & Co. had acquired the important Chiswell lead mines in southwest Virginia, and Austin moved there. His son, Stephen, was born soon afterward near the mines, in the present Wythe County.

Almost simultaneously with the arrival of Moses Austin in Richmond came Thomas Rutherfoord, an eighteen-year-old native of Scotland. Like so many men who rose to be leaders in the city's social and cultural life, Rutherfoord entered upon a mercantile career. In his case, as in numerous others, it was tobacco that attracted him and formed the basis of his fortune.

Nine years after his arrival in Richmond, young Rutherfoord had prospered so greatly that he bought a hundred-acre tract, just beyond the city limits and bounded on the east and west, respectively, by streets which later became First and Belvidere. He planned a large residence, and at first wished to place it at the tract's highest point, or exactly in the middle of F, later Franklin, Street. However, he decided not to follow his inclination in this regard, since that would have blocked the city's growth

westward—the direction in which it was obviously moving. So he placed
his house at what was later the northeast corner of Franklin and Adams
streets and added a pair of large outbuildings, two stories high, as well as a
stable. All these structures were built with bricks made from clay dug on
the estate. Rutherfoord would sell lots to relatives and friends.

William Radford, his brother-in-law, bought land just east of Rutherfoord, on the approximate site of what later became Linden Row. Hearing
that the General Assembly wanted to build a pententiary, Radford decided to sell his property to the state for that purpose. Rutherfoord
protested that a penitentiary would depreciate values in the whole area,
and offered to give the Commonwealth twelve of his hundred acres,
"beautifully situated and clothed with valuable timber." Radford's contract was accordingly canceled, and the state prison was built on the
proffered site—where it would stand for more than a century and three
quarters. Rutherfoord did not suffer severely for the loss of his twelve
acres. He was to become not only wealthy, but perhaps Richmond's
greatest business leader during the early decades of the nineteenth century, a man of broad cultural interests who exerted a profound influence.

Construction of the penitentiary on the property donated by Rutherfoord was begun as soon as possible, and Benjamin H. Latrobe, who had
come to Richmond shortly before, was engaged to design it. Latrobe, an
Englishman, had landed at Norfolk in 1796 and had moved to Richmond
some months later. He would become extremely distinguished, and a leading consultant in the designing of the Capitol at Washington.

Latrobe was high in praise of Virginia hospitality. "A Virginian welcome must be experienced to be understood," he wrote. "It includes everything that the best heart can prompt and the most luxurious country
afford."

The penitentiary he designed was placed "on a steep gravelly knoll
which overlooked the James River and was inhabited by snakes and graz-
ing cows." When opened in 1800, it embodied some of Thomas Jefferson's
enlightened penological concepts. The prison's location served to prevent
residential development along the nearby riverbank, since Richmonders
lacked enthusiasm for dwelling in the vicinity of a prison. The last
vestiges of Latrobe's original building were pulled down in 1928.

The penitentiary was for major criminals, whereas the city jail accommodated less hardened miscreants. This "cage for disorderly persons,"
three stories high, with a dome, was situated near the market at Seventeenth and Main streets, with stocks and whipping post in the rear. The
"cage" was open on three sides, except for iron gratings, and those within
were visible to passers-by. The need for such a facility was stressed by a
grand jury which found an excessive number "of vagrants, beggars, free
Negroes and runaway slaves" which "daily infest the streets and by night
plunder the inhabitants." The jury's findings also included a lamentation

concerning the state of public morals, with specific reference to "Negro dances where persons of all colors are too often assembled," a phenomenon not usually associated with the late eighteenth century.

Criminology everywhere was, of course, in a primitive state, and extremely harsh penalties prevailed. Hangings were carried out in public, and huge crowds came to witness these gruesome spectacles which, in Richmond, took place near Fifteenth Street, just north of Broad in the valley. The gallows there was more than ordinarily active, since condemned persons were brought to the capital from various parts of the Commonwealth. The fact that many more crimes carried the death penalty in that era than in later years increased the number of executions. Horse stealing, for example, was one of these capital offenses.

Punishments of slaves were severe. For the crime of larceny a Richmond slave was ordered "burnt in the left hand, which being done in the presence of the court, it is further ordered that . . . he be tied to the end of a cart and led through the Main Street, with a pair of cow's horns affixed to his forehead, and receive on his bare back one hundred lashes . . . well laid on." Other slaves had their ears cut off, in addition to being flogged. It should be borne in mind that penalties inflicted in Great Britain at the period upon freeborn Englishmen were every bit as harsh as these.

A less harrowing form of punishment, for what were termed "brabbing women," namely scolds or gossips, was provided in the ducking stool. As described by Mordecai, "a post was planted in the ground, on the margin of a pond or stream; on the top of this post a long pole fixed at its centre on a pivot, was made to revolve; at one end of the pole a chair was fastened. . . . The pole was turned so as to bring the incumbent over the water and was depressed sufficiently to dip her beneath the surface. This plunging bath was repeated until the patient was cooled—externally at least." This primitive form of feminine refrigeration had prevailed for more than a hundred years in Virginia, but it was abandoned early in the nineteenth century.

The problem of "brabbing women" was a minor one in Richmond during the 1790s. Of much greater concern to the white population was the fear of a slave uprising. The massacres in Santo Domingo caused widespread uneasiness, as refugees fled in terror from that Caribbean island. It would soon become obvious that fears of a slave insurrection in Richmond were far from groundless.

# FIVE

# Gabriel's Insurrection— Greatest Slave Plot in U.S. History

NAT TURNER'S INSURRECTION of 1831 in Southampton County, Virginia, is widely believed to have been the greatest and most significant slave conspiracy in the history of the United States. Yet a slave plot that occurred nearly a third of a century earlier, centering in the Richmond area and extending throughout much of the Commonwealth, was even more alarming to Virginia's white citizens. Led by a slave named Gabriel Prosser, it was known as Gabriel's Insurrection. Most Americans have never heard of it.

Thousands of blacks were involved in the Gabriel affair—which took place in 1800—and in the events that followed during the ensuing two years. The large number of participants contrasts with the small band of about sixty slaves who followed Nat Turner in his insurrection thirty-one years later. The attempted rebellion under Gabriel was designed to bring about a wholesale massacre of the whites, not only in Richmond but throughout the slaveholding areas of Virginia and beyond. In 1801 and 1802 there were other planned insurrections and intended massacres in half a dozen Virginia counties and several cities, as well as in a comparable number of counties just over the border in North Carolina.

The significance of Gabriel's planned uprising and the events that followed lies not so much in the failure of these efforts to butcher the slaveowners as in the fact that so much deep-seated hostility toward them was revealed.

The slaves did not hesitate to risk their lives in these desperate adventures. Even after Gabriel and some thirty-five of his followers had been hanged, further plots were hatched in both Virginia and North Carolina.

All these schemes were thwarted, several of them as a result of timely information furnished by bondsmen loyal to their owners—excellent evidence that there were slaves, undoubtedly a large number, who felt genuine affection for their masters and mistresses. At the same time, antagonism toward many slaveowners was shown to be great.

Rumors of impending insurrection had been heard off and on since the American Revolution, during which much emphasis had been placed on the "rights of man." Dr. William P. Palmer, a scholarly Richmond physician who was vice-president of the Virginia Historical Society and was responsible for inaugurating the *Calendar of Virginia State Papers*, took note of these rumors. In a series of articles for the Richmond *Times* in the late nineteenth century he declared that after the Revolution "a vague idea of future freedom seemed to permeate the entire slave community" of Virginia. He added that "at one time there was scarcely a quarter of the state in which there was not a feeling of insecurity . . . Richmond itself seemed to be quaking with apprehension." Appeals to the governor for arms as protection against possible uprisings were received by the executive from various directions.

The frightful massacres by the slaves of their often cruel French masters in Santo Domingo (Haiti), beginning in 1791, caused rumblings or revolt in various parts of Virginia and as far south as Louisiana. In July 1793 one hundred and thirty-seven square-rigged vessels, loaded with terrified and destitute French refugees, and escorted by French warships, arrived at Norfolk. A considerable number moved on to Richmond and other cities.

The manner in which the blacks had taken over in Santo Domingo by liquidating the whites caused apprehension in Virginia and other slave states. As one historian put it: "The fame of Toussaint L'Ouverture had spread to every corner of the Old Dominion. Around the cabin fires of slave-quarters excited Negro voices repeated again the saga of the black hero who had defied Napoleon himself to free his people."

White Richmonders asked themselves if the blacks had managed this coup in a Caribbean island, what was to prevent their attempting to do the same in Virginia or elsewhere?

A prominent white citizen of Richmond wrote Governor "Light-Horse Harry" Lee under date of July 21, 1793, that he had heard two Negroes talking of insurrection. He had gone quietly to a window in the darkness and had listened as one black told another of a plot "to kill the white people . . . between this and the fifteenth of October." The Negro called attention to the manner in which the blacks had slain the whites "in the French island and took it a little while ago."

John Marshall, the future Chief Justice, wrote Governor Lee in September of that year enclosing a communication concerning the situation in nearby Powhatan County. The letter stated that about three hundred slaves had met shortly before in the county, several Negro foremen "had run away," and the writer believed "the intended rising is true." As for Richmond, Mr. New, captain of the guard, had "a few men and guns" but not a "pound of shot," in case of trouble.

Other reports of a like nature came from the eastern shore, from Cumberland, Mathews, Elizabeth City and Warwick counties, and from Yorktown, Petersburg and Portsmouth. In the last-named place, four Negroes were found hanging from a cedar tree in the center of town. The Portsmouth citizen who communicated this news to the governor said the men had been executed by other Negroes, which may or may not have been correct.

The authorities were largely indifferent to these reports until an awareness of the realities roused them to action. In many areas, the militia were armed and held in readiness, other whites were supplied with weapons, and volunteer guards and patrols watched the movements of the slaves. The presence in Virginia of some five thousand white veterans of the Revolution also had its effect.

"The summer and autumn of 1793 was long remembered as one of the most trying periods of the state's history," Dr. William P. Palmer wrote a century later. The unrest among the slaves occurred despite the fact that after the Revolution their treatment had been markedly better. They were given more freedom to move about, and punishments inflicted on them were less severe.

After the rumblings of 1792 and 1793 were quelled, the slave population in Virginia was almost entirely quiet for seven years. Then, in the midst of this treacherous calm, pent-up resentments exploded in a far-reaching plot for wholesale massacre.

Although hundreds, if not thousands, of blacks were scheming for months to kill the whites, hardly a hint reached the ears of the latter until a few hours before the murders were to begin. The plans were laid in the Richmond area by slaves who were allowed to attend religious gatherings and barbecues, and were free to roam after nightfall. There were rendezvous of the conspirators at Sunday frolics, in taverns, in barns and in the kitchens of their masters and mistresses.

The leader of this widely ramified plot was a powerfully built twenty-four-year-old slave named Gabriel Prosser, the property of Thomas H. Prosser, who had a large plantation a few miles north of Richmond in a well-cultivated section of Henrico County. There were various other extensive plantations in this attractive region, owned by such families as the Winstons, Prices, Seldens, Mosbys, Sheppards, Youngs and Williamsons. Prosser's house, Brookfield, was less than a quarter of a mile from, and on the eastern side of, what was later called Brook Turnpike. It was just beyond the bridge over the brook, or Brook Run.

Brookfield has vanished and only two residences from that period are standing today in the area. One is Meadow Farm, the Sheppard home near Glen Allen, owned in 1800 by Mosby Sheppard, who had an important role in thwarting the uprising. A century and a half later it was occupied by his descendant, Major General Sheppard Crump, adjutant general of Virginia. The other dwelling surviving from that era is Brook Hill, home at that time of the Williamsons, and situated just across the brook from the Prosser plantation where Gabriel planned the rebellion. It was lived in for generations by the Stewart family, descendants of the Williamsons. On the death of the last of the Stewart ladies it became the home of their great-nephew, Joseph Bryan III, the author.

Gabriel was Thomas Prosser's most trusted slave. His brothers, Solomon and Martin, also were on the Prosser plantation. The killing was to begin with the Prosser family and spread to nearby plantations and then to much of the state.

Preparations had been careful and extensive throughout the whole Richmond-Petersburg region, and in Louisa and Caroline counties, the Charlottesville area and portions of lower Tidewater. James River watermen spread the word up and down that stream. A post rider whose route extended from Richmond to Amherst County enlisted recruits along the way. He also was active in the vicinity of the state arsenal at Point of Fork. A preacher in Gloucester County was a part of the plot.

All the foregoing participants were black, but there are excellent reasons for believing that at least one Frenchman, and probably two, were important to the enterprise. The slaves steadfastly refused to give the names of these men. However, Gabriel was known to have declared that a Frenchman "who was at the siege of Yorktown" would meet him at the brook and serve as commander on the first day of the revolt, after which he himself would take over. This Frenchman may well have been Charles Quersey, who had lived at the home of Francis Corbin in Caroline County a few years prior to the Gabriel plot. Gilbert, another slave who was a leader in the intended rebellion, was quoted as stating that Quersey frequently urged him and other blacks to rise and murder the whites. Quersey said he would help them and show them how to fight. Gilbert was informed that Quersey had been active in fomenting the Gabriel uprising.

The feeling was widespread that certain refugees from the island of Santo Domingo, both white and black, had important roles in planting the idea of insurrection in the minds of Virginia slaves. A number of free Negroes also are said to have been active in aiding with the plans.

Gabriel's right-hand man was a huge slave named Jack Bowler, 6 feet 5 inches tall, "straight made and perhaps as strong a man as any in the state." He had long hair, worn in a queue and twisted at the sides. The twenty-eight-year-old Bowler sought to lead the rebellion, but when a vote was called for, Gabriel was elected "General" by a large majority.

The slave Gilbert, a thoughtful man, was determined to go through with the plot, but said he could not bring himself to kill his master and mistress, William Young and his wife, since they had "raised him." He agreed, however, that they should be put to death.

Principal places of rendezvous for the plotters in those hot summer months of 1800 were at Young's Spring in the vicinity of Westbrook, at Prosser's blacksmith shop and at Half Sink, the Winston plantation on the Chickahominy River, embracing what later became the Ethelwood golf course.

Antagonism, even hatred, toward the whites was revealed at various parleys. Several slaves said they would have no hesitation in killing white people. One was quoted as saying that he could kill them "as free as eat."

Nothing less than revolution was envisioned. The first blow would fall on Saturday night, August 30. Martin, Gabriel's brother, pointed out that the country was at peace, the soldiers discharged, their "arms all put away" and "there are no patrols in the county." It seemed an ideal time to strike. "I can no longer bear what I have borne," Martin declared.

The number of slaves who had enrolled for the massacre cannot be determined with any exactitude. Gabriel claimed "nearly ten thousand" at one point, but this extravagant figure was apparently used to impress the slaves to whom he was speaking. That number, and many more, were expected to join him when the plot succeeded, but it seems certain that nothing like so many had enlisted at the outset. The secret nature of the plans, the absence of written records, the wide area over which the participating slaves were scattered, all combined to preclude accurate estimates of the number involved. Dr. Palmer held it to be "abundantly proved" that the plot's "ramifications extended over most of the slave-holding parts of the state."

Weapons were fashioned by the slaves in anticipation of the coup. There were frighteningly lethal swords made from scythes, as well as pikes, spears, knives, crossbows, clubs and bullets, plus stolen muskets and powder. The plan was to seize many additional arms at the Capitol in Richmond and others at the magazine, to release the convicts from the penitentiary, commandeer the treasury and gain control of the city. Gabriel or one of his agents had somehow managed to enter the Capitol on Sunday, when it was supposedly closed, and had found where the arms were stored.

Crucial to the success of the conspirators was the ingenious plan to move in the middle of the night and set fire to the wooden buildings along Richmond's waterfront at Rocketts. The whites would rush en masse from Shockoe Hill and Church Hill down to the river to put out the flames. Once they were fully occupied, slaves numbering perhaps a thousand would enter the city from the north. When the whites returned exhausted from fighting the conflagration, the blacks would engage them and wipe them out, if possible. The insurrectionists also planned to kidnap Governor James Monroe.

Vague rumors of impending trouble were heard in Richmond during August, but nobody was able to pinpoint them. Dr. James McClurg, Richmond's mayor, ordered temporary patrols, but the whites, by and large, remained in blissful ignorance of what was impending.

On Saturday, August 30, a strange phenomenon was noted. Whereas on Saturdays the slaves were accustomed to leave the surrounding areas for diversion in Richmond, it was observed that nearly all of them seemed to be going in the opposite direction. They were heading for Gabriel's prearranged meeting place just north of the brook.

Mosby Sheppard, one of the leading Henrico County planters, was sitting in his Meadow Farm counting room on that day when two slaves, Pharaoh and Tom, came in and nervously shut the door. They told him that the blacks planned to rise that night and kill him and all the other white people in the area. They would then proceed to Richmond and attempt to seize the city and murder its white population.

Sheppard got this alarming word to Governor Monroe at once. The latter called out all the militiamen who could be reached. He ordered them to guard the Capitol, the magazine and the penitentiary, and to patrol the roads leading into Richmond.

That afternoon dark clouds gathered in the west, thunder rolled and jagged lightning stabbed the sky. Rain fell—in sheets. It was a storm such as Virginia had seldom experienced. Roads were turned into quagmires, streams into roaring cataracts. The brook rose far out of its banks and became a foaming torrent. If the blacks had tried to cross it in either direction, they could not have done so. Disheartened by the rushing water and bottomless mud, and viewing the storm as a heavenly portent, Gabriel postponed the uprising until the next night. By then, the governor's patrols were covering the city and its environs so thoroughly that there was no chance for a successful uprising. The entire plan was abandoned and the leaders fled.

Most of them were rounded up promptly. In Henrico, where the vast majority were tried, legal procedures were strictly followed. James Rind, a highly respected lawyer, was named to represent the accused men and he did so conscientiously and ably. It is possible that there were irregularities in some of the few trials held elsewhere, although no convincing evidence to that effect has been produced.

The dimensions of the plot unfolded as various slaves turned state's evidence against their fellows. There were some conflicts as to details, but the general outlines of the conspiracy were clear. All agreed that the whites in a large area of Henrico were to be massacred, after which the slaves would march on Richmond and carry out their plan for wholesale arson and slaughter. There was some disagreement as to exactly what would happen once Richmond was in the hands of the black insurgents. Gabriel was aware that unless his plan achieved almost instant success, with the whites defeated and the city seized, there would be no mass uprising of the slaves. But if the city surrendered and the whites agreed to free their chattels, Gabriel planned to raise a white flag as a signal to blacks in the countryside to rise and join him. He would also "dine and drink with the merchants of the city." Whites whose lives were spared would "lose an arm," according to one version. Methodists, Quakers and Frenchmen would not be harmed, according to another. The prominent Mrs. David Meade Randolph, it was further reported, would be made Gabriel's "queen" because of her virtuosity as a cook.

Whatever the precise details of the plot, those who studied the evidence had no doubt as to its main outlines. Governor Monroe spoke positively to the General Assembly on December 5, 1800, four months after the scheme had been smashed.

"It was distinctly seen," said His Excellency, "that it [the conspiracy] embraced most of the slaves in this city and neighborhood, and that the combination extended to several of the adjacent counties, Hanover, Caroline, Louisa, Chesterfield, and to the neighborhood of Point of Fork; and there was good cause to believe that the knowledge of such a project pervaded other parts, if not the whole, of the state.

"The probability was if their first effort succeeded, we should see the town in flames, its inhabitants butchered and a scene of horror extending through the country."

The governor believed that someone other than the slaves had instigated the plot. He deemed it "strange that the slaves should embark in this novel and unexampled enterprise of their own accord." He suspected that they were "prompted to it by others who were invisible."

Most of the slaves who had been active in the plot were arrested within a few days of the conspiracy's collapse, but the two principal leaders, Gabriel and Jack Bowler, remained at large for weeks. Bowler was the first to be apprehended, but Gabriel managed to elude his pursuers until September 24. He hid in the swamps along the James below Richmond until the three-masted schooner *Mary* came down the river. Gabriel hailed the ship, and was taken aboard by Captain Richardson Taylor. Isham and Billy, two slaves who were serving in the crew, told Captain Taylor that they believed this was the man for whose capture a reward had been offered but Taylor, an anti-slavery Methodist, made no move to arrest his newly acquired passenger. When the ship arrived at Norfolk, Billy managed to get word of his suspicions to an acquaintance, and Gabriel was taken into custody by constables. Captain Taylor evidently had realized the slave's identity, but had been unwilling to turn him in.

Gabriel remained almost totally silent after his capture. He refused to tell Governor Monroe or anyone else details of the plot. He was tried and condemned to death.

About thirty-five slaves were executed, but this was a relatively small number, considering the hundreds if not thousands who were involved in the conspiracy. Not only so, but at least twelve were acquitted and several more were pardoned. Several pardons were granted on the petition of persons whom the condemned men admitted they had planned to kill. The clemency was on condition that those who received it be sold into slavery in the far South or the West Indies. Owners of executed slaves had to be compensated financially by the state for their loss. This may have tended to hold down the number of convictions.

John Randolph of Roanoke, who witnessed some of the trials, wrote a friend that "the executions have not been so numerous as might under such circumstances have been expected," but he added these pregnant words: "The accused have exhibited a spirit which, if it becomes general, must deluge the Southern country in blood. They manifested a sense of their rights and contempt of danger, and a thirst for revenge which portend the most unhappy consequences." A Richmond resident wrote one of the local newspapers that the condemned men "uniformly met death with fortitude."

The hangings were carried out at various points in Henrico, and also in Caroline and elsewhere, but the great majority were held in Richmond at the usual place of execution. This was a small clearing, surrounded by pines and undergrowth, just north of the intersection of today's Fifteenth and Broad streets. Crowds attended the hangings, and the doomed men went to their deaths "amid the singing of hymns and the wails of their fellow-slaves and friends."

Richmonders were profoundly affected by these tragic events, and for years thereafter they avoided passing by the place where the gibbets stood.

Governor Monroe's conduct throughout the crisis was exemplary. He leaned over backward to be fair, and was careful not to issue inflammatory statements. He resisted the appeals of citizens who were inclined to take the law into their own hands, among whom Joseph Jones of Petersburg was conspicuous. Jones, one of the leading citizens of Virginia, wrote the governor that "where there is any reason to believe that any person is concerned, they ought immediately to be hanged, quartered and hung upon trees on every road as a terror to the rest." He urged that trials be under martial law, since "if they are tryed by the Civil Law, perhaps there will not be one condemned; it will not do to be too scrupulous now." Monroe paid no attention to such hysterical appeals.

His friend Thomas Jefferson was a calming influence throughout. Like Monroe, Jefferson was opposed to slavery. He replied to Monroe's request for advice as follows: "The other states & the world at large will forever condemn us if we indulge a principle of revenge, or go one step beyond absolute necessity. They cannot lose sight of the rights of the two parties, & the object of the unsuccessful one."

Governor Monroe was determined to prevent Gabriel's desperate design from being revived. He ordered a "respectable force" to parade "Daily on the Capitol Square . . . that our strength might be known to the conspirators." The move was temporarily successful, but in his message to the General Assembly four months later the governor said: "What has happened may occur again at any time, with more fatal consequences, unless suitable measures are taken to prevent it."

George Tucker, youthful cousin of the famous St. George Tucker, was so concerned that he published a pamphlet. "The late extraordinary conspiracy . . . has waked those who were asleep," he wrote, and he went on to describe the situation in Virginia as "an eating sore" that was rapidly becoming worse.

The alarm was so general that a permanent guard was stationed at the Capitol. It remained there until the Civil War.

Governor Monroe's forebodings of further trouble were soon borne out. Despite the execution of Gabriel and his fellow conspirators, the fires of revolt had by no means been quenched.

There were definite evidences in late 1801 that all was far from serene in the cities and on the plantations. Monroe described some of the happenings in a message to the General Assembly in January 1802. He stated that "an alarm of a threatened insurrection among the slaves took place lately in Nottoway County which soon reached Petersburg . . . the publick danger proceeding from this . . . is daily increasing." Monroe expressed the view that "a variety of causes" were responsible, including "the contrast in the condition of the free Negroes and slaves, the growing sentiment of liberty existing in the minds of the latter, and the inadequacy of existing patrol laws."

The interception of a letter from a Negro named Frank Goode to a man named Roling Pointer in Powhatan County caused further apprehension. "We have agreed to begin at Jude's Ferry and put to death every man on both sides of the river to Richmond," said this missive. It declared, further, that "our traveling friend has got ten thousand in readiness to the night." Nothing of this magnitude developed, but there was decided slave unrest in that area, as well as in much of lower Tidewater and especially in the Southside.

Two slaves were executed in Brunswick County and another in Halifax, for involvement in plots to slay the whites. A third was hanged in Hanover County on a similar charge. Two slaves were sentenced to die in Norfolk when a plot to burn the city and massacre the white population was discovered. Governor Monroe granted the men a temporary reprieve, which brought a remonstrance from the mayor and 227 citizens of Norfolk, who signed a petition urging no further clemency. One of the men was hanged soon thereafter, but the other was transported out of the state.

In Williamsburg and Suffolk there was much unrest among the slaves, which the anxious whites took as signifying that an insurrection impended. A communication from Nansemond County to the governor stated that "our situation is truly awful."

Across the border in North Carolina there were threats of an uprising. From Hertford County came a letter "to the citizens of Nansemond County," Virginia, that "a horrid plot has been discovered amongst the Negroes of this county and the county of Bertie, which has for its object the total destruction of the whites . . . there is not a doubt remaining that such a plan does exist." A letter giving details had been found "in a cotton barrel in one of their cabins."

There were repercussions from these events in the Carolina counties of Camden, Currituck, Martin, Halifax and Pasquotank. Historians have estimated, on the basis of incomplete newspaper accounts, that at least five slaves were executed in North Carolina, with others lashed, branded and cropped. This last refers to the cropping of ears. It appears probable that the total number hanged was nearer fifteen than five.

Participation of white men in some of the Virginia slave plots of 1802 is apparently established. Documents from Halifax, Nottoway and Henrico counties seem to bear out this suspicion. Arthur, a slave on the plantation of William Farrar of Henrico, is supposed to have referred to "eight or ten white men" who were cooperating with him.

A certain amount of hysteria was involved in several of the above-mentioned alarms over the years in both Virginia and North Carolina, and some of the reports of planned insurrections were undoubtedly exaggerated. On the other hand, there was enough evidence of genuine conspiracy in both states, especially Virginia, to cause widespread and justifiable uneasiness.

This uneasiness was aroused only spasmodically in the years after 1802, until the Nat Turner outbreak of 1831. There were specific developments in 1808 and 1809, and Richmond seems to have been the center of these. Lieutenant Governor Alexander McRae informed the military on December 19 of the former year that he had satisfactory evidence, verbal and written, of an impending uprising, to take place during the following week. Samuel Pleasants, Jr., of Richmond published a circular "respecting insurrection of Negroes." The military was called out in the capital and remained on the alert until January 1. There were other similar warnings in Chesterfield County, as well as in Norfolk and the counties of Nelson and Albemarle.

Richmond was the center of further alarms in 1813. Mayor Robert Greenhow wrote that there were insurrectionary movements among the blacks, at the instigation of the British, with whom we were fighting the War of 1812. The mayor called out patrols and urged removal of the powder magazine to a safer place.

A conspiracy with greater potentialities was formed in 1815 and 1816 in Spotsylvania, Louisa and Orange counties. It was the work of a weird character named George Boxley, a white man who kept a country store. Boxley declared that a little white bird had brought him a holy message, directing him to deliver his fellow man from bondage. He persuaded many slaves to join him in a planned revolt, which was to involve an attack on Fredericksburg and then a march on Richmond. As had happened with several previous attempts at insurrection, a loyal slave informed her master of the plot. Many were arrested, including Boxley. He escaped and was never recaptured, but six slaves were hanged. Six others were sentenced to the same fate, but many whites appealed for clemency, and the blacks were reprieved and banished.

All this unrest among the slaves, especially that evidenced in Gabriel's attempted insurrection, caused a marked lessening of efforts by the whites to abolish chattel servitude. Such efforts had been actively pursued in the years following the Revolution, albeit without tangible results. But after 1800 the trend was the other way, and the Virginia Abolition Society ceased to function, as did all other such societies in the South. Not only so, but Virginia passed a law in 1806 providing that any slave who was freed had to leave the state within twelve months. This law was later modified to permit local courts to give certain manumitted slaves permission to remain, but passage of the harsh statute showed the tenor of the times.

A melancholy ballad, set to music, entitled "Gabriel's Defeat," is said to have been composed by a black, following the collapse of Gabriel's epochal rebellion. A reporter claimed to have heard it "at the dances of the whites and in the huts of the slaves." The song soon faded away and has not been heard for many years. Its mournful notes may well have provided an appropriate requiem for the revolt that failed.[1]

---

# SIX

# Flour, Tobacco, Politics, Parsons, Quoits and Aaron Burr

THE UNEXPECTED DEATH of George Washington brought profound sorrow to the people of Richmond. Coming as it did at the very end of the 1700s, his death seemed to symbolize the passing of one era and the beginning of another.

The capital of Virginia was quick to hold memorial services in honor of the great Virginian who had carried the nation to victory in the Revolution against tremendous odds and then, forgoing long-anticipated relaxation at his beloved Mount Vernon, served as the country's first President.

Governor James Monroe and his Council, Mayor George Nicholson and city dignitaries, soldiers of the Revolution and other citizens attended solemn ceremonies at the Capitol on December 18, 1799, four days after Washington's death. The Reverend John D. Blair, Presbyterian minister and chaplain of the House of Delegates, was the speaker. The governor and Council wore crape on their sleeves for thirty days, and nearly all Christmas festivities were dispensed with.

The year 1800 was the beginning of a new era for Richmond. Gabriel's thwarted insurrection caused widespread anxiety in the late summer and fall, but there would be significant advances in the coming years in education, industry, transportation and other fields. Much of this progress would be related to the fact that able and enterprising immigrants, future leaders in the city's business, professional and social life, had been crossing from Europe and settling in the little town. By the turn of the century there were important arrivals from Scotland, Ireland, France, Spain, Germany and Holland. They not only brought their own abilities to Richmond but gave it a more cosmopolitan air. In addition, plantation families were moving into Richmond and other Virginia cities, bringing with them the urbanity and sophistication which characterized the great landowners of that age.

Richmond was becoming a significant manufacturing center. The newly built canal around The Falls was in operation, and this was an incentive to users of water power. The Falls themselves were a source of such power, and mills were operated there before the construction of the canal. David Ross, an enterprising Scotsman, had built a flour mill at The Falls in the early 1790s. He called it the Columbia Mills. Other leaders in the industry at this time were Samuel Overton and Jean Auguste Marie Chevallié, a Frenchman who had come to this country after the Revolution as agent for the dramatist Beaumarchais in his claims against the United States for money advanced to the American cause.

Joseph Gallego, a Spaniard who was to become perhaps the greatest figure in Richmond's flour-milling history, began operations as early as 1796 and associated himself in the milling business with Chevallié. It was a natural combination, since the two men married sisters, Sarah and Mary Magee of Philadelphia. The Gallego-Chevallié mill burned about the year 1800, and the owners built a better and larger plant on the canal a mile above the city limits. It would soon be greatly expanded.

Other notable figures in the industry at this period were Thomas Rutherfoord, Philip Haxall and Edward Cunningham. Dr. Thomas S. Berry of the University of Richmond declared in his excellent article "The Rise of Flour Milling in Richmond" (*Virginia Magazine of History and Biography*, Oct. 1970) that "Three families or family groups succeeded in retaining the leading stakes in Richmond flour-mill ownership and management during much of the nineteenth century." They were: "The Gallego-Chevallié-Warwick-Barksdale group, the Haxall-Crenshaw group, and the Cunningham-Deane-Anderson group (Edward Cunningham and his sons, Edward Jr. and Richard, Francis B. Deane, Jr., and Richard Anderson). Except for the admission of Lewis D. Crenshaw into the Haxall firm in 1859, the Haxall properties went from father to son from 1809 to 1894. The Gallego Mills brand passed from Gallego, Richard and Company first to P. J. Chevallié and Company, then to (Abraham) Warwick and (William J.) Barksdale, and still later to Warner Moore and Company, without ever leaving the family group."

There was also the mill originally built by William Byrd II, and later taken over and enlarged by the Mayos. It was torn down in 1852 and rebuilt on a still larger scale by the firm of Dunlop, Moncure and Co., composed of James Dunlop, H. W. Moncure and Thomas W. McCance. Known as the Dunlop Mill, it continued in operation for nearly a century, and was functioning until fairly recent times as the Dixie Portland Flour Co.

Flour mills are much more prone to catch fire than most manufacturing plants, and the Richmond mills were no exception. The Gallego Mills seem to have gone up in flames on four different occasions over the years, and other mills burned from time to time. They were almost always rebuilt on a larger scale than before.

Richmond's flour-milling industry, along with its tobacco and other export businesses, suffered severely from President Jefferson's foreign trade embargo of 1808–9 and even more in the War of 1812. Commerce and industry got another setback in the serious depression of 1819.

With the extension of the James River and Kanawha Canal westward along the James in the 1830s and 1840s, and the building of the railroads at about the same period, wheat shipments poured into Richmond from the distant wheat-growing sections of Virginia.

Within a few decades, Richmond mills were shipping flour in huge quantities to South America and around Cape Horn to California. Baltimore's total production was somewhat larger than Richmond's, but Baltimore had several times as many flour manufactories. The Virginia city's enormous Gallego Mills, with nine hundred barrels a day at their peak, and its Haxall Mills with seven hundred, were the largest in the United States, some say in the world, until the Civil War. After that devastating conflict, Minneapolis mills took the lead.

Tobacco manufacture was the city's other principal industry. It went back for its origins to William Byrd I's tobacco warehouse in the wilderness at The Falls a century and a quarter before. For most of the intervening years the leaf served in place of currency, and tobacco warehouse receipts or produce were the customary means of exchange. When coins were used, they were likely to be Spanish doubloons or pieces of eight, Dutch florins, French écus or Turkish sequins. Such coins reached Richmond on the ships from many parts of the world that docked at Rocketts.

Manchester was a larger exporter of leaf tobacco in the early days than Richmond, since most of the leaf was grown on the southern side of the James. Thus the Manchester warehouses were more convenient to the growers than those north of the river. Furthermore, it saved the planters the toll on Mayo's Bridge to store their crops in Manchester and ship it from there.

Richmond not only was developing a tobacco-manufacturing industry; it was also shipping the "soverane herb" abroad. In 1819, when the first city directory was published, there were eleven tobacco-manufacturing plants in the city. Cigars were not yet made in any quantity in Richmond, and cigarettes would not be produced until after the Civil War. Chewing tobacco was all the rage, and the cuspidor a necessary article of furniture. The plugs were flavored wth spices and oils, sugar, rum and licorice. Famous brands such as Diadem of Old Virginia, Nature's Ultimatum and Christian's Comfort were yet to be developed, but the manufacture of "eatin' tobacco" was well on its way to becoming a mainstay of Richmond industry. Tobacco stemming was a significant operation as early as 1803. It employed children and servants who, the ingenious argument ran, would otherwise be idle.

In addition to flour and tobacco, products being manufactured in Richmond included iron, gunpowder, ceramics, beer, musical instruments, paper, cotton textiles, coaches, soap and candles. The little town's population was growing steadily—from 3,761 in 1790 to 5,737 in 1800, about half of whom were black.

Business had been carried on since the Revolution on a more or less chaotic basis, with no banking facilities and tobacco as the principal medium of exchange, plus the foreign coins that occasionally were available. This awkward arrangement could not be permitted to continue, and in 1804 the Bank of Virginia was chartered with headquarters in Richmond and branches in nine Virginia cities. Capital stock of $1,500,000 was quickly oversubscribed and Abraham B. Venable was chosen president with Dr. John Brockenbrough as cashier.

Despite the fact that some regarded banks as dangerous institutions, the Bank of Virginia was an immediate success. It was soon paying a 12 per cent dividend on stock quoted at 133⅓. Accordingly, in 1812 a group of Richmond businessmen, undaunted by the looming danger of war with Great Britain, organized the Farmers Bank of Virginia, with branches throughout the state, and capitalization of $2,000,000. Benjamin Hatcher was chosen president and William Nekervis cashier.

With the exception of Richmond branches of the controversial Bank of the United States, no other bank seems to have been established in the city until 1837.

Politics was hectic in Richmond at the turn of the century. The city was considered a Federalist stronghold, with John Marshall as the chief spokesman for that party, but Thomas Jefferson carried Richmond in the presidential contest of 1800 against Federalist John Adams, who was running for reelection. The Republicans called the Federalists Tories, aristocrats and British hirelings, while the Federalists struck back with "Jacobins, anarchists and sons of sedition." Jefferson was chosen President despite astounding abuse and misrepresentation—from which Adams was by no means immune. The press of that day was unbelievably scurrilous where politics was concerned. The clergy joined in the vituperation, and one of them declared that if elected, Jefferson would "destroy religion, introduce immorality and loosen the bonds of society." Jefferson was a deist, of course, just as were Washington and Madison.

President Adams was the victim of outrageous blasts from a drunken, vicious and depraved, albeit talented, Scotsman named James Thomson Callender, who had come to this country a few years before. For his defamation of Adams he was tried, under the Sedition Law, in Richmond's District Court before U. S. Supreme Court Justice Samuel P.

Chase, another flagrant partisan. He got nine months in jail and a $200 fine.

Thomas Jefferson had unwisely contributed money to Callender's earlier activities, and the latter bombarded Jefferson with letters from Richmond's none too salubrious bastille. Inveighing against "the stink of the place" and terming it "this den of wretchedness and horror," he appealed to the newly elected President to order his release. Soon after Jefferson was inaugurated, he did direct that Callender be set free, and he told him that his fine would be remitted. There was difficulty in implementing the latter commitment, and Jefferson ended by paying part of the amount from his own pocket. Callender never collected the remainder.

This outraged him, but he sought appointment as postmaster of Richmond as a reward for his services to Jefferson and the Republicans, as the party was then known. Callender failed to get the post, whereupon he turned on Jefferson in full fury, demanding what the latter termed "hush money." This got no results.

Callender then obtained an editorial position on the Richmond *Recorder*, a Federalist paper of no great reputation, and proceeded to put it on the map by blackguarding Jefferson. The slanders that are heard to this day concerning Jefferson's supposed brood of mulatto children at Monticello were broadcast by Callender in the columns of the *Recorder*. Federalist organs throughout the country leaped upon this juicy material and reprinted it widely. The *Recorder* became nationally known. Good-looking, light-skinned Sally Hemings was the slave at Monticello who was alleged to have been the mother of Jefferson's brood. She was the subject of ribald verses in the Boston *Gazette*, the first of which follow:

> Of all the damsels on the green,
> On mountain or in valley,
> A lass so luscious ne'er was seen,
> As the Monticellian Sally.

> Yankey doodle, who's the noodle?
> What wife were half so handy?
> To breed a flock of slaves for stock
> A blackamoor's the dandy.

The principal Jeffersonian authorities—Dumas Malone, Julian P. Boyd, Merrill Peterson and Douglass Adair—regard the charge that Jefferson had mulatto descendants as entirely without foundation. Yet the libel will not down, and Callender, more than any other person, is responsible.

He was drowned in three feet of water in the James River at Richmond in 1803, and the official verdict was that he was drunk.

Another Federalist foe of Jefferson was Augustine Davis, an early postmaster of Richmond. He was editor of the *Virginia Gazette and General*

*Advertiser* and operated the post office in the same building with the newspaper. Jefferson fired him as postmaster, a fact that did not diminish the hostility of the *Virginia Gazette* to the occupant of the White House.

The need for a strong newspaper in Richmond that would speak for the Republicans was obvious to Jefferson and his friend Judge Spencer Roane. The latter accordingly persuaded his young cousin, Thomas Ritchie, a schoolteacher and bookstore operator, to launch a Republican organ in Richmond. The result was the establishment of the Richmond *Enquirer* in 1804. Ritchie remained as editor for forty-one years, and became not only influential throughout Virginia but a power in the councils of the Republican, later the Democratic, party.

Judge Spencer Roane is a personality of great significance about whom more should be known. Like Thomas Ritchie he was a native of Essex County, and like Ritchie spent much of his life in Richmond. Described by a contemporary as "ugly and morose," Roane was a brilliant lawyer and jurist who, as a staunch States' Righter, represented the opposite school of thought from that of John Marshall. Roane would almost certainly have been named Chief Justice of the United States by President Jefferson if there had been a vacancy. President Adams chose Marshall for the post just before Jefferson took office.

Spencer Roane had been appointed to the Virginia Council of State at age twenty-two, to the General Court at twenty-seven, and to the Court of Appeals, the state's highest tribunal, at thirty-two. He remained on the last-named bench for twenty-seven years, and became its dominant member almost at once. He took the lead in defying the U. S. Supreme Court in 1815 in the case of *Martin* v. *Hunter's Lessee*, involving Fairfax lands. The nation's highest court overruled Virginia's highest court, but the latter refused unanimously to obey the Federal mandate.

Roane, Ritchie and Dr. John Brockenbrough, also a native of Essex County, were the leaders of what was known as the "Essex Junto" or the "Richmond Junto," which was enormously potent politically. Through the county courts and the officeholders dependent upon them, they were the controlling force in the councils of Virginia's Republican party for decades.[1] A notable aspect of their operations was that they were carried on so quietly, if not secretly, that few realized their full portent. Not only did this group dominate Republican politics in the state, but through Dr. Brockenbrough, who became president of the Bank of Virginia, it also was extremely powerful in banking circles.

Essential to an understanding of this era in Richmond's history is the fact that the barbaric, and illegal, practice of dueling was in its heyday, and the life of a politician and especially of a newspaper editor was a hazardous one. Meriwether Jones, editor of the Richmond *Examiner*, was hot-tempered and this caused him to be engaged frequently in duels. In one of these he was killed. John Daly Burk, the historian, had completed three volumes of his projected four-volume history of Virginia when he was slain in a similar encounter. Skelton Jones, Meriwether's brother, also on the Examiner's editorial staff and himself a duelist of note, undertook to complete Burk's history. Before he had gotten well started, he too fell, a victim of the "code duello."

Colonel John Mayo, the bridge-builder, was embroiled in a duel with William Penn of Amherst County, when Penn called him a "damned rascal" in the course of a political argument. Like many others, Colonel Mayo—with a wife and children—did not believe in dueling, but since the stupid notion was widely prevalent that anyone who refused a summons to the so-called "field of honor" was a coward, he met Penn the next day near Hanover Courthouse. Mayo was wounded in the leg and became so faint from the loss of blood that he was carried from the field. There the affair ended.

A few years later, two young Richmond law students, Wyndham Grymes and Keeling Terrell, became involved in an altercation which led to a challenge. Grymes fell mortally wounded. Much feeling against dueling was aroused by this tragic episode, but the practice continued for most of the nineteenth century, with many promising young men cut off in their prime.

In the religious realm, Richmond in and around the year 1800 cannot be said to have been well-served. The Episcopal Church had been disestablished throughout the state after having been recognized for nearly two centuries as the colony's official denomination. It was, therefore, in almost complete disarray, especially after its glebe lands were taken from it. The Jews had their small synagogue, opened in 1789. Methodist circuit riders held services in Richmond between 1790 and 1800, with their first meetings in the county courthouse on Main Street. However, Dr. W. Asbury Christian, the Methodist clergyman-historian, tells us that they "made so much noise with their singing and shouting that the people asked that the court house be closed to them." The Methodists accordingly built their own church at Franklin and Nineteenth streets. The revered Bishop Francis Asbury preached his last sermon there in 1816, a week before his death.

The hard-pressed and persecuted Baptists, some of whom had been jailed in earlier years for preaching as "unlicensed dissenters," erected a frame meetinghouse in 1800. Their leader was the forceful Elder John Courtney, and their house of worship was on the north side of Cary Street between Second and Third. This was soon outgrown, and a larger church was erected in 1804 at Broad and College streets, where the denomination worshiped thereafter. So popular did Elder Courtney become that he was elected chaplain of the House of Representatives over the famous Rev. John D. Blair.

Blair, one of the renowned "Two Parsons," of whom more will be said, had been holding Presbyterian services in the Capitol for some years, since there was no Presbyterian church. Dr. John Holt Rice, another eminent Presbyterian divine, decided in 1812 to establish a house of worship in the city. His first sermons were delivered in the Masonic Hall on East Franklin Street, and were so largely attended by members of various denominations that no auditorium in the city could hold them. The Rocketts Church was accordingly built at Main and Twenty-seventh Street extended. This was seen to be inadequate almost at once and another church was erected on the southside of Grace between Seventeenth and Eighteenth streets. It was completed in 1816, and was known as the "Pineapple Church" from an ornament on its steeple. We have here the genesis of today's First Presbyterian Church.

The Roman Catholics were few in numbers in these years, and the Abbé Dubois, a French priest of marked talents, was the first clergyman of that faith to hold mass in Richmond. This was in 1791–92, and masses had to be celebrated for some time in rented rooms or private homes, although the first mass ever celebrated in Richmond took place in the Capitol on invitation of the General Assembly. Joseph Gallego was a leader in seeking to provide more adequate physical facilities for the faithful, but it was not until 1816 that the Catholics leased the abandoned Rocketts Church from the Presbyterians. Nine years later they moved to a small wooden church at Fourth and Marshall streets. Then in 1832 Father Timothy O'Brien came to Richmond, and the cornerstone of St. Peter's was laid at Eighth and Grace streets. It was opened in 1835, and for many years served as the city's cathedral.

With no Protestant church, except what is now St. John's, functioning in Richmond in or about the year 1800, the Reverend John Buchanan and the Reverend John D. Blair, an Episcopalian and a Presbyterian, respectively, conducted services on alternate Sundays for all denominations at the Capitol. St. John's had declined to such an extent that services were held there only three times a year—at Christmas, Easter and Whitsunday. An attendance of a mere half-dozen persons was not uncommon.

The "Two Parsons," as they were universally known, were delightful personalities and congenial companions. There was nothing remotely resembling interdenominational rivalry between them. Both loved a good joke, and Blair was especially adept at light verse. Buchanan, a bachelor, inherited a substantial amount of money from his brother, and he handed most of his clerical fees over to Blair, whose income was so small that he had to supplement it on occasion by teaching school. Blair, for his part, teased Buchanan for his bachelorhood. In a letter to his friend he called upon the nymphs to sing to him of "life's gay morn," that he might haste to see the fair ones and "sing of love ere he grows old."

The "Two Parsons" led exemplary lives, but they were so jovial and companionable that a few of the more strait-laced brethren were shocked.

In the tradition of the eighteenth century, during which the parsons passed most of their lives, they were not averse to gathering round the flowing bowl, although there is no reason to believe that either indulged to excess. Yet in 1835, when both men were dead and the moral climate had become more austere, William Maxwell referred in his biography of John Holt Rice to "the gross impropriety of their clerical deportment."

Blair and Buchanan were important figures in the Buchanan Spring Quoit Club, which began functioning in the last decade of the eighteenth century and continued well into the nineteenth. The meeting place was on Buchanan's farm in the shade of great oaks, just beyond the present Hancock Street and near the 1000 block of today's West Broad. On Saturdays in spring, summer and fall some thirty of Richmond's leading citizens gathered there. The cool spring on the property was notable for its translucent purity, and the shade of the huge trees made it a place of restful quietude. The area was then beyond the city limits.

Wine, for some reason, was prohibited at the meetings, except on special occasions, but julep, punch or toddy were regular features, together with porter and ale. The meals were of monumental proportions.

They were consumed on a pine table covered by a shed, under the masterful ministrations of Jasper Crouch, a Negro major-domo. Retained originally by the Richmond Light Infantry Blues, who recognized his ability in roasting pigs, mixing punch and performing other culinary rites, Crouch presided over the club's gastronomical activities for many years. The Blues, founded in 1789, were given special privileges at the Buchanan farm. Their handsome thirty-two-gallon punch bowl of India china was a spectacular feature of their outings. It was filled with brandy, rum and Madeira, flavored with lemons and sugar and chilled with plenty of ice.

As for the Buchanan Spring Quoit Club, its members regularly consumed an astonishing array of meats, fowls, fish, eggs, vegetables, salads, cheeses and fruits, all washed down with assorted potations. It was natural, after such repasts, that the sated gentlemen wished to relax.

Quoits came next for those who were partial to that sport. John Marshall and Parson Blair were generally the leaders of the two contesting teams. All the other players used highly polished brass rings, but the Chief Justice, with his usual lack of ostentation, had heavy, rough iron rings which he hurled with great dexterity, in an effort to ring the peg or come as close to it as possible. For those not interested in quoits, conversation, with politics barred, was the order of the day. Such raconteurs and wits as William Wirt, John Wickham and Benjamin Watkins Leigh were particular stars here.

Long after the original members of the Buchanan Spring Quoit Club were dead, the Blues continued to meet on the Buchanan farm and to toast the memory of Parson Buchanan. And when Jasper Crouch, their master caterer, died, the company buried him with military honors.

One of the most famous residents of Richmond when the Buchanan Spring Quoit Club was in its heyday was George Wythe, but there is no record that he was a member. Undoubtedly Wythe attended on occasion, since he was widely beloved and John Marshall had been his pupil at the College of William and Mary. A signer of the Declaration of Independence and a law professor who taught not only Marshall but Thomas Jefferson, James Monroe and Henry Clay, Wythe was perhaps the most revered Virginian of his generation. He moved to Richmond in 1789 when the state's judicial system was reorganized and he was made its chancellor. He lived in a modest yellow wooden house, with a hip roof, at the southeast corner of what is now Fifth and Grace streets. Its garden extended to Franklin Street and embraced half of the square. Wythe was a childless widower of simple habits who took a cold shower every morning at dawn, winter and summer, with water drawn from his sixty-foot well. In the words of his long-time friend William Munford, "Many a time I have heard him catching his breath and almost shouting with the shock."

Wythe's private secretary was young Henry Clay, who had been born near Hanover Courthouse and had come to Richmond as a boy. After clerking in a store, Clay obtained work in the High Court of Chancery in the Capitol basement. A gawky, fifteen-year-old youth in ill-fitting clothes, he was laughed at when he first arrived, but he soon showed exceptional ability. Wythe was attracted to him and made him his amanuensis. Clay read law under the great teacher for several years, and acquired for him enormous admiration and respect. In 1797, however, Clay decided to cross the mountains and seek his fortune in the newly formed state of Kentucky, where he later became famous. Clay was highly regarded in Richmond throughout his public career, and in 1844 fashionable Clay Street was named for him. A statue of him stood in Capitol Square for nearly a century, and then was moved inside the building.

Chancellor Wythe lived in Richmond for seventeen years. In 1806 the town was profoundly shocked when, at age eighty, he was murdered by his grandnephew, George Wythe Sweeney, who put arsenic in his morning coffee. The old man died in his home, after lingering in agony for two weeks. A young mulatto boy who lived with him also died from the poisoned drink. Sweeney's motive is supposed to have been a desire to acquire his inheritance from his granduncle at once, since he was in serious financial trouble. But Wythe lived long enough to realize what had happened and to add a codicil to his will disinheriting Sweeney. The latter escaped punishment because the only convincing witness against him was a Negro woman whom Wythe had freed and who was his devoted servant. Under a Virginia law, ironically drafted by Wythe himself, a black person could not testify against a white person in court.

The lamented teacher, jurist and statesman was accorded impressive funeral services at the Capitol, with eulogy by the scholarly William Munford, translator of Homer. Burial was in St. John's churchyard.

In the following year, 1807, Richmond was the scene of the greatest trial of its kind in American history—that of Aaron Burr for treason, with Chief Justice Marshall presiding. In that day Supreme Court justices "rode the circuit" as part of their routine duties.

Vice-President Aaron Burr had killed Alexander Hamilton in a duel in 1804, and was therefore a fugitive from justice. He was also suspected of plotting to establish some kind of government beyond the Alleghenies, thus threatening dismemberment of the Union. On this latter charge he was arrested in the far South and brought to Richmond for trial.

President Jefferson was bitterly antagonistic to Burr, and he worked behind the scenes to obtain his conviction. Chief Justice Marshall, a political and personal foe of Jefferson, although they were cousins, was strongly inclined toward Burr. He was felt by many to lean toward the accused in his rulings.

A preliminary hearing was held in a room at the Eagle Tavern and Burr was admitted to bail. It was provided by two prominent Richmonders who happened to be in the tavern, Colonel Robert Gamble and Robert Taylor. Although Burr had on the shabby clothes he had worn on his long journey from the Deep South, his aristocratic manner is understood to have impressed the two gentlemen, who saw him pass through the tavern bar, under guard. They not only signed his bond for $5,000 but Taylor is said to have lent him $1,000 with which to buy some proper apparel.

Burr appeared next day, March 31, at the Capitol, where proceedings took place in the Hall of the House of Delegates. Justice Marshall fixed May 22 as the date when the case would be presented to the grand jury.

In the meantime, John Wickham, one of Burr's brilliant lawyers, a man who the Irish poet Tom Moore said was "fit to adorn any court," gave a dinner at his Richmond home. To it he invited both Aaron Burr and John Marshall, as well as other friends, some of whom would serve on either the grand or the petit jury. Marshall was so insensitive to the proprieties as to attend. Some claim that he did not know Burr would be present, but it seems incredible that his friend and neighbor Wickham would not have told him that Burr would be a guest.

At all events, there was a great stir over the episode, and Benjamin Watkins Leigh, then a young lawyer, wrote a parody on Gray's *Elegy* in which he contrasted the treatment accorded the poor with that given Burr. One stanza follows:

> Their lot forbade; nor circumscribed alone
> Their groveling vices, but their joys confined.
> To them luxurious banquets were unknown,
> With these *poor* rogues their *judge* had never dined.

Leigh's temerity in thus offending both the Chief Justice of the United States and the leader of the Richmond bar was typical of his courage and adherence to principle. As for Wickham, he demonstrated his ability to take criticism, for he is said to have exhibited a friendly attitude toward the young man after reading his clever verses. Leigh later married Julia Wickham, the attorney's daughter.

When the grand jury met the following month, John Randolph of Roanoke had been named foreman by Marshall. The latter was criticized for choosing Randolph, whose hostility to Jefferson was well-known, but Randolph was also quite antagonistic to Burr. Marshall appointed to the jury other men of great prominence, including Joseph C. Cabell, Littleton W. Tazewell, Dr. John Brockenbrough and James Barbour. In Marshall's behalf it must be pointed out that fourteen of the sixteen grand jurors were Republicans and only two were Federalists. Republicans, in general, were anti-Burr while many Federalists took the opposite side.

Counsel for the defense included not only Wickham but Edmund Randolph, Benjamin Botts and John Baker, as well as Luther Martin of Maryland, extremely able but known as "Old Brandy Bottle" because of his extreme predilection for alcohol.

The prosecution was led by George Hay, U. S. District Attorney, a competent lawyer but completely outshone by his scintillating and versatile associate, William Wirt, author of *The Letters of a British Spy*. The third member of the prosecution was Lieutenant Governor Alexander McRae, described as "an aggressive and alert Scotchman."

Thousands converged on Richmond by stagecoach, on horseback and in covered wagons when the news spread that the trial was about to begin. The taverns could not hold them, though they slept three in a bed; many spent the nights in or under their wagons, in tents or along the riverbank.

Among those in the throng was General Andrew Jackson, who had entertained Burr at his home The Hermitage, near Nashville, the previous year. Dressed in the attire of a backwoodsman, Jackson, who would normally be assumed to be sympathetic to Jefferson, loudly denounced the trial as "political persecution." Another defender of Burr who later achieved great prominence was young Washington Irving, then a correspondent for New York newspapers. He sent dispatches highly favorable to the accused which influenced opinion in the New York area. Irving was ecstatic in praise of Richmond hospitality.

Burr, too, had good reason to regard Richmonders as hospitable. While out on bail awaiting the meeting of the grand jury, the attractive and handsome man, whose father had been president of Princeton University, was entertained by many of Richmond's most prominent citizens. After he was indicted for treason on June 24, he spent two nights in Richmond's vermin-infested jail. He then was placed under guard in a brick house at the southwest corner of Ninth and Broad streets, but soon was removed to the recently constructed penitentiary. There he was given a suite of three rooms and every courtesy by his jailer. He wrote his daughter that servants from many Richmond homes constantly "arrived with messages, notes, inquiries, bringing oranges, lemons, pineapples, rasp-berries, apricots, cream, butter, ice and some ordinary articles." There were callers every day.

Court reconvened on August 3, for the purpose of impaneling a petit jury, and this took two weeks. Proceedings at the Capitol in connection with both the grand and the petit juries were attended by sweating throngs that overflowed the Hall of the House of Delegates and jammed the rotunda and corridors. Many frontiersmen in red woolen shirts and homespun trousers were there, virtually all of them convinced that Burr was guilty. The same feeling prevailed among most of the elegant aristo-crats, dressed in their black silk, knee breeches and silver buckles. It was one of the hottest summers on record, and in the steaming heat, between squirts of tobacco juice, high and low debated the pros and cons of the case.

Arguments by counsel were exceptionally able, and were listened to with rapt attention by the packed galleries. Wickham, Martin and Botts were the stars for the defense, with Wirt easily the central figure in the prosecution. In fact, Wirt's four-hour arraignment of Burr and defense of Harman Blennerhassett, also under indictment, has been cited ever since as an oratorical classic. A fragment, opening with the words "Who is Blen-nerhassett?", was declaimed from high school platforms for generations.

Although Burr was almost certainly guilty of trying to set up some sort of government in the West, the efforts of Wirt and his associates to prove it were of no avail. For Justice Marshall announced a definition of trea-son that tore the prosecution's case to shreds. He ruled that in order to prove Burr's guilt, it was necessary to show overt acts, with two wit-nesses present when each act was committed. The prosecution could ad-vance no such proof. It accordingly had to abandon its plans to put on the stand a whole array of witnesses, and the trial ended abruptly.

The jury was out only twenty-five minutes. Its verdict was: "We of the jury say that Aaron Burr is not proved guilty under this indictment by any evidence submitted to us. We therefore find him not guilty." This unu-sual type of verdict, said to have been acceptable only in Scotland, was vehemently protested as irregular by Burr and his counsel. Marshall there-upon directed that the clerk place on the record the words "Not Guilty."

In Burr's behalf, be it said that what he was apparently trying to do, namely dismember the Union, was not regarded in that era as so serious a crime as it would be today. Historian Thomas P. Abernethy clearly regards Burr as guilty, but he says in *The Burr Conspiracy*, "It was still widely ac-knowledged that states which had voluntarily entered the compact could easily withdraw from it." Notwithstanding the verdict, Burr remained under a stigma for the rest of his life.

# SEVEN

# Schools, Artists, Mansions, Race Tracks and Theaters

AT THE HEIGHT of the Burr trial there was added excitement in Richmond when the British frigate *Leopard* attacked the American cruiser *Chesapeake* off the Virginia capes. The attack grew out of Britain's resentment of the numerous desertions of British sailors to American ships, desertions that occurred, in part, because of American seamen's higher pay. When the *Chesapeake* refused to heed the *Leopard's* demand for permission to search her for deserters, the British ship fired a broadside without warning, killing three and wounding eighteen on board the American vessel. Riddled and taken by surprise, the *Chesapeake* had to lower her colors. The British came on board and carried off a deserter and several others.

Richmonders were furious, as was nearly everybody else in the United States. Indignant citizens came together at Virginia's Capitol, with Judge Spencer Roane presiding. President Jefferson directed all British warships to leave American waters, and when the British squadron in Hampton Roads failed to comply, state troops were ordered to that area by Governor William H. Cabell.

The Richmond Cavalry under Captain James Sheppard, the Richmond Light Infantry Blues under Captain William Richardson, and the Republican Blues under Captain Peyton Randolph set out for Hampton Roads. Bombardment and ultimate invasion by the British were feared, but when the British ships sailed away on July 28, the Richmond units returned.

President Jefferson was strongly opposed to war, if it could be honorably avoided, and he decided to implement his theory that economic pressure would be effective. In the last days of 1807, Congress accordingly passed his Embargo Act, prohibiting all exports from this country and banning the import of various British articles.

Coal exports from the Midlothian mines suffered severely as did the tobacco business, so heavily dependent on overseas trade. But many British goods could still be legally admitted, as evidenced by an advertisement in the *Enquirer* for March 8, 1808. The well-known firm of Ellis & Allen, under the heading "English Goods for Sale," offered a long list of such commodities. Among them were:

"Lady's fawn, brown and blue clothes, best London cassimeres and double mill'd blue and drab cloth, Princess cords, Constitution cords, velvets, corduroys and Thicksetts, Swansdowns, Toilenets and quilting for vests, Circassian and Tissue silks; gentlemen's silk hose, plain and ribbed; best shoes, with and without soals; misses cotton hose, ladies' elastic habits; gentlemen's best beaver and patent silk hats . . . new music for the pianoforte; Smith's bellows, anvils and vices; coal shovels and spades . . . some uncommonly large razors, warranted; elegant plate warmers, tea trays and waiters, double and treble gilt; spectacles, pebble eyes, set in silver . . . common hat pins; chimney horns and brass finger plates, handsome gilt dressing boxes and castors, brass commode handles . . ."

Sentiment was rising, however, against the purchase of British goods, and three months after the foregoing advertisement appeared, a mass meeting was held at the Capitol for the purpose of organizing a boycott and promoting domestic manufactures. James Monroe presided. It was unanimously agreed that at the ensuing Fourth of July celebration in Richmond, only clothes of American make would be worn and only domestic liquors consumed.

Yet, as time passed, Jefferson's embargo was conceded by nearly all to be a dismal failure, and it was repealed shortly before the end of the President's second term. The repeal was greeted with relief in Richmond, which celebrated the event with a dinner at the Bell Tavern.

Some months after Jefferson's retirement from the presidency in 1809, he appeared in Richmond to transact private business. With his usual lack of ceremony, he drove up unannounced to the Swan Tavern. News of his presence in the city spread rapidly, however, and a public reception at the Capitol was arranged. Dr. William Foushee was chairman and William Munford secretary. Dinners were given in his honor at the Swan and Eagle taverns with leading citizens in attendance. Governor John Tyler, James Monroe and others of like stature offered toasts. After a four-day sojourn in Richmond, Jefferson returned to Monticello.

One of the fortunate happenings of this period was the coming to Richmond of the artist St. Mémin. A French aristocrat who had fled the French Revolution, C. B. J. Fevret de St. Mémin arrived in the city at the height of the Burr trial and remained until early in the following year. In his studio at the northeast corner of Eleventh and Main he executed his famous profiles in black and white crayon with a pink paper background, using a device known as a physiognotrace. His list of sitters reads like a Who's Who of that era in Richmond, and it is due to St. Mémin that we have excellent likenesses of so large a number of Richmond's foremost judges, attorneys, doctors and merchants. Before he came to Richmond he had done portraits in various Northern cities, as well as in Alexandria and Fredericksburg, and he went later to Norfolk and Charleston. As Richard Beale Davis puts it: "The Virginia pictures show the queue and powdered horsehair wig of the gentlemen of middle age or more, the new-fashioned wind-blown Parisian-style locks of the younger men, the neat caps of the dignified matrons and tighter-fitting caps and voluminous dresses of the older ladies, and the romantic curls of the younger women."

The Sully family was another contributor to art in Richmond during the early Federal period. Lawrence Sully, who had studied at the Royal Academy in London, came to Richmond in 1792. He advertised that he would do miniatures, and also offered "all kinds of mourning, Fancy and Hair Devices, executed in the neatest manner." Seven years later, his younger brother, Thomas, arrived in the city to study under him. Lawrence was talented, but a devotee of the bottle. In a drunken brawl with sailors in 1804, he was killed and tossed into the James. Thomas took over the care of Lawrence's widow Sarah and her daughters. Two years later he and Sarah were married.

During the period from 1799 to 1806, Thomas Sully did portraits of important Richmonders. He also painted an eagle for the sign in front of the Eagle Tavern. He left the city in 1806 for the North, and never returned for a permament stay, but he came back frequently and did numerous portraits. He is described as "Richmond's favorite painter during his long life."

Robert Sully, nephew of Thomas, was also a painter. After studying in England for four years, he returned to Virginia in 1828, where he did some excellent portraits. His granddaughter, Miss Julia Sully, was long prominent in Richmond's social life.

Another artist who left his imprint on the city was John B. Martin. A native of Ireland who came to Richmond about 1817, Martin was a painter and engraver. His portrait of John Marshall hangs in the United States Supreme Court in Washington. He also did portraits of Major James Gibbon, Dr. John Brockenbrough and Dr. Moses D. Hoge, in whose church he was a ruling elder.

The Peticolas family was likewise significant in the early history of Richmond art. They arrived in the city in 1805 from France, via Pennsylvania. Philippe A. Peticolas, the father, taught music and miniature painting. His more talented son, Edward, was advertising at age fourteen that he was prepared to execute miniatures. Later he made several trips to Europe

1. William Byrd II, reluctant founder of Richmond, one of the most brilliant, sophisticated and talented men of his time. (Portrait attributed to Sir Godfrey Kneller.)

2. Four generations of the original Ege family, first dwellers in the Old Stone House, Richmond's oldest, are shown in this rare portrait about 1802. Left, Maria Dorothea Scherer, who in 1740 married Jacob Ege, the presumed builder of the house, into which they moved. Far right, their daughter, Elizabeth Ege, who married Gabriel Galt, proprietor of Galt's Tavern. Their daughter, Elizabeth, married Thomas Williamson, and the child is their son, Frederick.

3. Little-known watercolor of Belvidere, made in 1797 by Benjamin H. Latrobe, the famous architect who helped design some of the principal government buildings in Washington. Belvidere was built by William Byrd III in the middle or late 1750s, and burned a century later. It is shown in a thunderstorm with the James River in the background.

4. Recently discovered pastel of Mrs. John Marshall, the "dearest Polly" to whom the Chief Justice was deeply devoted during their married life of nearly half a century. She was much on young Marshall's mind when he was a student at the College of William and Mary. His classroom notes show "Polly Ambler" and "Polly" scribbled on the margins.

5. Meadow Farm near Glen Allen, the home of Mosby Sheppard, where two of his slaves tipped him off on August 30, 1800, to the fact that Gabriel's slave insurrection was slated to occur that night, with the slaughter of himself and all the other whites in the neighborhood. The blacks then planned to move on to nearby Richmond and kill the whites there. Mrs. Sheppard Crump, the present owner, has willed the property to Henrico County for a public park in memory of her husband.

6. Brook Hill, the only other dwelling in the area that survives from the time of the insurrection. The home in 1800 of the Williamson family, it was smaller than it is today, and situated just across the brook from the Prosser plantation Brookfield, where Gabriel planned the uprising.

7. The Reverend John Buchanan, one of the famous "Two Parsons" of the late eighteenth and early nineteenth centuries in Richmond. He was an Episcopalian, whereas the other parson, the Reverend John D. Blair, was a Presbyterian. Buchanan was better situated financially than Blair, and he gave many of his fees to his friend.

8. The Reverend John D. Blair, like the Reverend John Buchanan, was a convivial soul, loved a good joke and was adept at writing light verse. He and Buchanan alternated in holding services on Sunday at the Capitol in the early 1800s, since there was no Protestant church in the city except what was later known as St. John's. (Portrait by Cephas Thompson.)

9. Gilbert Hunt, the slave who was a hero of the terrible theater fire of 1811, is commemorated in a tablet in the portico of Monumental Episcopal Church, erected on the site of the tragedy. Hunt stood under a window of the burning building and caught about a dozen women as they were handed down to him by Dr. James D. McCaw. When McCaw had to jump to escape the roaring flames, Hunt pulled him to safety just before the wall collapsed.

10. This lovely aquatint of Richmond about 1832 by George Cooke is considered the most charming of all the early views of the city. The Capitol atop the hill in the background almost reminds one of the Acropolis in Athens. Behind it, to the reader's left, stands the old city hall, while at the base of the hill in the foreground is the winding James River & Kanawha Canal. The view is from what is now Hollywood Cemetery.

11. Thomas Ritchie, famous editor of the Richmond *Enquirer*, not only an immensely effective journalist but nationally influential in Democratic politics for several decades.

12. John Hampden Pleasants, exceptionally able editor of the Richmond *Whig*, and Ritchie's chief rival. He was killed in a duel by Thomas Ritchie, Jr., who falsely charged that he was about to found an abolitionist journal.

but always returned to Richmond, where he had quite a vogue as a portrait painter. Edward was the most famous member of the family, but he had several brothers and other relatives who were artists and musicians. Some were teachers.

Education in Richmond in the early 1800s was undergoing a change of emphasis, especially education for "females." In the preceding century there had often been a reluctance to instruct young ladies in anything more taxing to the brain than drawing, music, French or dancing. In the early 1700s—in England, at least—matters were particularly difficult. Joseph Addison, the English essayist, advised woman to "content herself with her natural talents, play at cards, make tea and visits, talk to her dog often, and to her company but sometimes."

A hundred years later, both in England and America, the tide was turning. The opening of the Richmond Female Academy in 1807, with a distinguished board and teaching staff, signaled a considerable shift of opinion in Virginia's capital on behalf of broader and more rigorous schooling for girls. The *Virginia Argus* of Richmond published with approval an article from the Lynchburg *Star* which said: "The outlines of the Richmond Female Academy bespeak a grand design, commencing a national reform and instruction in the right place. Enlighten and exalt the female mind and you forthwith banish from the world baseness, vice, villainy and ignorance." Great impetus was given this trend in the 1820s by James Mercer Garnett. He opened a superior school for girls at Elmwood, Essex County, which became famous. Garnett also lectured widely on behalf of the cause.

During these years, the schools for girls and young women in Richmond became definitely more demanding in their requirements and broader in their scholastic offerings. Such subjects as Latin, Greek, mathematics, history, geography and natural philosophy were frequently a part of the curriculum; even chemistry and astronomy were sometimes taught.

An excellent school that catered to both girls and boys was that of Louis H. Girardin, an accomplished French émigré. The sexes were educated under the same roof, although separately, for "co-education" in the modern sense did not exist in early Richmond. Children of many leading families were represented on the roster of Girardin's Academy.

On the faculty was Jean Charles Frémon, like Girardin a refugee from the French Revolution. He was employed to give young Mrs. John C. Pryor—the former Anne Whiting of Gloucester County—instruction in the "polite accomplishments." However, in the words of Wirt Armistead Cate, "he succeeded in less than a year in teaching her a subject not a part of any curriculum."

The whole town was rocked to its foundations in 1811 when Mrs. Pryor left with Frémon for the South, after the two had been surprised in what was termed "a compromising situation." Her prominent and aging husband, a veteran of the American Revolution, swore revenge. But the lovers remained out of reach, and eighteen months later, without benefit of marriage, Anne Whiting Pryor gave birth to a son, John Charles Frémon. He later added a "t" to his surname and became John Charles Frémont, the famous explorer of the West and in 1856 the first presidential nominee of the newly formed Republican party.

A well-known seminary for girls, which was attended by many from Richmond, was conducted for a decade in Warrenton, North Carolina, by Jacob Mordecai, father of Samuel Mordecai, author of *Richmond in By-Gone Days*. Before and after operating this school, Jacob Mordecai lived in Richmond.

Since there were still no street numbers in Richmond, the addresses of schools and every other type of establishment were given in such vague terms as "in the house lately occupied by Mrs. Broome on Shockoe Hill," "in Col. Bullock's house in the immediate neighborhood of Mr. Blair," or "on the west side of the creek in a yellow house once occupied by John Banks."

Library facilities in Richmond had their beginnings in these years, but they were always inadequate until well into the twentieth century. The Library Society of Richmond, which had been founded in 1784, was incorporated by the General Assembly in 1806. It gradually accumulated a collection of books for the benefit of its members, who paid an annual fee.

The number of springs that discharged their cool waters into the streets and squares of old Richmond was extraordinary. Samuel Mordecai says that in his youth "springs . . . flowed from various spots at the base of Shockoe Hill, along its whole extent from Fifth to Fourteenth Street. . . . There was a spring on almost every square west of the Capitol." He goes on to describe a scene that is hard for us to visualize today:

"Quite a rural and romantic spot was the square on the north side of Main Street between Sixth and Seventh—a steep hill, and a little valley shaded with forest trees; a spring, the water of which formed a pond for fishing and skating—the silence broken only by the singing of birds, the croaking of frogs and the sports of children."

There was no paving along Main Street immediately to the east of this bosky dell and as far as Ninth, a condition that remained unchanged until the Civil War. In fact, the *Virginia Patriot* of Richmond pronounced Main Street all the way to Rocketts "in a state disgraceful to civilized society." The paper declared that "there are holes in it almost deep enough to receive a hogshead of tobacco."

"Sad was the fate of the unlucky wight who, otherwise than on horseback, undertook to pass through the lower part of the city," ex-President John Tyler declared fifty years later in describing Richmond as he had known it in the early 1800s. And if it was so difficult to move about in broad daylight, consider the hazards at night. There were no gaslights on the streets, and those who tried to go from place to place on foot, on horseback or in a carriage were risking serious injury as they stumbled or bumped along over the ruts, gullies and ravines. Lanterns were called into play occasionally and seemed like fireflies in the gloom.

An attempt to provide illumination by gas, produced from wood and pit coal, was made in 1802 by an Englishman named Benjamin Henfrey. He erected a forty-foot brick tower for the purpose at Eleventh and Main streets and the apparatus functioned briefly, but failed to throw its beams a sufficient distance. The experiment was abandoned, although the tower stood at Eleventh and Main for many years. It might be termed the first lamppost in history to burn coal gas for municipal purposes. There would be no lighting of Richmond's streets by gas until 1851.

Capitol Square in the early 1800s was covered with gravel and weeds and was not enclosed, so that cows and goats moved in and out at will. The handsome iron fence around the square was not built until 1818. On each side of the Capitol was a horse rack. A shabby wooden barracks, occupied by the Public Guard and their families, stood on the site of the brick bell tower, which replaced it in 1824. Masculine shirts and feminine chemises hung from clotheslines, while children shouted, chickens cackled and pigs grunted.

The classic lines of the Capitol were marred by "Two lateral staircases of the heaviest Gothic structure that can be imagined," wrote Robert Gilmor, a visitor. The building was in need of repairs, as was the governor's mansion, Governor John Tyler, father of President Tyler, told the General Assembly.

The small wooden gubernatorial residence was "intolerable for a private family," he said, and there was "a cluster of dirty tenements immediately in front of the house." It apparently faced on Governor Street, then a country road heading westward along what was later Broad Street. The result of Tyler's representations was that the Capitol was tidied up and a new and much more commodious brick mansion, designed by Alexander Parris, was completed in 1814 on the site of the old one. When the legislature was in session, a five-gallon bowl of toddy punch was always available at the mansion for thirsty lawmakers.

Richmond had another annexation in 1810, which expanded the city to the east, north and west. This brought the total area to 2.4 square miles and the population to 9,785, including 3,748 slaves. The city had been divided shortly before into three wards, Jefferson, Madison and Monroe.

The municipal water supply came from springs and wells. Much of it was conveyed "by means of pipes sunk so low as to keep the water perfectly cool," Mayor David Bullock declared. He obtained permission from the state authorities to use the surplus water from two large springs on Capitol Hill "after supplying the Capitol and Barracks." Mayor Bullock promised in return to construct a reservoir nearby "at least 20 feet square," for use in case of fire.

Naming of streets went forward at this time. Capitol and Bank streets acquired those designations—the former because of its proximity to the statehouse and the latter because the Bank of Virginia was on it.

Communication between Richmond and other points was being facilitated by the inauguration of additional stagecoach service. Lines between Richmond and Staunton and Richmond and Hampton were announced. A coach left Richmond at 5 A.M. and reached Staunton at noon more than two days later. Another left Richmond for Hampton at 4 A.M. and arrived there the next day at 6 P.M.

Richmond apparently had a post office of some sort in the 1770s, but its first postmaster, James Hayes, was appointed in 1782. More than a quarter of a century later, a clerk under Postmaster William Foushee is said to have invented the individual box system for letter delivery. He was Thomas Brown, who long afterward became governor of Florida.[1] The post office in those years had no permanent home, and was housed in a newspaper plant, a hotel and a private residence. Finally, in 1859 the first customshouse and post office was completed on the Main Street site where it has remained for more than a century.

Richmond was an important port in the early 1800s, with square-riggers and coastwise schooners constantly taking on and discharging cargo along the small but teeming docks. Singing Negro stevedores and roustabouts rolled hogsheads of tobacco and barrels of flour onto the wharves for shipment to far places. Sailing vessels with English woolens and cutlery, French perfumes and wines, Brazilian coffee and East Indian spices discharged their freight. The pungent smell of pitch and tar mingled with that of golden Virginia leaf and aromatic cargoes from around the Horn.

Brawny sailors relaxed at nearby taverns from their long weeks at sea. Barrels of grog and puncheons of rum were ready to hand, and the tars sometimes were overzealous in their desire to put care aside. As, for example, when the *Argus* announced "with deepest regret" that "owing to the disorderly conduct of a few despicable wretches, heated (probably) by the fumes of whiskey, the peace of our town was much disturbed on Sunday evening." The military had to be called out to quell the "ruffians," and twenty or thirty were taken into custody.

The militiamen who arrested the riotous sailors got their weapons from the Virginia Manufactory of Arms. It had been built at the turn of the century under the direction of Captain John Clarke of Powhatan, a veteran of the Revolution. Not only muskets but pistols, swords and scabbards were made in the plant, which was situated on the bank of the canal below Gamble's Hill. A committee of the General Assembly pronounced the muskets superior to those made in Great Britain.

Sailors or others who did not wish to patronize taverns could purchase alcoholic refreshments in retail stores, such as that of William Patterson, who advertised "Madeira, Sherry, Port, Vidonia, Malaga, Cogniac Brandy, Holland Gin, St. Croix and Jamaica Rum." In addition, Patterson offered "French Gun-Powder and other Teas, Florence Oil, French Capers, Mustard in Bottles and Kegs, Cayenne, Spices, Raisins and Figs, New Orleans Sugar, Olives, Ginger, Lisbon Lemons, Irish linen, Genuine Spanish Segars, Green Coffee, and a few Dozen Grass Entry Matts."

Richmond's *bon vivants*, including John Marshall, John Wickham and William Wirt, patronized such alluring establishments as the above. The hospitality of these men was proverbial, but Marshall and Wirt put their guests more completely at ease than Wickham, whose dinners were stiffer and more formal.

Gentlemen's dress in the early years of the century rivaled that of the ladies in complexity. Many yards of muslin were wrapped around the throat with the aid of one's valet. If such a functionary was not available, the alternative was for the gentleman to attach one end of the so-called cravat to a bedpost, and then "revolve on his own periphery till he was wound up like the main spring of a watch or an Egyptian mummy." Those who could not afford the quantity of muslin involved in this operation could purchase a "pudding" or "pad," which formed the foundation for the cravat. An accessory to these gaudy habiliments was the snuffbox, which might be fancy or plain, as circumstances dictated. Among the avid takers of snuff was William Wirt, whose handling of the box was said to be exceptionally graceful.

Formal raiment was *de rigueur* for parties and balls in the early 1800s. For ordinary occasions, buckskin breeches and "fairtop boots" were considered the thing.

Male coiffure in that era was something special. Young men and boys let their hair grow until it fell around their shoulders. When they reached middle age, they began wearing it still longer and tying it up in a queue. When queues first became fashionable in the years following the Revolution, gentlemen put them up in silken bags, with the bag tied up close to the back of the neck. Later a tie or black ribbon was used instead of a bag. Men past middle age often were not satisfied with this relatively mundane arrangement, so they plaited their flowing locks, tied them at the extreme end, doubled them back, wrapped them with a long twisted cord and finally decorated the whole with a bow or black ribbon. "Nearly every old gentleman in Richmond had his hour for dressing his queue," said one writer. Queues continued to be worn in Richmond until about 1840.

One of the able attorneys in Richmond at this time was John Warden, a Scotsman. Ex-President Tyler declared in describing his distorted physiognomy and warped body that "his structure was seemingly reversed and everything out of place." Although his mouth was "enormously large . . . his tongue was too large for his mouth." Which led a wag to compose the following "epitaph":

> Reader tread lightly o'er his sod,
> For if he gapes, you are gone, by God.

The misshapen and satyr-like Warden was contemptuous of the state legislature at times, and on one occasion said that it did not have "sense enough to carry guts to a bear." For this transgression he was arrested by the sergeant at arms and required to retract the offending statement on his knees, in the presence of the Assembly. This he did, saying:

"Mr. Speaker, I confess that I did say that your honors were not fit to carry guts to a bear—I now retract that assertion and acknowledge that you are fit."

The houses in which Richmonders lived at this time were mainly of brick. The conflagration of 1787, when wooden houses burned like tinder, had taught them a lesson. Brick Row, the principal business section on Main Street, was one example, and the handsome residences erected in the Court End north of Broad and on Fifth Street north and south of Main were others. Fifth had become especially fashionable.

Moldavia, later to be associated with young Edgar Allan Poe, was built in 1800 at the southeast corner of Fifth and Main, by David Meade Randolph. He was then U.S. marshal for Virginia and an inventor of considerable talent. At various times he patented devices for making candles, drawing liquor and building ships, and he is credited with an invention that laid the foundations of the machine bootmaking industry. His wife Molly was also an inventor—in the culinary realm. Her cookbook was famous. Their home, Moldavia, was named for Molly and David. It was later sold to Joseph Gallego and then to John Allan, Poe's foster father.

The Hancock-Caskie house, which still stands at the northwest corner of Fifth and Main, was built only a few years later. Like so many of the mansions of that day, it had, in the words of Miss Mary Wingfield Scott, the preeminent authority, "besides a kitchen-wing, an icehouse, an office, a summer house, a smokehouse, servants' quarters, a well, a stable and a carriage-house, as well as the primitive outside plumbing arrangements that characterized Richmond's finest houses down into the eighteen-forties." All these auxiliary structures have long since disappeared, of course, not only from the Hancock-Caskie house but from the other surviving Richmond mansions of comparable importance. The most celebrated owner of the last-named residence, known in modern times as the Caskie house, was William Wirt, who finished his *Life of Patrick Henry* here and in 1826 declined an offer to become the first president of the University of Virginia. The house, in the mid-twentieth century, was headquarters for the

Red Cross and was then acquired by the William Byrd Branch of the Association for the Preservation of Virginia Antiquities.

Another impressive Fifth Street house, now vanished, was that of Joseph Marx, one of the Europeans who came to Richmond in the late eighteenth century and made important contributions to the city's cultural and business progress. Marx, whose father had been court physician to the Elector of Hanover, arrived in Richmond poor and unknown. He rose to a position of eminence and, in the words of the *Enquirer*, died "universally respected." His mansion, Hanover House, at 101 South Fifth Street, was built in 1813–14, almost simultaneously with the Wickham mansion at Eleventh and Clay, and was comparable to the latter in the opulence of its appointments.

Joseph Marx took as his bride Richea Myers, sister of another distinguished Jewish citizen, Samuel Myers. They had nine children, some of whom married into leading gentile families.

Marx was guardian for the children of Solomon Jacobs, who died in 1827. Jacobs had been acting mayor of Richmond, the only member of his faith to serve in that office. He also was Grand Master of Masons for the state of Virginia, the first Jew to be so chosen. His four children married prominent gentiles and joined Christian churches. Many leading Richmonders of today who do not follow Jewish religious practices have Jewish forebears. The fact may help to account for the cordial relations that have long existed in Richmond between members of the Jewish and non-Jewish communities.

Samuel Marx, son of Joseph, was a director of the James River and Kanawha Canal Company and president of the Bank of Virginia. Another son, Frederick, was a physician of eminence in Richmond, while a third, Charles, lived in Manchester, and Marx's Addition there was named either for him or his brother, the doctor.

Not far from Joseph Marx's Hanover House was Colonel Robert Gamble's Grey Castle, near the southwest corner of Fourth and Byrd. Built at the turn of the century for Colonel John Harvie, in accordance with designs of Benjamin H. Latrobe, it was purchased almost at once by Colonel Gamble. The latter had been born in Augusta County, served in the Revolution and became one of Richmond's most prominent merchants. He was killed in 1810 when a bundle of buffalo hides, tossed from the second story of a warehouse, so startled his horse that the animal reared, throwing him to the ground. Many years later, the Gamble mansion was the home of McGuire's University School. It was demolished in 1889.

Other significant houses were built on Fifth Street during these years, but all have disappeared, like those erected on the same street a decade or two earlier. One was that of Major James Gibbon, "the hero of Stony Point" in the Revolution. It stood just north of Main on Fifth, next door to the subsequently erected Second Presbyterian Church. Dr. Moses D.

Hoge, pastor of that church, lived in the Gibbon house for many years. Another notable residence on Fifth Street was that of William Munford at the southwest corner of its intersection with Canal.

Handsomest of all the mansions built in Richmond at this period was that of John Wickham at 1015 East Clay Street. Almost certainly designed by Robert Mills of Charleston, South Carolina, it included the most beautiful staircase in the city and one of the loveliest gardens. The youthful Wickham, a native of Long Island, had been jailed as a Tory in the Revolution, since he had enlisted in the British army. After the close of hostilities, he studied abroad and then briefly in Williamsburg. He moved to Richmond, where his extraordinary talents and polished manners carried him swiftly to the top of both the legal profession and Richmond society. He married Elizabeth McClurg, daughter of Dr. James McClurg, and they had seventeen children.

Another striking mansion in the immediate neighborhood also was designed by Robert Mills. It was the home of Dr. John Brockenbrough, later the White House of the Confederacy. It stood at Twelfth and Clay, was built a few years later than the Wickham house, and had only two stories at the time. Another was added at mid-century. Dr. Brockenbrough became acquainted with John Randolph of Roanoke when both were serving on the Aaron Burr grand jury, and Randolph visited Brockenbrough repeatedly thereafter. The Brockenbroughs were among the few people whom the waspish Randolph admired. He described Brockenbrough as "A one among men," and said of the latter's wife, Gabriella Harvie Brockenbrough, "There is a mind of a very high order: well improved and manners that a queen might envy." Randolph paid court to Maria Ward, "the love of his life," at the Brockenbroughs'. The romance was apparently going full blast when it was suddenly terminated by Miss Ward, and Randolph seems never to have recovered. Maria asked Mrs. Brockenbrough to see that Randolph's letters to her were burned after her death, with the seal unbroken.

Older than any of the above-mentioned houses is the Daniel Call house, built before 1796 at the southeast corner of Ninth and Broad streets. One of its first occupants was Jean Chevallié. Daniel Call, prominent attorney and brother-in-law of John Marshall, lived there for twenty-two years. In 1849 the house was put on rollers and moved to its present location at Madison and Grace streets, where in 1936 it was transformed into an undertaking establishment. Its present external appearance is not identical with that which it had in the late eighteenth century, and the interior has been greatly changed. Yet its preservation and adaptation for commercial purposes affords an example that might well be followed by other business establishments.

Entertainment of various kinds was available to Richmonders in the early 1800s. The Haymarket Gardens were well-established by that time, operated by Major John Pryor—the same whose young wife ran away with her French lover, Jean Charles Frémon, while the latter was teaching her "the polite accomplishments." The Gardens were located between Sixth and Eighth streets south of Arch, and extended to the river in a series of terraces. Also included was the square bounded by Seventh, Eighth, Byrd and Arch, so that there was room for a great variety of attractions and amusements. Among them was "the Riding Machine or Flying Gigs, wherein eight persons can be conveyed at the rate of two to five hundred yards in a minute . . . its effects are delightful to the riders and peculiarly efficacious to those of weak nervous habits." A thousand persons could be accommodated in the buildings surrounding the musical gallery, where musical events were staged. "The lower part of the Dancing House is also. open for entertainment when Balls, Ice Creams, Coffee Cake and all kinds of Fruit and the best of Liquors will be constantly provided," said an announcement. The gardens also offered "Sports of the Pit," namely cockfights, and there were other pits for bears. Quoits, bowling and shuffleboard were available, as well as stables for horses. One's horse could be "elegantly nicked for a guinea" and there was cropping and foxing in accord with the latest styles. From Haymarket Gardens one had an excellent view of the river's rocks and falls while strolling along the "broad walks with serpentine alleys."

The masquerade balls at the Gardens caused alarm in certain circles as being "dangerous to virtue." A writer in one of the newspapers expressed concern on this score, but was answered by another correspondent who viewed card parties as fraught with much greater peril, since "they afford many more opportunities for a display of those fopperies of love and habits of dissipation so fatal to the happiness of society."

There were other gardens similar to the Haymarket, albeit less extensive. Didier Colin, a Frenchman, bought nearly nineteen acres of land at the northern end of Eighth, Ninth and Tenth streets in 1792 and operated an amusement park called the French Garden for about a decade. Then there were the Falling Gardens, operated by a Quaker named James Lownes, and extending from Locust Alley to Fifteenth Street on both sides of Franklin. A special attraction was the bathhouse with both hot and cold water, at two shillings and sixpence the bath. There was also Jackson's Pleasure Garden at the northwest corner of Second and Leigh streets "illuminated with 2,000 variegated lamps." Another center of recreation was Vauxhall Island in the James, scene of countless picnics for three quarters of a century. Amusements in that era were much simpler and more bucolic than those of today.

Visits to friends usually lasted at least a week. Thomas Rutherfoord wrote in the summer of 1808 that he "determined to take a trip with my wife and such of our children as we could carry with us . . . spending two or three months with our friends in the country." He stopped with Colonel William Cabell at Union Hill, the Rives family at Oak Ridge, Colonel W. C. Nicholas at Warren and so on. A week or ten days was passed at each place.

Whether the Rutherfoords heard any mockingbirds such as were described by C. W. Janson, a contemporaneous visitor to Virginia, is not known. Janson wrote that a Frenchman "took great pains to encourage his wonderful warbler." After imitating other songsters, this mockingbird "descended to the brute creation, giving us the mewing of a cat, and the barking of a dog." The Frenchman "then led it to follow him in some French airs; and this was a prelude to another piece, consisting of a variety of Scotch airs and American popular tunes." Janson concludes, not surprisingly, "this concert . . . for variety and execution excited our wonder."

Richmonders a century and three quarters ago enjoyed the farm produce of surrounding regions, as they do today. Hanover watermelons, then as now, were regarded as a delicacy. "We remember in our boyhood," a prominent Richmonder wrote in the 1880s, "the watermelon carts in August, covered with thick-leaved limbs, passing through the streets."

Richmond was one of the greatest racing centers in the United States, beginning in the colonial era and continuing until the Civil War. The races were held under the auspices of the Richmond Jockey Club, which also sponsored sumptuous balls during the racing season. There were three tracks near the city. Fairfield in Henrico on the Mechanicsville Turnpike, the oldest, dated from the Revolution or earlier. Broad Rock, in Chesterfield, was on the site of McGuire Hospital, built during World War II, and Tree Hill was on Henrico's Tree Hill Farm. The heyday of Richmond racing seems to have been in the early years of the nineteenth century. Sir Augustus John Foster wrote at this period that horse racing in Virginia "is carried very far and gives rise to a good deal of gambling," but he noted that cockfighting was on the decline. "Quoits and nine-pins are much in fashion," he added, and also barbecues.

The importation of the famous horse Diomed from England about 1795 by Thomas Goode and Miles Selden raised the quality of American thoroughbreds to a marked degree. Diomed was the sire of such famous racers as Sir Archy, Florizel and Potomac. Some persons actually asserted that the death of Diomed in 1808 caused almost as much grief as the death of George Washington nearly a decade before.

Colonel John Tayloe III of Mount Airy was considered the leader of the Virginia turf, and the race between his Peacemaker and Colonel Ball's Florizel at Broad Rock in 1805 for $3,000 a side aroused enormous interest. Florizel won, but Tayloe's horses were often victorious. Expectation and Desdemona were among the famous racers from the Tayloe stable.

Richmond was for many years a leading theatrical center, beginning in the late eighteenth century. Prior to the erection of Quesnay's Academy a playhouse of sorts on lower Main Street near the market had been used.

However, the stage was regarded as dangerous to morals by certain elements of the population. Governor Benjamin Harrison helped to counteract this puritanical posture by declaring in 1784 that "a well-chosen play is amongst the first of moral lessons and tends greatly to inculcate and fix on the mind the most virtuous principles." Opposition continued, nonetheless, and this had to be overcome when Quesnay's Academy became available for theatrical performances.

The company of Hallam & Henry, led by the famous Lewis Hallam, Jr., opened at the Academy in 1789. The following year another excellent troupe, led by a Mr. Kidd, trod the boards at Quesnay's hall. A third celebrated group of thespians was the West-Bignall Company, which came to Richmond in 1790 and booked at the Academy. Thomas Wade West, the senior member of the organization, had Benjamin H. Latrobe design a combination hotel, theater and assembly for Richmond, but it was never built.

With the burning of Quesnay's Academy in 1798, it became necessary for plays to be held in the upper part of Old Market. Then a building at the northwest corner of Seventh and Cary streets, formerly Quarrier's carriage shop, was pressed into service. It was used for several years.

Finally a new brick theater was erected in 1806 on the site of the burned Academy. The city's standing in the theatrical world in those years may be partially grasped from the fact that in the late eighteenth and early nineteenth centuries twenty-four English plays were presented in Richmond for the first time in America.

The future mother of Edgar Allan Poe made her Richmond stage debut in 1804 at Quarrier's converted carriage shop. She was the daughter of Mrs. Elizabeth Arnold, an English actress who had come to Boston, after acting at London's Covent Garden. At the time of the daughter's initial appearance in Richmond, she was the wife of Charles D. Hopkins, a comedian. Following Hopkins' death she married David Poe, Jr., who came of a good Baltimore family and was a member of the troupe.

Elizabeth Arnold Poe was a pretty and exceptionally talented and versatile actress, with an almost incredible list of 201 roles. She was also a dancer and singer of ability. She appeared in Richmond to great acclaim off and on from 1804 to 1811.

She and her husband moved to Boston for three years after their marriage, and Edgar was born there in 1809. Her husband died soon afterward, leaving her with three small children. She was recognized already in Boston, New York, Norfolk, Charleston and Richmond as one of the foremost actresses of her time.

Elizabeth Poe was playing at the Richmond Theatre with the Placide Company in the autumn of 1811 when, at twenty-four years of age, she was stricken with a fatal disease. A benefit performance was given for her on October 9, and two days later she managed to enact the role of the Countess Winstersen in *The Stranger*. It was her final appearance.

In rapidly declining health and burdened with the care of her small children Edgar and Rosalie—the third child, Henry, was with his grandfather in Baltimore—the petite, dark-eyed widow was sorely in need of friends. She had them in abundance. Samuel Mordecai wrote his sister Rachel on November 2 that "the most fashionable place of resort" in the city is the chamber of Mrs. Poe, "a very handsome woman," and "the skill of cooks and nurses is exerted to procure her delicacies."

Yet Elizabeth Poe sank steadily. In the *Enquirer* for November 25 appeared an appeal in her behalf from an anonymous admirer, "To The Kind-Hearted of the City." Then in the same paper four days later was published the following:

## TO THE HUMANE HEART

On this night, *Mrs. Poe*, lingering on the bed of disease and surrounded by her children, asks your assistance and *asks it perhaps for the last time*. The Generosity of a Richmond Audience can need no other appeal. For particulars see the Bills of the Day.

This second "benefit" for Mrs. Poe was held at the theater, Mr. Placide explained, in consequence of her "serious and long-continued indisposition . . . and in compliance with the advice and solicitation of many of the most respectable families." He added: "Taking into consideration the state of her health and the probability of its being the last time she will ever receive the patronage of the public, the appreciation of another night for assistance will certainly be grateful to their feelings as it will give them an opportunity to display their benevolent remembrance."

Slightly more than a week later, on December 8, the winsome little actress died. The place of her death has been erroneously stated in numerous books to have been in lodgings on the north side of Main Street between Twenty-second and Twenty-third. Thanks to able researches by Elizabeth Valentine Huntley and Louise F. Catterall these theories have been proved wrong. While the exact location is not known, Mrs. Poe almost certainly passed away not far from the intersection of today's Ninth and Grace streets, occupied in late years by the Richmond Hotel. On that spot in 1811 stood the Washington Tavern, formerly the Indian Queen—lodging place of many of Mrs. Poe's fellow actors. She probably had rooms in or near the Washington Tavern. It was only four and a half blocks from the theater, whereas the address on lower Main Street was fifteen blocks away. On top of all else, Mrs. Huntley and Mrs. Catterall have shown that the small brick house on lower Main in which Mrs. Poe is said in various accounts to have died was not built until nearly two decades after her death.[2]

The mother of two-year-old Edgar Poe was buried in St. John's church-yard, in an unmarked grave. However, in 1885, an actor's memorial to Elizabeth Arnold Poe was placed, with appropriate ceremonies, in New York City. Finally, on April 10, 1928, a shaft was unveiled in St. John's churchyard by the University of Virginia's Raven Society and other organizations, at or near the spot where she was buried. On the stone are engraved the words written by her famous son:

". . . no earl was ever prouder of his earldom than he of the descent from a woman who, although well-born, hesitated not to consecrate to the drama her brief career of genius and beauty."

# EIGHT

# Fire, War and Depression

TRAGIC as was the death of young Elizabeth Arnold Poe on the threshold of what might have been one of the great careers in the history of the American stage, her fatal illness may have saved her from a fiery death. For less than three weeks after she died, the theater in which she had been appearing so frequently was consumed in a holocaust that wiped out seventy-two lives and shook Virginia and the nation.

It was the night after Christmas, 1811, and many of Richmond's most prominent citizens, in holiday mood, thronged the theater on Broad Street Hill. There had been forebodings when a comet streaked across the autumn sky and a mild earthquake rocked Richmond in mid-December, but these supposedly ominous phenomena were largely forgotten as Governor George W. Smith, former U. S. Senator Abraham B. Venable and some six hundred others crowded into the recently built playhouse.

All seemed to be going well, the principal play had been concluded, to applause, and the "after-piece," entitled *Raymond and Agnes or the Bleeding Nun*, was under way. A shift of scenery for the second act involved the removal of a chandelier. Instead of lowering it and extinguishing the flame, the stagehand raised it with the light still burning. A property man, seeing the danger, quickly gave the order, "Lower that lamp and blow it out!" The stagehand tried to comply, but the cords slipped from the trolley and became entangled. He jerked them, and the flame came into contact with the highly combustible scenery. It went up like a torch.

"The house is on fire!" was the dread cry of Hopkins Robertson, an actor, from the front of the stage. Pandemonium followed. Most of those in the pit were able to get out, but hundreds in the boxes stampeded for the narrow, winding stairs leading to the lone door through which they had entered, and which opened inward. In a frantic effort to avoid the leaping flames and the black, choking smoke they broke down the stairs and piled in heaps against the door. Many were crushed to death, others were burned beyond recognition or killed by the lethal carbon monoxide.

Governor Smith managed to reach a place of safety, but went back into the inferno to save a young lady he had brought to the theater. Both perished. Benjamin Botts, the distinguished young attorney of the Aaron Burr defense, got to the door but rushed back to find his wife, and both were consumed in the flames. Gallant young Lieutenant James Gibbon, son of Major Gibbon and veteran of the Tripolitan wars, had brought his sweetheart, the beautiful and talented Sally Conyers, to the play. When the fire broke out, Miss Conyers fainted in the crush, and Gibbon and his friend, John Lynch, picked her up. They were carrying her to the exit when Gibbon said, "Lynch, leave Sally to me. I am strong enough to carry her. You can save someone else." But the lovers were immediately engulfed in the deadly smoke and flame. Their charred bodies were identified by the buttons on Gibbon's uniform and by Sally's necklace.

One of the heroes of the disaster was Gilbert Hunt, a Negro slave. When Hunt reached the blazing building, people were jumping out of windows. He went at once to the nearby house of Sy Gilliat, a popular Negro fiddler, and begged Gilliat for a bed on which the panic-stricken playgoers could fall. Gilliat "positively refused."

Hunt then looked up and saw Dr. James D. McCaw "standing near one of the windows and calling to me to catch the ladies as he handed them down."

Hunt and McCaw were extraordinarily powerful men. Hunt was a muscular blacksmith and McCaw "might have been chosen by a sculptor for a model of Hercules." They succeeded in saving about a dozen of the women who were trapped in the building. It was now a roaring mass of flames and threatening to collapse.

McCaw had to jump for his life. "When he touched the ground, I thought he was dead," said Hunt. "He could not move . . . the wall was tottering like a drunken man, ready at any moment to fall. I heard him scream 'Will nobody save me?'. I rushed to him and bore him away to a place of safety." Dr. McCaw was made permanently lame by his injuries.

Abraham B. Venable, president of the Bank of Virginia, died in the fire, as did dozens of other well-known Richmonders. When news of the disaster spread, fathers, mothers, sisters and brothers rushed to the scene in an agony of suspense. The dead, dying and injured were being carried to nearby First Baptist Church.

Next day stunned and grieving citizens viewed the ghastly pile of mangled and burned corpses. The air was heavy with the odor of charred human flesh.

A mass meeting was held at the Capitol the same day for the purpose of passing resolutions and making funeral arrangements. John Marshall was named chairman of a committee to decide on a suitable memorial. Common Council authorized purchase of the site of the theater and arranged for burial of the dead on the very spot.

A funeral procession on Sunday, December 29, wound its way from lower Main Street to the Capitol and then to the scene of the catastrophe. Two large mahogany boxes containing the dead were deposited in a single grave where the pit of the theater had been. "Parson" Buchanan conducted the service and "Parson" Blair also took part.

Stores were closed for two days, citizens were asked to wear crape for a month and to abstain from all dancing; public shows and spectacles were forbidden for four months, with a fine of $6.66 per hour for violators. Theaters throughout Virginia closed voluntarily for various periods, and there was a sharp drop in theatergoing all over the nation. The tragedy was widely regarded as a sign from heaven and a punishment for sinful diversions. Preachers rang the changes on this theme. A Baltimore publication asked: "Is not the Playhouse the very exchange of harlots? The Players, generally speaking, who are they? Loose, debauched people."

It was decided that the most suitable memorial would be a church on the site of the tragedy. Robert Mills was selected as architect, and the church would be of the Episcopal denomination and named Monumental. The cornerstone was laid August 1, 1812. Subscriptions toward the cost of the building were made by leading citizens, most of whom gave $200.

Monumental Episcopal Church opened for worship May 4, 1814. A monument bearing the names of the seventy-two persons who lost their lives in the fire was erected on the portico over their common grave. The Reverend Richard Channing Moore of New York City was named rector of the church, and shortly thereafter was chosen Bishop of the Virginia Diocese. The Episcopal Church in the Old Dominion had been virtually defunct for years, but the building of Monumental and the coming of the Reverend Mr. Moore revived it. The new church was in what was then termed the West End of Richmond.

Richmond recovered during the ensuing year from the shock of the fire, and Thomas Rutherfoord recorded that there was "never . . . a winter of greater festivity than prevailed during that of 1812/13." A marine insurance company was organized and Richmond's first daily newspaper, the Daily Compiler, made its brief appearance.

Yet dark clouds hovered in the background, for war with Great Britain was drawing near. The British continued to seize American seamen on the high seas and otherwise to interfere with American commerce. Thomas Ritchie in the Enquirer repeatedly urged a declaration of war against the British, as did the influential Judge Spencer Roane. The General Assembly adopted a resolution on February 6, 1812, calling for war. On the recommendation of President Madison, Congress approved such a declaration four months later.

Governor James Barbour of Virginia called promptly for volunteers, and Richmond's young men rushed to enlist. Those who were not already enrolled in a military unit met at the Bell Tavern and formed four additional units of riflemen, artillerymen and mechanics. They began drilling regularly.

When the British fleet threatened Norfolk, all unnaturalized Britons in Richmond and its environs were ordered to leave for the upcountry. A company consisting chiefly of veterans of the American Revolution and commanded by Dr. William Foushee was formed. By the spring of 1813, the *Enquirer* was able to say that Richmond, which was the rendezvous for all military units from the West, had "more troops under arms" than at any time since the Revolution. The same paper published a letter from a British sergeant of Royal Marines who had been captured from the warship *Victorious* off Newport News, thanking the people of Virginia and "especially the gentlemen of Richmond" for the "very kind and strict attention shewn us."

Fearing invasion, Governor Barbour ordered several militia units from Richmond and vicinity to Norfolk and Hampton. It was also recommended that "every citizen . . . of capacity to carry a musket, do *immediately* supply himself with a musket, bayonet, cartridge box and at least six rounds of ammunition."

On September 20, 1813, the city was "brilliantly illuminated" in celebration of Commodore Perry's victory over the British at the Battle of Lake Erie. The name of Perry was "appropriately emblazoned in letters of fire."

When the British captured Washington and burned the White House in the late summer of 1814, there was great concern in Virginia's capital. Thomas P. Atkinson, a Richmond citizen, wrote years later that he had seldom seen such a "state of alarm," and that the British were expected in Richmond in three days. Dr. Thomas Massie, an assistant surgeon with the militia, arrived in the city on September 5, and found the town "in consternation, most of the inhabitants gone, goods, furniture, etc., remained." Massie added, "I do not think it improbable that Richmond will be a pile of ashes before the fall."

These forebodings were not realized, of course. Governor Barbour issued another call for volunteers, and there was such a response that "in two days after it was made he had to issue a second proclamation saying that he had more volunteers than he needed," Thomas Atkinson recalled. If the British ever had any idea of moving on Richmond, they dropped it. The war ended a few months later. There were celebrations in Richmond over Andrew Jackson's victory at the Battle of New Orleans, and the Treaty of Ghent which formally recognized that peace had returned.

Work had begun during the war on a U.S. government arsenal and foundry in Chesterfield County near Richmond for the casting of cannon. Called the Bellona Arsenal, after Greek mythology's "fire-eyed maid of

smoky war," it was completed in 1817. The construction was carried out
under the direction of the same John Clarke who had built the Virginia
Manufactory of Arms in Richmond. The arsenal was a cluster of massive
buildings along the old canal.

However, the Federal authorities decided to move the garrison, the machinery and other property to Fortress Monroe. Clarke then became the
owner of what was left. He made cannon for the U. S. Government.

During these years there was in Richmond an elevation east of Governor Street and between Ross and Broad streets known as Council Chamber Hill. On it stood a one-story brick building, in which the Council of
State had met during the Revolution. The structure was there as late as
1835, but then it disappeared, along with the mound on which it stood.
This entire area, says one Richmond writer, has been as completely
changed as though it had been hit by an atomic bomb.

At the foot of the mound a handsome mansion was built in 1808 by
Benjamin J. Harris. Called Clifton, and regarded as almost in the class
with the Wickham and Marx houses, it survived until 1905, albeit in a
much altered and considerably dilapidated state. Known in its latter years
as Clifton House, it served boarders long after Council Chamber Hill
behind it had been leveled. It then was used by recently founded Sheltering Arms Hospital.

An important building in downtown Richmond from the era of Clifton
was the new city hall. Designed by Robert Mills, with the aid of Maximilian Godefroy, and completed in 1818, the domed and columned structure was on the Capitol Street site facing Capitol Square, where later a
much larger city hall was built. City Council or the Common Hall had
been meeting in rented quarters and on the second floor of the city
market. It now was accommodated in the new municipal building along
with the other city offices and the courts.

Publication of the first City Directory in 1819 coincided almost exactly
with the completion of the municipal headquarters. In the same year the
Common Hall named Foushee, Adams, Jefferson, Madison, Monroe and
Henry streets.

Since houses were not numbered at that time, the distance of each from
the nearest corner is given in the directory. This was their official address.

It was coming to be realized that something would have to be done
about Capitol Square. The unimproved terrain, with cows, goats and pigs
browsing through the Jimson weed and chinquapin bushes, obviously left
much to be desired. Governor Wilson Cary Nicholas arranged for the sale
of two acres of unimproved land near the square for $80,000 and this
made fairly extensive improvements possible, not only in the square but in
the already dilapidated Capitol itself.

Maximilian Godefroy, the architect and engineer who, as already noted,
completed Robert Mills's design for the new city hall, had also been re-

tained to present plans for improving the square and repairing the Capitol. These plans were elaborate, and were violently opposed by some members of the General Assembly, one of whom termed Godefroy "a foreign adventurer, cast, God knows how, upon the surface of this happy country."

Godefroy, then living in Baltimore, was a Frenchman, exiled by Napoleon Bonaparte. Since his landscaping was essentially French, it was decidedly formal. His plan called for imported linden and chestnut trees, in straight lines on both sides of the Capitol. Marble basins with cascades also were in the design, together with other proposed changes, some of which were never carried out. The most important recommendation was for an ornamental iron fence entirely around the square. It was installed shortly thereafter by Paul-Alexis Sabbaton, and has lasted for well over a century and a half. The "vast ravine" in front of the Capitol was filled in.

The Capitol was in a deplorable state. One member of the General Assembly complained that legislators "daily see the interior of the building rotting, soaked, nay deluged in water by the deficiency of the exterior." In other words, the roof was leaking badly. Godefroy saw that a roof of durable slate was provided. Paint or stucco was applied to certain outside areas, and the clumsy, curving exterior staircases on each side of the building were replaced with simpler ones parallel to the wall. Completely new woodwork was installed throughout much of the Capitol's interior.

Simultaneously with the foregoing, a large new structure was being erected in the southeast corner of the square, at Eleventh and Bank streets, where the terrain was extremely rough. Authorization was given by the General Assembly for a brick building there, ninety-one by fifty feet. This was the Virginia Museum, the first major museum in the state.

The moving spirit behind the enterprise was James Warrell, an Englishman who had opened a dancing school in Richmond in 1799. Warrell devoted his attention for some years to terpsichorean diversions, but he also had marked artistic ability. He accordingly began painting, mostly portraits. Several were of well-known personages and were not without merit.

When Warrell launched his museum project, he had strong backing from Governor Nicholas and other leading citizens. He associated with himself in the enterprise Richard Lorton, brother of his first wife and a painter of miniatures. Subscriptions were successfully sought. The museum opened in 1817, and it advertised paintings by Rubens, Rembrandt and others, as well as cases of birds, shells, minerals and insects, bottled reptiles and Indian curiosities.

Later there were plaster cast replicas of famous masterpieces of sculpture, such as the Venus de' Medici and the Apollo Belvedere. Some were nude, and the more puritanical members of the community were scandalized. "The room containing them was considered by the fastidiously modest as forbidden ground," Mordecai wrote.

An astounding if not incredible phenomenon was recorded by the Richmond press. The only live specimen in the museum was a rattlesnake. A mouse was introduced into its cage with a view to beefing up the reptile's diet. The snake was slow to pounce, and the valorous mouse went into action. It leaped upon the lethargic rattler's head "and nibbled away so industriously as to cause his death." This saga of "mouse bites snake" is vouched for by Mordecai, apparently without tongue in cheek.

Warrell assembled a remarkable collection, all things considered, but the museum was never able to establish itself firmly. It went out of existence in the mid-1830s. Richmond, with a population of only 12,067 in 1820, simply could not support so ambitious a project indefinitely, especially since nearly half of its inhabitants were slaves or free blacks.

Slaves and free Negroes in Richmond in the early years of the century were occupied in various ways. Male and female chattels provided practically all the domestic service. Slaves were frequently hired out to such industries as flour and tobacco manufacturing and coal mining. Free Negroes also were employed in these factories. Much of the work on the canal locks at Westham was done by black labor. Advertisements seeking the services of Negro artisans and laborers appeared frequently in the Richmond newspapers.

Negro artisans also operated small businesses of their own. Among these were blacksmiths, barbers, coopers and shoemakers. A number of slaves were thus able to buy their freedom. Blacks who were already free could set up shop for themselves and acquire a fair amount of property, including slaves. Frederick Law Olmsted, a Northerner who traveled through the South in the 1850s and published a much-quoted book on the subject, wrote that at the current rate of wages, a free black might accumulate property faster in Virginia than any man in the North who depended solely on his labor. Richmond Negroes in the antebellum era could build or rent in almost any part of Richmond, if they had the money. This last is evidenced by a study of old landbooks.[1]

Some of Richmond's artisans became so proficient that the white community regarded them as virtually indispensable. When legislation passed in 1806 required all slaves who had been freed to leave Virginia within twelve months, there was often dismay among the whites. They took advantage of the loophole in the law that allowed them to petition for the exemption of any free Negro who was "of good character, sober, peaceable, orderly and industrious." Many free blacks who had become first-rate craftsmen and whose expertise was deemed essential by the whites were allowed to remain.

Perhaps the most remarkable free Negro of the era was Christopher McPherson. Born a slave in Fluvanna County, he rose to become principal storekeeper for his master, David Ross, a Scottish merchant. In that position, he had several whites under him. Ross freed McPherson in 1792. George Wythe gave him a letter of high recommendation and in 1800 Thomas Jefferson introduced him by letter to James Madison. McPherson wrote later: "I sat at Table Eve[ning] & morn[ing] with Mr. M. his lady & Company & enjoyed a full share of the Convers[ation]." Madison lent him horses to continue his journey.[2]

McPherson moved to Richmond and became clerk in the office of the High Court of Chancery. Investments in Henrico real estate were profitable for him. He sought to provide carriages for hire, but ran head on into a city ordinance passed in 1810 which provided that no "Negro or Mulatto shall be permitted to use the same [a carriage] except in the capacity of Maid or Servant to some Lady or Gentleman, hiring or riding therein." McPherson sought unsuccessfully to persuade the General Assembly to exempt him from the ordinance. He then tried to conduct a for-hire hack business anyway, with a white driver. This too was unsuccessful.

Obviously uninhibited by the firmly held conviction of most whites that free blacks should not "get out of line," he opened a "Night School for male adults of color . . . and with the consent of their owners, Slaves." McPherson placed an advertisement in the *Virginia Argus* recommending to "the people of color throughout the United States . . . to establish similar institutions." This was too much for the good burghers of Richmond. There was such an uproar that the paper yielded to pressure and discontinued the advertisement.

McPherson's fortunes began going steadily downhill. Their decline was accelerated by the fact that he had long entertained religious hallucinations which caused some to suspect his sanity. He moved to New York and died there.

Efforts to educate members of the black race ran counter to prevailing laws and customs. Yet some white Richmonders and other Virginians taught their slaves anyway.

William Munford was greatly impressed by a young slave named Beverley who had acquired an astonishing amount of learning. Beverley's slave mother had been taught to read and write by Munford's sisters, Mrs. Kennon and Mrs. Byrd, and the mother, in turn, had schooled her son. Munford declared that Beverley "is not content now unless he is reading Shakespeare or Homer, and he understands what he reads."

There was a "black aristocracy" in Richmond, composed mainly of butlers, coachmen and maids for the leading white families. Most of these servants were slaves, but they were proud of their positions and responsibilities. The butler presided over all lesser functionaries in the kitchen and dining room, while the coachman was lord of all that he surveyed in and around the stables. There was often great affection between these "house servants" and their white owners.

Preeminent among the black aristocrats was Sy Gilliat, the fiddler. He played for Richmond balls over a period of many years, dressed in an embroidered silk coat of faded lilac, breeches, silk stockings and shoes with large silver buckles. Gilliat had been fiddling in Williamsburg during the regime of Lord Botetourt, and his court dress was suspected of being one of the fifty suits left by His Lordship. He also wore a brown wig with side curls and a long queue.

It cannot have been generally known during his lifetime that he had refused to lend Gilbert Hunt a bed onto which victims trapped in the theater fire could jump—a refusal not made public by Hunt until 1859. Gilliat remained widely popular and respected. This despite the fact that he was discharged as sexton of St. John's Church when he was "suspected of partaking of the wine without the other ceremonies of the sacrament."

On his death in 1820, he was praised on every hand. The Richmond *Compiler* commented that he was "very celebrated as a Fiddler and much caressed by Polished Society, who will long deplore the loss of one so ingeniously skilled in his profession." Even "Parson" Blair was moved to compose one of his numerous bits of light verse, as follows:

Ye sons of mirth, attend his bier;
Sy's fiddle ye no more will hear.
A most obliging soul was he:
For modesty and harmless glee
    He rated high.

No more he'll guide the mazey dance,
While round & round the room ye prance.
    Alas, poor Sy!

One of those who undoubtedly danced to Sy's fiddle was the bewitching and talented Maria Mayo, the most celebrated Richmond belle of her time. So many superlatives were used in describing her that the lexicon of laudatory adjectives was well nigh exhausted. She appears to have been not only beautiful in both face and figure but intelligent, witty, cultivated, charming—and modest withal. Ireland's Tom Moore sat enthralled when she sang his famous composition "Believe Me If All Those Endearing Young Charms." Maria was reputed to have turned down scores of swains who sought to marry her before she accepted Winfield Scott, a major general at twenty-seven, 6 feet 5 inches tall and a national hero. They were wed in 1817 at Bellville, the magnificent home of her parents, Colonel and Mrs. John Mayo. Bellville, built by John Bell some years before, was said by Dr. William P. Palmer to have been "certainly the most elegant of all the mansions in and near Richmond." It was situated a short distance in front of the main building of old Richmond College, and was considered "in the country."

Colonel Mayo died the year following Maria's wedding. His funeral was doubtless conducted in the accepted manner of that time. Funerals were never held in churches, and black-bordered invitations were sent to friends and relatives, inviting them to the obsequies in the residence of the departed. On the day of the funeral, the furniture in the drawing room and all the family portraits were draped in white and tied up with rosettes and black ribbon. Cake and decanters of wine were on a table in a corner for those wishing refreshment. Sobriety prevailed, in contrast to the overindulgence in hard liquor that characterized many funerals in former times. When the body was taken to the cemetery, usually on the third day after death, the family and other mourners went in private carriages made available by friends, as there were no hacks for hire. The carriage drivers were required to wear white bands around their hats, tied up with black ribbon. No flowers were used either at the home or the grave; the coffin was sometimes covered with a black pall. Neither hearse nor carriages were allowed to enter the cemetery, and the pallbearers carried the coffin on a bier to the place of burial. The pallbearers shoveled the earth back into the grave after the coffin was lowered.

When such celebrated men such as Jefferson, Madison, Monroe and Marshall died, the mayor called a public meeting. A day was set aside for public mourning, and on that day all business houses were closed, minute guns were fired from sunrise to sunset, bells were tolled and a funeral oration was delivered by a selected citizen.

A funeral of a different sort during those years was that of Mrs. McClurg, wife of Dr. James McClurg, who had served several terms as mayor. Mrs. McClurg was descending the steep roadway on Governor's Hill near Capitol Square in her carriage when the horses became frightened, the driver fell from the box and the vehicle plunged wildly down the steep incline, catapulted across Main Street and crashed with great violence into one of the shops. Mrs. McClurg was killed and her two companions, Mrs. John Wickham, her daughter, and Mrs. Robert Gamble, both of whom were delicately described in the press as "in the most interesting of all situations," were badly hurt. The *Enquirer* commented that "no calamity since the destruction of the theatre has excited such thrilling commiseration."

Funerals were not held in churches during the second decade of the century, but citizens were more diligent than formerly in attending the regular church services. Older persons drove to the place of worship in their carriages, with driver and footman. Inside the sanctuary were heaters for cold weather, and some carried a heating device into the pew.

Getting to church was a decided chore for many Richmonders, for the ground was extremely uneven in several areas. The hills and valleys around the Capitol have been described. Broad Street was either sticky with mud or deep in dust until 1836, when the Richmond, Fredericksburg & Potomac Railroad put its tracks along that thoroughfare westward from the depot at Eighth. What we now know as Franklin Street was almost blocked in the vicinity of today's Madison and Henry by a declivity so deep as to be almost impassable. A wooden bridge a hundred yards long was built to aid pedestrians in crossing it. Carriages and wagons managed somehow to lurch through or around it. A few squares to the east, between today's First and Foushee streets, was a pond. No Richmond street was paved, and sidewalks were nonexistent, except on lower Main. Mayo's Bridge was far from being the indestructible span of later years. The bridge had been washing away at periodic intervals since colonial times. This happened again in 1814, 1816 and 1823 when high water carried off all or part of it.

Those who lived in such suburbs as Sydney or Shed Town had even more difficulty getting into the center of the city than those inside the corporate limits. Sydney was located southwest and southeast of today's Monroe Park, and was bounded, approximately, on the north by Monroe Park and Park Avenue (picturesquely named Scuffletown Road), on the west by Morris Street, on the south by Albemarle Street and on the east by Belvidere Street. Sydney was laid off originally in 1812 by Benjamin J. Harris, owner of Belvidere. The old Byrd estate was deteriorating, and Harris divided the huge property up into lots. He called it Sydney and offered the lots for sale. As time went on, certain adjacent areas were regarded as part of Sydney, so that the precise boundaries are difficult to determine. Shed Town (the origin of the name is obscure) was east of the city, and seems to have extended from today's Twenty-ninth to Thirty-second Street and from Clay to O Street.

Richmonders and other Virginians were still considering ways of making real George Washington's dream of linking Tidewater Virginia with the "western waters," namely the Ohio and the Mississippi rivers. The extent to which the James River was being used already may be seen in the figures for 1803. In that year, tolls were paid to the James River Company on 16,917 hogsheads of tobacco, 170,588 bushels of wheat, 58,183 barrels of flour, 34,348 bushels of corn and 2,022 coal boats, each with a capacity of 1,000 bushels. It was hoped to increase this river traffic enormously by linking the James with the Kanawha in what is now West Virginia. Once that link was created, the battle would be largely won, since the Kanawha flows into the Ohio.

With this ambitious plan in view, the General Assembly of 1812 appointed a commission, headed by Chief Justice Marshall, to "view James River from the town of Lynchburg to the mouth of Dunlop's Creek [on the site of Covington] . . . to mark out the best and most direct way from the mouth of said creek to the most convenient navigable point of Greenbrier River, and to view that river to its junction with New River, to the falls of the Great Kanawha." The munificent sum of $750 was appropriated to cover all costs of the expedition.

Marshall, then aged fifty-six, and five others set out September 1 from Lynchburg in a boat, and spent several months on the above-mentioned streams and in the territory between. They carried out their assignment, often in the face of considerable hardships. In their report to the General Assembly, on December 26, written by Marshall, they recommended that at a minimum, the James be made navigable to Dunlop's Creek, and that a turnpike be built across the Alleghenies. They also felt it desirable that the Greenbrier and New rivers be made navigable. All this was designed not only to channel commerce into Virginia, but to bring the Tidewater and Piedmont into closer relationship with the regions beyond the mountains.

Four years later, by means of locks, canals and sluices, the James had been improved from Richmond to Crow's Ferry, a distance of 220 miles. However, the General Assembly complained that the James River Company was rendering poor service, and that it had, among other things, "failed to make the canal from the Falls into Richmond capable of carrying traffic according to the terms specified in the charter." As a result, the state of Virginia bought the company in 1820, and it became a state enterprise.

A Board of Public Works had been created by the legislature in 1816, and a fund for internal improvements also was provided. This last gave great impetus to the plans for developing trade with the West, since the money was to be used exclusively for clearing the rivers and building canals and public highways.

Richmond was connected by stagecoach and ship with more and more cities, and service was speeded up. In 1819, two gentlemen left Philadelphia for Richmond, one by stage to Washington and Richmond, which took fifty-six hours and cost $25.50, and the other by boat to Norfolk and Richmond, which took ninety-two hours and cost $35. Coach service to Baltimore two years later by mail stage took thirty-three hours and cost $16. The journey to Petersburg could be made in a single day. The company advertised that its coaches were "all hung on steel springs, and go as easy as any private carriage." It was also made known that "families and private parties, averse to associating with strangers, may command all the seats at a small expense."

The invention of the steamboat was received with much excitement in Richmond, especially when the steamer *Powhatan* came into service between Richmond and Norfolk in 1816. The ship experienced various difficulties, however, and after being laid up three months for repairs, a boiler burst on her first trip thereafter, killing a fireman. The steamer *Richmond* began operations on the Richmond-Norfolk line in 1818. Since the channel was deeper on the Chesterfield side of the James, the wharf below Manchester was used. The ship left Manchester twice weekly at 1 P.M. and reached Norfolk at 7 A.M. the next day.

Travelers coming to Richmond in these years stayed at one of the numerous taverns. In 1817, however, the city's first hotel, the Union, was opened on the southwest corner of Nineteenth and Main, and was followed immediately by the Eagle, previously a tavern, on the south side of Main between Twelfth and Thirteenth. Prominent visitors had lodged at the Eagle Tavern since its opening in 1787, but like the other taverns, it was somewhat crude and almost exclusively for males. Hotels were more comfortable and catered to women as well as men. The Eagle burned in 1839, and the ruins were not cleared away and replaced by stores for six years.

An attraction for visitors to Richmond was the newly established market at the southeast corner of Sixth and Marshall streets. It was called the New Market when it opened in 1817, to distinguish it from the Old Market on lower Main. Seventeen years later it was extended to the northeast corner of Sixth and Marshall, so that it occupied both sides of Marshall Street at the intersection.

Only vegetables and meats were offered for sale at first, but flowers were soon on display. Jonquils, hyacinths, crocuses and tulips heralded the arrival of spring, and were succeeded by roses, iris, gladioli, marigolds, asters and chrysanthemums. As Christmas approached the market was gay with the holly's red berries and with mistletoe and running cedar. Negro women sold these flowers and Christmas greens over a period of many generations. In cold weather they often had their feet hidden in soapboxes, which sometimes contained tiny stoves.

Visitors to Richmond in search of theatrical entertainment were disappointed for eight years after the theater fire. The clergy were strongly opposed to building another playhouse because of the supposed relationship between the theater and vice. "Dissolute profligacy of the performers" was cited by the Richmond *Compiler* as the chief ground brought forward by opponents. The *Compiler* added that this attitude was not manifested solely by "canting and whining hypocrites," since the position was also taken by "many liberal and enlightened minds." Even Shakespeare was attacked for his "obscenities and vulgarities."

But these objections were registered by a minority of Richmonders, and in 1819 a new theater was opened on the southeast corner of Seventh and Broad streets. It was called simply The Theatre. Junius Brutus Booth made his American debut here two years later, and such other internationally famous actors as Edwin Forrest and Thomas Abthorpe Cooper appeared in productions. In 1838 the building was taken over by new management, given a thorough overhauling and rechristened The Marshall. Dramatic offerings were presented until the building burned in 1862. Richmond was known in the antebellum era as a leading center of the drama.

The Richmond Theatre had opened in 1819 simultaneously with the onset of the first major financial crisis in American history. The panic was nationwide, and Richmond was hit hard. The price of tobacco fell as low as $4 to $8 per hundred pounds and "some of the first families were reduced to a state of extreme embarrassment and distress." Real estate values plummeted. A house that was worth $5,000 in 1818 was worth only $2,500 a year later and $1,250 the year after that. Real estate speculation had been rampant in the "flush times" from 1816 to 1818, and many suffered heavy losses or were completely ruined when the bottom dropped out. Charles Ellis of the mercantile firm of Ellis & Allen wrote his brother in 1822 that business was bad and it was impossible to gain "more than a bare support."

A number of important mansions had been built in Richmond during the early 1800s, but construction came almost to a standstill. Richmond merchants were suffering so severely as late as 1831 that they called a meeting and drew up resolutions urging that the James River be linked as speedily as possible with the Kanawha. Business remained in the doldrums throughout most of the 1820s and 1830s.

# NINE

# Lafayette, Pirates, Slave Traders and the Canal

THE MARQUIS DE LAFAYETTE's visit to Richmond in 1824 was a long-remembered event. The sixty-seven-year-old soldier of the Revolution who, in 1777, had left his young wife in France, risked his life and spent some $200,000 of his fortune to aid the Continentals was a hero to every American. Hatred of the British, as well as zeal for the American cause, had motivated him. Jefferson wrote that he had "a canine appetite for popularity and fame." Yet none of this dampened the fervor with which he was welcomed and feted in Richmond and throughout the United States. Lafayette received "demonstrations of frenzied enthusiasm without a parallel in American history."

Elaborate preparations were made in Richmond, a city he had visited on three previous occasions. He was its defender twice in the spring of 1781 when the Virginia capital was threatened by Cornwallis. After peace was declared, in 1784, Lafayette was a guest there with George Washington, when both were entertained at dinner in Bowler's Tavern.

Now came his triumphal return to Richmond. He arrived at Rocketts from Yorktown and Norfolk on October 26, 1824, to the accompaniment of shouts from almost the entire population of the city and the firing of guns. A procession followed him from the dock to Main Street and along that thoroughfare to the Eagle Hotel, where the general and his son, Georges Washington Lafayette, had a suite of rooms. That evening a monumental repast was tendered the famous guest. It lasted from 5 P.M. to 11 P.M., probably a record, and included numerous courses and even more numerous toasts. Benjamin Watkins Leigh presided and Vice-President John C. Calhoun was present, along with Governor James Pleasants, Jr., and the leading citizens of Richmond. A bottle of malmsey wine, vintage of 1757, the year of Lafayette's birth, was presented to him.

Next morning, virtually all business was suspended and everything centered on the ceremonies in honor of the distinguished visitor. First was the parade from the Eagle Hotel to city hall, where Mayor John Adams welcomed Lafayette. The latter made a gracious response, and passed through one of the arches erected at the gates of Capitol Square, with "transparencies" at each honoring heroes of the Revolution. Chief Justice Marshall delivered the oration in the square, and the general was moved to the verge of tears. On guard at George Washington's old army tent, brought to Richmond for the occasion, were the Richmond Junior Volunteers, composed of youths too young to serve in the militia. Second in command of this "Morgan Legion" was Edgar Allan Poe, not quite sixteen. He had been elected lieutenant by his fellow legionnaires—a role not normally associated with one of history's most illustrious poets.

Lafayette dined at the governor's mansion, with other veterans of the Revolution, and refreshments were served to the crowd in the square. The general then reviewed a parade of military units from the porch of Dr. James Lyons' residence at the northwest corner of Seventh and Marshall streets. That night he was driven to the theater through brightly lighted streets—which contrasted sharply with the normal condition of no lights at all.

Next morning the indefatigable guest was once more at the city hall, where he was greeted by students from Mr. and Mrs. Turner's boarding school for females, who provided speeches and music. As the climax of these exercises, he was presented with a certificate of membership in the Virginia Bible Society.

Races at Tree Hill were next on the agenda of the Gallic nobleman, after which he was the dinner guest of the Jockey Club. That night there was an elaborate ball in his honor at the Eagle Hotel. The affair was held in the hotel court, which was covered over with canvas and floored with timber.

Young Innes C. Adams, who was there, described some of his adventures in a letter to a friend. "I danced with some of the greatest beauties in the room, such as Miss Delia Harris," he wrote. "I cut G. M. Mitchell out, for Miss Polly Clarke chose to dance with me also. . . . But still I did not neglect the ugly, for I danced with Miss Betsey Pollard and some others of the same nature. I also danced with some married ladies and I find that I have lost nothing by it, for I have been invited to not less than two parties since the ball from persons I scarcely knew before."

Lafayette visited Petersburg briefly. His distaste for slavery was made known in his conversation with Mayor Lewis Mabry. He told Mabry that he had planned to send a Richmond newspaper to his family in France, but an advertisement of fifty Negroes for sale changed his mind. "I did not wish them to see this thing," said he.

The former officer in the Continental Army was affectionate in greeting James Lafayette, the Negro who had won his freedom during the Revolution by exceptional services as a spy. "The black was recognized by him in the crowd," said the *Enquirer*, "called . . . by name and taken into his embrace."

The marquis was guest at still another Richmond dinner, this one at the Masonic Hall on East Franklin Street, with Chief Justice Marshall presiding. Next day he attended services in Monumental Church.

Finally, after a week's round of luncheons, dinners, receptions and balls Lafayette left Richmond for Monticello and a ten-day visit with Thomas Jefferson. The relaxing interlude was no doubt welcome.

A few months later, in January 1825, the tireless Frenchman returned to Richmond at the invitation of the General Assembly. He was again accompanied by his son, and was lodged at "Mrs. Richardson's boarding house" on the northeast corner of Eleventh and Main. He reviewed military units standing in the snow in front of his lodgings. An appearance before the legislature followed, after which the lawmakers tendered Lafayette a dinner at the Union Hotel. Next came a ball at the Eagle, after which he went back to Baltimore.

His death in 1834 was formally recognized in Richmond on July 4. An elaborate funeral procession wended its way from the Union Hotel to the First Baptist Church, with many military units in line and several ministers taking part at the church.

The hanging of three Spanish pirates in the city was a sensation of the year 1827. The piracy had been committed on an American ship plying between Cuba and the United States, and included wholesale murder by the three brigands. They were tried in the Hall of the House of Delegates before Chief Justice Marshall, and were sentenced to hang.

Thousands thronged the streets on August 17 when the doomed men, seated on their coffins and dressed in purple gowns with hoods over their heads and ropes around their necks, were driven in a wagon from the Henrico County jail to the place of execution. The vehicle with its macabre cargo, guarded by militia, passed along Main Street for more than a mile. The gallows had been moved westward from the former site near Fifteenth Street to a valley, since filled in, on the north side of the penitentiary.

An estimated seven thousand people were gathered on the slopes to witness the hangings. Such grim affairs were considered in that era to be almost festive occasions. The condemned men acknowledged their guilt at the gibbet, knelt in prayer and were sprinkled with holy water. Two Protestant clergymen then emerged before the multitude, the one to deliver a sermon on the wages of sin, the other to intone a prolonged prayer. At the conclusion of these rites, the trap was sprung. To the horror of the assembled thousands, two of the ropes broke and the men fell writhing to the ground. There were loud screams from onlookers, and some jumped to the conclusion that friends of the pirates had come to rescue them. The frightened portion of the audience departed precipitously. The two buccaneers were then tied to the crossbar again, and this time the rope held.

After the three dead men had been allowed to swing for an hour to satisfy the morbid crowd, they were buried nearby. But later in the same day it was decided to test the new theory that galvanic, or electric, shock would restore the dead to life. The bodies were accordingly dug up and taken to an armory, where the shock treatment was administered. This, of course, was completely futile.

The next major excitement in Richmond was the Constitutional Convention of 1829–30. The state had been torn for years with controversy between the east and the west. The latter section was increasingly discontented with its low representation in the General Assembly, with the small amount of public money spent in the region beyond the mountains and similar discriminatory practices. There were threats even then that what later became West Virginia would withdraw and form a separate state.

Pressure from the Shenandoah Valley and the lands farther westward forced the General Assembly to provide for a popular vote on whether to hold a constitutional convention at which all grievances would be considered. Richmond cast 90 votes against a convention and 81 for, but the state as a whole gave an affirmative majority of 5,230. The small number of voters is accounted for, in large measure, by the fact that only about one in four of white males over twenty-one years of age could cast a ballot, since the franchise was confined to freeholders, or owners of real estate. The West wanted white manhood suffrage.

The convention met at the Capitol in Richmond on October 5, 1829. The Hall of the House of Delegates where it convened was apparently an untidy place. Captain Basil Hall of the British navy visited the Capitol in 1828 and reported that the room in which the House met "did not appear to have been washed or swept since the Revolution." His wife wrote that "the floor where the members sat was actually flooded with their horrible spitting."

Richmond was crowded with visitors to the convention. Young men rode hundreds of miles on horseback from Kentucky, Tennessee and other states to witness the proceedings, and ministers of foreign powers came to the city for the occasion. These and others traveled from distant points to see what was termed "the last gathering of the giants"—James Madison, James Monroe, John Marshall and John Randolph of Roanoke. The first three were venerated and venerable statesmen of the revolutionary or post-revolutionary eras whose final appearance on the public stage gave the convention a unique quality. Eccentric John Randolph, not quite so aged as the others, was famous for his witty sallies and devastating ripostes. He, too, had only a few years to live.

James Monroe, in bad health and seriously strapped financially, was elected chairman despite his physical condition, reportedly because his friends wanted him to receive the double stipend which went to the convention's presiding officer. He served for a time, but then felt it necessary to resign the chairmanship.

James Madison, far from robust and almost inaudible, even at close range, admitted later that he got "buck ague" when he sought to address the convention. The members rose in a body and crowded round "the Father of the Constitution," in order to catch his words. But Madison told the official reporter later that "the knowledge that much was expected of me, the feebleness of my voice, the rush of the convention around me, unnerved and sealed my brain." He said he would give the reporter "the remarks I intended to make, but not that speech."

The appearance, especially the dress, of the four celebrities was a matter of comment. Madison's "dress was plain; his overcoat a faded brown surtout." Marshall's appearance "was revolutionary and patriarchal." The Chief Justice stood "tall in a long surtout of blue, with a face of genius and an eye of fire." He wore a style of dress that was completely outmoded. Monroe "was very wrinkled and weatherbeaten—ungraceful in attitude and gesture and his speeches only commonplace." Randolph's face was pale and withered, "but his eye radiant as a diamond." Tall, gaunt and bony, with a falsetto voice, he dressed in black throughout the convention, with crape on his hat and arm. The squire of Roanoke explained that he "wore mourning for the old Constitution of Virginia," adding that he expected the convention to preside over its death and burial.

Madison, Monroe and Marshall played relatively minor roles, with Marshall the most active, vigorous and conservative of the three. Randolph, equally conservative, spoke more frequently and was always the center of attention. Hugh Blair Grigsby, a twenty-three-year-old member of the convention, wrote years later: "The word passed through the city that Randolph was speaking, and soon, the House, the lobby and the gallery were crowded almost to suffocation. . . . The thrilling music of his speech fell upon the ear like the voice of a bird singing in the pause of the storm." Grigsby also declared that Randolph "inspired terror to a degree that even at this distance of time seems inexplicable . . . he seemed to paralyze alike the mind and body of his victim."

Differences over slavery were behind much of the debate between the east and the west. All but seven of the ninety-six delegates owned slaves, but all the large slaveowners were east of the mountains. Fierce arguments raged over the taxing of chattels and the low representation in the legislature of counties where few slaves lived. White manhood suffrage was also a bone of contention. Benjamin Watkins Leigh classed it with "the other plagues." Leigh was a major spokesman for the conservative east, and according to Grigsby, "his extraordinary oratorical displays not only dazzled the eyes of his fellow-citizens but created wonder and admiration throughout the Union."

With the return of the General Assembly to Richmond in early December, the convention had to vacate the Capitol and move to the First Baptist Church at College and Broad streets. After about a month's debate, the delegates voted on January 14 by 55 to 40 for the adoption of a constitution that suited no one completely. The west got few concessions and would have to wait for two more decades to obtain anything like real relief. The east was not happy over such slight concessions as were granted the west. At the spring elections the people of Virginia gave the new version of the organic law a majority of 10,500 in a total vote of about 42,000. Richmond supported the revised constitution, 301 to 19.

The west continued to agitate, and this kept intersectional relations in considerable turmoil. But in August 1831 an event in Southampton County, in the southeastern corner of the state near the North Carolina line, caused the people of Virginia to forget for a time that there was a controversy between the sections. This was Nat Turner's bloody slave insurrection.

The white population of Richmond and the entire state was filled with alarm when the slave Nat Turner led some sixty blacks in an orgy of killing that took the lives of nearly sixty whites, most of them women and children.

Captain Randolph Harrison of Richmond led his troop of light horse to the scene, but was unable to cover the eighty miles to Jerusalem, now Courtland, the county seat of Southampton, until the day after the massacre. By that time the Negro uprising had been effectively put down. The bugler for the light horse troop was a free Negro named Dick Gaines. He is described as tall and black, "a fine rider and striking figure as he appeared on horse back, bugle in hand, in his red jacket, sword and helmet, with its crest of white horse-hair falling over his broad shoulders."

Richmond's Fayette Artillery, with four pieces, also was ordered to the scene, but before it could get there was told to turn back. Its services were not required.

John Hampden Pleasants, editor of the Richmond *Whig*, was a member of the Richmond Light Horse, and described some of the events in Southampton County for his paper. He expressed shock over the barbarities perpetrated by Nat Turner and other slaves, as well as barbarities done in retaliation by the whites.

Unrest among Richmond slaves was feared when word of the Turner massacre was received, but the blacks were said to be altogether docile and "as astonished and indignant as were the whites."

However, the white population not only of Richmond but the entire

South was alarmed by the events in Southampton. Turner had been treated well by his master, and had apparently been satisfied with his lot. Yet he and his cohorts murdered not only his master and mistress and their baby, but scores of others. No wonder slaveowners everywhere feared uprisings of a similar nature. The memory of Gabriel, and his far more extensive plan for wholesale massacre, was also in their minds.

It was in this atmosphere that the General Assembly convened in late 1831. The frankest discussion of slavery that had yet occurred took place at that session.

The American Colonization Society had been formed in 1816, and Virginians had been more active in its affairs than citizens of any other state. U. S. Supreme Court Justice Bushrod Washington was its first president and Chief Justice John Marshall was president of the Virginia branch. The object of the organization was to colonize free Negroes in Africa. Liberia on Africa's west coast was chosen as the place to which the blacks should be sent.

The General Assembly of 1831–32 dealt at length with plans for colonizing Negroes on the Dark Continent and even with the complete abolition of slavery. Both the Richmond *Enquirer* and the *Whig* were arguing for the immediate or eventual elimination of the slave system. But the legislature ended by doing little or nothing toward that end. The time was felt not to be ripe.

Negroes, both slave and free, made up a vital part of Richmond's labor force, especially in the tobacco factories, the coal mines and the Tredegar Iron Works. In addition, black mechanics had a virtual monopoly in carpentry, masonry, shoemaking, cooperage and other trades prior to the Civil War. Whites considered it degrading to engage in the foregoing occupations, which left an almost clear field to the Negroes. Many white artisans left the state rather than compete with them.

The number of black employees in the Richmond and Manchester tobacco factories in 1833 was estimated by the *National Intelligencer* at from one to two thousand, with about the same number in the nearby coal mines. In the 1850s, Richmond's fifty-two tobacco factories employed about 3,400 slaves, who comprised practically the entire working force.

The singing of the Negroes in the tobacco factories was noted by many visitors, including William Cullen Bryant, the poet, who was then editor of the New York *Evening Post*. He came to Richmond and reported that song "sweetened the toil of slaves." An official of the plant told him that singing was encouraged by the management. "The boys work better while singing," he said. "Their tunes are all psalm tunes and the words are taken from hymn books."

A hospital for industrial slaves had been erected in Richmond by 1860. It had beds for forty patients and was staffed by four white physicians who insisted on cleanliness. The number of beds seems to have been by no means adequate. Insurance also was carried on the lives of some slaves engaged in hazardous industrial occupations. Here too the number of insured was only a small fraction of the whole. Richmond had two insurance companies that wrote this type of insurance, the American Life Insurance Company and the Valley Insurance Company.

The Tredegar, the most important single industrial plant in Richmond during the 1840s and 1850s, and especially during the Civil War, used a great deal of black labor, mostly slaves. They were either hired or bought outright. The Tredegar pioneered in various directions; it operated a hospital for slave employees and provided housing for them. The black historian Luther P. Jackson wrote that Joseph R. Anderson "stood ready to promote the advancement of any Negro slave who showed ambition." On the eve of the war, the Tredegar employed eight hundred blacks.

Earlier, the plant's reliance on Negro labor had brought a crisis. In 1847, the skilled white artisans became fearful that they would be replaced by blacks. They informed Anderson that they would not go to work until he removed slaves from certain jobs. He promptly addressed a letter to "my late workmen at the Tredegar," informing them that they had fired themselves. He also told those who were renting housing from him to vacate. He said he had had no intention of using Negro puddlers in the Tredegar rolling mill, nor had he planned to discharge any efficient workmen. But now, said he, the strikers had forced him to use Negro puddlers in both the Tredegar rolling mill and the Armory mill. That was the last time anybody struck at the Tredegar until the Civil War. Some Irish foundrymen struck for higher wages during the war and got them.

Slave auctions were frequent in Richmond during the antebellum years. Prior to 1846, the Bell Tavern, on the north side of Main just below Fifteenth, was the scene of a great many of these deplorable spectacles. Later the basement of Odd-Fellows Hall at Mayo and Franklin was the city's busiest slave mart.

The Richmond City Directory for 1852 listed twenty-eight "Negro traders." By 1860 the number involved in this nefarious business was much larger. The City Directory for that year listed eighteen "Negro traders," another eighteen who were termed "agents, general collecting" and thirty-three "auctioneers." Many of these merchants, with notable exceptions, dealt in human flesh and had their own private jails where the chattels were kept before going on the block. The slave business was carried on almost entirely in the area near East Franklin and Fifteenth streets. Five traders had their offices in the prestigious Exchange Hotel, the city's best, built in 1841 at Fourteenth and Franklin. During those years there were almost daily advertisements in the press that from twenty-five to fifty Negroes would be sold.[1]

Slave auctions were sometimes emotionally painful for onlookers, while at other times the sales went off with hardly a ripple. An Englishman who attended an auction in Richmond gave a detailed account of what he saw in *Chambers' Journal* for October 1853. He said, in part:

"There was an entire absence of emotion in the looks of men, women and children thus seated preparatory to being sold. This does not correspond with the ordinary accounts of slave-sales, which are represented as tearful and harrowing."

By contrast, John S. Wise tells in his remarkable book *The End of an Era* of having witnessed a Richmond auction when he was a boy, where a skinflint member of the General Assembly bought a mother but refused to buy her husband and two children. The mother was grief-stricken and in tears, as was the father. The legislator was adamant saying: "Thar ain't no way I could provide for gittin' the man and the young 'uns home, even if they was given to me. I think I'm doin' pretty well to save enough in one session to buy one nigger, much less a whole fambly."

It was a sickening performance. Just when it appeared that the mother was to be separated permanently from her husband and children, the lawyer for a recently deceased colonel whose estate was being settled by selling these slaves intervened. "By God!" he exclaimed, "I can't stand this . . . I am unable to make this purchase, but sooner than see them separated, I'll bankrupt myself. Mr. ——— I'll take Martha Ann off your hands, so as to buy her husband and children and keep them together." The sour old legislator whined that he should receive from the lawyer a sum a bit larger than he had paid for the mother; and this too was arranged. So the dramatic episode had a relatively pleasant ending after all.

Although the teaching of slaves to read and write was against the law, some bondsmen were instructed quietly by their owners or even in small schools. There was a published rumor in 1818 that "a society of [Richmond] ladies" had been organized for the purpose of teaching Negro children. Ten years later, a free black named Joseph Shippard announced that he had opened a school for other free blacks.

"Slaves in towns, and especially domestic servants do just as little as they like, and their masters and mistresses will not take the trouble to make them do more," James S. Buckingham, an English visitor to Richmond, wrote. "They live an easier life than many an English mechanic, farm-laborer or servant, as far as actual labor is concerned. In general, you see no stripes inflicted or blows struck or even harsh language used to the slaves in towns by anyone."

The Northerner Frederick L. Olmsted reported from Richmond: "As far as I have observed they [ the Negroes] are treated very kindly and even generously as servants, but their manner to white people is invariably either sullen, jocose or fawning.'"

Olmsted was impressed by the clothes worn in Richmond on Sunday by a certain class of blacks, saying that "in what I suppose to be the fashionable streets, there were many more well-dressed and highly-dressed colored people than whites; and among this dark gentry, the finest French clothes, embroidered waist-coats, patent-leather shoes, resplendent brooches, silk hats, kid gloves and *eau de mille fleurs*, were quite common." On the other hand, "the greater part of the colored people . . . seemed to be dressed in cast-off fine clothes of the white people."

Richmond streets at mid-century were considerably less rough than they had been two or three decades before; the jagged hills and valleys that had been so conspicuous a feature of the landscape had been leveled. Credit for this should go in large measure to Dr. John Adams, mayor of the city from 1819 to 1825, and one of its significant leaders and benefactors. His father was the Colonel Richard Adams who owned most of Church Hill and was a member of the General Assembly both before and after the Revolution. The prominence of this almost forgotten family may be seen when it is noted that Dr. John Adams' sister Sarah married Governor George W. Smith, who lost his life in the theater fire; another sister, Alice, married the brother of John Marshall, and still another sister, Ann, was wed to Colonel Mayo Carrington.

Mayor Adams seized every opportunity to use his official position in furtherance of forward-looking measures. A goodly portion of his fortune was spent to that end. He built the Union Hotel, Richmond's first— designed by Otis Manson, the earliest Richmond-born architect of note— and he and John Enders constructed several other brick buildings on lower Main. He erected what was later the Van Lew mansion on Church Hill. Dr. Adams succeeded in inaugurating stage service to various cities. Adams Street is named for him.

Neither Mayor Adams nor anyone else could do much to stop the rock battles between the youths of "Butchertown" in the Seventeenth Street Valley, also known as Adams Valley, and those higher up on Shockoe Hill. These "Butcher Cats" and "Hill Cats" carried on their feuds for generations. Some of the participants were seriously injured.

Farther to the west, on what is now West Broad Street, but beyond the city limits of that day, was "Screamersville," a batch of shoddy structures standing in the mud. They were grogshops and cheap boarding houses, patronized by the lowest classes. "They kept the night hideous by their orgies, and to their own diabolical noises was added the night-long clamor of barking curs," wrote Dr. William P. Palmer. He added that "the dissipated, reckless and reprobate of both sexes and of all colors congregated there." Richmond boasted only three policemen at the time, and since Screamersville was just over the county line, the miscreants in that sinkhole were almost beyond both arrest and redemption.

Street names in Richmond during several decades of the nineteenth century caused much confusion. The *Compiler* was one of those who complained. It declared in 1839 that "we are compelled to say 'E or Main Street' while H Street is denominated 'Main Street, Shockoe Hill.'" It

went on to assert that "Cary Street is never called by its letter." The newspaper urged that since the existing system of using both letters and numbers was bewildering to both local citizens and strangers, names should be
substituted for letters. Five years later, in 1844, the Common Hall
officially rechristened a number of the principal thoroughfares, as follows:
A—Adams; B—Byrd; C—Canal; D—Cary; E—Main; F—Franklin; G—
Giles; H—Broad; I—Marshall; K—Clay; and L—Leigh. These names have
remained unaltered to the present day, with the exception of Giles, which
was changed to Grace almost at once. The presence of so many churches
on that street is believed to be the reason for the selection of the
name "Grace." The Common Hall decreed that the new street names be
printed on corner houses.

Richmond was termed "the healthiest city of its size in America and
perhaps in the world" by Dr. John P. Little in his history of the town
which appeared in 1851. He gave statistics showing that deaths in Richmond were about one in seventy, compared with one in thirty-seven in
New York, one in forty-five in Philadelphia, one in thirty-six in Charleston, S.C., one in forty in London and one in nineteen in Liverpool. This
despite the fact that there were severe cholera epidemics in Richmond in
1832, when 498 died, and in 1849, when the disease took 129 lives. The
General Assembly became so alarmed in the latter year that it held its session at Fauquier Springs.

Richmond doctors during the first two or three decades of the nineteenth century traveled on horseback to see their patients rather than in
carriages. They apparently relied heavily on calomel in their practice, as
evidenced by verses published in the *Enquirer* in 1825. Two stanzas follow:

> Howe'er their patients do complain
> Of head, or heart, or nerve or rein,
> Of fever, thirst or temper fell
> The medicine still is calomel.

> And when I do resign my breath,
> Pray let me die a natural death,
> And bid you all a long farewell,
> Without one dose of calomel.

"Domineering insolence was by no means unknown among the old-time
doctors of Richmond," Dr. William H. Taylor, of the Medical College of
Virginia faculty, wrote in 1908. "It was not a very strange thing for the
doctor to take possession of the patient's home, to go storming through it,
to demolish with his own hands obnoxious articles of food or drink, plates,
dishes, cups and saucers, and even beds, and to make himself such a portent and such a terror that when he hove in sight consternation fell upon

the habitation, the women rolled themselves together as a scroll and the children fled into a back alley." It is difficult to believe that many physicians behaved in this fashion. Certainly one who did not was Dr. Lawrence Roane Waring, to whom Dr. Taylor paid a moving tribute. Dr. Waring died in 1869, aged forty-two, from overwork among the poor. "A vast procession," consisting to a large extent of the disadvantaged and the poverty-stricken, followed his body to the grave. Several meetings of citizens were then held and a substantial sum was raised, despite the straitened circumstances of nearly everyone during Reconstruction. A plot near the grave of President Monroe was purchased, the body was moved there and a 16-foot granite shaft erected "by grateful and loving friends" for "the good Samaritan who gave his life for the cause of humanity."

Dr. Waring was a noteworthy personality in his day, and there were nonmedical men from the antebellum years who deserve mention. One of these was Peter Francisco, the herculean veteran of the Revolution. Francisco, of either Portuguese or Spanish descent, had landed from a ship at City Point, now Hopewell, aged five or six. His antecedents were altogether mysterious. With the outbreak of the Revolution about a decade later, when he was sixteen, he enlisted as a private and performed legendary feats with his huge sword. At the end of his life he was sergeant at arms of the Virginia House of Delegates. Judge Peter Johnston, under whom he had served in the war, appeared in support of his application. Judge Johnston said he had "no doubt that Peter had killed more of the British . . . than any ten men in the American army, and that if he could eat gold dust, the legislature ought to feed him on it." Francisco served as sergeant at arms for six years, and had his residence in Richmond. A prominent citizen reported seeing him "grasp a stout man by the collar with his left hand, raising him from the floor with perfect ease, and walk him out of the House for having improperly intruded." Francisco died in 1831 and was buried with military honors in Shockoe Cemetery. Peter Francisco Day is observed annually in Virginia, Massachusetts and Rhode Island on the anniversary of the Battle of Guilford Courthouse, in which the 260-pound soldier is said to have killed eleven British fighting men. An eighteen-cent stamp in Francisco's honor was issued in 1975 by the U. S. Post Office.

Another citizen of foreign birth who spent some years in Richmond and went on to national prominence was Isaac Leeser, who came to the city in 1824, aged seventeen, from his native Germany. He worked in his uncle's store during the day and studied and wrote at night. Leeser published two articles in the Richmond *Whig* replying to an attack on the Jews in a London magazine. In Richmond he also wrote his preface to *The Jews and the Mosaic Law*. Leeser left in 1829 for Philadelphia to become rabbi of the oldest congregation in America. He is recognized as the founder of the Jewish press in this country and as a pioneer of the Jewish pulpit.

Richmond was the home for nearly a decade of Francis Walker Gilmer, whom Jefferson termed "the best-educated subject we have raised since the Revolution." Gilmer was in Richmond from 1811 to 1814 studying law under William Wirt, and he returned to the city to practice that profession from 1818 to 1824. A noteworthy event of this period was a near-duel with Robert Stanard. Gilmer struck Stanard in the face when the latter said something in court that he considered offensive. In 1824 Gilmer declined Jefferson's offer to become the first professor of law at the soon-to-be-opened University of Virginia, but he visited Europe on a successful quest for professors at the institution. After suffering for years with tuberculosis, Gilmer died at age thirty-five, the greater part of his magnificent promise unfulfilled. He wrote the pathetic epitaph for his tomb at Penn Park, Albemarle County, where he was born:

> Pray, Stranger, allow one who never had peace while he lived
> The sad Immunities of the Grave,
> Silence and Repose.

Another man of great prominence in Richmond who is now almost completely forgotten is Andrew Stevenson. He practiced law in the city after his graduation from William and Mary in the early years of the century. He served later as Speaker of the Virginia House of Delegates (1812–15), Speaker of the House of Representatives (1827–34), and U. S. Minister to Great Britain (1836–41). Stevenson was a member of the politically powerful Richmond Junto, along with Thomas Ritchie, Spencer Roane and others. After completing his service at the Court of St. James's, he retired to his estate, Blenheim, in Albemarle County. Stevenson then was elected president of the Virginia Society of Agriculture and rector of the University of Virginia. Of a scholarly turn of mind, he had a library numbering 3,511 volumes at his death.

Gustavus A. Myers was another Richmonder of genuine stature. He was not only an attorney of exceptional ability and prominence but a man of literary attainments as well. His one-act interlude *Nature and Philosophy* was "performed on two continents for over twenty-five years." He served for nearly a third of a century on the City Council, and for twelve years (1843–55) was its president. Myers was also president of the Richmond Club and a member of the Virginia Historical Society's executive committee. A man of unusual wit and charm, he was an intimate friend of Judah P. Benjamin when the latter served in the Confederate Cabinet. Myers' wife was a daughter of Governor William B. Giles. She was Episcopalian and he Jewish. They have numerous descendants in Richmond.

A friend of Gustavus Myers was William H. Macfarland, the "founding father" of what many years later became the United Virginia Bank. Macfarland was president at various times of the Farmers Bank of Virginia, and of the Planters National and the State Bank of Virginia. In 1836 he delivered the oration at the Capitol in honor of James Madison, who had just died. Shortly thereafter he was elected lieutenant governor of Virginia. A gifted and versatile man he was active in the cause of education and other civic movements. When such eminent visitors as Daniel Webster, President Millard Fillmore and the Prince of Wales came to Richmond, William Macfarland was chairman of the welcoming committee or he occupied some other comparably important post. As a member of the Virginia Convention of 1861, he strove to keep the Old Dominion in the Union, but in the final showdown cast his vote for secession.

Macfarland was a leading advocate of railroad development as a better means of transportation than the James River and Kanawha Canal. The James River Company, which operated the canal, was under state control from 1820 to 1835, and the waterway was extended thirty miles into Goochland County. It became obvious, however, that the enterprise would never be completed all the way to the Kanawha under the aegis of the state, so in 1835 a joint stock company was organized. This was the James River and Kanawha Company, for which the Commonwealth subscribed three fifths of the stock.

There was stiff opposition from Norfolk, Petersburg and Fredericksburg, which were competing with Richmond. The Norfolk *Beacon* urged the construction of one of the new steam railroads along the James instead of a canal. So did Claudius Crozet, a veteran of Napoleon's army who came to this country in 1816 and was named Virginia's state engineer in 1823. (He lived in Richmond's Crozet House at First and Main streets from 1828 to 1832.) Some advocates of railroads were seeking to prevent Richmond from developing as a port, with the aid of the canal. Richmond, in turn, was not anxious to see the port of Norfolk prosper at its expense. Others were sincerely convinced that the future lay with the railroads, as turned out to be the case.

After many battles in and out of the General Assembly, the money was forthcoming to build the canal as far as Lynchburg. Ceremonies marking the completion of the waterway to that city were held there in 1840. The orator of the occasion rose to such heights that he lost his balance and fell into the canal.

Seven years later the Assembly provided for connecting the waterway at Richmond with the James below the falls through the Richmond dock, and authorized the company to borrow $350,000 for the purpose. It took seven more years and an additional $500,000 to finish the job. This Richmond dock and tidewater connection extended for a mile along the north side of the river. There was a series of locks and basins extending from the main canal basin to the upper end of the dock, with a ship canal linking them to the river at Rocketts.

The Richmond dock was easily the most profitable operation of the James River and Kanawha Company. In 1855, the year following its completion, 1,217 boats and vessels entered the dock and 1,377 departed from it. Included among the incoming vessels were sixty New York packets, forty Baltimore packets and twenty-nine Boston packets with assorted cargoes. This traffic rose steadily and was about 50 per cent greater in 1860. After the Civil War it declined drastically, owing largely to competition with the railways. By 1851 the canal had been extended as far as Buchanan, Botetourt County, but the much anticipated link with the Kanawha River did not materialize until the Chesapeake and Ohio Railroad provided an all-rail connection some years after Appomattox, when the canal had gone out of business.

Richmonders found travel on the canal's passenger packets delightful at first, but the gentry are said to have preferred other means of transportation after 1855. In traveling to Lynchburg, for example, they went by train to Farmville and by stagecoach the rest of the way. It took thirty-three hours to reach Lynchburg via the canal. Passenger packets left Richmond every other day for Buchanan, via Lynchburg; every other day for Columbia, and every other day for Scottsville. Horses or mules pulled the canal boat along the towpath, and travelers could sit on deck in good weather and watch the world go by. There was a bar below to soothe them in case the weather was bad, and also if it was good. Freight packets plied the waterway in large numbers, and total tonnage in 1859 was more than three times that of the Richmond and Danville Railroad, the state's principal rail carrier. It took freight barges on the canal three and a half days to reach Lynchburg from Richmond.

The canal played yet another role in the lives of antebellum Richmonders. They were fond of strolling along its banks at twilight beside the murmuring waters of the river. The canal promenade extended from the foot of Fifth Street westward for miles. As the shadows lengthened, dusk melted into darkness and quiet reigned along the stream, Richmonders of all ages found surcease there from the cares of the day.

# TEN

# Edgar Allan Poe in Richmond

A FAMILIAR figure in Richmond from time to time during the 1820s, 1830s and 1840s was Edgar Allan Poe. Upon the death of his mother in 1811 when he was less than three years old, Edgar was taken into the household of John Allan, a member of the mercantile firm of Ellis & Allan. The boy was given the middle name of Allan, although he was not related to the family.

Poe was "beautiful, yet brave and manly for one so young," and "a leader among his playmates," Thomas Ellis wrote many years later. Charles Ellis, partner of John Allan and father of Tom, said Poe was "trained in all the habits of the most polished society," and he added that "there was not a brighter, more graceful or more attractive boy in the city." Young Edgar attended Monumental Episcopal Church with his foster parents.

Frustration, poverty and near-starvation in later years changed Poe's personality. His break with John Allan in the mid-1820s contributed to this dramatic metamorphosis. He once termed "the want of parental affection . . . the heaviest of my trials."

When the orphaned boy joined the household of the childless Allans, they were living over the Ellis & Allan store at the northeast corner of Thirteenth and Main. It was not unusual in Richmond at the time to live over one's store, although the well-to-do merchants had their commodious residences, complete with garden, stable and other dependencies. The Allans went to England in 1816 and remained five years, taking Edgar with them. The boy was there from ages six to eleven. Allan was interested in opening an English branch of his firm.

Upon the return of the Allans, they lived for nearly a year in the home of Charles Ellis, on the southwest corner of Second and Franklin. Poe played as a boy in Ellis' "enchanted garden." The garden, with its jasmine and roses, its myrtle and honeysuckle, its flowering shrubs and twittering birds, was across Franklin on the site of the eastern half of today's Linden Row. The linden trees which lined the block gave their name to Linden Square and to the handsome row of ten Greek Revival houses built there in the mid-nineteenth century.

On leaving the Ellis home, the Allans took a "long low cottage house on Fifth Street, fronting west, between Marshall and Clay Streets." They moved thence to a house at the northwest corner of Fourteenth Street and Tobacco Alley, and were there in 1825 when Allan's uncle, William Galt, a prominent Richmond merchant, died and left him a fortune.

Allan promptly purchased the handsome house, Moldavia, at the southeast corner of Fifth and Main. It had been bought from the David Meade Randolphs by Joseph Gallego, the wealthy miller, who lived there until his death in 1818. Gallego never recovered from his wife's death in the devastating theater fire of 1811.

Poe was now sixteen and preparing for college. He had attended various schools in England and Scotland, and then had spent two years in the fashionable Richmond school of Joseph H. Clarke, of Trinity College, Dublin, where he demonstrated considerable facility in Latin, Greek and declamation. In 1823 he was entered in the well-known school of William Burke, and again was an exceptional student.

Thomas Ellis wrote vividly from his recollection of Poe at this period:

"No boy ever had greater influence over me than he had. He was, indeed, a leader among boys; but my admiration for him scarcely knew bounds; the consequence was, he led me to do many a forbidden thing, for which I was punished. The only whipping I ever knew Mr. Allan to give him was for carrying me out into fields and woods beyond Belvidere one Saturday, and keeping me there all day until after dark, without anybody at home knowing where we were, and for shooting a lot of domestic fowls, belonging to the proprietor of Belvidere. . . . He taught me to shoot, to swim, and to skate, to play bandy, etc; and I ought to mention that he once saved me from drowning—for having thrown me into the falls headlong, that I might strike out for myself, he presently found it necessary to come to my help, or it would have been too late."

Poe was fond of sports. One friend of his youth said he was "a swift runner, a wonderful leaper," and "a boxer with slight training." Certainly he was an excellent swimmer; his six-mile swim in the James from Richmond to Warwick, against a strong tide, attests this fact. Robert G. Cabell and Robert Stanard, two of his boyhood chums, accompanied him in a boat or along the bank; Robert Mayo tried to swim the distance with him but gave up at Tree Hill, about halfway. The day was extremely hot, and teen-aged Edgar Poe emerged from the water with blistered face, neck and back. In later years he wrote concerning this exploit when someone referred to it in the press:

"The writer seems to compare my swim with that of Lord Byron [across the Hellespont], whereas there can be no comparison between them. Any swimmer 'in the falls' in my days would have swum the Hellespont and thought nothing of the matter. I swam from Ludlow's Wharf to Warwick (six miles), in a hot June sun, against one of the strongest tides ever known in the river. It would have been a feat comparatively easy to swim twenty miles in still water. I would not think much of attempting to swim the British Channel from Dover to Calais."

Allowing for a certain amount of braggadocio in the foregoing, the fact remains that Edgar performed an extraordinary feat.

As the well-knit youth of medium height with unusually broad forehead, white skin and brilliant eyes of hazel gray grew to manhood, his stormy and tragic career began to unfold. During those years he came under the spell of two Richmond women, Jane Stith Craig Stanard, the inspiration of his memorable poem "To Helen," and Elmira Royster, who may have been his "Lenore."

Jane Stanard was the mother of Poe's friend "Rob" Stanard. She would die insane at thirty in 1824 and her grave is to be seen today in Shockoe Cemetery. But in earlier years the radiant vision of Jane Stanard by the "brilliant window-niche" of her house on Ninth Street opposite Capitol Square evoked an image in the mind and heart of Edgar Poe that later was made imperishable in one of the world's great lyric poems. Edgar's adoration of Mrs. Stanard was that of a boy barely in his teens for an older married woman. His feeling for Elmira Royster was altogether different.

Jane Stanard's youth had been spent in the home of her parents, the Adam Craigs, at 1812 East Grace Street, one of the two or three oldest houses standing in Richmond in the late twentieth century, and built in the 1780s. As the birthplace of "Poe's Helen," it has an especial attraction and charm.

Poe paid court to Elmira Royster before going off to the University of Virginia at age seventeen. They were engaged when he left for college, she said many years later. During his ten months there he wrote her many letters, all of which were intercepted by her father "because we were too young," Elmira declared. She was sixteen at the time, and hearing nothing from Edgar married A. Barret Shelton the following year. He was older and a person of means and social standing. Some of Richmond's elite regarded Poe slightly askance because his mother had been an actress.

When Poe returned from the university, in December 1826, he was shocked to find that his letters had never reached his fiancée and that their romance was over. Worse still was the growing breach with his foster father, made almost inevitable by the latter's refusal to provide him with the absolute minimum in funds to cover essential expenses at Charlottesville. Allan had been generous in paying for his earlier education in England and Richmond and had often expressed affection for the boy, but he suddenly became parsimonious in the extreme when Edgar entered college. This despite the fact that Allan was then wealthy, whereas he had been badly pressed for money during the depression which struck in 1819.

Allan had no reason to complain of Edgar's scholastic record at the university, for it was excellent. His courses were exclusively in ancient and modern languages. And while there was a great deal of riotous conduct at the institution during that session, and some fifty students sought by the sheriff "traveled off into the woods and mountains, taking their beds and provisions with them"—as Poe put it in a letter to Allan—he himself was not among them. Nor do faculty records indicate that he was guilty of any misconduct at all.

What he did do, as he admitted, was to gamble, in the hope of taking care of his essential university bills, as well as some rather extravagant purchases of clothes. He lost heavily, and some have placed his total indebtedness to students and others at $2,500, but this is probably too high. He also drank at times, and being unusually susceptible to alcohol's effects, he was often thought to have consumed more than was actually the case.

Why Allan became so bitterly hostile to his ward is rather difficult to understand. Poe said his foster father wrote him early in the university session "in terms of the utmost abuse, . . . because I could not contrive to pay $150 [in university fees] with $110"—which was all that Allan provided him with when he entered the institution. Granted that Edgar was not without faults, and that he may have done something of which we are not aware, Allan's attitude is a mystery. A possible explanation is that Edgar, who loved Mrs. Allan dearly, found out that Allan was a philanderer. If so, this could have caused his foster father's antagonism. "Jock" Allan sired several illegitimate children by a Mrs. Wills. He provided for them in his will, while leaving Edgar nothing.

Mrs. Allan, the former Frances Keeling Valentine, was a pretty woman of good family, and extremely fond of Edgar. She was understanding and helpful through his many trials. But she was in frail health much of the time and of a nervous disposition. Thus she was unable to counteract the hostility of her domineering husband toward the boy, and Edgar was desperately unhappy. In March 1827, a few months following his return from the university, he enlisted in the United States Army under the name of Edgar A. Perry.

After two years in the service, during which he rose to the highest noncommissioned rank, that of sergeant major, and was unreservedly commended by his superiors, he obtained an honorable discharge.

Toward the end of this period, Mrs. Allan died. Allan refused to finance the boy's education further, and Poe decided to apply for entrance to the United States Military Academy. This was far from being an educational institution congenial to his temperament—he had published two small

books of poems while in the army and was determined to publish others—
but he was trying to make the best of an unsatisfactory situation. Fortunately, his record in the service was such that he was successful in his application to the Academy.

During his stay at West Point (July 1830 to March 1831), he did well
in his studies, was already familiar with the drill from his army experience
and was well-liked by the cadets. But creative literary work was virtually
impossible, and this was his all-consuming passion. Furthermore, his relations with Allan remained bitter, with no financial support from that
quarter.

Poe's letters to his foster father were often movingly pathetic, and Allan
failed sadly to appreciate his artistic temperament. At the same time, the
older man was understandably infuriated when Poe had the bad taste to
write a friend that "Mr. Allan is not very often sober." Poe's letter was for-
warded to Allan after Poe reached West Point, and its effect on their already strained relations can be imagined. By this time it was clear that the
two men could never be congenial, and while Allan is rightly subject to severe criticism, Poe was by no means blameless.

The youth decided that he must leave West Point, so he got himself
dismissed by deliberately disobeying the rules. He went to live in Baltimore with his aunt, Mrs. Maria Poe Clemm, and published a third volume of poems. He also began writing prose tales. But once again he was in
tragic circumstances. John Pendleton Kennedy, the Baltimore novelist,
came to his aid. "I found him in a state of starvation," Kennedy wrote in
his journal after Poe's death. "I gave him clothing, free access to my table
and the use of a horse for exercise." Kennedy was instrumental in obtaining publication of several stories by Poe in the *Southern Literary Messenger* at Richmond. Despite his admiration for Poe, he wrote that the latter
was "irregular, eccentric and querulous."

The *Messenger* had been established in 1834 by Thomas W. White, a
Richmond printer, for the laudable purpose of raising the level of Southern letters. He himself was without literary ability, but he secured as editorial consultant James E. Heath, a Richmond novelist who later wrote an
excellent play. Heath, often called the magazine's "first editor," although
he apparently did not actually have the title, served without pay until the
following year.

Poe by that time was in correspondence with White concerning work
on the magazine. He expressed himself as anxious to return to Richmond,
and said he would accept congenial duties on the *Messenger* if the salary
were "the merest trifle." John Allan had died in 1834, which may have increased Poe's desire to return to the city where he had spent much of his
youth.

The twenty-six-year-old Poe came to Richmond at White's invitation
and plunged into his work on the magazine. The *Messenger*'s offices were

on the second floor of a building at the southeast corner of Fifteenth and Main. Poe lived in a cheap boardinghouse and was far from happy. He was desperately in love with his thirteen-year-old cousin, Virginia Clemm, and agonizingly fearful that he would lose her. His letter to his Aunt Maria, Virginia's mother, is one of the most moving outpourings that can be imagined. Too long to be reproduced here, it begins, "I am blinded with tears while writing this letter—I have no wish to live another hour. . . . Oh God have mercy on me!" There is much more in this vein. Poe then goes on to say:

"I had procured a sweet little house in a retired section of Church Hill —newly done up with a large garden and every convenience—at only $5 per month. I have been dreaming every day & night since of the rapture I should feel in seeing my only friends—all I love on earth with me there; the pride I would take in making you both comfor[table] & in calling her my wife. But the dream is over. . . . What have I *to live for?* Among strangers with *not one soul to love me.*"

At another point Poe says that "every one here receives me with open arms," which hardly comports with his description of himself as "among strangers." However, he was obviously greatly overwrought and apparently on the verge of suicide. Yet the letter does not read as if written by a man under the influence of alcohol, although Poe certainly went on sprees from time to time. There is no reason to believe that he was ever addicted to drugs.

His aunt's reply to his impassioned communication is not of record, but evidently the situation was by no means as hopeless as he feared. For less than a month later he was in Baltimore, at which time a marriage license was taken out for himself and Virginia. The ceremony was not performed until subsequently in Richmond, when another license was issued, but Poe's apprehensions as to Virginia's attitude toward him are seen to have been groundless.

Yet much of the time he was in a state of profound depression, even when he was about to marry Virginia and his fortunes were otherwise greatly improved. "I am wretched and know not why," he wrote his friend John P. Kennedy. "Convince me that it is . . . at all necessary to live."

The fact seems to be, as Poe's finest biographer, Arthur Hobson Quinn, declares, that he was "fighting the most desperate conflict that any man can face, the struggle for sanity." There was mental instability in his family, and he appears to have been aghast at the thought that he might be adjudged insane. It was an era when "lunatics" were locked up in asylums and forgotten.

Poe was able to persuade his Aunt Maria and Virginia to join him in Richmond, and they were all installed in Mrs. James Yarrington's boardinghouse at Twelfth and Bank streets, fronting Capitol Square. Board for the three was $9 a week.

13. The widow Elmira Royster Shelton said that as Elmira Royster she was engaged to Edgar Allan Poe at age sixteen, when Poe went off to the University of Virginia. The romance died, but was renewed in the last months of Poe's life. Elmira may have been the woman to whom Poe referred as his "lost Lenore."

14. Edgar Allan Poe's marriage license when he was wed in Richmond to his cousin, Virginia Clemm. She was not quite fourteen, but the license shows that Thomas W. Cleland, a friend, made affidavit that Virginia was "of the full age of twenty-one."

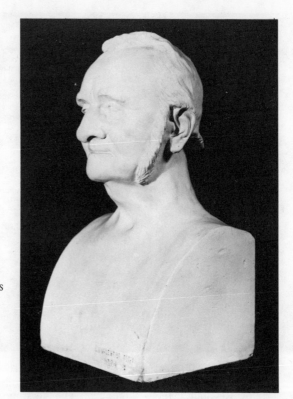

15. Samuel B. Mordecai, whose book *Richmond in By-Gone Days* is the most delightful of all the accounts of the city's early years, is shown in a bust by Edward V. Valentine.

16. The Reverend Moses D. Hoge, one of the most eminent divines in Virginia history, was pastor of Second Presbyterian Church for more than half a century.

17. The Thirteenth Street Bridge, built in 1860 over the James River & Kanawha Canal, was restored recently in handsome and accurate fashion by Reynolds Metals Company. The keystone bears the initials of the builders, R. Barton Haxall and Lewis D. Crenshaw.

18. Dr. George W. Bagby, one of the most charming writers on old Virginia scenes and personalities, was Richmond correspondent for a number of Southern newspapers during the Civil War. Poor health compelled him to resign from the Confederate Army, but not until he had performed the almost incredible feat of sleeping through the first Battle of Manassas.

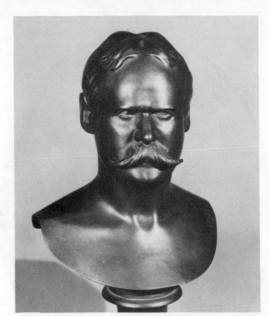

19. Bust of the brilliantly versatile Innes Randolph, made by Randolph himself. Author of *The Good Old Rebel*, he was an officer in the Confederate Army for four years, and also was a musician, music critic, poet, sculptor and wit.

20. The Robertson Hospital at the northwest corner of Third and Main streets, usually known as Captain Sally Tompkins' Hospital. Young Sally Tompkins turned the residence of Judge John Robertson into a place where Confederate wounded were extremely well cared for, and was made a captain in the Confederate Army. From a drawing by Elmo Jones.

21. Constance Cary, later Mrs. Burton Harrison, whose good looks and talent made her a central figure in Richmond during the war, is shown in an unpublished miniature. She was gifted as a writer and amateur actress.

22. Hetty Cary, most famous beauty in Richmond during the Civil War, married Brigadier General John Pegram in January 1865, in St. Paul's Episcopal Church. He was killed shortly thereafter at the front, and three weeks to the day from her wedding she knelt in St. Paul's beside his coffin. The miniature is published here for the first time.

23. Brigadier General John Pegram of Richmond won Hetty Cary's hand, and after their wedding they went to his headquarters in a farmhouse in front of Petersburg. Soon thereafter he was killed leading a charge. She returned to Richmond in the freight car that carried his body.

24. Richmond falls, April 3, 1865, to an obbligato of burning buildings and exploding shells and powder magazines. Soldiers and citizens are shown evacuating the doomed city across Mayo's Bridge. A Currier & Ives print.

Poe's morale was improved by the presence of the ladies, but he was still subject to fits of profound melancholy. He also was being warned by White of the *Messenger* against further drinking. Yet his bouts with the bottle were not as frequent as many suppose. James Southall Wilson, one of the leading authorities on all aspects of Poe's career, says that "from the summer of 1835 to January, 1837 at most three and possibly only two irregularities from intoxication on Poe's part came to the attention of Thomas W. White." It must be borne in mind, however, that when Poe "fell from the water wagon," he fell with a dull thud. "He was an ill man for days and even weeks," says Wilson.

White warned Poe sternly in September 1835 that should he "again sip the juice," he would be fired. It is difficult to believe that alcohol interfered tremendously with Poe's performance on the magazine, for he was writing all the critical and literary notices, and doing them extremely well. In December White announced that he, White, was being assisted by "a gentleman of distinguished literary talents," and that "journals on every side . . . have rung the praises of his uniquely original vein of imagination, and of humorous, delicate satire."

Poe was, in fact, attracting national attention already with his slashing book reviews and critical articles, as well as with his highly original short stories. In January 1836 he wrote his friend Kennedy in Baltimore, "I am in every respect comfortable and happy." While this euphoria was not to endure, since Poe, like most geniuses, had a mercurial temperament, he was viewing the world through rose-tinted glasses at that particular moment. He mentioned that his annual income from the *Messenger* was $800 and that he had been promised an increase to $1,000.

Poe was married to Virginia in May at Mrs. Yarrington's boardinghouse, and this also helped his morale, at least temporarily. The bride was not quite fourteen, but Thomas W. Cleland, a friend, swore, when the license was obtained, that she was twenty-one. The Presbyterian clergyman, the Reverend Amasa Converse, raised no objections. Virginia, though beautiful, was necessarily immature, and she has always remained a somewhat shadowy personality. But Poe loved her devotedly until her death. She was equally steadfast in her love for him.

On their return from a brief honeymoon in Petersburg, Poe was again absorbed in the *Messenger*. He continued to write criticism, stories and poems that showed great originality. The magazine's circulation zoomed to about thirty-five hundred, as contrasted with five hundred when he joined the staff. Yet White refused to give him complete control of policy, with the result that Poe was acutely dissatisfied. White reproved him again for drinking. All this combined to cause his resignation in January 1837.

He had been at the helm of the magazine for about eighteen months, and had raised it from a publication of limited reputation to recognition as one of the foremost journals in the land. Poe had written 112 book reviews for the *Messenger*, contributed 8 hitherto unpublished stories and 7 unpublished poems, while reprinting others. In addition, he handled a considerable correspondence, supervised the make-up of the publication, read proof and addressed the monthly issues.[1]

As editor of the magazine he did not hesitate to discuss controversial topics of the day. For example, he defended slavery. He also advocated free public education for the state of Virginia, saying that, in view of the absence of public schools, the Commonwealth's "once great name is becoming, in the North, a bye-word for imbecility."

Generally speaking, however, Poe's writings, both then and later, were far removed from the contemporary scene. His stories and poems were often concerned with eerie and blood-chilling themes—with, in the words of Van Wyck Brooks, "gloom, despair, sepulchral thoughts, grim fantasies and the fear of impending mental decay." Poe's world was "overhung with the sable wings of lunacy, perversity, hysteria, of sickness, hypochondria, ruin, dissolution and death." He was pathetically neurotic and on the verge of madness at times, especially in his last years. These somber traits may have been, in some degree, inherited, but they certainly stemmed, in part, from the frustrations and torments that beset him during most of his adult life. The normality of his early behavior and his ability to become a sergeant major in the army are in vivid contrast to his later eccentricities and his literary preoccupation with horror, terror and the grave.

When Poe resigned from the *Messenger* in January 1837, he returned to New York, taking his wife and aunt with him. Mrs. Clemm opened a boardinghouse, and William Gowans, a Scot who spent eight months there, wrote later in praise of Poe's sobriety, hard work and gentlemanly demeanor during that time. He also described Virginia as "of matchless beauty and loveliness" whose "eye could match that of any houri, and her face defy the genius of a Canova to imitate." Captain Mayne Reid, the novelist, a constant visitor to Poe's home in 1843, described Virginia as "angelically beautiful in person and not less beautiful in spirit. . . . We, the friends of the poet, used to talk of her high qualities." She was then about twenty-one years of age.

The country was in the grip of a depression when Poe went to New York in 1837, and he was unable to obtain steady employment. He accordingly took his family to Philadelphia, in the hope of finding an outlet for his talents. A position on the staff of the *Gentleman's Magazine* became available, and Poe worked there as co-editor for about a year. But he quarreled violently with William E. Burton, the proprietor, and resigned in 1840. Poe had an unfortunate way of making enemies of the very persons who could help him most. His needlessly sarcastic and biting critiques of books by certain prominent authors are important examples of this.

After leaving the *Gentleman's Magazine*, Poe obtained an editorial position on *Graham's Magazine*, also in Philadelphia. He remained there for slightly more than a year.

During this latter period, in January 1842, his beloved Virginia ruptured a blood vessel while singing at the piano. She lingered for five years, and her life was despaired of on several occasions. The emotional strain on the highly sensitive Poe can be imagined. According to one friend of the family, he contracted "brain fever brought on by extreme suffering of mind and body—actual want and hunger and cold having been borne by this heroic husband in order to supply food, medicine and comforts to his dying wife."

Poe, Virginia and Mrs. Clemm returned to New York in 1843, with hardly enough money to pay the railroad fare. Virginia finally died in January 1847, in their cottage at Fordham. Poe's drinking seems to have been understandably greater during this period.

He visited Richmond briefly in 1848, for the first time in more than a decade. Hardly anything is known of his movements. A near-duel with John M. Daniel, the fiery editor of the Richmond *Examiner*, was a highlight of his stay, but the circumstances of this encounter are vague.

Poe came back to Richmond the following summer for the last visit of his life and lodged at the Swan Tavern. Whereas he was said by John R. Thompson, editor of the *Southern Literary Messenger*, to have gone on a prolonged drinking bout during his sojourn the year before, this time he joined the Sons of Temperance and, except for two reported lapses, apparently remained sober.

The now famous poet was received with marked enthusiasm and generous hospitality. Robert Stanard, Robert Cabell and Robert Sully, his boyhood friends, greeted him warmly. Susan Archer Talley, later Mrs. Louis Weiss, saw him on several occasions at Talavera, her parent's farmhouse which many years later became 2315 West Grace Street—still standing in 1976. Talavera, in 1849, was in the suburbs, as was nearby Duncan Lodge, the home of the Mackenzies. Mrs. Weiss wrote long afterward that Poe "spent his mornings in town, but in the evenings would generally drive out to Duncan Lodge [which stood on West Broad Street between today's Lodge and Mackenzie streets]. He liked the half-country neighborhood, and would sometimes join us on our sunset rambles in the romantic old Hermitage grounds." Mrs. Weiss described in detail a visit by Poe to Talavera in 1849, on a "pleasant though slightly drizzly morning in the latter part of September." They discussed "The Raven" and both agreed that it had imperfections. Susan was emphatic in her criticism of certain phrases.

Poverty still dogged Poe's footsteps, despite his rising fame. He wrote Mrs. Clemm, "I have been invited out a great deal—but could seldom go, on account of not having a dress coat."

A "large and enthusiastic" audience greeted him at the Exchange Hotel on August 17, when he lectured on "The Poetic Principle" and read "The Raven." Admission was only twenty-five cents, so that the receipts cannot have added up to much. However, Poe was so strapped for funds that any small sum was welcomed. "I *never* was received with so much enthusiasm," he wrote Mrs. Clemm. "The papers have done nothing but praise me before the lecture and since." He delivered the lecture in Norfolk, to applause, and then returned to Richmond and repeated it. There was general agreement that Poe's voice as a lecturer was exceptionally melodious and had an indefinable quality that gave it a special charm.

During his last visit to Richmond he renewed his courtship of Elmira Royster Shelton, then a widow. The forty-year-old Poe, whose letters to Elmira from the University of Virginia nearly a quarter of a century before had been intercepted, pressed his suit with renewed ardor. The widow Shelton lived at 2407 East Grace Street, a house standing in 1976. During the early part of his visit to Richmond, Poe was often seen mounting the steps to Elmira's front door. Then for several weeks the visits ceased mysteriously, only to be resumed in September. He spent the evening of September 26 at Elmira's, but was not feeling well. She was not engaged to him at that time, she said years afterward, but they had "an understanding." Poe thought they were going to be married.

Despite his malaise, he left for Baltimore by boat the following morning, expecting to return. His subsequent movements are altogether mysterious. He dropped out of sight for six days, and was found semiconscious near a Baltimore polling place where an election was being held. His clothing had been stolen and he was wearing shoddy garments. Poe was taken to a hospital, where he died on October 7. His last words were "God help my poor soul."

Thus ended the star-crossed career of perhaps the most tragic figure in Richmond's history. Born in Boston because his actor-parents happened to be in that city, he called himself "a Virginian" and regarded Richmond as "home." James Southall Wilson said he had "the most brilliant and variously gifted mind that America had yet produced . . . of enormous energy and creative fire." Despite poverty, ill-health and long-continued emotional strain, he produced in two decades about seventeen volumes. They include some of the loveliest lyric poems and most original short stories in the language, together with a great body of incisive critical writing. Conan Doyle termed him "the inventor of the detective story." Poe's ingenuity and imagination were matched by his exquisite choice of words, words as musical as the notes of a symphony. His prose often gives forth the sounds of poetry, and the names of the characters in his writings have a flowing and rhythmic quality—Ligeia, Israfel, Lenore, Ulalume and Annabel Lee.

Edgar Allan Poe was at times his own worst enemy, for like many greatly gifted men he was temperamental and unstable. Yet the creative passion within him was never quenched, and he left a literary legacy that will live.

ELEVEN

# Richmond's Leadership
# Before the Civil War

VIRGINIA's two greatest newspaper editors of the nineteenth century were
Thomas Ritchie of the Richmond *Enquirer* and John Hampden Pleasants
of the Richmond *Whig*. Almost from the time that Ritchie established
the *Enquirer* in 1804, he was recognized as a journalistic genius. The paper
became the Bible of the Democrats, and its editor one of the movers and
shakers in the national councils of the party. Thomas Jefferson wrote in
1823 from his mountaintop, "I read but a single newspaper, Ritchie's
*Enquirer*, the best that has been or is published in America."

Young John Hampden Pleasants, the son of Governor James Pleasants,
may have learned of this Jeffersonian dictum in Lynchburg, where he had
established and was editing the *Virginian*. At all events, he concluded that
the capital of the state should have an organ for the Whigs as a foil to the
ably edited mouthpiece of the Democrats. So in 1824, the Richmond
*Whig* came from the presses under his editorship. Pleasants soon made a
strong impact with his paper, and Ritchie had an altogether worthy competitor.

Those were the days of personal journalism and of absurdly partisan
newspapers, in which the candidate of the party to which the paper vowed
adherence was depicted as possessing every conceivable virtue and his opponent as probably guilty of both venality and imbecility. Henry Clay, for
example, whom the *Enquirer* delighted to excoriate, was termed by the
*Whig* "the nearest approximation of human intellect to the divine."

Although dueling was in its heyday, Ritchie and Pleasants managed, despite caustic remarks about each other in their papers, to avoid a resort to
"pistols at ten paces." Pleasants, much the younger and more caustic of
the two, actually termed Ritchie an "impotent dotard and driveller" without bringing a challenge.

Pleasants was excessively shy and unwilling to make public appearances, whereas "Father Ritchie," as he came to be known, was the speaker or toastmaster on many public occasions.

Both men were well in advance of current thinking on various important issues. Both were highly critical of the slave system in the 1830s and its effects on Southern attitudes and Southern progress. Pleasants maintained his critical posture longer than Ritchie. Both papers declared in the 1840s that an infusion of Northerners would benefit Virginia and tend to lift Virginians out of their lethargy. Fairer representation in the General Assembly for the western counties of the state was advocated by the two papers. The *Enquirer* and the *Whig* repeatedly and earnestly urged the establishment of public schools throughout the Commonwealth, and declared that educational opportunities ought to be made available not only to white males but also to "females." The papers wished to improve and elevate the status of women in society.[1] Ritchie actually hinted that he might even tolerate the idea of woman suffrage.

The place of women was in a state of flux. An anonymous college president, who was evidently the Reverend Adam P. Empie of William and Mary, published a letter of advice to his daughter in the *Southern Literary Messenger* in 1835, expressing a viewpoint that was passing away. Dr. Empie advised his daughter—who was about to be married—that she must never oppose her husband, never show displeasure, no matter what he might do. She should repose entire confidence in her mate, and always assume that he would know best. "A difference with your husband ought to be considered the greatest calamity," said the father, who added that a woman who permitted such differences to occur could expect to lose her husband's love. Few parents admonished their offspring in such categorical terms in the mid-nineteenth century, but woman's "place" was still quite definitely "in the home," rather than in the public arena.

At the same time, as noted in an earlier chapter, the view was coming to be held that women should be given opportunities for broader intellectual development. "It was desirable," as Ann F. Scott has written, "that wives have something more on their minds than the best recipe for scuppernong wine or the most effective treatment for measles." There were numerous evidences of mounting support for more adequate educational facilities for women, and the Richmond *Enquirer* and *Whig* were leaders in this movement.

Thomas Ritchie retired as editor of the *Enquirer* in 1845 and moved to Washington, at the urging of newly elected President James K. Polk, whom Pleasants and the *Whig* termed "a fifth-rate lawyer and pettifogging politician." Ritchie took over the editorship of the Washington *Union*, and left the *Enquirer* in the hands of his sons.

One of these, Thomas Ritchie, Jr., got into a bitter editorial controversy with Pleasants over slavery. Pleasants still maintained his highly critical attitude toward the institution, but there was no truth in the *Enquirer's* charge that he planned to found an abolitionist journal. In the heated exchange over his false allegation, Thomas Ritchie, Jr., termed the editor of the *Whig* "a coward."

Pleasants was opposed in principle to the code duello, but in that era men felt that they must act when publicly charged with cowardice. Pleasants sent a message to Ritchie that he would meet him at sunrise on the Chesterfield side of the James, two hundred yards above the cotton mill, on February 24, 1846, prepared to shoot him on sight. This unorthodox type of challenge was accepted by Ritchie, who was an experienced duelist, whereas Pleasants was wholly inexperienced.

The latter was determined to "vindicate his honor" by showing his courage under fire, but not to harm Ritchie. Hence when the men faced each other in the gray dawn beside the James, he wasted his bullets in the air. Ritchie, on the other hand, shot with deadly aim and wounded him mortally. He lingered long enough to praise his opponent's bravery and to ask that Ritchie not be prosecuted. In his dying moments the forty-nine-year-old Pleasants gasped out, "What a damned immolation, to be such slaves to public opinion!"

Virginia and the South had lost an eloquent and courageous spokesman in an era when such men were all too rare. The "code of honor" had claimed another victim.

In the year following Pleasants' tragic death, there appeared on the Richmond scene an editor cast in a different mold—twenty-two-year-old John Moncure Daniel of the Richmond *Examiner*. This young man set out deliberately to attack almost every prominent citizen of Virginia, thus making himself widely known, and also widely hated. His brash editorials attracted attention throughout the Old Dominion and in other states. Daniel's journalistic career was interrupted in 1853 when he accepted an appointment as United States representative to the Court of Sardinia, where he remained for seven years. Upon the secession of South Carolina, he returned to Richmond and resumed his editorial post. Daniel again edited the *Examiner* with superlative style and reckless abandon until his untimely death from tuberculosis at the end of March 1865, on the eve of Lee's surrender at Appomattox.

Richmond editors were in the thick of the mounting controversy over slavery in the 1850s, as armed conflict between the sections drew nearer. Representative Preston Brooks of South Carolina caned abolitionist Senator Charles Sumner of Massachusetts into unconsciousness while the latter was seated defenseless at his desk in the Senate, because Sumner had delivered an offensive attack on a relative of Brooks. The savage assault on Sumner was applauded by many Southern papers. The Richmond *Enquirer* declared, "Our approbation . . . is entire and unreserved. . . . It was a proper act, done at the proper time and in the proper place." The

Richmond *Examiner* remarked that "far from blaming Mr. Brooks, we are disposed to regard him as a conservative gentleman seeking to restore the lost dignity of the Senate."

Inside the state, controversy flared over more locally significant issues. Henry A. Wise, a pungent phrasemaker, described Negroes on one occasion as "ebo-shinned and gizzard-footed." Talented Robert Ridgeway of the *Whig* referred to Wise thereafter as "Old Gizzard Foot" or "Old Gizzard." When Wise, a Democrat, was elected governor in 1856, Ridgeway declared in the *Whig* that in choosing him, the Democratic party had abandoned its old-time policy of choosing an idiot as governor, and had named a lunatic as well. All this led O. Jennings Wise, Henry Wise's son, to call on Ridgeway at his office and administer a caning. Ridgeway challenged him to a duel, but it was somehow averted. Jennings Wise, editor of the *Enquirer*, fought eight duels in the two years immediately preceding the outbreak of the Civil War.

In open dissent from the partisanship of the local press, a newspaper was founded at Richmond in 1850 that proclaimed its political nonpartisanship. This was the *Dispatch*, with James A. Cowardin as proprietor and Hugh R. Pleasants, a brother of John Hampden Pleasants, as editor.

Cowardin was described as "genial, full of wit and vivacious." He was evidently an able journalist, for within a decade he was boasting that the *Dispatch* had eighteen thousand circulation, or more than all the other Richmond papers combined. Like the rival journals of the period, it was full of advertisements for quack medicines. Though nonpartisan politically, the paper could be tart in its comments on men and affairs. For example, when a rural citizen spoke disparagingly of the morality of cities, the *Dispatch* observed that "the country is not without vice," and went on to declare that "there is probably more scandal and gossiping in a small town in 24 hours than there has been in London or New York for the last 100 years."

Richmond's two antebellum historians had contrasting views of the city's press. Dr. John P. Little wrote that the influence of Richmond's newspapers throughout Virginia "is more powerful than the press of any other city in any other state." They evidenced "a high order of talent," he said. But Samuel Mordecai had no words of praise for the Richmond papers and declared: "It is much to be deplored that many editors of the present day, instead of endeavoring to form or to reform and to refine the taste of their readers, are too apt to pander to the grossness of the least intelligent of them, and in many instances to render their sheets unfit for the perusal of a family circle."

Mordecai's sensibilities were perhaps more delicate than most. For instance, he wrote with respect to the use of profanity that it was now "scarcely heard in respectable society" whereas it was "very prevalent among gentlemen of the past generation." "D——d," wrote he, was no longer "the term by which to express admiration of a good fellow or detestation of a rascal."

In other words, it was not "respectable" in Richmond in the 1850s to declare that "Richmond is a d——d prosperous manufacturing center," although such was indeed the case. Richmond was the industrial center of the South and the region's wealthiest city, based on per capita property valuation.[2] It was the nation's, and perhaps the world's, largest manufacturer of tobacco and, as we have seen, the nation's second largest flour milling center.[3] The city was also the leading coffee port in the country, since the fleets of ships that carried vast quantities of flour to South America from Richmond's mills returned bringing the fragrant bean.[4] In addition to Richmond's preeminence in tobacco manufacture, half of the tobacco grown in Virginia and North Carolina was marketed in the city.[5] Richmond at this time, as previously noted, was "the wealthiest city of its size in America and perhaps the world." Not only so, but its dynamic quality is evidenced in the fact that its population jumped from 27,000 to 38,000 between 1850 and 1860, an increase of 37 per cent, the largest in Richmond's history.

Over against the rocketing prosperity of Richmond in the last decade before the Civil War was the catastrophic collapse of the silkworm boom shortly before. Attempts to produce raw silk in Virginia from the mulberry tree and the silkworm had been unsuccessful in the seventeenth century. The effort was revived in 1837 when Thomas M. Randolph presented a report to the General Assembly advocating a state bounty for the culture of silk.

Grievously exaggerated predictions were made by imported so-called experts as to the profits that might be expected from silk manufacture in Richmond. The *Enquirer* went so far as to say that annual yields of up to $1,000 an acre might be anticipated. Other forecasts put the probable per acre return at from $200 to $500. Richmonders mortgaged their homes to buy trees by the thousand and silkworm eggs by the million. The eggs were white, gray, yellow or speckled, which made for a special "sales pitch." It was even claimed that five separate crops of worms could be raised in a single twelvemonth.

But within a few years it became evident that the idea of getting rich from silk manufacture in Richmond was a sad illusion. The trees were not as hardy as represented and the worms were uncooperative. The whole process was found to be more complicated and difficult than was realized. The silkworm bubble burst with lamentable results for the investors.

Those who put their money into the making of chewing tobacco during these years were much more fortunate. Mastication of the leaf was widespread among males, a fact noted without enthusiasm by foreign visitors. One of these suggested that our national emblem should be the spittoon rather than the eagle.

William Barret was among the Richmonders who became wealthy in
this branch of industry. His fortune was based principally on a brand
called "Negro Head," huge quantities of which were sold in England and
Australia. The Myers Brothers, Colonel Samuel S. and William R., turned
out plug in large quantities under such brand names as "Little Swan
Rough and Ready" and "Darling Fanny Pan Cake." John Enders was another rich tobacconist. His life was cut short when he fell while superin-
tending the building of a warehouse. Robert A. Mayo was also a prosperous Richmond producer of the plug.

However, the leading leaf manufacturer in Virginia and North Carolina
prior to the Civil War was James Thomas, Jr. He came to Richmond as a
poor youth from Caroline County and by 1860 had the largest tobacco
factory in the city. Among his brands were "Nature's Ultimatum,"
"Diadem of Old Virginia" and "Wedding Cake." Thomas was a leading
Baptist layman, and was so hospitable to visiting clergymen that his handsome home at 112 East Grace Street was called "the Baptist hotel." Built
in 1853, it stood until 1937, and was the first of the pretentious mansions
erected by tobacco men and others in the 1850s.

Richmond's tobacco factories, with the mellow singing of Negro
workers serving as a stimulus to production, reached their peak in the decade before the war. The flour mills also achieved new highs, with output
of some 400,000 barrels annually. In heavy industry, the Tredegar Iron
Works had become the city's mainstay. Other ironmakers also were in operation and several cotton mills had sprung up.

Chesterfield coal was a boon to Richmond industry. The mines were
going full blast during this period and extensive use was being made of
free Negroes in the labor force. The blacks worked side by side with English, Scottish, Irish and Welsh miners, apparently without friction. There
were two serious explosions in the mines; one in 1839 took fifty-four lives
and another in 1855 wiped out fifty-five more.

The James River and Kanawha Canal was losing business to the railroads. The first rail carrier in Virginia was the Chesterfield railroad, which
began operations in 1831, hauling coal from the Midlothian mines to
Manchester. Mule-power and the force of gravity combined to make the
road function. Seven years later the steam-operated Richmond & Petersburg Railroad began hauling coal over the same route. It was the parent of
the Atlantic Coast Line.

Attention was focused meanwhile on the building of the Richmond,
Fredericksburg & Potomac Railroad. The first twenty miles, reaching almost to the South Anna River, was finished in 1836. A hundred and fifty
guests of the road made the initial trip, to the accompaniment of band
music. The twenty-mile journey took an hour and thirty-one minutes.

The R.F.& P. had its Richmond terminus on Broad Street at Eighth,
and the trains roared down the middle of that thoroughfare on a track

that was well above street level. This novel state of things was the subject of much adverse comment.

The situation was almost unbelievable. The railway management, Dr. Little declared in his history, "actually allows passengers to land their cars in the middle of the street, without shelter from the pelting rain or burning sun, in the midst of noisy porters and hack drivers, and then to pass through mud and dust to the sidewalk."

Two early presidents of the R.F.& P. were brothers, Moncure and Conway Robinson. Moncure (1802–91), an engineer and railroad builder, attracted attention throughout America and Europe. He built the bridge over the James for the Richmond & Petersburg Railroad and the Philadelphia & Reading Railroad, with a tunnel 1,932 feet long and a spectacular stone bridge. Robinson refused an invitation from the czar of Russia to supervise construction of the Russian railway system.

His brother, Conway Robinson (1805–84), was notable as a legal scholar and historian. As a member of City Council, he performed other important cultural services. For example, he led in arranging for the establishment of the Athenaeum in the Richmond Academy Building at the southeast corner of Tenth and Marshall streets. The Athenaeum not only made rooms available to the Virginia Historical and Philosophical Society and the Richmond Library free of charge, but it was also used for lectures and concerts. In addition, Conway Robinson had much to do with establishing Richmond's antebellum park system, including Monroe, Gamble's Hill and Libby Hill parks.

Railroads serving Richmond also included the Virginia Central, later the Chesapeake & Ohio—which connected Richmond with Staunton and Jackson's River (Clifton Forge) via Colonel Claudius Crozet's notable tunnel through the Blue Ridge. Then, too, there was the Richmond & Danville, which linked the capital with the latter city, and the Richmond & York River, which ran to West Point and was the means, among other things of bringing York River oysters to Richmond tables.

White Sulphur Springs was the most fashionable of the mountain resorts in the western part of the state patronized by Richmonders. Before the Virginia Central got into operation, the long and difficult journey had to be made by canal boat and stagecoach, or by stagecoach or private conveyance. When rail travel all the way to the White became a reality soon after the war, that resort and others nearby were especially popular.

Young male Richmonders courted sloe-eyed belles at these watering places during horseback rides or on strolls in the moonlight beside murmuring streams. The accepted procedure for such wooing contrasted drastically with that of later times. As Mary Virginia Hawes of Richmond put it in her autobiography, written under the pen name of Marion Harland: "For a man to touch a lady's arm or shoulder to attract her attention was an unpardonable liberty. If a pair were seen to 'hold hands,' it was taken for granted that they were engaged." However, engagements were never announced and every effort was made to keep them secret.

While transportation from Richmond to other parts of Virginia was being speeded up, something similar was happening inside the city. The Richmond Omnibus Coach Company announced in 1833 that it was ready to provide service along Main Street from the docks at Rocketts westward as far as "the Banks," i.e. on Main just below Capitol Square. Passengers and baggage would also be conveyed to and from the various hotels and boardinghouses and "the steamboats." More comprehensive city omnibus service was provided in 1847 by A. Perkins and Company.

Richmond was involved in the "log cabin and hard cider" presidential campaign of Virginia-born William Henry Harrison and John Tyler in 1840. A block-long log cabin was erected in Shockoe Bottom and served as headquarters for the Whigs. Daniel Webster—who stopped at the Powhatan House at the southeast corner of Eleventh and Broad, the city's finest —spoke for two hours and a half at the Capitol. Two other pro-Harrison orators followed him. President Harrison died the following April less than a month after his inauguration and a Richmond merchant advertised "Ladies Mourning Shoes," to be worn "as a tribute of respect."

When controversy with Mexico over the annexation of Texas brought the United States to the verge of war, a volunteer company was formed in Richmond. The Blues, Grays, Fayette Artillery, Rangers and Marshall Guards also held themselves in readiness. The declaration of war came in 1846, and Richmond units left for the fighting zone. At the end of the conflict, the returning heroes were welcomed in the city with parades and dinners. A century later, Thomas Lomax Hunter, Richmond *Times-Dispatch* columnist, aptly termed the war with Mexico "an expedition in search of real estate."

Richmond had barely finished celebrating this successful quest when the city was caught up in the California gold rush fever of 1849. Many Richmond men set out on almost interminable trips around Cape Horn or on equally dangerous and arduous journeys via the Isthmus of Panama, in the hope of finding quick riches. A writer in a local newspaper reported, "We heard two pretty girls lamenting the departure of 'so large a share of the young beaux of Richmond.'"

When the city's seekers after gold finally reached the Pacific coast, they found themselves in a dog-eat-dog scramble with similar adventurers from all parts of the United States, as well as from England, France, Australia and China. The whole ill-conceived scheme was a monumental fiasco insofar as Richmond was concerned, and the city's frustrated participants returned from the coast sadder, wiser and poorer.

Almost simultaneously with the departure of the "forty-niners," a new Richmond cemetery called Hollywood was dedicated. The ceremony took place on June 25, 1849, and Oliver P. Baldwin, a journalist who later became editor of the *Dispatch*, was the orator of the occasion. St. John's churchyard and Shockoe Cemetery in the center of town were filling up rapidly, and it had become necessary to find additional land for a burying ground. Yet, despite the spectacular beauty of the Hollywood tract, much opposition arose. It was claimed that the promoters were merely trying to make money and that corpses buried in proximity to the city water works would contaminate the municipal water supply. Some also contended that the "noise and tumult of the falls" would disturb the dead. In view of these and other objections, the sale of cemetery lots proceeded with glacial slowness. Finally, after several acres nearest the water works were sold to the city, opposition died down, and Hollywood became Richmond's principal burial ground.

Richmond College was becoming firmly established during these years. In 1834, the widowed Mrs. Philip Haxall had sold her handsome mansion, Columbia, at today's Lombardy and Grace streets, to the Virginia Baptist Education Society. This organization was conducting a seminary for Baptist ministers on Spring Farm at the head of Hermitage Road, and was anxious for more commodious quarters. In 1840, the seminary, which had moved to Columbia, was transformed into a liberal arts institution, Richmond College. Mrs. Haxall had prided herself on her beautiful trees, shrubs and flowers, and took satisfaction in serving to guests five varieties of nuts—walnut, hickory, chestnut, pecan and filbert—all grown on the estate. The Richmond College students occupied this sylvan setting, but they were cramped for space. The entire institution was housed in the Columbia mansion and the small brick outbuildings. The Reverend Robert Ryland, one of the remarkable men of his time, was the first president, and he remained in that office for thirty-four years. James Thomas, Jr., was the college's greatest benefactor during the antebellum era.

The women's branch of Richmond College had its inception in the Richmond Female Institute, established in 1854 under Baptist auspices, with the Reverend Basil Manly as president. The institute was housed in a large building at Tenth and Marshall streets which accommodated 250 students. There were both preparatory and collegiate departments. Later called the Woman's College, it was one of two centers of learning in or near Richmond that provided anything remotely resembling today's brand of higher education for women.

An institution of a different type was the nonsectarian home for "virtuous and indigent females" operated by the Female Humane Association. This organization had been founded in 1807, but it had no adequate quarters until Edmund Walls, who had come to Richmond as a poor Irish boy and made a fortune, died and left the association a substantial sum. The building was completed in 1843. Many years later the organization moved to Highland Park and changed its name to the Memorial Home for Girls. An agreement was made subsequently with the Children's Memorial

Clinic, whereby the assets and facilities of the Memorial Home for Girls would be used for a study and treatment home. The name of the latter organization was changed to the Memorial Foundation and later to the Memorial Foundation for Children.

The 1840s witnessed important developments affecting various Richmond churches. About a quarter of a century after Monumental Episcopal was built on the site of the dreadful theater fire of 1811, certain prominent members decided that they wanted to erect another Episcopal church "farther west." The reasons for this decision are not altogether clear, since St. Paul's, the church in question, is only three blocks to the westward. At all events, handsome St. Paul's was built at Ninth and Grace streets in 1845, and many of Monumental's members went over to the new congregation.

Centenary Methodist dates from these years, and is the oldest Methodist church now standing in the city. Its house of worship near Fifth and Grace was completed in 1843, and has been enlarged more than once. Broad Street Methodist Church erected its handsome building at Tenth and Broad in 1859. It stood there for more than a century until its demolition following the property's sale to the city, which needed space for the Civic Center. Perhaps Broad Street Church's greatest pulpit orator, and one of the foremost such orators in any denomination, was the dynamic Dr. James A. Duncan, pastor during the Civil War.

Richmond's Jews had been worshiping in the cramped quarters of Beth Shalome synagogue on East Nineteenth Street, and then in a fairly commodious temple on Mayo (later Ballard) Street. In 1841, German Jews organized Beth Ahabah, and Rabbi M. J. Michelbacher came from Philadelphia in 1846 to take charge. Two years later the temple's new home was erected on Eleventh Street between Marshall and Clay. Beth Shalome merged with Beth Ahabah, which then represented the Reform branch of Judaism, in 1898. Several other Jewish congregations would be established in future years, notably conservative Temple Beth-El. Founded in 1931, it attained the largest membership among Richmond synagogues.

The mid-1840s witnessed the founding of Second Presbyterian Church. First Presbyterian had been established earlier, as an outgrowth of the leadership of Dr. John Holt Rice. Second Presbyterian Church erected its house of worship on Fifth Street just north of Main in modified Gothic style. The Reverend Moses D. Hoge was chosen its first pastor; he would remain in that post for more than half a century, and become the most noted clergyman of his time in Richmond.

The Presbyterian Church, like the Methodist and Baptist churches, split into Northern and Southern branches during the antebellum years. The mounting controversy over slavery was the cause.

First Baptist Church at Broad and College streets found itself rent asunder in 1841, but not for the same reason. Its large membership was overwhelmingly black, and the blacks wanted a church of their own. The law forbade Negroes to assemble for worship, except under a white minister, but these Negroes preferred that arrangement to having a mixed congregation. So the whites withdrew and formed what we know today as First Baptist. They built a handsome church in modified Greek Revival style at Twelfth and Broad. The Reverend Jeremiah Bell Jeter was the pastor. He forbade the use of instrumental music as being ungodly.

The first white pastor of the solidly black Baptist church two blocks to the east—which changed its name to First African Baptist—was Dr. Robert Ryland, president of Richmond College. Dr. Ryland was far ahead of his time in the area of race relations, a fact that caused him to be viewed askance by many whites. He remained pastor of the church until 1866.

"In 1852 Richmond was terrified by a series of murders of white children by their Negro nurses," writes Blanche Sydnor White in her history of First Baptist. In that year a slave, Jane Williams, a member of First African Church, confessed to the slaying of her sleeping mistress, Mrs. Joseph P. Winston, and the latter's child. She was sentenced to hang.

The doomed woman was driven across the city in a wagon. Her pastor, Dr. Ryland, accompanied her on the entire journey, and when the wagon reached the gallows, he addressed the crowd of almost six thousand that had come to witness the execution. The clergyman implored his hearers to have mercy for a fellow creature, sinful though she might be. He then offered up "a fervent prayer for her immortal soul."

"Never before," said a Richmond newspaper, "did religious ceremonies fall upon more unwilling ears."

Jane Williams went to her death with complete composure. And the Reverend Robert Ryland, heedless of public opinion when he felt a principle to be involved, went back to his duties at First African Church and Richmond College.

# TWELVE

# On the Edge of the Precipice

RICHMOND had no public schools or public library, in the modern sense, before the Civil War, but there were many cultivated citizens in the town. Fine private libraries existed in abundance, and a remarkable number of well-stocked bookstores. Richmond also boasted private academies and seminaries of the highest quality. The city's newspapers were among the best, while the *Southern Literary Messenger* was unsurpassed in its field.

Internationally known lecturers on literary and scientific subjects came to Richmond and were greeted by large and appreciative audiences. Plays and concerts in the city were of excellent caliber and well-attended.

While Richmond did not have what we today would call a public library, hardly any other city did either. Furthermore, Richmond's substantial black population was largely illiterate, and hence had slight need for a library. White artisans were few in number. The rest of the population was served by the Richmond Library Association, whose books were available to those who paid annual dues, and the State Library, whose collection of fourteen thousand volumes was praised by Charles Dickens. In 1852, when the Athenaeum opened, the city tendered one of its rooms to the Library Association, plus $150 a year, on condition that its collection be made available to every citizen.

Establishment of the Virginia Historical and Philosophical Society at Richmond in 1831 evidenced the intellectual concerns of leading Richmonders and other Virginians. John Marshall was the organization's first president. During its early years the society interested itself in both the natural philosophy and the history of the state, and specimens of iron and copper were collected along with the writings of Captain John Smith, William Byrd and other eminent Virginians. But during succeeding decades, emphasis in the organization became so exclusively historical that the name was changed in 1870 to the Virginia Historical Society, and has so remained.

Richmonders were excited in 1842 by a visit from Charles Dickens and his wife. They arrived from Washington on March 17 "in the cars," as the saying was, and took lodgings at the Exchange Hotel. Dickens accepted an invitation to a *petit souper* in his honor at the Exchange, attended by about a hundred gentlemen. Thomas Ritchie presided, as he so often did on such occasions. His remarks were in good taste when he expressed regret that Virginia had no Irving or Bryant to present the eminent English novelist. But when he said that Virginia had produced statesmen "who never indulged in works of the imagination, in the charms of romance, or the mere beauties of the *belles-lettres*," he made future generations wince. The word "mere" could hardly have been more out of place. It was, unfortunately, in accord with the prevailing view in many parts of the country that a "mere man of letters" was wasting his time and talents.

Dickens apparently evidenced no resentment over Ritchie's remarks, and his response was warm and cordial. The dinner closed with a toast that harked back to *Oliver Twist:* "Charles Dickens, the 'artful dodger,'; he has dodged Philadelphia and Baltimore, but he could not dodge the Old Dominion."

Before Dickens left the city, Dr. Francis H. Deane, a prominent Richmond physician, requested him to write an epitaph for a child, Charles Thornton, who had died. The famous author complied, and mailed a beautiful and touching inscription to Dr. Deane from Cincinnati. It was placed on the stone over the little boy's grave in Cumberland County.[1]

But when Dickens got back to England, he wrote in blistering terms of what he had seen in Richmond. The institution of slavery was so revolting to him that he returned to it again and again, and he seemed incapable of finding anything good in a people who tolerated it. Dickens noted "gloom and dejection" and an "air of ruin and decay" wherever "slavery sits brooding." Both inside and outside Richmond he found "a darkness—not of skin but of mind—which meets the stranger's eye at every turn." In writing the book, *American Notes*, which contained these observations, he helped himself to considerable material from Theodore Weld's abolitionist opus *Slavery As It Is* without bothering to acknowledge his source.

William Makepeace Thackeray, the other internationally famous English novelist of the era, came to Richmond in 1853 for a series of lectures, and was most favorably impressed. In contrast to Dickens, he found the Negroes "well cared for, adequately fed and obviously happy." He added that he was "delighted with the comfortable, friendly, cheery little town—the most picturesque I have seen in America."

Thackeray was the guest of the Robert C. Stanards in their handsome home at the southeast corner of Sixth and Grace streets. This was the Stanard who had been Poe's boyhood friend, the son of Poe's "Helen."

Richmonders were entranced by Thackeray and remained so, in contrast to their resentment of Dickens, as is apparent from the following comment of John R. Thompson in the *Southern Literary Messenger*, of which he was then editor:

"When Mr. Dickens came here, he was feted, toasted and almost worshipped; his laughing at our manners, ungratefully sneering at our well-meant attentions, and abusing us when he had departed, proved a littleness of spirit and that Mr. Dickens was a low-bred man. . . . Mr. Thackeray in his visit has acted differently, for he is a gentleman."

A somewhat embarrassing episode occurred, however, involving Thackeray's secretary, Eyre Crowe, whose sketches of American scenes, made on the trip, are intriguing. Crowe decided to sketch a Richmond slave auction. The proceedings were under way when he arrived, and he sat down and began to draw. Suddenly he became aware that the bidding had stopped and that he was the center of attention. The whites gazed at him balefully, apparently taking him for an abolitionist. They refused to bid further as long as he was present. Crowe did not wish to seem to be running away, so he made a leisurely exit, remarking, "You may turn me away, but I can recollect all that I have seen." Thackeray wrote a friend, "Crowe has been very imprudent." Nothing further was heard of the incident.

The great English novelist made a splendid impression in Richmond, and was again welcomed in the city three years later when he delivered additional lectures.

Another British visitor to Richmond caused tremendous excitement and something closely approaching mob scenes. He was the nineteen-year-old Prince of Wales, later King Edward VII, traveling under the name of "Baron Renfrew." The youthful prince arrived on October 7, 1860, accompanied by a large retinue which included the Duke of Newcastle, the Earl of St. Germain, Lord Lyons and Lord Hinchingbrook. "Richmond, in the eager demonstration of its assembled thousands, eclipsed every other place the Prince had visited," wrote the correspondent of the New York *Herald*.

The foregoing statement appears justified, for from the time when "Baron Renfrew" arrived at the Exchange Hotel in the late afternoon of October 7 until he departed on the morning of October 9, his comings and goings were followed by huge crowds. The hotel was surrounded by expectant Richmonders when he arrived, and he had to fight his way to the door. After reaching that point, he found himself confronted by a throng that jammed the lobby and hallways, and he had great difficulty getting to his apartment. The prince was guest of honor at the hotel that evening at a private dinner of fabulous proportions. It lasted for four hours.

When word got out that the young heir to the British throne would attend the Sunday morning service next day at St. Paul's Episcopal Church, a crowd estimated at five thousand persons stampeded to the sanctuary and filled every seat, as well as nearby streets and adjacent portions of

Capitol Square. Persons inside the church clambered up on the pews to get a better view of the prince, to the shocked amazement of many Richmonders, and, no doubt, that of the royal visitor.

After the service, Governor John Letcher escorted His Royal Highness on a tour of the Capitol. Again the crowd surged around the prince and his party, so that progress was difficult. That afternoon the visitors were taken to Hollywood Cemetery and the tomb of President James Monroe, whose body had been brought to Richmond from New York in 1858, and then to St. John's Church. The prince left the next morning by special train from the R.F.& P. station at Eighth and Broad. He waved goodbye to the throng that turned out to have a last look at the man who would someday succeed his mother, Queen Victoria, and reign over what was then the mightiest empire on earth.

When H.R.H. Albert Edward's fellow citizen, William M. Thackeray, was lecturing in Richmond, he was interviewed by John Esten Cooke, then an aspiring young novelist who was supposedly practicing law. Actually, Cooke seems to have spent most of his time writing, and doing it with astonishing facility. During the year 1854, for example, he turned out three novels, one of which was *The Virginia Comedians*, perhaps his best. While the quality of Cooke's work was extraordinary, considering the speed with which he worked, it suffered from a lack of revision. Before the outbreak of the Civil War and while still in his twenties, Cooke was nationally known. He served through that conflict, and wrote well of some of its principal figures. His *Surry of Eagle's Nest* is one of the finest of the Civil War novels.

Cooke was the only novelist in Richmond of anything like national stature in the pre-war years. John R. Thompson was a talented minor poet. John Calvin Metcalf rated his translation of Nadaud's poem "Carcassonne" as "a classic," and his "Ashby" and "Music in Camp" as "notable war poems." Thompson was editor of the *Southern Literary Messenger* from 1847 to 1860, and in the words of James Southall Wilson, that was the period of the magazine's "greatest influence and reputation." The *Messenger* had been brought to the attention of the country by Edgar Allan Poe, and after Poe had resigned the editorship, James Silk Buckingham, a well-known English traveler and writer, said in the early 1840s that the magazine contained "as many well-written articles as any similar publication in England."

In the sphere of painting and sculpture, Richmond was not as much of a center as it had been several decades earlier, but there was still significant achievement. John B. Martin, James W. Ford and William J. Hubard did good work in the city at that period, as did Robert and Matthew Sully, who lived elsewhere but visited Richmond to pursue their profession of portrait painting. There was considerable interest in art, and for so small a center of population, a creditable amount of artistic activity.

In the late 1850s, Hubard abandoned painting and devoted himself to the reproduction of Houdon's Washington in bronze. When the war broke out, he used his foundry to cast cannon for the Confederacy. An explosion there injured him fatally.

Richmond did not produce a notable actor, dramatist or musician at mid-century. On the other hand, it maintained its reputation as a city where fine dramatic and musical productions were well-attended. The Marshall Theatre was the scene of most of these, but Odd-Fellows Hall, erected in 1842, was a serious rival. Then in 1853, Robert A. Mayo bought the abandoned First Presbyterian Church on the north side of Franklin between Thirteenth and Fourteenth, and remodeled it to seat 1,500 persons. It was called Metropolitan Hall, and a great variety of events, mainly musical, were held there.

A long line of internationally known actors and actresses trod the boards in Richmond during the century's middle years. Junius Brutus Booth, who had made his American debut in the city in 1821, returned many times, as did his son, Edwin, a favorite with Richmond audiences. Edwin's brother, John Wilkes Booth, who would assassinate Abraham Lincoln, also appeared in Richmond productions. Other celebrated actors and actresses who were seen in Virginia's capital were Joseph Jefferson, the elder John Drew, Edwin Forrest, James W. Wallack, Jr., Fanny Morant and Agnes Robertson.

One night in 1850, Junius Brutus Booth was unfortunately quite drunk, at the very time when he was supposed to be making a much-advertised appearance in *Richard III*. The Marshall Theatre was packed and the curtain was about to rise, when the announcement was made that Mr. Booth had "mysteriously disappeared" and there would be no play. The management stated subsequently that Booth would not be allowed to appear there again during the season. However, seventy-six prominent citizens petitioned that the order be rescinded. Their request was granted, and $500 was deposited by the management with Gustavus A. Myers as a guarantee that Booth would not again fail to show. Some years later, when he almost fell during a play, it was quickly made known from the stage that a dray had run over his foot earlier that day, lest the audience "attribute it to some other cause."[2]

Blackface minstrels had become popular during the era, thanks largely to Thomas D. Rice and his "Jim Crow" act. He first presented the act in Louisville, and gave it in Richmond in 1840 and many times thereafter. The act included the "Jim Crow Song," from which stems the "Jim Crow" phrase of today.

Among the internationally distinguished musicians who appeared in Richmond during the middle years of the century were Camillo Sivori, Therese Parodi, Sigismond Thalberg, Ole Bull and his wife, Amelia Patti. With the last-named pair was nine-year-old Adelina Patti, whose blood relationship to Amelia, if any, was unknown. At all events, the child, who would later become the world-renowned opera star, sang "Comin' Through the Rye" and operatic selections, to great acclaim. Ole Bull returned to the city several times, once with the youthful Adelina.

The greatest musical sensation of the era in Richmond was the concert given in 1850 at the Marshall Theatre by Jenny Lind, "the Swedish Nightingale." P. T. Barnum was her impresario, with the result that advance publicity was unprecedented. It included a rumor, possibly planted by Barnum himself, that Jenny had contributed $1,000 to the abolitionists. This, of course, caused a frightful uproar and demands that she be forbidden to appear. The rumor was quashed, but interest had been centered on Miss Lind to such a degree that there was a complete sellout, with some tickets going as high as $105 and none less than $8, for a total of more than $12,000.

The concert was received with thunderous applause. The enraptured critic from the *Whig* compared the singer's voice to "a stream of pearls flowing into a golden basin," and added that "God has vouchsafed this voice to teach us the melody eternal in heaven." However, even Barnum could not bring himself to say that Jenny was pretty. He settled for "genial, whole-souled, generous and merry."

Music and the drama were in their heyday in Richmond during these years, but horse racing, so important a diversion in earlier times, had declined sadly. Mordecai, writing in 1856, declared that "the sports of the turf have so degenerated of late years that few ladies of the present generation ever saw a race." He added that "the field is now chiefly in possession of a class, termed in softened phrase, 'sporting characters,' in the same way that Negro-traders are called 'speculators.' Exclusive of the racing, the field presents a scene of the lowest gambling and dissipation." But the sprightly chronicler of *Richmond in By-Gone Days* was not entirely pessimistic. He thought he saw "a prospect of the sport being more respectably patronized and conducted."

Education for young Richmonders was a constant concern during these years. Conventions designed to bring about a statewide system of public schools were held at Richmond in 1841, 1845, 1856 and 1857. The Richmond *Enquirer* and *Whig* were ardent advocates of this objective. James Mercer Garnett of Essex County presided over the first of the conventions, Governor James McDowell of Rockbridge County over the second and Governor Henry A. Wise over the last two. Yet it was impossible to persuade the General Assembly to provide the necessary statewide system of taxation. A majority of Richmond's leaders shared the aversion of most eastern Virginians to a system of general taxes for the education of all.

An institution called the Lancasterian School had been in operation in Richmond since 1816, based on a system of such schools in England. Most of its pupils were poor, but a few were not. There was only one trained teacher, under this system, and the older pupils taught the younger ones. The newly built Richmond school was situated just north of Marshall and west of Fifteenth Street. The city donated the site and appropriated to the school $600 annually. The existing city-operated free schools for indigents were done away with and their functions merged into the Lancasterian School. Unfortunately, a new jail was built immediately opposite, which did not enhance the neighborhood's desirability for children. Furthermore, this was "Butchertown," where the proletarian "Butcher Cats" carried on their perennial warfare with brickbats and rocks against the better-circumstanced "Hill Cats" on the heights to the west.

After the adoption of the new state constitution in 1851, emphasizing the importance of public education, Richmond's City Council voted to establish a free primary school in each of the three wards. This was done and the schools were operated with a $1,000 appropriation from the Council and $200 from the state's Literary Fund. All the pupils appear to have been from poor families. The system was coordinated with the Lancasterian School, which became strictly a high school, supplementing the primary schools in the wards. Such was Richmond's "public school system" before the Civil War. By contrast, Norfolk, Portsmouth and Fredericksburg had fully operative systems in the late 1850s, as did six counties in Tidewater and four beyond the Alleghenies, plus the city of Wheeling.

The Richmond Academy had been operating for about a decade and a half in 1850. Founded in 1803, with great hopes and some thousands of dollars in the till, it made the mistake of choosing the wrong site on a hill in Henrico County a quarter of a mile beyond the city almshouse. The result, as Margaret Meagher writes in her valuable *History of Education in Richmond*, was that "from 1803 until 1835, the Academy existed as a mouldering brick basement." Revived in the latter year, after many vicissitudes, and with the distinguished Dr. Socrates Maupin as headmaster, the institution finally got off the ground at a new site, Tenth and Marshall streets. It functioned there under such eminent headmasters as William Burke and Claudius Crozet. Then in 1850 the school became inoperative, and the city bought the building. The structure was rechristened the Athenaeum, where, as previously noted, the public was given access to the book collection of the Richmond Library Association. It also was the scene of important public lectures. In 1853, furthermore, the Council set forth plans for transforming the Athenaeum into a central high school or academy, to be the focus of an authentic system of public education. But this was not to be. The property became too valuable, and in what Mordecai terms "a paroxysm of municipal frugality" the Council sold it in 1858 for $25,000. The building was demolished and dwellings were erected on the site.

Private schools continued to flourish in Richmond. Those for boys were sometimes stern in their disciplinary mandates. The antebellum experience of Dr. William H. Taylor of the Medical College of Virginia faculty is perhaps not altogether typical, for he may have been more than ordinarily obstreperous in his youth. Yet the bizarre chastisements visited upon him indicate that the "rod" was regarded as an indispensable adjunct to learning. Dr. Taylor wrote:

"I myself have had experience of switches, leather straps, detached and fastened wooden handles, slate frames, rulers, pieces of chalk (not the modern crayons but substantial chunks . . . ), dictionaries . . . obscure and mysterious articles belonging to female apparel, hands, fists, and sometimes the knees and feet of my instructors."

One of the best of the private schools for boys was William Burke's. Whether disciplinary measures such as the foregoing were invoked there is not known. Burke's school was opened in 1821 and continued until 1852. Edgar Allan Poe was only one of the sons of prominent Richmonders who were enrolled. Burke, born in Ireland, was a man of genuine learning and great ability as a schoolmaster.

Another boys' school of standing was that of L. S. Squire, a New Englander. Opened in 1845, it operated at various locations until 1898, and continuously under Headmaster Squire.

Among schools for girls, that of Miss Jessie Gordon, afterward Mrs. W. O. English, was exceptional. It opened in 1855 and continued into the eighties.

Another notable school for girls was that of Mrs. Anna Maria Mead, which operated under her direction from 1831 to 1853, first at Sixth and Marshall streets and then at 3 East Grace Street. When Mrs. Mead retired, one of her teachers, Hubert P. Lefebvre, took charge. The same building on East Grace was occupied later by the Richmond Female Seminary, also known as "Powell's School" after its founder John H. Powell, and not to be confused with the earlier school of D. Lee Powell.

Lee Powell's Southern Female Institute, founded in 1850, attained particular distinction. It provided a curriculum for women that was hardly distinguishable from that provided for men. Like several other excellent schools, it began in Linden Row—the two westernmost houses—but moved to other addresses. An early advertisement declared that the Institute sought "to elevate the standard of female education," and that it was "modeled after the University of Virginia and the Virginia Military Institute."

The Southern Female Institute, which operated until 1874, is not to be confused with the Richmond Female Institute, founded in 1854, to which reference was made in the preceding chapter. From the latter institution, many years later, grew today's Westhampton College of the University of Richmond.

The girls' school operated by the Pegram ladies at 106 and 108 Linden

Row from about 1855 to 1866 should be noted. Mrs. James W. Pegram, the widow of General Pegram, and her daughter, Mary, who later became the second wife of General Joseph R. Anderson of the Tredegar, were in charge. Miss Mary Pegram had an especially striking and stimulating personality, and these qualities were reflected in the fine standing of the school.

On another level of education, the Medical Department of Hampden-Sydney College opened at Richmond in 1838 in the Union Hotel, at Nineteenth and Main. The doctors of the city—as they have often been since—were divided into several rival groups. A bitter controversy broke out between these medical factions over the filling of a newly created chair in the Medical Department. The Hampden-Sydney trustees became involved, and there was a dreadful uproar. The trustees finally became so disgusted that they severed all relations with their medical wing. The General Assembly, at its session of 1854, accordingly chartered the orphan department as the Medical College of Virginia, supported by the state.

For its first session, the Medical College had on its faculty the internationally known Dr. Charles E. Brown-Séquard. The inimitable Dr. William H. Taylor was one of his pupils, and he recounts an experiment of the learned man, as follows:

"In studying the phenomena of digestion, he let down into his stomach pieces of food tied to the end of strings, and therewith fished up material for subjection to the processes of science. . . . At length the constant titillation of the organ turned him into a sort of cow, his food as fast as he got it down insisted on coming back into his mouth to be chewed over and over again. A disorder of this kind . . . would make any other man hang himself."

The Hampden-Sydney Medical Department had moved from the Union Hotel in 1845, and into the newly erected Egyptian Building. This structure was designed by Thomas S. Stewart of Philadelphia, the architect of St. Paul's Episcopal Church, and is said to be the best example of the Egyptian architectural style in this country. Why Stewart chose this style is not clear. Almost all the activities of the college were centered in this one building until the 1890s.

An institution founded at Richmond in 1846, the Richmond Male Orphan Asylum, now the Richmond Home for Boys, is understood to be the oldest continuously operated boys' home in the United States.

In the political realm, demands for more representation in the state legislature were mounting from the western regions of the Commonwealth. The Shenandoah Valley and the areas beyond also wanted white manhood suffrage and popular election of the governor and other officials. The convention of 1829-30 had refused to provide the desired relief.

Responding to these pressures, Virginia's political leadership consented to a referendum on the question whether a convention should be called.

The vote was held, and the advocates won by a majority of two and a half to one. Richmond voted in favor by five to one.

The Constitutional Convention of 1850–51 met on October 14, 1850, at the Capitol, but had to move in January to the Universalist Church on Mayo Street when the General Assembly came to town. The convention returned to the Capitol when the legislature adjourned. Its presiding officer was John Y. Mason of Southampton County, who had served in the convention of 1829–30 and was a former Secretary of the Navy and U. S. Attorney General.

Henry A. Wise of Accomack, who would soon be elected governor, was easily the conclave's principal orator. He spoke on every subject, and on the much-debated problem involving the basis for representation in the General Assembly he held the floor continuously for five days. The galleries were crowded throughout, despite the fact that Junius Brutus Booth was playing Hamlet in Richmond at the time.

There were distinguished men among the convention delegates, but the over-all average was far below that of Virginia's earlier constitutional conventions—evidence that the level of statesmanship in the Old Dominion was declining. As with most such conclaves, the majority of the members were lawyers, 97 out of 135. This proliferation of legal talent was likened by a contemporary writer to "the plagues of the Egyptians." Historian Little, a physician, attended as an observer and was similarly unenthusiastic over the number of lawyer-delegates. He wrote that when members of that profession "are collected in large numbers, they never fail to do mischief."

The Richmond delegation to the "Reform Convention," as it was called, included John A. Meredith, Robert C. Stanard and James Lyons, all well-known lawyers. Lyons was often termed the handsomest and most elegant gentleman of his day, and, in the words of Judge George L. Christian, was "a man of the finest presence that I ever saw." Lyons urged the popular election of governors, as demanded by the west, but said he would vote to allow the west to secede from Virginia and form another state, rather than support change in the basis on which it was represented—or underrepresented—in the General Assembly. Delegates from the West were talking openly of disunion.

The final breakaway of West Virginia was postponed for more than a decade as a result of the concessions made at the convention. The west was allotted 83 of the 152 seats in the House, but got only 20 of the 50 seats in the Senate.

Every white male twenty-one years of age was given the right to vote, a victory for the trans-Allegheny region, as was the newly instituted popular election of the governor and other state officials.

Richmond found its electorate increased by 45 per cent, and was allotted two additional seats in the General Assembly. The city voted overwhelmingly to ratify the new constitution, as did the state as a whole.

Richmond's city charter was amended in 1851 to provide—in accordance with the prevailing trend—for the popular election of the mayor, recorder, high constable, collector and other municipal officers. These had previously been chosen by the Council and Board of Aldermen. This general form of government would be retained by the city for almost a century. Richmond was divided into five wards instead of three, and it acquired its first fire engine. General William Lambert, who had been the mayor since 1840, was again chosen, by vote of the people. He served until shortly before his death in 1853, and was succeeded by Joseph Mayo. The latter occupied the office until just after the Civil War.

Politically, Richmond was a Whig stronghold. When Henry A. Wise, a Democrat, ran successfully for governor in 1854, he lost the city overwhelmingly. His son, John S. Wise, wrote long afterward that Richmond "was the stronghold of Know-Nothingism in Virginia," and that since his father was running on an anti-Know-Nothing platform he got less than 25 per cent of the Richmond vote. Virginia's capital, the younger Wise wrote, "was the abode of that class who proclaimed that they were Whigs, and that 'Whigs knew each other by the instincts of gentlemen.'" It seems probable that highly conservative Richmond was opposed to Wise because of his championship of white manhood suffrage and public schools rather than because of any appreciable support in the city for the Know-Nothings, who made a fetish of disliking foreigners and Roman Catholics.

Richmond, John S. Wise also wrote, "was admittedly the center of a society unsurpassed in all America for wealth, refinement and culture." He added that "nearly every distinguished foreigner felt that his view of America was incomplete unless he spent some time in the capital of the Mother of States and Statesmen. Soldiers, authors, sculptors, artists, actors and statesmen sought Richmond then as surely as today [in the late nineties] they visit New York and Boston."

Hardly any visitors to Richmond stopped at a hotel, Wise declared, because the private establishments were so large and their openhanded hospitality was so great.

Many prominent persons came to the city on February 22, 1850, to take part in or to witness the laying of the cornerstone for Thomas Crawford's equestrian statue of George Washington in Capitol Square. Plans for the memorial had been lagging, when the Virginia Historical and Philosophical Society sent a committee before the General Assembly to urge that arrangements be made for the cornerstone-laying. This was accordingly set for Washington's birthday, 1850. The exercises were preceded by a parade a mile and a half long. President Zachary Taylor, Vice-President Millard Fillmore, ex-President John Tyler and several members of Taylor's Cabinet were at the head of the procession, with Governor John B. Floyd as chief marshal. Virginia-born President Taylor addressed the ten thousand persons who crowded the square or viewed the proceedings from nearby windows and housetops.

Everybody seemed happy except young John Moncure Daniel, the ever caustic editor of the Richmond *Examiner*, who raspingly noted the "essential stupidity" of the entire proceeding. The conveyance in which the principal dignitaries rode in the parade was "a vulgar open carriage, fit only for a snob or parvenue," the *Examiner* said. The Masons, who laid the cornerstone, "went through their mummeries—winding up the same with a most doleful and lonesome psalm tune . . . several brass bands performed with unexampled fury in alarming propinquity to one another," and "the Sons of Temperance, remarkable for their red noses and faces, made their appearance . . . in great force."

More than seven years passed before the completed statue arrived by ship from Munich, Germany. With it came the tragic news that Thomas Crawford, its forty-seven-year-old sculptor, had died of a malignant brain tumor. The statue was hauled from lower Main Street with ropes pulled by thousands of Richmonders to its pedestal in Capitol Square. The formal unveiling came on February 22, 1858. Again there was a huge parade with many dignitaries in line, including U. S. Senator R. M. T. Hunter, the orator of the occasion; Governor Wise, General Winfield Scott, the Virginia Military Institute cadets and others. An observer commented on the far from impressive appearance of a Major Thomas J. Jackson, who accompanied the cadets. "His old blue forage-cap sat on the back of his head, and he stood like a horse 'sprung' at the knees." His commands "were given in a piping, whining tone." There is little here to suggest the immortal "Stonewall," then an obscure member of the VMI faculty.

Crawford completed only two of the six figures surrounding the Washington statue, those of Jefferson and Henry. The others were executed by Randolph Rogers.

Opinions have differed down the years as to the merits of Crawford's Washington. There is apparent unanimity concerning the superlative quality of Houdon's Washington inside the Capitol, but while some connoisseurs praise Crawford's work in the highest terms, others do not. Lorado Taft wrote scathingly in his *History of American Sculpture* that Crawford's equestrian Washington "is so bad . . . that the approaching traveler can scarcely trust his eyes." One of those who disagrees strongly is F. D. Cossitt, the knowledgeable and objective art critic for the Richmond *Times-Dispatch*. He terms the work "a marvel of dignity and Gallic grace."

In addition to unveiling the Washington monument, those in charge of Capitol Square made two other important changes there, pursuant to the designs of John Notman of Philadelphia. One was the scrapping of the ultra-formal landscaping and the substitution of native trees for the European varieties placed in accordance with the plan of the Frenchman

Godefroy. A visitor termed the Godefroy square "nice and prim, as if under the special guardianship of some maiden lady of antique age, cleanly habits and vinegar countenance."

The other notable change was the erection in 1846 of the General Court Building in the southeastern corner of the square, on the site of the defunct museum. Sessions were held there of the General Court, the Supreme Court of Appeals and the circuit courts of Richmond and Henrico. The records of these tribunals were stored in the building.

A significant bit of construction nearby was that of the post office and customhouse on Main Street. Completed in 1859, it was the core of Richmond's main post office building for more than a century. Prior to 1859, the post office had been housed in various structures, including the museum building and the Exchange Hotel. The customhouse had been for many years in a warehouse on Fifteenth Street near Cary. Still another important addition in the 1850s was the Ballard House, built by the owner of the Exchange Hotel, John P. Ballard, and connected with the Exchange by a bridge over Franklin Street at the second-floor level.

The classical style of architecture, exemplified first in Thomas Jefferson's Capitol, was seen in Richmond residences in the early nineteenth century. It was not until 1834, however, that what Miss Mary Wingfield Scott terms "the first real mansion of the Greek period" was erected. This was the Abraham Warwick house at 503 East Grace Street, which stood until 1937. One block to the east was the Robert Stanard house—later the Westmoreland Club—built in 1839 and likewise demolished in 1937. It became impossible to maintain these fine residences in the center of Richmond's most important retail district.

Greek Revival houses standing in 1976 include the David M. Branch house at 1 West Main Street (1841), for many years the home of the novelist Ellen Glasgow; the Norman Stewart house, 707 East Franklin, (1844), the occasional wartime residence of General Robert E. Lee; the William Barret house, 15 South Fifth Street (1844); the William F. Taylor house, 110 West Franklin Street (1844), in modern times the Mayo Memorial Church House; and the eight Linden Row houses, 100–118 East Franklin Street (1847 and 1853). Several attractive Greek Revival houses on Church Hill have been restored by the Historic Richmond Foundation, of which more later.

Taste in architecture underwent a startling change during the 1850s. The best example would seem to be the Bolling Haxall house, 221 East Franklin, for many recent years the home of the Woman's Club. Other examples are Morson Row, three houses at 219–223 Governor Street, and the William H. Grant house, 1008 East Clay Street, long the home of Sheltering Arms Hospital. These structures all exhibit many curves, especially over the windows, whereas the Greek Revival style emphasizes the straight line.

Handsome ironwork enhanced the appearance of the city's houses in the 1840s, 1850s and 1870s. Much of it was made in Richmond. Fences in front of the Bolling Haxall house, referred to above, and St. Paul's Episcopal Church are excellent examples. Numerous iron front verandahs and balconies might also be mentioned. The iron fronts on Main Street business houses came after the Civil War.

Those who rightly deplore the tearing down of old buildings in our own day may be wryly comforted when they remember that Mordecai expressed himself similarly in the second edition of his book on Richmond, published in 1860. Referring to a house which had been demolished, he said that most of the old buildings noted by him in his first edition (1856) were gone by 1859.

The same chronicler was pleased to point out, however, that many handsome churches had been built in Richmond during his lifetime. He mentioned that whereas in his youth the city had only one church, St. John's, by 1860 it had "nearly forty."

The fact that Richmond had "never seen a mob" was attributed in 1851 by Dr. John P. Little, the historian, to the influence of the churches.

Seeking more open space for the citizenry, the municipality acquired land in 1851 for three parks. Names were not given them until 1859, but the property was bought at the earlier date for what became Jefferson Square (now Libby Hill), Madison Square (Gamble's Hill) and Monroe Square (originally Western Square). Conway Robinson, one of the foremost men of the era, and a member of the City Council, is believed to have been largely responsible.

Western Square in 1851 was a field of blackberry bushes and scrub pines. The first annual fair of the Virginia Agricultural Society was held there in 1854, and because of these annual expositions, the square was known for many years as the Fair Grounds. As if to compensate for the badly deteriorating racing events on the tracks below Richmond, a circular racecourse was laid off on the grounds, embracing part of today's Franklin Street and a bit of territory to the north of it.

In an effort to provide better communication with the area to the west of Richmond, the General Assembly incorporated the Westham Plank Road. Shares of stock at $25 each were sold in the amount of $20,000, for the construction of a plank road along the Westham or River Road to the intersection with Three Chopt Road. It was stipulated that the new thoroughfare must be at least fifteen feet wide, "and not less than eight feet thereof was to be covered with plank." Tolls could be levied when half of the road was completed.

A remarkable phenomenon of the period was the large number of Germans who came to settle in Richmond. "During several years immediately preceding the Civil War the German element in the state capital accounted for almost 25 per cent of the total white population," Klaus

Wust writes in *The Virginia Germans*. Among them were "artisans and mechanics, artists and engineers, adventurers and traders." Burghart Hassel founded the German-language Richmond *Anzeiger* in 1853; it soon became a daily and lasted for over sixty years. Albert Stein designed Richmond's first water works. A. W. Nolting and Emil O. Nolting were important to the city's overseas tobacco trade. William Thalhimer opened a shop in 1842 that grew into the great department store of today. Louis Rueger operated the Lafayette Saloon at Ninth and Bank streets, on the site, in more modern times, of Rueger's Hotel. William Flegenheimer and Oswald Heinrich were refugees from political upheavals in Germany. Flegenheimer, an expert penman, inscribed the Ordinance of Secession in 1861. Heinrich became a teacher and architect.

The Germans soon established a couple of breweries in Richmond. The product thereof was consumed in various German-operated taverns, where the patrons relaxed from the cares of the day with a Seidel and songs from the Bavarian Alps or the banks of the Rhine. Out of these lager-inspired renditions grew the Gesang-Verein Virginia, founded in 1852, the city's oldest musical organization. It was going strong nearly a century and a quarter later, with a rousing annual event called the *Oktoberfest*.

A tragic happening of the year 1854 was the loss in the sinking of the steamship *Arctic* in the North Atlantic of Dr. Carter Page Johnson. This almost forgotten thirty-two-year-old Richmond surgeon, the son of Chapman Johnson, had made a reputation far beyond that of many older men in the medical profession. An M.A. of the University of Virginia at eighteen and an M.D. of the medical school in Richmond, then a part of Hampden-Sydney College, at twenty, Johnson was apparently destined for national fame. After a surgical career of less than six years, he made so large an impact that Henry Smith in his *System of Operative Surgery*, containing the most significant articles published by American surgeons, included six by Johnson. This was more than for any Virginia surgeon except Dr. Peter Mettauer, a much older man. Just before young Johnson embarked for Europe, where he visited various medical centers, he was elected president of the Medical Society of Virginia. It was upon his return a few months later on the *Arctic* that this Richmonder of great achievement and even greater promise was drowned in the worst sea disaster of the nineteenth century.[3]

An extraordinary event of these years was the finding of a 23¾ carat diamond at the southwest corner of today's Ninth and Perry streets, South Richmond. The gem was turned up in 1854 by a workman who was leveling a hill. Benjamin Moore, the finder, sold it for a reported $1,500 to a Captain Dewey. After being cut, the diamond was bought for $6,000 by John Morrissey, who became heavyweight boxing champion of the world a few years later.[4]

One of the most tremendous snowstorms in Virginia history occurred January 22–23, 1857. It blanketed Richmond and nearby areas under two to three feet of snow, with drifts of six to eight feet. Dr. Joseph E. Cox, a prominent Chesterfield County physician, tried to reach a patient in this blizzard, with temperatures reported at 18 degrees below zero. With him in his buggy was his son-in-law, Robert C. Traylor. The singletree of the buggy broke, and the two men set out on foot. They never arrived. Dr. Cox was found next day frozen to death and Traylor died soon afterward. The storm has been known ever since as "Cox's Snow."

Race relations during the fifties had their surprising aspects. There was the amazing funeral in 1854 of sixty-three-year-old Joseph Abrams, a black clergyman, whose obsequies were said by the *Dispatch* of June 7, 1854, to have been the largest held in Richmond down to that time. Eight thousand people were estimated by the paper to have crowded into and around First African Baptist Church during the ceremonies, and more than fifty carriages followed the hearse to the grave. Assuming that the mourners were nearly all black, we have here almost two thirds of the entire black population of the city. These figures as to eight thousand mourners and over fifty carriages were repeated in the *American Baptist Memorial* for 1854 and 1855.

What is the explanation for this almost incredible demonstration of grief and devotion? No one has been able to provide an even remotely adequate answer. Abrams could not serve as pastor or preach in any church after 1831, under legislation passed following the Nat Turner insurrection. Hence his activities were confined to conducting funerals, preaching in homes and offering prayers in churches, some of which were so long as to be virtual sermons. He was a preacher of exceptional power and was for many years a deacon of First African Church. None of which explains the enormous crowd at his funeral. No notice of his death on June 4 can be found in any Richmond newspaper until June 6, when readers of the *Dispatch* learned that he had died and that the funeral would be at 11 A.M. on that day. His friends must have heard by grapevine of his passing. And how did blacks, who were mainly slaves, manage to get more than fifty carriages? It is all a great mystery.

Tension was mounting in Richmond and elsewhere in the South, over the slavery issue. *Uncle Tom's Cabin* put the entire region on the defensive, and there was anxiety over possible slave insurrections. Yet a traveler reported that "in Richmond almost every slave-child is learning to read," despite the fact that such teaching was against the law. Free Negroes had many businesses of their own. By 1860 they owned and operated seven grocery stores, three confectioneries, two fruit shops, fifteen barbershops and an excellent livery stable. One free Negro family in four owned property.[5]

A free Negro who had his own blacksmith shop was Gilbert Hunt, hero of the 1811 theater fire. As a slave, Hunt also had been courageous in fighting a fire at the penitentiary and he had rendered good service in the War of 1812. There was talk in those years of obtaining his emancipation, but nothing came of it. He himself finally bought his freedom with $800 earned as a blacksmith. In 1859, when he was an old man and still operating his blacksmith shop, a movement was launched to show the community's appreciation of his brave and unselfish contributions. The Richmond *Whig* and a young man named Philip Barrett joined forces to that end. Barrett interviewed the elderly Negro and wrote a pamphlet entitled "Gilbert Hunt, the City Blacksmith." The *Whig* carried laudatory editorials, and urged Richmonders to buy the pamphlet. Many did, and Gilbert Hunt was finally given tangible evidence of Richmond's gratitude. More recently, a tablet in Hunt's memory was placed on the portico of Monumental Church, site of the theater fire.

Negro slaves were escaping to the North from Richmond and other parts of Virginia during these years, although nothing like so many as was claimed by the abolitionists. One such escapee was Henry Brown of Richmond, who squeezed himself into a box 3 feet 1 inch long, 2 feet wide and 2 feet 6 inches deep. Anti-slavery friends shipped him and the box to Philadelphia. Although it bore the words "This Side Up With Care," Brown was upside down during a part of the journey. Yet he did not appear fatigued when he emerged several days later in Philadelphia from his horribly cramped quarters, according to the Boston *Traveler*. He was known thereafter as "Box" Brown.

Intersectional feeling was rising in the 1850s, and most of the Protestant ministers of Richmond signed an appeal for calm and a more dispassionate view of the differences between North and South. "They received little encouragement from the excited press of Richmond," says Wirt Armistead Cate.

The City Council adopted a comprehensive "Ordinance Concerning Negroes" in 1859, listing numerous restrictions, many of which were already set forth in earlier ordinances. This enactment, which was similar to those adopted in other Southern cities, provided that "no Negro shall walk or be in the Capitol Square or in the grounds adjacent to the City Spring, City Hall or Athenaeum," except for the purpose of attending a white person, or serving an owner or employer. Slaves were forbidden to ride in a licensed hack or carriage without the written consent of their owners. It was provided, further, that "No Negro shall smoke tobacco . . . on any public street or public place." Negroes were not only forbidden to "speak aloud any blasphemous or indecent word"; they were also not permitted to "make any loud or offensive noise by conversation or otherwise in any streets or other public place." Not more than five Negroes could stand "at the corner of a street or public alley." The penalty for violating the foregoing prohibitions was, in most cases, thirty-nine lashes. If a white whipped a black unlawfully, he was subject to a fine of up to $20.

One might suppose that with such exceptionally stringent regulations covering their every movement, the Negroes of Richmond would be unhappy, if not surly and resentful. But various visitors testified to the contrary. One of these was the Reverend Nehemiah Adams, a New England abolitionist, who was astonished to find that "if the colored people of Savannah, Columbia and Richmond are not happy people, I have never seen any."

Intersectional animosities were drastically increased in 1859 when John Brown made his raid on Harpers Ferry, in the hope of setting off a slave insurrection. Governor Wise ordered militia units from Richmond to the scene. When they arrived, they found that a unit of U. S. Marines, commanded by Colonel Robert E. Lee, had captured Brown and his small band, barricaded in the engine house. The Richmond militiamen returned to their home base.

Some weeks later, after Brown had been tried and condemned to death, Governor Wise received a telegram saying that five hundred armed men were marching from Wheeling to free Brown and his fellow prisoners. Richmond militia units were again ordered to Harpers Ferry, but they found on their arrival that it was a false alarm.

With the Richmond Grays on this expedition went John Wilkes Booth. He had been appearing off and on for several years at the Marshall Theatre in Richmond, although overshadowed by his more talented brother, Edwin. John Wilkes was not a member of the Grays, but he had gone on several outings with that organization. When it was ordered to Harpers Ferry, Booth somehow managed to enlist and go along. Thus the erratic actor, who was emotionally involved as a strong partisan of the South, witnessed the hanging of Brown. Philip Whitlock of the Grays was standing near Booth when the trap was sprung. The future assassin of Abraham Lincoln turned white, said Whitlock, and called for "a good stiff drink of whiskey."

Whitlock, who was within fifty feet of Brown when he was hanged, flatly denied the report circulated in the North that Brown, on his way to the scaffold, kissed a Negro baby. Not a single Negro was in sight, said Whitlock. Similar testimony was given by Dr. William P. Palmer, who was present as a member of the newly organized Richmond Howitzers. Palmer said he witnessed "the proceedings from the time the culprit left the door of the jail . . . until he swung from the gibbet," and that Brown did not kiss any Negro woman or baby. An artist's conception of the condemned man emerging from the jail and embracing a Negro infant in its mother's arms was widely circulated.

President Lincoln and the great majority of Northern newspapers expressed no sympathy for Brown and his ill-starred expedition. Yet a small group of articulate Northern extremists praised him extravagantly as a martyr. In fact, a group of well-known New Englanders, terming themselves the Secret Six, had been furnishing Brown with money and arms.

All this caused Richmonders and other Southerners to become increasingly bitter. Among those who reacted in this fashion were the Southern-born medical students in Northern institutions. When John Brown's coffin was carried through the streets of Philadelphia, where most of these students were in medical school, fights broke out with the "rough elements of the city." Many students were injured and some were jailed. They decided to leave for the South. Those at Jefferson Medical College, where young Dr. Hunter McGuire was a teacher, numbered 119, and there were 15 others in the University of Pennsylvania Medical School. Dr. McGuire telegraphed the Medical College of Virginia, asking on what terms these men would be admitted to that institution. The reply came at once that they would be matriculated free of charge and given full credit for work done in the North.

A train bearing them and other Southern students to congenial territory below Mason and Dixon's Line reached Richmond in December 1859. They were met at the station by a brass band and an enthusiastic crowd and marched to Capitol Square, where Governor Wise addressed them. They then were guests at a banquet at the Columbian Hotel, attended by some six hundred persons. The Medical College admitted 140 of the students, approximately trebling its enrollment. Among the enrollees were a few who came from Northern medical schools other than those in Philadelphia. Some of the students proceeded on to various cities in the Deep South.

Events were moving rapidly toward the sundering conflict of the sixties. Governor Wise, addressing the General Assembly, proclaimed: "We must take up arms! The issue is too essential to be compromised."

The majority of Richmonders and other Virginians were not ready to follow Wise's advice. They were being swept inexorably on, but they were anxious to avoid armed hostilities by all honorable means. Yet storm clouds were black on the horizon and Richmond, only slightly more than a hundred miles south of Washington, was certain to be in the eye of the oncoming hurricane.

# THIRTEEN

# Inside the Confederate Citadel

RICHMOND in 1860 was overwhelmingly opposed to secession, as was Virginia, but strident voices were being heard in the capital urging the breakup of the Union.

The *Southern Literary Messenger*, under John R. Thompson, had sought with considerable consistency to allay hostility between the sections, but when George W. Bagby took that journal's editorial helm, its tone underwent a drastic reversal. Bagby was primarily a humorist and gentle satirist whose essays on life in the Old South are delightfully nostalgic. But the John Brown raid and other manifestations of Northern antagonism turned him into a bellicose secessionist. He began advocating withdrawal from the Union months before the bombardment of Fort Sumter.

Defense of slavery, Bagby argued in the *Messenger*, was defense of "republican institutions." Thus he echoed one of the more preposterous contentions advanced three decades before in the Virginia Convention of 1829–30. Bagby also delivered judgments concerning Northern civilization that were sharply at variance with those he expressed after the war, when he made a tour of the region. In the febrile atmosphere of 1860–61, he wrote that "not a breeze blows from the Northern hills but bears upon its wings taints of crime and vice, to reek and stink, and stink and reek upon our Southern plains."

The people of Richmond, despite such inflammatory exhortations, sought to calm intersectional feeling. Richmonders were mainly Whigs, and hence Unionists. Their situation was a difficult one, for Richmond newspapers, especially John M. Daniel's *Examiner*, were inflaming the public mind. And there were such appeals to irrationality as the advertisement in a local paper wherein a citizen offered to be one of a hundred "gentlemen" to give $100 for U. S. Secretary of State Seward's head, and $25 each for the heads of a long list of Yankee "traitors," including

Horace Greeley, Charles Sumner, Wendell Phillips and Henry Ward
Beecher.

John Letcher, a strong Unionist, had been elected governor just before
the John Brown raid. In his inaugural address in 1860, Letcher proposed
that the Virginia legislature invite the other states to a national convention for a discussion of the best means of calming the mounting animosity
between the sections. His suggestion was ignored. When Abraham Lincoln was elected President later in the year, Letcher and others were still
striving to prevent the breakup of the Union. But in December the fire-
eating South Carolina convention voted unanimously to secede, and by
February 1, 1861, six other "cotton states" had taken similar action. The
provisional government of the Confederate States of America was formed,
with the capital at Montgomery, Alabama, Jefferson Davis as President
and Alexander H. Stephens as Vice-President.

In the face of these events, Virginia still sought to prevent the oncoming catastrophe, and Richmond joined in the effort. Governor Letcher
called a special session of the General Assembly and that body invited the
then thirty-four states of the Union, including the seven that had seceded,
to attend a "peace conference" in Washington. It was a complete failure.
The states that had established a separate government refused to send delegates, while the Radical Republicans, at the other end of the political
spectrum, rejoiced at the convention's impotence. The Richmond *Examiner* denounced the gathering as seeking to bring dishonor on the Old Dominion, and termed Virginia delegates George W. Summers and William
Cabell Rives, both ardent Unionists, "consummate traitors."

The same paper also advanced the dictum that it was "simply untrue
that Northern men were as brave as Southern men," since "their foremost
and most admired" had been "kicked, caned and cowhided as unresist-
ingly as spaniel dogs."

Not to be outdone, Isaac L. Cary of Richmond declared that the
"hellhounds of the North are the most contemptible and detestable of all
God's creation . . . vile wretches whose honor consists in low cunning,
slander, Puritanical conceit and thieving." Comparable appraisals of
Southerners were being uttered by well-known citizens of the North.

Virginia called a convention at Richmond to consider what action to
take in the crisis. Delegates elected from the city were Marmaduke Johnson, William H. Macfarland and George Wythe Randolph. The first two
were for the Union and the third against it. The convention met on February 13 and the prevailing sentiment was decidedly Unionist. After considerable debate, a vote on April 4 showed the delegates to be 88 to 45
against secession. The fact that seven Southern states had left the Union
was not enough to shake the Old Dominion's determination.

The *Examiner* published an editorial entitled "The Parliament of
Beasts" in which it described various prominent Unionist members of the

convention as animals, such as "the Jackass from Petersburg, the Hyena from Monongalia, the curly-headed Poodle from Richmond." Colonel Marmaduke Johnson was "the sleek fat pony from Richmond, who neighed submission; one master for him would be as good as another; what he went in for was good feeding, and he believed he could get that from Old Abe as well as anybody else."

The stir created by this editorial can be imagined. One result was that Colonel Johnson encountered editor Daniel in broad daylight on Franklin Street and began shooting. Daniel returned the fire. Neither man was hit. A duel would almost certainly have resulted, had not the court placed Johnson under a $3,000 bond to keep the peace.

On April 12, cannon boomed along the battery in Charleston and shells exploded on Fort Sumter. In the face of this overt act against the U. S. Army garrison inside the fort, the Virginia convention stood firm. Next day it sent a delegation to Washington to confer with President Lincoln in the hope of warding off disaster. While the delegation was in Washington, Sumter fell.

Wild rejoicing in Richmond greeted the news. The hysterical populace was swept off its feet, the Fayette Artillery fired a hundred-gun salute in Capitol Square, Confederate flags fluttered from windows and rockets lit up the sky. Still the convention demurred. When an excited crowd surged over to the governor's mansion, "Honest John" Letcher remained calm. He reminded the superheated citizens that Virginia was still in the Union.

Richmond ladies were among the most ardent secessionists of all. The girls at the Richmond Female Institute raised the Confederate flag on April 14, and claimed that it was the first to be displayed in the city. When hostilities actually began, the ardor of Southern belles for the secessionist cause was such that many suitors were informed in no uncertain terms that unless they wore the uniform of the Confederacy, they would have to look elsewhere for feminine companionship.

The fateful turning point in the intersectional crisis came on April 15 when President Lincoln called for 75,000 volunteers, including 8,000 from Virginia, to put down the rebellion in the Deep South. Next day a so-called People's Convention met in Richmond's Metropolitan Hall, with a doorkeeper carrying a drawn sword, and some four hundred delegates, representing nearly every county in the Commonwealth. Its purpose was to pressure the Virginia convention, meeting at the Capitol, into withdrawing from the Union. The latter gathering up to that time had been strongly Unionist, but it was greatly influenced by Lincoln's demand. It asked for one more day to make up its mind, and the People's Convention agreed.

The Virginia convention thereupon reached its final decision. Delegates who on April 4 had stood 88 to 45 against secession voted 88 to 55 in favor of it. All three Richmond delegates stood with the majority. The news was conveyed to the People's Convention in Metropolitan Hall, and that assemblage shook the rafters with its cheers. Lincoln's call on Virginia to provide volunteers for the purpose of subjugating the seceding states had united the Old Dominion in determination to fight to the end.

Near-pandemonium reigned in the city, once the final decision was announced. The action of the convention would have to be ratified by the people, but this was a mere formality. (Virginia's vote the following month was 4 to 1 for secession. Only four Richmonders voted no.)

Business came virtually to a standstill as soon as the convention adjourned, and all attention was focused on preparations for the conflict that loomed ahead. The greatest torchlight procession in Richmond's history wound through the streets on the night of April 19. With thousands of men and women in line, bands playing the new Southern airs, singing marchers joining in, the Southern Cross blazing from dozens of windows, Roman candles lighting up the sky and rockets piercing the darkness, it was a thrilling sight. Governor Letcher was now entirely wedded to the cause, and the Confederate banner floated from the Capitol. There were shouts that Confederate forces would be in Washington in thirty to sixty days.

An embarrassing episode the following Sunday showed how disorganized Richmond was and how far Virginia was from "marching on Washington." Richmond was aroused to great excitement by the sudden tolling of the bell in Capitol Square, portending some grave emergency. Militia units rushed for their guns and martial individuals grabbed everything from squirrel rifles to derringers. The *Pawnee*, a small Federal gunboat, was reported steaming up the James to bombard Richmond. Artillery and infantry units marched off down Main Street to fire on the intruder. It all turned out to be a false alarm, based on the misreading of a telegram.

The near-panic created by the reported approach of a single gunboat brought home to thoughtful Richmonders the fact that a vast amount of preparation was necessary before the South, or Virginia, was ready to cope with the greatly superior manpower, wealth and industrial capacity of the North. Colonel Robert E. Lee, who had just declined a formal offer to command the Northern armies, was one of those who was fully aware of the odds.

Although strongly opposed to secession, prior to Lincoln's appeal for Virginia troops, Lee, who owned not a single slave, gave up stately Arlington and impoverished himself and his family to cast his lot with the land of his birth. He recognized from the first that it was a well-nigh hopeless cause.

Lee came to Richmond on April 22 at the invitation of Governor Letcher and accepted the post of major general commanding the Virginia forces. Fifty-four years old, with a black mustache, erect and handsome, he gave a modest and brief speech of acceptance that greatly impressed the Convention.

It devolved upon him at once to whip an army into shape from the raw but eager recruits who began pouring into Richmond from all parts of the South. He set up offices in Mechanics Hall on Ninth Street, just north of Main. Lee's commands were sometimes sharp and his temper short. Colonels who displeased him in those hectic days when so much had to be done in so little time emerged from his presence shaken by his reprimands.

Lee's personality was far removed from the imaginary marble image that evolved in so many minds as the years passed. All who have studied his career objectively agree that he was a man of noble character, profound patriotism and deep dedication. Yet he was a human being and hence not completely flawless. Lee lost his temper at times when under great pressure. He was rude on one occasion to General Wade Hampton, whom he greatly admired, simply because ill-health, personal tragedy and military stress had strained his normally great self-control to the breaking point. Further evidence of his human qualities is seen in his frank admission of susceptibility to the charms of pretty women. Lee corresponded in an entirely proper way with several of them. He had a gentle sense of humor and a great love of children.[1]

The young men who were arriving in Richmond from all over the South to be trained under Lee's supervision ranged from the sons of wealthy Charleston aristocrats or Mississippi planters, bringing trunks and body servants, to the gaily dressed Louisiana Zouaves, many of whom had lately emerged from New Orleans jails, and who swaggered about with bowie knives, causing the Richmond citizenry to have a care for their wallets and their hen houses. A Richmond unit known for its elite membership from the "best families" was Company F, 21st Virginia Regiment. Many of its members refused to take commissions and remained as privates in Company F, at least for a few months, in order to encourage others to volunteer.

Cadets of the Virginia Military Institute aided in drilling the eager would-be soldiers, who were often crack shots in the hunting field but didn't know "squads right" from "present arms." Editor George W. Bagby was one of these. He had been among the first to enlist, although wholly unmilitary and suffering from chronic dyspepsia. He was dreadfully annoyed at being ordered about by a "fat little cadet, young enough to be my son." "He made me sick," Bagby added in disgust.

The city was being overrun by soldiers, adventurers, speculators, gamblers, prostitutes and every other type of person who gravitates in wartime to the place "where the action is." Richmond shortly before had been a small, somewhat sleepy town of just under 38,000 inhabitants, of whom 11,699 were slaves and 2,576 free blacks. In a few months its population would be twice as big and far more heterogeneous.

The newly built Spotswood Hotel at the southeast corner of Eighth and Main was the center of things—the place where Confederate officers, government officials and their wives congregated, and where the latest rumors and gossip proliferated. A decidedly unusual event occurred when a drunken soldier from one of the Carolinas rode his horse through the Spotswood bar. "How he scattered people and things right and left!" wrote Mary Boykin Chesnut in her fascinating diary, kept throughout the war, and one of the most sprightly sources of information concerning men, women and events.

The new Fair Grounds on West Broad Street, behind what many years later was the site of Broad Street Station, became Camp Lee, and was the scene of feverish drilling, marching and countermarching. Ladies drove out in their carriages to this area well beyond the city limits bearing cakes and sweetmeats for the toiling young men.

The Virginia Secession Convention invited President Jefferson Davis on April 27 to move the Confederate capital from Montgomery to Richmond, and the invitation was accepted. There were various reasons for making Richmond the Confederate seat of government in addition to the fact that the hotels in Montgomery were said to be unspeakably bad. One of the best was that Richmond was the site of the Tredegar Iron Works, much the most important industry of the kind between the Potomac and the Rio Grande, and comparable for Confederate purposes to the Krupp Works in Germany.

President Davis arrived in Richmond May 29 and was driven to the flag-draped Spotswood, which would be his place of residence until he moved into the Confederate White House at Twelfth and Clay streets. That handsome structure's most recent owner, Lewis D. Crenshaw, wealthy flour manufacturer and builder of the Spotswood, had sold the mansion to Richmond's government for $35,000. The city offered it to the Confederate President free of charge "for the duration," but he declined the gift. The Confederacy rented the building from the municipality.

Arrival of the Davises and the Confederate Cabinet from various parts of the South was greeted without enthusiasm by Richmond's upper crust. Some elements of high society were said to have reacted "much as the Roman patricians felt at the impending arrival of the leading families of the Goths." Yet Thomas C. DeLeon, chronicler of many happenings in the wartime capital, declared that Richmond's hospitality was much superior to Montgomery's, and that "everyone connected with the government remarked the vast difference." The Alabamians, he said, privately regarded these connected with the Confederate government as "social brigands come to rob their society of all that was pure in it."

Jefferson Davis was a self-made man whose forebears were undistinguished. Mrs. Davis, on the contrary, was the former Varina Howell of a well-known Mississippi family. But there were few patricians in the new government, and no Virginians, as yet, in high places. This last was readily understandable, since President Davis, Vice-President Stephens and the Cabinet were all chosen before Virginia seceded. President Davis had gracious, gentlemanly manners, but some of those around him were less polished. Mrs. Davis possessed unusual charm and was a cordial and witty hostess.

As a West Pointer, veteran of the conflict with Mexico and former Secretary of War, Davis, like Lee, was aware that the South faced a desperate uphill battle. Mrs. Chesnut reported a conversation with him in June 1861, in which "his tone was not sanguine" and "there was a sad refrain running through it all." Davis thought it would be a long war and "only fools doubted the courage of the Yankees."

Preparations for the defense of Richmond were launched on a modest scale by the City Council, which gave assistance to local military units and appropriated $5,000 as a starter toward the building of defenses. Redoubts were begun at several points on the outskirts. Street cleaners were put to work building the fortifications and unemployed free Negroes were seized on the streets for similar tasks. Later the blacks were paid $11 a month, the compensation of a private in the Confederate Army. The Richmond Home Artillery, commanded by Captain Thomas H. Ellis, was organized and equipped.

General Lee succeeded during seven weeks of intensive work in putting together Virginia units totalling some 40,000 men. They were far from fully trained, but they had learned some of the rudiments of warfare and were in improved physical condition. With the prospect of imminent invasion of Virginia from the north, these troops were promptly absorbed into the Confederate forces.

A slight skirmish at Big Bethel, on the lower peninsula, in which the greatly outnumbered Confederates were the winners, was proof to excited Richmonders of the prevailing notion that one Rebel could handle several Yankees. The Richmond Howitzers used their artillery to good advantage in this engagement.

Meanwhile the Union Army was readying its invasion of northern Virginia. On July 16, U. S. General Irvin McDowell crossed the Potomac with 35,000 men. The Battle of Manassas, or Bull Run, took place five days later. It was the first major engagement of the war and a victory for the South. Richmonders rushed to the conclusion that Confederate troops would move swiftly into Washington.

Nothing of the sort happened, of course. President Davis, who had been present on the field of Manassas, gave a huge crowd outside the Spotswood Hotel a report immediately upon his return. He warned that hard fighting lay ahead. Yet it was difficult in the afterglow of the first great Southern victory to suppress the optimism that pervaded the Confederate capital.

But when trains bearing hundreds of seriously wounded chugged into the station at Eighth and Broad in the pouring rain, the city was suddenly made aware of the grim realities. Here were men wrapped in bloody bandages, shot through the body or with an arm or leg missing, men blinded or moaning in pain. Anguished relatives at the station looked in the storm, with the aid of flickering lanterns, for husbands, sons or brothers. Would they find them there or on one of the trains loaded with the coffins of the dead?

The bodies of General Barnard Bee of South Carolina and Colonel F. S. Bartow of Georgia were accorded special honors. It was Bee who cried out to his retreating men in that critical hour at Manassas, "There stands Jackson like a stone wall!" Coffins bearing the officers were taken to the Capitol as the "Dead March" from *Saul* sounded through the streets. That mournful dirge would be heard during the ensuing four years as thousands of Virginians went to their deaths on the battlefields and were laid to rest in Hollywood and Oakwood cemeteries.

Richmond was almost wholly unprepared to care for the wounded who came flooding in. The new city almshouse became General Hospital No. 1. Dozens of private homes were thrown open by their owners to the ailing Confederate fighting men, and the women of the community were indefatigable in their attentions. Facilities and equipment of every sort were in short supply, if not completely lacking. Medicines, beds, blankets, bandages and nurses were sought in all possible places. The doctors and the ladies of Richmond performed heroically for long hours and under extremely difficult circumstances. The soldiers were made as comfortable as possible. A zealous young woman approached one of them and asked if she could do something for him—bathe his face, for example. "Yes, miss," the soldier replied wearily but politely. "It's been washed seventeen times already, but go ahead."

One of the homes that was made available for the wounded was that of Judge John Robertson at the northwest corner of Third and Main. This large frame house was empty, since the judge had sent his family to the country. The furniture was rearranged, cots were brought in and twenty-five men were cared for.

Twenty-seven-year-old Sally Tompkins made this Robertson Hospital famous. She took charge, rallied a group of prominent ladies as helpers and achieved such an extraordinary record that she was made a captain in the Confederate Army by special order of President Jefferson Davis.

Captain Sally Tompkins, a demure lady who never married, thus became one of the famous women of her time. The chief surgeon in her hospital throughout most of the war was Dr. A. Y. P. Garnett, who left a lucrative practice in Washington, D.C., to cast his lot with the South. So extraordinary was the efficiency of Captain Sally, Dr. Garnett and their associates that many of the most desperate cases were sent to their hospital. Of the 1,333 wounded men admitted there during the war, only 73 died.

The former mansion, Columbia, at today's Lombardy and Grace streets, then the principal building of Richmond College, was thrown into service as a hospital. Bloodstains were visible on the floor for many years.

Federal prisoners captured at Manassas and brought to Richmond in the summer of 1861 were a problem. Among them was Congressman Alfred Ely of Rochester, New York, one of the eager noncombatants who had gone out from Washington in holiday mood to witness what they regarded as the certain defeat of the Rebels.

With Richmond crowded to the eaves already, and the influx growing steadily, space had to be found for these captives. The hastily converted prison for Federal officers was a warehouse and ship chandlery on the north bank of the James, owned by the Luther Libby estate—known to fame thereafter as Libby Prison. The noncoms and privates were placed in tents, under guard, on Belle Isle in the river. Numerous prisoners were sent to other Southern states from Richmond, but from 1,400 to 1,800 were retained in the city until the end of 1861.

Many criticisms were heard then and later of the lack of adequate care for these and other prisoners taken by the Confederates. Richmond's prisons had to be improvised by inexperienced officials from warehouses and other such structures. Furthermore, there were shortages of nearly all necessities in the city and throughout the Confederacy for the Southern people and their families, as well as the Southern soldiers.

The year 1862 opened inauspiciously with the death of the venerable ex-President John Tyler on January 18. He had been one of the most fervent advocates of peace before secession was decreed, and he was then elected to the Confederate Congress from Richmond. The body of this man, who had been a much more effective President of the United States than many today realize, was borne to his grave in Hollywood by a long procession of mourners, following largely attended services at St. Paul's Episcopal Church.

In February, a disaster at Roanoke Island, North Carolina, cast gloom over the city. A much too small Confederate force was charged with garrisoning Roanoke Island against overwhelmingly superior Federal units. Warnings to General Benjamin Huger, commander of the Norfolk District that included the island, went unheeded. General Henry A. Wise, in command of Confederate forces at Roanoke, was also unsuccessful in persuading Secretary of War Judah P. Benjamin that additional help was essential. The result was that almost the entire Confederate force was lost. Not many were killed, but 2,675 were captured, including two companies of the Richmond Blues, and thirty-two heavy guns. Among the slain was the Blues' recklessly brave Captain O. Jennings Wise, son of the general.

Captain Wise's funeral from St. James Episcopal Church at Fifth and

Marshall streets brought an almost unprecedented outpouring of grieving citizens, from the highest to the lowest. Hundreds were unable to get into the church and stood outside in the snow and slush, as the coffin, wrapped in the flags of Virginia and the Confederacy, and bearing the dead soldier's cap and sword, was carried into the sanctuary. Thousands viewed its sad passage to Hollywood.

Even before the Roanoke Island calamity, there had been much bickering and squabbling in the Confederate government, involving President Davis and his Cabinet. When the casualty lists came in from Roanoke Island, the situation was intensified. Secretary of War Judah P. Benjamin got most of the blame in the public mind. He served for only six months as Secretary of War—he had been Attorney General and would later serve as Secretary of State—and he exhibited great executive ability in all three posts. But he was without military experience and he had the misfortune to hold the war portfolio when Roanoke Island fell. General Huger was more to blame, but Benjamin was the more obvious target for Richmonders. He was shortly succeeded as Secretary of War by George Wythe Randolph, grandson of Thomas Jefferson, who had had military experience. However, Randolph remained in the post for only eight months and James A. Seddon, a Virginia-born civilian, was named. He was an able man, but with an ashen complexion, said to resemble "an exhumed corpse after a month's interment."

At this stage and throughout the war, there were sharp differences of opinion concerning the personality, qualifications and performance of President Davis. George W. Bagby wrote in his diary early in the conflict that he was "cold, haughty, peevish, narrow-minded, pig-headed, *malignant*," but few others except the editors of the *Examiner* and the *Whig* went to such extremes. The *Dispatch* referred to Davis at the time of his inauguration as "the impersonation of the principles and spirit of the free and valiant people over whom he has been called to preside." On the whole, Davis was not a popular figure until after the war.

He was formally inaugurated in a deluge of rain on February 22, a few days after the funeral of Jennings Wise. The soggy and chilled multitude huddled under umbrellas in Capitol Square. A few of the more fortunate viewed the ceremony, which took place at the Washington monument, from windows in the Capitol and other comfortable points of vantage.

The weather intensified the atmosphere of depression, and there was also bad news from the "West," where Forts Henry and Donelson on the Tennessee River had fallen to Union forces. The prevailing despondency seemed to be heightened when Mrs. Davis, setting out for the ceremonies, found "walking solemnly, and with faces of unbroken gloom, four Negroes in black clothes, on either side of her carriage, wearing gloves of white cotton." She asked the coachman the meaning of this, and he replied, "This, madam, is the way we always does in Richmond at funerals and sich-like."

Mrs. Davis told Constance Cary, whose words we are quoting, that she was almost grieved to have to "order the pall-bearers away, so proud were they of their dignified position."

Miss Cary—who would marry Burton Harrison, President Davis' private secretary, after the war—wrote that the President and his wife "made a most favorable impression on all Richmond." Other observers agreed, especially as to Mrs. Davis. The President, who was plagued with bad health throughout his years in the Confederate White House—a fact accounting for much of his apparent peevishness—looked thin and pale.

Constance Cary and her cousins, the sisters Hetty and Jennie Cary, all fervent and fearless Confederate sympathizers, were known as the "Cary Invincibles." Hetty and Jennie were living in Baltimore at the outbreak of the war. Jennie set James Ryder Randall's new poem, "Maryland, My Maryland," to the now familiar air of an old German song, "Lauriger Horatius," and it swept the South. Hetty, one of the most beautiful women of her time, sang it in Baltimore and often during the war years at social gatherings and in Confederate Army camps. She waved a smuggled Confederate banner from the window of her father's home while Union troops were marching past, and had to leave the city under threat of immediate arrest and confinement in a Northern prison. Hetty and Jennie accordingly hid drugs and other articles needed by the Confederacy in their clothing and ran the blockade, accompanied by their brother.

The Cary girls were among the liveliest and most charming citizens of Richmond throughout the war. Constance was active in amateur theatricals, held mainly in private homes, for which she revealed considerable talent. As the languishing Lydia in *The Rivals*, she made an especial hit.

Such diversions helped lift the morale of the capital in dark days. The theater at Seventh and Broad streets entertained large crowds and had little difficulty providing adequate programs. The house was full nearly every night, and President Davis and his Cabinet came often, according to the manager, Mrs. McGill, widow of a Confederate officer. The theater burned in January 1862, but was soon rebuilt and called the New Richmond Theatre.

"Connie" Cary contributed a column called "Blockade Correspondence" to the widely read *Southern Illustrated News* of Richmond. Possessed of literary talent—she published numerous novels and short stories after the war—Miss Cary's observations on life in hard-pressed Richmond were amusing and informative. They were read by Confederate women who were having increasing difficulty with their wardrobes. "Blockade Correspondence" provided suggestions for altering and renovating old garments in a manner to conform as nearly as might be to the latest Paris styles.

The beauty of Constance's cousin, Hetty, was such that while her face cannot be said to have "launched a thousand ships," it was gazed upon by enraptured swains throughout the whole area. Confederate officers in squads and platoons sought her hand. An idea of her charms may be had from the following rhapsody penned by the awe-struck correspondent of the New Orleans *Crescent*:

"Look well at her, for you have never seen, and will probably never see again, so beautiful a woman! Observe her magnificent form, her rounded arms, her neck and shoulders, perfect as if from the sculptor's chisel, her auburn hair, the poise of her well-shaped head. Saw you ever such color in a woman's cheek? And she is not less intelligent than she is beautiful. . . . It is worth a king's ransom, a lifetime of trouble, to look at one such woman."

On a more mundane note, experiments were going forward during the summer of 1861 in a portable metal bathtub in the home of Robert H. Maury, 1105 East Clay Street. The house had been built in 1846 by the famous educator Dr. Socrates Maupin, a founder of the Medical College of Virginia in 1838 and later chairman of the University of Virginia faculty for sixteen years. Commander Matthew Fontaine Maury, the "Pathfinder of the Seas," and cousin of Robert Maury, had a bedroom in the house, and was working on methods of exploding small charges of powder under water. He finally came up with a torpedo that wreaked havoc among Union warships. The U. S. Secretary of War said after Appomattox that the North had lost "more vessels by torpedoes than from all other causes."

A resident of Richmond during much of the war was Anna Mathilda McNeill Whistler, a native of Wilmington, North Carolina, mother of James Abbott McNeill Whistler, and subject of his famous portrait "Whistler's Mother," now in the Louvre. Anna Whistler's other son, Dr. William Whistler, was a Confederate surgeon, and they were in the beleaguered city together. She ran the blockade in 1863 and joined James Whistler in London. He painted the beautiful and moving portrait of her a few years later.

The spring of 1862 found the Confederacy's fortunes at a low ebb. Since Manassas, there had been a succession of Confederate defeats. President Davis rammed a conscription bill through Congress over violent opposition. The measure also provided for holding in the army men who had enlisted for twelve months and whose enlistments were expiring.

In Richmond, the atmosphere was depressing. Added to the losses in the field was the fact that rowdyism, drunkenness and crime were widespread. The city was crowded with soldiers on leave, plus questionable characters of all sorts. The situation was symbolized by a near-riot in the gallery of Metropolitan Hall, involving a brawl between "brazen women" and "unprincipled men" who yelled, cursed and discharged firearms.

Anticipating the need for drastic action, the Confederate Congress, on recommendation of President Davis, passed a bill in secret session, authorizing martial law in Richmond. It included suspension of the writ of habeas corpus, and Davis put it into effect March 1. Passports were required for persons leaving the city. General John G. Winder took charge of administering military rule in Richmond and outside it for a distance of ten miles. There was much complaining against the arbitrary actions of his agents. His first general order forbade sales of liquor, except with a physician's prescription, and closed all saloons and distilleries. "It was not long," writes one historian, "before Winder's detectives were forging prescriptions for brandy, drinking the brandy and then arresting the unfortunate apothecaries who had sold it to them."

The idea of martial law and conscription was shocking to many in Richmond, despite the fact that the Confederacy was in a fight for survival. Eccentric, ruggedly independent John Minor Botts, always his own man and an unremitting foe of secession, raised such a storm that he was locked up in jail for eight weeks.

He was let out only on condition that he would reside far from Richmond and keep his opinions to himself. He left for Culpeper County, where he remained on his farm for the rest of the war, proclaiming himself "neutral" and suffering depredations from soldiers of both the Northern and Southern armies.

Spies were circulating in Richmond on a large scale, and the plans of the Confederates seemed to be known in Washington almost as soon as they were made. J. B. Jones, the War Department clerk, wrote in his famous diary that General Joseph E. Johnston told President Davis "the enemy not only knew everything going on within our lines, but seemed absolutely to know what we intended doing in the future, as if the most secret counsels of the cabinet were divulged." The New York *Herald* appeared with such accurate information as to the size of all Confederate forces, with names and grades of the general officers, that the Secretary of War said his own department could not have furnished a more accurate list. "Who is the traitor?" rhetorically asked Jones.

The first spy to be caught and executed in Richmond was Timothy Webster, masquerading as an Englishman, but actually a Northern agent. He was hanged in April 1862. The following November, John Richardson, alias Louis Napoleon, was the first person hanged for counterfeiting Confederate notes.

General Robert E. Lee, who had lived in the Spotswood Hotel when he first came to Richmond, was offered a house at 707 East Franklin Street for his military home by John Stewart of Brook Hill, Henrico County. He accepted, and used it from time to time during the war as a stopping place on his brief visits to the city. At first, Mrs. Lee stayed elsewhere in Richmond, and 707 was turned into bachelor's quarters for the general's son, Custis Lee, and other young Confederate officers. Called "The Mess," it was a lively place for these men, when back from the front, and also for army friends in need of a place to sleep.

Mrs. Lee, who was severely crippled with arthritis and confined to a wheelchair, decided late in 1863 that she wanted to move to 707 East Franklin. The general sought to dissuade her, for there were stairs in the house, difficult for her to negotiate. He also knew what a blow it would be to Custis and the other members of "The Mess," who would have to go elsewhere. However, Mrs. Lee was determined to make the move, so her husband wrote his cousin, requesting him to "go down there and help disperse the club," adding, "The members are all aghast." But they had to move out, and Mrs. Lee took charge in January 1864, to remain until the war was over.

The Richmond City Council had sought a few months before to provide General Lee and his family with a rent-free house. (John Stewart was supposedly renting No. 707 to the Lees, but after the war Stewart refused to accept anything but Confederate money in payment.) When word of the City Council's Plan to present him with living quarters reached Lee, he respectfully declined "the generous offer," and suggested that any available funds be devoted to "the relief of the families of our soldiers in the field."

The City Council became disturbed the previous year over what it felt to be a lack of concern on the part of the Confederate and state governments for Richmond's protection. Councilman Thomas H. Wynne, one of the remarkable men of that era, who has been almost completely forgotten, presented a resolution early in 1862. It was evident, he said, that neither the Confederate nor the state government was doing or is "likely to do" anything for the protection of Richmond. Wynne proposed "prompt and efficient action" to prevent "the capture of our city." The Council adopted the resolution and appropriated $50,000 for land and river defenses. Two months later it made available $50,000 more for river defenses and an equal sum to equip Richmond volunteers for the Confederate service. This was none too soon. General McClellan and his Union host would soon be hammering at the gates.

As the enemy approached, nonslaveholders were sometimes more belligerent than slaveholders. The attitude of the uncultured white was exemplified in the utterances of two women. One was quoted by Judith McGuire in her volume of wartime memories, *The Diary of a Refugee*. Mrs. McGuire met a "very plain-looking woman in a store," and asked her why her fifty-four-year-old husband was enlisting when her three sons had gone to the colors already.

"Them wretches must be drove away," said the bellicose lady.

"Did you want your sons to go?" asked Mrs. McGuire.

"Want 'em to go!" she exclaimed. "Yes, if they hadn't a-gone, they shouldn't a-stayed whar I was. But they wanted to go, my sons did. . . . Them Yankees must not come a-nigh Richmond; if they does, I will fight 'em myself."

25. Two women in deep mourning move among Richmond's ruins, typifying the blasting of Confederate hopes and the end of the Confederacy.

26. Five years after Richmond's fall, April 27, 1870, another tragedy overwhelmed the city. The crush of people in the courtroom on the top floor of
the Capitol caused the floor to collapse, plunging hundreds forty feet to the
ground below. Sixty-two persons were killed and 251 others injured. The
scene is here depicted for *Harper's Weekly* by Richmond's W. L. Sheppard.

27. The Reverend John Jasper, most famous black preacher in Richmond's history, by virtue of his sermon "The Sun Do Move." Leading whites flocked to Sixth Mt. Zion Baptist Church to hear this noted deliverance. Verbal pyrotechnics were a part of it, and he rushed around the pulpit "with his ankle in his hand," laughed, sang and shouted. Jasper said he delivered the sermon 250 times.

28. Mary Triplett, a stunning blonde and one of the great belles of her day, was the innocent cause of the famous duel between John B. Mordecai and Page McCarty, two of the most prominent young men in Richmond. Mordecai was mortally wounded. The trouble started when a bit of harmless verse about "Mary" appeared in a Richmond newspaper.

29. John B. Mordecai, who in 1873 was fatally wounded in a duel with his onetime friend Page McCarty. Mordecai and McCarty got into a heated argument at the bar of the Richmond Club, and Mordecai knocked McCarty down. A challenge to "the field of honor" was the inevitable outcome in that era.

30. Page McCarty, Richmond journalist, like John B. Mordecai had been, or was, in love with Mary Triplett. McCarty was severely wounded in the duel with Mordecai, and never recovered fully. He seemed for the rest of his life to be filled with remorse over the killing of his erstwhile friend.

31. Edward V. Valentine, sculptor of many Confederate heroes, whose masterpiece is the recumbent statue of Robert E. Lee in the chapel at Lexington. He is shown at about the time when he did the Lee statue.

32. John Peyton McGuire, founder and principal of McGuire's University School in Richmond, and one of the noted schoolmasters of his era.

33. Joseph Bryan, one of the fore-most Virginians of his time, is shown as he looked as a relatively young man in 1878. Bryan was notable as a businessman and news-paper publisher, and also as a churchman and civic leader.

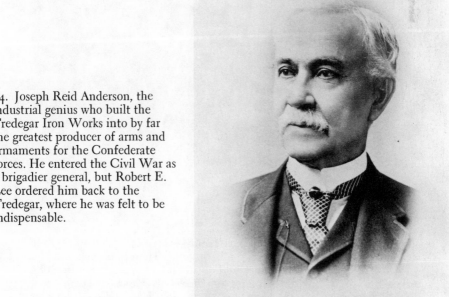

34. Joseph Reid Anderson, the industrial genius who built the Tredegar Iron Works into by far the greatest producer of arms and armaments for the Confederate forces. He entered the Civil War as a brigadier general, but Robert E. Lee ordered him back to the Tredegar, where he was felt to be indispensable.

35. Four generations of the Branch family—three of whom were presidents of the Merchants National Bank. Seated is Thomas Branch, founder and first president of the bank, holding his infant great-grandson, John Aiken Branch, in his lap. Standing, on the left is Thomas Branch's son, John P. Branch, second president, and on the right his grandson, John Kerr Branch, the third president.

Some months later, another woman was commenting on the Confederate success at Big Bethel. "Provi*dence* is fightin' our battles for us," she exclaimed. "The Lord *is* with us, and thar's his handwritin'—*jest as plain.*"

The spirit of these two women of humble birth was in sharp contrast to that of the Confederate Congress, which decamped from Richmond precipitously in the face of the oncoming storm. Much ridicule was heaped upon the fleeing statesmen. The *Whig* said they had gone by canal boat for fear of railroad accidents, and that they had been furnished with an escort of ladies to protect them from snakes and bullfrogs.

Mrs. Davis and several wives of Confederate cabinet members departed for safer climes in North Carolina and Georgia. In fairness to Mrs. Davis, it should be noted that her husband insisted that she leave with the children.

President Davis himself had no thought of abandoning Richmond, nor did the City Council or the Virginia General Assembly. Both bodies resolved that they would stand any loss of life or property. Instead of adjourning, the Virginia legislature remained in almost continuous session, and voted to burn the city rather than let it fall into enemy hands. Plans were made for blowing up the Capitol and the statue of Washington in the square.[2]

This determination to go down fighting was not universal, as already noted. The passport office was crowded with persons who suddenly found business elsewhere. The always scathing *Examiner* declared, "When we speak of the people of Richmond . . . we do not include the Rats. We do not include the contemptible sneaks who care more about their own rickety carcasses than for the independence, the destiny and the existence of the Confederacy."

The building of fortifications against the approaching attack went on apace. Blacks were still being picked up and put to work on them. Some who attempted to escape were shot, a Richmond newspaper declared.

There was an improvement in morale as the crisis approached. Two church conventions were held quietly in the city the latter half of May 1862. The proprietors of Richmond's numerous gambling "hells" patriotically decided to close for a time, on the ground that too many officers were being lured from their duties. They also voted $20,000 toward the cost of articles needed by the thousands of wounded who were expected once the two armies clashed.

The tramp of Confederate infantry and the gallop of horsemen was heard in Richmond, as units of Longstreet's "walking division" and "Jeb" Stuart's cavalry passed down Franklin Street and through the city, en route to the peninsula, there to join Joseph E. Johnston, in his effort to stop McClellan. On such occasions, the ladies lining the curb pressed flowers or articles of food into the hands of the grimy, mud-stained, often barefooted men as they passed, and waved handkerchiefs from windows, while the bands played "Dixie."

A boyish-looking young man was waving to the passing troops, one of whom noticed him and called out, "Come right along, sonny! Here's a little muskit fer ye!"

"All right, boys," cheerily replied the youth, "have you got a leg for me too?" And, as Thomas C. DeLeon related it, "Colonel F. stuck the shortest of stumps on the window sill.

"With one impulse the battalion halted; faced to the window, and spontaneously came to 'Present!', as the ringing Rebel Yell rattled the windows of that block."

Bombardment of Richmond from the river by Federal warships was feared, and extremely ingenious fortifications were hastily erected downstream at Drewry's Bluff under Captain W. W. Blackford's direction. Enemy vessels arrived there on May 15, with the ironclad *Monitor* in the van. But Confederate artillery on the heights was so effective that the Union vessels fell back toward Norfolk, then in Union hands. Richmond breathed a sigh of relief.

The city could not relax for long. McClellan's army, greatly outnumbering Johnston's, was moving slowly toward Richmond through the Chickahominy swamps. McClellan's forces became divided, and Johnston attacked. Two days of bloody fighting followed, during which a large percentage of Richmond's population thronged the heights in the city's eastern end to listen to the roar of the cannon and view the distant battlefield with anxious hearts. The engagement was costly to the South in killed, wounded and missing. Among the wounded was General Johnston, who was knocked from his horse by a shell fragment, and was brought to a house on Church Hill to recuperate.

Johnston's wound made it necessary for President Davis to choose a commander to replace him, and he appointed Robert E. Lee. The appointment brought few cheers, for Lee had been on an impossible mission in the western mountains and then had been engaged on the unspectacular job of fortifying Charleston and Savannah. "Granny" Lee was one of the contemptuous epithets hurled at him by the *Examiner*. When he promptly set to work erecting vital fortifications in front of Richmond, he was sneered at as the "King of Spades."

It now devolved upon Lee to organize his numerically inferior and weakened forces in a way to stop the oncoming Union Army. Seven Pines had increased McClellan's determination to take Richmond.

Confederate wounded, meanwhile, were being brought to the city in great numbers. Manassas had given Richmond a taste of what was to come, but Seven Pines was on a far larger scale. Some 4,700 had to be cared for, and there were no adequate facilities. The maimed and the suffering came to Richmond over the rough roads, in hacks, wagons and ambulances, swathed in bloody bandages and groaning in pain. Many died on their arrival for lack of attention, since no such avalanche of wounded had ever descended upon the city. The great Chimborazo Hospital on Chimborazo Hill and Winder Hospital on Cary Street in the far west end had been got into operation, but there were still shortages of practically everything. These hospitals could not accommodate as many patients as they did later, when Chimborazo became the largest hospital in the world.

The doctors and women of Richmond worked around the clock in an effort to meet the overwhelming need. Not only homes but empty storerooms and stores along Main Street were made available and fitted out with bunks. Citizens put aside their dinners for the benefit of the suffering, and servants with trays were seen in the streets en route to the hospitals.

The ladies of Richmond, like those elsewhere throughout the South, performed heroically. They were tireless in visiting the wounded. Although unaccustomed to such work, and reared in comfort, they bathed the men's bleeding wounds, washed the gore and mud from their hair and beards and wrote letters home for them. The odors that filled the hospitals were often sickening, and some of the ladies fainted. But they carried on.

Yet the monuments that rose across the South after the war were almost always to the men who fought, not to the women who tended the wounded and kept the families together behind the lines, often under extremely difficult circumstances. The women frequently bore tremendous burdens, while constantly worried for the safety of their husbands or sons. Comparing the sacrifices made by the men and women of the South during the conflict, Bell I. Wiley, the noted Civil War historian, says of the women, "Unquestionably, theirs was the greater sacrifice."

Gravediggers worked feverishly in Richmond after the Battle of Seven Pines in an attempt to bury the almost one thousand Confederates who were killed in that engagement. The burial of officers was to the accompaniment of the "Dead March" and muffled drums, which could be heard in the streets at any hour of the day or night. Men in the ranks were buried with little or no ceremony, sometimes in hastily dug graves where the rain soon washed away the thin layer of earth.

Richmond was bracing itself for the next attack by McClellan when Jeb Stuart electrified the South with his three-day ride entirely around McClellan's army, beginning and ending at the Confederate capital. He did it with the loss of only one man, young Captain William Latané. "The Burial of Latané," illustrating the simple ceremony at the young cavalryman's grave in Hanover County, still hangs in Richmond homes.

Stuart's unique achievement, combined with the sensational victories of "Stonewall" Jackson in the Shenandoah Valley, lifted the morale of hardpressed Richmond. Long committed to the offensive, Lee decided to attack, as he so often did, despite the fact that he always had less total manpower and firepower than the North. The Seven Days battles followed. There was a relatively minor battle on June 25, but then came the action at Mechanicsville, on June 26, followed by the desperate encounters that continued on through Gaines's Mill, Savage's Station and Frayser's Farm, and ended at Malvern Hill on July 1. Lee's brilliant strategy and tactics compelled McClellan to retreat to the safety of Harrison's Landing. Richmond was saved, but at huge cost.

Once more the flood of Confederate wounded engulfed the city, in greater volume than ever. Some 16,000 men had been maimed or mutilated since the fighting began at Seven Pines a month before, and practically all of them had to be cared for in Richmond. Then there were the thousands of Federal prisoners who had to be put somewhere. Libby Prison and Belle Isle became more and more crowded.

Richmond's fifty hospitals, large and small—most of which were in churches, lecture rooms, private homes or vacant buildings—were jammed to overflowing. The great Chimborazo and Winder hospitals took the bulk of the patients and were constantly expanding to carry heavier and heavier burdens.

The surgeons and the women of Richmond were again tireless in their attentions to the suffering men. Some of the wounded came limping on foot, black with powder and stained with blood. Others were brought into the city in every conceivable type of conveyance from carriages to carts. When nothing else was available for a bed, they had to lie on rough boards until the overworked medical men could get to them. Some did not live that long. Pew cushions were taken from churches and pillows from private homes to make the wounded more comfortable. Carpets and curtains were cut up for blankets.

Amputations were carried on day and night, with or without anesthetics. Chloroform was in short supply, because of the blockade, and the men had to grit their teeth or take a shot of brandy if no anesthetic was available. Legs and arms were piled outside the rooms where surgery was performed. Whole areas of Richmond were pervaded with "the vapors of the charnel house," one woman reported.

Mrs. Pryor, wife of General Roger A. Pryor, was working in a hospital during the Seven Days when she fainted on seeing the red stump of an amputated arm. However, she said she found herself "thoroughly reinstated" with the staff when she appeared not long afterward, accompanied by a man carrying "a basket of clean, well-rolled bandages." They were made from her tablecloths, sheets, dimity counterpanes and chintz furniture covers. Later, her fine linen underwear and table napkins were cut into lengths two inches wide by the sewing circle at the Spotswood to form "pointed wedges" for surgeons' compresses.

Mrs. Pryor remarked on the ghastly sight of open wagons piled with the dead. From one "a stiff arm was raised, and shook as it was driven down the street, as though the dead owner appealed to heaven for vengeance."

On a less macabre note, she described the report of John, General Pryor's body servant, concerning his master's situation one morning during the Seven Days. Mrs. Pryor asked John if her husband had had a comfortable night.

"He sholy did," was the reassuring reply. "Marse Roger cert'nly was comfortable las' night. He slep' on de field twixt two daid horses!"

Richmond was the principal hospital center of the South. The organization of its numerous hospitals by Confederate Surgeon General Samuel Preston Moore was extraordinarily efficient, especially when one considers the fact that he was short of practically everything, and the shortages increased as the blockade tightened. Instruments, medicines, drugs and equipment were either too scarce, too few or nonexistent. Great ingenuity was shown in using such things as green persimmon juice as a styptic, hemlock for opium and wild cherry for digitalis. Pieces of soft pine wood served as probes for bullets, while tourniquets were made from pliant tree bark.

Most remarkable of Richmond's hospitals was Chimborazo, through which passed 76,000 patients during the war. The mortality rate, despite the difficulties described above, was only slightly over 9 per cent, a figure not equaled in military hospitals until World War II.[3]

Chimborazo was organized in late 1861, and it developed ultimately into 150 well-ventilated single-story buildings, each 100 by 30 feet. There were also 100 "Sibley tents" in which eight to ten convalescents could be cared for. Five large icehouses, a Russian bathhouse, a bakery, a brewery and hundreds of cows and goats made up this huge establishment. An excellent system of sewage disposal was another notable feature. All this was developed and managed with superb skill by Dr. James B. McCaw, a man with great medical understanding as well as exceptional administrative ability.

Winder Hospital on Cary Street in the city's western outskirts was organized in April 1862, and had a capacity of 4,800 beds. It covered 125 acres but was barren of grass and trees. A dairy, bakery, icehouse and gardens worked by convalescents were part of the establishment. The bakery's surplus capacity was disposed of to the prisoners at Libby Prison and Belle Isle.

Other important hospitals in and near the city included Stuart, Camp Jackson and Howard's Grove. As such substantial institutions came into operation, dozens of temporary havens for the wounded set up in churches, stores and homes were closed. Twenty hospitals for Confederate soldiers were functioning in 1863; by the following year the number had fallen to thirteen.

One reason for the success of Chimborazo Hospital was the work done there by Phoebe Yates Pember, chief matron of Hospital No. 2, one of the institution's five "divisions." This brave and highly competent woman came from a cultured Jewish family in Charleston, South Carolina. The chief surgeon viewed her arrival with some skepticism, fearing "petticoat rule." He soon found how able and dedicated she was. Phoebe Pember worked backbreaking hours caring for the wounded. As custodian of the hospital's barrel of whiskey, she had to defend it against the depredations of thirsty patients. Among these was a group of half-drunken thugs who laid hands on her roughly and demanded access to the barrel. She pulled a pistol from her pocket, and they beat a hasty retreat.

Mrs. Pember's memoir, A Southern Woman's Story, is a vivid and well-written account of her experiences. She declares that when her entire hospital was reserved for Virginians, she was much pleased, since they were "the very best class of men in the field, intelligent, manly and reasonable, with more civilized tastes."

There were many hardships in the hospital as the war wore on, and "privations had to be endured which tried body and soul." The thermometer in February 1863 went to ten below zero and the river was frozen hard. Both in February and March nearly a foot of snow fell. There were troubles then and at other times with rats. "Epicures sometimes manage to entrap them," Mrs. Pember wrote, "and secure a nice broil for supper, declaring that their flesh was superior to squirrel meat."

After McClellan was driven from the outskirts of Richmond in the summer of 1862, there was no more jeering at Robert E. Lee as "Granny" or the "King of Spades." He and Stonewall Jackson were the heroes of the South. Morale in Richmond took a sharp upturn.

An outbreak of smallpox late in the year caused problems. There were 169 cases in the smallpox hospital at Twenty-fifth and Cary streets on December 20, of whom 40 were convalescent. It was stated in February 1863 that of 102 cases at Howard's Grove Hospital in the suburbs, 24 had died. Widespread vaccination was ordered, with the city paying the cost for those who could not afford it. The disease was brought under control.

City Council also was concerned for Richmond's disadvantaged, in view of food shortages and rising costs. It appropriated $20,000 in late 1862 "for the relief of the destitute poor during the coming winter," and similar amounts until the end of the war.

The municipal authorities were anxious to provide better lighting for Richmond's streets. Gaslights had been installed at certain points about a decade before, but these were few and far between. A councilman complained in November 1862 that the people of the city had been "in total darkness for three months." Stabbings, garrotings, robberies and other crimes throve in this Stygian atmosphere. Even when the lighting was somewhat improved, the crimes continued.

The city issued $300,000 of its own paper money in 1862, in denominations of 10, 25, 30, 50, 60 and 75 cents.

Richmonders who suffered from anxieties incident to the war had to relax sometimes, or the strain would have been too great. The salon of Mrs. Robert C. Stanard was a place for surcease from cares. A charming widow, she lived until 1862 in her handsome mansion at Sixth and Grace streets. In that year she sold it to William H. Macfarland and moved to the northeast corner of Eighth and Franklin, a site occupied in modern times by the rear of the Federal Reserve Bank. In both houses she entertained "everybody who was anybody"—members of the Confederate Cabinet, high-ranking officers of the army and foreign visitors. Her "salon" was much sought after, and one of her guests, decades later, recalled the sparkling conversation and the delicious taste of her "hot muffins and broiled chicken."

The Mosaic Club was another center for "getting away from it all." It had no fixed address or membership, and was simply an informal meeting of such congenial souls as were back from the front, in whatever home was available. The pleasure was doubled if one of the members happened to have real coffee or some other rare beverage or dish, smuggled through the blockade.

Innes Randolph was a bright star of this intangible group of kindred spirits, most of whom were exceptionally talented. A major on Stuart's staff, Randolph is said to have written and sung the first draft of his renowned ditty "The Good Old Rebel" at one of the Mosaic Club's sessions. He could reel off extemporaneous verse on almost any subject, and was musically gifted as well. Captain John Hampden Chamberlayne, described as "colossal in originality," later editor of the Richmond *State*, was another member of the circle.

John R. Thompson, editor and poet, was in the club until he went through the blockade to London in 1864 and became the influential chief writer for the *Index*, organ of the Confederacy in Great Britain. Captain John Esten Cooke, novelist and historian, was a participant when he could get back to Richmond from service with Stuart. Sometimes he brought along the famous Jeb, with his jovial manner and baritone voice. General John Pegram, "a delightful and artistic whistler," was another who took part, as did Colonel Albert T. Bledsoe, Confederate Assistant Secretary of War until President Davis sent him on a mission to London. Page McCarty, prominent in Richmond journalism after the war, but remembered chiefly for his fateful duel with John Mordecai, was another talented participant. There were occasions when ladies were a part of the Mosaic, as when Miss Mattie Paul exhibited her considerable abilities at the piano.

George W. Bagby was also a leader in the club. He had to resign from the army because of his chronic dyspepsia, and became the wartime Richmond correspondent of more than twenty papers throughout the South. Bagby was termed by a Florida editor "literally the best newspaper writer in the Confederate States." His modest editorial sanctum was described as "the Will's Coffee House of the war wits," who scribbled bits of original verse on his "cartridge-paper table-cloth."

Bagby served in an editorial capacity with both the *Whig* and the *Examiner*, and he echoed enthusiastically their anti-Davis views. The *Examiner* was the more scathing of the two, for in addition to the blistering diatribes of editor John M. Daniel against the President of the Confederacy, there was the constant carping of associate editor Edward A. Pollard against both the President and Mrs. Davis. If Mrs. Davis entertained, she was not sacrificing sufficiently for the cause. If she thereupon reduced her entertaining, she was being stingy.

As the crisis deepened for the Confederacy, there appeared opportunely in Richmond, about a month after the defeat at Gettysburg, a humorous weekly, *Southern Punch*. Edited by James W. Overall, it twitted high and low in lighthearted fashion. Editor Overall was a member of the militia, and he spoofed all militiamen as being averse to encountering any Yankees whatsoever. The magazine also heckled the officers who came to Richmond for dances and flirtations. The touch was generally deft, but whenever *Southern Punch* mentioned President Lincoln, it was heavy-handedly abusive.

Thousands of Negroes were at work on the Richmond fortifications in late 1862 and early 1863. J. B. Jones estimated that ten thousand were thus engaged. Two or three thousand more were working on the Piedmont Railroad.

Some blacks were secret operatives for the Union, even in the Confederate White House. For example, Mary Elizabeth Bowser, an intelligent free black, was provided with excellent references by Miss Elizabeth Van Lew, a native Richmonder of Northern parentage, and herself a spy. Miss Bowser was given a post by Mrs. Jefferson Davis on her staff, and she relayed important information, picked up in overheard conversations, to Betty Van Lew. The latter transmitted it by secret underground to the North.[4]

The White House had unhappy experiences with its black staff. The butler and the coachman decamped for Union territory, and an attempt was made to burn the place down. Shavings and a bundle of faggots were found blazing in the basement next to a woodpile.

Miss Van Lew was a small woman with snapping blue eyes and superior intelligence, who hated slavery passionately and was known to be sympathetic to the Union. By flattering officials she got a permit to visit the prisoners in Libby, and she went there almost daily with food, books and other supplies. By behaving and dressing in an odd manner, she created the impression that she was feeble-minded, and children jeered at her in the streets as "Crazy Bet." This "helps me in my work," she noted in her diary. Whether she aided the 109 prisoners who escaped from Libby in a mass exodus through a tunnel is unknown, although many have credited her with doing so. She did have a secret room in her handsome mansion on Church Hill, and escaped prisoners were occasionally hidden there. General U. S. Grant wrote her, "You have sent me the most valuable information received from Richmond during the war."[5]

Although Betty Van Lew was watched constantly, she was never surprised in any act of overt espionage. Other spies were caught from time to time and hanged at Camp Lee. That was also the place for executing deserters. These hangings and shootings were watched by the morbidly curious.

Speculators and profiteers were numerous, but they were not hanged or even imprisoned. A law was passed in 1864 against importation through the blockade of nonessential luxuries, but it was violated on all sides. Some of Richmond's leading citizens were engaged in the importation of forbidden perfumes, silk stockings, gowns and liquors at enormous profit, when weapons, ammunition, medicines and drugs were sorely needed.[6]

Food speculators were greedy and ruthless. They bought up huge quantities of flour, sugar, bacon, salt and other staples and stored them in warehouses, knowing that the longer they held them, the more money they would bring. Farmers kept their produce from the market until they could obtain higher prices. Many Richmonders meanwhile were on the edge of starvation. President Davis pronounced these extortionists "worse enemies of the Confederacy than if found in arms among the invading forces." Governor Letcher declared that the profiteering and extortion "embraces to a greater or less extent all interests—agricultural, mercantile and professional." A year later, Governor William ("Extra Billy") Smith, who had succeeded him, was protesting all over again, but to no avail. The practices continued until Richmond fell.

The suffering of the poor erupted in widespread disorder in the spring of 1863. Known as the "Bread Riot," it began quietly on April 2 with a meeting of women in the Belvidere Baptist Church on Oregon Hill. They marched to Capitol Square, and were joined en route by others of like kidney. Their leader was a tall Amazon named Mary Jackson, with a white feather in her hat. The feather was an oriflamme for the hungry women, as they poured down into Main Street behind Mrs. Jackson and began looting food shops. Then they decided to grab pretty much everything in sight, for a distance of some ten blocks, and jewelry, clothing and millinery were seized through smashed windows. All this caused such a furor that Mayor Mayo and Governor Letcher tried to calm the mob. But the pillaging continued until President Davis arrived, mounted a dray, and told the crowd that the troops had orders to fire if it did not disperse in five minutes. Davis took out his watch, the soldiers stood with guns at the ready, and the minutes ticked away. Just as the time was about to expire, the crowd broke up.

The Richmond newspapers were requested by the Confederate authorities not to mention the Bread Riot. The *Dispatch*, accordingly, carried a powerful discussion of "Sufferings in the North." The always cantankerous *Examiner*, uncooperative as ever, published an account of the event, but described the participants as "Prostitutes, professional thieves, Irish and Yankee hags, gallows birds. . . ." There were similar outbreaks in other Southern cities during the war, but none so severe as Richmond's. However, nothing of the sort occurred thereafter in the Confederate capital, although the food shortages grew worse. One cause of the shortages was the incredible bungling of Commissary General Lucius B. Northrop. He should have been fired early in the action but was kept on by President Davis almost until the bitter end.

Richmond presented sharp contrasts between luxury and poverty. Some citizens who had been wealthy were living in damp basements and making a heroic effort to keep from starving. Others were dining on canvasback ducks and oysters, terrapin and rare wines. Much of the high living was done in the numerous gambling houses with blockade-running connections. Occasionally, too, Mrs. Davis would have an excellent dinner of several courses and champagne. Her friend, Mrs. Chesnut, would do likewise. The latter was reproved more than once by her husband, Colonel Chesnut, for setting so bad an example. Criticism was heard of the partying that went on in some private homes and the gambling houses in the last year of the war, but there was a fairly general realization by then that the Confederacy was doomed. After the retreat from Gettysburg in July 1863, and the simultaneous fall of Vicksburg, hope faded. Many took the view that both Richmond and the Confederacy probably would not survive, so they might as well have one final fling.

Some of Richmond's most prominent young people organized a "Starvation Club" and had parties where no refreshments were served. They chipped in to hire musicians for dancing—"dancing on the edge of the grave," they called it.

Among the picturesque figures in Richmond were Major Heros von Borcke, the huge Prussian cavalryman who came over to fight for the South and serve as J. E. B. Stuart's adjutant general, and General John B. Hood, blond leader of the Texas Brigade. Von Borcke was finally wounded in the throat and invalided from active service. Hood, who lost a leg at Chickamauga, was deeply in love with Sally Buchanan ("Buck") Preston, and the ups and downs of that tempestuous affair are graphically recounted by Mrs. Chesnut.

Prostitution was widespread in wartime Richmond. The population in 1864 was estimated at 128,000, as against just under 38,000 three years before. The city was overrun by rootless people of all sorts—soldiers on leave, refugees from the war-torn areas, spies, thieves and adventurers. The prostitutes came pouring in on the eve of the Seven Days battles, and they stayed. An entire block on Locust Alley, in the area to the southeast of the Exchange Hotel, where many gambling houses also were located, was given over to the red-light district. The mayor wrote in 1864, "Never was a place more changed than Richmond. Go to the Capitol Square any afternoon and you may see these women promenading up and down the shady walks, jostling respectable ladies into the gutter . . . or leaning upon the arms of Confederate officers." Soldiers on leave from the battlefields headed for the barrooms, got drunk on cheap whiskey and then were preyed upon by the army of rouged streetwalkers. Venereal disease was a serious problem.

Throughout the four years, the Tredegar Iron Works, at the foot of Gamble's Hill between the river and the canal, was the mainstay of the Confederate war effort. Proximity of the Chesterfield coal mines was a godsend, insofar as production was concerned, but the smoke from the Tredegar chimneys permeated the atmosphere in a manner that would have grieved modern ecologists. Joseph R. Anderson, the dynamic head of the Tredegar, went to the field early in the war as a brigadier general, but General Lee felt that he could not be spared from the management of the South's most vital industry, and he returned to Richmond for the remainder of the conflict.

The bulk of the *Merrimack*'s armor was cast at the Tredegar, along with rifled guns for the ship, not to mention hundreds of other guns, huge quantities of ammunition, railroad iron and so on. Large numbers of Negroes were employed, many in highly responsible positions. The magnitude of the operation may be glimpsed from the fact that in 1863, in order to keep the more than two thousand free and slave workers and their families adequately fed, it was necessary to accumulate over 300,000 pounds of bacon, 600,000 to 700,000 pounds of beef and 40,000 bushels of corn, plus corn and hay for horses and mules. There was a constant shortage of workers and also of raw materials, notably pig iron. For these reasons, the works never operated at more than one third of capacity. Employees of the company and conscripts formed the Tredegar Battalion which served in Richmond and also on the front lines.

Josiah Gorgas, Confederate chief of ordnance, was another production genius in the sphere of small arms and equipment. He introduced an innovation by employing white women in his laboratories and arsenals. An explosion in the ordnance laboratory on Brown's Island was a tragic event of early 1863. Thirty-five persons were killed and many others injured.

The Virginia State Armory in Richmond on the canal made muskets, and the Bellona Arsenal across the river in Chesterfield County turned out ordnance. There were also fourteen foundries and machine shops, four rolling mills and fifty small iron and metal works.

The value of those products to the Confederacy fell suddenly in May

1863, when Stonewall Jackson died from wounds received at the Battle of Chancellorsville. The whole South was plunged into gloom by the news. Jackson's body came to Richmond by train, and thousands followed the bier to the governor's mansion. It lay all night, with the moonlight falling on the strong, ashen face. Next morning it was taken through the streets in a plumed hearse, with all Richmond mourning and many in tears. Three brass bands in front of the hearse played dirges, and the general's riderless horse followed. Next came wounded soldiers from the "Stonewall Brigade," many other military units and the highest civilian dignitaries. Jackson then lay in state at the Capitol, his coffin garlanded with spring flowers. Twenty thousand sorrowing citizens passed and looked for the last time on the face of the Confederacy's greatest idol.[7] His body was taken by train and canal boat to Lexington, and buried in the cemetery there.

The Confederacy would never recover from the loss of Stonewall Jackson. Richmond's spirits sank with those of the entire South. They rose again when Lee invaded Maryland and Pennsylvania and met Meade at Gettysburg. But with Jackson gone, victory eluded Lee. Confederate fortunes thenceforth were downhill, and Richmond morale fell accordingly.

The price of everything was mounting to astronomical heights. Boots were $100 a pair in September 1863, and ordinary shoes $60. Wood was $40 a cord, butter $4 a pound, bacon $2.75 to $3, chickens $2.50 to $7 a pair, snaps $1 a quart, tomatoes 50 cents to $1 and country soap $1 to $1.50 a pound.

"We are in a half-starving condition," J. B. Jones wrote in his diary. "I have lost twenty pounds and my wife and children are emaciated to some extent. Still I hear no murmuring." A few months later, he added: "We are a shabby-looking people now—gaunt, and many in rags."

On Christmas Day, 1863, Jones declared that his family had gone to church but that he had to remain behind, since "it would not be safe to leave the house unoccupied; robberies and murders are daily perpetrated."

With Richmonders short of food and many other necessities, the Federal prisoners at Libby and Belle Isle were also suffering. About four thousand officers were crammed into Libby and perhaps twice as many privates crowded onto Belle Isle. Four thousand prisoners were accordingly transferred to Danville in late 1863 to relieve the congestion.

In an attempt to free the prisoners remaining in Richmond and perhaps achieve other results, twenty-one-year-old Colonel Ulrich Dahlgren attacked the city in March 1864. Coming down the River Road from the west with three hundred picked cavalrymen, he was met beyond the outskirts of the town on today's Cary Street Road by about three hundred members of the Home Guard. This motley group of overage men and young boys managed to drive off the intruders with rifle fire. Dahlgren's force veered around Richmond and headed for lower Tidewater. Dahlgren himself was killed in King and Queen County when he encountered units of the 9th Virginia Cavalry. Papers were found on his body declaring that Richmond "must be destroyed and Jeff Davis and his cabinet killed." There were suspicious factors with respect to these documents, including the misspelling of Dahlgren's supposed signature on one of them. Controversy has raged ever since over their authenticity. Virgil Carrington Jones, who has made the most intensive study, believes they were genuine. Others contend that they were Confederate forgeries.

The disposition of Dahlgren's body involved a series of mysterious events, with Miss Elizabeth Van Lew as the mastermind. Dahlgren was buried secretly by Confederate authorities below Oakwood Cemetery, Richmond, but the grave was discovered by agents of Miss Van Lew. They dug up the body at night and took it in a cart, covered with young peach trees, to the Henrico County home of Robert Orrock near Hungary, now Laurel. Orrock was a Scottish-born Union sympathizer who soon thereafter became a paid Union agent. Dahlgren's body remained in its grave on Orrock's farm for more than a year, while baffled Confederate officials sought vainly for it. After the war, it was exhumed, taken to Philadelphia and buried there in the Dahlgren family plot.

Dahlgren had been driven from the suburbs of Richmond in March 1864, but U. S. Grant was about to mount his massive offensive against the dwindling forces of Lee. He crossed the Rapidan on May 4, heading toward the Confederate capital. Anticipating this crisis, the Confederate Congress had suspended the writ of habeas corpus once more, and Jefferson Davis was accorded virtual dictatorial powers. Orders were given that everyone who could possibly do so should leave the city, as it might be shelled at any moment. All schools were closed.

The roar of the guns on the nearby front lines was heard night and day. Citizens became accustomed to the "eternal cannonade." The wounded came in an avalanche from such sanguinary fields as the Wilderness, Spotsylvania and Cold Harbor, and scores lay on the pavement around the station on Broad Street. Their wounds had often been hastily bandaged with strips of coarse homespun cotton "on which the blood had congealed and stiffened until every crease cut like a knife." The men were carried to the hospitals as promptly as possible.

One of those stricken fatally and brought to Richmond was General J. E. B. Stuart. In a cavalry battle near Yellow Tavern, six miles north of the city, the jaunty, picturesque and intrepid leader was shot through the liver as he charged bravely into the melee firing his pistol and rallying his men. In agony, he was taken to the house of his brother-in-law, Dr. Charles Brewer, at 206 West Grace Street.

Word spread through Richmond that Stuart was dying. A crowd, many of whom were weeping, gathered outside the house, on the sidewalk and in the street. Almost exactly a year before Stonewall Jackson had been lost, and now the *beau sabreur* of the Confederacy was sinking fast. Jefferson Davis called. Stuart told him that he was willing to die if God and his country felt that he had fulfilled his destiny and done his duty. Major Heros von Borcke, Stuart's Prussian-born adjutant general, knelt by the bed, his huge frame wracked with sobs. The windows rattled with the sound of the guns.

Stuart knew that he could last only a few hours, and he longed to see his wife. She was trying frantically to reach his bedside from Hanover County, but the Federals were between her and Richmond. She finally arrived late in the day, but thirty-one-year-old James Ewell Brown Stuart had fought his last fight. The funeral from St. James's Episcopal Church brought another great crowd of mourning citizens. "At the head of the coffin sat the soldier who had rescued him, all battle-stained and soiled," wrote Judith McGuire, "and nearby the members of his staff, who all adored him." Once more there was the sorrowful procession to Hollywood.

Two weeks before, another tragedy had overwhelmed the Confederate White House. Five-year-old "Joe" Davis, whom Mrs. Davis called "the most beautiful and brightest of my children," climbed up on the railing of the porch outside the east front of the building, lost his balance and fell to the brick pavement below. He died almost instantly. His father, who had been suffering paralyzing pain which, it was feared, might cause total blindness or even death, walked the floor all night. Joe's funeral was from St. Paul's Episcopal Church. At the cemetery hundreds of school children heaped flowers on the grave.

John M. Daniel of the *Examiner* never tired of belaboring the Confederate government. Most of those whom he assailed were too busy or too indifferent to challenge him, but E. C. Elmore, the Confederate treasurer, was unwilling to take Daniel's slurs. He summoned the editor to a duel, and they met at 5:30 A.M., August 17, 1864, on Dill's Farm, Henrico County. Daniel fought, although unable to use his pistol arm, and was wounded in the leg. If ever an editor invited challenge, it was the vituperative and sarcastic but utterly fearless Daniel. One observer wrote forty years later, "It does honor to humanity to think that some of his victims had sufficient self-control to challenge him to the field of honor instead of going after him with a meat cleaver." Daniel kept urging heroic efforts upon the Confederate forces and people while abusing Confederate officialdom.

Prospects for a Southern victory were growing increasingly hopeless as the year 1864 waned. Lee's genius and the fighting spirit of his men were not enough to compensate for the enormous disparity in manpower and resources with which they were confronted. Richmond knew that the sun of the Confederacy was sinking.

# FOURTEEN

## Rendezvous with Disaster

THE LAST WINTER of the war found the Confederate capital shabby and down-at-heel, its people hungry and cold, its houses in need of paint, its crime-ridden streets dirty and unlighted.

The shivering and starving Confederate soldiers defending Petersburg—the last bastion in front of Richmond, and the key to its survival—were often without shoes or overcoats in the sleet and snow. Lee wrote his family in January that in most regiments only about fifty men had shoes.

Richmond had determined that its defenders should have something special for Christmas. A campaign for contributions of food and money was launched in the city's newspapers, and dinner in the trenches was set for January 2, 1865. Hams, chickens and turkeys came out of hiding and gifts of money were made. Letters to the press from soldiers warned against trusting any of the viands to the commissaries. "Quartermaster and commissary are considered synonymous with scoundrel," wrote one. So these questionable individuals were bypassed, the dinners were cooked in the kitchens of the Ballard House and the provisions packed in boxes and barrels. Beef, ham, mutton, shoat, fowl and sausage were included. Distribution was made along the thirty-mile line in front of Petersburg. Most of the soldiers received some of this Christmas cheer as they stood guard in the icy trenches.

During that same January, gorgeous, titian-haired Hetty Cary was wed in St. Paul's Church to handsome Brigadier General John Pegram. Several happenings, such as a mirror breaking, a horse rearing en route to the church and a wedding veil tearing at the door as Hetty stooped to pick up her handkerchief, seemed ominous of things to come. But the happy bride and groom were in no mood to be troubled by such portents. They went for their honeymoon to General Pegram's headquarters in a farmhouse near Hatcher's Run in front of Petersburg. Shortly thereafter Pegram was killed leading a charge. His blood stained the snow that carpeted the field. Hetty came back to Richmond in the freight car that brought her husband's body. Exactly three weeks after she had stood with John Pegram in St. Paul's as his bride, she knelt beside his coffin in the chancel.

Tragedy upon tragedy was engulfing the Confederate capital. There had been no more popular and admired young man in Richmond than John Pegram. His brother, William, was equally popular and highly regarded. They were sons of the widowed Mrs. James W. Pegram, who operated a school for girls in Linden Row. Less than two months after his brother was killed, "Willie" Pegram, a colonel of artillery at twenty-three, was mortally wounded at Five Forks. With him in his dying moments was his adjutant, Captain W. Gordon McCabe, later the famous schoolmaster, who pronounced William Pegram "the most superb soldier in all the world." It was one more shattering blow to the Army of Northern Virginia.

That army had been reeling for months under the shock of Grant's relentless pounding. Outnumbered and outgunned throughout the war, it was unable to stand the irreplaceable losses in men and matériel inflicted upon it by the well-equipped and virtually inexhaustible manpower of the North.

In the hope of ending hostilities on terms acceptable to both sides, a conference was held in February on a ship in Hampton Roads. Participants were President Lincoln and Secretary of State Seward on the one hand, and a Confederate commission consisting of Vice-President Alexander H. Stephens, Robert M. T. Hunter, president pro tem of the Confederate Senate, and Assistant Secretary of War and former U. S. Supreme Court Justice John A. Campbell on the other. Hopes were high in war-weary Richmond that peace might be at hand. Nothing came of it. Each side insisted on terms completely unacceptable to the other.

Richmonders were again close to despair. Like the men on the front lines many were near starvation and scantily clad in one of Virginia's bitterest winters. A young officer in the city for a wedding described the scene: "People without overcoats met one another upon the streets and talked over the prospects of peace, with their teeth chattering, their thin garments buttoned over their chests, their shoulders drawn up, their gloveless hands sunk deep into their pockets for warmth."

In this crisis, the idea of enlisting Negro troops was brought forward. The *Enquirer* suggested it in the fall of 1864, and General Lee embraced the plan. He proposed that 200,000 slaves be placed in the army as combat troops, in return for their freedom after the war. In a letter to Congress, Lee said that the blacks "furnish a more promising material than many armies of which we read in history." Under Lee's urging, Congress passed legislation, but without guaranteeing freedom for the fighting slaves at the end of hostilities. The law, such as it was, passed on March 13, too late to have any appreciable results. While it was being discussed, Richmond slaves began leaving in large numbers for the North.

Two companies of blacks were recruited from the employees of Richmond hospitals, and they paraded, without uniforms, in Capitol Square on March 22. The *Dispatch* commented that they were not, as far as it knew, in the Confederate military service, and added that their unmilitary bearing was in great contrast to "the squad of Major Turner's colored troops neatly uniformed and showing a good, soldierly carriage."

During these days, John M. Daniel, long plagued by poor health, was sinking fast. The brilliant and mercurial editor of the *Examiner* died on March 30, just before the curtain went down on the Confederacy.

Courageous President Davis seemed, at times, to feel that even if Lee's lines were broken in front of Petersburg, his forces cut to pieces and Richmond given up, the South could fight on to some sort of acceptable conclusion. This view was not shared by Mrs. Davis, who saw that the cause was lost. She begged her husband to let her remain at his side, but he insisted that she leave with the children at the end of March. Davis told his wife, with emotion, "I do not expect to survive the end of constitutional liberty," which sounded as if he too foresaw the end of the Confederacy. When he said goodbye to his family at the railroad station, his wife wrote later that "it was evident he thought he was looking his last upon us." Two of the children clung to him convulsively. Finally, the group pulled out for South Carolina in the dilapidated coach.

A few days later word came to President Davis from General Lee that Petersburg was about to fall and that Richmond would have to be evacuated. The message reached Davis on April 2 while he was attending Sunday morning services at St. Paul's Church. He left at once for his office, tense and pale. The congregation, sensing the worst, was asked by Dr. Charles Minnegerode, the rector, to remain until the end of the service. This they did.

At Second Presbyterian, Dr. Moses D. Hoge received word simultaneously that the city would have to be evacuated. Dr. Hoge, who had run the blockade to England in order to bring back thousands of Bibles, bade an eloquent farewell to his congregation. He expressed the belief that they would never again meet there for worship.

By the time church services ended, the word had spread that Richmond could no longer be defended. Citizens began making hurried preparations for getting out of town before the arrival of the onrushing Union forces. They saw government officials and clerks frantically packing records or burning them. The few trains still operating were reserved for President Davis and members of his official family, who were leaving for Danville, taking with them the Confederacy's gold supply and important papers.

Uncertain as to what the Northern troops, especially black ones, would do when they took Richmond, thousands of citizens, especially women, decided to flee. The banks were open and depositors drew out such valuables as they had. Millions of dollars in worthless paper was burned in a bonfire on Capitol Square.

The fleeing citizenry set out in whatever conveyances they could find—canal boats, hacks, carriages or wagons, on horseback or on foot—going either to the west or across the still standing bridges to the south. Most of them had no specific destination; they were simply determined to get out of Richmond before it was taken by the Federals. Many others decided to stay and await whatever fate was in store.

It had been determined long before that if Richmond fell, the stocks of tobacco should be burned to prevent their falling into enemy hands. Orders to this effect had been issued and General Richard S. Ewell prepared to carry them out. Mayor Mayo protested that the fire might spread and cause a general conflagration. The protest did not reach Ewell, and a subordinate refused to listen.

The torch was applied and the tobacco warehouses began to burn. The air, at that time, was still, and there appeared to be no danger of the fire's spreading. But soon a strong wind sprang up from the south and blew sparks and burning fragments toward the business district. Buildings near the tobacco warehouses caught fire, and the flames, fanned by the wind, spread to other structures. Soon there was a roaring inferno.

This was sufficiently terrifying. The fires, burning through the night, shed a lurid glow upon stricken Richmond. Then shortly before dawn, a series of violent explosions in the river shook the city and broke windows as far away as two miles. The Confederate warships, with their loaded magazines, were being blown up by their officers.

Soon there was another and more tremendous explosion on the northern edge of town near the city almshouse. The great powder magazine there went up with a reverberating roar. Had it not been situated in a small ravine, the loss of life would have been staggering. As it was, eleven paupers were killed. Virginia Military Institute cadets had been using the almshouse for barracks since the destruction of the institute by U. S. General David Hunter the previous year, but they had fortunately been ordered to the front, and were not in the building when the explosion took place. It wrecked half of the almshouse and totally destroyed small nearby structures. The northern wall of Shockoe Cemetery was leveled, and there was the sound of tinkling glass all over town, as windows were shattered.

The noise of these explosions in the dawn alarmed the people of Richmond. Some imagined that they were being bombarded by the Yankees, and many poured into the streets. Desperate and disreputable characters emerged from hiding. The guards at the penitentiary fled and 350 convicts escaped. When the authorities tried to fight the mounting flames, they found the hoses had been cut. They also caught convicts and other sinister individuals setting fire to buildings.

Looting began. Stores and warehouses were broken into and food, cloth-ing, jewelry and supplies of all sorts were carried off. In order to prevent large stocks of whiskey from falling into the hands of the mob, officials or-dered the tops of the barrels staved in and the liquor poured into the gut-ters. The rabble dipped it up in cups, pans, or any other available vessels. Some lapped it up, lying prone. They drank freely, and as most of them had empty stomachs, they got drunk in short order. Pillaging mounted to a higher crescendo as the white and black drink-crazed looters fought with one another for the spoils.

In the hospitals patients who had been bedridden for months, profess-ing to be unable to move, suddenly found their legs. Phoebe Pember went through her wards at Chimborazo Hospital, in the hope of rendering as-sistance, and found them empty. "The miracles of the New Testament had been reenacted," she wrote, with tongue in cheek. "The lame, the halt and the blind had been cured."

Another gigantic explosion rocked the city at around 8 A.M., when the arsenal, with its hundreds of thousands of artillery shells, blew up. The air was filled for hours with the hissing, exploding projectiles, adding to the prevailing hazards. Bursts from the shells reverberated through the city and illuminated the darkness caused by the dense smoke from the fires. Shell fragments fell throughout Richmond. Miraculously, casualties were few.

Great numbers of Negroes prayed quietly for a Northern victory. De-spite outward manifestations of loyalty to the whites, and the faithfulness with which the vast majority of slaves protected their "white folks," espe-cially on the plantations, most slaves were inwardly anxious for freedom.[1]

At the same time, there were such striking examples of devotion to their owners as was given by a young slave woman who was encountered walk-ing toward Richmond while the city was going up in flames, to a thun-derous obbligato of bursting shells.

"I'm gwine to town to hunt my young mistress," the slave told Emma Mordecai, who recorded it in her diary. "I'd risk my life to git her from dem terrible Yankees."

A bucket brigade was formed for the protection of the Lee house at 707 East Franklin. Flames licked past Eighth and Franklin and the house next door was burning. The front of the Lee house caught fire. Yet Mrs. Lee could not be persuaded to leave, although the Confederate government had departed for Danville and people were fleeing the city in droves. A carriage was sent for her but she refused to budge.

The fire was spreading over a wide area, partly because a portion of Shockoe warehouse was covered with bituminous paper or canvas. Flam-ing flakes of this material were blown by the high wind for great distances, to stick "like Greek fire to every neighboring roof and cornice and gable." Dr. William P. Palmer, who witnessed the scene, was confident that the

General Court Building, for example, would have survived except for these "floating firebrands." The court building, in Capitol Square, had a shingle roof, and the same was true of many other structures. Their shingles were more than ordinarily inflammable, since the weather had been warm and dry.

The court building contained not only irreplaceable records of several of the highest courts, but those of many Tidewater counties, which had been stored there for safekeeping during the war. Palmer calls the loss of these records "the most serious ever sustained by the state. . . . The several burnings of Jamestown, the destruction of the old capitol at Williamsburg, or even the terrible catastrophe at the Richmond Theatre in 1811 . . . did not equal in importance this disaster."

The three bridges across the James had not yet been destroyed by the Confederates, and refugees poured over Mayo's Bridge into Manchester carrying such effects as they could in wagons, carts, buggies or other conveyances. The last military units also went over. When this headlong exodus was completed, Mayo's and the two railroad bridges were fired.

With Richmond's business district going up in smoke, shells detonating overhead and hundreds of terrified people huddled in Capitol Square, Mrs. Robert C. Stanard sat calmly on a trunk outside her doomed residence at Eighth and Franklin. Dressed in her finest, she viewed the holocaust through her lorgnette and refused assistance. The handsome widow whose "salon" had been so important a feature of wartime Richmond was salvaging what she could in her trunk and hoping for better days.

The City Council appointed a committee to accompany Mayor Mayo in surrendering the city to the Federals. Those chosen were William H. Macfarland, Judge W. H. Lyons, Judge W. H. Halyburton, Judge John A. Meredith and Loftin Ellett.

Early in the morning of April 3, the eighty-year-old mayor and several members of the committee set out quietly in a dilapidated hack, pulled by a bony horse, for the Union lines. Passing along Main Street, they dodged the burning buildings and rampaging mobs, and traveled eastward. Realizing that they had no white flag to wave at the enemy, they cut off a couple of their own shirttails, pinned them together and tied them to a staff.

Near the junction of Osborne Turnpike and New Market Road, between 6:30 and 7 A.M., they met U. S. Army Majors Atherton H. Stevens, Jr., and Emmons E. Graves. Mayo handed Stevens a note addressed to the "General Commanding the United States Army in Front of Richmond," which said: "The Army of the Confederate Government having abandoned the City of Richmond, I respectfully request that you will take possession of it with an organized force, to preserve order and protect women and children."

This was tantamount to surrender, but Mayo and his delegation returned to the city behind the entering Federals, and formally capitulated to U. S. General Godfrey Weitzel at eight-fifteen at the city hall.

The victorious Union Army came into burning Richmond via Main Street as shells continued to explode overhead. The flames were so hot that the whiskers of some soldiers were singed. The looting mobs paused to watch the well-dressed, splendidly equipped cavalry, artillery and infantry pass. The sleek, well-fed horses were in sharp contrast to the starving animals with the Confederate forces. The blue-uniformed infantrymen marched in serried ranks, while on an ironic note their band burst into the strains of "Dixie."

Negroes went wild as the Northern soldiers moved along Main and then up Governor Street to the Capitol. Such fervent ejaculations as "Bless de Lord!", "Glory hallelujah!", "We's free, we's free!" were heard on all sides. The blacks were packed so tightly in front of the oncoming troops that it was difficult for the latter to move forward. The exuberant former slaves shouted, prayed and embraced the knees of the horses, hailing the Negro cavalrymen as deliverers.[2]

Major Stevens led the way with his cavalry to the Capitol, and hoisted two guidons on the roof. There is conflicting evidence as to who first raised the Stars and Stripes. General George F. Shepley claimed the honor. So did a Negro youth, Richard G. Forrester, who said he hid the American flag that was taken down when Virginia seceded, kept it in his home at College and Marshall streets and ran it up on the Capitol when Federal troops entered Richmond. U. S. Lieutenant Royal B. Prescott saw a flag whipping from the pole at about 7:30 A.M., and was told by Forrester that he had hoisted it.

With smoke and burning fragments sweeping across Capitol Square, General Weitzel went to the Capitol portico with General Edward H. Ripley, General Charles Devens and the division commanders of the XXV Corps of Negro troops. Mayor Mayo and other city officials were there. The conflagration roared on unchecked.

Weitzel directed Ripley to begin at once putting out the fire and restoring order. Since the hoses had been cut by the mob, Union soldiers were set to work tearing down walls and destroying buildings to create a fire break. By the end of the day, the situation was under control. Pillaging had also been stopped.

But the heart of the business district had been wiped out. Nine hundred buildings, including some 230 of the best business houses, were gone, with their contents, plus three bridges across the James, the Henrico County courthouse, the General Court Building, two railroad depots, several tobacco warehouses, all the banks, the state armory and a church. Main Street between Ninth and Fourteenth gave the appearance of utter ruin. Only the granite customhouse, where the Confederate government had its principal offices, was still standing for a distance of seven blocks on both

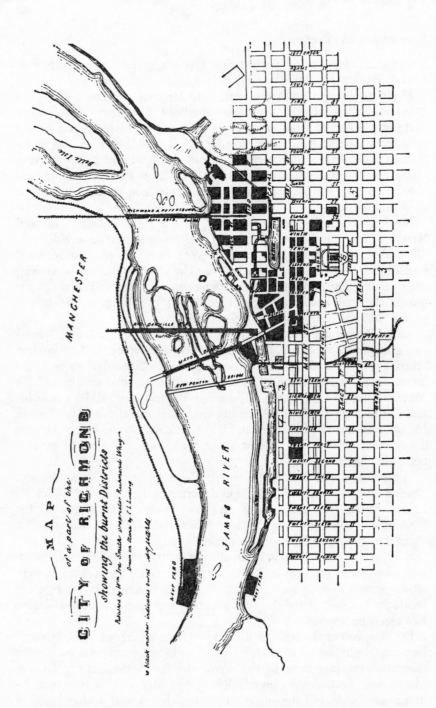

(3) Richmond's business district, along Main Street and below it to the river, was virtually wiped out in the fire of April 2–3, 1865, as the black squares on the map make plain. There was also considerable destruction between Main and Franklin, and some even north of Franklin. All three bridges over the James were burned.

sides of Main Street. Almost everything from Cary Street to the river between Fourth and Fifteenth was destroyed. This was also the case along
Franklin and Bank from Eighth to Thirteenth.

General Weitzel described pathetic scenes in Capitol Square. "It was
covered," said he, "with women and children who had fled there to escape
the fire. Some of them had saved a few articles of furniture, but most had
only a few articles of bedding, such as a quilt, blanket or pillow, and were
lying upon them. Their poor faces were perfect pictures of utter despair. It
was a sight that would have melted a heart of stone."

The Union commander ordered all Northern troops, white and black,
to behave with utmost correctness and protect citizens and property.
These orders were carried out. There was universal praise for the conduct
of the Union troops. Thousands of black soldiers were billeted at Camp
Lee and strict discipline was maintained. Mrs. Robert E. Lee remained in
her scorched house and told her husband later, "It is impossible to
describe the kind attentions of the Union soldiers."

On April 4, President Lincoln appeared suddenly in Richmond after
sailing upriver from City Point. Many of the older inhabitants had retired
on the previous day to their homes, with shutters drawn, leaving the
streets to the Northern troops and the Negroes. The tall, gangling President walked from Rocketts in the dust and unseasonable heat up Main
Street, holding his young son "Tad" by the hand. Escaped convicts and
other shady characters made his passage a dangerous one, since his only
guard was a detachment of a dozen crewmen from his ship, the *River
Queen*. U. S. Admiral David D. Porter accompanied him. Dense puffs of
smoke floated from fires still burning near the Tredegar.

Lincoln's progress was slow, for he was surrounded by exultant and ad-
miring blacks who had been waiting for years to greet "Marse Linkum."
He said later that the streets were "alive with the colored race. They
seemed to spring from the earth, they came tumbling and shouting from
over the hill and from the water side." Some fell on their knees in expres-
sions of gratitude. "Many poor whites joined the throng and sent up their
shouts with the rest," according to Admiral Porter.

Porter also related that "a beautiful girl came from the sidewalk and
presented Lincoln with a large bouquet of roses." On it was a card, "From
Eva to the Liberator of the Slaves."

It took half an hour for the procession to reach Libby Prison. As the
marchers walked past, there were shouts of "Pull it down!" but Lincoln
said, "No, leave it as a monument." (It was privately purchased in 1889,
razed and transported to Chicago. Portions were lost in Indiana when the
train wrecked.)

The procession turned north at Fourteenth Street to Franklin, avoiding
debris on Main, and moved westward to Governor Street. A detachment
of cavalry arrived and led the way along Twelfth to the former White
House of the Confederacy.

Lincoln was weary and thirsty on his arrival there. He asked for a glass of water, rested a short time in a chair and then took a look around the premises. He conferred with Weitzel, who had his headquarters in the White House, and Weitzel's officers. All except Lincoln took powerful swigs from a bottle of whiskey brought by a servant.

After lunch the President expressed a desire to talk with leading Richmonders. Assistant Secretary of War John A. Campbell and Joseph R. Anderson of the Tredegar accordingly conferred with him. The Army of Northern Virginia was still in the field, although hard pressed, and there had been no hint of Lee's surrender, which would take place six days later at Appomattox. President Lincoln was conciliatory, and asked Judge Campbell to visit him the next day on the *Malvern*, Admiral Porter's flagship. Campbell accepted.

Later that afternoon, Lincoln drove around Richmond in an open carriage, escorted by Negro cavalry, with bands heralding his passage. He visited the Capitol, and found "dreadful disorder" in the legislative halls, wrote Admiral Porter. "Members' tables were upset, bales of Confederate script were lying about the floor, and many official documents of some value were scattered about." Liberated blacks greeted Lincoln everywhere, and some whites joined in the welcome. He spent the night on the *Malvern*.

Next morning Judge Campbell took with him to the ship Gustavus A. Myers, a leading lawyer of Richmond. Campbell and Myers were much impressed with President Lincoln's generous and magnanimous spirit. His terms included restoration of the Union, abolition of slavery and the disbanding of all hostile forces. Property would be restored to those who laid down their arms, and no oath of allegiance would be required. Myers wrote later that the conference was conducted "with entire civility and good humor."

Four fifths of Richmond's food supply had been destroyed in the fire, and stark hunger confronted the people. Proud women, often dressed in black and heavily veiled, in mourning for loved ones lost in the war, swallowed their pride and went to Capitol Square to accept the Federal handouts of corn meal and codfish. It was the only menu the victors could provide in the early days immediately following the city's fall. In order to get those scanty rations, ladies reared in comfort had to stand in line among sweaty, pushing crowds of ex-slaves, free blacks and rootless white panhandlers.

The Federal authorities were considerate and helpful to the limit of their abilities. The Relief Commission reported issuance of 128,132 rations during the first seventeen days of the occupation. At least one third of the population was driven to the "humiliation of subsisting alone on supplies of food furnished them by the conquerors."

The business district was reeking with the smell of charred and smoldering timbers. Many of the walls still standing like ghosts in the devastated area were knocked down by the Union troops in the interest of safety. The debris and rubbish that filled the streets was pushed aside to permit passage of vehicles.

Yankee traders, newspaper correspondents, curiosity seekers and others flooded in behind the troops. The traders set up shop in such empty stores as could be found. They offered canned goods, but hardly any Richmonders had money with which to buy.

In the midst of these desolate scenes, the city was slowly pulling itself together when suddenly another blow fell. It was signaled by cannon fire lighting the night sky above Camp Jackson. Lee had surrendered at Appomattox.

Most Richmonders recognized that this meant the end of Confederate resistance, although some pointed hopefully to the fact that Joseph E. Johnston's army was still in the field. But with the Army of Northern Virginia only a memory, it was clear to realists that the end had come.

The surrender on April 9 took place exactly a week after Lee's message to President Davis that Richmond would have to be evacuated. Fire and disaster had overwhelmed the Confederate capital in the intervening days. Twelve thousand Union troops had marched through the city on April 8, portending no good for Lee's army. And now came the capitulation of the proud remnant of that indomitable force of fighting men. The jubilant victors fired a hundred guns in Capitol Square.

Six days went by, and there was no direct word from Lee. Then all at once a forlorn caravan appeared in the drenching rain on the pontoon bridge across the James. The weary and worn commander of the Army of Northern Virginia was riding his famous war horse Traveller, his hat and clothing were soaked, and several officers who accompanied him were equally waterlogged. Behind them rumbled the rickety ambulance that served General Lee for his campaign kit. Behind that came two or three wagons, pulled by gaunt and jaded horses. The canvas top of one was missing, and a sagging, dripping old quilt was in its place.

Arrival of the group at the bridge was noted at once and crowds gathered quickly. Cheers rang out and hats were thrown into the air when Lee hove into view. Union soldiers joined heartily in the tribute of respect to this man who had held them at bay for four years against overwhelming odds. There were tears from those who saw the grizzled warrior as the symbol of the fallen Confederacy. He lifted his hat time and again in acknowledgment of the tributes. Finally he arrived at his residence, 707 East Franklin Street, where a throng awaited him. These citizens of Richmond, young and old, hoped to take his hand or touch his uniform. Some were sobbing. Lee himself was deeply moved and on the verge of losing his self-control. He grasped as many hands as he could, then made his way through the gate and up the steps. Bowing to the crowd, he entered the house and closed the door.

It was a sad hour for the onetime capital of the Confederacy, but further calamities lay ahead. On April 15, the day that Lee returned from Appomattox, news of President Lincoln's assassination reached the city. It was the ultimate disaster—for Richmond, Virginia and the South. Civil and military leaders from the Potomac to the Rio Grande united in condemning the murder. The wise and tolerant policies enunciated by President Lincoln would now be superseded by those of the vengeful Northern radicals.

The future seemed bleak indeed for devastated, bankrupt Richmond, its people hungry and disconsolate, its soldiers returning penniless from the front, and many of its finest young men killed, or maimed for life.

# FIFTEEN

# Up from the Ruins

GLOOM and depression gripped Richmond after the surrender. Thieves, murderers and pickpockets swarmed in the streets. The prevailing feeling of despair was intensified when suspicions were expressed in certain Northern quarters that Jefferson Davis and other Confederate leaders were somehow responsible for Lincoln's death. This was, of course, absurd, but Northern radicals were looking for an excuse to punish the South to the limit.

Orders were accordingly issued forbidding as many as three former Confederates to stand on any Richmond street corner, lest they engage in further "conspiracies." No Confederate insignia could be worn, with the result that a former soldier who had only his battered Confederate coat had to cut off the buttons or cover them with cloth.

Many citizens talked of emigrating to Canada, Europe or Latin America. General Lee argued strongly against this, saying that all should remain in Virginia and help to build her up again. That was the course he himself followed. But some were determined to leave, and did so. Others were granted permission to depart from Richmond for foreign lands, when suddenly the Federal official in charge revoked the permission, and they had to stay. It was fortunate for the city, since these leaders were important to its gradual rebuilding.

Confederate veterans back from Appomattox, including members of the most prominent Richmond families, went to work cleaning bricks in the wrecked district, or undertook equally lowly tasks.

The victorious Union armies passed through Richmond in early May. The Army of the Potomac, fifty thousand strong, was reviewed from the city hall portico by Generals Meade and Halleck on May 1. It required most of the day for the blue line to pass. Then came a large part of Sherman's army, and on the following day Sheridan rode through at the head of eight or nine thousand cavalrymen.

Negroes were flooding into Richmond and other cities from the country districts. An estimated fifteen thousand blacks came to the former Confederate capital, doubling its black population. Many of these newcomers believed vaguely that they would be cared for indefinitely by "Marse Linkum" or his agents. As one of Emma Mordecai's former slaves put it, "All de land belongs to de Yankees now, and dey gwine to divide it out 'mong de colored people. De kitchen of de big house is ma share. I helped built hit."

Another ex-slave was heard to say: "Dis what you call freedom! Can't get no wuck, and got ter feed and clothe yo'sef."

Many blacks realized that although they were free, they had to work for a living. Often they took jobs with the Federal authorities. Some raked up and hauled away debris; others cleaned the docks or loaded ships. Cooks were glad to obtain employment with Union officers.

A group of freedmen interviewed by a New York *Times* reporter wanted to work, but understandably not for Confederate money. One expressed a desire for "de money dat you has," and added, "Dis chile'd like to hab a heap o'dat."

It was often easier for blacks to get work than whites. Ex-slaves were known to bring their impoverished former masters or mistresses Federal greenbacks and food from the U. S. Commissary. It was clear that there were strong ties of affection between many onetime slaves and their erstwhile owners. On the other hand, there was the sudden departure of old family retainers who had been deemed to be content with their lot. A delegation of Richmond blacks called on President Andrew Johnson in June 1865, claiming that their condition was worse than it had been under slavery. Johnson told them that matters were in a state of transition, and asked them to be patient and await the working out of solutions.

General Lee was still in Richmond, but he found the constant stream of callers too great a strain on his failing health. In late June he and Mrs. Lee moved to a modest home, Derwent, in Powhatan County.

Susan Archer Weiss returned to what was left of Talavera, the estate on Richmond's outskirts where she and Poe had discussed "The Raven" in 1849. She found "a bare and lonely house in the midst of encircling fortifications . . . every outbuilding had disappeared . . . all the beautiful trees were gone; greenhouses, orchard, vineyard . . . swept away."

The universal presence in Richmond of Federal troops was something of a tranquilizer for the criminal elements who had been running amuck in the city. Harvey M. Watterson, who was sent to Richmond by President Johnson to report on conditions, declared, "You may walk the streets for days and not witness one act of disorder or violence."

The Freedmen's Bureau, a Federal agency established throughout the South to feed, protect and educate the former slaves, opened for business in Richmond. Schoolteachers came down from the North to instruct the blacks. Those in charge of these activities were idealistic in the extreme, but too frequently were lacking in understanding. Yet they provided food, medical care and schooling for thousands of blacks who were in need. Establishment of the Richmond Institute and the Richmond Normal and High School for the benefit of the Negroes was a direct outgrowth of their activities.

The provisional governor of Virginia, Francis H. Pierpont, arrived in Richmond on May 26. He was a sincere and honest man who understood the situation far better than some others who occupied important posts. Pierpont sought conscientiously to alleviate the sufferings of all the people, both white and black.

Among those in dire need of help were the returning Confederate soldiers who had been confined in Northern prisons. These haggard, weak and often ill men, clad in hardly more than rags, staggered into town after somehow making their slow and tortuous way back to the South.

Governor Pierpont got the city government into operation by reinstating Mayor Mayo and all the other municipal officials. He appointed David J. Saunders, president of the City Council, manager of the gas and water works. He also gratified most white Virginians by saying: "You cannot govern a state under a republican form of government when nineteen-twentieths of the people are disfranchised and cannot hold office."

As Richmond's business community struggled to recover from the shock of the fire, efforts to establish a bank were got under way within two weeks of the conflagration. Robert A. Lancaster, Wellington Goddin, Horace L. Kent, Franklin Stearns and Charles Palmer were the moving spirits. It was necessary to have the cooperation of Northern business interests, and this was provided by Hamilton G. Fant, a partner in a Washington banking firm, and a group of associates, each of whom bought stock.

Here we have the beginnings of the First National Bank of Richmond. The stockholders met in Washington on April 24 and elected Fant, the largest stockholder, president. Eight other stockholders, all non-Richmonders, were chosen directors. A few weeks later, it was decided to name four Richmonders to the board of directors, in place of four of those initially chosen. These were Messrs. Goddin, Kent, Stearns and Palmer from the original group that had met to form the bank.

The First National opened for business on May 10, and was located in a small room in the fire-blackened customhouse and post office, the only structure standing in the financial district. During that month General Robert E. Lee opened an account.

Richmonders held a meeting at the Capitol on June 20 with a view to devising some means of aiding those who had lost everything in the fire. A ruling by the U. S. Attorney General dashed their hopes. He held that persons owning more than $20,000 worth of property who had not been pardoned or taken the loyalty oath could not sell their property, negotiate a bill of exchange, execute a promissory note or raise money by means of a mortgage.

A delegation went to Washington in the hope of persuading President Johnson to reverse this ruling and institute policies that would permit the rebuilding of Richmond. They received little encouragement. Johnson, who later became much more moderate in his policy, told them that Southerners worth over $20,000 had given too much assistance to the "rebellion." At about this time, "Thad" Stevens of Pennsylvania, one of the most rabid of the radicals in Congress, was advocating confiscation of all "rebel" property and its distribution to the Negroes.

Fighting between Federal soldiers and Negroes occurred frequently in Richmond. Two soldiers shot a black through the head, leaving him for dead near the old Fair Grounds after robbing him of two watches and five dollars, according to the *Dispatch*.

The Virginia press was almost unanimous in opposition to Negro suffrage. The Richmond *Times* said, for example: "The former masters of the Negroes in Virginia have no feeling of unkindness toward them, and they will give them all the encouragement they deserve, but they will not permit them to exercise the right of suffrage, nor will they treat them as anything but 'free Negroes.' They are laborers who are to be paid for their services . . . but vote they shall not."

However outmoded and unfair such views appear today, they were widely held in that era. This is understandable when one bears in mind that the blacks had for two centuries been the slaves of the whites; then suddenly they were not only free but the Federal government was in some respects placing these largely illiterate persons above their former masters. It should be remembered also that eight Northern states refused between 1863 and 1868 to grant Negroes the right to vote.

The Richmond *Enquirer* and *Dispatch* were particularly slow to change their ways. For example, the *Enquirer*'s accounts of proceedings in police court affecting the blacks were sprinkled with such phrases as "forlorn, degraded and sulky eboshins," "bullet-headed, brazen-faced lady of color," "kinky-headed culprit" and "flat-nosed, asp-eyed little darkey."

A correspondent of the New York *Nation* found the Virginia Negroes "decidedly more intelligent than the Negroes of Southern Georgia and South Carolina." He added that they "evince their superiority by their language, dress and alertness of demeanor."

The Virginia General Assembly was urged by Governor Pierpont in 1866 to approve the Fourteenth Amendment, but it refused by an almost unanimous vote. Nine other Southern states also refused. The ten were accordingly punished by the congressional radicals, robbed of their identities and termed "military districts." General John M. Schofield was put in charge of Virginia, which was Military District No. 1. Fortunately Schofield, like Pierpont, was an honest and understanding man.

The right of Negroes to ride on streetcars and railroads was in dispute. Blacks were forbidden under Virginia law to use the horse-drawn cars at all, until the Federal Civil Rights Act was passed in 1866. After that enactment, two classes of cars were established—one for white ladies and their escorts and one for all others, regardless of race or sex. As a result, Richmond blacks engaged in riotous demonstrations in April 1866. A year later there was a major riot, stemming in part from the streetcar situation, and stimulated by incendiary oratory from radical whites and Negroes. Three policemen were badly injured, and a company of Federal troops, with fixed bayonets, was called out by General Schofield to disperse the rioters.

Next day another Negro mob tried to take from the police a Negro who had been arrested for being drunk and disorderly. Blacks threw stones at and fired upon the officers. Federal troops were again called out to restore order. They were then stationed throughout the city to prevent a recurrence.

Richmond's Memorial Day was inaugurated during the spring of 1866. The Oakwood Memorial Association and Hollywood Memorial Association were organized at that time. The Oakwood Association was formed April 19 and held ceremonies in St. John's Episcopal Church May 10, the anniversary of Stonewall Jackson's death. Several speakers delivered addresses. Most business houses closed and hung crape on their doors with the inscription "In Honor of Stonewall Jackson and the Confederate Dead." The Richmond Light Infantry Blues marched to Oakwood and Hollywood cemeteries and placed flowers on the graves of their fallen comrades.

The Hollywood Memorial Association observed Memorial Day on May 31, thus instituting a custom that has survived to the present. Some eight hundred Confederate soldiers and others, under Major Thomas A. Brander, went to Hollywood several days before and set to work cleaning up the Confederate section. Business was suspended on May 31, and a long procession formed in the vicinity of Grace Episcopal Church at Foushee and Main streets, and moved to Hollywood. In line were the First Virginia Regiment, three companies of Howitzers, the Grays, the Fayette Artillery, the Otey, Crenshaw, Purcell, Letcher and Marye batteries and other units. Many vehicles and citizens on foot followed. More than eleven hundred graves of Confederate soldiers were strewn with flowers.

Although Richmond businessmen had been rebuffed in June 1865 in their efforts to begin rebuilding the city's ruined district, the process was somehow gotten under way shortly thereafter. So much so that the *Whig* reported in early October that no fewer than a hundred buildings were under construction. This truly amazing upsurge could not have been accomplished without the aid of Northern capital, since Richmond and Virginia were without such resources. Just how the financing was obtained has never been made public.

The Tredegar works escaped the flames in 1865, thanks to the Tredegar Battalion which barred the way when a mob of escaped convicts or other like elements sought to burn the place down. General Joseph R. Anderson had the foresight during the war to ship quantities of cotton to London. After the fighting was over, he and his associates at the Tredegar realized $190,000 in greenbacks for the cotton, and this enabled them to take the first steps toward getting the great plant back into full production. It had been severely damaged by fire in 1863, and wartime depreciation necessitated considerable rebuilding and renovation. As early as August 1865 the Tredegar began operations.

The Gallego and Haxall mills burned and had to be rebuilt. The Dunlop and Crenshaw mills survived, but wheat from the devastated areas of Virginia was slow in reaching them.

Organization of the Planters National Bank in December 1865 was additional evidence that Richmond was getting back on its feet. The Planters was announced as successor to the Farmers Bank of Virginia, which had gone down with the Confederacy. Samuel C. Robinson was first president and the stockholders were mostly Richmonders. William H. Macfarland, who had been president of the Farmers before the war, was involved in so many business and civic matters that he could not accept the presidency of the new institution at the outset, although he did so soon afterward. Macfarland headed the City Council at the time, and was carrying other civic responsibilities. He resigned as president of the Planters Bank in 1870 and organized a competing institution, the State Bank of Virginia, of which he was also president.

Another significant figure in Richmond's revival was Thomas Branch, who moved from Petersburg to Richmond in 1865. He and his family became leaders in Richmond banking and finance. Thomas Branch was the era's largest benefactor of Virginia's Methodist Church.

Banks were refusing to make loans of less than sixty days' duration in the autumn of 1866, and three years later the minimum was ninety days. The rate was 1¼ to 1½ per cent per month. The scarcity of currency kept interest rates high. Eleven banks were operating in Richmond by midsummer 1867.

Tobacco manufacture, vital to the city before the war, was gradually resumed. Like General Joseph R. Anderson, James Thomas, Jr., Richmond's leading antebellum manufacturer of the leaf, had arranged shrewdly for an overseas account, to be collected at the close of hostilities. Immediately after the bombardment of Fort Sumter, Thomas had shipped all available manufactured tobacco abroad, with the stipulation that he not be paid for it until peace returned. He was estimated to have lost over a million dollars in the war, but his overseas account enabled him to recover and build another fortune. Thomas was a central figure in the revival of Richmond's tobacco industry, the city's most important in the postbellum years. By 1870, there were thirty-eight tobacco factories employing nearly four thousand hands.

No industry made a quicker comeback after the war than the railroads. Five roads connected Richmond with other sections of the state, and all were ripped up by the Union armies to a greater or lesser degree. They were the Richmond, Fredericksburg & Potomac; the Virginia Central; Richmond & Danville; Richmond & Petersburg; and Richmond & York River. Railroad men lost no time in going into action with a view to rebuilding the destroyed carriers. The Virginia Central, under the presidency of Edmund Fontaine, actually got back into operation all the way to Jackson River by late July 1865, although it had suffered almost total destruction in tracks, bridges and cars. The various roads added little new mileage in the early years, but several consolidations were effected.

The James River & Kanawha Canal was to some extent a casualty of the war, although it had been apparent that the canal could not compete on even terms with the railroads. Sheridan's cavalry inflicted severe damage on the waterway from Scottsville to a point within thirty miles of Richmond. In addition, the company's Richmond offices sustained great losses in the evacuation fire. The inevitable end was postponed for some years, but the James River & Kanawha Canal Company finally went out of business in 1880.

Steamship service between Richmond and Norfolk was resumed soon after the surrender.

Inside Richmond, omnibus service was offered from Brook Avenue to Rocketts, beginning in June 1865, with horse-drawn buses leaving each end of the line every fifteen minutes. Horse-drawn streetcars were put back into service in December 1866, operating from Eighth to Twenty-eighth Street.

Despite defeat in the war and the burning of the city, there was occasional gaiety and laughter, as Richmond rose slowly from the ashes. In fact, the young were at times so noisy in evidencing their mirth that a matron who wrote in 1867 of her youth half a century before was shocked. "I confess I have sometimes of late years been startled by a burst of laughter from a pretty young girl," the Richmond belle of 1817 declared in a magazine article. She said, furthermore, that she was "somewhat pained by hearing a group of wild girls and clever young men talking in tones better suited to the mill than a drawing room." The matron added that when she was young "the loud laugh was considered ungraceful and slang words abominable."

On a different level of behavior, the Richmond gangs known as "cats" were having rock battles in all parts of town. Such sinister aggregations as the Gamble Hill Cats, Oregon Hill Cats, Sidney Cats, Brook Road Cats, Basin Bank Cats, First Street Cats, Second Street Cats, Fourth Street Horribles, Fifth Street Cats, Shockoe Hill Cats, Butchertown Cats, Old Market Cats, Church Hill Cats, Clyde Row Gang, Hobo Gang and Park Sparrows, who roosted in the vicinity of Monroe Park, were among those engaged in this internecine warfare. In Manchester another group of rock battlers was operating. Among them were the Terrapin Hill Cats, Baconsville Cats, Diamond Hill Cats, Swamp Poodle Cats, Marx's Field Cats, Hull Street Gang and Decatur Street Gang.

The Butchertown Cats felt so disadvantaged in their historic and long-continued feud with the Shockoe Hill Cats on the heights above that they devised a powerful slingshot capable of heaving half a brick for long distances. Even pistols and shotguns were at times brought into play by various gangs. The result was that there were tragedies, and such a community outcry arose that the battles were more or less terminated. They were revived in milder form a couple of decades later.

Jefferson Davis was brought to Richmond in May 1867 to stand trial on a charge of treason. He had been confined in Fort Monroe for two years, part of the time in irons. Davis had been indicted at Norfolk, with U. S. District Judge John C. Underwood of New York on the bench. Underwood delivered a charge to the grand jury which made various absurd statements concerning Richmond, including one that "licentiousness" had been so prevalent in the city that "probably a majority of the births were illegitimate." The Richmond *Whig* lashed back by terming Underwood an "ignorant blockhead" and "malignant blackguard." The judge retorted by blaming the Richmond press for "the murders, lusts, assassinations, violent and ungoverned passions" which he said prevailed in the Confederate capital. The jurist also declared that in Richmond "the fashionable and popular pulpit had been so prostituted that its full fed ministering gay Lotharios generally recommended the worship of what they most respected—pleasure, property and power." The *Whig* snorted in reply that these assertions were "the most wantonly mendacious, brutally libellous utterances that ever came from the bench in any civilized country."

Jefferson Davis, broken in health and greatly enfeebled by his confinement, came to Richmond for his anticipated trial in the custody of General Henry S. Burton, commandant at Fort Monroe, and stopped at the Spotswood Hotel, Eighth and Main streets. The Spotswood had been almost miraculously spared in the fire two years before.

A huge crowd filled the street in front of the hotel and in the vicinity of the customhouse where the case was to be heard. Davis had been unpopular during the closing years of the war, but his long imprisonment and the inhumane treatment he had received caused him to be regarded now with reverence and even affection.

He was represented by a remarkable array of eminent Northern attorneys, who had come to the conclusion that he was being treated with great injustice and offered their services. The list included Charles O'Conor of New York, probably the leader of the American bar; George Shea of New York; and William Read of Philadelphia. John Randolph Tucker, who had served as attorney general of Virginia, also was one of the defense counsel, together with Judge Robert Ould and James Lyons, both of Richmond. The prosecution was headed by U. S. Attorney General William M. Evarts.

O'Conor requested that the trial proceed at once, but the government declared that this was impossible. Judge Underwood, perhaps impressed by the fact that Davis was represented by such distinguished Northern counsel, said the defendant would be admitted to bail in the sum of $100,000. The bail bond was promptly signed by such onetime foes of the Confederate President as Horace Greeley, editor of the New York *Tribune*, and Gerrit Smith, New York reformer and foe of slavery. Another New Yorker who signed was Cornelius Vanderbilt.

As soon as the court announced that Davis would be admitted to bail, someone ran to a window and shouted to the crowd below on Main Street, "The President is bailed!" A mighty roar of applause greeted the news.

When the formalities were completed and Davis was released from custody, he was escorted to his carriage on Bank Street by Charles O'Conor and Judge Ould. As the three men emerged from the building, they were greeted with "that fierce yell which was first heard at Manassas, and had been the note of victory at Cold Harbor, at Chancellorsville, the Wilderness and wherever battle was fiercest." The "rebel yell" reverberated again as the carriage passed along Main Street to the Spotswood.

Silence fell upon the crowd as the vehicle stopped at the hotel door. Then, as Davis rose from his seat to alight, a deep voice boomed the order, "Hats off, Virginians!" Thousands of men uncovered, as a gesture of respect for the brave man who had led them through four years of desperate conflict and then had suffered for two more years in prison. Jefferson Davis was never tried by the Federal authorities.

The hectic atmosphere that prevailed in Richmond at this time may be glimpsed in an English visitor's account of an attempt by a Richmond editor to "cowhide a New York contemporary." The two men struggled "until their heads went through a glass door in the office of the principal hotel."

While there were complaints in some quarters that former slaves were extremely reluctant to take jobs, many whites were showing a similar aversion to toil. The *Enquirer* said that whereas most whites were "diligently at work . . . others are occupied with vain lamentations and wailing." A few years later the *Whig* declared that idleness among whites had "attained alarming proportions." The paper stated that "they seem to have no further object, desire or hope than to get a 'place' to avoid manual labor."

Industrial training was needed for the blacks, but they appeared to resent the proposed apprenticeship system on the theory that it was a substitute for slavery. This attitude was a serious obstacle in the way of their obtaining work in the mechanical trades.

However, the freedmen were quick to establish small business enterprises, such as barbershops, restaurants, retail stores and real estate operations. They also were active as hack drivers, contractors and undertakers. By 1870 they had deposited in the Freedmen's Bank a total of $318,913, with a balance on that date of over $84,000. Real estate with an assessed value of nearly $1,000,000 had been accumulated, much more than in any other Virginia city.

Interracial feeling was intense at times. Richmond blacks announced in 1866 that they would celebrate the anniversary of the Emancipation Proclamation. Shortly thereafter, the Second African Church burned down. It was believed that hostile whites were responsible.

Yet there was a substantial reservoir of good will between the races during Reconstruction, despite the efforts of agitators and demagogues to foment trouble. Occasional violent outbreaks, such as the Richmond streetcar riots, were by no means typical.

Negroes were nowhere admitted to public inns and hotels. They were allowed in the theaters, but were not permitted to sit in the "dress circle." On the railroads, blacks were usually segregated in the front smoking car. Several who were ejected from first-class coaches filed suit under the Civil Rights Act and were awarded monetary damages.

Carpetbaggers from the North were organizing the blacks by means of a secret society known as the Union League. That agency worked with the Freedmen's Bureau in marshaling the blacks for political activities. Fraternal orders in large numbers also sprang up among the freedmen, and became a dominant influence in their social life. There were more than thirty of these secret orders in Richmond in 1866, and the number increased rapidly thereafter.

At this point there entered upon the Richmond scene an unprincipled rabble-rouser named James W. Hunnicutt. Born in South Carolina, he had lived in Fredericksburg before the war, where he was a slaveowner and secessionist. After Appomattox, Hunnicutt was suddenly metamorphosed into a violent hater of all slaveowners and an advocate of unrestricted Negro suffrage. The New York press quickly became aware of his noxious and evil characteristics. A reporter for the New York World wrote that "none who gaze upon that countenance, so full of cunning and malignity, can ever forget it."

Hunnicutt edited a Richmond journal called the New Nation. He and another radical named Wardwell organized five hundred Negroes who were living in the former Chimborazo Hospital into a military unit, armed them with muskets and sabers, and began drilling them every night. The two agitators also roused the blacks with inflammatory speeches. The group was growing so rapidly that U. S. General A. H. Terry seized their arms and ordered them to disband.

With a view to electing "a loyal governor and loyal congressmen," Hunnicutt summoned the Republicans of Virginia to a convention in Richmond in April 1867. There were 210 delegates, 160 of whom were black.

A group of conservative Negroes in Richmond, led by Solon Johnson, sought opinions from white leaders as to the best course. A meeting of both races was accordingly held in the Richmond Theatre, and Raleigh T. Daniel, prominent attorney, and others spoke. Cooperation with the white leadership was advised. The results were negligible, as the convention of Republican radicals met two days later at the First African Church, with Hunnicutt in complete control.

The convention urged that "rebels" be deprived of all their property and their rights. Both in the church and in Capitol Square Hunnicutt and others delivered incendiary harangues. He urged the Negroes, even boys of ten and girls of twelve, to put the torch to the houses of the whites. During this period a New England agitator, Zedikiah K. Hayward, was arrested for inciting the blacks to "acts of violence, insurrection and war." General Schofield had to call out the militia on several occasions to maintain order.

Another convention of Republican radicals was summoned for August at the First African Church. Its purpose was to review the actions of the April conclave. Richmond Negroes, obeying the orders of Hunnicutt, packed the church. John Minor Botts, who had served a term in jail during the war for his Unionist views, and was far more liberal than the average white Virginian, was refused admittance. Only fifty whites—those who had sat in the April convention—were allowed inside. Negroes who expressed a willingness to cooperate with whites were barred.

Later, Botts was allowed to address the convention. He advised the blacks to work with any respectable whites who were willing to join the Republican party and accept its principles. Fields Cook, a Richmond Negro, endorsed this viewpoint. It did not prevail. The convention approved all acts of Congress, however radical. A delegate who offered a resolution opposing confiscation of the lands of those who served in the Confederate forces was shouted down.

Solon Johnson, who had sought to guide his fellow blacks toward a program of working with the whites, continued to follow that policy. Robert Hobson, another Richmond Negro, led in forming "Conservative Colored Men's Clubs" which attempted to bring the races together instead of driving them apart.

These events preceded the nomination and election of delegates to a constitutional convention called for December. The mass meeting for nominating the Richmond delegation took place in Capitol Square on October 13. Tobacco factories were closed for the day to permit the workmen to attend. Radicals were in complete control. A party consisting of former Democrats and Whigs calling itself Conservatives put forward the names of Governor Pierpont and Franklin Stearns. Stearns, like Botts, had served a term in jail during the war because of his Union sympathies. But this Conservative ticket was steamrollered, and neither Pierpont nor Stearns was nominated. The successful slate was composed of Judge Underwood, whose tirades against Richmond and its inhabitants had infuriated virtually every white in the city; the cold-eyed, fanatical Hunnicutt; "Irish Jim" Morrissey, proprietor of a "low groggery" patronized chiefly by Negroes, and staunch ally of Hunnicutt; and two blacks—Lewis Lindsay and Joseph Cox.

Lindsay was a militant, all-out advocate of Negro rights—a shrewd individual who would speak with great frequency and at excessive length in the convention. He was a janitor at the customhouse, and later led a well-known brass band in Richmond. Cox was termed in the New York *World* "by far the most worthy man in the Richmond delegation," and in the Richmond *Dispatch* "the most moderate man on the Radical ticket." The latter paper said Cox enjoyed "the entire confidence of his colored friends and is infinitely superior in many respects to the men who head the ticket," namely Underwood and Hunnicutt. Cox, like Lindsay, was employed at the customhouse.

When the election was held, the polls were kept open in Richmond for three days, and well into the night on the third day, to enable the blacks to get out their full vote. There was disorder at times, and troops dispersed a mob. Many former Confederates were pronounced ineligible to exercise the ballot, and only 5,382 whites registered in Richmond as against 6,284 blacks. The latter were also successful in getting a larger percentage of their registrants to the polls. The inevitable result was a victory for the entire Radical party slate.

The convention met in the Hall of the House of Delegates on December 3, 1867, with Judge Underwood presiding. No such gathering had ever been seen in Virginia. The hostile Richmond newspapers lost no time in terming it the "Convention of Kangaroos," the "Black Crook Convention" and the "Bones and Banjo Convention." New York was heavily represented among the delegates, with thirteen natives of that state. There were also representatives from Ohio, Massachusetts and Pennsylvania, as well as England, Canada, Scotland and Ireland. The Northern delegates were mainly former Union soldiers who had come to Virginia as invaders. The convention was composed largely of these carpetbaggers, plus white scalawags, i.e. Virginia citizens who sided with the Radicals, and black Virginia delegates. There was a minority of white Virginia Conservatives, almost entirely from the Northern section of the state, the Shenandoah Valley and the southwest. Richmond, the Southside and Tidewater were represented overwhelmingly by delegates strongly hostile to all former Confederates and slaveowners.

The correspondent of the Staunton *Spectator* wrote in January 1868 that "the white Radicals are a motley crew; some of them have apparently little more intelligence than the Negroes." (The blacks, it should be said, had been mostly slaves, and under the law, slaves could not be taught to read and write, although this law was sometimes violated.) White members "rise to pints of order," the Staunton correspondent wrote from the convention hall. He also described a dialogue between a white Radical and a black delegate. The former asked the latter to allow him the floor for a minute. "No," replied the freedman, "I ain't gwine to 'low you nary a minute." He added that he had "sot here and hern 'em talk about taxation. . . ."

A Radical white delegate expressed himself as strongly favoring a capitation tax, but opposing a poll tax. When a "mischievous Conservative" asked him to explain the difference between the two levies, he advanced the remarkable dictum that "a capitation tax is on the head" but "a poll tax is for roads."

U. S. General Benjamin F. Butler, known as "Beast" for his exploits in New Orleans during the war, was invited to speak in Richmond while the convention was in progress. Butler was reputed, rightly or wrongly, to have walked off with quantities of silver spoons while in the Louisiana metropolis. Delegate Jacob N. Liggitt of Rockingham accordingly introduced a resolution in the convention warning the citizens of Richmond "to observe more than ordinary vigilance in the preservation of their plate and silverware."

Butler spoke at the First African Church, which was crowded to the eaves with blacks. A Richmond newspaper commented as follows:

### THE BEAST

Butler spoke, chairman Wardwell smiled, mob applauded. Sublime occasion! Hen-roost and pig-sty thieves forgot their avocation, and chickens and pigs for two hours slept in undisturbed security, while the petty pliers of small trades vied with each other in doing homage to the more successful rascal!

The "Underwood Convention" completed its work, but Hunnicutt's demagoguery was too much for even that bizarre gathering, and his influence waned. However, this had little effect on the outcome, for a constitution was drafted and approved that would unquestionably have placed Virginia under "Negro rule" had it been adopted by the people in its original form.

General Schofield, commander of Military District No. 1, and Horace Greeley of the New York *Tribune* agreed that no Union party could be built in the South on any such basis. Schofield wrote General U. S. Grant to that effect, and ordered postponement of the scheduled popular election for approval or rejection of the constitution.

In the meantime, a group of leading Virginians, headed by Alexander H. H. Stuart of Staunton, and known as the Committee of Nine, embarked upon a bold course. They suggested a plan for "universal suffrage and universal amnesty," under which they agreed that all blacks would be allowed the ballot, but stipulated in return that the disfranchisement and test-oath clauses of the constitution were to be voted on separately from the main body of that document. These clauses, if adopted, would keep the vast majority of former Confederates from both voting and holding office.

One Richmonder, James Neeson, a native of southwest Virginia, was on the Committee of Nine. The committee's program was regarded as highly objectionable by many Conservatives, who could not bring themselves to accept the idea of universal Negro suffrage. Yet nearly all of them finally came to the conclusion that there was no satisfactory alternative. The Committee of Nine succeeded in getting President Grant's approval of the plan, and he obtained the approval of Congress.

The Conservatives set to work for the purpose not only of defeating the disfranchisement and test-oath clauses in the referendum, but also of electing a Conservative governor and legislature. Their gubernatorial nominee was Gilbert C. Walker, a moderate New York Republican who had moved to Norfolk during the war. The radical Republicans named former Union General H. H. Wells of New York, who had succeeded Pierpont as provisional governor of Virginia. The campaign was hard fought, and both sides used improper methods. Much of the Virginia press, led by the Richmond *Enquirer*, advocated the discharge of Negro workingmen who voted the Republican ticket. Such threats were made by employers in Richmond and other cities.

Shortly before the election on July 6, 1869, a group of about 250 Conservative Richmond blacks who were supporting Walker held a barbecue and invited a number of white leaders. The object was to promote white-black cooperation for the good of both. A crowd was standing on a suspension bridge linking two islands in the James River when the bridge collapsed. Several persons were killed and many injured. Among the dead was the banker and civic leader Colonel James R. Branch, Conservative nominee for the U. S. Senate. The procession from St. Paul's Church to his grave in Hollywood was said to have been nearly two miles long.

The results of the election were as cheering to Richmond as the death of Colonel Branch was depressing. The test-oath and disfranchising clauses were badly defeated, the rest of the constitution was approved almost unanimously. Walker was elected governor and an overwhelmingly Conservative legislature was chosen. Richmond voters backed Walker by a small majority and stood against the objectionable clauses by a somewhat better majority. The large black vote in Richmond accounted for the closeness of the election in the city.

The "Underwood Constitution," so-called because Judge Underwood presided over the convention, was not as bad as might have been expected. Most of the Richmond press damned it regularly for years, as did many Richmonders. The fact is, however, that once it was divested of the disfranchising and test-oath features, the document had a good deal to recommend it.

First, it provided for a statewide system of public schools, something Virginia had never had. It also established the secret ballot, which had not previously been in effect. There were changes in the tax structure that were both good and bad, but the organic law's new incarnation was far from being the monstrosity its critics were fond of describing.

Education in Richmond, both on the public school and the college level, took an upturn during the years following Appomattox. Richmond College, used as a hospital during the war, opened again on October 1, 1866, with ninety students and five professors. The Medical College of Virginia, which had never ceased operations, and was the only medical school in the Confederacy of which this was true, was able to function on a more adequate scale. Virginia Union University had its origins in 1867 in what had been Lumpkin's slave jail. Its parent institution was the Richmond Institute, established by the Freedmen's Bureau. It evolved into Richmond Theological Seminary, a school for training black clergymen. The seminary moved in 1870 from the former jail to what had been the Union Hotel, a Confederate military hospital during the war. Out of this grew the Virginia Union University that we know today.

The idea of providing a system of public schools, supported by general taxation, had been fought by many Richmonders and other conservative Virginians before and after the war. The Richmond *Whig*, normally more forward-looking than most of the Richmond newspapers during the years immediately following the close of hostilities, was one of those that expressed opposition. Public schools were "a Yankee error," the *Whig* declared in 1866.

A group of Richmond citizens, apparently acting under the impetus of the Freedmen's Bureau, petitioned City Council in April 1869 to provide a citywide system of public schools. This was several months before the voters of Virginia ratified the new constitution, calling for a statewide system. By the fall of that year, following the referendum, a City School Board was organized, with Andrew H. Washburn, one of the teachers working under the Freedmen's Bureau, as city superintendent.[1]

A notable private school was founded in Richmond six months after Lee's surrender by John Peyton McGuire, Jr., a Confederate veteran and son of the Reverend John Peyton McGuire, headmaster of Episcopal High School at the outbreak of the war. The school began on a small scale at Fifth and Cary streets, and moved half a dozen times before locating over a bar, market and plumber's shop at the northeast corner of Belvidere and Main streets. This site, which was within a few feet of the tracks of all north- and southbound trains along Belvidere, would hardly be regarded today as ideal for the instruction of youth. Yet it was occupied from 1888 to 1914, at the height of the school's fame—excellent evidence that a high level of scholastic achievement does not necessarily go hand in hand with lavish and expensive equipment. The beloved and admired principal, known to his boys as "Old Boss," was not only an inspiring teacher, but he had for his guiding star the principle that nothing counted so much as character, and that honorable conduct was the *sine qua non* of a gentleman. More will be said of McGuire's University School in a later chapter.

The newspapers of Richmond were almost completely wiped out in the evacuation fire of 1865, but several were got back into operation within a short time. A few papers were temporarily suppressed by the Federal authorities for expressing sentiments which the latter did not approve. There were no fewer than seven morning papers in Richmond and one evening paper in the period following the war.

Newspaper editors often went armed as they walked about the Richmond streets, as did many of their readers. Gunfire in broad daylight was not unknown. Reference has been made to the exchange of shots on Franklin Street between John M. Daniel of the *Examiner* and Marmaduke Johnson. Robert Dixon, clerk of the Confederate House of Representatives, was fatally shot on Bank Street in 1863 by Robert S. Forde. Three years later, J. M. Hanna of the *Examiner* and R. D. Ogden, stage manager of the Richmond Theatre, exercised their shooting irons on each other in Seventh Street. Neither was hit, but both were hauled into court.

The most sensational of such *rencontres* occurred in January 1866 in the rotunda of the Capitol while the General Assembly was in session. The fusillade grew out of articles in the *Examiner* critical of the publishers of the *Enquirer*. Henry Rives Pollard of the *Examiner* and Nathaniel Tyler and William D. Coleman, the *Enquirer's* publishers, were the participants. "The three gentlemen drew their pistols," says the account in the *Dispatch* of January 6, "and Mr. Pollard took his stand behind the statue of Washington and commenced firing." Pollard's fire "was returned by Mr. Coleman with a single barrel pistol," whereas "Mr. Tyler did not fire." No one was wounded, but a bullet knocked the marble tassel from Washington's cane. Pollard was tried and reprimanded by the House of Delegates.[2]

This same Henry Rives Pollard, brother of Edward A. Pollard, the even more celebrated journalist of that era, was shot and killed two years later at the corner of Fourteenth and Main streets. Pollard, aged thirty-five, was then editor of a journal called *Southern Opinion*, which had published material deeply resented by a Richmond citizen, James Grant. It involved Grant's sister. Grant stationed himself in a second-story window across from the entrance to Pollard's office, and killed him instantly with a load of buckshot as he was approaching the door. It took the jury only forty minutes to acquit the assassin.

The years immediately following the war were years of struggle in which nearly everybody had difficulty making ends meet. For example, Dr. Hunter McGuire built up a large practice in Richmond soon after leaving the Confederate service, but hardly any of his patients had money with which to pay medical bills. He said the only way he managed to keep going was by means of the fees he got for serving as a surgeon at duels between Union officers. He got $100 per duel.

The mood during Reconstruction was often one of discouragement and depression. Traveling lecturers were much sought after, especially those who might be able to cheer the populace up with humorous disquisitions. George W. Bagby was perhaps the most popular of these. His "Bacon and Greens" lecture was frequently in demand.

During these years, Miss Elizabeth Van Lew lived in her Church Hill mansion, shunned by nearly everybody because of her record as a Civil War spy. President U. S. Grant gave tangible evidence that he appreciated her services by appointing her postmistress of Richmond only fifteen days after his inauguration in 1869. She served for eight years, and some of the Richmond press, surprisingly, praised her for her efficiency. She then went to Washington, where she was employed in the Post Office Department. When Grover Cleveland assumed the presidency, she lost her position and returned to Richmond. Betty Van Lew was in financial straits, but these were relieved by Colonel Paul Revere of Massachusetts, whom she had befriended when he was in Libby Prison. Finally, she lived alone with her niece and forty cats. In 1900, she died, and Massachusetts admirers marked her grave in Shockoe Cemetery with the following:

ELIZABETH VAN LEW

1818    1900

She risked everything that is dear to man—friends, fortune, comfort, health, life itself, all for the one absorbing desire of her heart, that slavery might be abolished and the Union preserved.

THIS BOULDER
FROM THE CAPITOL HILL IN BOSTON
IS A TRIBUTE FROM HER
MASSACHUSETTS FRIENDS

Reconstruction in Virginia came to an end in January 1870, although Charles Sumner of Massachusetts described the Old Dominion as "smoking with rebellion." The Federal garrison was withdrawn from Richmond, and Military District No. 1 was no more.

Morale in Richmond took an upturn. The city's population was shown in the census of 1870 to be just over 51,000, as against less than 38,000 a decade before. The city contained nearly 28,000 whites and slightly more than 23,000 Negroes.

Although military rule had ended, there were significant vestiges of Reconstruction. This was evident in the controversy that erupted over the governance of Richmond. The Conservative-controlled General Assembly authorized Governor Walker to appoint a new City Council. That body elected as mayor Henry K. Ellyson, publisher of the *Dispatch*. But George Chahoon of New York, who had been serving as mayor, refused to vacate the office. There followed a period in which two rival mayors and rival police forces tried to gain control, and there was a chaotic state of affairs. Ellyson deputized Conservatives as members of his force of gendarmes and they surrounded Chahoon and his followers in a police station, cutting them off from food and water. U. S. General E. R. S. Canby, acting without authority, sent three companies of soldiers from Camp Grant to release Chahoon, and the Ellyson forces retreated. Chahoon and his largely black police then got control of another police station. This dispute finally landed in the Virginia Supreme Court of Appeals. That tribunal convened to hear the case April 27, 1870, on the top floor of the Capitol. Hundreds of persons crowded every foot of space in the courtroom and the gallery.

Just as the proceedings were about to begin, there was a loud cracking noise and the gallery gave way under the weight of the crowd. It fell onto the courtroom floor, along with its struggling mass of people. This additional burden caused that floor to collapse, hurling everybody in the courtroom through the ceiling of the Hall of the House of Delegates a distance of some forty feet to the ground level below. Hundreds of men fell, along with bricks, splintered planks, iron bars, plaster, desks and chairs. Shrieks and moans were heard through the dense cloud of dust that billowed up and made it impossible to see who was dead and who had survived. Many were crushed to death, others were suffocated. When the cloud lifted, human forms covered with dust and blood were revealed. They were carried or they staggered to the Capitol lawn, where they were often unrecognizable until the dirt and gore was cleaned from their faces.

There was pandemonium in and around Capitol Square. Wives, mothers, relatives and friends rushed to the scene, as did every doctor within reach. Ambulances, hacks, carriages and other vehicles were commandeered to take the wounded to hospitals or their homes. The dead were placed temporarily in the Senate chamber or under the trees in the square.

Sixty-two men lost their lives and 251 others were injured. There were no women in the courtroom at the time. It was a disaster almost comparable to the theater fire of fifty-nine years before. If the House of Delegates had been in session, nearly all of its members probably would have been killed.

Among the dead were Patrick Henry Aylett, grandson of Patrick Henry and prominent attorney and journalist; Powhatan Roberts, attorney; J. W. D. Bland, black senator from Prince Edward; John Turner, member of the House of Delegates from Page County; and Major Samuel Hairston of Henry County.

Henry K. Ellyson and George Chahoon, the rival mayors, were both injured, as were Thomas S. Bocock of Lynchburg, Speaker of the House of Delegates; W. Dallas Chesterman and W. C. Elam, journalists; George L. Christian, attorney; Peachy L. Grattan, reporter for the Court of Appeals; Robert R. Howison, historian; Judge John A. Meredith; and ex-Governor H. H. Wells.

Richmond was aghast over this tragedy, as was the entire state. The city had been recovering slowly from the war and its aftermath, but another disaster had struck. All business houses were closed, and many hung crape on their doors. Street vehicles also displayed crape, as did railroad trains coming into Richmond. New York, Baltimore, Washington and other cities took up collections for the relief of Virginia's capital.

In the near-hysteria that prevailed, resolutions were offered in the State Senate calling for demolition of the Capitol and the erection of another. Fortunately, this idea was abandoned, and it was decided to rebuild and strengthen the shattered structure. However, the catastrophe caused the municipal authorities to pull down their handsome city hall, on the theory that it was unsafe. It turned out to be extremely sturdy, but by then the building had been wrecked beyond recall.

The members of the Virginia Supreme Court of Appeals were uninjured in the Capitol disaster, since they had not entered the hall, but were about to do so, when the floor fell.

They convened two days after the crash, and rendered a decision favorable to the Ellyson administration. It was installed, but a month later an election was held, at the court's direction, and the Chahoon forces won. However, the messenger carrying the ballot box from the precinct that cast the biggest vote for Chahoon was attacked in broad daylight and robbed of the ballots. The Election Commission, dominated by Conservatives, recognized only the remaining returns, and awarded the contest to Ellyson. Still another election was called, and the Conservatives apparently won, although the Radicals charged widespread skulduggery. A.

M. Keiley was elected mayor this time around. Some months later, Conservatives sent Chahoon to prison on charges of implication in a forgery. He was later pardoned by Governor Walker, reportedly on condition that he leave the state.[3]

A protracted drought troubled Richmond and Virginia in the summer and early fall of 1870. Suddenly, in the western areas of the Commonwealth there were enormous downpours of rain that caused the James to rise rapidly to almost unprecedented heights. Mayo's Bridge, battered by floods for nearly a century, was washed away once more, and the surging waters carried houses, mills, timbers, furniture and trees downstream. Lower Main Street from Fifteenth to Seventeenth was several feet under water, and a "large schooner" was put into service to ferry passengers across. There was tremendous property damage along the river front.

The city was beginning to recover from this calamity when news came that Robert E. Lee had died in Lexington on October 12. Richmond's grief was profound and unashamed. Bells tolled throughout the city next day from 6 A.M. to 6 P.M. and business was halted. Public buildings and private residences by the hundreds hung crape, and even the United States flag on the customhouse was lowered to half-mast. The City Council chamber was draped in mourning for six months. A memorial service was held in First Presbyterian Church, at which Jefferson Davis spoke and many of Lee's former officers and soldiers were present. The movement to erect a monument in Richmond to the great Confederate leader was begun.

The year 1870 was brought to a close by the burning of the Spotswood Hotel on Christmas Eve. At least eight persons died, four more were missing and never accounted for, and numerous others were injured. The Spotswood had played a major role during its decade of existence. Most of the Confederate dignitaries had stopped there, and Union generals did likewise after Richmond fell. Cause of the fire was never discovered. The menu for next day's Christmas dinner was saved from the flames, and would seem to be proof that there was no shortage of food in Richmond at that time. Partridges, roasts, fish, lobster, goose, duck, calf's head and venison were among the entrees, along with salads and cold dishes, plus thirteen vegetables, ten pastries and six desserts. The price was omitted, and of course the meal was never served.

"The Year of Disasters" was the term applied to 1870, in view of the foregoing series of calamities, beginning with the lethal collapse of the courtroom floor in the Capitol, and continuing on through the drought, the flood, the death of Lee and the burning of the Spotswood.

Yet Richmond's morale seems to have held up well. Robert Somers, an Englishman who visited the city near the end of the year, wrote:

"There is no dejection, no loss of honorable pride, and little repining at the bitter consequences of the war, but a resolve, more deeply felt than strongly expressed, not only to accept the situation, but to turn it to account of improvement, and to build up anew the prosperity of the old commonwealth, which the Virginians love with an ardor and a faith in the future hardly credible in a community so greatly shattered."

# SIXTEEN

## Putting the War Behind

RICHMOND held its first large postwar Fourth of July celebration in 1871. Independence Day had gone virtually unobserved in the city since the South's surrender. Bitterness and grief were so poignant and widespread that the people couldn't bring themselves to hold elaborate ceremonies based on the concept of national unity.

But when July 4, 1871, arrived, sentiment was changing. The Glorious Fourth was appropriately observed with fireworks and oratory. W. Dallas Chesterman wrote that the sight of young Richmonders "making independence speeches and drinking American cocktails" was the final evidence that "the past had been left behind, the reconstruction successfully completed, and the era of good feeling and reconciliation finally and fully restored."

Edward A. Pollard, who had found nothing good in the Union, the constitution or the liberated Negro, underwent an almost total change of heart. He said in 1868 that he had seen the strength of the national government during the years of conflict, and that this had inspired in him and other Southerners a feeling of national unity. Two years later, in *Lippincott's Magazine*, he was unrestrained in his tributes to the freedmen— their industry, thrift and sobriety, and their desire for education. He admitted that all this was directly contrary to what he had confidently predicted would happen when the slaves were emancipated.

The optimism of 1871 was shattered in 1873 when a financial and business panic hit the entire country. Bankruptcy of serveral Northern railroads that were heavily indebted to the Tredegar Iron Works for railroad iron and other equipment threw the Richmond concern into a receivership. Joseph R. Anderson acted as receiver until 1879, at which time it was announced that the Tredegar's debt had been successfully funded. The panic of 1873 had numerous other serious effects in Richmond. Two

36. First faculty of the University College of Medicine, 1894. Front row: left to right: Dr. Thomas J. Moore, Dr. Hunter H. McGuire, president, Dr. L. M. Cowardin. Second row: Dr. William S. Gordon, Dr. J. Allison Hodges, Dr. Jacob Michaux, Dr. Joseph A. White. Third row: T. Wilber Chelf, Dr. Landon B. Edwards, Dr. Moses D. Hoge, Jr., Dr. Charles L. Steel, Dr. Charles H. Chalkley. Fourth row: Dr. Paulus Irving, Dr. Stuart McGuire, Dr. John F. Winn. Rear row: Dr. Charles V. Carrington, Dr. James N. Ellis, Dr. Edward McGuire, Tom Haskins, morgue attendant, and Dr. John Dunn.

37. Capitol Square in the nineties under a blanket of snow, before the
eastern and western wings were added.

38. Sir Moses Ezekiel, the most famous sculptor Virginia has produced. He lived in Rome for many years, and was decorated by the Emperor of Germany and two kings of Italy. He was, however, proudest of all that he fought at the Battle of New Market with the VMI cadets.

39. Wedding party at Algoma, Buckingham County, for the marriage in 1888 of Miss Katy Logan and Dr. Henry Dixon Bruns of New Orleans, with many prominent Richmonders present.

Front row, left to right: John Skelton Williams with Mul Logan in his lap, Patrick H. C. Cabell, Thomas Adkins, Edward W. Scott, Charles Stringfellow, Beverley B. Munford, William C. Bentley.

Second row: Miss Minnie Cox (later Mrs. Samuel C. Graham), Miss Virginia Archer, Miss Elise Strother (later Mrs. Frederic W. Scott), Miss Elise Williams, Miss Lulu Logan (later Mrs. William C. Bentley). The small girls behind this row are Lily Logan (later Mrs. Albert Morrill) and Lena Logan (later Mrs. Douglas Forsythe).

Third row: Dr. Charles Minnegerode, rector of St. Paul's Church, Richmond; Miss Fannie Silvey, Cabell Robinson, Miss Bertha Leeds, Miss Florine Nolting (later Mrs. E. B. Thomason), Miss Bessie Lay (later Mrs. George C. Lafferty), Miss Frances Scott, General T. M. Logan, Miss Margaret Logan (later Mrs. Hartwell Cabell), Miss Martha Snead, Miss Mary McCaw, Miss Cyane Williams (later Mrs. E. L. Bemiss), Miss Katy Logan (in black, the bride), Thomas N. Carter, Dr. Henry Dixon Bruns (with sideburns, the groom), E. L. Bemiss and George Snowden, VMI cadet.

Back row: John F. Alexander of New York, Miss Mary Cox (later Mrs. Richmond T. Minor), Miss Anna Boykin and Eugene C. Massie.

40. Mrs. Charles Dana Gibson, née Irene Langhorne, one of the greatest beauties in Virginia history, is shown in a hitherto unpublished crayon portrait by her husband, the famous creator of the "Gibson girl." Irene's marriage in 1895 to the noted artist from Massachusetts in St. Paul's Church was the social event of the season.

41. Mrs. James Brown Potter, née May Handy of Richmond, was Irene Langhorne's only serious rival among the Gay Nineties belles at White Sulphur Springs and other resorts. May Handy was as fabulously beautiful as Irene Langhorne. The suitors for both numbered in the dozens.

42. Miss Elizabeth Van Lew, the noted Union spy during the Civil War, is shown in the garden of her Richmond mansion. The historic and picturesque structure was demolished after her death, pursuant to a stupid decision of the City School Board that the site was needed for a public school.

43. What was left of the famous Swan Tavern on the north side of Broad Street between Eighth and Ninth is shown in this photograph taken in 1903. Erected in the late eighteenth century, its guests included Patrick Henry, James Madison, George Mason, Edmund Pendleton, Thomas Jefferson and Edgar Allan Poe.

44. Part of the parade down Franklin Street at the Confederate reunion of 1907. The ladies are members of the United Daughters of the Confederacy, and the bearded gentleman is, of course, a Confederate veteran. The monuments to General J. E. B. Stuart and President Jefferson Davis were unveiled at this reunion, which was attended by thousands of veterans and their families.

45. John Powell, the internationally known pianist and composer, in a little-known portrait painted when he was a young man.

46. Mrs. Benjamin B. (Lila Meade) Valentine, the only woman who has been honored with a memorial tablet in Virginia's Capitol. She was a pioneer in the fields of education, race relations, health and women's rights.

small banks failed, several manufacturing plants closed and many people were thrown out of work. There was suffering, and the City Council and other organizations tried to help those in want. As late as 1877 the crisis was by no means over, as indicated by the fact that there were approximately 175 applicants for every vacancy on the police force.

Women who had lost husbands, sons or brothers in the war still wore heavy mourning. A visitor who happened to be in Richmond on Memorial Day said he saw "thousands of ladies dressed in black wander silently and tearfully among the graves."

Despite the mourning and the low state of business there was occasional gaiety on Richmond's "seven hills." The city has often been compared to Rome with its seven hills, but there has been no agreement as to which Richmond hills are meant. Among those mentioned are Church Hill, Gamble's Hill, Oregon Hill, Shockoe Hill, Libby Hill, Chimborazo Hill, Navy Hill, Union Hill and Maddox Hill.

The Richmond German, an aristocratic organization devoted to terpsichorean enjoyments, was founded in 1870 in the home of Mr. and Mrs. John H. Montague in Linden Row, with Mr. Montague as the first president. The word "German" has no Teutonic connotations and signifies an ultra-formal dance with "figures." The first German, held in the Montague home shortly after the founding, is described by Eda Carter Williams, as follows:

"The gentlemen came in their 'Prince Alberts' which had been laid away during the war years. The etiquette was to be strictly ordered. Ladies wore gowns ingeniously renovated from pre-war finery. White gloves were obligatory, for no gentleman would have dreamed of taking a lady's hand or enclosing her 18-inch waist with bare hands. At least a foot of daylight must come between the partners as they whirled, swooped, reversed and stepped to a polka, a schottische or a Strauss waltz."

However, there were several Germans in Richmond during the late years of the century. There was the Monday German, which was the oldest, and there were the Tuesday and Friday Germans, often with overlapping memberships.

Episcopal Bishop Francis M. Whittle was sorely troubled by the dancing that went on in Richmond during these years. From the pulpit of Monumental Church he denounced the round dance and the waltz, and declared that "this scandal is not to be tolerated." The bishop added that he understood the "dreadful and sinful habit of intemperance appears to be on the increase, even among members of the Episcopal Church." Bishop Whittle also shook up the parishioners by prohibiting flowers in the churches at Easter.[1]

The German element in Richmond was lively and addicted to music, dancing and beer. Members of the Gesang-Verein Virginia raised their voices in song each week at Saenger Hall on Seventh Street. A *Saengerfest* was held in 1873, with German singing societies from New York, Philadelphia, Baltimore and Washington as guests. Parades, concerts and brass bands were on the program, and the exuberant Teutons appeared in full regalia.

Richmond's Germania Maennerchor sponsored dances on a regular basis, with programs printed in German. A program for a *Masken Ball* on March 7, 1876, shows a *Tanz-Programm* which included no fewer than eighteen dances, and followed a *Concert-Programm* of fifteen numbers. The dances were polonaises, polkas, mazurkas, schottisches, waltzes, quadrilles, varsoviennes and "galops." Edward Lehr was chairman of both the arrangements and dance committees.

Two well-known men's clubs, the Westmoreland and Richmond Club, were founded. The Westmoreland, which dated from 1877, continued for sixty years, most of the time in the former Stanard-Macfarland residence at Sixth and Grace streets. The Virginia accents heard in these sanctuaries for males were remarked upon by a visitor from the North. He said that educated and refined people actually pronounced door "doah" and floor "floah," while they "almost invariably allude to our late unpleasantness as the 'waw.'"

The Richmond Club at the northwest corner of Third and Franklin was the scene of a fateful encounter in 1873 between two of the city's most popular and admired young men, John B. Mordecai and Page McCarty. It led to a duel in which Mordecai was mortally wounded and McCarty sustained physical and psychological damage from which he never recovered.

The beautiful Mary Triplett was the innocent cause of this tragic encounter. She was one of Richmond's dazzling belles, a classic blonde whom a contemporary described as "a veritable daughter of the Gods, divinely fair and most divinely tall . . . with wondrous expressive eyes." She and Mattie Ould were the two reigning beauties of that particular era, both in Richmond and at the White Sulphur Springs. Miss Ould was not only lovely to look upon but her wit was famous. When a lawyer noted for his tall tales and bibulous habits boasted that he had earned a $30,000 fee and spent it all on a single spree, Mattie commented, paraphrasing Gray's "Elegy," that she might doubt the "storied earn" but she found it easy to credit the "animated bust."

John Mordecai, nephew of Samuel Mordecai, was deeply in love with Mary Triplett, and a bit of verse appeared one morning in the *Enquirer* which roused him to anger. It read as follows:

*The First Figure in the German*
When Mary's queenly form I press, in Strauss's latest waltz
I would as well her lips caress, although those lips be false.
For still with fire love tips his darts, and kindles up anew

The flame which once consumed my heart, when those dear lips were true.
Of form so fair, of faith so faint, if truth were only in her,
Though she'd be the sweetest saint, I'd still feel like a sinner.

Mordecai took great offense at the lines, and accused McCarty of having written them. Mordecai was paying court to Mary Triplett at the time, whereas McCarty was said to have been engaged to her previously. McCarty admitted his authorship, but said he was referring to another Mary, and the matter seemed to blow over. But a young woman with a vicious tongue began circulating the report that McCarty had written the lines about Mary Triplett and had been afraid to admit it. McCarty was "put in a terrible fury."

He and Mordecai happened to meet soon thereafter in the bar of the Richmond Club, and heated words were exchanged. Mordecai knocked McCarty down with a terrific blow in the face and threw himself on him, pinning him to the floor. They were separated by friends, but in those days such an event made a summons to "the field of honor" inevitable.

They met on May 9 at six o'clock in the late afternoon behind Oakwood Cemetery. Both men had served in the Confederate forces and they were calm as they looked into one another's gun barrels. Neither was hit at the first fire but both went down after the second. Seriously wounded, they lay on the ground for several hours, while their surgeons and seconds worked on them and sent for carriages to take them back to Richmond. Much time was spent in whittling fence rails to place across the carriage seats, so the suffering men could be in a recumbent position. Meanwhile, Chief of Police Poe arrived and arrested everybody concerned except the two surgeons, Dr. Hunter McGuire and Dr. J. Dorsey Cullen.

Mordecai was taken to the home of his uncle, Major E. T. D. Myers, at the southeast corner of Belvidere and Franklin streets. He lingered there in great pain until May 14, and in his dying moments gave one of his seconds, William L. ("Buck") Royall, a message "for his sweetheart"—presumably Mary Triplett, although Royall mentions no name in his *Reminiscences*.

McCarty was fined $500 and sentenced to jail, but his health was such that Governor Kemper ruled that he would not have to serve the sentence. He finally recovered from his physical wound, but was never the same again. Once joyous, witty and outgoing, he became morose and withdrawn, seemingly haunted for the rest of his life with remorse over the killing of his onetime friend.

The seconds in the duel had been admitted to bail immediately after the event, but they were all clapped into jail on charges of murder when Mordecai died. These were some of Richmond's most prominent citizens —William R. Trigg and William L. Royall, seconds for Mordecai, and Colonel W. B. Tabb and John S. Meredith for McCarty. They stayed in jail for more than a month, making unsuccessful efforts to obtain their release. Finally they got out through the good offices of Judge B. W. Lacy of New Kent County, and were placed under bond of $5,000 each. They were all acquitted later.

Mary Triplett, worshiped by adoring swains for a decade, married Philip Haxall on April 14 of the following year, in the home of her widowed mother, with the Reverend Charles Minnegerode performing the ceremony. One week later, on the night of April 21, fire broke out in the Haxall, Crenshaw Mills—owned in part by Philip Haxall. The mills were destroyed but were later rebuilt. Mary Triplett Haxall continued to be a sensation at the White Sulphur and the Rockbridge Alum for more than a dozen years. She died childless, of a sudden heart attack, in 1890. Mattie Ould, the other great belle of the era, married Oliver Schoolcraft, and died in childbirth the following year. Her favorite song had been "Under the Daisies"; they sang it at her funeral and planted daisies on her grave.[2]

Completion of the Ninth Street Bridge across the James was a noteworthy event of 1873. Baptism by immersion of fifty-five Negroes in the millrace at the Richmond end of the span by the Reverend John Jasper, a black Baptist preacher, was the principal event incident to the opening. Jasper would soon become nationally famous by virtue of his sermon "The Sun Do Move."

The manufacture of chewing tobacco and the milling of flour went forward in Richmond on a substantial scale, despite the depression. When the cigarette came into vogue a few years later, cigarette manufacture was added, and the making of plug became less and less important. The city's flour mills were operating at a good pace, although they had lost many of their markets, at least temporarily, during the Civil War. The Gallego Mills, rebuilt since the fire of 1865, were producing 1,500 barrels a day. However, Minneapolis millers got into full production a few years later, and took away some of Richmond's business.

Coal mining continued to be an important resource in the Richmond area during the years immediately following Appomattox. The U.S. census for 1870 showed that four active mines in the Richmond basin produced more than 60,000 tons—nearly all of the coal mined in Virginia that year. In 1873, however, coal was discovered in Tazewell County, and the fields of southwest Virginia and West Virginia became steadily more significant. By 1904 continuous production had ceased in the Richmond basin. It was only intermittent thereafter.

The Valentine family founded an important Richmond industry in the latter part of the nineteenth century, based on a formula for beef extract. Mann S. Valentine, the first member of the family to settle in Richmond, came to the city at age twenty from his home in King William County. He was given charge of the penitentiary commissary, and managed it with much skill. With his demonstrated talent for trade he entered the dry goods business, and was highly successful. Valentine built a handsome combined residence and store in 1850, with the residence fronting on Capitol Street and the store on Broad at Ninth. Part of the large structure was later the Park Hotel.

His son, Mann S. Valentine II, inherited his father's business acumen and was even more devoted to literature, art, music, history and science. It was he who devised the beef extract formula which restored the family fortune wrecked in the war—a formula known and praised on five continents. Valentine's Meat Juice first made its appearance on a small scale in Richmond in 1871, and six years later was so successful that the company opened a large new plant. Its business grew rapidly, and the Empress of Russia wrote to express her thanks for meat juice used in the Russo-Turkish War. After President Garfield was shot in 1881, it was announced that he had been having the extract for breakfast, with toast. Valentine's Meat Juice soon was winning international awards in this country and Europe. It was used on expeditions to both the North and South Pole.

After Richmond had passed through the hectic Reconstruction era, the city was involved in the jarring controversies over building and consolidating railroads and "readjusting" the public debt. Throughout the period, General William Mahone, the "Hero of the Crater" in the Civil War and a consummate politician, was a central figure.

Mahone's war record won the high commendation of General Robert E. Lee, but his small stature—he weighed only about a hundred pounds—and his squeaky voice made his military prowess seem incongruous. He early manifested a genius for politics and railroad building that catapulted him to the forefront in Virginia.

Richmond was a railroad center of astonishing importance in the years immediately following the war. In 1868, the city received nearly 13,000,000 pounds of freight—almost as much as Philadelphia, Baltimore and Norfolk combined. The following year the total was 18,725,000 pounds—more than the three above-mentioned cities put together, and exceeded only by New York.[3] The explanation may lie, at least partially, in abnormally large consignments of materials for rebuilding Richmond's burnt district.

Richmond business and shipping interests fought Mahone's plan for consolidating several small railroads, on the theory that consolidation was primarily for the upbuilding of Norfolk and would damage Richmond. They also contended that it would be harmful to their trade with Lynchburg. The legislature, nevertheless, approved Mahone's plan overwhelmingly, and the Atlantic, Mississippi & Ohio came into being. It linked the Atlantic Ocean with the Ohio and Mississippi rivers, passing from Norfolk to Bristol via Petersburg and Lynchburg. Supporters of the consolidation argued that it did no serious damage to Richmond, and showed that much of the freight carried by the A.M.&O. came to Virginia's capital. The A.M.&O. went into the hands of receivers in 1876, as a result of the business depression, and the new purchasers changed the name to Norfolk & Western.

Railroad facilities in Richmond were often criticized. This was especially true of the R.F.&P. railroad tracks along Broad Street westward from Eighth. The arrangement had been objected to for thirty years, and had been brought before the Council several times. Finally, in 1873 one of the horses drawing a streetcar was frightened by a railroad locomotive and ran away. The streetcar ran over a Richmond man, Thomas Crummitt, and killed him. A mob formed, marched westward to Screamersville, placed logs across the railroad tracks and threatened to kill the first R.F.& P. engineer who tried to pass. They were tearing up the rails when police appeared and dispersed them. The use of steam locomotives on Broad Street was forbidden by the Council in 1874, and the cars were pulled down the street thereafter by horses, with a Negro driver blowing a tin horn on the front platform. The tracks were not removed until the middle nineties.

The R.F. & P.'s Byrd Street Station at Byrd and Eighth, where the trains from New York to Florida stopped, had only rudimentary facilities, and none of the other depots in the city was adequate, even by the standards of that day. The Byrd Street Station was reached from the north through a 600-foot tunnel under Gamble's Hill. Later, Elba Station, a small facility, was built at Broad and Pine, and was in use until handsome Broad Street Station was constructed in 1919.

The building of a 4,000-foot tunnel under Church Hill by the Chesapeake & Ohio Railway, to connect with its marine terminus at Rocketts Landing, was a noteworthy enterprise of the seventies. State and municipal bodies were largely subservient to the railroads in that era, and Richmond's City Council seldom mustered up the courage to buck the carriers. The city's lawmakers offered to provide $200,000 toward the tunnel's construction, but the C.&O. pronounced the sum unsatisfactory. Council met at once in special session, greatly increased the amount and rescinded the conditions originally stipulated.

Various accidents, one of them fatal, plagued the builders of the tunnel. A dangerous fissure opened on Twenty-fourth Street, and those living nearby were told to evacuate. Flames from broken gas mains shed a lurid glow over the scene at night, and there was danger of setting fire to adjacent houses. Then the tunnel collapsed, with a sound "like musketry," between Twenty-fourth and Twenty-fifth streets, and a huge hole opened which wrecked three houses and permanently damaged Third Presbyterian Church. Despite all this, the tunnel was completed in the winter of 1873–74. Direct rail traffic between western Virginia and Newport News was thus inaugurated. A trestle skirting Church Hill near the James was substituted for the tunnel in 1901.

Steamer connections via James River with Norfolk and New York were good in the seventies. The Virginia Steamship Company and the Old Dominion Company were rival operators. Most of the vessels were wooden, but "iron ships" were coming into use. Both passenger and freight were carried. The latter included not only fruits and vegetables but manufactured articles and such commodities as copper and marble.

Although the Atlantic, Mississippi & Ohio Railroad went into the hands of receivers in 1876, and General Mahone lost control of it, he was soon in the center of the political stage as a candidate for governor. "Readjustment" of the state's $45,000,000 antebellum debt was the principal issue stressed by the "king of the lobby," as the pint-size general was known. He didn't win the governorship himself, but he elected his man to office a short time later, got control of the General Assembly and kept the state in turmoil for years.

Mahone and his followers argued that it was absolutely impossible for a devastated and impoverished state to pay the $45,000,000 pre-war debt in full, and that it was unreasonable to expect poor whites and Negroes, especially the latter, who had no part in contracting the debt, to be taxed for its liquidation. Much of the amount—which had been borrowed before 1861 to build railroads, canals and turnpikes—was owed to bondholders in the North, whose armies had wrecked a large part of Virginia during the Civil War. Adequate financing of the newly established public school system would be out of the question if the debt were paid in full. Mahone and his followers wanted to scale it down.

But many sincere and high-minded Virginians, especially in Richmond, felt that this was a debt of honor, and that any scaling down would be unthinkable. Those who took this position called themselves Funders. They formed a Committee of Thirty-nine in the city "to preserve the credit of the state" and advocate payment in full. Robert Beverley was chairman, with William L. Royall, attorney for the bondholders and the group's leading spirit, as secretary. The committee included several prominent clergymen—the Reverends Moses D. Hoge, Joshua Peterkin and Jeremiah Bell Jeter.

The Richmond *Dispatch* and the recently established Richmond *State* were the Funders' two principal journalistic supporters. Captain John Hampden Chamberlayne founded the *State* in 1876, and although he died six years later at age forty-three, he made a great impact with his paper during that brief period.

Mahone had bought control of the *Whig*, and W. C. Elam, a caustic North Carolinian, was its editor. Elam argued the case for readjustment of the debt with considerable ability and no little vituperation. He was involved in several duels. One was with Colonel Thomas Smith, son of Governor "Extra Billy" Smith, which took place back of Oakwood Cemetery. Another was with Richard F. Beirne, co-editor with Chamberlayne of the *State*. In the first of these two encounters, a bullet split the bone in Elam's chin, broke his jaw, knocked out four teeth and lodged under his tongue. In the second, fought two years later near Waynesboro, Elam was wounded in the thigh. Despite all this, he never toned down his editorials in the slightest, nor did his rival editors.

Beirne agreed to fight a duel with H. H. Riddleberger, the "Gamecock of the Valley," near Ashland. Beirne forgot to bring the caps for the pistols, and the encounter was accordingly called off. On the same day Riddleberger met Richmond's newly elected congressman, George D. Wise, "on the field of honor" near Atlee. Neither was hit, and Riddleberger spoke that night at a political rally in Richmond. Wise, a nephew of Henry A. Wise, served four terms in Congress as the city's representative.

The ferocious language used in newspaper editorials during these years seems almost unbelievable today, especially when one considers that the users thereof were liable at any moment to be challenged to "pistols at ten paces." Such words and phrases as "scoundrel," "traitor," "conceited ass," "renegade Virginian" and "cowardly liar" were tossed about with utter abandon. Consider the torrid exchange between twenty-seven-year-old Richard F. Beirne of the *State* and forty-seven-year-old W. C. Elam of Mahone's *Whig*, which led to the above-mentioned duel between them. Beirne wrote:

"In making this comment on Boss Mahone, we wish it to be distinctly understood by all his corrupt henchmen that what we say and have said of him we mean and have meant of them personally, individually and collectively, and in any other sense they may choose to feel. A more vicious, corrupt and degraded gang never followed any adventurer than those who hang about the petty boss."

Elam retorted:

"Not only does the *State* lie, but its 'editor and owner' lies, and the poor creature who may have actually written the article in question also lies—all jointly and severally—deliberately, knowingly, maliciously and with the inevitable cowardice that is always yoked with insolent bravado."

Dueling was so scandalously prevalent in and around Richmond, despite the law which forbade it, that the General Assembly strengthened the anti-dueling statute in 1882. It added a proviso that any elected or appointed state official, including members of the legislature, must take an oath not to engage in one of these affairs, directly or indirectly, i.e. as a "second," and that any such official who violated this oath would lose his office and become ineligible to hold office thereafter. These encounters under the code duello were mainly brought about by heated controversies between Funders and Readjusters.

The effort of Richmond's so-called "Bourbons," who constituted the Funder leadership, to organize a statewide Society to Preserve the Credit of the State was a failure. The organization disappeared from view in a short time.

Yet the emergence of this society in 1878 paved the way for the organization of the Readjuster party the following year. Not only so, but the campaign of 1879 ended in a thumping victory for that party. Mahone and his cohorts captured 56 of the 100 seats in the House and 29 of 40 in the Senate. Two years later, William E. Cameron, the Mahone candidate, was elected governor. From 1879 until 1883 Mahone dominated the political scene in Virginia, and the Richmond Bourbons gnashed their teeth in wrath and frustration. They foresaw dire things for the Commonwealth under Mahone's leadership. Certainly he was a brazen autocrat whose methods were both dictatorial and devious. Yet during his regime the debt was scaled down to a reasonable figure and the credit of the state was not destroyed; the public schools which had been closing in many areas for lack of funds were kept open, the teachers were paid, the whipping post and poll tax were abolished and the Normal and Collegiate Institute for Negroes was established at Petersburg, as was the Central Hospital for mentally afflicted blacks.

Mahone achieved his victories at the polls with the indispensable aid of the Negro vote. In return, he delivered on his promises to the blacks. He did not promise them high political office, and they did not attain such office when he was in control of affairs in Virginia. Mahone fought the candidacy of John Mercer Langston, the only Negro ever elected to Congress from Virginia, and supported one of Langston's white opponents. In Richmond, blacks were named doorkeepers in the House and Senate, replacing the Confederate veterans who held the posts, and two were named to the City School Board. Blacks also were given clerkships in several state departments, and Governor Cameron chose one as his messenger. Black teachers were appointed to teach in black schools. This hardly equates with the "Negro rule" that was so fearsomely predicted by Mahone's foes throughout that era.

Blacks were disfranchised on a wholesale scale by a law passed in 1876 which provided that any person convicted of petty larceny would lose his vote. In Richmond Hustings Court about one thousand Negroes were disfranchised between 1870 and 1892 because of felony or petty larceny convictions, and in Richmond Police Court another thousand were rendered ineligible between 1877 and 1892 by virtue of petty larceny convictions.

As for the attitude of the whites toward Negro education, Edward King, a Northern writer who came to Richmond in 1873–74, declared that "no one thinks of refusing to aid the Negro in obtaining his education, although he contributes little or nothing toward the school tax." The foregoing is not strictly accurate, but it indicates that there was considerable sentiment among whites for providing adequate schooling for blacks. A total of 3,300 Negroes were enrolled in the Richmond public schools for the session of 1870–71.

The Richmond Colored Normal School, established by the Freedmen's

Bureau soon after the war, remained in operation and was expanded in 1873, when a larger building was constructed on North Twelfth Street. Raza M. Manly, a Vermonter who had served as a Union Army chaplain, was the principal. He gave the building with its contents, valued at $25,000, to the city in 1876. In return, the city promised to maintain and develop the institution as a high and normal school for the training of Negro teachers. Manly was retained as principal. The school achieved a remarkable standard of excellence for the period, and produced a number of prominent and successful graduates. Its name was changed to Colored Normal and High School in 1886. During the period from 1869 to 1900, the city of Richmond built four schools for blacks. Enrollment for those years was almost 50 per cent less than the black school population.

All public schools for whites were taken over by the municipality in 1870, and in the following year became a part of the newly established state system of schools. James H. Binford, who became city superintendent in 1870, evidenced a devotion and dedication comparable to that of the able William H. Ruffner, the first state superintendent of public instruction. Death cut short Binford's career in 1876, but he had done much to lay the foundations of Richmond's school system, and to build acceptance in the city for public education. There was widespread opposition to the concept, not only in Virginia but elsewhere. For example, the Richmond *Standard*, edited by G. Watson James, quoted with approval in 1880 an article in the *North American Review* entitled "The Public School Failure." The newspaper agreed with the article's author that public schools should be maintained only on the elementary level, and that parents should be responsible for everything else.

Despite such sentiments, construction of a high school was an early priority in Richmond. Facilities were primitive until the new home of the Richmond High School was opened in 1873 at 805 East Marshall Street, where later the George Wythe Junior High School stood. It was often difficult in those years to get teachers for the public schools. Certain members of prominent Richmond families impoverished by the war gladly took teaching positions.

Both the white and black schools suffered severely following the depression of 1873. Not only were times hard, but the Funders argued that payments on the state's public debt should supersede those for the maintenance of the public school system. That system, never adequately financed during the era, was starved to such a degree that schools were shutting down and teachers were unpaid. However, with the reduction of the debt, under the leadership of the Readjusters, the school system received appropriations more consonant with its importance to the Commonwealth.

Several notable private schools sprang up during these years. John Henry Powell, kinsman of D. Lee Powell who had operated the Southern Female Institute before the war, established the Richmond Female Seminary in 1873. Often known simply as "Powell's School," it would rank to-day "as a junior college of the highest standard," in the opinion of Margaret Meagher, historian of Richmond's schools. The seminary continued until 1903, nearly all of that time at 3 East Grace Street—a structure later used for thirty years as the Home for Needy Confederate Women. The school was under the direction of Mr. Powell until his death in 1901. There were students in the boarding department from all parts of the South, and some Northern states. Powell's four daughters taught at one time or another in the institution. John Powell, the celebrated pianist, was his son.

A famous school for boys was that of Mrs. Annie Colston Camm, which opened in 1873 and continued until 1902. It was considered a "feeder" for Norwood's University School, established in 1864 by Thomas Norwood and Thomas Price, and operated until Norwood's death in 1892. At that time the Norwood school was taken over by George M. Nolley, and operated as Nolley's Classical School until 1909.

Elementary instruction for both boys and girls was furnished by Miss Simonia Roberts for twenty years, beginning in 1881. "Miss Sye," as she was known, had a pedagogical methodology that was unique. The girls were called "pinkies" and the boys "busters" and they sat on opposite sides of the room, with the teacher, wielding a monitory ruler, in the middle. A "stool of repentance" in the corner was brought into play when a "pinkie" or "buster" became obstreperous. The alphabet, the multiplication table and Roman numerals were all made the subject of jingles by Miss Sye, as in the following:

> b—a bay, b—e bee, b—i bicky bi
> b—o bow, bicky bi bow
> b—u, bicky—bi bew . . .

Whatever the cosmic significance of the foregoing, a Richmond grandmother who had attended Miss Sye's in her extreme youth repeated the foregoing at once from memory in 1974 when the school was mentioned.

Miss Maria Blair was another important personality in the world of Richmond education. She had a school of her own for only a few years, but she taught literature and history of art in several other institutions, and made a lasting impression. Her successor on the faculty of Powell's in 1898 was Miss Augusta T. Daniel, who for twenty-two years had operated an excellent boarding and day school for girls. Another well-known institution for young ladies was that of Miss Lizzie Grattan, daughter of Peachy R. Grattan, which functioned for twenty-eight years, beginning in 1869.

The official seal of the City of Richmond was the subject of a report in 1872 which showed that the seal's history had been a most erratic one. A number of different designs were used from the time of Richmond's incorporation as a city in 1782, and the report said: "No two of these seals were exactly alike. But worse than this, not one of them has any legal sanction." On top of all else, the date "July 19, 1782" was on many of them, but it had no real significance. It was merely the day when the Common Hall or Council approved a motion to appoint a committee to choose a seal. A design was not actually approved until 1806. Yet neither this nor any other design seemed to stick for long. The city fathers were continually changing it.

Following the report of 1872, the Council adopted an ordinance that provided for "a sitting female figure, clothed in classic costume, wearing a mural crown; in her left hand a bundle of tobacco leaves, which rest upon her lap; at her feet a river flowing to her left, on the banks of which are shown mining operations, iron works and a steam engine . . . above her head the ,tto *Sic itur ad astra* ["Such is the way to the stars," from Virgil's *Aeneid*] . . . and this inscription: 'Richmond, Va., Founded by William Byrd. MDCCXXXVII.'"

Other seals of varying design have been adopted by the Council since then. The City Code of 1963 contains the following specifications, which have been followed, with minor variations, since the early twentieth century, and were still in use in 1976:

"A female figure typifying robed justice, bearing scales in the left hand and carrying a drawn sword in the right hand; the inner and upper semi-circle to contain the motto SIC ITUR AD ASTRA . . . and under the figure . . . the words 'City of Richmond, July 19, 1782', being the seal used by the city prior to October, 1872." The meaningless July 19 date is thus specified once more.

Councilman Thomas H. Wynne was chairman of the committee which reported on the history of the seal in 1872. Wynne was a self-made man who attended the Lancasterian School and went to work at age thirteen. He rose to become president of a railroad and two iron manufacturing companies, publisher of several newspapers, a member of the General Assembly and president of City Council, the author of important books on colonial Virginia and secretary of the Virginia Historical Society. On his death in 1875, the state legislature passed resolutions praising his work as a statesman and historian, adjourned in his memory and attended his funeral, as did the mayor and Council. All trains leaving Richmond on the day of the obsequies were draped in black.

General George E. Pickett, famous for the charge of his division at Gettysburg, died this same year in Norfolk, and his body was brought to Richmond for burial in Hollywood. It lay in state at the Capitol and was then carried to the cemetery. Pickett's war horse and members of his division were in the long procession to the grave. Among those in line were several black militia units. There had been controversy over this, but General Joseph E. Johnston and others were successful in arranging for their participation.

But that controversy was mild by comparison with the one which erupted almost simultaneously over the request of the same Negro units to take part in the parade two days later, incident to the unveiling of the statue of Stonewall Jackson in Capitol Square. The statue, "presented by English gentlemen," had been pulled through the streets from Rocketts by hundreds of Jackson's old soldiers and others. The unveiling was on October 26, 1875, with a huge parade and elaborate ceremonies. General Jubal A. Early, a fiery, profane and totally "unreconstructed rebel," was outraged over the idea that blacks would march in the procession. "Old Jube" wrote Governor Kemper angrily demanding that they be prevented from participating. Kemper shot back that the program was fixed, "all hell can't change it," and that the Negro units would march. For some unexplained reason, the units didn't show up.

The parade and the subsequent ceremonies in Capitol Square were among the most impressive in the city's history. The widow of General Jackson and their daughter Julia were among the honored guests. The Reverend Moses D. Hoge was the orator of the occasion.

Among those on the speaker's stand was young Bishop James Gibbons of the Roman Catholic Diocese of Richmond. He had come to the city in 1872 from the Diocese of North Carolina, where he had made a remarkable record. An exponent of religious amity, he had preached there, by invitation, in Masonic lodge rooms and Protestant churches. In Richmond his influence was again in the direction of interfaith understanding, and it was in Richmond that he wrote his greatly admired book *The Faith of Our Fathers*, which sold two million copies during his lifetime. He also was instrumental in establishing the Little Sisters of the Poor. Bishop Gibbons left Richmond in 1877 to become Archbishop of Baltimore, and then Cardinal Gibbons, one of the most distinguished clergymen in the history of the United States. He returned to Richmond over the years for various important ceremonies.

A clergyman of an entirely different type was the Reverend John Jasper, the Negro preacher to whom reference has been made. Born a slave, the youngest of twenty-four children, and self-educated by studying a "New York speller" at night, he became one of the masterful pulpit orators of his time. His rudimentary education was evident, but governors, judges, legislators and other prominent persons in all walks of life came to hear him deliver his famous sermon "The Sun Do Move." Jasper's church was the Sixth Mt. Zion Baptist at 14 West Duval Street, still standing in 1976.

His biographer, the Reverend William E. Hatcher, an eminent white Baptist divine, wrote: "His imagination was preeminent. A matchless painter was he . . . [but] his vocabulary was poverty itself, his grammar a riot of errors, his pronunciation a dialectical wreck, his gestures wild and unmeaning . . . [yet] his entire frame seemed to glow in a living light, and almost wordlessly he wrought his miracles."

Jasper is said to have preached "The Sun Do Move" 250 times, and his reputation spread throughout the United States. The church and nearby streets were sometimes filled hours before the service.

"He circled 'round the pulpit with his ankle in his hand," wrote Dr. Hatcher, "and laughed and sang and shouted and acted about a dozen characters within the space of three minutes." How he got around the pulpit "with his ankle in his hand" was not explained. At all events, Jasper captivated his listeners. He was strikingly handsome, dignified in bearing and aristocratic in manner. His argument that the sun moves around the earth was based solely on the Bible, which to him was "the sum and substance of all knowledge."

One of the arguments he used is contained in the following extract from his sermon:

"Joshwer . . . asked de Lord ter issure a speshul order dat de sun hol' up erwhile an dat de moon furnish plenty uv moonshine down on de lowes' part uv de fightin' groun's. . . . Joshwer . . . tell de sun to stan' still tel he cud finish his job. Wat did de sun do? Did he glar down in fi-ry wrath an' say: 'What you talkin' 'bout my stoppin' for, Joshwer? I ain't navur started yit. Bin here all de time, an' it wud smash up evything if I wuz ter start'? Naw, he ain' say dat. But wat de Bible say? Dat's wat I ax ter know. It say it wuz at de voice uv Joshwer dat it stopped. I don' say it stopt; t'ain't fer Jasper to say dat, but de Bible, de Book uv Gord, say so. But I say dis; nuthin' kin stop until it hez fust startid. So I knows whut I'se talkin' 'bout. . . ."

Another passage cited by Jasper was, "From de risin' uv de sun even unter de goin' down uv de same, My name shall be great 'mong de Gentiles." This scriptural reference proved "movement" on the part of the sun, said he. "How do dat suit yer?" he asked his hearers triumphantly. "It look lak dat ort ter fix it. Dis time it is de Lord uv hosts Hissef dat is doin' de talkin'. Ain't dat clear nuff fer yer? De Lord pity dese doubtin' Thomasses."[4]

Significant visitors came to Richmond during these years. One was a sixteen-year-old Negro youth who had somehow made his way four hundred miles from Malden, West Virginia, and arrived in Richmond hungry and penniless. He crawled under a wooden sidewalk, and slept there several nights, working during the daytime on the docks. Finally he made enough money to get to Hampton Institute. His name was Booker T. Washington. A quarter of a century later he would return to Richmond as one of the most famous men of his era, and would address the General Assembly, the City Council and leaders of both races.

Oscar Wilde was another visitor to Richmond. He came in 1882, on his lecture tour of the United States. The noted aesthete, whose mannerisms had been satirized the previous year in the Gilbert and Sullivan operetta *Patience*, appeared for his Richmond lecture in knee breeches and ruffled shirt, with a large sunflower in his lapel, and his hair down to his shoulders. Some two hundred Richmonders heard his witty discussion of "Decorative Art."

Various forms of artistic endeavor were under way in Richmond. Edward V. Valentine executed his recumbent statue of Robert E. Lee for the chapel in Lexington, and it was unveiled there to great acclaim in 1883. Lee had come to Richmond in 1870 for a physical examination, and allowed Valentine to make detailed measurements for a bust. The sculptor followed him back to Lexington, and began actual modeling. The bust was cast June 20, less than four months before Lee's death. Valentine was the natural choice for the full-length recumbent statue.

He had studied in Europe, and returned to Richmond in 1865. His studio on Leigh Street between Eighth and Ninth was the scene of much activity. Among his works were busts of such Confederate figures as Matthew Fontaine Maury, John H. Mosby, Albert Sidney Johnston, Joseph E. Johnston and J. E. B. Stuart. Also statues of Thomas Jefferson for the Jefferson Hotel, of General Williams C. Wickham for Monroe Park, of Lee for Washington's Statuary Hall and of Andromache and Astyanax for the Columbian Exposition in Chicago. Valentine lived until 1930. He did no sculpture after 1910, but was fairly active until the end of his life as president of the Virginia Historical Society and in other ways.

William L. Sheppard was another Richmonder who achieved national recognition as an artist in the postbellum years. After serving in the Confederate Army, he studied in London and Paris. His charming sketches of life in the South appeared in the best magazines, and in *Battles and Leaders of the Civil War*. He also illustrated books by such authors as John Esten Cooke, William Dean Howells and Thomas Nelson Page. Sheppard did several works of sculpture, among them the statues of General A. P. Hill over Hill's grave at Hermitage Road and Laburnum Avenue, and of Governor "Extra Billy" Smith in Capitol Square. The monument to the Richmond Howitzers at Park Avenue and Harrison Street was done by him, with Morgan P. Robinson, afterward state archivist, as the model. Sheppard also executed the Confederate Soldiers and Sailors monument on Libby Hill.

John A. Elder, a native Fredericksburger, is an artist identified with Richmond who achieved a wide reputation. He studied five years in Europe before the Civil War, but was back in Virginia when the fighting began. Elder enlisted and saw much active service. His "Battle of the Crater," an engagement in which he participated, is the best-known of his war paintings. He lived most of the postwar years in Richmond, and painted numerous portraits, including many of Confederate generals.

Richmond was a significant musical center during the 1870s and 1880s, and musical events were continued until after the turn of the century. The Mozart Association was organized in 1876, and from that year until 1887 it presented a weekly musicale, first under the direction of Jacob Reinhardt, and then under Pierre and Caroline Bernard, who had come to the city with the English Opera Company. The Thursday night concerts, operas and operettas presented by the Mozart Association were leading social events. The organization achieved a membership of from 1,500 to 2,000 in the 1880s. Prominent Richmond businessmen were officers and members of the association, and some played in the musicales. Professional musicians also were employed. The Mozart Academy of Music was dedicated with considerable fanfare in 1886. It was situated on Eighth Street between Grace and Franklin. Governor Fitzhugh Lee attended the ceremonies and General Bradley T. Johnson, first president of the Mozart Association, spoke.

But the Mozart Association, seemingly in its heyday, gradually gave way to the Wednesday Club, founded in 1893. The Mozart began holding its musicales only twice monthly, and they ceased entirely in 1897. Meanwhile the Wednesday Club was organizing its May Festivals, which included two or three days of concerts by the Wednesday Club Chorus, plus guest orchestras and internationally known musicians. These events continued for more than a quarter of a century, but music became a less significant element in the life of Richmond after 1900.

The James River flood of 1870 had been one of the worst in history, but that of 1877 seems to have equaled or surpassed it. Mayo's Bridge, for the umpteenth time, was carried downstream toward Chesapeake Bay, and enormous damage was done all over again to the river front and lower Main Street, where boats once more had to be brought into play.

Along the stream, at this time, the James River & Kanawha Canal had gradually ceased to function, and in 1879–80 the Richmond & Allegheny Railroad laid its tracks on the canal's towpath. This line to Clifton Forge would become the James River Division of the Chesapeake & Ohio.

The centennial of the surrender of the British at Yorktown was celebrated in Richmond with elaborate ceremonies. Many Richmonders attended the cornerstone laying of the monument at Yorktown, and then on October 22, 1881, the city's observance began. Among those present were descendants of revolutionary Generals Lafayette, Rochambeau and von Steuben, along with the governors of Maine and Georgia and military units from half a dozen states. The observance continued for several days, and included exercises in Capitol Square, a torchlight procession and historic tableaux, plus a "trades parade" in which every important business enterprise in Richmond was represented by a float.

Richmond's population in 1880 was 63,600, of whom 27,832, or 43.7 per cent, were black. By 1890, the population had grown to 81,388, of whom 32,330, or 39.6 per cent, were black, a drop of 4.1 percentage points. The proportion of Negroes to whites was falling in the United States as a whole, mainly because of massive immigration of whites from Europe.

Richmond in 1880 was one of only ten cities in the South with more than 25,000 population. A decade later, there were nineteen such cities. Virginia and the South were still overwhelmingly rural, but the urban trend was slowly getting under way.

Richmond had electric trolley cars, the first commercially successful system of such cars in the world. The inventor was Frank J. Sprague, a New York engineer, and the builder A. Langstaff Johnston of Richmond. The city's horse-drawn cars were phased out and the dazzling new contraptions were put in their place. Forty of them went into operation in May 1888, and it took five men to operate each car. They generated no less than seven horsepower. The first line went from Harrison and Main to Church Hill, passing over to Franklin and along that thoroughfare from Seventh to Ninth, down Ninth to Bank, and along Bank to Twelfth, thence back to Franklin and eastward to Church Hill.

During the thirty years following the Civil War (1865–95), twenty-five blacks served in the two branches of the Richmond City Council, eighteen of them in the decade 1880–90. For some years the entire eight-man Jackson Ward delegation, from the black residential and business area north of Broad Street, was black. The last group of Negroes to serve in the Council did so between 1892 and 1896. By 1900 there were no blacks in either the Board of Aldermen or the Common Council.

Relations between blacks and whites on the Council were said to be better than those between the races in the state legislature. The black councilmen and aldermen obtained various benefits for members of their race in Richmond, according to Thomas E. Walton, who wrote an M.A. thesis on "The Negro in Richmond, 1880–1890" for Howard University. Among benefits he lists "a new school building, fuel for the Negro poor, an armory for Negro troops, improved streets in the Negro section and better street lighting." Black members of the Council included graduates of the Howard Law School, the Yale Law School and the University of Michigan Medical School.

John Mitchell, Jr., editor and publisher of the Richmond *Planet*, of whom more will be said later, was the most prominent and militant member from the black community. Josiah Crump, a postal clerk, served several terms on the Board of Aldermen, and at his death in 1890 resolutions of high praise were adopted by his fellow aldermen, who attended his funeral in a body and asked the Common Council to do likewise. His chair and desk were draped in black for thirty days.

A note of intersectional amity was struck in 1885 when General U. S. Grant died. His magnanimous conduct at Appomattox and after caused him to be much admired in the South. Business was suspended in Richmond on the day of his funeral, the city's flags were at half-mast and the Howitzers fired a salute. Governor Cameron and his staff, with four companies of Virginia militia, attended the obsequies in New York.

Richmond's steady industrial progress was accompanied by a sharp rise in the strength of organized labor in the city. Most of the unions were affiliated with the Knights of Labor, a national organization. They entered local politics on a big scale, and in 1886 were sufficiently successful in the councilmanic elections to win temporary control of the city government.

That same year the Knights of Labor held their national convention in Richmond. The Knights insisted on "social equality" for blacks, and this caused a considerable stir. There were Negro delegates from various areas, but reservations for them could not be made at Murphy's Hotel. A Negro delegate referred in a speech to racial "superstitions" in the South, which added to the tension. A ball was called off because of the determination of the blacks to participate, and there were problems over seating them in the theaters.[5]

Perhaps the most sensational murder trial in Richmond's history occurred in the late 1880s, when Thomas J. Cluverius of King and Queen County was tried in Richmond for the death of Fannie Lillian Madison of King William. The body of the young girl, eight months pregnant, was found floating in the Richmond city reservoir. Nearby on the ground was a watch key that was traced to Cluverius. There was other evidence. Enormous interest was focused on the case. Cluverius was convicted and sentenced to hang. The event took place in the yard of the Richmond city jail. Frank Cunningham "sang several beautiful songs before the march to the gallows." The jail yard was jammed and the nearby roofs were crowded, while thousands thronged the adjacent area. It was the last of the great public hangings in Richmond. The electric chair soon replaced the gallows.

Times were still hard, but there were relaxing moments, as when the Negro cart drivers from Hanover County arrived in the summer with watermelons. Their melodious voices echoed through the streets with "Watermillions! I got um, green rind an' red meat, an' full o' juice an' so sweet!"; or "All dat got money, come up an' buy, dose dat got none stan' back an' cry, kase I'se got watermillions!"

Little barelegged and barefooted black boys appeared in springtime crying "Fresh feesh! Fresh feesh!" Their musical accents mingled with those of the Negro newsboys hawking the evening papers. And in the winter months, the oyster man and the charcoal burner were heard peddling their wares. Before the James River & Kanawha Canal ceased to function, there was additional melody with the arrival of the canal boat, heralded by mellifluous notes on the long horn or trumpet carried by each vessel.

Life was leisurely. Since there were no quick lunch counters or cafeterias, only expensive downtown restaurants, the average business or professional man went home from his office to three o'clock "dinner." He went on foot if he lived nearby, or by buggy or horse-drawn streetcar. After consuming the solid midday repast, he returned to his desk, and often remained until rather late. If he needed a between-meal snack, he could patronize the "cake man" who made a regular tour of the larger establishments. Or he might seek surcease in one of the numerous saloons. There were no fewer than 163 of these emporiums in the city in 1883.

Conversation was one of the leading diversions during these years. One of the topics could well have been an episode involving the Vicomte de Sigour, French consul in Richmond. He and Madame de Sigour rented the Barret house at Fifth and Cary streets, and the vicomte was seen kissing the French maid. When a busybody mentioned the matter to *la comtesse* (née Johnson, of Connecticut), she replied, "I don't care whom he kisses provided he doesn't kiss *me!*"

Architecture in Richmond during the postbellum era contrasted sharply with that of earlier years. Expensive residences built in the eighties and nineties were in the prevailing late-Victorian style. Termed "costly monstrosities" by at least one authority in the mid-twentieth century, they have lately come to be regarded as possessing genuine merit. Salient examples of the style are the Lewis Ginter house at Shafer and Franklin, which served for a time as Richmond's first public library and then became the administration building of Virginia Commonwealth University; and the E. A. Saunders house—across Shafer from the Ginter house—once the home of Lieutenant Governor Joseph E. Willard, and also used today by V.C.U. Other notable structures erected in Richmond during this period were the iron front business houses in the 1100 block of East Main Street.

The builder of one of the charming antebellum houses on Franklin Street, Horace L. Kent, died in 1872. He was a Northerner by birth who had been bitterly opposed to secession. One of his daughters had been an ardent Confederate sympathizer, and he pointedly left her in his will $250,000 in worthless Confederate bonds and emancipated slaves. The Kent home, at First and Franklin, was purchased by the Charles Talbotts and then by the Granville Valentines, who enlarged it considerably in 1904. Known as the Kent-Valentine house, it was purchased in 1973 by the Garden Club of Virginia for its headquarters.

A scandal of the 1870s and 1880s revolved about the practice of robbing graves in Oakwood Cemetery to provide cadavers for students at the Medical College of Virginia and the University of Virginia Medical School. "Respectable teachers of anatomy" at both institutions were involved, although the robbing of graves was a felony. "The principal figure in the oft-repeated spectacle of grave robbing was the . . . Negro janitor," Dr. Wyndham B. Blanton writes in his *Medicine in Virginia in the Nineteenth Century.* "Armed with pick, spade and lantern, the grave-digger fared forth, alone or accompanied by a few adventurous medical students. A dark night, a sack, a cart and a shallow grave were all he needed." In 1880, it was discovered that no fewer than forty graves in Oakwood Cemetery had been recently relieved of their contents.

Many of the bodies were shipped by rail to the University of Virginia in coal oil barrels. The ghoulish facts were duly chronicled in the Richmond press. At least one doctor at the Medical College was arrested, along with two students and miscellaneous Negroes directly involved in the enterprise. The *Whig* reported that "Chris" Baker, a Negro employee of the Medical College and a "noted resurrectionist," was arrested on Leigh Street with a cadaver in a wheelbarrow.

Finally, in 1884 the General Assembly established an Anatomical Board to distribute "unclaimed dead bodies" of convicts, paupers and the like to be used "for the advancement of medical science." Thus ended the saga of Oakwood Cemetery and its ghouls.

A significant development in the medical field was the opening of the Retreat for the Sick in 1877. Richmond had no general hospital, and the city almshouse was the only available haven for the ill. A public-spirited lady, Mrs. Annabel Ravenscroft Jenkins, saw the need, and the Retreat opened in the Hospital Building of the Medical College of Virginia at 1225 East Marshall Street. The faculty of the college served as the medical and surgical staffs. The Retreat was described in its catalogue as "an unendowed charitable institution, the only one of its kind in the South." It moved to a nearby location in 1883 and then in 1919 to its present site, 2621 Grove Avenue, which has been greatly enlarged. The name was changed in recent years to Retreat Hospital. The institution is unique in Richmond, and perhaps in the United States, in that it has always had three types of patients—those who can pay nothing, those who can pay something and those who can pay in full. There is complete confidentiality as to the various categories.

The political scene during the early 1880s was hectic, but triumphs were in the offing for the Democrats. First came their sweep in the General Assembly elections of 1883, when they won back control of the legislature from Mahone. Great was the rejoicing in Richmond, and there was a spectacular demonstration with General Thomas L. Rosser in command. Fireworks, bonfires and a torchlight procession were evidences of Democratic exuberance. Half a dozen orators from inside and outside the state spouted on the city hall lot. A year later, Grover Cleveland was elected President—the first Democrat to occupy the White House since before the Civil War—and the jubilation in Richmond was unrestrained. Then in 1885 Fitzhugh Lee, a Democrat, won the governorship, and the dominance of Mahone on Capitol Hill was ended once and for all. When General Robert E. Lee's popular nephew was inaugurated, there was a ball at the First Regiment Armory at which hundreds of Democrats and their ladies danced all night, to the music of two brass bands. There was a general lack of inter-party bitterness in the excitement of the hour, and outgoing Governor Cameron and John S. Wise, Lee's defeated opponent, were special guests. Yet the final ousting of William Mahone from power was nowhere more fervently celebrated than in conservative Richmond.

# SEVENTEEN

# The Not Always Gay Nineties

THE LAST DECADE of the dying nineteenth century is often referred to as "the Gay Nineties." It was indeed the era of gay blades and blushing belles, of mustache cups and high-button shoes, derby hats and wing-collars, Confederate reunions and excursions to Buckroe Beach, buggy rides, trolley rides and skating parties on the ice. It was the era of the famously beautiful Irene Langhorne and May Handy, of the Gibson girl and bicycles-built-for-two, of trips to the "White" with trysts in the gloaming and masked balls in the Old White Hotel. And every November there were high jinks at the University of Virginia-North Carolina football game at the field on West Broad Street.

Most of this seems "gay" enough, in the old-fashioned sense. On the other hand, the nineties were marked by the serious financial panic and depression of 1893, which caused suffering, unemployment and bankrupt-cies in Richmond for years. Unveiling of the statue of Robert E. Lee in 1890 brought an unprecedented turnout of Civil War figures, but there were startling attacks on Lee and all Confederates in the Negro news-paper, the Richmond *Planet.* Race relations had deteriorated. Further-more, today's youth probably would have found the diversions of the nine-ties utterly boring. No motion pictures, radio, television or automobiles, no rock festivals or pot smoking parties. "Females" wore "rats" in their hair, no "make-up" on their faces, and had hourglass figures with skirts practically on the ground. Legs were "limbs," and "holding hands" was regarded as exceptionally daring. There was mud in Richmond's James River drinking water at all times.

The decade opened with the unveiling of the equestrian statue of Lee, an event to which the South had looked forward for a quarter of a cen-tury. The artist was the noted French sculptor Jean Antonin Mercié, and the cost was $77,000, a sum raised by the Southern people from their slender resources. The campaign for funds had got off to a shaky start in the seventies, when an organization formed for the purpose by the always bellicose General Jubal A. Early ran head on into another organization, the Ladies' Hollywood Memorial Association, which was equally determined to lead the movement. It took some years to calm down the two organizations and get them working together under a legislative act that created a new agency.

There were controversies, too, over the choice of a sculptor. A competition in 1886 resulted in an award to a "Yankee" artist from Ohio. Whereupon General Early wrote Governor Fitzhugh Lee that "if the statue of General Lee be erected after that model," he (Early) would "get together all the surviving members of the Second Corps and blow it up with dynamite." Another competition brought the much-admired model by Mercié. It showed Lee seated on Traveller.

Choice of a site was not achieved without contention. Hollywood Cemetery, Libby Hill, Capitol Square, Monroe Park and Gamble's Hill had their backers. Finally the site at today's Monument and Allen avenues was decided upon. It was then an open field where cows grazed. The land was given by Otway S. Allen, a prominent citizen and Confederate veteran. There was unhappiness from various quarters over the selection of this site beyond the city limits. The Lynchburg *News* protested placement of the monument in "a remote and inaccessible suburb of Richmond."

Governor Lee was upset when he discovered that the model called for a statue and pedestal measuring some ten feet less overall from bottom to top than Washington's equestrian statue in Capitol Square. He insisted that Mercié alter his design and place Robert E. Lee not one inch lower than George Washington. The sculptor was unhappy over this, but he complied. Enlargement of the figure of Lee and his horse added $6,000 to the cost.

Extremely sour notes concerning the entire project issued from the Richmond *Planet,* owned and edited by Negro Councilman John Mitchell, Jr. Mitchell not only argued vehemently in the Council against the $10,000 appropriation toward expenses of the unveiling, but the paper echoed his sentiments. "The men who talk most about the valor of Lee and the blood of the brave Confederate dead are those who never smelt powder," snarled the *Planet.* "Most of them were at a table, either on top or under it, when the war was going on." The paper declared on the day of the unveiling, May 31, 1890, that the entire proceeding handed down a "legacy of treason and blood" to future generations, and left no doubt that "the loyalty so often expressed penetrates no deeper than the surface." There was more in the same vein. However strong one's disagreement with Mitchell's sentiments, his courage in expressing them at a time when lynchings were at their height cannot be denied.

The vast majority of Richmonders probably were unaware of the

*Planet's* editorial blasts. Certainly the unveiling was one of the great events in the city's history. Wagons carrying the statue had been pulled to the site with ropes by hundreds of citizens, as with the Washington statue in 1858. The parade preceding the unveiling found 50 Confederate generals in line, together with 15,000 Confederate veterans from every Southern state and 10,000 other citizens. Governor Fitzhugh Lee was chief marshal, and the parade took two hours and a half to pass a given point.

Colonel Archer Anderson, who would succeed his father, General Joseph R. Anderson, in two years as head of the Tredegar, was the principal orator for the unveiling. He was a polished speaker, an able business executive and an accomplished scholar and linguist who had studied at the University of Berlin. He rose in the Civil War from the rank of private in Richmond's famous Company F to the post of adjutant general in the Army of Tennessee. In his address, Colonel Anderson expressed unbounded admiration for Lee, while at the same time voicing forward-looking sentiments in tune with those of the younger postwar generation of Southerners.

The monument did not long remain outside Richmond's corporate limits. Annexation in 1892 brought into the city 292 acres of West End territory, including the tract on which Lee and Traveller stood. Because of the depression of 1893, there was little building on newly created Monument Avenue until the early 1900s, but some forty-four houses, many of them unusually handsome, rose there in the first decade of the century.

Various Northern newspapers commented favorably on the monument and the ceremonies accompanying it, but the Philadelphia *North American* compared Lee to Benedict Arnold, and the New York *Mail & Express* urged that Congress forbid the setting up of any more monuments to Confederate heroes or display of the Confederate flag.

Yet posts of the Grand Army of the Republic, composed of former Union soldiers, had been coming to Richmond for social visits, had been welcomed enthusiastically and had left with high praise for their ex-Confederate hosts. The Trenton, New Jersey, post published an account of its visit in 1881, saying that Mayor William C. Carrington's words of welcome were so moving that "every man among us felt the tears trickling down his cheeks." It went on to declare that they shed tears again as they prepared two days later "to part from those we have learned to love." At about the same time, Company A of the Richmond Light Infantry Blues went to Washington for the unveiling of the monument to Union General George H. Thomas, of Virginia, "the Rock of Chickamauga." When it was proposed to build a Home for Confederate Veterans on the Robinson farm in Henrico County, facing what later became "the Boulevard" in Richmond's West End, the first contributor was the G.A.R. post in Newark, New Jersey, which sent $100 in gold. Shortly thereafter General U. S. Grant forwarded his check for $500.

Another event affecting the Confederacy during these years was the effort of the City School Board to tear down the Confederate White House. The building had been used for eighteen years to house the Central School, and the board concluded that it was unsuited for such purposes. That august body desired to erect a "suitable" school on the site. Fortunately for history and posterity, Alderman John B. Cary grasped the stupidity of this suggestion. He proposed that the city put its new school building elsewhere, and that the White House of the Confederacy be turned over to the recently formed Confederate Memorial Literary Society for use as a Confederate museum. The plan was adopted, and the museum was dedicated in 1896.

While the Confederate White House was being saved, Libby Prison was being taken down, piece by piece, and transported to the Chicago World's Fair. It never came back.

A monument to General A. P. Hill, whose name was on the lips of both Lee and Jackson in their dying moments, was unveiled on Memorial Day, 1892, at today's Laburnum Avenue and Hermitage Road. The ceremony was preceded by an elaborate parade. Hill's body was removed later from Hollywood and placed under the monument.

Mrs. John Stewart of Brook Hill and her daughters gave the Lee house at 707 East Franklin Street to the Virginia Historical Society in 1893 for its headquarters. The society's *Virginia Magazine of History and Biography* was founded soon afterward, under the editorship of Philip A. Bruce.

Richmond was recovering steadily from the ravages of the war. "Fitz" Lee's election as governor had signalized the end of the time-consuming and divisive political battles over readjustment of the state's public debt, and enabled the business leaders of the city to unite in rebuilding its shattered fortunes. Governor Lee himself was more open-minded and progressive than many of the so-called Bourbons or ultra-conservatives.

Richmond's population in 1890 was in excess of 81,000—more than double the figure of 1860. The depression of 1873 had been weathered, and the city was showing considerable *élan*. Tobacco and flour manufacture were still thriving, while other industries had been added and were providing greater diversity.

The city's steady recovery was accelerated by the emergence of several young men who had served in the Confederate Army, and who became masterful leaders and innovators in subsequent years. Conspicuous among them were Joseph Bryan, Lewis Ginter and James H. Dooley. They joined with such successful men of the antebellum era as Joseph R. Anderson and James Thomas, Jr.

Young "Joe" Bryan, who had served gallantly in Mosby's Rangers, entered upon the practice of law in Richmond, after studying the subject under the celebrated John B. Minor at the University of Virginia. One of Bryan's early business ventures was in cooperation with John Stewart (his father-in-law), James H. Dooley, John P. Branch, Frederic R. Scott and others. They united in setting up the Richmond & West Point Terminal Railway and Warehouse Company in 1880. It was a holding company, and never actually operated a single railroad. It had an almost incredibly checkered career. Yet, in the final analysis, and with the aid of J. P. Morgan, it contributed importantly to Richmond's development as a railroad center.

Joseph Bryan was best-known as a newspaper publisher although his business and civic activities were manifold. For instance, he was president of the Richmond Locomotive Works, which he and William R. Trigg developed from the Tanner & Delaney Machine Works into an operation employing three thousand men. It manufactured locomotives for various railroads in this and other countries, including Finland. The highly successful concern was sold later to the American Locomotive Company of New York, and Bryan became managing director of the Richmond branch.

Bryan's newspaper career began when the struggling and money-losing *Times* was dumped into his lap by Major Ginter in 1887. Neither Ginter nor Bryan knew anything about newspaper publishing, and Ginter soon concluded that he had had enough. He gave the *Times* to Bryan. Despite Bryan's lack of experience in any aspect of journalism, he soon transformed the paper into an important organ of opinion. The Cowardin-Ellyson *Dispatch* had long been entrenched as the largest and most widely read paper in Virginia. The *Times*, under the new management, became a stiff competitor. It was the first paper in the South to install that revolutionary but now outmoded machine the Mergenthaler Linotype. The *Times* was also fearless in taking positions on highly controversial issues.

One such issue was the corruption in Virginia elections. "I had rather see the Democrats take shotguns and drive the Negroes from the polls than to see our young men taught to cheat," Bryan declared. The *Times* was a strong advocate of electoral reform. It was also uncompromising in its opposition to William Jennings Bryan and his "free silver" doctrine. By the time the presidential election of 1896 arrived, the *Times* had seven thousand circulation, but its searing attack on Bryan and "free silver" cost it a large percentage of its readers. On election night, a roaring mob formed outside the office of the paper, shouting imprecations. Joseph Bryan did not flinch. He and his paper maintained to the end that "free silver," despite its popularity with the masses, was sheer imbecility. W. J. Bryan carried Richmond.

One of Joseph Bryan's greatest contributions to the public weal was his refusal in 1893 to fight a duel. He not only refused; he turned the challenger, Jefferson D. Wallace, over to the police, and denounced dueling as "barbarous and absurd." That was the end of dueling in Virginia. It was on its way out already, for John S. Wise, another Confederate veteran whose courage was well-known, had publicly refused nine years before to fight Page McCarty. Wise denounced dueling as murder.

Bryan's friend Lewis Ginter was one of Richmond's foremost benefactors and business leaders. Born in New York of Dutch immigrant parents named Guenther, he came to Richmond in the early 1840s, aged eighteen, and opened a small shop selling "fine linens." He showed extraordinary ingenuity, especially in the attractive packaging of his merchandise, a talent that was crucial to attainment of his subsequent position as one of the preeminent figures in the development of America's tobacco industry.

Ginter's pre-war dry goods business prospered remarkably, but when the fighting began, he entered the Confederate service. He made an exceptional record and rose to the rank of major. With the return of peace, he attempted unsuccessfully to reestablish his business, and for a number of years faced the hardships and difficulties that confronted so many former Confederate soldiers. He finally took a job in the middle seventies with the Richmond tobacco firm of John F. Allen & Company. Ginter persuaded Allen to make the newfangled smoke called a "cigarette," and to make it from Virginia tobacco. The firm of Allen & Ginter was formed in 1875, with this object in view. Soon it was turning out "Richmond Gems" —hand-rolled by twenty women—apparently the first prepackaged cigarettes ever made.

Thanks largely to Ginter's genius in packaging and merchandising, the business was phenomenally successful. Soon Allen & Ginter had offices in London, Paris and Berlin. When James B. ("Buck") Duke obtained exclusive rights to the recently invented Bonsack cigarette-making machine for his American Tobacco Company, Ginter decided to join the company as a subsidiary, holding $7,500,000 of the stock. Irish-born John Allen had retired some years before from his partnership with Ginter. A highly cultivated man and ardent music lover, Allen devoted much of his time and means to promoting the city's musical appreciation and advancement.

Ginter was offered the presidency of the American Tobacco Company, but he declined. A lifelong bachelor, he remained in Richmond, contributing to the city's upbuilding and entertaining his friends in his $250,000 brownstone city mansion at Shafer and Franklin streets and his handsome country·residence, Westbrook. His fortune was estimated at $12,000,000, a huge sum for those times. He spent most of it in ways that promoted the advancement of his adopted city, and at his death in 1897 it was said to have dwindled to around $2,000,000. He developed Ginter Park as a fine residential area, and reportedly chose this Northside section rather than a tract in the West End so that residents would not have to drive downtown in their buggies with the sun in their faces, and similarly back home in the afternoon.

Widely traveled in Europe, a lover of art and an accomplished pianist,

Mayor Ginter became acutely aware of the need for a fine hotel in Richmond. He accordingly invested an estimated $500,000 to $1,500,000 in the design, construction and furnishing of the Hotel Jefferson. It was the most impressive and attractive hostelry in the South, with towers modeled on those of the Giralda in Seville, a spectacular lobby and luxurious and tasteful furnishings and appointments. Leading citizens sought to place a plaque in the hotel, celebrating the all-important contribution of Major Ginter in bringing the Jefferson into existence, but the modest man refused to allow it.

When Union Theological Seminary decided to move from Hampden-Sydney, Major Ginter, an Episcopalian, gave the Presbyterian institution a choice $25,000 tract of nearly twelve acres in Ginter Park, and the seminary opened there in 1898. However, Ginter declined to contribute $10,000 to the rebuilding of the rotunda at the University of Virginia after it burned in 1895, saying that his interests were "in Richmond, first, last and always." He retained the astonishing habit throughout his life of using the double negative, saying that he did it for added emphasis. Few men in Richmond's long history have done so much for the city's advancement.[1]

Others contributed significantly to the tobacco industry in Richmond in the late nineteenth century. Peter Mayo, Alexander Cameron, James B. Pace, Joseph G. Dill, Dr. R. A. Patterson and T. C. Williams were all highly successful. In 1891, there were 120 large and small tobacco factories in Richmond with 8,820 employees. The Negro hands in these plants were still singing at their work, as in antebellum days.

"Old plantation melodies and expressive Negro hymns follow each other in rapid succession," said a writer in *Harper's Weekly*, "and the work goes all the faster for them. The music is generally a monotonous recitative by a single voice, followed by a grand chorus of a hundred or more voices, each perfect in its part. There is an intense musical rivalry between the hands of the several factories, and the acquisition of a good soloist by any one of them is hailed with joy."

The same writer was greatly impressed with Richmond's recovery since Appomattox, and commented on the passing of the Old South, as follows: "The new order has taken its place, and foremost among its promoters and supporters stands Richmond, a leader of the industrial South, as 25 years ago she was of the Confederate South." Joaquin Miller, the "poet of the Sierras," described Richmond as "roaring with progress."

Among the industries noted in *Harper's Weekly* was the Richmond Cedar Works, which claimed to have the "largest and best-equipped woodenware factory in the world," and the Randolph Paper Box Factory, "the largest maker of paper boxes for druggists' use" in the United States, if not on the globe.

One of the ablest and most innovative of all the city's industrialists,

Joseph R. Anderson, died in 1892. The Tredegar had become prosperous
again under his leadership and that of his son. General Anderson was
much more than an industrialist, however; he was a leader in the civic and
religious life of Richmond. His pillared house on Franklin Street, on the
site subsequently occupied by the Jefferson Hotel, was an important social
center. The crowd at his funeral from St. Paul's, where he had been senior warden for many years, was said by the *Dispatch* to have been "the
largest ever seen at a private funeral in Richmond." The entire working
force of the Tredegar, white and black, marched from Monroe Park to the
church, bearing huge floral banners they had obtained for the occasion.
General Anderson's constant concern for the men and women of the
Tredegar was thus recognized. Virtually the entire city joined the
Tredegar workers in tribute.

The body of Jefferson Davis, who died in New Orleans in 1889, was
brought to Richmond four years later for reburial in Hollywood. The
closed casket lay in state at the Capitol. It was then taken to the cemetery, followed by a procession that included Mrs. Davis and her daughters,
"Winnie" and Margaret, as well as numerous Confederate generals, several governors of Southern states and thousands of citizens. The crowd at
the grave was estimated at from 20,000 to 25,000.

A Confederate veteran who had come up rapidly in Richmond's business world and was now an extremely wealthy man was James H. Dooley.
Railroads, real estate and steel were the principal ingredients of his fortune. By 1890 it was large enough for him to buy a hundred acres to the
west of Richmond overlooking the James. He christened it Maymont in
honor of his wife, the former Sallie May of Lunenburg County. There
he built an enormously expensive, typically Victorian mansion, and surrounded it with truly fabulous and extraordinarily beautiful plantings of
trees, flowers and shrubs from all over the world.

Dooley was small of stature and ramrod straight, with a keen mind and
nonexistent sense of humor. His right wrist had been shattered in the
Civil War, and never healed properly. He struggled all the rest of his life
to use the wrist and hand to the maximum degree possible, and usually
carried a cane in order to steady the hand.

The final years of the century saw Richmond recovering from the crash
of 1893. The Haxall-Crenshaw flour mills had gone into receivership almost at once, and there were business failures over a period of several
years—as many as fifty-two in 1897. But by 1899 the time was felt to be
ripe for the opening of a shipyard in Richmond. William R. Trigg, prominent industrialist, took the lead in this venture, and the Talbott Iron
Works on the river was converted into the Trigg Shipbuilding Company.
Contracts for two U. S. Navy torpedo boats, the *Stockton* and the
*Shubrick*, were obtained and the *Shubrick* was launched a year later, with
President William McKinley and the members of his Cabinet on hand,

plus some 30,000 onlookers. A million-dollar contract for a navy cruiser came through almost at once, and by 1900 five war vessels were under construction.

Despite these favorable factors, the yard got into financial difficulties— in large measure, it appears, because of the declining health of its founder, "Willie" Trigg. The company went into receivership at the end of 1902, and Trigg died a few months later. The shipyard never got back into operation.

The position of women in business and industry was improving. They were being employed in large numbers in the tobacco factories, especially those making cigarettes. Women were also useful as telephone switchboard operators. The first woman to strike out on her own in an important way in the mercantile field was Mrs. Jane King. Her successful ice business relied on consignments of ice by ship from Maine. Mrs. Belva A. Lockwood was the first Richmond woman to be issued a license to practice law. She entered the profession in 1894.

The perennial problem of how to make the James River more accessible to larger ships was again to the fore, and a joint committee of the Chamber of Commerce and City Council submitted arguments in favor of deepening the channel from 16 feet at low tide to 22 feet. During the year ended December 31, 1898, a total of 811 ships entered and cleared at the Richmond customhouse, not including "the large number of vessels engaged in the coastwise trade."

Medical affairs in Richmond were in a state of turmoil most of the time for the entire second half of the nineteenth century. A pleasant interlude was the founding, in 1889, of the Sheltering Arms Hospital. The founder was Miss Rebekah Peterkin, daughter of the Reverend Joshua Peterkin, rector of St. James's Episcopal Church. After a few years in the Clifton house on Fourteenth Street, the hospital moved to the Grant house at 1008 East Clay, where it remained until 1965. It moved in that year to new quarters on Palmyra Avenue adjoining Richmond Memorial Hospital. As the only free general hospital in Virginia, the Sheltering Arms has met a real need in caring for thousands of patients unable to pay. The great majority are under sixty years of age, and hence ineligible for Medicare. Free service is rendered by physicians, and a vast amount is done by a volunteer force of ladies. More than 60,000 patients had been given treatment without cost by 1974.

Two by-products of the Sheltering Arms in the early 1900s were Pine Camp Hospital for tubercular patients and the Virginia Home for Incurables, now the Virginia Home. When a girl who was a patient at the Sheltering Arms was found to be tubercular, Miss Frances Branch Scott, president of the hospital board for twenty-six years, called a meeting of her friends and the idea of Pine Camp was born. The Richmond Tuberculosis Association was another outgrowth of that activity. At about this time it

was decided that Sheltering Arms could no longer care for incurable patients. Miss Mary Greenhow, a board member who had been permanently
crippled from a fall, was accordingly instrumental in launching the Virginia Homes for Incurables.

But let us return to the acrimonious wrangling between the various
medical factions in Richmond. The death of a prominent Richmond
woman in childbirth in 1875 became the subject of charges and coun-
tercharges on the floor of the Richmond Academy of Medicine. Each of
the two major participants in the controversy had treated the patient and
each claimed the other was guilty of unethical conduct. There were heated
exchanges. At one meeting, a threatening gesture by one doctor caused another to throw a pocketknife at him. There was such a furor that the
police were called. Four members of the Academy were put under $2,500
bond to keep the peace for twelve months.

Reorganization of the Medical College after the Civil War was not
achieved without wounding certain sensibilities. Furthermore, various doctors at the institution became violently hostile to their colleagues in the
Richmond Academy of Medicine. Several prominent physicians resigned
from the Academy. The controversy was seething when Readjuster Governor Cameron poured gasoline on the fire by trying to replace the entire Medical College board. When his appointees sought to take over,
they were met with force by several faculty members, backed by the
police. The latter hauled a particularly combative appointee off to jail.
The matter was finally carried to the Virginia Supreme Court of Appeals,
which decided unanimously that the governor had exceeded his authority
in seeking to oust the MCV board.

So much antagonism was caused by all this that a rival to the Richmond Academy of Medicine was formed called the Richmond Medical
and Surgical Society. For a decade the city had two hostile and competing
organizations. They finally got together in 1890.

Yet those who imagined that tranquillity and harmony had descended at
last upon the medical profession in Richmond were in for a rude awaken-
ing. A brand-new institution, the University College of Medicine, was
founded in 1893, in direct competition with the Medical College of Virginia.[2]

The new institution was first called the College of Physicians and Surgeons, but the name was soon changed to University College of Medicine.
The founder was Dr. Hunter H. McGuire, of whom Dr. Wyndham B.
Blanton has written in his authoritative medical history, "For thirty-five
years after the war no one seriously challenged his reputation as leading
surgeon in the South." Dr. McGuire would be elected president of both
the American Medical Association and the American Surgical Association,
and after his death his statue would be placed in Capitol Square.

The dominant figure in the Medical College of Virginia was Dr. George

Ben Johnston, head of the Department of Surgery, who would later be chosen president of the American Surgical Association. It has long been believed that Drs. Johnston and McGuire were rancorous personal enemies, but this has been denied by Dr. Stuart McGuire, distinguished son of Dr. Hunter McGuire. The elder McGuire and Dr. Johnston were the heads of two surgical groups in Richmond, and their followers and patients seem to have been responsible for the long-continued antagonism that prevailed. Dr. Stuart McGuire quoted his father as saying that Dr. Johnston and he had never had a quarrel; that "the trouble had been made by their respective patients" and that "his patients and Dr. Johnston's patients had by their loyalty really divided the city." Dr. Stuart McGuire went on to say: "My father ended our conversation with the statement that Dr. Johnston was an able surgeon and a good man, and that if I ever needed advice I should not hesitate to go to him."[3]

Despite the foregoing, the intensity of the bitterness between the University College of Medicine and the Medical College of Virginia was almost unbelievable. The competition seems to have benefited the latter institution, but the rivalry was such that, in the words of Dr. Stuart McGuire, "runners were sent by both colleges to meet incoming trains and try to secure students, and other undignified measures were resorted to." Aid from the state treasury was sought by the privately operated University College of Medicine, and when this was denied the institution tried unsuccessfully to put an end to the support long accorded MCV by the state.[4]

Following Dr. Hunter McGuire's death in 1900, his son was chosen president of UCM. He found the "antagonism and bitterness intolerable" and determined to end it. A merger of UCM and MCV was finally effected in 1913, thanks in no small degree to what Dr. McGuire termed "Dr. Johnston's cooperation and good judgment, and his sound advice during this difficult period."

The first president of the consolidated institution was Dr. Samuel Chiles Mitchell, then president of the University of South Carolina—previously and thereafter one of the most beloved teachers at the University of Richmond. Dr. Mitchell served only one year as president of MCV, but during that time he managed to assuage some of the prevailing animosities. In 1914 Dr. Stuart McGuire became dean and executive officer.

Throughout all the wrangling and squabbling in Richmond's medical profession, one man retained the good will of both sides. He was Dr. William H. Taylor, to whom reference has been made in previous chapters. Witty, erudite Dr. Taylor was famous for his quips. Coroner of Richmond for forty-five years and a member of the MCV faculty for almost as long, he was chosen chairman of the faculty when the intramural brawling was at its height, since he was "the only man that both sides would speak to." He explained this by saying that as coroner he "meddled with no doctor's patients until the doctor himself had finished with them."

Dr. Taylor was so nearsighted that he could read only with the aid of a magnifying glass, but he was nonetheless highly literate and possessed of a delightful literary style. A lifelong bachelor, he viewed the ladies with a jaundiced eye. His lecture on the subject to his class at MCV began with the somewhat pungent observation that "woman is inferior physically, mentally and morally to man," that her qualities "require us to class her as infantine," and that "she has not succeeded in obscuring her descent from the ape to the extent that her brother has done." Another salient declaration was that woman "is squatty and fatty, and is built up with a variety of exaggerated spheres, cones and cylinders strung together." These unchivalrous observations in the "age of chivalry" did not endear Dr. Taylor to the fair sex.

In another area of education in Richmond, there was an important development. Richmond College chose a president in 1895 in the person of young, scholarly Frederic W. Boatwright, aged twenty-seven. He had been teaching modern languages at the college, studying in Germany and evidencing exceptional ability. Some faculty members wished to retain the "chairman of the faculty" system and were opposed to anyone's election as president. Others felt that Boatwright, who had sat in their classes and was less than half their ages, was too young. Several resigned. Some students and alumni also believed that the trustees had erred grievously in selecting this junior professor with no administrative experience. He would soon prove how wrong they were. Boatwright plunged into his task and grew a beard to counteract his youthful appearance.

Like other Southern colleges and universities, Richmond College had had a hard struggle to survive in the years following the Civil War. A small cadre of devoted teachers kept the institution alive. Dr. Tiberius Gracchus Jones (whose brothers were named Cincinnatus, Telemachus and Ulysses) was chosen president after the resignation of Dr. Robert Ryland in 1866. He served for three years, and then the college decided to operate with a chairman of the faculty. Dr. Bennet Puryear and Dr. Herbert Harris alternated in this position. Dr. Harris, professor of Greek, was, in the words of Mrs. Samuel Chiles Mitchell, by common consent "the bright particular star of the college." Other eminent members of the small teaching staff included Dr. Charles H. Winston, physics, and Dr. Edmund Harrison, Latin.

Special mention should be made of Dr. J. L. M. Curry, who served on the faculty from 1868 to 1881 as professor of English, philosophy and law, and who went on to become agent for both the Peabody and Slater Funds for the development of public schools in the South. In this capacity he promoted the Richmond public schools in significant ways. He also served as president of the Richmond College trustees and as ambassador to Spain. His devotion to the college was deep and lasting, and at his request, his funeral was held there in 1903, followed by burial in Hollywood.

Removal of Union Theological Seminary from Hampden-Sydney to Richmond in 1898 and its establishment on land donated by Major Ginter have been noted. The seminary came to Richmond primarily because the larger community would offer students greater practical experience in religious work and additional cultural opportunities. Leadership in making the move was taken by the brilliant Dr. Walter W. Moore, who was elected as the seminary's first president in 1904. An additional thirty-four acres was acquired. In 1908, the Presbyterian School of Christian Education had its beginnings. In that year, a two-year course was offered at the seminary, without charge, to young women wishing to prepare themselves for mission work at home and abroad. Out of this developed the General Assembly Training School, now the School of Christian Education.

Almost simultaneously with the opening of Union Seminary in Richmond came the founding of Virginia Union University for blacks. It was the result of a merger in 1899 between Wayland College and Seminary and Richmond Theological Institute. These schools had their earliest beginnings in 1867 in Lumpkin's former slave jail, on Fifteenth Street between Franklin and Broad. The jail was in the center of a half-acre tract, and was one of four buildings used by Lumpkin in his slave business before the war. The Richmond Theological Institute rented the barred structure for $1,000 a year. The school moved in 1870 to the old Union Hotel at Nineteenth and Main, which had been renamed the United States Hotel. The building was remodeled to meet the school's requirements. It remained there until ground was broken in 1898 on the present site of Virginia Union. Hartshorn Memorial College for girls was founded in 1883 in Ebenezer Baptist Church by the Reverend J. C. Hartshorn of Providence, Rhode Island. He provided $20,000, and buildings were erected at Leigh and Lombardy streets, on the site of the subsequent Maggie Walker High School.

Richmond was badly in need of a new city hall. The handsome and sturdy structure that had served for most of the century had been pulled down in 1874, in the hysterical aftermath of the Capitol disaster, on the theory that it too might collapse. The business of the municipality had been conducted thereafter for nearly two decades in a temporary building, and it was essential that more adquate quarters be provided. Councilman Andrew Pizzini introduced an ordinance in 1882 calling for a referendum on the erection of a new city hall, to cost $300,000. The people voted approval, and the winning design was that of nationally known Elijah E. Myers of Detroit. It called for a structure of American High Victorian Gothic. When bids were let, the lowest was $369,000. It was therefore decided to construct the elaborate hall with day labor, under the direction of Colonel W. E. Cutshaw, city engineer, a one-legged Confederate veteran and able member of his profession.

A tablet commemorating Colonel Cutshaw's services describes him as "a man of physical as well as moral courage, integrity, iron will, character and vision," and declares that during his service as city engineer "this City Hall was erected, and parks, tree-lined streets, a sewer system and a public water supply had their beginnings."

It took until 1894 to finish the city hall, and instead of $369,000, the low bid in the middle eighties, the cost was $1,318,000. Nobody seemed to know why the amount was so astronomical. The use of unskilled labor may have had something to do with it, and the stone construction and unusual style of architecture were expensive. Nobody dreamed of intimating that Colonel Cutshaw profited personally, but there were allegations of waste and even graft. No charges were ever preferred.

The death of Mann S. Valentine II in 1892 ended the career of one of Richmond's most talented and public-spirited citizens. In his will he provided an endowment of $50,000 to establish a museum in his handsome residence at Eleventh and Clay streets, the former home of John Wickham, one of the finest mansions of the Federal period in the United States. Valentine had amassed a remarkable collection of books, manuscripts, prints, pictures, portraits of Virginians by Virginia artists and articles having to do with archaeology and anthropology, especially those relating to the Indians. The house itself, built in 1812, is an architectural gem, with the most beautiful circular staircase in Richmond, fine woodwork, elegant door and window trim, cornices and mahogany doors, together with the loveliest old garden in the city. This last contains, among other things, flowering pomegranates, the most ancient magnolia in Richmond, planted by Wickham in 1805, and a Victorian fountain. The museum was opened in 1898. Negroes were admitted on certain days of the week.

Richmond blacks had been making progress since the Civil War. In fact, *The Negro in Virginia*, published in 1940, declares: "From 1890 to 1920—when John Mitchell [Jr.] and Giles B. Jackson were acknowledged leaders in Negro fraternal, political, financial and publishing circles—Richmond was considered the most important center of Negro business activity in the world." The account goes on to state that "many Negro-owned establishments successfully competed with white businesses," and it mentions livery stables, shoe stores, haberdasheries, barbershops and restaurants "operated by Negroes for white patrons." Blacks also conducted "the most efficient laundry in the city."

The first bank organized anywhere by Negroes was opened in Richmond in 1888 under the leadership of William W. Browne, as the Savings Bank of the Grand Fountain United Order of True Reformers. It grew and expanded and apparently prospered enormously until 1910, when it failed spectacularly in an atmosphere of scandal.[5]

However, the St. Luke's Penny Savings Bank, organized in 1903 by Mrs.

Maggie L. Walker, one of the ablest women of her time, survives today in the successful Consolidated Bank & Trust Company, oldest bank in the nation operated by blacks. Mrs. Walker was the first woman in the United States to be president of a bank.

The bank she founded was the outgrowth of her work with the Independent Order of St. Luke. Such fraternal orders were important in the lives of Richmond blacks. She developed and expanded this ailing organization to an amazing degree, serving as its grand secretary for more than a quarter of a century. Under her leadership, the savings bank was organized and a bank building constructed, while membership in the order increased substantially. A headquarters building for the organization was acquired, and a newspaper, the *Saint Luke Herald*, of which she was editor, was founded. A juvenile branch of the order was formed, and thousands of children were enrolled in thrift clubs and given instruction in morals and hygiene. At the end of her quarter of a century of leadership in 1924, over $8,000,000 of insurance was in force, more than $1,000,000 in death benefits had been paid, and there was a surplus in the treasury of nearly $400,000. A mass meeting packed the City Auditorium in appreciation of Mrs. Walker's effective and dedicated leadership.

In addition to Richmond's priority in the founding of banks by Negroes, there was the establishment in the Virginia capital in 1893 of the oldest of all the Negro life insurance companies, the Southern Aid and Insurance Company. It was still doing business in 1976 as the Southern Aid Life Insurance Company, Inc.

Many Negroes were moving into Richmond and other cities in the final decade of the nineteenth century. Numerous skilled mechanics had been trained on the plantations before the Civil War, and they were able to put that training to good use. The 1890 census showed that Virginia Negroes were being employed in large numbers on the railroads, in saw and planing mills, and as carpenters and joiners, blacksmiths and wheelwrights, brickmasons and potters. There were also numerous boot and shoe makers and repairers, iron and steel workers and textile mill employees. As in earlier years, blacks made up the major portion of the work force in tobacco factories, and they were heavily engaged in domestic service.

A group of white Richmonders terming themselves the Powhatan Club appeared before the City School Board in 1892 and urged that the eighty-four Negro teachers in the public schools be removed and their positions given to white teachers. The board refused, saying that the black teachers were capable, painstaking and conscientious, and that they could do more effective work with the Negro pupils than white teachers.

The black leader who did most to prevent such injustices as that attempted by the Powhatan Club was John Mitchell, Jr. In the Richmond *Planet* he did not hesitate to assail the whites, as evidenced by his caustic comments at the time of the Lee monument's unveiling. Mitchell was also quick to point out injustice in the courts, as when a white man was fined $25 for shooting a Negro and a Negro got five years for threatening a white man.

Mitchell denounced segregation, in an era when to do so was not only almost unprecedented for a black, but risky as well. There were sixty-one lynchings in Virginia between 1880 and 1894. Mitchell conducted a veritable anti-lynching crusade, and was widely quoted in the Northern press. Not only so, but when a black named Richard Walker was lynched in Prince Edward County, Mitchell announced in the *Planet* that he would make a personal investigation on the ground. He was warned, in a letter containing a piece of rope, that if he came to Prince Edward, he too would be "strung up." He went, carrying "a brace of Smith & Wesson revolvers," and although thrown into jail for a few hours, was not otherwise harmed.

Mitchell was a participant in a particularly piquant episode in 1895. He dined with Governor Charles T. O'Ferrall and Mayor Richard M. Taylor at the governor's mansion, along with a black member of the Massachusetts legislature. This was six years before President Theodore Roosevelt brought down a storm of denunciation on his head from Virginia and all other Southern states when he had Booker T. Washington to lunch at the White House.

The background of the forgotten episode involving the two Negroes who dined with the governor is as follows: O'Ferrall received a letter from Massachusetts advising him that a committee of that state's legislature would be visiting Richmond. He accordingly invited the group to dine at the mansion. There is conflicting evidence as to whether O'Ferrall knew that a Negro was in the Massachusetts delegation. At all events, there was general agreement that the governor carried off the dinner without evidencing signs of embarrassment or dismay. Robert Teamoh, the Negro, was not only treated hospitably, but O'Ferrall invited Mayor Taylor and Alderman John Mitchell, Jr., to join the party. Mitchell spoke glowingly of the dinner in the *Planet* the following week. The *Dispatch* and the *Times*, not surprisingly, took a quite different view, and the *Dispatch* characteristically assailed the "meanness, treachery and ingratitude" displayed by Teamoh and Mitchell in presenting themselves to the governor's lunch table. There were repercussions outside Virginia. Demagogic "Tom" Watson of Georgia observed that Governor O'Ferrall sat down and dined at the same table with John Mitchell, Jr., "just as natural as if he was a human being."

F. W. Darling of the Massachusetts delegation wrote the *Times* that O'Ferrall had told him he knew Teamoh was to be a member of the party. O'Ferrall thereupon wrote Darling that he had had no advance knowledge of this, and that had he been aware that the Negro was coming, he would not have invited the group to the mansion for a meal. At all events, excitement over the unprecedented event died down rather quickly.

The fraudulent methods being used in Richmond elections were an open scandal. In 1888, for example, Congressman George D. Wise was "counted in" by the Democrats in his contest with Edmund Waddill, Jr., his Republican opponent. The notorious tactic of delaying blacks at the polls by asking them interminable questions or otherwise preventing them from ever reaching the ballot box had been employed. Wise had been given an alleged majority of 261, but Waddill contended that about seven hundred Negroes had been left standing in line in Jackson Ward when the polls closed. He contested Wise's supposed victory and the congressional committee voted to seat him. Waddill served one term, and later was appointed to the bench of the U. S. District Court and then to the U. S. Circuit Court of Appeals. He sat on those tribunals for a total of twenty-three years.

As long as the victims of electoral thieveries and frauds were blacks, devious methods were tolerated by most Virginians. But when whites began cheating whites, as in the Wise-Waddill contest, the matter seemed more serious. The Democrats were in almost complete control of Virginia's electoral machinery, thanks to the Anderson-McCormick and Walton laws, passed in the 1880s and 1890s. Now, however, the methods used had become so flagrant that leaders of the party became either frightened or conscience-stricken. Furthermore, the Richmond *Times* was hammering at the prevailing crookedness. It was perhaps worst in Southside Virginia and the southwest, but Richmond was almost as bad.

The technique of delaying black voters at the polls in Richmond's Jackson Ward by asking them innumerable ridiculous questions was being used regularly. In an 1896 election, six hundred blacks were still in line when the polls closed. Negroes began going to the voting booths at midnight and waiting there, in order to be sure of casting their ballots next day. Electoral skulduggery with the blacks was facilitated by the fact that as late as 1890 nearly half of the Negroes in Richmond could neither read nor write.

John Mitchell, Jr., was defeated for reelection to the Board of Aldermen from Jackson Ward in 1896. Fraud was used against him, of course, but another factor in his defeat was a split in the Negro vote, owing to animosities that Mitchell had aroused among the blacks. However, his elimination as an alderman did not lessen the vigor of his incisive and well-written editorials in the *Planet*.

The calling of the Constitutional Convention of 1901–2, largely for the purpose of disfranchising most of the blacks, was assailed by Mitchell. Many white leaders professed to have convinced themselves that if Negroes could be kept from the polls, Virginia elections would suddenly become pure and undefiled. The *Planet* scorned the whole scheme. Referring to white fears of black domination, Mitchell observed caustically that the Negro had been kept from voting for more than a decade, and if "this illegal body can do any more disfranchising . . . or make a dead man any 'deader' after he is dead, then the country will look with interest upon this experiment."

An ally of Mitchell during the nineties was a prominent white Richmonder, Lewis Harvie Blair. Member of an old family, a well-to-do businessman and Confederate veteran, Blair astonished his fellow citizens by publishing a book entitled *Prosperity of the South Dependent upon the Elevation of the Negro*. In this volume, which appeared in 1889—it had been published in installments shortly before in a New York magazine—Blair advocated the abolition of racial segregation in all walks of life, and pointed to the many obvious injustices from which the blacks were suffering. For unexplained reasons, Blair reversed his position completely in the early years of the twentieth century, demanding "segregation of the Negro . . . as a lower form of man."

During the decade or more in which Blair and Mitchell were advocating the elimination of segregation in the schools and all other areas, race relations in Richmond and Virginia were deteriorating steadily. The segregation system had been much less rigid in the seventies and eighties. Streetcars and railroads were not segregated during these decades, but during the nineties leading whites were beginning to advocate separation of the races on these carriers. The *Dispatch*, for example, declared that "the Negroes are daily becoming more aggressive, daily making themselves more offensive to the white ladies, and daily increasing the demand . . . for separate cars." In his annual report for 1891, J. C. Hill, state railroad commissioner, urged that legislation be enacted to require separation of the races in railway cars. After much discussion, this law was passed in 1900. Four years later similar legislation was passed covering streetcars. One reason for these enactments was the shift in the position of the *Times*, which had been more moderate on the race issue than the *Dispatch*. But by the turn of the century the *Times* had reached the conclusion that segregation of the races was essential "in every relation of Southern life," and that "God Almighty drew the color line and it cannot be obliterated."

John Mitchell, Jr., was extremely unhappy over these developments, as were many other Negro leaders. The *Planet* advanced the thesis that "Jim Crow beds are more necessary in the Southland than Jim Crow cars . . . and that white men who are so anxious to be separate from colored men must also be made to separate from colored women." He suggested that those who professed to be so concerned about the "purity of the white race" secure the enactment of a law making it a felony for a white man to keep a black mistress. All of which had no appreciable effect on the trend of events.

When the Spanish-American War broke out in 1898, two battalions of Negro militia from Virginia, constituting the 6th Regiment, were among the first to volunteer. Most of the 1st Battalion was from Richmond, and its headquarters was in the city. The Negro militiamen had practically no financial support from the state, and "to a great extent depended upon private contributions from Negro citizens for the purchase of equipment and uniforms."

A sharp controversy arose over whether the two battalions would be allowed to serve in the war under their black officers. Governor J. Hoge Tyler decided that these officers would be retained, but that a young white West Pointer, Richard C. Croxton, would command the regiment with the rank of lieutenant colonel. Strongly objecting to this arrangement, the Richmond *Planet* sounded the slogan, "No officers, no fight." The plan, nevertheless, was put into effect.

Competence of the black units was called into question by officials, and the 2nd Battalion, headquartered in Petersburg, was given a particularly bad report. All this caused a general lowering of morale and a desire to be mustered out of the service. Nine officers of the 2nd Battalion resigned, and a mass meeting of blacks was held in Richmond in an effort to persuade the Secretary of War to fill these vacancies from the ranks of the regiment. The Secretary passed the buck to the governor of Virginia, who filled eight of the nine vacancies with white officers, and quoted Colonel Croxton as saying that there were no black men in the ranks with sufficient education and ability to fill the positions. This caused a near mutiny.

The frustrated and unhappy mood of the black volunteers was intensified by their transfer to a camp near Macon, Georgia. Discrimination and Jim Crowism there surpassed anything they had experienced. In a public park on the edge of Macon they saw a sign "No Dogs and Niggers Allowed in Here." One of their number was shot dead by a streetcar conductor when he refused to move his seat to the colored section. The conductor was acquitted, the verdict being "justifiable homicide." All this caused extreme bitterness among members of the 6th Virginia, and they decided to return to civilian life. They were accordingly mustered out of service. That was the end of the Old Dominion's black militia regiment, units of which had been formed in Richmond a quarter of a century before.[6]

White units of the Virginia militia, including companies of the Richmond Blues and Grays, had a happier experience in the Spanish-American War, although they did not see any active fighting. A number died from "embalmed beef" and typhoid fever. Fitzhugh Lee, who was U.S. consul general at Havana when the conflict broke out, was named a major general in the U. S. Volunteers—striking evidence that intersectional animosities were cooling.

Negro morale in Richmond, which had been falling as a result of the treatment of the city's black soldiers, was lifted temporarily by an event that occurred at Murphy's Hotel in 1899. John L. Sullivan, ex-heavyweight boxing champion of the world, became angry with William Miller, the waiter who was serving him breakfast. Alcohol-soaked "John L.," probably breathing Bourbon, despite the early hour, shouted at Miller that he had "killed two coons the night before and that Miller was going to be the third." Whereupon Miller hurled a hot coffeepot into Sullivan's face, knocking him "cold." Miller "took a vacation" immediately, at the urging of the hotel management. He returned some days later to find himself a hero. Contributions totaling more than $3,000 poured in from admirers, and William L. ("Buck") Royall, prominent attorney and chief editorial writer of the *Times*, presented him with a silver coffeepot, inscribed "To the World's Champion Coffee Pot Fighter." Miller took his $3,000 and opened Miller's Hotel for Negro patrons. It operated for many years.

An institution in Richmond for generations after the Civil War, as well as before it, was the Negro mammy. She would not fit into today's race relationships, and blacks of the late twentieth century apparently would prefer that no mention be made of her existence. But she was too important to be ignored, too widely beloved to be forgotten. James Branch Cabell wrote that in the late nineteenth century, "a mammy still ruled over every household in which there were children." And he went on to say:

"In no part of Richmond were mammies infrequent; but it was in Monroe Park that you noted them in full panoply. To every bench there would be two or three mammies; alongside most of the benches sprawled a baby carriage. . . .

"These ladies wore white caps and large white aprons, befrilled proudly. . . . Each one of them some twenty years earlier had been a slave; but now they were tyrants . . . none dared to assail the authority of the mammies of Richmond within the borders of their several kingdoms; and this was especially true of the parents who paid to each one of them ten dollars a month."

Cordiality among the religious denominations of Richmond continued in the tradition established by the "two parsons" in the early 1800s. Brilliant young Rabbi Edward N. Calisch, who had come to Temple Beth Ahabah at age twenty-six, invited Dr. R. P. Kerr, pastor of First Presbyterian Church, to deliver the Thanksgiving Day sermon at the temple in 1893. Dr. Kerr preached and also assisted in the religious service. Two years later, by invitation, the Traveler's Protective Association attended services in a body at Temple Beth Ahabah, the first time that a non-Jewish organization had done so. When Major Lewis Ginter died, he made generous bequests to Jewish charitable agencies.

William Lovenstein was a Jewish leader in that era. He fought as a member of the Richmond Blues in the Civil War, and then represented

Richmond in the General Assembly for twenty-three years, rising to the position of president pro tem of the Senate.

A picturesque Richmonder was Dr. Bennett W. Green, author of the *Word-Book of Virginia Speech*. Dr. Green walked westward to the Lee monument, winter and summer, rain or shine, every day at 4 P.M. and saluted the great commander. Dr. W. Gordon McCabe, the noted schoolmaster, trained his sons to salute the statue whenever they passed it.

An enormous Confederate reunion in 1896 brought dozens of Confederate generals and thousands of Confederate veterans from throughout the South. Entertainment lasted for days, and included music by Polk Miller of Richmond and his Old South Quartette, receptions at the White House of the Confederacy and the governor's mansion, copious oratory and a gargantuan parade. There were loud cheers for a group of veterans, apparently former inhabitants of a Northern prison, who carried a banner with the words "43 Days on Rotten Corn Meal, Cats and Pickle."

Henry James, Anglo-American novelist, came to Richmond a few years later, and his observations, as recorded in his book *The American Scene*, were none too complimentary. He mentioned the "high elegance" of the equestrian monument to Washington, but saw the monument to Lee as "some precious pearl of ocean washed up on a rude bare strand." Lee "looked off into desolate space," wrote James. "He does well . . . to appear to see as far, and to overlook as many things." The cause for which Lee fought James termed "the very heaven of futility."

By contrast, Matthew Arnold, who had lectured in Richmond some years previously, wrote his daughter of his delight in the city and his reception there. "One gentleman came in twenty miles on an engine to hear me," he said. Arnold, among other things, was rhapsodical over Richmond's batter cakes and batter bread.

The city's, and the state's, foremost postbellum literary figure was Thomas Nelson Page. He practiced law for eighteen years, but his literary inclinations overcame his interest in the legal profession. When his story "Marse Chan" appeared in the *Century Magazine* in 1884 and created a sensation, his career as a writer was launched. Page's long series of novels and stories followed. Perfumed with magnolias and bathed in Southern moonlight, they created a much more favorable picture of the Old South than had previously appeared in Northern publications. It was a one-dimensional picture, since the darker aspects of slavery were glossed over or ignored entirely. But Page's work showed genuine literary artistry, and his writings were instrumental in lessening prejudice against the South. As ambassador to Italy he also contributed to better international understanding.

W. Gordon McCabe was a less well-known literary figure than Page, but his school for boys, conducted for thirty years in Petersburg and then for six years in his native Richmond, made him one of the foremost figures in America in the field of secondary education. McCabe was termed by Dr. John C. Metcalf "the outstanding Richmond poet and essayist of the war and postwar days." He was for many years president of the Virginia Historical Society, and contributed frequently to literary and historical publications.

Two newspapermen, W. Dallas Chesterman and his son, Evan R. Chesterman, were journalists of exceptional talent. Dr. William H. Taylor, writing on "Unremembered Men of Letters," paid special tribute to Dallas Chesterman as an editorial writer of peculiar grace. "He could invest very small and commonplace things with an unsuspected charm and unimagined interest," Taylor wrote.

Evan Chesterman conducted a column called "The Idle Reporter" in several different Richmond newspapers, beginning in the early nineties and continuing through the first decade of the twentieth century. It was in lighter vein and charmingly written, but also informative as to customs and habits of Richmonders during the period. Chesterman knew everybody and went everywhere. He was private secretary to Governor O' Ferrall early in his newspaper career, and he kept on writing, then and later.

An interesting fact revealed by him was that in the seventies there were four or five deer in Capitol Square. "Most of them became the victims of dogs," he wrote, but a stag named George survived until the age of four and frequently came into the Capitol. George "undertook one day to swallow an Irish potato, and becoming choked, breathed his last."

"The Idle Reporter" was aghast in the pre-automobile era over the hazards encountered in Richmond traffic. "You can take your choice between being pulverized by an electric car, beaten to jelly by horses' hoofs, or cut into slices by the tires of bicycles," said he. "A thousand times a day I expect to be hurled to destruction."

Sarah Bernhardt arrived in town for a performance of *Camille*. "The divine Sarah" came in a private car, accompanied by forty-three members of her entourage, together with four servants, a St. Bernard, a mastiff, a parrot and 140 trunks. Both the *Dispatch* and the *Southern Churchman* regarded the play *Camille* as demoralizing, "especially upon the young and pure mind." The *Churchman* expressed dismay that although the plot "turned upon adultery," not a single member of the audience got up and left "in protest against nastiness that sends to hell."

Richmond had two sensational beauties in the nineties—Irene Langhorne and May Handy.

Irene was one of several lovely daughters of Chiswell Dabney Langhorne, Confederate veteran and tobacco auctioneer. He originated the yammering sales pitch still used at auctions of the leaf. Langhorne went into the railroad business afterward and made a fortune. In addition to Irene there was another daughter, Nancy, later Lady Astor, the first woman to serve in Britain's House of Commons. The Langhornes lived at the southwest corner of Adams and Grace streets, in a house no longer standing. It was incorporated into Dr. Allison Hodges' Hygeia Hospital, a building subsequently destroyed by fire.

"I'm afraid we were rather hooligans," Lady Astor wrote in her old age. She and her sisters had a goat cart and raced about the streets. One well-known citizen, apparently John Powell, the pianist, told his friend "Nannie" Astor long afterward that as a youth he had been afraid to pass her house for fear the Langhorne sisters would throw stones at him.

Irene was so stunningly beautiful that even as a schoolgirl there were paragraphs in the newspapers concerning the gorgeous young lady who was growing up in Richmond. When a New York paper published her picture, her father was furious and threatened to make a special trip to Gotham for the purpose of shooting the editor. It was not considered proper for a young girl to be thus mentioned in the public prints.

Irene Langhorne was a sensation at White Sulphur Springs at the age of sixteen. All agree that wherever she went, she was the center of attention. There was agreement, too, that she was entirely unspoiled by the adulation. She is supposed to have had sixty-two proposals of marriage before she accepted Charles Dana Gibson of Massachusetts, creator of the Gibson girl. Her father was both irate and profane at the prospect of her marriage to that "damned charcoal artist." However, the wedding took place at St. Paul's in 1895 as the highlight of the social season. The Richmond *State* gave the nuptials more than two columns on page 1.

Irene's vivacious sister, Nancy, was a belle herself of no mean dimensions, as she admitted in her above-mentioned memoir. She carefully recorded sixteen proposals from Americans, Englishmen and Frenchmen. Earlier, at age fourteen, she fell in love with St. George Bryan of Richmond, who was "eighteen and very good looking" and "whistled beautifully." "Our romance consisted mainly in our going for rides together," Lady Astor wrote. "It lasted quite a few years, but then it just faded out."

May Handy, daughter of Captain and Mrs. Edward Handy, was a fabulous beauty. Mrs. Edward Handy was also the mother—by her first marriage, to Judge Robert Ould—of the lovely and witty Mattie Ould. May Handy was even better-looking than her half sister, but few could hope to equal Mattie at clever repartee.

A special variety of violet was named for May Handy by a Richmond florist, and Franklin Street was on tiptoe whenever she stolled past, wearing a bouquet of the flowers. At White Sulphur Springs she was Irene Langhorne's only serious rival for attention, and at Bar Harbor, Newport and Saratoga her admirers were innumerable. The University of Virginia annual for 1895, dedicated "To Southern Womanhood, Ever the Inspiration and Support of Southern Chivalry," carried a full-page picture of her, but there was no name beneath it. Taboos against publicizing "females" doubtless dictated the omission, but everybody knew at once that it was the incomparable May Handy. When a few years later she married James Brown Potter, a New York banker who had been divorced, there was uneasy agitation among the lorgnettes.

The nineties at "the White" witnessed the rise to fame of a young man named Jo Lane Stern. A native of Caroline County, Virginia, he had served the Confederacy as a boy telegrapher, and then had graduated from Washington College during the presidency of Robert E. Lee. Stern began leading Germans and devising fancy maneuvers on the dance floor at the Old White Hotel in the late seventies. By the nineties the season there had not really "begun" until he arrived. His virtuosity as a leader of balls, masked and otherwise, was such that the belles and beaux waited eagerly to learn of his latest ingenuities. Percival Reniers has described some of them for us:

"The National Figure, in which the ladies carried drums suspended from their shoulders and beat a tattoo while their partners waved flags; the Butterfly Figure, in which the ladies fluttered about waving their great wings of chiffon and the gentlemen pursued them with nets; the Slipper Figure, in which the favors were tiny silver slippers filled with candy and *not* champagne; the Coach-and-Four Figure, with the gentlemen driving the ladies harnessed four abreast and covered with jingle bells, around the ballroom."

So great was Jo Lane Stern's fame that he was soon commandeered to lead the Richmond German, a role which he filled for more than half a century. A Richmond lawyer of ability, he also served at one time as adjutant general of Virginia, which caused him to be addressed as "General" Stern. A lifelong bachelor, Stern was noted as a potent wielder of the lightning riposte. On his death at age eighty-three, the Richmond *News Leader* declared with some exaggeration that "his ready wit and flashing repartee were more renowned than those of any Richmonder since the days of Innes Randolph."

Richmond's preferred residential areas in the nineties were along Franklin and Grace streets, and also on Cary and Main streets from Foushee to Fifth, together with South Third Street. Franklin ended at Lombardy and Grace at the eastern gate of the Richmond College grounds. Both were hardly describable as streets as they neared their western termini. Similarly, Broad Street was merely a wide country road after it passed the intersection with Hancock. Beyond that point there were tall trees at intervals on both sides until the road reached the Fair Grounds.

Grove Road, later rechristened Grove Avenue, was highly regarded for residential purposes. It was a fashionable driveway, tree-lined, and bordered by comfortable homes on large lots. Much farther to the west, the River Road, later known as Cary Street Road, connected with Three Chopt Road, whose name derived from the notches cut into the trees in the early days when the rough trail traversed an uncharted wilderness.

Trolley rides for picnics in the park were among the diversions of the nineties. Or a trip to Pizzini's confectionery, on Broad Street to the east of Murphy's Hotel, was a welcome interlude. There, under handsome chandeliers and on marble floors, one could enjoy cooling ices or munch candies and fruit. Pizzini's, of which Captain Andrew Pizzini was the proprietor, furnished the sweets for Richmond's fashionable suppers.

Ladies often received formally on a certain day of each week, and light refreshments were served. The parlor where such receptions took place was an awesome affair, with small and uncomfortable gilt chairs and an equally uncomfortable horsehair-covered sofa, with antimacassars protecting its back and arms. On the wall was the inevitable picture of General Lee, and perhaps "the Burial of Latané." Calling cards were *de rigueur*, and anyone who was invited to a party or reception was expected to call within a reasonable time, leaving a card if the host or hostess was not at home.

Adjoining the parlor was the "back parlor," today's living room or family room. A feature there was often a "pot-bellied" Latrobe stove. Fitted into the fireplace, it heated that room and perhaps another, as well as the room above. The anthracite coal fire within glowed cheerfully through the isinglass panes in front.

Under a long-standing custom in the nineteenth century, married women addressed their husbands regularly as "Mr." When the husband died, the widow wore deep black for years.

The century's last decade was signalized near its end by perhaps the worst snowstorm in Richmond's history. The great blizzard of 1899 struck the city on February 6, and howled for fifty-five hours. The avalanche of flakes came down in marrow-piercing blasts, and piled up to a depth of seventeen inches on the level and from three to eight feet in drifts. There was also heavy sleet, which added to the hazards and damage.

Everything was brought to a standstill. Streetcars and trains stopped running, there was no mail, and the schools closed. There had been zero temperatures for thirteen days, breaking previous records. When the weather finally moderated, and Richmond dug itself out of the drifts, rain began falling. The ice in the river melted, and smashed against Mayo's Bridge, tearing it from its piers all over again. There were floods on lower Main. Things began getting back to normal by February 15, when the streetcars and railroad trains began operating. Schools opened two days later.

The decade ended on a characteristic note. The United Daughters of the Confederacy held their national convention in Richmond. Mrs. Norman V. Randolph, active for many years in the organization, was president of the host chapter. A carved angel over the grave of Varina Anne ("Winnie") Davis, the "Daughter of the Confederacy," was unveiled by the U.D.C., which had raised the funds for it. "Winnie," who had died the previous year, had been born in the Confederate White House in 1864. A statue of Jefferson Davis, the gift of his widow, was unveiled at his grave nearby. There was a parade of veterans and military units, and Beverley B. Munford, Richmond attorney and historian, delivered the address. J. H. Reagan, sole surviving member of the Confederate Cabinet, also spoke, as did General Fitzhugh Lee.

Confederate flags were everywhere, in tribute to those who had fought for the South, but there were no hints of disloyalty to the Stars and Stripes. The North and South had united the year before in the war with Spain, in which "Fitz" Lee served as a major general. Richmonders, along with other Southerners, were back in the Union.

# EIGHTEEN

# Moving into the New Century

RICHMOND was moving strongly ahead as the new century dawned. Morale was improving, and the business depression was fading from men's minds. The *Dispatch* declared on January 1, 1901, that the year just ended had "not been surpassed during the past hundred years, probably, as a year of natural advancement along every line that makes a city great."

Richmond was expanding as a railroad center. Two important railway stations were about to be built—the handsome Chesapeake & Ohio-Seaboard Air Line depot on Main Street between Fifteenth and Sixteenth, and the Southern Railway station at Fourteenth and Mill.

The first train from Tampa, Florida, over the newly completed S.A.L. reached Richmond on June 2, 1900, and was greeted by a welcoming throng. Drawn by two engines made by the Richmond Locomotive Works, and carrying many of the city's leaders, the train crossed a new bridge over the James and steamed into Richmond, to an obbligato of guns fired by the Howitzers. John Skelton Williams, one of Richmond's foremost financiers, later Comptroller of the Currency under Woodrow Wilson, was president of the Seaboard. His small son John Skelton, Jr., drove the golden spike that signaled the completion of the railroad.

A significant Richmond industry not heretofore noted was the quarrying of granite on the southern side of the river. Stone used in the State, War and Navy Building in Washington came from the Westham Quarry upriver from Forest Hill Park. The structure in Washington was the most elaborate building of granite in the United States at the time, and the largest in the world under one roof. These quarries also furnished most of the stone for Richmond's city hall, completed in 1894, and that for the soldiers' and sailors' monument unveiled on Libby Hill the same year. The McIntosh Quarry near Granite in Chesterfield County provided the material for the steps and approaches to the Capitol at Richmond when the wings were added in 1906.

The death in 1900 of Colonel Charles O'B. Cowardin, proprietor and editor in chief of the *Dispatch* brought sorrow to the city. "Charlie" Cowardin was only forty-eight when he succumbed to typhoid fever. The son of James A. Cowardin, who founded the paper in 1850, Colonel Cowardin had been chief of staff to four governors, president of the Westmoreland Club and a leader in musical circles. He was famous as a raconteur. The New York *Sun* commented after his death that he was "one of the two great story-tellers of this country." Another paper declared that on a visit to New York he had been "delightful, engaging and inimitable" and had sung "a ballad of his own composition."

John L. Williams & Sons bought the *Dispatch* from the Cowardin estate, and in 1903 Joseph Bryan acquired it from the Williams interests. He combined it with the *Times* to form the *Times-Dispatch*. Bryan sold the colorless but profitable *Leader* to John L. Williams & Sons, who owned the *News*, and they put the two together. Thus the *News Leader*, afternoon competitor of the *Times-Dispatch*, came into being. John Stewart Bryan and associates bought the *News Leader* in 1909.

Joseph Bryan's energy and drive were almost unbelievable. His diary for this period shows him in New York several times a month, and also traveling to Philadelphia, Washington, Norfolk, Birmingham, Hot Springs, Gloucester and other places, usually in connection with business, but also on civic and religious matters. Typhoid fever in 1900 weakened his heart, but he never slowed down. His strenuous life finally put the heart under too great a strain, and he died in 1908, aged sixty-three. There were tributes such as have seldom been accorded a private citizen. Persons in all walks of life, both white and black, grieved over his passing. An association of citizens erected a statue of him in Monroe Park. On it were the words "The character of the citizen is the strength of the state."

Mrs. Bryan, on behalf of herself and her four sons, presented some 200 acres to the city as a memorial to her husband. The City Council named it Joseph Bryan Park, and after Mrs. Bryan's death erected a gateway to the park in her honor.

The burning of the Jefferson Hotel in March 1901 was a calamity for Richmond. The Jefferson had not only been the center of the city's social life since its opening in 1895, but it had also been a great asset to the business community. The fire started at about 10 P.M. from defective electric wiring, and while nobody was killed or even injured, the handsome structure's magnificent lobby with its regal stairway was a total wreck. There was also serious damage elsewhere from the flames, and from water and smoke in the building. Henry Lee Valentine rushed to the scene and organized a group of about a hundred men who worked all night carrying out the beautiful paintings, bronzes, furniture and bric-a-brac. In bringing

47. Giles B. Jackson, prominent Richmond lawyer who organized the Negro Exhibit at the Jamestown Exhibition of 1907, and worked quietly with Booker T. Washington to break down segregation. He was personally acquainted with several U.S. Presidents.

48. Mrs. Maggie L. Walker, first woman in the United States to be president of a bank, and one of the ablest women of her time in Virginia. The bank she organized and headed in 1903 survives today in the Consolidated Bank & Trust Company.

49. Members of the fourth form at the 1910–11 session of the Richmond Academy, many of whom grew up to be leading Richmond citizens —

First row: A. Churchill Young, Jr., Louis M. Latane, Frederic W. Scott, Henry S. Raab, Ramon D. Garcin, Charles H. Thompson, Jr.

Second row: W. Wymond Cabell, John Gordon Wallace, James M. Taylor, Malcolm U. Pitt, E. Lee Roden, Jr., R. Millington Blankenship, Melville E. Sullivan.

Third row: Isaac Diggs, Jr., William A. Chambers, Jr., James B. Patton, Jr., William E. Chapin, Jr., Roger M. Millhiser, A. Beirne Blair, Jr., T. Ashby Miller, Jr., Hill Montague, Jr., B. H. Ellington, Jr.

Fourth row: M. Osborne Jones, Dalton Taylor, Charles B. Robertson, Jr., Charles H. McGee, Thomas T. Mayo, Preston T. Bronaugh, Robert M. Sharp.

50. Miss Ellen Glasgow, in a portrait painted by Prince Pierre Troubetzkoy in the winter of 1912–13. It hung in her Richmond home and then was given to the American Academy of Arts and Letters.

51. Miss Virginia Randolph (Miss Jennie) Ellett, famous headmistress of girls' schools in Richmond, including St. Catherine's, shown in her latter years.

52. "Justice John" Crutchfield, the picturesque and erratic Police Court justice, whose colorful personality was the basis for a Broadway play, *The Virginia Judge*. He was also the first judge of a Juvenile Court in Virginia, and his work on that bench drew high praise.

53. Mr. and Mrs. Benjamin J. Lambert, Jr., well-known Richmond caterers, are shown surrounded by their seven successful children. Left to right: Dr. Benjamin J. Lambert III, Abbot J. Lambert, Mrs. Elizabeth L. Johns of Alexandria, Va., John A. Lambert, Mrs. Anne Scott Johnson, Leonard W. Lambert and Richard A. Lambert. Mrs. Lambert was Virginia Mother of the Year for 1974.

54. Rabbi Edward N. Calisch of Temple Beth Ahabah, for decades Richmond's most prominent spiritual leader, an eloquent speaker on many religious and civic occasions.

55. Mayor J. Fulmer Bright, who served for sixteen years, longer than any mayor in the city's history. Ultraconservative, he fought all innovations in Richmond's outmoded form of government. In his will he made generous bequests to many religious and civic groups.

56. Booker T. Bradshaw, a foremost businessman and constructive citizen, vice-chairman of the City School Board during the difficult early years of integration.

57. Beautiful garden of the Valentine Museum, with the historic Wick-
ham-Valentine house in the background. The mansion was built in 1812
by John Wickham, learned and polished defense counsel for Aaron Burr
in his trial for treason five years before.

58. The "enchanted garden" of the Edgar Allan Poe Museum, with rear view of the Old Stone House, built about 1739; from a drawing by Elmo Jones. The view is from the loggia constructed of bricks from the demolished former home of the *Southern Literary Messenger*, made famous by Poe.

59. Statue in aluminum of Bill ("Bojangles") Robinson, the renowned tap dancer, by John Temple Witt of Richmond, the only statue of a black in the city. The square where it stands has been named for Robinson.

out Edward V. Valentine's marble statue of Thomas Jefferson, they inadvertently broke the head off, but this was soon repaired by the sculptor. It was not until 1907 that the Jefferson was got back into full operation. A company headed by Joseph Bryan achieved this, and added not only an auditorium for conventions but a pool with live alligators. The alligators were a unique feature of the lobby for decades.

One of the most picturesque figures in Richmond during the late nineteenth and early twentieth centuries was "Justice John" Crutchfield, who presided over Police Court for nearly a third of a century. A Confederate veteran, the son of a native-born Englishman who had sat on the Hustings Court bench, Justice John was "a good deal of a clown and exhibitionist," says a Richmond lawyer who knew him. Always dressed in a turned-down collar and black string bow tie, he squirted tobacco juice in the general direction of a huge cuspidor, and rendered verdicts that often bore little relation to the evidence. Justice John invariably called blacks "niggers." His two great aversions were blacks from North Carolina and lawyers.

In 1888, when Crutchfield was first appointed to the bench, he sat in a building at the corner of East Franklin and Mayo streets. Upon completion of the city hall, he moved to that building's basement. His colorful and erratic behavior made him known over a wide area. Visitors to the city came to his court as though to a side show, and Walter Kelley wrote a play, *The Virginia Judge,* in which a character closely resembling Justice John was the central figure.

General John A. Cutchins, who served as city director of public safety after Crutchfield's time, says in his *Memories of Old Richmond* that Justice John was "worth fifty policemen." General Cutchins recognized the oddities in the justice's *modus operandi* while feeling at the same time that the very name of Crutchfield "struck terror to the hearts of criminals."

A frequently repeated dialogue in the Crutchfield court was as follows:

"Nigger, where you from?"

"Nawth Ca'lina, judge."

"I thought so. Thirty days."

In the justice's behalf it should be said that some of these North Carolina defendants had been before him previously and had police records. He did not always give them thirty days automatically simply because they were from Tarheelia.

Justice John delighted in "bawling out" lawyers in his court. He was not a lawyer, and he made it clear that he found members of that profession a nuisance and a hindrance to the proper operation of his tribunal. More than once he burst out at attorneys before him approximately as follows:

"Git out of here! If you lawyers will just quit talking and pestering me, I'll decide this case like it ought to be."

Justice John was completely unpredictable. A drunk would be brought in off the street, and the judge would say, "Bailiff, give this man a stiff

drink of whiskey to steady him up and let him go home." Or a drunk
would fall flat on his face in front of the justice, who would yell: "What
do you mean coming into my court drunk? Case dismissed!" Or he would
give a man and his wife an absurdly severe sentence of thirty days for engaging in fisticuffs with each other on the street. The foregoing are all actual cases, vouched for by John H. Gwathmey in his book *Justice John*.

Despite Justice Crutchfield's attitude toward the Negro race, Giles B.
Jackson, the city's leading black lawyer, presented him with a handsome
silver service on his sixty-ninth birthday, on behalf of black clergymen and
other leading black citizens. Jackson paid an affectionate tribute to the justice in appreciation of the contribution he was felt to have made in building a better Negro citizenry.

When the juvenile division of Richmond Police Court was created in
1912, Crutchfield presided over it for three years, sitting in the afternoon.
He was the first judge of a juvenile court in Virginia. Those who observed
his demeanor on that bench believed that it contrasted sharply with the
attitude exhibited by him earlier in the day in Police Court. This was
noted by both Judge J. Hoge Ricks, who later sat as judge of the Richmond Juvenile and Domestic Relations Court, and the Reverend J. J.
Scherer, long the beloved pastor of First English Lutheran Church, and
assistant judge of the court. They remarked on the compassion and wis-
dom shown by Justice John when dealing with youthful offenders.

Adoption of the state consitution of 1901–2, with its restrictions on the
franchise, had an impact in various directions, including the voting power
of Jackson Ward, where the blacks were concentrated. In 1896 there had
been 2,983 black voters in the ward and 789 white voters. After the new
constitution went into effect, only 33 black voters managed to register. A
number of blacks presented evidence that their fathers were Confederate
veterans. Attorney General William A. Anderson ruled at once that illegitimate Negroes were not eligible to register, even if they could prove that
their fathers were Confederates. This despite the fact that the new constitution provided that sons of veterans could vote. Another blow fell in
1903. The wards of the city were reapportioned, and the territory that had
been Jackson Ward was divided up and distributed among the other
wards. On top of all else, the Republicans began excluding blacks from
their councils and boasting that they were "lily-white."

These happenings were highly discouraging to such black leaders as
John Mitchell Jr., of the *Planet* and Giles B. Jackson. Mitchell, as we have
seen, had been militant in his denunciation of the many discriminatory
laws and rulings against the blacks. By contrast, Jackson, like Virginia-
born Booker T. Washington, had been outwardly conciliatory. Mitchell
decided that immediate justice for the Negro was unobtainable, and that
he would have to adjust to the situation. He kept the *Planet*, but was
much less aggressive thereafter, and founded the Mechanics Savings Bank

in 1902. As for Jackson, he remained seemingly cooperative with the whites, while working with Booker T. Washington behind the scenes to break down the entire segregation system in the courts.[1]

Extremely significant in this connection is a letter written to Washington by Jackson under date of January 24, 1901 (now in the Library of Congress), concerning arrangements for Washington's address in Richmond the following month before the governor, the General Assembly and other dignitaries. This address had been announced as under the auspices of the National Negro Business League, a conservative organization, highly regarded by whites. Actually, as Jackson makes clear in his letter, after paying Washington's expenses and other incidental bills, two thirds of the remaining sum realized from the lecture would go to finance the fight against segregation.

John Mitchell, for his part, was busy with his new bank—the depository for the Knights of Pythias, of which he was grand chancellor for Virginia. He was for many years the only black member of the American Bankers' Association. Addressing the association in 1904 at the Waldorf-Astoria Hotel in New York, he said, "I love the white man of the South . . . there is no quarrel between me and him." He got a standing ovation. Mitchell had decided that the wisest course for the blacks was to conciliate the whites and build a strong but separate black economy.[2]

He did not, however, completely abandon militancy, for in the year that he addressed the bankers in New York he organized a boycott of the streetcars in Richmond to protest segregation on the vehicles. Similar boycotts were being tried in a number of other Southern cities. The Virginia Passenger & Power Company, which operated the Richmond cars, was the only traction company in Virginia that was enforcing segregation. The blacks, exhorted by Mitchell, boycotted the cars on a considerable scale for several months, walking to their destinations. "Fish salt, fish grease and witch hazel" were reported in great demand for aching feet. Later in the year, the *Planet* exclaimed: "The street car company is busted: three cheers for the Richmond Negroes." Stockholders had indeed asked that receivers be appointed, and the petition had been granted.

But the company had gone through a devastating strike the year before by its motormen and conductors, and this apparently was the principal factor in the receivership. Violence broke out and there was gunfire, with threats to burn car barns and bridges. A number of persons were injured and one was killed. Sixteen companies of militia were called out from Richmond and other Virginia cities. The strike continued for two months, and business in Richmond was severely damaged.

All this, combined with the boycott by blacks, caused the Virginia Passenger & Power Company to go bankrupt. The Virginia Railway & Power Company was incorporated in 1909 and acquired the properties of the defunct concern. As for the blacks, the law which had permitted streetcar companies to use their own judgment in separating the races was amended in 1906 to make segregation mandatory.

An extraordinary development in the sphere of race relations was the little-known activity of William L. Royall in his last years to combat residential segregation in Richmond. Royall, who as chief editorial writer for the *Times* and in his private capacity had campaigned vigorously for disfranchisement of the blacks, cooperated quietly with the National Association for the Advancement of Colored People against restrictions imposed on Negroes in their selection of a place of residence—as shown by correspondence in the NAACP files.[3]

The Negro exhibit at the Jamestown Exposition of 1907 was something of a sensation, and Giles Jackson was the man whose idea it was and who made it a reality. He obtained an appropriation of $100,000 from the Federal government toward the expenses of the exhibit, and traveled widely in helping to raise another $100,000. The state of North Carolina appropriated $5,000, but neither Virginia nor any other state appropriated anything.

The Negro exhibit was visited by a total of approximately 750,000 persons, at a rate of from 3,000 to 12,000 a day, by actual count. There were agricultural and business exhibits, musical scores, needlework, paintings, inventions, three hundred books and other evidences of black progress. President Theodore Roosevelt, who attended the exposition, took in the Negro exhibit and was much impressed. When he stopped off in Richmond en route back to Washington, he went out of his way to congratulate Giles Jackson. The President drove to exhibit headquarters at 528 East Broad Street and called for "Mr. Giles B. Jackson." The latter hurried down from his second-floor office and stood at the President's carriage. Roosevelt congratulated him not only on the Jamestown exhibit but on the banks and other business enterprises in Richmond operated by blacks. "I am glad as an American for what you are doing," said "T.R." Jackson bowed acknowledgment, and there were cheers as the President moved on to a reception in Capitol Square.

Giles Jackson collaborated with another remarkable Richmond black, the Reverend Daniel Webster Davis, in the writing of *The Industrial History of the Negro Race in the United States*, used for many years in the Richmond public schools. Most of the book was apparently written by Davis, who was Baptist minister, public school teacher, poet and orator *par excellence*. Like Jackson, Davis was outwardly conciliatory in his attitude toward the whites. The book is extremely mild in its criticism of slavery and it denies that the South fought to preserve "the peculiar institution." However, Davis, like Jackson, was vehement in his private condemnation of slavery and of the Negro's lowly status after emancipation. He was also active in private efforts to bring about a change. When he died prematurely in 1913 at age fifty-one, his funeral at First African Baptist Church was said by the *Planet* to have drawn the largest crowd in the church's history. "A solid wall of humanity blocked streets and adjoining yards," said the paper.[4] Whether the funeral was in fact larger than that of the Reverend Joseph Abrams from the same church in 1854, as described in Chapter Twelve, it is impossible to say.

Another able and dedicated Negro, Miss Virginia E. Randolph, was evidencing extraordinary qualities of heart and mind during these years. Born in Richmond, Miss Randolph was a teacher in one of the Henrico County schools for Negroes. Jackson Davis, then Henrico school superintendent and later a high official of the General Education Board, wrote in 1908 that "in her own school she has accomplished many of the results in industrial work that we now hope for in all schools." Miss Randolph was accordingly appointed industrial teacher for all the county's Negro schools, in which capacity she rendered sacrificial service. As a result, funds from the Jeanes Foundation were made available, and the system she had established was extended to other areas of rural Virginia, and eventually to the entire South.

Her salary was $40 a month, and from this meager sum she had to hire a horse and buggy, in order to reach the twenty-three schools under her charge. She left home at 6:30 A.M., and arrived on the return trip at about 9 P.M. The roads were abominable and she sometimes traveled in rain, sleet or snow. Her amazing versatility and ingenuity may be grasped from the following activities at various schools listed in her first report:

"Fenced the yard, set out hedges, set out trees, white-washed the trees and fence; taught laundry work, sewing, needlework, carpentry and making of shuck mats; planted flowers, planted and tended a school garden; raised money for the school, built a wood house, cleaned school grounds, rooted up stumps, ploughed up ground and graveled walk."

Many years after Virginia Randolph's death, her body was moved to the grounds of a small museum near the Virginia Randolph Training Center on Mountain Road, on the site of the one-room school in Henrico County where she began her teaching career. A bronze bust of her is there, together with letters, personal items, documents and memorabilia.

Her modest sphere of operations in rural schools was in contrast to the magnificent Roman Catholic Cathedral of the Sacred Heart, a gift of Thomas Fortune Ryan, the New York financier and Virginia native. Its consecration was a highlight of the year 1906. Ryan and his wife were present for the elaborate ceremonies, as was Cardinal Gibbons, always a beloved figure in Richmond. About a dozen archbishops, bishops and monsignors also were in attendance. The cornerstone, laid three years before, had been cut from solid rock on the Mount of Olives in the Garden of Gethsemane.

Richmond acquired a city auditorium of sorts the following year, when the West End Market at Cary and Cherry streets, erected in 1890, was converted into a hall where large gatherings or concerts could be held. It was hardly more than a barn with seats, and many were embarrassed at having world-famous musicians and divas, such as Paderewski, Galli-Curci and Geraldine Farrar, perform there. Plans for a better auditorium were formulated in 1914, when the Ford Hotel, on the lot across Eleventh Street from the city hall, was bought by the municipality and pulled down. A committee recommended construction on the site of a large building, containing not only an auditorium but a library, courtrooms and offices. The grandiose plan was never carried out, perhaps because of uncertainties created by the outbreak of World War I.

Richmond's facilities in these and other areas were the subject of an article in *Collier's* magazine by Julian Street. He also quoted the epitaph in Hollywood of James E. Valentine, a locomotive engineer killed in a collision. Street said it was "almost as well-known as the monuments erected there [in the cemetery] in memory of the great." The engineer's epitaph follows:

> Until the brakes are turned on Time
> Life's throttle valve shut down,
> He wakes to pilot in the crew
> That wear the martyr's crown.
>
> On schedule time on upper grade,
> Along the homeward section,
> He lands his train in God's roundhouse
> The morn of resurrection.
>
> His time all full; no wages docked;
> His name on God's payroll,
> And transportation through to Heaven,
> A free pass for his soul.

Also during these years a young Richmonder, Allan Hirsh, the son of Mr. and Mrs. Sampson Hirsh of the 800 block of West Franklin Street, composed the famous "Boola Boola" song of Yale University. Hirsh was a student at Yale when he wrote "Boola Boola." It was the official song of the state of Connecticut for many years.

The annual University of Virginia-North Carolina Thanksgiving Day football game on the field north of Broad between Allen and Lombardy always created excitement. This despite the fact that there was considerable sentiment for abolishing the sport, injuries and deaths were becoming so frequent. A University of Georgia football player had been fatally injured in 1897 in Atlanta when playing against the University of Virginia. Legislation was introduced in the Virginia General Assembly to outlaw football, but it was defeated. The University of Georgia authorities voted to abandon the sport and construct a huge bicycle track on their playing field. This action was evidently rescinded later.

The controversy in Virginia was greatly intensified in 1909 when Archer Christian of Richmond, playing in the University of Virginia backfield against Georgetown University in Washington, was fatally injured. The body of this much-admired young man was brought to the home of his parents, Mr. and Mrs. Andrew H. Christian, at 204 West Franklin Street. In attendance at the funeral from St. Paul's Church were delegations of students from both Georgetown and Virginia, together with a packed congregation of other mourners. An outburst of letters to the editor demanded that football be abolished. Nothing was done, of course, except that a few changes were made in the rules to reduce the hazards of the game.

Two more Confederate monuments, those to J. E. B. Stuart and Jefferson Davis, were unveiled on Monument Avenue almost simultaneously in 1907. The ceremonies were combined with a week-long Confederate reunion, the biggest of them all, with eighteen thousand veterans in attendance. These occasions were accorded an almost incredible amount of publicity in the Richmond press. It was not unusual for the entire front page and fifteen or more other pages to be devoted to the program and the events and personalities involved.

The Stuart monument by Fred Moynihan, showing the dashing cavalryman astride his high-stepping horse, with a jaunty plume in his hat, was unveiled with appropriate fanfare. The parade and oratory were repeated a few days later when the veil was drawn from the Davis monument. It had been designed by William C. Noland and executed by Edward V. Valentine. The cornerstone was first placed in Monroe Park in 1896, a site selected by Mrs. Davis. It was moved later to Monument Avenue.

An honored guest at the Davis monument's unveiling was James A. Jones, Davis' Negro-Indian valet and coachman. Jones was nearby when the Confederate President was captured at Irwinville, Georgia, in May 1865, wearing a type of cloak and shawl worn by both sexes. These garments were slanderously described in some Northern circles as a female disguise. Jones was always loud in denying the accusation.

An excellent book on the Civil War was written by Carlton McCarthy, who served as mayor of Richmond from 1904 to 1908. It was entitled *Soldier Life, Army of Northern Virginia*. However, Mayor McCarthy's ideas as to the proprieties were less widely acceptable than his account of his experiences in the Confederate Army. Those ideas were extremely strict, even for the early 1900s. He embarked on a crusade to force all department stores to have only fully clothed mannequins in their windows. Stockingless store window ladies wearing "unmentionables" were out. His Honor also bore down on "mashers" who ogled ladies when they exposed a bit of ankle while getting on streetcars. A constructive development of his administration was the annexation in 1906 of territory containing twelve thousand persons on the eastern and western edges of the city.

Congressman John Lamb, who represented Richmond and the Third District from 1897 to 1913, was instrumental in securing the return to the South of the captured Confederate battle flags held by the North. President Cleveland had tried unsuccessfully seventeen years before to bring this about.

The United Daughters of the Confederacy, with Mrs. J. Enders Robinson of Richmond as their first historian-general, announced an essay contest in 1908 that turned out to be a resounding fiasco. The contest was limited to students at Teachers College, Columbia University, New York, and President Edwin A. Alderman of the University of Virginia and Professor C. Alphonso Smith, then dean of the Graduate School at the University of North Carolina, were judges. The theme was "Robert E. Lee: A Present Estimate." Before the U.D.C. realized what was happening, the judges awarded the $100 first prize to a lady from Minnesota who made numerous highly heretical statements. One of them was: "Robert E. Lee was a traitor in that he sacrificed all to aid the enemies of his country." Another was that "the South was intellectually dead; most of its people were densely ignorant." The reaction of the Daughters of the Confederacy to these assertions may be imagined. Under heavy fire, Drs. Alderman and Smith protested that "the prize was for an essay, not a eulogy." The fuming Daughters were not appeased.

The Protestant Episcopal Church held its forty-fifth triennial convention at Richmond in the fall of 1907, with Rt. Rev. A. F. Winnington-Ingram, Bishop of London, preaching the opening sermon. Among the delegates was J. Pierpont Morgan. Lewis L. Strauss, who became one of the most eminent men ever to grow up in Richmond, serving as chairman of the U. S. Atomic Energy Commission and president of the Institute for Advanced Study at Princeton, New Jersey, recorded his boyhood impressions of Morgan in his book *Men and Decisions*. "For that brief visit," wrote Rear Admiral Strauss, "he had taken one of the stately houses of the city, staffed it, brought down his own transportation—a barouche and horses, complete with tophatted coachman and footman on the box. I remember standing goggle-eyed with a crowd of other small boys along the curb across Franklin Street to see the great man arrive and depart, with the footman hopping down to open the carriage door for him and unfold the little iron steps."

Miss Grace Arents was far from being as fabulously wealthy as Morgan, but she was a philanthropist who deserves to be remembered. The favorite niece of Major Lewis Ginter, she was left a substantial sum by her uncle. With it she made numerous benefactions, especially in the Oregon Hill area. The handsome Gothic St. Andrew's Episcopal Church was built entirely at her expense, as were the Grace Arents Public Free Library and the Arents Public School. She and her two sisters also provided St. Thomas Episcopal Church with three lots on which that house of worship was erected. And finally, she created the Lewis Ginter Botanical Gardens at Blooemdaal Farm in the Lakeside area.

Unlike Miss Arents, Dr. Ennion G. Williams of Richmond was not wealthy, but he gave himself to the cause of public health in a manner that evoked the admiration and gratitude of the entire state. Appointed Virginia's first state health commissioner, and reappointed by every succeeding governor, he served from 1908 until his death in 1931. Dr. Williams took the post at a salary of $3,600 a year, a fraction of his income as a practicing physician. When seeking to obtain from the General Assembly an appropriation for the eradication of typhoid fever, a great scourge at the time, he told the lawmakers that if there was a question of appropriating money to fight typhoid or to pay his salary, he would prefer that his salary be eliminated. He got the appropriation, and typhoid was effectively attacked. Dr. Williams also did much to eradicate malaria and tuberculosis and to improve sanitary conditions in the public schools. He was instrumental in obtaining funds for the appointment of Richmond's first city bacteriologist, Dr. E. C. Levy, later city director of public welfare and president of the American Public Health Association. Dr. Williams frequently took no vacation. He suffered a coronary attack, but was back at his desk as soon as possible, working with no visible letup. When he died at age fifty-seven, the Richmond Academy of Medicine adopted extraordinarily laudatory resolutions evidencing its poignant sense of loss.

Dr. Williams was fortunate in having the assistance in public health work of three dedicated women of gentle birth, the Misses Sadie H. Cabaniss, Agnes D. Randolph and Nannie J. Minor. These ladies entered the emerging profession of nursing despite the tradition that it was somehow improper for young women to be involved in any profession except teaching. None of the three was a Richmond native, but as is stated in *The First 125 Years*, a history of the Medical College of Virginia, "Miss Minor, Miss Cabaniss and Miss Randolph, the intrepid three, began a new era of social work in Richmond." They founded the Nurses' Settlement for work among the poor, and out of this grew the Instructive Visiting Nurse Association. Miss Minor was director of the I.V.N.A. for twenty years, and then for ten years was director of Public Health Nursing for the State Board of Health. Miss Cabaniss was the founder of nursing education under the Nightingale Plan at the Medical College in 1895. She later became director of the I.V.N.A. and then the first rural public health nurse in the state. Miss Randolph was graduated in 1914 in the first group of nurses to receive their diplomas from MCV. She soon became executive secretary of the Virginia Tuberculosis Association, and was later transferred to the staff of the State Board of Health, where she organized the

Tuberculosis Bureau. Miss Randolph is credited with doing more to reduce the deathrate from tuberculosis in Virginia than any other person.

On the subject of medical care, it is interesting to note that in 1913, hospital rooms in Richmond ranged from $2.25 to $5 a day, and that this scale changed only slightly in the next twenty years. In a different area, the Jefferson Hotel, finest in the South, advertised rooms at "$1.50 and up."

Two other aristocratic, able and socially conscious Richmond women were directing attention in the early 1900s to shortcomings in such spheres as education, race relations, health and women's rights. They were Mrs. Benjamin B. (Lila Meade) Valentine and Mrs. Beverley B. (Mary-Cook Branch) Munford. Both were endowed with intellectual curiosity and breadth of vision far ahead of their time.

The Richmond Education Association was formed in 1900 in the home of Mrs. Valentine, with Mrs. Munford among the leaders. It sought to raise the low level of the public schools. Establishment of the Instructive Visiting Nurse Association was influenced importantly by a meeting in that same home two years later. Mrs. Valentine and Mrs. Munford also were active in the famous May Campaign of 1905 for better schools throughout Virginia, and in the founding of the Co-operative Education Association, a statewide agency.

Lila Valentine shrewdly focused attention on the horrifying rats and filth in Richmond's only high school, and the result was a new school. She worked effectively in the field of tuberculosis eradication. An ardent suffragist, she was chosen first president of the Equal Suffrage League of Virginia, and was shunned by many friends in consequence. So conspicuous were Mrs. Valentine's dedication and leadership that a marble plaque to her memory was placed in the Capitol. She is the only woman thus honored.

Mrs. Munford led for many years in the effort to obtain admission of women to the University of Virginia. She almost succeeded in 1916, losing in the General Assembly by only two votes, but women were not admitted on the same basis as men until long after her death. A tablet at the university commemorates her devoted service.

The crusade launched by Mrs. Valentine against the filthy conditions in the Richmond High School resulted in the building of the John Marshall High School, but the City School Board tried to tear down the adjacent home of John Marshall to provide a larger playground. This scheme was thwarted by an outburst of popular indignation.

The Old Stone House, most ancient dwelling in Richmond, also was in danger of being pulled down in 1911. It is due to the generosity of Mr. and Mrs. Granville G. Valentine that the structure was acquired by the Association for the Preservation of Virginia Antiquities. Some years later, Mr. and Mrs. Archer Jones conceived the idea of transforming it into a shrine to Edgar Allan Poe. This concept was beautifully executed. The stone house was tidied up, the piles of rubbish behind it were cleared away and a charming garden was created. In the center was placed a fountain, and at the foot a loggia built of bricks from the demolished building at Fifteenth and Main that had housed the *Southern Literary Messenger*, made famous by Poe. The latter is not known to have been associated in any way with the Old Stone House during his lifetime, but the ensemble includes a fascinating museum containing important relics and mementos of his tempestuous and tragic career.

The cities of Richmond and Manchester finally merged in 1910, following more than half a century of spasmodic negotiation. The population was now 127,000. A delegation from South Richmond, headed by Mayor Henry A. Maurice, drove across the river on April 15 in five official automobiles to Richmond's city hall, bearing a floral key. They were greeted by Mayor David C. Richardson of Richmond. Manchester became Washington Ward.

Communication across the river was soon facilitated by the construction of a handsome new Mayo's Bridge of concrete and steel, replacing the rickety span which, from time immemorial, had been battered and swept away by floods. The new bridge, still standing in 1976 and apparently good for many more years, has survived all assaults of the raging James.

Simultaneously with the commencement of construction of the bridge in 1911, Richmond's City Council reduced the number of wards from eight to four—Jefferson, Madison, Clay and Lee. These four wards were retained thereafter, albeit with shifting boundaries as the city expanded. Such expansion took place in 1914, when Richmond annexed areas on all four sides of the consolidated municipality, especially on the Southside and Northside. The city's area was more than doubled, and now totaled nearly twenty-three square miles. The population was in excess of 145,000.

A drastic but short-lived change in Richmond's form of government took place during these years. An Administrative Board of five members elected by the people was created, effective January 1, 1913. The members received salaries of $5,000, and furnished the city's administrative leadership. This experiment was not successful, and five years later the board was abolished by an overwhelming popular vote, approving a charter change that provided for the "strong mayor" form of government.

Other innovations in government, albeit on the national level, were in the offing as Woodrow Wilson launched his campaign for the presidency in 1912. He was persuaded to come to Richmond by a committee that included two of his former college-mates at the University of Virginia— Archibald W. Patterson of Richmond and Dean Richard Heath Dabney of the university faculty. Special trains on the Chesapeake & Ohio brought hundreds of backers from Staunton and Charlottesville. Wilson began by speaking to students at Richmond College in the forenoon. He then appeared briefly before each branch of the General Assembly in turn. That night he spoke to a capacity audience at the City Auditorium, and attacked "machine rule." The result was that he antagonized the members of Virginia's dominant Martin machine, headed by U. S. Senator Thomas S. Martin, and created hostility for his candidacy in the Virginia delegation at the upcoming Baltimore convention.

The founding of Chamberlayne's School for boys in a large frame house on Grove Avenue—number 3311 at that time, and later 3211—was an important event of those years. The headmaster was Dr. Churchill G. Chamberlayne, son of John Hampden Chamberlayne and holder of numerous degrees, including an M.A. and Ph.D. from the German University of Halle-Wittenberg. Dr. Chamberlayne understood boys and when his school opened in 1911 with sixteen of them, and Dabney S. Lancaster as assistant headmaster, it was the beginning of a notable adventure in the field of secondary education. The Chamberlayne School remained on Grove Avenue, well outside of town, for three years, and then moved much farther out, truly "in the country," to a site near Stop 25 on the Westhampton streetcar line. In his history of the school, DeWitt Hankins has described the arrival of the students via the trolley:

"The young men . . . in short pants, long black stockings, high shoes, and carrying assorted styles of book bags, bounded off the car and took their way north on what is now Henri Road. . . . Tall pines, broomsedge and rabbit tobacco grew where there are now solid blocks of homes."

At least twice a year, Dr. Chamberlayne repeated the saying of his old schoolmaster, W. Gordon McCabe, "We cannot all be scholars, but we can all be gentlemen."

The school was bought by the Episcopal Diocese of Virginia in 1920, and the name changed to St. Christopher's, with Dr. Chamberlayne remaining as headmaster until his death in 1939. Tributes poured in at his passing, and there were sincere references to his character, personality, ability and sense of humor. St. Christopher's is recognized as one of the country's top preparatory schools.

Dr. John Page Williams, a Richmond-born Rhodes scholar, was the next headmaster. Hampden-Sydney College conferred on him the honorary degree of D.Litt. before he relinquished the post at the end of eleven years to become dean of church schools in the Episcopal Diocese of Virginia.

Dr. Robert W. Bugg, longtime member of the St. Christopher's teaching staff, succeeded Williams, and served for thirteen years. When he retired at age sixty-five there were many testimonials of esteem and affection. "Integrity" was felt to be the keynote of his leadership. Bugg had been a noted teacher of mathematics, and Hampden-Sydney conferred on him the degree of D.Sc.

He was succeeded by Warren P. Elmer, Jr., director of Princeton

University's placement bureau. When Elmer resigned eight years later, Bishop Robert F. Gibson and Dr. T. N. P. Johns, chairman of the trustees, said he had "stimulated students, faculty, parents, alumni and board members toward an awareness of changing conditions."

George J. McVey, assistant headmaster, was elevated to succeed Elmer, and is carrying on the school's traditions effectively.

Another school for boys, Richmond Academy, was established in 1902 by the authorities of Richmond College. For fourteen years it operated in a building bordering Stuart Circle where Stuart Circle Hospital was subsequently erected. William L. Prince, later dean of men at the University of Richmond, served as head of the school from 1905 to 1918. In the latter year Richmond Academy went out of existence, after affording a high grade of instruction to many sons of leading citizens.

Richmond College and Westhampton College—the latter institution was originally the Richmond Female Institute and then the Woman's College—traveled westward in 1914 from their respective locations on West Grace Street and East Marshall. They moved to their beautiful campus in Henrico County but it was not beautiful then. Certain members of the Richmond College board actually threatened to get a court injuction to prevent the move. The lake was derided as "an old duck pond," and it was disfigured by trees that had been chopped down and left in the water. Two abandoned farms on each side of the lake had made the land "gullied and galled." There were cabins where Westhampton College now stands. However, President Boatwright and a majority of the Richmond College board wisely insisted on the move. In 1920 Richmond College became the University of Richmond. It included the two above-mentioned institutions and the T. C. Williams Law School, endowed by the T. C. Williams family. The university also had been aided financially by the U. S. Government, which made $25,000 available in compensation for damage done to the West Grace Street property by Union soldiers during the Civil War and for the property's rental.

A statewide referendum on the adoption of prohibition was another notable event of 1914. The spark plug behind the drive for a "dry" Virginia was the Reverend James Cannon, Jr., a devious and immensely able Methodist divine who spoke for the Anti-Saloon League and kindred agencies. He had founded the Richmond *Virginian*, a daily newspaper, four years previously, largely for the purpose of getting a state "dry" law through the General Assembly, subject to subsequent approval by the people. The Assembly passed the law.

The Richmond *Times-Dispatch, News Leader* and *Evening Journal* were all strongly opposed to prohibition and in favor of local option. Their relations with Dr. Cannon were strained, to put it mildly. They exchanged verbal brickbats with the doctor at frequent intervals.

The foes of legalized aridity organized the Association for Local Self-

Government, headed by the highly respected Judge George L. Christian. It included many leading business and professional men, such as Dr. Stuart McGuire, Henry St. George Tucker, candidate for governor in 1909, and Egbert G. Leigh, Jr., Richmond manufacturer and one of the most cultivated gentlemen of his time. The association rented an entire floor of a downtown office building and began sending out dignified speakers and equally dignified literature. By contrast, Cannon and his allies appealed to the emotions rather than the intellect. They rang the changes on the terrible effects of alcoholism, pictured starving babies whose fathers spent their all in saloons, and attacked the foes of prohibition as allies of the liquor interests and of "the fallen women, the debauchers, the panderers, the pimps, the white-slave dealers, the gamblers, the thieves, and slaves of appetite and passion." Cannon mobilized the evangelical clergy and their congregations and the Woman's Christian Temperance Union. He contended that prohibition was opposed primarily by "high society folks" who loved to drink in their exclusive clubs. Their motto, he said, was "Give us liquor or give us death!"

On election night there was near-hysteria at Seventh and Grace streets, where some five thousand persons were gathered to see and hear the returns thrown on a screen by the Anti-Saloon League. Hundreds joined in singing hymns, others wept and prayed as the results showed a sweeping victory for statewide prohibition. Richmond managed to withstand the stampede, but the state as a whole went overwhelmingly the other way.

Just before the law became effective in 1916, Richmonders who were disenchanted with the enactment laid in maximum supplies of alcoholic beverages. When those supplies were exhausted many leading citizens, including dry-voting politicians and pillars in the churches, did business with bootleggers.

At this time, two natives of Richmond who were to become greatly distinguished novelists, Ellen Glasgow and James Branch Cabell, had crossed the threshold of their illustrious careers. Both were out of sympathy with many beliefs, prejudices and customs of the era.

Miss Glasgow published her first book, *The Descendant*, in 1897 when she was only twenty-two. From the outset, as she once wrote, she was "in revolt against the formal, the false, the affected, the sentimental and the pretentious in Southern writing." There were raised eyebrows and whisperings behind the teacups when this well-reared young Richmond woman began writing about lower-class farmers, illegitimate babies and other subjects not previously discussed by Richmond writers or in the best Richmond circles.

Furthermore, Miss Glasgow herself declared in her posthumously published autobiographical work, *The Woman Within*, that she had fallen in love at first sight with a much older married New Yorker, who was the great love of her life, and who died seven years later, in 1905. She also had various other suitors, was engaged twice, and was far from the shut-in spinster that nearly everybody had taken her to be. The revelations in *The Woman Within*, published in 1954, nearly a decade after her death, rocked Richmond.

Miss Glasgow set out to write, in her novels, a "social history of Virginia" from the years just before the Civil War down to and including her own lifetime. Dr. Jay B. Hubbell, author of the definitive work, *The South in Southern Literature*, feels that she succeeded exceptionally well. He places Miss Glasgow's novels at the top among twentieth-century Southern writers. More will be said of her in subsequent chapters.

James Branch Cabell, the other superlative ornament of American letters from this period, was graduated from the College of William and Mary in 1898 as its most brilliant student. His career was clouded by unjust charges of homosexuality, of which he was acquitted, along with other students, following a faculty investigation. A couple of years later, while serving as a reporter on a Richmond newspaper, he received another blow when widespread gossip connected him with a murder committed almost in front of his home at 511 West Franklin Street. The murder victim was "Jack" Scott, prominent bachelor man-about-town, who was killed by blows on the head after he had left the Commonwealth Club at 401 West Franklin, at 1:45 A.M. Scott fell dying in front of the E. T. D. Myers house at Belvidere and Franklin. There was a feverish investigation by the police and the Pinkerton detective agency, and vast publicity in the press, but the whole affair was suddenly and mysteriously hushed up. Some prominent person or persons evidently did not wish the facts to come out. It was proved later that Cabell had nothing whatever to do with the crime.[5]

But he now had passed, as a youth, through two highly traumatic experiences, and these had inevitably affected his sensitive nature and his subsequent literary career. As Edgar E. MacDonald has written, "It would be difficult to find an American writer whose environment played a larger role in creating those stresses which result in literature."

Cabell went to New York, and worked for two years as a reporter on the *Herald*, covering Harlem, among other things. He returned to Richmond, and spent a decade studying the genealogy of the Branch family and publishing two books on the subject. Then he worked for two years in the office of a West Virginia coal mine. But his real métier was the writing of fiction and essays, and to these forms he then turned. Cabell came back to Richmond, where he was to remain. He achieved financial security in 1913 when he married Priscilla Bradley Shepherd, a well-to-do widow with five children. Cabell's subsequent literary career will be discussed hereafter.

Miss Mary Johnston, a native of Botetourt County, had written several well-received historical novels when she moved to Richmond in 1902.

Some of her best-known works were produced in the Virginia capital, before she moved on to Warm Springs. She published *Lewis Rand* when living at 110 East Franklin Street in Linden Row. Miss Johnston's *Hagar* was a ringing appeal for women's rights, a movement in which she had been active with Lila Meade Valentine and others. Miss Johnston's "contribution to the American historical novel," writes Dr. John C. Metcalf, "is one of the most notable in our fiction."

A Richmond-born sculptor who grew up in straitened circumstances in the lowly neighborhood near the Old Market was living in Rome during the 1890s and early 1900s, on intimate terms with many of the great men of that era, including Franz Liszt and Cardinal Hohenlohe. He was Moses Ezekiel, who had fought with the VMI cadets at New Market in the Civil War. While at the Institute, he became well-acquainted with General Robert E. Lee, then president of nearby Washington College. Lee said to him, "I hope you will be an artist, as it seems to me that you are cut out for one." Ezekiel took the advice and somehow managed to finance studies in Berlin, where, at the end of three years, he won the Michael-Beers Prize, never before awarded to a foreigner. This relieved his financial stress.

Ezekiel went to Rome and set up a studio in the Baths of Diocletian. He remained there for more than thirty years, moving in the highest circles of society. Knighted by Emperor William I of Germany and King Humbert I and King Victor Emmanuel II of Italy, he was thereafter known as Sir Moses Ezekiel. Always proudest of his career at VMI, he presented the statue of "Virginia Mourning Her Dead" to the Institute at a cost of some $7,000 to himself. He also did the statue of Stonewall Jackson at VMI, the original of which is in Charleston, West Virginia.

Ezekiel is Virginia's foremost sculptor. "His art forms a link between mid-Victorian smugness and twentieth century searching," says one critic. At his request, upon his death in 1917, he was buried in Arlington Cemetery, near the Confederate monument which he executed, and with the following epitaph:

Moses J. Ezekiel
Sergeant Company C
Battalion of Cadets
of the
Virginia Military Institute

An Indiana-born sculptor who made his home in Richmond for most of his life, and who became perhaps the leading sculptor of the Lost Cause, was F. William Sievers. When he got the commission for the Lee monument at Gettysburg in 1910, Sievers decided to live permanently in Richmond. His statue, known as the Virginia Memorial, shows Lee seated on Traveller, watching the immortal charge of Pickett's division across the open field over which it moved toward the serried guns on Cemetery Ridge.

Sievers executed many other well-known monuments and busts. These include the Stonewall Jackson and Matthew Fontaine Maury statues on Monument Avenue in Richmond; the busts of James Madison, Patrick Henry, Sam Houston and Zachary Taylor in the Capitol, and the bas-relief of Bishop Francis Asbury on the wall of a building at 1900 East Franklin.

The musical career of a young Richmonder, John Powell, was a sensation of the early 1900s. After graduating with high honors from the University of Virginia, he studied piano for several years in Vienna under Leschetizky. Next came loudly acclaimed concerts in Paris, Vienna and London. His successful New York debut was in 1913. The following year in London, Moisevitch played the world premiere of Powell's striking composition for the piano, the *Sonata Teutonica*. Zimbalist hailed his violin concerto as "the most beautiful concerto for the violin written since Brahms."

Folk tunes, as part of an indigenous musical culture, were deemed by Powell to be of enormous importance, and he incorporated these tunes into many of his compositions, including *Rhapsodie Nègre*, one of the most admired of them all. Powell played *Rhapsodie Nègre* with many of the leading orchestras in this country and Europe.

His career as a concert pianist was virtually wrecked when he refused, as a matter of principle, to join the Musicians' Union. John Powell was a man of the most intense feelings, with convictions that nothing could shake. His blue eyes flashed fire as he discussed this or any other subject which moved him deeply. He became heavily involved in efforts to maintain segregation of the races, and gave a great deal of time to this matter, at further cost to his musicianship. Whereas in Vienna as a young man he had been instrumental in opening membership in his *Turnverein* to Jewish musicians, two decades later, in the twenties, he took an ultra-rightist position on black-white relations, and lobbied in the General Assembly on behalf of highly restrictive legislation affecting the blacks. His quest for folk-tunes also absorbed a vast amount of his time, and led him into remote byways of the Virginia and North Carolina mountains.

After fifteen years of composition, he completed his *Symphony in A*, commissioned by the National Federation of Music Clubs. Into this monumental work he wove the folk music that had engaged his attention for decades. John Powell was the greatest musician Virginia has produced. He would have been even greater but for the intensely held convictions that distracted him and hampered his musical career.

In the first decade and a half of the century, and for a considerably longer period, the men and women of Richmond divided the downtown business area. Broad Street was the city's shopping thoroughfare, frequented chiefly by ladies, while Main Street with its financial district was the haven for males. In between were Grace and Franklin, which were purely residential. Gradually stores and shops began to appear on these streets, until over a period of several decades the "downtown" portion of Grace and Franklin became almost entirely commercial. Fine antebellum mansions were bulldozed to make way for "progress."

The Miller & Rhoads and Thalhimers department stores were nothing like so large in those early years of the century, and they had no branches. Shopping centers in the suburbs also were unknown, but there were neighborhood grocery and drug stores. Shoppers usually came downtown on the streetcar if they did not live within walking distance. "Walking distance" was not what it is today; people believed in using their feet.

A popular Broad Street place of rendezvous for young blades and their "dates" was T. A. Miller's drugstore, on a site now occupied by Miller & Rhoads. A claret limeade was a special treat there, or perhaps a banana split. Hellstern's, at Seventh and Broad streets, sold superlative ice cream by the pint, quart or gallon. Over at the Sixth Street Market, in the Sixth and Marshall area, housewives shopped for particular varieties of meats, groceries, pastries and flowers.

Then, as now, the southern side of Broad had most of the better stores and shops. The saloons were on the northern side, which lowered the tone. Furthermore, the south side was said to receive a bit more sun in winter and more shade in summer, which the lady shoppers found pleasant. In succeeding years, the "wrong side of Broad," as it had come to be known, continued to be less elegant than the other side, although there has been some definite upgrading.

Along Broad and other streets were seen the early automobiles, primitive affairs that had no self-starters and had to be cranked up by hand; they were also blessed with tires that frequently blew out or were punctured. Powered by gasoline, steam or electricity, the cars sputtered, coughed, wheezed and backfired. The Model T Ford, representing a great advance, appeared on Richmond streets in 1907, costing $850. There were fewer than two hundred privately owned automobiles in the city in 1913.

A three-day Virginia Endurance Contest for automobiles was sponsored in 1910 by the *Times-Dispatch*. The cars would try to reach Washington the first day, Charlottesville the second and return to Richmond the third. It was stipulated that no car would be permitted to chug to Washington in less than ten hours, so that there could be "no question of danger to persons or property on the roads over which the cars pass." An average speed of 12.5 miles per hour was called for in the rules. Given the roads of that day, with their bottomless ruts and mudholes, this was not quite as ridiculous as it may seem. A general holiday was observed in every town on the route of the cavalcade.

At the head of the procession were E. D. Hotchkiss, Jr., in a Stevens-Duryea, Dr. Stuart McGuire in an Olds and John Aiken Branch in a Packard. There were twenty-three participants, and Miss Anna Dunlop of

Petersburg, with a perfect record, was the winner. Seven other women drivers took part, which for 1910 was nothing less than astounding.

The remarkable status of women at the period may be glimpsed in the announcement of two insurance companies to their Richmond policy-holders that they made "no extra charge" for insuring women's lives. And about 1910, when a woman was seen smoking a cigarette at the newly established Country Club of Virginia, it set the town on its ear. As late as 1924, women were forbidden to smoke in the Miller & Rhoads tearoom.

Ladies who walked home in the early 1900s from services at St. Paul's Episcopal Church on Sunday morning past the Westmoreland Club were supposed never to turn their heads in the club's direction. Any who did so would be "talked about as being very bold and unladylike," General John A. Cutchins writes. The approved feminine costume was gored skirts, shirtwaists and leg-of-mutton sleeves, with a hat that was sometimes large and sometimes small. Richmond women in the early 1900s wore no make-up, and were supposed to be "pale and interesting." Sunburn was exactly what they didn't want, and they carried parasols in order not to acquire it.

Those in search of painted ladies could find them on Mayo Street, where the city's legally recognized red-light district was located for the first two decades of the century. The name was changed to Ballard Street at about the time when such districts were outlawed. Ballard intersected Broad near Fourteenth, but it has now been obliterated by extensive construction.

Trolley cars were the city's principal means of transportation. The fare was five cents, as compared with the ten-cent tariff on the earlier horse-drawn vehicles. Each car had a conductor and a motorman. Carriages were seen less and less as the motor age dawned. Colonel Archer Anderson was driven daily by his coachman to his office at the Tredegar until his death in 1918, although many of his friends had cars. His widow used her handsome victoria until her passing ten years later. City Engineer Charles E. Bolling continued to drive each day in his buggy to his home on West Grace Street for lunch until well into the 1920s. Few other horse-drawn equipages were on the streets. With the growing volume of motorcars, this means of locomotion was not only slow but hazardous.

In the early twentieth century, Richmond was still a leading theatrical and musical center, a position it was not able to maintain in later decades. "In a single week, one could see vaudeville at the Lyric, a Broadway success at the Academy, a concert at the Richmond Municipal Auditorium and a stock company at the Empire or Bijou," Edith Lindeman wrote in one of her perceptive articles in the *Times-Dispatch*. There were thirty-four theaters of all kinds in Richmond in 1913 as compared with twenty-seven in 1971, when the city was twice as big.

The movies had come into their own during the century's first two decades. A nickel would get you in to see Pearl White in *The Perils of Pauline* or Charlie Chaplin in *The Kid*. If you had another nickel you could revel in candy or peanuts. Some of the motion picture houses lacked comforts and conveniences. One ingenious owner provided a primitive form of air conditioning for the sweltering customers by putting electric fans behind tubs of ice.

In addition to spending time watching the "flicks," the boys of that era engaged in occasional rock battles with rival gangs, as their fathers had done before them. Also, there was the lively custom of purloining ash barrels to have a bonfire at Christmas time. A group in the lower Fan District, known as the "Bumtown Gang," showed particular virtuosity here. Boys who later became bank presidents, judges and other staid business and professional men were leaders in carrying off the barrels. They staged an annual bonfire near a huge oak on the 1200 block of Park Avenue that lasted from Christmas Eve to New Year's Day.

Citizens naturally became irate over the loss of their barrels, for the ashes then had to be dumped in the back yard where the ash man refused to pick them up. The Bumtown Gang worked out a solution. They went from house to house in the Fan District, soliciting contributions to buy cord wood for their bonfire, and promising each contributor that there would be no further larceny of his ash barrel. It worked. The boys kept their word scrupulously, cord wood blazed throughout Christmas week on the 1200 block of Park and everybody was happy. By the time the youths finally stopped lighting bonfires, they had a surplus in the treasury, which they gave to charity.

Since time immemorial, Richmond's water supply had been muddy, like the James whence it came. Many families had private filters or they drove to one of the clear springs and collected drinking water in bottles. The city finally provided a filter system of its own in 1909. Operated in connection with the Byrd Park Reservoir, it solved the problem for a decade and a half.

But drinking water seemed a minor matter when, in 1914, the great powers of Europe stood on the edge of war. The pistol of the Bosnian Serb terrorist Princip cracked in Sarajevo on June 28, and Archduke Franz Ferdinand, heir to the Austro-Hungarian throne, fell mortally wounded. An inexorable series of events was set in motion, culminating in declarations of war by the major European powers. There followed the Battle of the Marne and other epochal happenings, all of which engaged the eager attention of Richmonders.

They were strongly sympathetic to Great Britain, whence came most of their forebears, and its ally France. In a few short years units from Richmond would be fighting beside the British "Tommies" and the French *poilus,* but in 1914 they were content to watch the conflict from the sidelines. Suddenly a German U-boat surfaced in Hampton Roads, and the people of Richmond were made aware that the war was not three thousand miles away, but almost in their front yard. It would draw ever nearer.

# NINETEEN

# World War I, Cabell, Glasgow and the Roaring Twenties

RICHMONDERS and most other Americans were outraged, and many wanted to declare war on Germany at once when a German submarine sank the great British liner *Lusitania* without warning on May 7, 1915, off the Irish coast. One hundred and twenty-four Americans were among the 1,198 persons who lost their lives. Outraged Richmonders did not know that the *Lusitania* was carrying 4,927 boxes of .303 caliber rifle ammunition to the British fighting forces. Advertisements placed in the New York press by the German embassy in Washington had warned that persons who embarked on ships sailing the North Atlantic did so "at their own risk." However, the Germans certainly should have given the passengers and crew of the *Lusitania* a chance to get into the lifeboats.

War against Germany was not formally declared by the United States for nearly two years, but it became increasingly obvious that America would be drawn in. A company for Home Defense was accordingly organized by Richmond business and professional men, against the day when the city's established military organizations, one of which served on the Mexican border in 1916, would be ordered into the U. S. Army.

These units were mustered into the service in the spring of 1917, following the declaration of war on April 6, and volunteers flooded into the recruiting stations. Camp Lee near Petersburg was constructed in three months to accommodate 45,000 men, and some Richmond units went there for training. Soldiers on leave poured into Richmond, and the city did its best to make them welcome and comfortable. The local chapter of the Red Cross became active in turning out bandages and other supplies. Richmonders cooperated wholeheartedly in the observance of "meatless" and "wheatless" days, in order that the soldiers on the front lines and the starving European civilians might be adequately fed. About 8,000 Richmonders served in the armed forces during the conflict and 251 died.

Draft dodgers and deserters were few, for most people were convinced that Kaiser Wilhelm II of Germany had launched the war with a view to conquering Europe, if not the world. This oversimplified view of the conflict was widely held until several years after peace was restored and the archives of the various powers could be examined. German atrocities in Belgium roused the people of Richmond and the rest of the country to fever pitch.

After America's formal declaration of belligerency, the Tredegar went full blast in supplying the United States Army and Navy with munitions. Prior to the entry of the United States into the war, it had made projectiles for the British. The Richmond branch of the American Locomotive Company installed new machinery and began turning out shells as early as 1916. Near the close of hostilities there was a great demand for railroad locomotives, and the company went back to building them. At Sandston, just outside the city, a powder plant employed some three thousand workers.

The Richmond Academy of Medicine was quick to form a base hospital for service overseas. Dr. Stuart McGuire, the famous surgeon, closed St. Luke's Hospital, founded by his even more famous father, "for the duration," and headed Base Hospital 45. It included many leading Richmond doctors, among them forty members of the Medical College faculty. Because of a lifetime affliction (tuberculosis of the spine), Dr. McGuire always wore a heavy and uncomfortable body brace whenever he was active. Yet he carried on his arduous duties to the satisfaction of everyone, and rose to the rank of colonel. Serving under him were Major W. Lowndes Peple and Major J. Garnett Nelson. Base Hospital 45 was established at Toul, France, and the services it provided were given the highest praise by U. S. Surgeon General Ireland.

Because of strong anti-German feeling, Richmonders of German birth, such as August Dietz, the highly regarded head of the Dietz Printing Company, were snubbed and insulted. The Germania Life Insurance Company felt it necessary to change its name to the Guardian Life Insurance Company. Sauerkraut became "liberty cabbage," and the artist who did the comic strip "The Katzenjammer Kids" temporarily gave it a new name. This hysteria did not die down fully until the coming of peace.

Richmond College students formed a reserve unit and moved from Westhampton back to the old campus on West Grace Street. They were housed in empty St. Luke's Hospital and drilled by army officers. Four Liberty Loan drives were held, beginning in June 1917 and ending with the fourth in September 1918. John Kerr Branch was chairman of each. Richmond went far "over the top" in all four, and led the entire country in the first two, oversubscribing its $7,000,000 quota by 79 per cent in the first and its $8,460,000 quota by 138 per cent in the second. *Richmond*, the magazine of the Chamber of Commerce, exhorted the citizenry, saying that the first Liberty Loan was "America's answer to the barbarities of the Kaiser," and the second was "for equipping our sons and brothers with arms to fight the terrible Hun." This was also the tone of Richmond's newspapers and of the American press generally. A Victory Loan was announced in April 1919, with Herbert W. Jackson in charge. It, too, was oversubscribed.

The deadly influenza epidemic of 1918 which swept the country, taking tens of thousands of lives, struck Richmond with devastating force. The disease broke out at Camp Lee on the ominous date of Friday, September 13, and five hundred soldiers died within four weeks. The "flu" spread to Richmond with lightning speed, and by early October the municipal authorities had closed all churches, schools and theaters. John Marshall High School was converted into an emergency hospital for one thousand patients and other schoolhouses were pressed into service for the care of the sick. A railroad strike stopped the trains and large numbers of coffins accumulated on station platforms. Florence B. Decker says in her biography of her husband, Dr. Henry W. Decker, that she and Dr. Decker saw coffins "piled to the eaves" at Richmond's Main Street Station. The rail strike also brought a fuel shortage, and this caused many influenza patients to contract fatal pneumonia. On top of all else, rumors circulated that the Germans were spreading the flu germs. By Armistice Day, November 11, the worst of the epidemic was over, but there were occasional cases throughout the winter. More than eight hundred Richmonders died.

Armistice Day was greeted in the city with vast enthusiasm and uninhibited rejoicing. The news of Germany's surrender came in the middle of the night, and by 4 A.M. factory whistles were blowing throughout Richmond. Before daylight trucks loaded with young people began roaring about the city, tooting horns and ringing bells. Everything closed for the day—factories, stores, schools and offices—and Broad Street was a mass of cheering, flag-waving humanity. There was a parade led by the band from Camp Lee, with the John Marshall High School cadet corps and others taking part.

When, in the succeeding months, Richmond's soldiers, sailors and aviators returned from the war, they were feted with parades, speeches and banquets. Marshal Ferdinand Foch, generalissimo of the Allied armies, visited the city on Armistice Day, 1921. He received a welcome such as had seldom been accorded in Richmond to any hero. Cannon boomed and virtually the entire population turned out to cheer him as he passed down Broad Street from the railway station to Capitol Square. A great military parade followed, and there was a banquet in the marshal's honor at the Jefferson Hotel with Eppa Hunton, Jr., as toastmaster. Foch visited one of the battlefields of the Seven Days, and a young newspaper editor named Douglas S. Freeman who acted as guide amazed those present with his intimate knowledge of the terrain and the movements of the opposing forces.

Many Richmond clergymen were active in various patriotic capacities during World War I, but none was more zealous in the cause than Rabbi Edward N. Calisch of Temple Beth Ahabah. Although in his fifties, he volunteered for a chaplaincy, but was rejected because of age. He spoke in half a dozen states in Liberty Loan and Red Cross drives, and his rare eloquence did much to form public opinion.

Dr. Calisch had come to Beth Ahabah in 1891, aged twenty-six, when the congregation worshipped on North Eleventh Street. In 1904 it laid the cornerstone for its handsome new home at Ryland and Franklin. Calisch took an M.A. degree from the University of Virginia during that year, and a Ph.D. four years later. In order to complete the work for these degrees he traveled to Charlottesville each week on the Chesapeake & Ohio Railroad, changed trains at Gordonsville and waited there for two hours in the middle of the night.

He served his congregation for more than half a century, and for decades was probably the most prominent religious leader in Richmond. Members of all faiths looked to him for guidance, and he was the speaker at countless community functions and interdenominational gatherings. He served as president of the Central Conference of American Rabbis, and delivered the prayer at Mount Vernon on the centennial of George Washington's death.

Richmond achieved a triumph in 1914, when the city was chosen as the site of the Fifth Federal Reserve Bank, in competition with much larger Baltimore. For this and other reasons, the city came out of World War I with enhanced business prestige. During these years the Chamber of Commerce boasted that Richmond had the largest cigarette factory, cigar factory, woodworking plant, mica mills, baking powder factory and plant for reproducing antique furniture in the entire world. It also said the city could boast of the largest blotting paper industry and fertilizer factory in the United States; and the biggest bank, insurance company, book publishing house, florist establishment, paper bag factory and mail order house in the South. During the decade from 1910 to 1920, the population jumped from 127,000 to 171,000, an increase of 34.5 per cent. A goodly part was accounted for by the annexation of 12.21 square miles in 1914.

Richmond was the site of an automobile-manufacturing plant, the Kline Kar Corporation, located on the Boulevard. It operated from 1912 to 1923. The Kline Kar was built of parts assembled from all over the country, and it sold well. Two racing cars, "Jimmie" and "Jimmie Jr.," took part in races at tracks along the East Coast, and received considerable publicity. But mass production methods furnished too much competition for the company's James A. Kline, and he went out of business.

In banking during these years, the preeminent figure was John M. Miller, Jr., president of First National Bank and then of the consolidated First & Merchants National Bank. Beginning as a bank runner in his native Lynchburg, he rose in 1916 to the presidency of Virginia's largest banking institution. He remained in that post until 1939, and then served as chairman of the board until his death in 1948. His trademark was an unlighted cigar, which he carried at virtually all hours.

John M. Miller, Jr., was not only the outstanding banker in Richmond; he was regarded as a leader over a much wider area, comprising several states. In 1927, he all but predicted the great financial panic that broke less than two years later, saying that "we may look for failures, fraud and scandal to develop in the next few years, and doubtless many with the sale of securities." He was the only Southern banker summoned to Washington when President F. D. Roosevelt ordered the nation's banks closed in March 1933. Expecting to remain for one day, he found it necessary to stay for three, without any baggage or change of clothes.

Owing to his unusually conservative policies, he had kept his bank strong and liquid. He was appointed by Roosevelt as head of the National Recovery Administration (NRA) for Virginia, and was a leader in many other civic and community activities.

Miller also did much, as a director of corporations, to promote Richmond's business prosperity, and to bring new industries to the city. A notable advance in this connection was the construction in 1918 at Ampthill, on the James just below Richmond, of a rayon-manufacturing plant, the first of several large units of the E. I. du Pont de Nemours Company. They employ thousands.

At about this time, in 1926, it was announced that U. S. Customs receipts at Richmond passed the $2,000,000 mark for the first time. The figure in 1897 had been $20,000. The Chamber of Commerce was excited over this convincing evidence of Richmond's development as a port.

The chamber was distressed over the death of Giles B. Jackson, the Negro lawyer. For the first time in its history, the chamber passed resolutions of sorrow on the death of a nonmember. The resolutions praised Jackson's "work for harmony between the white and colored races and his indefatigable efforts for the material advancement of the colored people." They went on to declare that "his influence should be lasting and his example emulated." The News Leader joined the chorus, saying editorially that Jackson "had the patience of the pioneers and the courage of heroes." Neither the News Leader nor the chamber had the remotest notion that Jackson had been working secretly for a quarter of a century to break down the segregation laws, as noted in the previous chapter. Had they known this, the comment, one may be sure, would have been far different. Certainly the chamber would not have said that his example should be "emulated." The breaking down of the segregation laws was just about the last thing the white people of Richmond wanted in the mid-1920s.

Giles Jackson was indeed an extraordinary man. He was said to have known personally President U. S. Grant and every succeeding President, down to and including Coolidge. President McKinley made him an honorary colonel so that he might command a regiment of Negro cavalry at his inauguration, and Theodore Roosevelt renewed the commission.

John Mitchell, Jr., the prominent black contemporary of Giles Jackson, came upon hard times. The dapper, well-dressed Mitchell, with his long-tailed coat, striped trousers and diamond stickpin, found his Mechanics Savings Bank in serious trouble. It was closed in 1922 by the state, and the state bank examiner declared that the causes of its closing included "an unsound credit and investment policy, mismanagement, falsification of records and dishonesty." Dr. Abram L. Harris, the Richmond-born black author of *The Negro as Capitalist,* from which the foregoing quotation is taken, goes on to say: "Although Mitchell was indicted, the criminal prosecution was quashed. . . . It seems that Mitchell made good the claims against him and as a result died virtually a poor man." It was a sad ending for the former bank president and once militant editor of the *Planet.* That publication was taken over in 1938 by the *Afro-American.*

In earlier days, Mitchell had striven to better the opportunities for blacks. The need for such betterment was made especially manifest when a study of the Negro in Richmond was published in 1927, with evidence of discrimination in many fields. In education, health and welfare the facilities available to blacks were not even remotely comparable to those for whites. The magnitude of the discrimination came as a surprise to many. Blacks whose opinions were sought in the survey mentioned dilapidated housing and unpaved or poorly cared for streets as their chief grievances. A smaller number mentioned the segregation system.

The percentage of blacks in the city's population had been declining steadily since 1870, when it was 45 per cent. By 1910 it had dropped to 36.6, and by 1927 to under 29 per cent, according to census estimates. However, there were nearly 56,000 Negroes in Richmond in the last-named year. Their teachers at all levels were paid much less than the white teachers for comparable work, but this would soon be corrected. Illiteracy among blacks was fourteen times as high as among native whites. Illegitimacy, crime and disease were vastly greater.

A study of wage scales in twelve of Richmond's basic industries employing 4,229 black men and 2,503 black women—and a good many whites—showed the highest weekly rate of pay was $18.54 (paper products), and the lowest $12.87 (tobacco). Hours ranged from over eight to over ten per day, with half a day off on Saturday. Few Negroes had jobs in the better-paying industries. The average wage of domestics in one-servant homes was $8.09 per week and in two-servant homes $12.08 per week. Most were furnished with meals and uniforms. Of course, the dollar bought several times as much as it does today.

It was not clear what the blacks wanted the whites to do about some of the existing discrimination. A petition from Negroes to the City School Board asking appointment of black principals for the black schools—there were none—was met with another petition, also signed by blacks and supported by black teachers, opposing any such appointments. No such principals were named at that time. Josephus Simpson, a black, writing in the magazine *Opportunity*, declared that the great majority of Richmond's black teachers and parents did not want Negro principals.

Despite the manifest handicaps and disabilities under which Richmond blacks suffered, there was a degree of cordiality between them and the whites which many in other regions may find surprising. Evidence of this is seen in the reception accorded the Negro Elks when they held their national convention at Richmond in 1925. It was their first convention in a Southern city, and they were greatly pleased with their reception. Segregation ordinances were suspended temporarily, Jim Crow regulations in streetcars and restaurants were forgotten, and front porches were made available by many white residents to Negroes who wished to watch the immense parade of eighty thousand gaudily uniformed Elks.

Henry Lincoln Johnson, national president of the Elks, responded to the welcomes from Governor E. Lee Trinkle and Mayor J. Fulmer Bright as follows:

"We met in Boston, the governor of the state sent a substitute and the mayor of the city sent his secretary to welcome us. We went to Chicago. The mayor of that city sent a substitute and the governor of the state sent his regrets.

"This is the first time in the history of this fraternity that we have heard words of welcome from a chief executive of a state. We assure your excellency that we came to this city with no misgivings at all. We shall go with happy recollections. . . . We are on ancestral ground. . . . I feel like shouting, 'Governor, oh Governor, safe at home!' "

The Negro Elks, as noted above, had been free to use the Richmond streetcars without being Jim Crowed. The cars were back in operation, following a strike in 1922, during which jitneys took up the slack. These automobiles, operated at the time by the Richmond Central Trades and Labor Council, traveled between the West End and downtown. Jitneys had been introduced in the city as far back as 1914, and they were much to the fore during the streetcar strike. A nineteen-inch snowfall greatly complicated Richmond's transportation problem. Finally the strike was settled, and an ordinance was passed by the Council putting an end to the jitneys. They had been cutting into the revenues of the Virginia Railway & Power Company.

The year 1922 also was marked by the death of Major James H. Dooley.

The Richmond multimillionaire left Maymont, with its mansion and extensive grounds, to Mrs. Dooley for life, with the understanding that it would go to the city on her death. Major Dooley also bequested $3,000,000 to the Roman Catholic Sisters of Charity for the construction of two girls' orphanages. At the time, it was the largest single bequest made to Catholic charities in the United States. St. Joseph's Villa was accordingly built on the Washington Highway outside the Richmond city limits. Dooley also left $25,000 to the Medical College of Virginia for the enlargement of the Dooley Children's Hospital, previously established by him. Swannanoa, the huge mansion he built on the crest of the Blue Ridge near Afton, went to Mrs. Dooley.

A notable milestone in Richmond's history was the acquisition in 1924 of the city's first free public library, in the modern sense. Richmond was the last city of its size in the country to build and operate such an institution.

The Rosemary Library, founded by Thomas Nelson Page as a memorial to his wife, had opened in the early nineties, but users had to pay dues. For most of its twenty-five-year life, the small collection was located at the southwest corner of Fourth and Franklin streets. It was a fashionable rendezvous; ladies brought fancy work.

Andrew Carnegie offered the city $100,000 in 1901 for a public library open to all, if the municipality would provide $10,000 a year for maintenance. Richmond did not accept the offer. Many Richmonders apparently felt that a library was a luxury, and that other public services were more essential.

The City Council was again indifferent to the need in 1922 when an ordinance was introduced appropriating $350,000 for a library, accompanied by a petition bearing ten thousand signatures. The Council took the view that there were "more important demands for funds."

But there was now a large, well-organized, determined bloc of citizens who had formed the Richmond Library Association, successor to the earlier Richmond Education Association, in which Professor John C. Metcalf, Mrs. B. B. Munford and the Reverend Dr. W. Russell Bowie were prominent. The Library Association chose John Stewart Bryan, publisher of the *News Leader*, as president and Mrs. Edmund C. (Kate Pleasants) Minor, one of the ablest and most socially conscious women in Richmond, as vice-president. The Richmond-First Club and other agencies joined the fight. The almost immediate result was that the Council approved a $200,000 bond issue. In 1924 the Lewis Ginter mansion at Shafer and Franklin was bought for $112,000. The city's first public library opened there in the fall of that year. Mr. Bryan, whose efforts had been so essential to victory, was the first chairman of the City Library Board, and served in that capacity for a decade and a half.

The Ginter mansion was not well-suited to the needs of a modern library, but it was far superior to anything the city had had in the past. Operations there had hardly gotten under way when Mrs. James H. Dooley died and left $500,000 to the city for the erection of a public library in memory of her husband. First and Franklin was chosen as the site, and work was begun. The new Dooley Memorial Library opened in 1930, and provided much more adequate service than had ever been provided before. A small branch for Negroes began operating in 1925 in the Phyllis Wheatley Y.W.C.A. at 515 North Seventh Street. Soon thereafter, the larger Rosa D. Bowser branch, named for the first black woman to teach in Richmond's public schools, opened at oo Clay Street.

One of the advocates of a public library for Richmond was Mayor George Ainslie. Elected in 1912, the handsome, dapper chief executive of the city began urging the establishment of such an institution almost as soon as he took office, succeeding David C. Richardson. His administration lasted for twelve years. The "strong mayor" type of municipal government was adopted during that time, and the mayor became more than a figurehead occupied mainly with greeting prominent visitors. Ainslie's service ended when he was defeated for reelection by Dr. J. Fulmer Bright.

Important events, such as wars, elections, criminal trials or sports events were covered in those days in newspaper "extras." Election news also was flashed on a screen on the fronts of newspaper buildings. Radio was barely coming into use and television was far in the future. The public depended on the papers for prompt information. An extra might appear at any time of the day or night, and newsboys would sell it on the streets, crying their wares. There was hot competition to be first with an extra when big news was breaking.

Baseball scoreboards were operated annually during the world series by the *Times-Dispatch* and *News Leader*. A baseball diamond was rigged up on the wall of each newspaper, with movable figures representing the players. When the batter made a base hit, a bell would ring and the figure at bat would move to the proper base, while any base runners would advance. Excited crowds jammed the street to follow the heroic feats of Rogers Hornsby or Walter Johnson. Radio Station WRVA was established in 1925 by Larus & Brother Company, but it would be a good many years before the games were broadcast over this 50,000-watt station.

There was also interest in "dance marathons." In one such Richmond event, three couples were still on their feet at the end of two days and nights, and not surprisingly had sunken cheeks, red, swollen eyes and drooping mouths. The winning couple kept going for more than seventy-two hours. Flagpole sitters likewise competed in various cities.

This was the "jazz age," signalized by "flappers," John Held cartoons, Stutz Bearcat automobiles, raccoon coats, hip flasks, "cawn" whiskey, charred kegs, home brew and bathtub gin. Undoubtedly the phrase "flaming youth" was apropos at times during the Roaring Twenties; yet the carryings-on between the sexes were not at all comparable to those of the 1970s, when many college students were living and sleeping together in dormitories with administration acquiescence, abortions were legal and the use of drugs was prevalent.

The follies and foibles of Richmonders, both young and old, were incisively viewed in the novels of Ellen Glasgow and James Branch Cabell. Both had a low opinion of the intellectual capacities and concerns of most of their fellow citizens, an attitude no doubt related to the unimpressive sales that their books enjoyed in the city. Miss Glasgow wrote:

"I have known intimately, in the South at least, few persons really interested in books more profound than 'sweet stories.' My closest friends, with the exception of James Cabell, still read as lightly as they speculate, and this description applies as accurately to the social order in which I was born."

She also declared that "there was only one key to unlock modern Richmond, and that key was golden." Miss Glasgow went on to say that "anybody from anywhere who could afford to give a larger party became automatically, as it were, a social leader."

Cabell slyly satirized the inhabitants of Richmond in his writings about a remote place of his invention in medieval France called Poictesme. Many Richmonders failed to grasp the fact that the irony was directed at them.

However, the judgments of both Cabell and Glasgow with respect to the slight intellectual concerns of Richmonders seem unduly harsh. A city that boasted of two such writers as they, together with Douglas S. Freeman, plus the magazine *The Reviewer*, was far from intellectually dead. Freeman and *The Reviewer* will be discussed hereafter.

Cabell's beautiful yet esoteric prose had appealed to a limited circle until the attempted suppression in 1919 of his novel, *Jurgen*, by the New York Society for the Suppression of Vice. The publicity accompanying this event, and the subsequent court ruling that the book could not be taken off the market because of alleged obscenities, made the Richmond author a national figure. Almost simultaneously H. L. Mencken published his scathing essay on the South entitled "The Sahara of the Bozart." This roweling broadside created a gargantuan stir, and in it Mencken singled out Cabell, with considerable exaggeration, as the only Southern novelist worth mentioning. The two circumstances combined to project the Richmonder to the forefront of American letters.

Miss Glasgow's fame also was rising during this period, and her novel *Barren Ground* was hailed by the critics. It was a dark and somewhat depressing chronicle, but it was soon followed by *The Romantic Comedians*, a light and diverting work satirizing what she regarded as the weaknesses of the male, especially the male genus as found in Queenborough, her thinly disguised name for Richmond. *The Romantic Comedians* was a huge commercial and critical success, and was followed by *They Stooped to Folly*, another ironic view of Queenborough and its citizens. This too was well received, although not quite so well as *The Romantic Comedians.*

During these years Miss Glasgow was having a serious love affair with Henry W. Anderson, a leading Richmond attorney, to whom she became engaged. The ups and downs of their involvement were only dimly known to Richmonders until the publication of her posthumous work, *The Woman Within.* There she made a number of revelations which were the subject of amazed comments in the city for months.

It was from this book, as noted in the preceding chapter, that the public first learned of Miss Glasgow's deep involvement with an unidentified married New Yorker who died in 1905, after their affair had gone on for seven years. She also told in its pages of her tempestuous engagement to Henry Anderson. She was betrothed to the Richmond attorney when he enlisted in the American Red Cross at the outbreak of World War I and left for Romania. There he apparently became infatuated with the beautiful Queen Marie. She conferred three decorations upon him, and on taking his final leave, he "had fallen on his knees before her and kissed the hem of her skirt," Miss Glasgow wrote bitingly when she read of the event in Queen Marie's autobiography. The queen had identified the chivalrous gentleman merely as "a Southern colonel," but Miss Glasgow took it for granted that this was the man who had asked her to marry him before he left for the Balkans, and who had become a lieutenant colonel in the Red Cross.

They continued to see each other at fairly regular intervals after Anderson returned to Richmond, but it was never again the same. As she put it in *The Woman Within*, "for seventeen months out of twenty-one years we were happy together." Most of the happiness ended when Queen Marie came between them.

Miss Glasgow tells us that at one point she was on the verge of suicide over the breaking of the engagement, and that she took so many sleeping pills one night that "sleep or death, it did not matter." As things turned out, it was only sleep, and she resumed seeing her former fiancé.

The inner turmoil caused by the termination of her betrothal to Anderson was reflected in much of her writing, as she herself conceded. She also told of her overwhelming grief on the death of her pedigreed Sealyham, "Jeremy"—given her by Anderson. The lively little dog, who was accustomed to greet guests at the door, died in 1929, and his death brought her such sorrow that she "often awoke in the night with stabbing pains in her heart." Jeremy had had a long illness, during which Miss Glasgow consulted specialists in New York and Philadelphia, and had the noted Richmond surgeon Dr. Stuart McGuire do the operation, rather than a veterinarian. When his bill came, bearing the words "Services for dog," she was incensed. She felt that it should have read "Services for Mr. Jeremy Glasgow."[1] It seems probable that the death of Jeremy crushed her more completely than the passing of any member of her family.

All this emotional tension may well have affected her disposition, at least temporarily, for Frank N. Doubleday, her publisher during these years, is eloquent in describing her temperamental behavior. In his *Memoirs of a Publisher* Doubleday declares that Ellen Glasgow was "about the hardest thing to get along with since Eve was made from Adam's rib." He speaks of letters from her "screeching with ill nature," and adds, "She writes such a terrible hand that it is impossible to read most of the insults, but you can bet your life that they are there."

This, it must be said, was not the image of Miss Glasgow that her Richmond friends or the public had. She seemed a gracious lady who entertained charmingly in her antebellum home at First and Main streets. True, she suffered from almost lifelong deafness, a great trial to her, and she used an apparently unique type of hearing aid, a hollow, silvery device on the end of a cord. One had to talk into this apparatus in conversing with her. After making an observation, she would extend the tube in one's direction, and it was important to respond quickly. Miss Glasgow appeared outwardly cheerful, however, and happy in the company of guests.

Cabell, on the other hand, was not at all socially inclined. He was aloof and withdrawn, an introvert who disliked crowds, seldom appeared in public and never spoke from a platform. He entertained occasionally, but his wife did most of the talking. Cabell was happiest when alone upstairs with his typewriter and his books. His aim, he said, was to "write perfectly of beautiful happenings," and he added, "I burn with generous indignation over the world's pigheadedness and injustice at no time whatever. I do not expect anyone to be intelligent or large-hearted." Man, to him, was "an ape reft of his tail and grown rusty at climbing," and he delighted in exposing what he saw as the simian inanities and puerilities of the human race. In doing so he achieved great critical acclaim. Vernon Louis Parrington termed Cabell "one of the great masters of English prose, the supreme comic spirit thus far granted us. . . individual and incomparable."

Despite his supercilious and anti-social attitudes, Cabell was somehow persuaded to edit three issues of a little magazine, *The Reviewer*, founded in Richmond by Emily Clark, Hunter Stagg, Margaret Freeman (many years later, the second Mrs. Cabell) and Mary Dallas Street.

The story of *The Reviewer* is an extraordinary one. The founders began the operation with a total bankroll of $200.75. Miss Clark, society editor of the *News Leader*, and Stagg, who conducted a book column for one of the papers, were to look after the editorial side, and Miss Freeman promised to wangle a few advertisements.

A large group of nationally and internationally known writers were somehow persuaded to contribute without compensation. H. L. Mencken, who, like Cabell, gave the impression in his writings of not being willing to help anybody do anything at any time, was constantly lending assistance and advice. Cabell and Miss Glasgow also provided valuable aid. The small publication was suddenly getting national notice, and no wonder. Consider the following partial list of contributors, all of whom were paid "in fame, not specie": Hervey Allen, John Galsworthy, Paul Green, Joseph Hergesheimer, DuBose Heyward, Gerald W. Johnson, Mary Johnston, Amy Lowell, Robert Nathan, Julia Peterkin, Josephine Pinckney, Burton Rascoe, Agnes Repplier, Amélie Rives, Gertrude Stein, Allen Tate, Louis Untermeyer, Carl Van Vechten and Elinor Wylie, not to mention Cabell, Mencken and Glasgow.

How could such a list have been put together when the magazine was able to pay absolutely nothing to writers? Cabell, Mencken and Hergesheimer approached their friends for contributions, apparently presenting the argument that *The Reviewer* was a trail-blazing enterprise bringing enlightenment to "The Sahara of the Bozart." Emily Clark also wrote to possible contributors. The little magazine made literary history, and was a significant factor in the South's intellectual renascence. It appeared at irregular intervals from early 1921 to late 1924, and then moved to Chapel Hill, North Carolina, where it expired the following year.

Another magazine published briefly in Richmond was the *Black Swan*. Founded as a journal to promote the Windsor Farms development, it became an independent publication in 1929, under the editorship of T. Beverly Campbell. During its remaining two years of life, short stories from the *Black Swan* were selected by both the O. Henry and O'Brien annual best short story compilations. The magazine was a victim of the Depression.

Three Richmond writers—Margaret Prescott Montague, Pernet Patterson and Helena Lefroy Caperton—were especially talented in the field of the short story. Their work was represented in the annual collections of "best" short stories.

Henry Sydnor Harrison, a Tennessean, came to Richmond in the early 1900s and joined the editorial staff of the Richmond *Times-Dispatch*, where he became chief editorial writer and a paragrapher of national repute. He also wrote a number of novels, notably *Queed* and *V.V.'s Eyes*.

Henry W. Anderson, the Richmond attorney who had so large a part in the life of Ellen Glasgow, ran for governor of Virginia on the Republican ticket in 1921. Miss Glasgow was still seeing him regularly, although on what seems to have been a platonic basis. She entered enthusiastically into his campaign for governor, while remaining entirely in the background.

Anderson was running against E. Lee Trinkle, the nominee of the Democratic machine. That organization, under the leadership of U. S. Senator Thomas S. Martin, who died in 1919, had become ingrown and unresponsive to public needs, and Anderson put on a campaign that shook up the politicians and roused the people generally. He knew that he had no chance of election, but accepted the nomination as a public duty. Anderson represented the better element in Virginia's struggling Republican party, in contrast to C. Bascom Slemp of Big Stone Gap, who spoke for the seekers after "political pie."

Colonel Anderson's campaign technique was decidedly unorthodox. Instead of slapping backs and osculating babies at political rallies, he arrived for his scheduled addresses impeccably attired with his pince-nez on his nose and in a foreign car driven by a liveried chauffeur. The latter opened the door for the colonel, who strode to the platform, said his say, bowed to his audience and entered the car for the return trip as the chauffeur held the door open once more.[2]

The Republican party in Virginia had become "lily-white," and so proclaimed itself in the platform on which Anderson ran. It was made plain to the blacks that they would not be named to public office or be allowed to participate in its councils. The idea was to disassociate the Virginia G.O.P. in the public mind from the Republicans who had worked hand in hand with the blacks during the Reconstruction era, and from the threats at that time, real or imagined, to "white supremacy." The blacks were much discouraged over this turn of events. In retaliation, they bolted and nominated John Mitchell, Jr., the Richmond banker, for governor on an all-black ticket.

One of the ablest men of his time, Colonel Anderson put the Democrats on the defensive by pointing to obvious weaknesses in the state government, which they dominated completely, and by exposing some of their questionable practices. It is not too much to say that he helped to bring about the reforms that took place in the late 1920s under Governor Harry F. Byrd. In the election, Anderson got one third of the 210,000 votes cast, a reasonably good showing. John Mitchell, Jr., and his "lily-blacks" polled about 5,000.

Anderson became prominent in the councils of the Republican party in the United States, and his name was twice advanced for Vice-President at the party's national conventions. He is understood to have been seriously considered for the U. S. Supreme Court by President Herbert Hoover, but the appointment seems to have been prevented by the two senators from Virginia and C. Bascom Slemp. Leaders of Virginia's Democratic "organization" were decidedly lacking in enthusiasm for Colonel Anderson, in view, among other things, of his absurd statement in 1927 that "Virginia has the most tyrannical government of any state since the Stuarts were driven from England, and the most inefficient of any state in the Western Hemisphere, not excepting Mexico, Nicaragua and Venezuela." Anderson was named by President Hoover to the National Commission on Law Observance and Enforcement, usually known as the Wickersham Commission, which studied the workings, or nonworkings, of the prohibition law. Decorations came to him during and after World War I, not only from Romania and Queen Marie but also from Italy, France, Serbia, Greece, Montenegro, Russia and Czechoslovakia. He stated in a letter to Marjorie Kinnan Rawlings, the novelist, that he had been offered the crown of Albania, but had rejected it.[3]

Far from Albania, in a small Tennessee town, a historic drama was unfolding in the mid-1920s. John T. Scopes, a teacher in the Dayton, Tennessee, high school, was on trial for instructing his pupils in the doctrine of evolution, and the repercussions were felt in all corners of America, not least in Richmond. The formidable Dr. George W. McDaniel, pastor of Richmond's First Baptist Church, was on the war-path in uncompromising opposition to Scopes and to acceptance of Darwin's evolutionary hypothesis. As president of the Southern Baptist Convention in 1926, Dr. McDaniel declared in his annual message to that body, "I am happy to believe that this convention accepts Genesis as teaching that man was a special creation of God, and rejects every theory, evolution or other, which teaches that man originated in, or came by way of, a lower animal ancestry." The convention adopted this declaration as a statement of its beliefs.

The Reverend R. H. Pitt, revered editor of the Baptist *Religious Herald*, leaped into the fray, saying: "There isn't an intelligent Baptist 21 years old . . . who would be willing, if he stopped to think about it, to give his approval of the declaration . . . that the first chapter of Genesis is literally true. If the first chapters of Genesis are to be taken as literal history, then, of course, the world was made in six days. That is what the record says. No intelligent person in full age in our time believes that the world was made in six days."

Dr. Pitt was a bulwark in Virginia against the passage of anti-evolution legislation, such as was introduced in every Southern state except Virginia, and passed in Tennessee, Arkansas and Mississippi, while almost passing in others. He also had much to do with defeating the "Bible bill" introduced in the Old Dominion, which sought to make Bible reading compulsory in the public schools. Dr. Pitt fought the measure as "an unholy alliance of state and church." This time Dr. George W. McDaniel was on his side and a powerful force in opposition to the bill. So were the Dover Baptist Association, which included Richmond at that time, and numerous other Baptist associations.

The bill was supported by an agency calling itself the Patriotic Welfare Committee, representing the Ku-Klux Klan and certain other orders. The committee also made a spectacle of itself by opposing the erection of the Christopher Columbus statue which stands in Byrd Park. The Italian-Americans of Richmond had generously offered to pay for the monument, but the Patriotic Welfare Committee appeared in opposition before a committee of the Council. Columbus, they said, was a "foreigner," the organizations sponsoring the statue were "sectarian," i.e. Roman Catholic, and Columbus didn't discover America anyway. An illiterate statement setting forth the foregoing was read. The terrorized councilmanic committee actually voted to reject the statue, and the rebel yell resounded through the chamber. But there was such a furor that the rejection was overridden when the matter reached the Council, and the monument was accepted. Italian-Americans from throughout the United States came to Richmond for the unveiling on Columbus Day, 1925.

The Klan was a sinister force in many American states and cities during the 1920s. It never became as powerful in Richmond or Virginia as it did in many other places, but it played a role. When Governor Alfred E. Smith of New York, a Roman Catholic, ran for President in 1928 against Herbert Hoover, the Klan was a definite factor in carrying both Richmond and Virginia for the Republican nominee. Anti-Catholic prejudice was the major cause of Smith's defeat, along with the fact that he was opposed to prohibition. Sentiment on both issues changed radically in subsequent years, but Smith could not surmount these handicaps at this period in America's history, and Virginia went to the G.O.P. for the first time since Reconstruction.

Richmond and Virginia returned to the Democratic column the following year when John Garland Pollard ran for governor on the Democratic ticket against William Moseley Brown, a Washington & Lee professor. Brown was the candidate of what were called the "Hoovercrats," a combination of Republicans and anti-Smith Democrats, the latter shepherded into the fold by Bishop James Cannon, Jr. Pollard swept the city and state by large majorities.

The election of 1928 occurred sixty-three years after the burning of Richmond at the close of the Civil War, but Confederate memories were still strong in the city. Two more statues of Confederate heroes were unveiled on Monument Avenue at about this time—Stonewall Jackson in 1919 and Matthew Fontaine Maury in 1929. The Confederate veterans in the nearby Old Soldiers' Home are said to have insisted that since Lee seated on Traveller faced southward from the avenue, Jackson on Little Sorrel should look northward into the eye of the foe, and their wish was granted. The Jackson and Maury monuments are by F. William Sievers, who stated that the Maury was easily his favorite among all his sculptures.

Battle Abbey, a handsome building in the Greek Revival style, and a memorial to the men and women of the Confederacy, was dedicated in 1921. The idea of such a memorial was first suggested in 1892 by U. S. Senator John W. Daniel of Lynchburg in an address to Confederate veterans in New Orleans.[4] Charles Broadway Rouss, Virginia-born veteran, offered sometime thereafter to contribute $100,000, on condition that the people of the South provided an equal amount. The City of Richmond came forward with $50,000, and the State of Virginia donated the site. Thomas F. Ryan paid for the Confederate murals by Charles Hoffbauer.

The cornerstone was laid in 1912, and the building was virtually finished by 1914. But Hoffbauer, a noted French artist, went off to fight for France on the outbreak of the world war, leaving the murals incomplete. He served on the front lines throughout the conflict, and when he returned in 1919 to resume work on the paintings, he felt compelled to wipe out all that he had done and begin over again. His experiences in battle had given him an entirely new concept of war, he said. Hoffbauer worked tirelessly and with enormous zeal. Finally his task was completed, and Battle Abbey was opened to the public. The French artist's paintings, in the classical tradition, grace the walls of the south wing. They show Lee, Jackson, Stuart, Mosby and other Southern commanders, with bugles sounding, cavalry charging, cannon firing and Jackson's ragged "foot cavalry" passing in review before their leader. In the other wing, where more recently Confederate battle flags from many fields have hung, there was the million-dollar collection of paintings given to the Commonwealth by John Barton Payne, later the nucleus of the exceptionally valuable holdings of the Virginia Museum of Fine Arts. Behind Battle Abbey, handsome grounds, enclosed in elegant magnolia and box, were laid out under the direction of a well-known landscape designer, Warren H. Manning of Boston.

John Buchan, the distinguished British historian, visited Richmond in 1924 and wrote the Confederate Museum that the city's "memorials of the War Between the States are conceived with such dignity and simplicity that they are infinitely the most impressive things I saw on the American continent." Almost simultaneously, the chargé d'affaires of El Salvador at Washington declared that "Monument Avenue is destined in the course of time to become known as the most beautiful avenue in the world."

Two years later the Virginia flag taken down from the pole atop the Capitol by a Federal officer on April 3, 1865, was returned to Richmond by the officer's grandson. The flag had been made by two sisters, the Misses Sallie Munford, later Mrs. Charles H. Talbott, and Margaret Munford. Governor "Extra Billy" Smith asked the two young ladies to make the flag as a replacement for the badly worn banner then flying from the Capitol. When the relic was returned sixty-two years later, Mrs. Talbott was present at the ceremonies in the old Hall of the House of Delegates, and identified the flag as the one she and her sister had made during the Civil War.

Various homes on Franklin Street westward from the now-vanished structure in which the Munford sisters stitched the flag in the sixties were taken over many years later by Richmond Professional Institute. The institute had its origins in 1917 on the third floor at 1112 Capitol Street, over the old Juvenile and Domestic Relations Court, and was called the Richmond School of Social Work and Public Health. Its founder was Dr. Henry H. Hibbs, an able young man who affords one of the foremost examples in Richmond's history of how to make bricks without straw.

With no financial resources of his own, he persuaded John M. Miller, Jr., president of the First National Bank, to approach friends for assistance. Miller was attracted by Hibbs's plan for "training nurses to take doctors' places" in World War I. During and immediately after the war, $73,000 was raised in this way. Another man who provided much counsel and leadership was the Reverend J. J. Scherer, Jr., of First English Lutheran Church. He served as board chairman until his death nearly forty years later. The school became part of the College of William and Mary in 1925, and took the name of Richmond Professional Institute in 1939, but no state funds were made available until 1940.

Purchase of the Saunders-Willard house at Shafer and Franklin streets for all the school's operations was made possible through a financial campaign headed by T. M. Carrington. Nearly $100,000 was raised. Three years later, in 1928, the School of Art was opened under the leadership of Miss Theresa Pollak in the loft of what had been the Saunders-Willard stable. Miss Pollak, the moving spirit in the school for decades, retired in 1970 after nearly forty years of service. By then, the School of Art had expanded into the School of the Arts at Virginia Commonwealth University, one of the largest and best such schools in the United States.

The use of stables and stable lofts, as well as the Victorian mansions to which these substantial outbuildings were attached, was a vital element in the expansion of the Richmond School of Social Work and Public Health. Since the school lacked funds for new construction, the purchase of nineteenth- and early twentieth-century residences for use as classrooms and dormitories was carried out whenever money could somehow be obtained. It was all part of the ingenious plan of Dr. Henry Hibbs.

Another imaginative educator came on the Richmond scene at about this time. He was Dr. William T. Sanger, who was elected president of the Medical College of Virginia in 1925. Dr. Sanger was then secretary of the State Board of Education. The college was in danger of losing its accreditation at the hands of the Council on Medical Education and Hospitals of the American Medical Association, and indeed, was on the verge of collapse. Dr. Stuart McGuire, president of the institution since 1919, had been carrying a superhuman load as executive head of the college, while continuing his large surgical practice and directing the affairs of St. Luke's Hospital. He was among the first to urge the election of a full-time president.

There was no longer any hope on the part of MCV that the University of Virginia Medical School would be moved to Richmond and combined with it—a proposal discussed off and on for twenty years, and frequently in heated terms. This plan, strongly fought by the University of Virginia, was defeated once and for all by the General Assembly in 1922.

Upon taking over, Sanger set about strengthening MCV in various directions. Things began to move at a furious clip. The new president's initial accomplishments are outlined in the college history, *The First 125 Years*, as follows:

"After ten months in office, Dr. Sanger reported . . . $300,000 raised of a million dollar goal; $20,000 increase in the annual state appropriation; assurance of a new laboratory and outpatient clinic building; a new dormitory for nurses; organization of the School of Nursing as an integral part of the college with its own dean; appointment of the first full-time professor of medicine, Dr. William Branch Porter; better supervision and improvement of teaching; extension of the pharmacy curriculum under Dean [Wortley F.] Rudd from two to three years; Class A rating for the School of Dentistry; and reorganization of the central administration of the institution through creation of the administrative council."

The foregoing is a sample of the administrative drive demonstrated by Sanger throughout his years as president of MCV.

A notable development in the sphere of secondary education occurred in Richmond in 1917 with the founding of St. Catherine's School for Girls. The school had its origins in 1890, when Miss Virginia Randolph Ellett, universally known as "Miss Jennie," and one of the great teachers of her time, began holding classes in the dining room of a boarding house at 109 East Grace Street. She moved twice more before establishing a country day school in Westhampton in 1917. Three years later it was incorporated into the system of diocesan schools of the Episcopal Church, with the name St. Catherine's. Miss Jennie relinquished the post of headmistress at this time to Miss Rosalie Noland, who served until the selection of Miss Louisa Bacot (later Mrs. Jeffrey R. Brackett) in 1924. Mrs. Brackett was an effective headmistress until her retirement in 1947. Enrollment enjoyed spectacular growth during her twenty-three years as the school's administrative head, and the same was true of the physical plant.

Miss Jennie retained her affiliation with St. Catherine's until her death in 1939. She was greatly admired by her pupils, who felt that she gave them a desire for learning that remained with them throughout their lives. Several teachers on her staff were also exceptionally gifted, including Miss Louisa ("Miss Lulie") Blair and Miss Edmonia Lancaster, whose specialties were Shakespeare and Latin, respectively.

Nancy, Lady Astor, was a pupil of Miss Jennie, and when it was decided by other pupils many years later to provide their former teacher with an automobile, Lady Astor cabled: "Mechanize Miss Jennie. Get her a chauffeur. Send bills to me."

At age seventy, Miss Ellett did not regard herself as fully educated, so she took a course at Oxford. She was the guest of Lady Astor during her so-journ in England.

In a beautiful and well-written tribute to Miss Ellett, Mrs. Wyndham B. (Natalie) Blanton, one of her ablest pupils, noted that, with all her brilliance and dedication, she had her faults. "Not everyone understood her recognition of the power of wealth and social prestige, tools in her day as they are in ours," said Mrs. Blanton. "There is no doubt that she used them, but aways to build."

Miss Susanna P. Turner, a lieutenant-colonel in the Women's Army Corps during World War II, succeeded Mrs. Brackett as headmistress in 1947, and served ably for eighteen years. Enrollment increased, the curriculum was expanded and new buildings were added. Deeply idealistic, Miss Turner resigned to join the staff of a mission school in Liberia.

Robert W. Trusdell, who had headed a school in Savannah, Georgia, succeeded Miss Turner. During his eight years at St. Catherine's the curriculum was revised and several new buildings added.

Michael S. Churchman was chosen in 1974 after Trusdell resigned. Headmaster of a girl's school in Denver, Colorado, Fulbright exchange teacher in another girl's school in England, and a former executive of the Marshall Plan in Europe, he brought to the post a broad outlook and wide experience.

In 1915, two years before St. Catherine's was established, another fine school for girls, Collegiate, was founded. Miss Mary Carter Anderson was headmistress and Miss Helen Baker assistant headmistress. The Stratford School, launched in 1906 by Mr. and Mrs. E. L. Bemiss, merged with Collegiate in 1917. A large number of students from Miss Morris' School also joined Collegiate the following year. Collegiate had begun operations at 1133 West Franklin Street, but in 1917 built more adequate quarters at 1619 Monument Avenue.

E. L. Bemiss came to the school's rescue in 1920 when Miss Baker, the assistant headmistress, was forced into bankruptcy. He enlisted the aid of other businessmen, and this group kept the institution going. Two years later, the Presbyterian League of Richmond purchased the property and operated the school, with Bemiss always active in its affairs. However, Collegiate was never affiliated officially with the Presbyterian Church. Members of various religious denominations serve on its Board of Trustees.

Miss Catherine Stauffer was named headmistress in 1940, and two years later became Mrs. William M. Flippen. She served with distinction until her retirement in 1972.

A large tract of property on River Road opposite Mooreland Farms was given to the school by J. Louis Reynolds, who subsequently donated additional acreage. The result was the establishment there of the Collegiate Country Day School, with pupils in the kindergarten and lower grades, while instruction for the higher grades continued for the time being on Monument Avenue. The two merged in 1960 and moved to the River Road site, and by then boys as well as girls were being enrolled. Malcolm U. Pitt, Jr., succcessful principal of Richmond's Albert H. Hill School, was chosen headmaster for boys, and Mrs. Flippen continued as headmistress for girls. E. Angus Powell, Richmond business executive, headed a drive for funds that netted the remarkable sum of $1,150,000, and The Collegiate Schools, as they are now known, were well on their way. Malcolm U. Pitt, Jr., was elevated to president of the schools in 1972.

The oldest cadet corps in Richmond is that of Benedictine High School at 300 North Sheppard Street. Founded in 1911 by Benedictine monks and conducted by that ancient Roman Catholic order, the school requires all students to participate in the military program. Benedictine has been classified as a "military institute" by the U. S. Department of the Army, the top classification granted to a high school.

As with St. Christopher's, discussed in the preceding chapter, St. Catherine's and The Collegiate Schools, nearly all Benedictine graduates go on to college. There is a healthy atmosphere of discipline at Benedictine, and every cadet must wear a coat and tie when not in uniform. Long hair and weird male coiffures are not allowed.

St. Gertrude's High School for girls, nearby at 3201 Stuart Avenue, was founded in 1922 by the Benedictine sisters. Like Benedictine, it is a day school; each has between three hundred and four hundred students.

Marymount School, with a somewhat smaller enrollment, is a Roman Catholic day school for girls, founded in 1952 by the religious of the Sacred Heart of Mary. It is situated at Paxton, the handsome former residence of John Skelton Williams, 5219 Cary Street Road. The great majority of students at both Marymount and St. Gertrude's are college-bound.

In another cultural realm, that of music, the Wednesday Club continued to function in the early 1900s, but a group of Richmond ladies, headed by Mrs. Channing M. Ward, decided in 1916 to form the Musicians Club. It began with thirty members and rose ultimately to eleven hundred. Internationally renowned artists were brought to Richmond each year. Concerts by local virtuosos and singers stimulated study and fine performance. During World War I the club gave semi-weekly concerts at Camp Lee.

The art of playing the piano or the violin throve in Richmond during these years but the art of digging tunnels was less successful. The C.&O. Railroad sought in 1925 to reopen the tunnel dug through Church Hill in the 1870s, but 400 feet of it collapsed with a train inside, together with a number of workmen. Two of them were killed and two others were never found. The effort was abandoned and the tunnel containing the train was sealed.

More successful was the walling in of Shockoe Creek, which had been flooding Shockoe Valley in heavy rainstorms, with devastating results.

Allen J. Saville was City Director of Public Works from 1920 to 1924, and performed with unusual ability. In the latter year he resigned, went into private business, and carried out various important projects, including the development of Windsor Farms for T. C. Williams, Jr. He was also an admired leader in civic affairs.

The 500-acre Windsor Farms tract contained only one residence, the early nineteenth-century house Windsor, which was later pulled down. Streets were laid out in a circular design to avoid stereotyped patterns, and were given names redolent of the English countryside. Houses had to meet certain minimum standards and be of Georgian architecture or in a style harmonizing with it.

Two ancient English country houses were brought across the ocean piece by piece in the late 1920s and reerected in Windsor Farms. Since one was deteriorating rapidly and the other was about to be demolished by the English, the latter found their removal to this country acceptable.

Agecroft Hall, a fifteenth-century manor house near Manchester, was transported to Richmond by T. C. Williams, Jr., for his residence, and rebuilt on rolling hills overlooking the James. The oriel window above the entrance and the splendid mullioned bay window in the two-story high great hall are striking features of this typical English gentleman's dwelling of centuries ago.

On the adjacent tract, Alexander W. Weddell, ambassador to Spain and the Argentine, put together substantial portions of Warwick Priory in partial reproduction of Sulgrave Manor, ancestral English home of the Washingtons.

Warwick Priory, situated on the northern edge of the town of Warwick, had begun as the priory of St. Sepulchre in the twelfth century. It underwent various changes, and in the sixteenth century, when Henry VIII seized the monasteries, he transferred the property to one of his favorites, Thomas Hawkins, also known as Fisher. The latter rebuilt and expanded it into a stately manor house, known as The Priory. In 1572 Queen Elizabeth came to sojourn briefly at nearby Warwick Castle, and the Earl and Countess of Warwick moved out and went to The Priory. The queen suddenly betook herself thence one evening and joined the earl and countess at supper. Thomas Hawkins, the owner, was upstairs "grievously vexed with the gout." Elizabeth "after a little repast, rose again and went to visit the good man of the house," who "would have kneeled," but "Her Majesty would not suffer it," knowing the suffering that would thereby be caused to the gentleman's aching joints. The queen wished him a speedy recovery and departed.

When The Priory entered its new incarnation in Richmond some three and a half centuries later, it was rechristened Virginia House by the Weddells. They had their Richmond home there for about two decades, but were tragically killed on New Year's Day, 1948, in a Missouri train wreck. They left Virginia House to the Virginia Historical Society, and also provided an endowment of $950,000 for that organization.

The bringing of Agecroft Hall and Warwick Priory to Richmond was not the only excitement in the late 1920s. There was also the fire in the governor's mansion at Christmas time, 1926, when five-year-old Billy Trinkle, son of Governor and Mrs. Trinkle, brandished a sparkler under the Christmas tree and set it ablaze. The flames spread, and Mrs. Trinkle was severely burned, while Billy's older brother had to leap from an upstairs window. Considerable damage was done to the building, and to valuable paintings, which were later restored.

The following autumn Charles A. Lindbergh, who had made his epochal solo flight across the Atlantic a few months before in the *Spirit of St. Louis,* flew to Richmond in his famous plane for the dedication of Richard Evelyn Byrd Field, the municipal airport. Young Lindbergh was received with almost hysterical acclaim, and was entertained at a huge dinner at the Hotel Jefferson.

Capitol Square was being tinkered with all over again during this period. It was suffering at the hands of a remarkably obtuse superintendent of buildings and grounds. Terming the charming old brick walks "out of date," this individual proceeded to replace many of them with concrete. Bewildered by the green patina on the bronze statues of George Washington and the six smaller figures surrounding the monument's base, the superintendent ordered them painted black. Horrified officials were able to halt the desecration before it was actually begun.

Richmond's tallest skyscraper as of that time, the twenty-two-story Central National Bank Building on Broad Street near Third, was completed in 1930. The twelve-story Mutual Building and nineteen-story First National Bank Building in the Main Street financial district had been built in 1904 and 1913, respectively.

The Central National Bank, headed by William H. Schwarzschild, was well on the way toward carrying out its ambitious plan when the great stock market crash of 1929 shook the country and the world. A grim joke in circulation at the building's opening a year later was to the effect that it had been finished just in time for those in charge to jump from the top floor.

Men ruined by the collapse of the market and of business generally were indeed jumping from buildings in other cities. There would be plenty of suffering in Richmond, but conditions were never as bad in the Virginia capital as in the vast majority of urban areas.

A mania for getting rich quick by various means, including wild speculation in stocks and real estate, had brought the country to the brink of total disaster. Things would never be the same again. The Roaring Twenties had passed into history, and Richmond braced itself for the hard years ahead.

# TWENTY

# The Great Depression
# and World War II

THE MAGNITUDE of the catastrophe which the stock market crash of 1929 portended was not apparent at first in Richmond, or elsewhere. Leaders in and out of government intoned regularly that American business was "fundamentally sound" and that the skies would soon become brighter. But conditions grew steadily worse.

Fortunately for Richmond, the city's huge tobacco industry not only maintained its position, it expanded. Scarcely anybody seems to have stopped smoking, and women were taking up the habit in increasing numbers. Some persons smoked more than before, but many switched to cheaper brands. The stability of tobacco manufacture, more than anything else, kept Richmond from plunging into such depths of unemployment and suffering as overwhelmed Birmingham, for example, where the collapse of the steel industry, around which the city's entire economy revolved, had devastating effects.

But tobacco wasn't "everything" in Richmond. The city had a well-balanced economy, and the rayon plants, like the tobacco factories, expanded production, although many other factories were cutting back or shutting down. Rayon was in special demand since silk was too costly for most buyers during the Depression.

As the crisis deepened, more and more businesses failed, with consequent joblessness and suffering. Many who had plunged in the market on a 10 per cent margin were ruined. Avid speculators in real estate lost everything. Thousands wondered where their next meal was coming from.

Federal agencies were set up in 1933 to meet the emergency, and accomplished much in providing a subsistence income for the unemployed. First the federally financed Virginia Emergency Relief Administration created work on improvements around schools, sanitary facilities, airport projects, parks and streets. Then the Works Progress Administration (WPA) offered needy persons jobs on small construction projects, such as the rehabilitation of school buildings and other public structures, the laying of sewers, digging of drainage ditches and so on. Writers, musicians, artists and teachers also were given employment in their respective fields. There was a limit of $25,000 per project.

The Public Works Administration (PWA) built much larger and more expensive structures, thus providing further job opportunities. The Lee Bridge over the James, Virginia State Library, Maggie L. Walker High School and Medical College of Virginia Hospital are examples of what PWA did for the city's sagging economy. In each case, PWA provided nearly half the cost. The Virginia Museum of Fine Arts also was constructed at this time. John Barton Payne had given his million-dollar collection of paintings to the state, and he added $100,000 for a museum building, on condition that the sum be matched. Governor John Garland Pollard managed to scrounge $100,000 from the Federal government and private sources.

When newly inaugurated President Franklin D. Roosevelt closed all the banks in the United States for four days in March 1933, one Richmond institution, American Bank & Trust, was not permitted to open when the closing order was lifted. Another blow to the community was the failure of Frederick E. Nolting & Company, a highly regarded brokerage house specializing in real estate mortgage bonds. Yet there were fewer such failures in Richmond than in most cities.

In 1932–33 Richmond's unemployed numbered about eleven thousand. Seeking to capitalize on this situation, a diminutive New York Communist named Abe Tomkin came to town and organized an Unemployed Council, composed mainly of Negroes. Tomkin was joined by another white agitator, Thomas H. Stone of Richmond. They attracted little attention at first.

But the insignificant band was pounced upon by Mayor J. Fulmer Bright and hounded in almost every conceivable way. The police arrested Tomkin and Stone on the flimsiest pretext and no pretext. When they sought an audience with the mayor, for example, the latter ordered officers to "take these men by the scruff of the neck and the seat of the pants and throw them out of here." Another such encounter, involving a similarly unceremonious exit from the City Social Service Bureau, was eloquently described by one of those ejected:

"We got th'owed in and then we got th'owed out. I've been in all kinds of trouble, this-a-way, that-a-way and the other way, but it appeared to me that the policemen got more excited that afternoon than I've ever seen them get before. Two or three of them got hold of me and I thought I was in a windstorm. The detectives was railroading Comrade Stone down the steps."

All this persecution of the agitators brought many to their side who otherwise would have paid no attention. At first their meetings were attended by a mere handful, but as time wore on and the uproar mounted, more and more turned out, until finally at least six hundred persons, mainly blacks, were on hand to hear Stone denounce "the Scotts and the Branches," as well as practically all other wealthy Richmond families, in rabble-rousing appeals.

Tomkin, Stone et al. were arrested so many times that it was difficult to keep track. The Richmond press defended them against this treatment, whereupon the mayor and police chief "severed relations" with the newspapers and refused to deal with them. The *Times-Dispatch* got a court order giving the press access to warrants and police blotters.

Nearly all those arrested were fined or sentenced in Police Court, despite the spurious nature of the charges. They appealed to Hustings Court, where Judge John L. Ingram, an able and courageous man, threw out every case except one. In that, the defendant was convicted by a jury and fined $20. Judge Ingram remitted the fine.

The municipal authorities became so jittery over the Red Menace that they grew positively hysterical. For no reason at all, a truckload of police, swinging nightsticks, would dash up to a street corner in downtown Richmond, leap from the conveyance and begin rushing about in search of Soviet agents. Finding none, they would climb sheepishly into their truck and clatter back to the police station. This happened not once but several times, to the astonishment of gaping citizens.

Things calmed down for a bit, but in the winter Stone and his cohorts returned to the attack. They requested permission for a "hunger march" through the city, but a permit was denied. "Hunger marches" were being held in various parts of the country. The would-be Richmond marchers had no permit, but they decided to walk around city hall anyway. It was snowing hard, and about a hundred persons circled the building, which was heavily guarded by police, inside and out. After the marchers had made the circuit half a dozen times, Stone tried to make a speech. He was clubbed on the head and arrested. Convicted in Police Court, he appealed, and all charges were dismissed.

Tomkin finally departed Richmond for good. Stone also subsided. They seem to have concluded that the Depression in the city, although extremely serious, was not shot through with sufficient misery and despair for their efforts to succeed. Probably, too, they felt that conservative Richmond was barren ground for Marxist propaganda. The city's image suffered greatly, however, from the nationwide publicity given Mayor Bright's illegal persecution of the little band of agitators. Bright was often a reasonable and courteous man, but he had inflexible views on some subjects which nobody could change. The "Communist threat" was one of these.

As the Depression deepened, many of the jobless had no money with which to buy fuel. They were accordingly allowed to haul coal without charge from the strip deposits near Robious, Chesterfield County, in any vehicle they could command. Lines of wagons, hacks, buggies or "tin lizzies" from Richmond and nearby points took advantage of this opportunity. At the bottom of the Depression in 1934–35 the average number of people receiving relief in Richmond was 17,598. The total for Norfolk was just over 15,000.

One of the most constructive activities of this dismal era, and one that provided food, fuel and shelter for the destitute was the Citizens' Service Exchange, established in 1933 by the Richmond Council of Social Agencies. It gave the unemployed an opportunity to meet necessities by working. The report of the Service Exchange for 1937 describes the system as follows:

"Scrip has been used as the medium of exchange since the organization started. One scrip is equivalent to one hour's work. The scrip is redeemed only in the store operated by the Exchange. Nothing produced by the workers is sold for cash; we work on the barter system. For instance, the shoemaker may exchange his labor for wood, and the wood-cutter may exhange his labor for a repair job on his shoes or for any other commodities or services produced."

In the five years since the Exchange was organized, work had been provided for 11,912 persons. These were men and women who couldn't get work elsewhere, many of whom had never been on relief. Often they were trained by the Exchange for useful jobs, and as a result, in numerous instances they managed to maintain their morale.

The Citizens' Service Exchange remained in operation until 1945, years after the Depression ended, when it was transformed into a Richmond branch of the Goodwill Industries, a national organization which concentrates on aiding and rehabilitating the handicapped. A. H. ("Dutch") Herrmann, first president of the Citizens' Service Exchange in 1933, remained as head of that organization and of the Goodwill Industries until his retirement in 1966, one third of a century. Herrmann was one of many Richmonders who rendered sacrificial service to the destitute during the Great Depression.

The alarming decline in business and tax revenues was a major factor in bringing about the repeal of prohibition on state and national levels. Legalized sale, it was argued, would provide employment in various directions and help fill the shrinking coffers of the commonwealth and the country. As it was, bootleggers were riding around in Cadillacs while the public treasury suffered. This was wholly aside from prohibition's fostering of lawlessness, hypocrisy and corruption on a gigantic scale.

Two years before the Eighteenth Amendment was repealed, Chief Justice Charles Evans Hughes came to Richmond for an address, and expressed a desire to place a wreath on the grave of John Marshall in Shockoe Cemetery. The ceremony was duly arranged, but it was thrown into disarray when containers of bootleg whiskey were found reposing in the sarcophagus on Marshall's grave.

The episode sheds light on the technique of the bootleg trade, which used every conceivable place of concealment for its wares. There were several prominent bootleggers in Richmond whose telephone numbers were well-known, and who delivered by the case or the keg at practically all hours of the day or night. The merchandise might be raw "white lightning" in Mason jars, fresh from the mountain still, or less scarifying whiskey in a charred keg. The raw "corn" could be aged by placing it in a keg or by putting charcoal sticks into the jars, and leaving them for several months. The raw stuff was loaded with fusel oil, and potent enough to knock the drinker's head off. An astonishing amount of this "white mule" was consumed, nevertheless. Frequent arrests were made of small-fry bootleggers, but the big boys seldom were touched, leading to the conclusion that somebody was being bought off.

The Richmond newspapers, which were violently opposed to statewide prohibition when it was adopted in 1914, became temporary converts to it, in its modified form, after the quart-a-month law was enacted by the General Assembly in 1916. When it had been in effect for a year, they pronounced the system an unqualified success. But with the advent of nationwide prohibition, all spirits, wine and beer were outlawed, and the Richmond press became highly critical. Liquor-running gangsters in the big cities, such as Al Capone; prohibition agents who shot down innocent persons on the merest suspicion; and widespread lawlessness and corruption caused the newspapers to reverse their position.

A particular gadfly of the "drys" was Thomas Lomax Hunter, a *Times-Dispatch* columnist who wrote under the heading, "As It Appears to the Cavalier." His scathing references to prohibitionists as "moral mercenaries" and "Hessian soldiers of the cross" quite naturally infuriated them. Hunter also declared that the prohibition laws "succeeded in making the largest army of law violators ever mobilized on this footstool of God." "Prohibition never stopped me from taking a drink," quoth the Cavalier, "and I never encountered a man whom it had stopped from taking a drink." Furthermore, Hunter proclaimed, "I am for the open saloon, openly arrived at." Such pronunciamentos brought cries of outrage from Bishop James Cannon, Jr., and his allies.

Although there were tens of thousands of speak-easies in New York City where illegal usquebaugh could be purchased, there were none in Richmond, unless a few were operating in Jackson Ward. Drinking Richmonders had whiskey delivered to their homes or offices. A smaller num-

60. U. S. Supreme Court Justice Lewis F. Powell, Jr., the first Virginian to serve on the nation's highest tribunal in more than a century. Drafted for the post, he has made an exceptional record in his few years on the bench.

61. Prominent Richmonders are smiling because two of them have jus
made a $2,000,000 gift to Virginia Union University in its drive for fund:
Left to right, seated, James C. Wheat, nationally known investmen
banker, and Dr. Frank S. Royal, physician, co-chairmen of the drive. Stanc
ing, at left, Dr. Allix B. James, president of the university, Sydney Lewi:
leading Richmond businessman, and Mrs. Lewis, who made the gift.

62. Four Richmond authors attend the St. Christopher's School Boo
Fair. Tom Wolfe is seated, and standing behind him, left to right, are Tor
Hale, the Reverend John S. Spong and J. Harvie Wilkinson III.

63. State Senator L. Douglas Wilder, at left, the first black elected to the Virginia Senate in this century, smiles as he is "roasted" at a dinner in his honor. At right is Vice-Mayor Henry L. Marsh III, and in the center, Mrs. Rosalie Clark, who presided.

64. Shirley MacLaine and Warren Beatty, sister and brother, shown as the future movie stars were growing up in their native Richmond.

65. Self-caricature by the late Fred O. Seibel, widely reprinted cartoonist for the Richmond *Times-Dispatch*.

67. Self-caricature by Jeff Mac-Nelly, Pulitzer-prize-winning cartoonist for the Richmond *News Leader*.

66. Caricature by Fred O. Seibel of Charles MacDowell, columnist and Washington correspondent of the Richmond *Times-Dispatch*.

68. Caricature by Jeff MacNelly of the late Charles (Mike) Houston, Richmond *News Leader* columnist.

69. In this view of Richmond's skyline, with the James River in the foreground, the extent of the city's recovery from the burning of its business district in 1865 can be grasped. Note also that whereas the Capitol dominated the scene a century ago and for many years thereafter, it is now completely obscured by high buildings. Tobacco Row, which rose along the river for decades, has disappeared. The tallest structure on the far right is the new home of the First & Merchants National Bank, and on the far left is the Central National Bank. A view of the new city hall, slightly to the right of the picture's center, is cut off by a building in front of it, and hardly more than the mast on top of the white stone structure is visible.

70. The beginnings of A. H. Robins Company, one of the nation's leading pharmaceutical firms, are shown here. A. H. Robins is standing with his small grandson, E. Claiborne Robins, in front of his modest pharmacy. Claiborne Robins later developed the company to its present preeminence.

71. The huge new Richmond home of Philip Morris, biggest cigarette factory in the world, and costing over $200,000,000, much admired for its architectural excellence and its many innovations. The designer is internationally famous Gordon Bunshaft of Skidmore, Owings & Merrill, the firm which also designed the striking Reynolds Metals Executive Office and General Office buildings in Richmond.

ber made wine or beer in their basements, as yeasty odors or vinous exhalations permeated the premises.

Winston Churchill came to visit the Civil War battlefields during the era, and was the guest of Governor Harry F. Byrd at the mansion. Admiral Cary T. Grayson warned the governor that Churchill would not be comfortable without a quart of brandy a day. Byrd was a "dry" and kept no such drinkables in the mansion, but Virginia hospitality required that he gratify his guest. Suspecting that John Stewart Bryan, publisher of the *News Leader*, had a well-stocked cellar, acquired before the drought descended, Byrd made an urgent call to his friend, explaining the problem. Bryan promptly supplied the brandy. There were other bizarre aspects of Churchill's visit. He walked around the mansion in his shorts, and he mistook one of the other guests, R. Gray Williams, a leading Virginia lawyer, for the butler, and gave him a quarter to go out and get him a newspaper. Williams got the paper and pocketed the quarter as a souvenir.

After repeal of prohibition was voted in 1933, it was decided unofficially in Richmond that beer of 3.2 per cent alcoholic content could be sold, pending the meeting of the General Assembly which would levy a tax on it and otherwise prepare for the demise of the "noble experiment." Hurried orders for lager were dispatched to Milwaukee and St. Louis.

When the Alcoholic Beverage Control Board was established in Virginia, Richmond's principal bootlegger, who catered to the "silk stocking" trade, got a job as inspector for the board. It was a post for which he was undoubtedly qualified, and in which he apparently rendered good service. Another well-known merchant of illegal spirits was soliciting funds some years later for the Y.M.C.A.

In 1932, on the eve of prohibition's repeal, the thin gray line of Confederate veterans from throughout the South held their last reunion in Richmond. They were lavishly entertained, and presumably a certain amount of ardent spirits was covertly provided. But only some two thousand of the feeble old men were able to attend.

The last of the Confederates in the Soldiers' Home on the Boulevard died in 1941. For more than half a century, the veterans in their faded gray uniforms could be seen smoking their pipes and swapping yarns or strolling about under the trees. There had been approximately 150 pensioners when the home opened in 1885, and twice that number when the institution was in its heyday. But as time went on, death made heavy inroads.

The little frame chapel, which still stands, was built with funds contributed by the veterans. About 1,700 were buried from it. Demolition of the other buildings began in 1941, following the death of the last inmate. The Virginia Museum of Fine Arts and its grounds occupy the site today.

The Valentine Museum came into its own at this time. Granville G. Valentine, son of Mann Valentine, the founder, took the lead in arrange-

ing the purchase of the three adjacent buildings, so that the collections
could be transferred there and the mansion restored to its pristine condition and furnished as a dwelling to illustrate Richmond architecture and
social life in the late eighteenth and nineteenth centuries. Miss Helen
McCormack became director of the reorganized institution in 1930, and it
was under her dynamic and imaginative leadership that the museum entered a brand-new and more useful phase. Later, the antebellum Brans-
ford-Cecil house was moved from Fifth Street to become part of the ensemble.

The Valentine is recognized today as the principal repository for materials relating to the city of Richmond. Its library contains a huge collection of manuscripts, documents, books and photographs. The Textile Resource and Research Center includes costumes from every period of the
city's history. Paintings, drawings and photographs are on view or in the
files. A comprehensive expansion program was carried forward under
Robert B. Mayo, who became director in 1966 and resigned in 1975. The
Junior Center was organized, with the assistance of the Junior League, and
this extends the work of the museum into the schools and provides cultural events for both black and white.

A group of intrepid Richmonders decided in 1932, in the depth of the
Depression, to launch a symphony orchestra. There had been a series of
discouragements in the 1920s, when public interest in concerts waned.
The attempt to establish an orchestra at the worst possible time was evidence of supreme confidence, if not audacity. Wheeler Beckett, a young
American conductor, was retained as its leader, and the organization struggled along for four years. It succumbed to the financial stringencies that
wrecked virtually all such enterprises.

Almost simultaneously with the founding of the symphony Virginia
dedicated its memorial to the dead of World War I. A memorial library
had first been decided upon, but that plan was discarded in favor of a
carillon at Richmond, suggested by Granville G. Valentine. With Valentine as chairman of a Virginia Citizens' Carillon Committee, $75,000
was raised by public subscription. The General Assembly appropriated
$250,000 for the building and the city donated a site in Byrd Park. Thou-
sands of visitors, including representatives of fourteen Allied nations, came
to Richmond for the dedication, October 15, 1932. After an impressive parade, Anton Brees, internationally famous carillonneur, gave a concert.

The Westmoreland Club was staggering along during these years. The
Depression made it difficult for the members to pay dues, and prohibition
hampered conviviality. The property at Sixth and Franklin was extremely
valuable for commercial purposes, and as early as 1920 the Westmoreland
sought to merge with the Commonwealth Club. The Virginia Supreme
Court of Appeals ruled the following year that the merger could not be
consummated because thirty-three Westmoreland members voted against

it. But by the 1930s the handwriting was on the wall for the West-moreland, founded in 1877. The Commonwealth had been launched in 1890 at Franklin and Monroe streets, and was in a more prosperous condition. It had brought in the members of the Richmond Club, oldest of such organizations in the city, and that club went out of existence. When the Depression struck, the Westmoreland members found it impossible to continue operations, and they merged with the Commonwealth in 1937. These two clubs had been the scene of many a festive dinner and wassail, and their walls had echoed to the repartee of such wits as J. St. George Bryan, Charles Cotesworth Pinckney, Egbert G. Leigh, Jr., Dr. W. T. Oppenhimer and John T. ("Jake") Anderson.

The older organization's fine collection of portraits of Civil War heroes was turned over to the Commonwealth, where they now hang. The handsome and historic Westmoreland clubhouse was torn down to make way for a commercial establishment.

The Commonwealth Club has had two famous Negro major-domos, Henry Yancey in earlier days, and William Rush, who retired in 1945. The courtly Henry knew everybody who was anybody during his lengthy regime, and then Rush, a celebrity in his own right, took his place. Rush was particularly famous for his delectable dish, corn meal cakes with oysters and Smithfield ham, under glass, and for his impeccable rendition of Lee's farewell to the Army of Northern Virginia. He said he memorized the latter late one night in the early 1900s, following the dinner given by University of Virginia alumni to Dr. Edwin A. Alderman, the institution's newly elected president. Rush said he consumed various "heel taps" after the party had broken up, and feeling at peace with the world, sat down in the library. Taking a book from the shelf, he thumbed through it and his eye fell upon Lee's farewell. He thereupon committed it to memory. His recital of Lee's words was a frequent feature of Commonwealth Club entertainments thereafter.

The Depression caused many financial problems for the City of Richmond. The Richmond-First Club, founded in 1919 for the purpose of studying and improving the municipal government, decided to launch an intensive analysis. It was begun in 1933 under the presidency of Lloyd C. Bird, and lasted for two years. Upon its completion, the large stack of detailed reports was condensed and coordinated by Dr. Raymond B. Pinchbeck of the University of Richmond. The material then was published serially in the *News Leader* and also in pamphlet form. It demonstrated the impossibility of having modern, efficient government with a two-chamber council consisting of twenty councilmen and twelve aldermen elected by wards, and showed that an average of fifty days was required to get anything through the two chambers. The report also urged numerous other reforms, practically all of which were opposed by both the mayor and the Council.

T. Coleman Andrews, a prominent young certified public accountant, was retained in 1936 to make a survey of the city's accounting procedures. He reported that Richmond could save at least $200,000 a year by retaining a purchasing agent, and made numerous other recommendations. Mayor Bright, who declared repeatedly that Richmond had "a splendid government," although it had not changed appreciably since the eighteenth century, opposed centralized purchasing and just about any other reform. He said that if Richmond was the last city in the United States to retain the two-chamber "strong mayor" form, he would favor its retention.

Andrews was elected city comptroller and soon got into a row with the mayor. He discharged various employees in the finance and gas and water offices, and urged adoption of the city manager form with a one-chamber council. Wholesale waste and inefficiency were disclosed by him during his two-year term. All this provided significant impetus for the adoption of the new city charter approved a decade later.

Mayor Bright's ideas concerning the proprieties were as ultra-conservative as his attitudes on municipal government. Like Mayor Carlton McCarthy in the early years of the century, he felt that certain public displays were indecent. One of these was a Bull Durham tobacco billboard entitled "Her Hero," showing a cow gazing lovingly at a bull. The mayor sent painters around the city with orders to paint out the bull's masculine attributes.

Bright's outmoded views, especially his refusal to make any concessions whatever to modern trends in municipal government, finally caught up with him. He was defeated for reelection in 1940, but only after he had served sixteen years, longer than any other mayor in Richmond's history. He was uncompromising to the end. When, in the early 1950s, the worldwide Communist propaganda network stirred up a global uproar over the execution of the so-called "Martinsville Seven"—blacks convicted of the mass rape of a white woman—Bright, a retired brigadier general in the Virginia National Guard, offered his services. He appeared in the office of Governor John S. Battle wearing his National Guard overcoat and armed to the teeth.

When Dr. Bright died a few years later, he was extraordinarily generous in his bequests to charitable and religious organizations of all races and creeds, and he provided for the establishment of a public park in "my beloved city." He was a man of fine impulses, which were often misdirected.

Gordon B. Ambler, a Richmond lawyer, was the candidate who defeated Bright for reelection in 1940. Ambler helped markedly to bring modern government to Richmond by running on a platform which included a plank urging that the people of the city be given "an opportunity to have an outright showdown between a modern, up-to-date, progressive type of government and an obsolete reactionary type." He was elected overwhelmingly, and even Bright considered this a mandate for sweeping change. But while the new mayor was able to institute centralized purchasing and other reforms, the two-chamber council succeeded in thwarting all his attempts to have a popular referendum. A major annexation in 1942, bringing in new territory on all sides of the city, raised the area to just under 40 square miles and the population to 208,039. Ambler did not offer for reelection. The long-sought referendum would come two years after he went out of office.

A breakthrough in the interracial sphere came in 1936 when a Richmond black, A. S. Richardson, became the first Negro in the history of Virginia to be named to the staff of the State Department of Education. His title was Assistant Supervisor of Negro Education. For fifteen years his office was in a building separated by a considerable distance from the white staff members. Despite this separation, Richardson saw his appointment as one of several developments heralding the upgrading of education for blacks in Richmond and throughout the Commonwealth. Equalization of teachers' pay for blacks and whites was accomplished in 1945, pursuant to a permanent injunction against discrimination issued by U. S. District Judge Robert N. Pollard of Richmond. Later, the average pay of blacks was slightly higher than that of whites, the black teachers tended to have longer tenure and more degrees.

Installation of a Negro, Mrs. Ethel T. Overby, in 1933 as principal of Elba School, the first black woman to be put in charge of a public school in Richmond, was another milestone. When Maggie Walker High School opened in 1938, James E. Segear became the city's first back high school principal. Within a fairly short time all Negro schools in the city would have such principals, despite the opposition of some blacks.

Negro participation in Democratic primaries was assured by 1936, as a result of court orders. However, indifference on the part of black voters, including many clergymen and business and professional men, resulted for years in a low vote. Then, too, blacks had tended over a long period to vote Republican. Negroes did become aroused in 1940 on behalf of Gordon B. Ambler when Ambler ran for mayor against J. Fulmer Bright. Under Bright's leadership there were only 281 Negroes on the municipal payroll in 1937 out of a total of 3,304, and 273 of these were schoolteachers. Conditions were largely the same three years later. Mayor Bright had been antagonistic to the race in other respects. A concerted voter registration drive was conducted in the 1940 contest, and about 2,400 Negroes were qualified. They went almost solidly for Ambler and helped to swell his margin of victory.

Social status among blacks was determined by occupation, with a line separating "white collar" from "blue collar" workers, according to *The Negro in Virginia*, published in 1940 under the sponsorship of Hampton Institute. This study goes on to say:

"The tradition of the gay 'nineties, when the term F.F.N.V's (First

Families of Negro Virginia) was used, is still strong in Negro Virginia 'high society.' A constant round of teas, bridge parties and 'dawn dances' provides diversion for the 'elite,' which is made up largely of the professional classes. Such groups in every city sponsor 'closed balls,' strictly formal, whose guest lists are limited to the Negro '400.'"

In Richmond and other Virginia cities the blacks also found pleasure in belonging to such social clubs as the Congenial Matrons, the Saps Social Club, the Dukes and Duchesses, the Big Fifty, the Duckie-Wuckies, the We Moderns, the Violet Art Circle and the So Whats, as well as various Fleur de Lis societies.

An influential black leader in Richmond's intellectual circles was the Reverend Gordon B. Hancock, holder of advanced degrees from Colgate and Harvard, student at Oxford and Cambridge, member of the Virginia Union faculty, columnist in the Negro press and pastor of Moore Street Baptist Church. He was one of the two principal instigators of a conference of leading Southern blacks at Durham, North Carolina, in 1942, designed to formulate a program for better race relations and improved Negro opportunities. It was followed by a biracial conference in Atlanta, and then by another such gathering in Richmond. Out of all this grew the Southern Regional Council, with headquarters in Atlanta, which replaced the Commission on Interracial Cooperation.

Dr. Hancock strove to obtain from Southern whites sufficient concessions to keep overall direction of interracial trends in the hands of Southern blacks. "It makes a world of difference to the cause of race relations," he said, "whether the capital of the Negro race is in New York City or Atlanta."

The *Times-Dispatch* sought to aid in keeping the Negro "capital" in Atlanta, by advocating abolition of segregation on streetcars and buses. The proposal, made November 13, 1943, received acclaim in the Northern press and none at all in the Southern, except for a favorable response in a small Kinston, North Carolina, paper. Letters to the *Times-Dispatch* poured in from white readers, and were three to one in favor of the proposal. But the General Assembly did nothing, and interracial tension mounted.

A further cause of tension was the introduction at successive legislative sessions of "barber bills," the object of which was to eliminate Negro barbers and give white barbers control of the trade. Blacks enjoyed a virtual monopoly in earlier days, but white barbers infiltrated gradually. As early as 1900, the "Idle Reporter" wrote in the *Dispatch* that a "barber bill" had been introduced in the legislature, providing examinations for those desiring to wield the shears and razors. By the 1930s it was evident that the purpose was to force blacks out by setting up a licensing board and asking trick questions, such as "Where is the arrector pili muscle located and what is its function?" and "How many hairs are there to the square inch on the average scalp?" Once the Negroes were driven out, prices could be doubled. The scheme was thwarted by repeated ventilations in the white press. Years later a bill was got through, but it was a genuine health measure and apparently fair to all.

In another, and quite different, sphere of race relations the radio program "Amos 'n' Andy," presenting episodes involving supposed Negro characters, was a sensation. With 40,000,000 listeners at the height of its fame, the program attracted what was said to be the most colossal fan mail ever recorded. Freeman F. Gosden, who took the part of Amos, was a native Richmonder.

A governor of Virginia more friendly to Negro progress than his predecessors was James H. Price, the only citizen of Richmond ever elected to the governorship. Handsome, gregarious Lieutenant Governor Price, who had served seven terms in the House of Delegates, was not a Byrd "organization" man, and he looked with favor on the Roosevelt "New Deal." But he was so popular throughout the Commonwealth that the "organization" despaired of defeating him for the state's highest office, and accepted his candidacy grudgingly. When Price took office as governor in 1938, the hostile, Byrd-dominated General Assembly proceeded to slaughter his program. "Jim" Price died suddenly of a stroke at age sixty-one the year following the expiration of his gubernatorial term.

One of the most celebrated Richmond citizens of any era was Dr. Douglas S. Freeman, a native of Lynchburg, editor of the *News Leader* from 1915 until his retirement in 1949, and author of Pulitzer Prize-winning biographies of Robert E. Lee and George Washington.

Freeman was brilliantly able, versatile and indefatigable. For decades he rose at 2:30 A.M., saluted the statue of Robert E. Lee on Monument Avenue en route to his office, and worked steadily there and at his home until bedtime at 7:30 P.M. A vast number of newspaper editorials and numerous books poured from his pen. Two daily radio programs on current events and a Sunday radio sermon, together with countless public addresses, were delivered over a long period. Freeman conducted a weekly current events class for more than a third of a century and a class in journalism at Columbia University for seven years.

He almost never attended purely social functions. To him, work was recreation. Practically nobody called him "Douglas" or "Doug"; it was always "Dr. Freeman." He was not only a Johns Hopkins University Ph.D.; he had honorary doctorates from many of the principal centers of higher learning in this country. He budgeted his time in the most incredible way. Beginning in 1926, every hour that he spent researching and writing his books was meticulously set down. He recorded 6,100 hours on *R. E. Lee*, after he began keeping track, 7,121 on *Lee's Lieutenants* and 15,693 on *George Washington*.

Freeman was a director of several large corporations whose board meet-

ings took him to New York about twice a month. He lectured regularly to
the armed services on leadership and strategy. Each year he traveled about
20,000 miles.

J. Ambler Johnston, another remarkable and versatile Richmonder, who
knew Freeman almost throughout his adult life, commented on how old
he always looked. "At twenty-five he appeared fifty-five," said Johnston.
The two men roamed the Civil War battlefields together and Johnston
succeeded Freeman as the authority on those in Virginia. They were
jointly responsible for the initial marking of the battlefields around Richmond, and thus created the nucleus for the National Battlefield Park System.

Freeman was writing his masterful books on the Civil War during the
years when Ellen Glasgow and James Branch Cabell were producing their
superlative fiction. It would be difficult to name an American city which,
at any time in this century, had three such significant literary figures living
and working simultaneously within its borders.

And there were other writers of distinction in Richmond. Clifford Dowdey had published his much-admired novel *Bugles Blow No More*, as well
as other works of fiction. He then made an auspicious entry into the field
of historical writing with *Experiment in Rebellion* and *The Land They
Fought For*. After Freeman's death in 1953 at age sixty-seven, Dowdey became the recognized authority on the Army of Northern Virginia,
publishing a series of highly regarded works on the Seven Days, Gettysburg, a one-volume life of Lee and related subjects. He also produced historical studies of the colonial era.

Mary Wingfield Scott's two scholarly works, *Houses of Old Richmond*
and *Old Richmond Neighborhoods*, are classics of their kind. Published in
1941 and 1950, respectively, they are indispensable to all students of the
city's past.

Mrs. Ralph T. (Louise F.) Catterall, whose unequaled knowledge of
Richmond's history has been of enormous help to all those interested in
the subject, was the author of the unsigned and immensely useful volume
*Richmond Portraits, in an Exhibition of Makers of Richmond, 1737–1860*,
published by the Valentine Museum in 1949.

Dr. Hamilton J. Eckenrode, a native Fredericksburger, wrote significant
books on Virginia's role in the American Revolution and Reconstruction,
and later produced other historical and biographical works. He was state
historian for twenty-two years and supervised the creation of Virginia's excellent system of historical highway markers.

Rebecca Yancey Williams' *The Vanishing Virginian* appeared on the
eve of our entry into World War II. This light hearted account of her
early life in Lynchburg went into many editions and was a welcome interlude for the grim news from the European battle fronts.

A tragic loss was the death of Dr. Maude H. Woodfin, acting dean and professor of history at Westhampton College. She edited one of the diaries of William Byrd II and planned a major work on the three William Byrds.

Four Richmond blacks achieved wide reputations. They were Bill ("Bojangles") Robinson, Leslie G. Bolling, George H. Ben Johnson and Charles S. Gilpin.

Robinson, the most famous tap dancer of his time, was befriended as a young boy by Justice John Crutchfield. At the age of seven, Bill was orphaned and placed in charge of his ailing grandmother. Crutchfield learned that the grandmother was in straits herself, and unable to care properly for the child. He visited the home and took Bill to live in his house until a satisfactory guardian could be found. This was about the year 1885. When Robinson grew up, he became a star on Broadway and in motion pictures. His "dance on the stairs" was unique. In 1937 he was chosen "the outstanding stage and screen star of the year." Robinson made millions but he spent or gave away all that he made. He combined generous impulses with a hot temper; knife and razor scars on his body bore testimony to the latter trait. He raised enormous sums for charitable causes by his dancing. When he died, his liabilities exceeded his assets.

Always loyal to his home town of Richmond, Bojangles paid for a traffic light at the corner of Adams and Leigh streets where a number of accidents had occurred. It was draped in black during his New York funeral in 1949. An aluminum statue of him by John Temple Witt of Richmond was erected in 1973 on a plot at the same intersection. The area was named "Bill 'Bojangles' Robinson Square" in honor of the first black man to be memorialized by a statue in Richmond.

In the sphere of painting, a Richmond black who won acclaim was George H. Ben Johnson. One of his portraits was exhibited at the Barrington Galleries in London, and his works are in the permanent collections of the Virginia Museum of Fine Arts, the Valentine Museum, Virginia Union University and Virginia State College. He was for twenty-seven years a mail carrier.

Leslie G. Bolling, a porter in Richmond, was another black artist. He achieved his reputation as a sculptor in wood, and annually for years the Harmon Foundation sponsored a touring exhibit of his works to American art centers. He had exhibits at the Smithsonian Institution, the William B. Cox Galleries in New York and the Texas Centennial. Bolling's carvings were done with a sharp penknife, and the results were so extraordinary that their "robustness of style" was compared to that of Diego Rivera's murals.

Charles Gilpin was a famous Richmond black from a slightly earlier era. When penniless and jobless he was chosen by Eugene O'Neill for the title role in his play *Emperor Jones*. Gilpin played the role superbly for two years, and was awarded the Spingarn Medal. Shortly thereafter he was voted one of the ten best actors of the year by the New York Drama League, the first time this honor had been accorded a Negro.

A Richmond black who has made a conspicuous contribution to civic advancement and better interracial relations is Booker T. Bradshaw. His business career began when he and Clarence L. Townes decided to salvage something from the wreckage of the National Benefit Life Insurance Company, which collapsed in the Depression. After raising $10,000 collateral and $2,500 working capital they were in a position to begin reinsuring the Virginia business of the defunct company. The Virginia Mutual Benefit Life Insurance Company was accordingly organized, with Bradshaw as president and treasurer. It grew steadily and has been highly successful.

Booker Bradshaw is one of Richmond's leading citizens. Vice-chairman of the City School Board in the difficult years when the school system was being integrated, pursuant to the U. S. Supreme Court's order of 1954, he also served on the board of the Virginia State Library, and on those of Virginia Union University and Virginia State College, being rector of the latter institution. During World War II and for a total of twenty-five years he served as chairman of Draft Board No. 55, and in 1966 was given the Richmond-First Club's Good Government award.

His son Booker T. Bradshaw, Jr., a *cum laude* graduate of Harvard and graduate of Britain's Academy of Dramatic Art, speaks three foreign languages and sings in nine. He appeared on his own show over the British Broadcasting Corporation, giving seven of his own songs. He is a successful Hollywood screen writer and actor.

Business growth was almost nonexistent in Richmond during the worst years of the Depression, but conditions soon began to improve. While the nation's industrial volume was dropping 16.7 per cent between 1929 and 1939, Richmond's was rising an extraordinary 59 per cent, much the best record of any city in the United States.[1]

An important element in Richmond's forward surge was the decision of Reynolds Metals Company in 1938 to move its executive offices to Richmond from New York. Two decades later Reynolds would open its strikingly handsome headquarters office building on West Broad Street, and would move its general sales office from Louisville to Richmond.

Another significant development was the completion in 1940 of the Deepwater Terminal, on a 333-acre tract south of the James a few miles below the city. Cost of the entire installation was $1,750,000, a mere fraction of what it would have been a few years later. Channel depth at the terminal was 25 feet. The city has been trying ever since to obtain Federal financing in deepening the channel to 35 feet all the way to Chesapeake Bay. The lack of such depth has been a major handicap in developing additional ocean-going commerce.

In the cultural and business field an important event of 1940 was the merger of the *Times-Dispatch* and *News Leader*. Rival Richmond papers —the *Virginian, Evening Dispatch* and *Journal*—had fallen by the wayside. The economics of the situation dictated the merger of the two remaining papers in a city the size of Richmond, although both managements regretted the necessity. Skyrocketing costs of labor and materials made it essential to have a combined operation, in accordance with the steady trend throughout the United States. John Stewart Bryan, publisher of the *News Leader*, one of the foremost Virginians of his time and later president of the College of William and Mary, became publisher of the two papers. Douglas S. Freeman remained as editor of the *News Leader*, and Virginius Dabney of the *Times-Dispatch*. Both would serve in their respective posts for about a third of a century.

Richmond was paralyzed in January 1940 by the worst blizzard since 1908. Sixteen inches of snow fell in the city, amid howling winds, and 21.6 inches at Byrd Airport. Streetcars and buses came to a standstill, most stores failed to open, schools were closed, mail deliveries halted, and persons who got to work at all had to stumble through snowdrifts, use skis or travel in wagons or on horseback. The mercury went to eleven below zero at Byrd Airport and to eight below twenty-four hours later. Richmond dug itself gradually out of the drifts as temperatures moderated.

Almost exactly three years later, in January 1943, the worst sleet storm in half a century struck. Breaking under the weight of the ice, hundreds of tree limbs cracked in the night like pistol shots. Even large trees were uprooted, 32,000 were damaged, and streetcar and bus traffic was blocked. Electric and telephone lines were down, and dangerous wires lay exposed in the streets. Thousands were without light or heat. It took days to remove fallen trees and limbs and get things moving again.

Another calamity hit Richmond the following year. The Jefferson Hotel had its second serious fire since 1900. Seven lives were lost and the flames were barely checked before getting completely out of control. Mrs. James H. Price, widow of Governor Price, and State Senator Aubrey Weaver of Front Royal were among those who died. Several other prominent members of the General Assembly barely escaped. This was the worst fire in the city since the destruction of the Lexington Hotel at the southwest corner of Twelfth and Main in 1922. Twelve persons died in that blaze.

Richmond said goodbye during that same year to one of its famous secondary schools, McGuire's. Its founder, John Peyton McGuire, had been succeeded upon his death in 1906 by his son, John Peyton McGuire, the third of that name. The first of the line, as previously noted, was headmaster of the Episcopal High School at the outbreak of the Civil War. The third of these McGuires was also a great teacher and inspiring leader.

He moved the school in 1914 from its quarters over a bar, market and plumber's shop at Belvidere and Main to a frame building on Idlewood Avenue overlooking Byrd Park. His unwillingness to press parents for tuition and other bills, on the theory that a gentleman would certainly pay if he could, caused untold financial losses to the school, especially during the Depression. McGuire's finally closed in 1942, when the headmaster's age, ill-health and fiscal worries made it impossible for him to carry on.

Alumni of the school soon discovered that Mr. McGuire was badly strapped financially, largely because of his goodness of heart in not pressing for payment of outstanding obligations. They made up a substantial purse which relieved him of monetary anxieties in his last years. McGuire's University School had enrolled more than ten thousand students since its founding seventy-seven years before, and had trained many of Richmond's leaders.

Large numbers of these young men would serve in World War II, a conflict that was rapidly approaching in the late 1930s. The powder keg exploded when Adolf Hitler sent his screaming Stukas and roaring Panzers into Poland on September 1, 1939.

The people of Richmond and the rest of the United States were deeply divided as to the proper course for America, and large numbers were determined to stay out of the conflict, if that could be done with honor. The war was banned as a topic of discussion in the Richmond public schools, and Superintendent Jesse H. Binford ordered teachers to maintain a strictly nonpartisan attitude.

Yet the valor of the British in standing up to the Nazi air attack aroused the unrestrained admiration of Richmonders, whose forebears came largely from the British Isles. Soon the people of the city, along with most other Americans, were strongly favoring President Roosevelt's shipment of surplus arms and fifty overage destroyers to the hard-pressed people of the beleaguered island.

With France collapsing in the face of the Nazi blitzkrieg, a hundred citizens met at the Commonwealth Club and formed the Richmond branch of the Committee to Defend America by Aiding the Allies. Oliver J. Sands was chairman. A large majority of the city's inhabitants apparently were unreservedly in favor of all-out material aid to Britain and France, but opposed to sending troops. Arrangements for finding homes in Richmond for refugee English and Scottish children went foward under the direction of the Reverend Vincent C. Franks, rector of St. Paul's Episcopal Church. Peacetime conscription was enacted by Congress in September 1940, as the Battle of Britain moved toward its crescendo. Colonel Mills F. Neal of Richmond was put in charge of Virginia's Selective Service, a post he would hold until early in 1945. Eight local boards were formed.

Three armories were fitted up to furnish sleeping facilities for servicemen on leave, the Blues' and Grays' for whites and the Howitzers' for blacks. Soldiers of the 29th Division presented the show *Snap It Up Again* at the Mosque before a packed house. A feature was the singing of "Ballad for Americans" by a chorus of two hundred voices.

This number, which became famous, was the work of John LaTouche, a talented young Richmond-born composer of songs and ballads that were spectacularly successful on Broadway. He had graduated from Richmond's John Marshall High School at age fifteen and composed "Ballad for Americans" seven years later. Heedless of his health, LaTouche worked at all hours, with no regard for the clock. A massive heart attack carried him off at age thirty-nine.

The United States appeared to be headed for involvement in the European conflict, but strong disagreements continued as to the proper course for the nation. Then, without warning, Japan attacked Pearl Harbor and, in the words of the *Times-Dispatch*, America was "shocked into unity on a single Sunday afternoon."

The news came suddenly over the radio at 2:26 P.M., December 7, 1941, as Richmonders were relaxing after their Sunday dinners. Newspaper extras with black headlines soon were being cried by the newsboys. Almost at once, men began lining up at the Navy recruiting office.

Next day, the 29th Division, which included the Richmond Blues, Grays and Howitzers, was leaving North Carolina, where it had been on maneuvers. The long line took four hours to pass through Richmond, en route to Fort George G. Meade, Maryland. The men were loudly cheered by tens of thousands, who showered them with candy, cigarettes and sandwiches. Regimental bands played in Capitol Square and Monroe Park, as Governor Price reviewed the division. Strangely enough, this was the only occasion during the entire war when the people of Virginia's capital had an opportunity to salute a large body of troops. Units of the 29th would cover themselves with glory on the beaches of Normandy, spearheading the invasion of Hitler's "Fortress Europe."

Richmonders were ready to follow the lead of the President in girding at once for war. The city had the largest total industrial production in the South.[2] Iron and steel manufacture was not the principal industry, but it was important, with the Tredegar Company still an outstanding producer of war matériel. The Tredegar would receive a number of Army and Navy citations during the conflict. Richmond manufactured one third of the nation's cigarettes, and this output would be greatly increased to satisfy the cravings of the fighting men. In fact, Richmond civilians would have difficulty at times buying cigarettes for themselves.

No great new wartime industries were established in the city, but many plants already there were expanded and converted to wartime purposes. For example, the Crawford Manufacturing Company turned to making 12-pound suits of armor for the protection of infantrymen's heart, lungs, stomach and kidneys, and flak suits for flyers. Friedman-Marks Clothing Company made Army and Navy trousers and Navy pea jackets; B. T. Crump Company, jungle hammocks, woolen sleeping bags, barrack bags and pistol holders; Reynolds Metals, aluminum baffling devices to render enemy detection operations ineffective; while Richmond Chick Hatchery produced vast quantities of chicken parts, mostly for overseas comsumption. Kingan & Company built a large addition to meet the extraordinary service and Lend-Lease demands for its ham, bacon, beef, pork and lard.

The Tredegar was always effective in producing shells and other wartime necessities, but its *modus operandi* was sometimes quaint, to put it mildly. An article published in the *Saturday Evening Post* in 1943 declared that Paul E. Miller, who succeeded Archer Anderson, Jr., as president, had no telephone in his office.

"The only outside phone . . . is a booth fifty feet from the president's desk," wrote Pete Martin in the magazine. "When there is a call for him, he gets up and walks down the hall to take it."

"Another time-honored custom," the article went on, "is for the president to open all mail. 'That way you know what's going on around the place and you don't have to call a meeting to find out what the other men are doing,' he says."

All of which is not quite as astonishing as the practice described as having been followed until after 1900 by W. R. Trainham, vice-president and treasurer. "As the keeper of the books, he figured the payroll in shillings and pence, then translated it into dollars and cents when payments were made," Pete Martin declared.

As the United States moved into active belligerence, feeling was strong against Germans and Japs, but there were few absurdities involving Richmond's German-Americans comparable to those of 1917–18. The principal episode of this sort was the whispering campaign against Nolde Brothers Bakery. Nazis were poisoning the bread at Nolde's and other bakeries with German names, according to these nonsensical reports. Nolde's took full-page advertisements in Richmond and Norfolk papers to refute them.

The Byrd Airport and the Deepwater Terminal were taken over by the armed forces. The airport became the Richmond Army Air Base and the terminal the Richmond Reconsignment Depot, where carloads of war matériel were received and broken up into smaller units for shipment to the front. This depot coordinated its activities with the enormous distribution center constructed on the Bellwood and Parker tracts some eight miles below Richmond. An idea of the latter's magnitude may be partially grasped from the fact that in March 1945 more than 350,000,000 pounds of supplies for the armed services were shipped in and out of the depot, with more than 850 freight cars dispatched and received in a single day. Some 2,500 German and Italian war prisoners worked there.

Richmonders became acutely aware on June 15, 1942, that they were in a war when some of them vacationing at Virginia Beach witnessed the torpedoing of two U.S. merchant vessels by a German submarine a few miles offshore.

Rationing of essential foods and other things, such as automobiles, tires, gasoline and fuel oil began in that year. Most citizens obeyed the regulations, but there were the inevitable chiselers who patronized the black market. The stealing or counterfeiting of ration coupons caused occasional scandals. Prices were regulated by the Office of Price Administration (OPA), with former Mayor J. Fulmer Bright as state administrator. Dean Raymond B. Pinchbeck of the University of Richmond was State Food Czar.

Many citizens planted Victory gardens. Intensive drives to salvage scrap metal, rubber, tin, toothpaste tubes and other materials useful in the war effort were launched under the state chairmanship of Frederic W. Scott of Richmond. He was also in charge of gasoline coupon rationing.

Orders were issued that the speed limit for autos on the open road was thirty-five miles an hour and that the maximum temperature in houses must be sixty-five degrees. Reporters checked government buildings in the city and found thermostats registering seventy-seven degrees and up, with the highest temperature of all in the fuel-regulating agency. A fuel shortage in January 1945 caused renewed orders for conservation. A check disclosed that OPA headquarters was "the hottest place in town."

War bond drives were organized early in the war, and there were seven in all, with Morton G. Thalhimer, Richmond's outstanding realtor who would be chosen by John D. Rockefeller, Jr., to do much important work for Colonial Williamsburg, as city chairman. A grand total of $434,000,000 in bonds was purchased in the seven drives, greatly exceeding the city's quota of $294,000,000. Purchases by banks brought the over-all total of bond sales in Richmond to no less than $868,000,000.

The possibility that the city might be bombed from the air by the Germans caused the setting up of a system of air raid wardens, with practice blackouts, black cloth for window covers at night and sirens at strategic points. Air raid spotters were stationed throughout Richmond and nearby areas scanning the skies. It was forbidden to publish weather forecasts, lest this aid the enemy in planning bombing raids.

At the request of the War Department, the 45th General Hospital was organized for service overseas. Dr. Carrington Williams, one of the distinguished surgeons of his time and a veteran of Base Hospital 45 in World War I, was in charge. However, he was disqualified for overseas service by reason of physical disability, and Dr. John Powell Williams, a notable internist, succeeded him briefly until a doctor from the regular army took over. The unit, which included doctors and nurses from the Medical College of Virginia, served in North Africa and Italy, and was officially commended for "superior performance . . . and outstanding devotion to duty." Absence of so many prominent physicians and surgeons left a shortage of medical personnel in Richmond.

There was also a scarcity of males to fill many jobs, and women were pressed into service as factory workers, elevator operators, bank runners, grocery clerks and in other capacities.

The University of Richmond made an important contribution. Hundreds of pilots were trained there, and when this task was completed the Navy's V-12 program was instituted.

Ground was broken in 1943 for a $5,000,000 Army hospital at Broad Rock Road and Belt Boulevard, to accommodate 1,750 wounded. It subsequently became the McGuire General Hospital.

Rumors of impending race riots swept Virginia in July 1943, including reports that all the ice picks were being bought up by blacks with a view to attacking the whites under cover of darkness. Such canards were even more widespread in Norfolk, Newport News and Petersburg than in Richmond. Adjutant General E. E. Goodwyn readied troops for immediate service, but nothing happened.

Richmond had three Medal of Honor winners, two of whom survived. Sergeant Ernest H. Dervishian received the nation's highest military decoration for "prodigious courage and combat skill" in the Fifth Army's breakout from the Anzio beachhead in Italy. He captured forty Germans and three machine-gun nests. Lieutenant James W. Monteith, Jr., performed deeds of tremendous heroism in the D-day landing at Colleville-sur-Mer, Normandy. He was killed as he led in destroying several enemy gun positions with grenades under heavy fire. The Richmond alumni of his alma mater, Virginia Polytechnic Institute, give an annual leadership award in his honor to a VPI senior. Commander George L. Street III performed one of the great naval feats of the war when he took his submarine into a Korean harbor and torpedoed a Japanese ammunition ship and two enemy patrol freighters. Street had previously been awarded the Navy Cross, the Navy's highest decoration. He and Dervishian received heroes' welcomes on their return to Richmond.

On the civilian front, Walter S. Robertson, Richmond investment banker, rendered exceptional service overseas, first as head of the U. S. Lend-Lease mission to Australia, and then as counselor of economic affairs at Chungking, China, with the rank of minister. Robertson would later serve with ability and dedication as Assistant Secretary of State for Far Eastern Affairs and as a delegate to the United Nations General Assembly.

Richmond had been represented for twelve years in Congress by Andrew J. Montague, former governor of Virginia. Highly regarded in Washington and mentioned for a place on the U. S. Supreme Court, Montague was old and feeble when he ran for reelection in 1936. He barely defeated young Dave E. Satterfield, Jr., Richmond's Commonwealth's attorney for a dozen years. A few months later, Montague died, and Satterfield succeeded him.

Dave Satterfield gave the district able representation until 1944, when he resigned to become general counsel for the Life Insurance Association of America. Two years later, Richmond was shocked when he died suddenly at age fifty-two when visiting the city for the Christmas holidays. He had been succeeded in Congress by J. Vaughan Gary.

During most of the war, young Colonel Frank McCarthy of Richmond served as secretary of the general staff, and then briefly as Assistant Secretary of State. He would later become a leading motion picture producer in Hollywood. McCarthy was succeeded as secretary of the general staff by equally youthful H. Merrill Pasco, also of Richmond.

The desperate conflict with the Axis powers was drawing to a close in early 1945. American and British forces were smashing across Germany, and Americans were capturing one Pacific island after another, en route to Japan. The death of President Roosevelt on the eve of victory stunned the nation and the world, but the Allies drove relentlessly ahead.

Hitler's Nazis surrendered on May 7, and Richmond took the news with relative calm. It was realized that the war in the Pacific was still to be won. Largely attended religious services were held.

American airmen opened a new era by dropping atomic bombs on Hiroshima and Nagasaki, and a few days later, August 14, Japan surrendered. This time there was unrestrained joy in Richmond. Broad Street was a mass of tooting horns, singing men and women, exuberant "gobs" and exultant "G.I.'s." Some grabbed the first girl they saw and kissed her fervently. The jubilation and revelry went on far into the night.

History's greatest war had ended in victory for the United States and its allies. About 725 Richmonders had given their lives, nearly three times as many as died in World War I, when American involvement was much briefer.

The Richmond Blues, Grays and Howitzers did not return to the city as single units. They had been scattered throughout the Army midway of the war, and those who survived came back to this country with the units to which they had been assigned. There were no parades of returning soldiers in Richmond.

With peace declared the city buckled down to the task of recovering from the strains and dislocations of more than four years of conflict. In the economic sphere, Virginia's capital had fared better than most cities, but there were gold stars in the windows of some 725 homes, and thousands of Richmonders, many of them maimed for life, had returned with battle wounds. As in the country's other wars, Richmond had made its contribution.

# TWENTY-ONE

# The Postwar Years

A NEW ERA in municipal government for Richmond was ushered in almost immediately following the end of the war. The long-sought popular referendum on the adoption of a city manager form with a one-chamber council, to replace the bunglesome two-chamber council and "strong mayor" system which nearly everybody else had abandoned, was held.

The recently formed Richmond Citizens Association, with Richard H. Hardesty, a candy manufacturer, as its first president, put on a concerted drive to win supporters for the plan to modernize the city government. Ed P. Phillips, machinery distributor, and Dean Charles W. Florence of Virginia Union University were campaign managers.

The result was that former Mayor J. Fulmer Bright's "splendid form of government" went down the drain. First, a charter commission was elected by popular vote, with the Richmond Citizens Association slate, dedicated to reform, winning by about four to one. W. Stirling King, who had urged adoption of the new governmental form during his five years on the Board of Aldermen, led the winning ticket. Lewis F. Powell, Jr., who would serve later as president of the American Bar Association and justice of the U. S. Supreme Court, also received a large vote and was chosen commission chairman.

The charter, when drafted, was submitted to a referendum on November 4, 1947, and in the largest turnout in any municipal election held down to that time, was ratified, 21,567 to 8,060. A nine-member Council, elected at large on a nonpartisan basis, with no primary, and a city manager chosen by the Council, to serve at its pleasure, were salient provisions. Modern financial management was also provided, and there was, overall, much more effective and efficient service for citizens. The mayor, a member of the Council and elected by it, enjoyed less authority than before. While his chief functions, under the charter, were to preside over meetings of the Council and represent the municipality on ceremonial occasions, the mayor could be, and often was, influential in unofficial ways. W. Stirling King was elected the first incumbent of the office under the new charter, and Sherwood Reeder the first city manager.

Reeder got the new government off to a good start, and Richmond was chosen an All-America City by the National Municipal League and the Minneapolis *Star & Tribune.* The city's credit rating rose from AA to AAA. Reeder served until 1953, when he resigned to accept another position.

He was succeeded by Horace H. Edwards, former city attorney and mayor, and unsuccessful candidate for governor. Edwards' previous experience in city affairs stood him in good stead, but it was feared that his political background would lessen his effectiveness. As a matter of fact, he made some admirable nonpolitical appointments. Also, during his thirteen years as city manager the Civic Center took shape. This included a new Health-Safety-Welfare Building costing over $5,000,000, the beginnings of an eighteen-story city hall, and plans for an 11,791-seat Coliseum. Handsome new school buildings, such as John Marshall and George Wythe High and East End Middle School, were erected. Four branch libraries were built, and the library system was thrown open to blacks in 1947, by action of the Richmond Public Library Board, making Richmond one of the first cities in the South to take this action. The following year, Oliver W. Hill, a black attorney, was elected to the Council, Richmond's first black councilman in modern times. There would be several others in succeeding years, including Winfred Mundle and Henry L. Marsh III, both vice-mayors.

When the U. S. Supreme Court handed down its historic school desegregation opinion in 1954, Richmond, like other cities, knew it was headed for drastic change. It was fortunate in having H. I. Willett as city superintendent of public schools and Lewis F. Powell, Jr., as chairman of the school board. Both were able and courageous men. Willett had just served a term as president of the American Association of School Administrators. Booker T. Bradshaw, one of Richmond's foremost Negro businessmen, was vice-chairman of the school board and a stabilizing force. The city's black leadership was unusually mature, interracial relations had always been relatively good in Richmond, the local institutions of higher learning provided a sophisticated outlook and members of both races had a prevailingly conservative approach to problems.

However, all was not invariably serene with Richmond's race relations during these years. "Selective buying," a polite term for "boycott," was practiced, with picket lines, against Richmond's two major department stores until they agreed to serve blacks on the same basis as whites. Serious tension mounted on this and other occasions, and there was the possibility of a riot at the time of the Martin Luther King assassination. But good sense prevailed. In contrast to schools in the cities of Norfolk and Charlottesville, and the counties of Warren and Prince Edward, Richmond's schools were kept open. They were integrated gradually at first and then more rapidly.

While these things were happening, the barriers to blacks were coming down in Richmond in such areas as hotels, restaurants and motion picture houses, and on intracity buses. Negro firemen and policemen were appointed. Black police officers with limited jurisdiction had been named by Mayor W. C. Herbert, who served briefly until his death in 1946, after rendering excellent service as Director of Public Safety. For decades, voting by blacks in Richmond had been on the same basis as voting by whites.

The city forged ahead of most Southern municipalities in the status enjoyed by its Negro citizens. The great majority of whites were not happy over the rapid advance of the blacks into areas formerly closed to them, but they realized that a new day was coming and they did not believe in defying the courts. Integration went steadily forward, so much so that the liberal Washington *Post* published an article in 1962, covering almost a full page, and bearing the headline "Richmond Quietly Leads Way in Race Relations." Famous journalist Arthur Krock, writing two years later in the New York *Times*, pronounced Richmond "a model for every town, city and county in the United States." In 1966, Jack Greenberg, attorney for the legal defense and educational fund of the National Association for the Advancement of Colored People, hailed the "giant stride" Richmond had taken voluntarily toward complete desegregation. Phi Beta Sigma Fraternity, virtually all-black, held its national convention in the city in 1967, and Dr. Charles W. Hill of Beverly Hills, California, a delegate, wrote that he had traveled in 127 foreign countries, and "Richmond is the greatest community for good public relations on the globe . . . true brotherhood in action." He added that it was "the unanimous consensus that Richmond is the most hospitable city in America." These statements were contained in a letter to C. L. Townes, leading black businessman.

The National Association for the Advancement of Colored People and the U. S. Civil Rights Commission reported in the 1950s and 1960s, respectively, that they had found no significant racially motivated impediments to Negro voting anywhere in Virginia. In Richmond there were voting precincts whose officials were all white, some that were mixed and some that were all black. Until its repeal by Federal action in the middle sixties, the poll tax served as a voting deterrent for both races. But the principal reason for the relatively low turnout of Richmond blacks at the polls was indifference.

Blacks founded the Crusade for Voters in 1956 to stimulate greater participation by Negroes in the electoral process by getting them to register, organizing them by precincts, endorsing candidates and transporting voters to the polls. Dr. William S. Thornton, a black podiatrist, has been the leading spirit in the organization since its establishment, and was its head for many years.

Black voting increased markedly in Richmond when the Crusade began operations. The organization has its slates of candidates in municipal elections as well as in contests for the General Assembly and statewide office. The Crusade bills candidates, after it endorses them. On the average, councilmanic endorsees are charged $500, Assembly candidates $1,500 and aspirants for statewide office $2,500.[1]

Results on Election Day in predominantly black Richmond precincts clearly show the power of the Crusade in delivering support for its favorites. In 1968, it endorsed ony five persons for City Council, instead of the usual nine, and came close to electing all five, which would have given it control. But while the agency sharply increased the number of Negro voters in Richmond, and its endorsement is worth much to political aspirants, the Crusade is by no means successful in every instance. Nor is the percentage of black voters in the city as large as one would expect, given the intensive effort put forth. Many blacks are still uninterested.

The Richmond Citizens Association had been in operation for a decade when the Crusade began functioning. The association elected eight of the nine candidates it endorsed in 1948 and 1950, and six of nine in each of the next four elections. By 1958, however, questions were being raised as to whether the organization was dominated too completely by the West End's business and professional elite. Critics felt that blacks and labor were not adequately represented in the association's top echelons and membership. Furthermore, the Crusade was getting up steam, and its competition was being distinctly felt.

In 1963 the conclusion was reached that the Richmond Citizens Association had served an extremely useful purpose, but that another organization with a somewhat different emphasis and personnel was needed. So Richmond Forward was founded, with Thomas C. Boushall as president. Some six months later, Richmond Forward attacked the City Council for two years of "ineptness, bungling, bickering, indecision and inaction." The organization put on a drive for the June 1964 election and elected enough members to give it a majority. Such councilmen as James C. Wheat, Henry R. Miller III and B. A. Cephas were added.

However, in 1966 Howard H. Carwile was elected to the Council, and the place was in an uproar a good part of the time thereafter. Carwile was a sharecropper's son from Charlotte County who said he lived on lard sandwiches and seventy-five cents a week while studying for his law degree during the Depression. Possessed of a remarkable vocabulary and an alliterative speaking style, he startled his hearers with such sentences as "This horrendous hunk of hokum sears my soul and agitates my abdomen."

Carwile's election to the Council followed eighteen unsuccessful tries

for public office. He won with Crusade support, but with typical unpredict-
ability reversed his field a few years later by attacking school busing and
other causes beloved of the Crusade, and lost practically all his black followers. Carwile decided to run for the House of Delegates in 1973 from
Richmond and Henrico, and managed to defeat Dr. William Ferguson
Reid, who had entered the House in 1968 as the first black elected to that
body since Reconstruction. Vowing to "raise hell" as soon as he got into
the General Assembly, he was unable to create anything like the stir in the
hundred-member House that he had produced in the nine-member Council. He was defeated for reelection in 1975.

The Richmond Citizens Association and Richmond Forward experienced great difficulty in getting the best-qualified citizens to run for the
Council. Service there is so time-consuming that many of the ablest business and professional men were unable or unwilling to make the race.
Then, too, a large percentage of those who might otherwise have been
available were ineligible by reason of residence outside the corporate
limits.

Efforts were made by the city to merge with some of these suburban
areas or to annex them. After the substantial annexation of 1942, nothing
further was done toward expanding the city's boundaries until the attempt
to merge with Henrico in 1961. Alan S. Donnahoe, executive vice-
president of Richmond Newspapers and later president of Media General,
masterminded the effort behind the scenes. An intensive and well-
organized campaign was put on, under the chairmanship of Andrew J.
Brent, and it was hoped that the county's citizens would see the advantage
of a combined operation. But while Henrico's Tuckahoe district voted for
the plan, the rest of the county went strongly against it, and the attempt
failed. Richmond, by contrast, went pro-merger by well over two to one.

Merger having been rejected by Henrico, Richmond instituted annexation proceedings. The court took more than three years to decide, and it
finally ruled that Richmond could have about seventeen square miles of
Henrico with 45,000 population, far less than was sought, and that the
city would have to pay the county $55,000,000. The Council turned down
the proposition, deeming the monetary cost too high. Today, the overwhelming consensus, in light of subsequent events which could not have
been foreseen, is that the city fathers should have accepted the proposal.

Richmond was fortunate in the caliber of its Council during these years
and in its mayors and city managers. Upon the retirement of Horace Edwards from the latter post, Alan F. Kiepper came from Atlanta to succeed
him. Kiepper served four and a half years, and contributed markedly to
the city's forward surge. The *Times-Dispatch* termed him "dynamic, imaginative and prudent." He left to return to Atlanta as city manager, and
was succeeded in 1972 by his thirty-two-year-old assistant, William J.
Leidinger, who is built along the lines of a professional football tackle,

and was actually a taxi-squad place kicker for the Washington Redskins. He has been discharging his duties with ability.

Eleven mayors have served the city since the adoption of the new charter, in the following order: W. Stirling King, T. Nelson Parker, Edward E. Haddock, Thomas P. Bryan, F. Henry Garber, A. Scott Anderson, Claude W. Woodward, Eleanor P. Sheppard, Morrill M. Crowe, Phil J. Bagley, Jr., and Thomas J. Bliley, Jr. Each was in office for two years, with the exception of Crowe, who served four years, and Bliley, who has served five. Bliley was caught in the litigation over the annexation of Chesterfield territory in 1970, which prevented new councilmanic elections from being held until the case was resolved. The Crowe and Bliley administrations were especially fruitful for the city. The charming Mrs. Sheppard also deserves special mention as Richmond's first woman mayor. She acquired so large a following that she was elected to several terms in the House of Delegates.

The racial trend in Richmond during the sixties and early seventies was similar to that in many other localities, i.e. the blacks were moving in and the whites were moving out. There was a great shuffling about of pupils in the public schools, most of them bused to remote parts of the city, at great expenditure of time, money and trouble, but the percentage of integration was largely unchanged.

In 1950, before the Supreme Court's school decision in *Brown v Board of Education*, there were 33,106 pupils in Richmond's public schools, of whom 19,797 were white and 13,309 black, or just over 40 per cent black. By 1970, the number of pupils had risen to 48,013, but the white total had fallen to 17,364, well below that of twenty years before, while the black figure had leaped to 30,649, or nearly 64 per cent. Five years later it was 78 per cent.

Individual schools had been completely transformed, insofar as their racial composition was concerned. Thomas Jefferson and John Marshall high schools, once all-white, were from 80 to 90 per cent black. The level of scholastic performance at Thomas Jefferson, in particular, was sharply down. Once rated among the finest high schools in the Southeast, it had become merely one of many. J. E. B. Stuart School went from all-white to all-black in a few years, Binford Junior High from all-white to lopsidedly black, Mary Munford from all-white to 96 per cent black.

Schools in the almost solidly black East End received infusions of white pupils as a result of busing, but all such institutions, including Armstrong and John F. Kennedy high schools and East End and Mosby middle schools, remained predominantly black.

An effort by the Richmond School Board to combine the city's schools with the preponderantly white schools of Henrico and Chesterfield was blocked by the U. S. Supreme Court after U. S. District Judge Robert R. Merhige, Jr., ordered the merger.

In the sphere of higher education, Dr. Frederic W. Boatwright retired as president of the University of Richmond in 1946, after fifty-one years in office. His running controversy with a small group of Virginia Baptists, chiefly Dr. George W. McDaniel, pastor of Richmond's First Church, was a notable feature of his presidency. Boatwright was seeking larger contributions from the denomination, while at the same time maintaining a greater degree of independence. As an example of attempts at denominational control, the Baptist General Association of Virginia in 1921 asked the trustees of the college "whether all faculty members assent to the cardinal doctrines of the Baptist faith; whether the school permits hazing; whether the school permits dancing on school property." Boatwright succeeded in advancing the institution in important directions, despite these harassments. In 1932, on the centennial of the college's founding, Dr. Douglas S. Freeman, rector of the institution for many years, declared in the Richmond *News Leader* that Boatwright "had done immeasurably more for the school than any other individual ever connected with it."[2]

When Dr. Boatwright retired in 1946, he was succeeded by Dr. George M. Modlin, who came to the institution from Princeton University. Modlin was an admirable choice. He not only was a fine administrator; he was tactful and effective in handling the Baptists. He ingratiated himself with the Richmond community, serving, among other things, as president of the Richmond Chamber of Commerce. Modlin ran a "tight ship," and during the widespread campus upheavals of the late 1960s and early 1970s, things were quiet at the University of Richmond.

Perhaps George Modlin's greatest contribution was in persuading E. Claiborne Robins, the Richmond pharmaceutical manufacturer, to make a $50,000,000 gift to the university—at that time the largest such personal contribution in the history of American education. Robins subsequently made the condition that $10,000,000 of the amount would have to be matched. The gift was also conditioned on the termination of Baptist control over university policy. Both objectives were achieved.

Modlin retired in 1971 and was chosen chancellor. He was succeeded as president by E. Bruce Heilman, an experienced educator and administrator who was selected primarily as a man who could raise enough money to undergird the financial structure of the institution—the essential need at that time. In this Dr. Heilman was phenomenally successful. By late 1975 he and his associates had raised more than $27,000,000, and the University of Richmond was well on its way to becoming one of the superior privately financed institutions of its type in this country.

In another area of higher education, the Medical College of Virginia advanced steadily during the three decades when it was under the leadership of President William T. Sanger. The latter's employment of Dr. William Branch Porter in the mid-1920s as the first full-time professor of medicine was strongly opposed by many in the city's medical community.

"The critics were incensed not so much by Dr. Porter's appointment," Sanger wrote in his reminiscences, "but by the principle of whole-time professors in general." Sanger went ahead, nevertheless, and appointed Dr. I. A. Bigger the first full-time professor of surgery. Drs. Porter and Bigger made important contributions to the progress of the college and to medicine and surgery in the state. Another notable member of the faculty, and its last clinician to serve without pay, was Dr. H. Hudnall Ware, Jr. He was one of the first obstetricians and gynecologists in Virginia, and chairman of the Department of Obstetrics and Gynecology at MCV for a quarter of a century.

MCV's steady advance over the years may be seen in the fact that whereas in 1925 the resident and intern staff numbered sixteen, by 1975 it numbered several hundred. The college has been one of the nation's leaders in kidney and heart transplants.

Some of the MCV board were opposed in 1937 to accepting federal loans and grants. This opposition was overcome, and completion of the new hospital three years later, with the aid of PWA funds, was the result. Since then, large annual federal grants have been essential to the institution's growth and performance.

When Sanger retired as president in 1956, he was succeeded by Dr. R. Blackwell Smith of the faculty, a noted pharmacologist. During Smith's twelve-year tenure, MCV progressed in various directions. The Medical School was enlarged, the faculty strengthened, graduate study extended and important new buildings added.

Union Theological Seminary also made impressive advances during the century's middle years. Largest of the Southern Presbyterian seminaries, its teaching staff is notable for scholarship. UTS was listed in a recent issue of *Change* magazine among the top ten seminaries in the United States.

Dr. Benjamin R. Lacy, one of the most beloved men of his time, succeeded to the presidency in 1926, on the death of Dr. Walter W. Moore. He served for thirty years, and during those three decades the faculty and student body doubled in size, the physical plant improved and expanded and the endowment increased substantially.

Upon Dr. Lacy's retirement, Dr. James A. Jones was chosen president. He served until his untimely death ten years later. A man of great personal charm, Dr. Jones achieved extensive curricular improvements, increases in faculty and additions to the physical plant.

Dr. Fred R. Stair was named to succeed him, and a major achievement has been the formation of the Richmond Theological Center, composed of the Virginia Union School of Theology, the Presbyterian School of Christian Education and the seminary. Students may cross-register in courses, office space is shared and the libraries have been amalgamated. A single student association has been formed. The seminary's liberal attitude toward blacks goes back to 1927, when they were enrolled in the graduate school—so that UTS apparently is the first educational institution in the South to abandon segregation. In addition, qualified women have been admitted since 1957 as candidates for the B.D. degree. Notable members of the faculty in recent decades include Dr. John Bright, world-famous Old Testament scholar; Dr. Ernest T. Thompson, much-admired author of numerous books and editor of church publications; the late Dr. William Taliaferro Thompson, pioneer in pastoral theology and one of the truly great teachers; and Dr. John Newton Thomas, erudite M.A. and Ph.D. of the University of Edinburgh and student at the University of Berlin, who has served on boards of several institutions of higher learning.

Virginia Union University also has made remarkable progress, and in the face of handicaps that beset predominantly black colleges and universities. Dr. Allix B. James, its able president, is highly regarded by members of all races and creeds. He and his faculty are credited with a major role in preventing riots and disorders in Richmond in recent years when many cities were unable to avoid these upheavals.

Virginia Union is an accredited, coeducational, church-related liberal arts and sciences institution. More than two dozen states and a number of foreign countries are represented among its 1,400 students. Graduates include many of the leading blacks in the United States. The university offers the B.A., B.S. and Master of Divinity degrees. Standards and curricular offerings have been dramatically expanded and improved in recent years. The university is conducting a campaign for funds, and by late 1975, had raised $7,500,000.

Dr. Dorothy N. Cowling, the university's admired vice-president for administrative affairs, was named in 1975 to head a biracial planning effort for a national black cultural center in Richmond. The plan calls for this center to combine a historical archive, a library, a center for the performing arts and other facilities. Location is to be on land donated by the Roman Catholic Diocese of Richmond, in the area bounded by First, Second, Duval and Jackson streets.

Richmond's newly created institution, Virginia Commonwealth University, is the latest addition to the educational scene. VCU came into being in 1968, in response to the need for a state-supported, urban-oriented university offering the M.A., M.S., Ph.D., M.D. and D.D.S. degrees and other specialized professional instruction. It is a combination of the Medical College of Virginia and Richmond Professional Institute, and has more than 17,000 students, on a "head count" basis. Of these, 9,300, including 5,000 adults, attend the Evening College. VCU's Evening College is the second largest school of its kind in the United States.

Union of MCV and RPI was the result of recommendations made by several study groups. The Virginia Higher Education Study Commission, headed by State Senator Lloyd C. Bird, recommended to the General Assembly of 1966 that a state-supported university "with a substantial graduate school" be established in the Richmond metropolitan area. A separate study by Dr. Joseph C. Robert of the University of Richmond on behalf of the seven centers of learning in the Richmond area reached somewhat similar conclusions. The 1966 General Assembly accordingly created a fifteen-member commission to undertake a comprehensive study. Edward A. Wayne, president of the Federal Reserve Bank of Richmond, was appointed chairman, and the commission rendered a comprehensive report recommending that MCV and RPI be combined to form Virginia Commonwealth University. Special emphasis was placed upon the need for an urban-oriented institution, addressing itself intensively to distinctively urban problems.

First president of the new institution was Dr. Warren W. Brandt, under whom the institution was strengthened in many directions. He resigned after five years to accept another presidency and was succeeded at VCU in 1975 by able Dr. T. Edward Temple. VCU had by no means reached its full potential, and the future seemed bright as Temple took over.

Cooperation among educational institutions in Richmond and over a much wider area of Virginia is promoted by the University Center, established in the city soon after World War II, largely at the urging of Dr. William T. Sanger. The Center was unable to obtain all the financing it had hoped for, and its scope had to be limited accordingly. Its principal activity over the years has been bringing prominent lecturers to the campuses.

Another cultural advance was the chartering of the Richmond Opera Group in 1946, reorganized in 1975 as the Richmond Civic Opera Association. It provided operettas, pop concerts and pageants in the Lyric Theater—later the WRVA Theater—until the building's demolition in 1963. Since then it has had to limit itself to performances at Dogwood Dell in Byrd Park, in cooperation with the City Department of Recreation and Parks, and an annual Christmas opera at the Mosque. The latter structure, built in 1926 by the Shriners of Acca Temple, was purchased by the city fourteen years later as a civic auditorium.

The Richmond Symphony was revived in 1957, after the failure of its predecessor in the Depression. The founder and moving spirit was the late Brigadier General Vincent Meyer, Rtd. He served as president for four years and was succeeded by Edmund A. Rennolds, Jr., who has been exceptionally active in the organization's affairs. Edgar Schenkman was the orchestra's first conductor, and when he resigned after thirteen years, Jacques Houtmann took over. Richmond's symphony is one of the best among cities of its class.

A leading figure for decades in Richmond musical circles has been Mrs. William R. (Emma Gray) Trigg, Jr. She headed the Federal government's relief project for unemployed musicians in the Depression, was active in the founding of both symphonies, and has been a leader in virtually every similar endeavor in the city for half a century. In collaboration with Elizabeth Bull Maury, who wrote the music, Emma Gray Trigg did the book and lyrics for three operettas presented by the Richmond Opera Group. She is a poet of exceptional gifts, as several volumes of her poetry attest, and is withal one of Richmond's striking personalities.

Florence Robertson, following the death of her long-time teacher John Powell, became the city's most celebrated resident musician. She has gained national attention as piano soloist with leading symphonies.

Three Richmond-born blacks have gone on to fame as orchestra conductors. Paul Freeman, a Ph.D. of the Eastman School of Music, has been conductor in residence of the Detroit Symphony since 1970, and has made numerous guest appearances with major orchestras in this country and Europe. He is the winner of two awards in international competition. Isaiah Jackson III, thirty-year-old conductor of the Rochester Philharmonic since 1973, made his European debut by occupying the podium of the Vienna Symphony. A *cum laude* graduate of Harvard in Russian studies, he has done graduate work at the Juilliard School and elsewhere. Jackson has appeared as guest conductor with many U.S. orchestras. Dr. Leon E. Thompson, director of youth activities for the New York Philharmonic Orchestra, has a doctorate in conducting from the University of Southern California, and has conducted some of the greatest symphonies. He is a graduate of Richmond's Armstrong High School.

Research into Virginia's rich past was greatly stimulated when the Virginia Historical Society acquired Battle Abbey in 1946 from the Confederate Memorial Association, and added a commodious, fireproof and architecturally harmonious annex. In these modern surroundings, the society's 3,500,000 manuscripts, more than 200,000 printed books and pamphlets, thousands of maps and other such materials were made far more accessible to the scholars and researchers who have been flooding in from all over the United States and various foreign countries. Additional treasures of the organization include its unrivaled collection of Confederate battle flags, the finest and most complete exhibit of Confederate small arms in existence and the largest assemblage of historical portraiture south of Washington. Its *Virginia Magazine of History and Biography*, edited by W. M. E. Rachal, ranks with the best publications of its type in this country. Director of the society is the able John M. Jennings.

The internationally acclaimed man of letters Douglas S. Freeman retired as editor of the *News Leader* in 1949 to devote more time to his multi-volume life of George Washington. Four years later, with the biography unfinished, he died suddenly of a heart attack. The seventh and final volume on Washington was completed admirably by Mary Wells Ashworth of Richmond and J. A. Carroll.

When Dr. Freeman died, his physicians, the distinguished Drs. William

H. Higgins and William H. Higgins, Jr., found that he had left a note for them in which he said he had been having chest pains for weeks, but had not told them, for fear they would put him to bed and thus prevent him from completing the *Washington*. Freeman was thoughtfully absolving them of any blame, in case of his death, but they were of the opinion that had they known of his condition, they might have altered the course of his disease by sharply limiting his daily activities. Thus, instead of preventing his completion of the Washington biography, they might have made it possible for him to finish this and other biographical and historical works.

Freeman was succeeded as editor of the *News Leader* by youthful James Jackson Kilpatrick, a native of Oklahoma. A more vivid and colorful writer than Freeman, "Jack" Kilpatrick's editorial page struck sparks. He was especially effective in promoting and popularizing the doctrine of "interposition," which had been exhumed from long-gone political battles of earlier centuries, and under which the state was supposed to be able to "interpose" its sovereign authority between itself and the Federal government.

The doctrine was used to buttress Virginia's "massive resistance" to the U. S. Supreme Court's integration decision of 1954. Kilpatrick wrote friends that he realized "interposition" would not stand up in the courts.[3] However, his crusade in its behalf was so successful that resolutions approving interposition were overwhelmingly adopted in the legislatures of Virginia and several other Southern states. The whole thing blew up in 1959 when both the state and federal courts ruled that the obstructionist legislation enacted by Virginia was unconstitutional.

Kilpatrick resigned as editor in 1967, after sixteen years in the post, to write a syndicated Washington column and appear on television and the lecture platform.

He was one of numerous members or former members of the *News Leader* or *Times-Dispatch* staffs who published books of fiction or nonfiction—mostly the latter—which, in the main, were well-received by the critics. Among these authors were Douglas S. Freeman, John Stewart Bryan, Joseph Bryan III, Cabell Phillips, Henry Sydnor Harrison, Roy C. Flannagan, Virgil Carrington Jones, John J. Corson, Louis D. Rubin, Jr., John M. Patterson, James C. Burke, Alan Matthews, Parke Rouse, Jr., Charles McDowell, Guy Friddell, F. Earle Lutz, Garry Wills, Richard J. Whalen, Edward Grimsley, Clifford Dowdey, Green Peyton, Charles Houston, Frances Leigh Williams, Emily Clark, Elizabeth Copeland Norfleet, John H. Gwathmey, Scott Hart, Maria Williams Minor, Louise Ellyson, Isabel Dunn, Rhea Talley Stewart, Thomas Howard, David D. Ryan and Beverly L. Britton. It would be difficult to name any two papers of comparable size in the United States with so impressive a list. In addition, Roger Mudd, the nationally known CBS broadcaster, is a *News Leader* alumnus. Fred O. Seibel, the widely reprinted cartoonist, was on the staff of the

*Times-Dispatch* for several decades. Jeff MacNelly, the *News Leader* cartoonist, got the Pulitzer Prize in 1972.

Richmond is one of the prime retail book markets in this country, and is so recognized by the American Booksellers Association. On a per-capita basis, Richmond far surpasses in book sales all cities in the Southeast between Washington and Atlanta, and may even surpass Atlanta. It has no remotely close rival in Virginia.

Excellent regional books are published in Richmond by Whittet & Shepperson and Dietz Press. William Byrd Press, which formerly produced books for leading university presses, has been issuing only a few specialized volumes of late and concentrating on magazine publication. It absorbed the highly regarded regional book publishing firm of Garrett & Massie a few years ago.

Despite Richmond's obvious concern for books, James Branch Cabell's works sold there hardly at all in his declining years. Even when he wrote pungently of life in the city, his books were widely ignored.

One of his works that should have proved of avid interest to Richmonders but had virtually no sales was *As I Remember It*. In a chapter of that volume, Cabell skewered Ellen Glasgow with delicious irony because of her uncalled-for discussion in *The Woman Within* of the long-forgotten and discredited rumors that he was a homosexual and a murderer. She had been angered by his review of her book *A Certain Measure*, and while she made it plain that she held him to be innocent of the ancient allegations, her revival of this irresponsible gossip infuriated him. His fury was heightened by the fact that when she was ill and he spent months at her bedside going over two of her books, revising and rewriting, she made no public acknowledgment of this kindly and, indeed, indispensable assistance. His essay in rebuttal is a classic of gallant, tongue-in-cheek tributes to "a great lady," artfully combined with devastating raillery concerning her faults and foibles.

Cabell's fame remains alive in critical circles, and the new library at Virginia Commonwealth University in Richmond is named for him. The Cabell Society, a national group that concerns itself primarily with the fantasy in his books, meets periodically. For about three years it published *The Cabellian*, a journal devoted to his writings.

Miss Glasgow's fame is nurtured effectively by the Ellen Glasgow Society, organized in 1974 in Richmond. It issues a newsletter and seeks to keep Miss Glasgow's works in print. Dr. Edgar E. MacDonald of Randolph Macon College was the prime mover in its founding. An impressive centennial symposium commemorating the novelist's birth was held at Mary Baldwin College in 1973. Eight books devoted exclusively to analyzing her and her writings have appeared in the past decade and a half.

Easily the most celebrated Richmond-born author writing today is Tom Wolfe. Readers of his highly original and wholly unacademic prose might not guess that he is a Yale Ph.D. who, incidentally, pitched somewhat earlier on the Washington & Lee and St. Christopher's baseball teams. In his series of remarkable books, Wolfe "has caught the spirit of the tumultuous 1960s in much the way that Fitzgerald caught the Twenties, Steinbeck the Thirties and Hemingway the era of the Spanish Civil War," Maurice Duke, book editor of the *Times-Dispatch*, has written.

Wolfe is one of the foremost creators of and most eloquent spokesmen for what is termed "the new journalism." In his book of that name, he explains with profound scholarship, obviously based on much reading, the precise nature of this unorthodox approach to the journalistic profession. And more recently in *The Painted Word* he has assailed some of the more grotesque aspects of modern art in terms that stirred a tornado of controversy.

Frances Leigh Williams is a scholarly Richmonder who has produced books of permanent significance. Her *Matthew Fontaine Maury: Scientist of the Sea* is the definitive life of the "Pathfinder of the Seas," and her forthcoming one-volume multi-biography, *A Founding Family: The Pinckneys of South Carolina*, seems certain to receive enthusiastic acclaim.

Exceptional distinction as a contributor to leading magazines and as a magazine executive has been attained by Joseph Bryan III, who also is the author of several well-received books, including *Admiral Halsey's Story, Aircraft Carrier, Mission Beyond Darkness* and *The Sword Over the Mantel*. He was managing editor of *Town & Country* and associate editor of the *Saturday Evening Post* in his early and middle thirties. Since 1940 he has been a free lance. In addition to his books, "Joe" Bryan has contributed over one hundred articles to the better magazines.

J. Harvie Wilkinson III, a brilliant young member of the University of Virginia law faculty, is a Richmonder who produced a top-flight and widely quoted historical work in his early twenties. This was *Harry Byrd and the Changing Face of Virginia Politics*. He followed it a few years later with an exceptionally able study, *Serving Justice: A Supreme Court Clerk's View*.

Another youthful Richmonder who is making a name for himself, specifically as an authority on the Civil War period, is Emory M. Thomas of the University of Georgia faculty. His *The Confederate State of Richmond, The American War and Peace* and *The Confederacy as a Revolutionary Experience* are all valuable contributions.

Welford D. Taylor, professor of English at the University of Richmond, broke new ground with his book *Amélie Rives*, and shed light on the career of Sherwood Anderson by editing *The Buck Fever Papers*. He was general editor of *Virginia Authors, Past and Present*, with Maurice Duke of VCU as bibliographical editor.

It is perhaps not generally realized that Morris Markey, who originated the "Reporter at Large" feature for *The New Yorker* and was a leading member of the magazine's staff almost from its founding, grew up in Richmond and attended John Marshall High School. He left the city soon thereafter. Markey wrote several excellent books.

Among poets, Dabney Stuart of the Washington & Lee faculty and Sarah Lockwood are the best of the younger group. Other notable Richmond writers of poetry, in addition to Emma Gray Trigg, are Natalie Blanton, Ulrich Troubetzkoy, Anne Page Johns and Brodie Herndon. James Branch Cabell wrote excellent poetry as did Florence Dickinson Stearns.

The writing of verse in Richmond and over a wide area of the United States is being stimulated by the VCU Series for Contemporary Poetry, sponsored by Virginia Commonwealth University and the University Press of Virginia. It is one of five such award programs in this country, and Walton Beacham of the VCU English faculty is general editor.

No Richmonder has won a Pulitzer Prize for poetry, but several have won the prize in other categories, as follows: in biography, Douglas S. Freeman, for R. E. Lee, 1935, and George Washington, 1958, the latter a posthumous award shared by Mary Wells Ashworth, co-author of Volume VII; David J. Mays, for Edmund Pendleton, 1953. For the novel, Ellen Glasgow, In This Our Life, 1942; for newspaper editorials, Virginius Dabney, Richmond Times-Dispatch, 1948; for newspaper cartoons, Jeff Mac-Nelly, Richmond News Leader, 1972.

In the realm of the arts, Richmond has a conspicuous asset in the Virginia Museum of Fine Arts. The museum developed spectacularly under the twenty-year direction of Leslie Cheek, Jr., and it went forward steadily under his successor, James M. Brown. It offers an almost unparalleled variety of cultural opportunities for an institution of its type, not only in its valuable collections of paintings, sculpture, jewels and articles of historical value, but also through its offerings in music, drama and the dance. The museum's artmobiles and its chapters and affiliates throughout Virginia give it a particularly broad impact on the life of the state. All this might be said to be, to some extent, a culmination of early efforts by Miss Adele Clark and Miss Nora Houston to stimulate artistic concerns in Richmond.

Greatly contributing to the current artistic burgeoning in the city is the School of the Arts at Virginia Commonwealth University. Acknowledged to be one of the best such schools in the United States, and also one of the largest, its faculty and students are prime factors in Richmond's artistic advance.

A number of Richmond artists enjoy national reputations. The list includes Nell Blaine, Jack Beal, Robert Gwathmey, Theresa Pollak, Bernard Perlin, Edmund Minor Archer and Jewett Campbell. Most of them are living elsewhere, but all are Richmond-born except Campbell. Two Richmond portrait painters, Hugo Stevens and David Silvette, are in great demand.

Another branch of art is furthered in the city by the Richmond Ballet, which for decades has furnished opportunities for the development of talented dancers.

The Federated Arts Council of Richmond, with several dozen organizations as participating members and another dozen as associate members, sponsors an annual Festival of the Arts at Dogwood Dell in Byrd Park. The Council also gives an award each year to the Richmonder who is deemed to have made the greatest contribution to the arts.

In addition to being an art center, Richmond is a city of churches. Well-known bishops, pastors and rabbis of earlier years have been mentioned in previous chapters. A revered figure in more modern times was Bishop Henry St. George Tucker, for nearly a quarter of a century an Episcopal missionary to Japan, and for a decade of that time Bishop of Kyoto. He became Bishop of Virginia in 1927 and presiding bishop of the Episcopal Church in 1937, serving in the latter position for nine years. During two of those years he was also president of the Federal Council of Churches of Christ in America. Bishop Tucker was the most eminent divine ever born in Virginia. A familiar sight on the streets of Richmond for decades, his simple piety, lack of ostentation and keen sense of humor, especially when laughing at himself, endeared him to all.

Clergymen, since retired, who served their congregations in Richmond with distinction for more than a quarter of a century include Dr. Theodore F. Adams, president of the Baptist World Alliance and pastor of the First Baptist Church, largest Southern Baptist congregation in the state; Rabbi Ariel Goldburg, whose Temple Beth Ahabah is the largest Reform congregation between Washington and Atlanta; and Dr. Reno S. Harp, Jr., whose St. Stephen's is the largest church in the Episcopal Diocese of Virginia. Bishop John J. Russell, a man of great personal charm, who presided over the Roman Catholic Diocese of Virginia for a decade and a half, did much to promote cordial relations between Catholics, Protestants and Jews. Dr. George S. Reamey, editor of the *Virginia Methodist Advocate* for thirty years, was a leader among the Methodists.

The postwar era in Richmond saw the rise of a number of business leaders who became nationally known, and whose contribution to the city's commercial and industrial advancement has been phenomenal.

Their contribution was facilitated by the fact that when the Axis powers surrendered in 1945, Richmond's business posture was excellent. There were no important flash-in-the-pan industries in the city—only established plants that had expanded during the war. Richmond seems to have maintained its position as "the fastest growing industrial center in the nation."[4] Residential and business construction zoomed. Reynolds Metals, headed by Richard S. Reynolds, Jr., constructed its $10,000,000 office building, one of the handsomest structures of the kind in the country, and a $5,500,000 extrusion plant in Chesterfield County. The Willow Lawn

Shopping Center, first in the Richmond area and largest at that time between Washington and Atlanta, got into operation. Living costs in the city increased nearly 40 per cent over those of the pre-war years, but this was 6 per cent below the national average.

Significant impetus for the city's forward surge was contributed by Thomas C. Boushall of the Bank of Virginia, who, by common consent, is Richmond's preeminent banker since the passing of John M. Miller, Jr. Innovative and imaginative beyond any of his competitors, Tom Boushall broke new ground in both consumer banking and branch banking. He fought the Virginia Bankers' Association for fourteen years on the issue of "branching" and won a clean-cut victory.

Another superlative business leader is James C. Wheat, who has developed Wheat, First Securities into the foremost investment banking firm in the Southeast. This despite the fact that Jim Wheat is blind. His is one of the amazing accomplishments of the era. In 1950, his firm had a total of five employees; today it has several hundred in two dozen offices spread over three states. In addition to being a business genius, Wheat is an expert fisherman for sailfish and marlin; he formerly rode to hounds, jumping fences with the best of them; has actually shot a few ducks as a huntsman, and is a poker player of great gifts, using a braille deck.

Floyd D. Gottwald is still another Richmonder who has had a stunning impact on the business world. As president of Albemarle Paper Company, he borrowed no less than $200,000,000 in 1962 and purchased the far larger Ethyl Corporation from General Motors and Standard Oil of New Jersey. Truly, "Jonah swallowed the whale" in this almost unprecedented operation. Ethyl functions today on a worldwide basis in the fields of chemicals, plastics, metals and paper, and has its Richmond headquarters in a handsome colonial-style complex of buildings. Gottwald, who grew up without means in Richmond's East End, has been a generous contributor to Montrose Baptist Church, to which he belonged in his youth and for many years thereafter. His other quiet philanthropies have been numerous.

The storybook success of E. Claiborne Robins parallels that of Floyd Gottwald. His grandfather, Albert H. Robins, had a small apothecary shop at 200 East Marshall Street. Before and during the Depression, Claiborne's indomitable widowed mother, by dint of tremendous effort, kept the small operation going. Young Robins worked his way through the University of Richmond and the MCV School of Pharmacy, and then took charge of the business. It lost $500 the first year, made $100 the second, and then began expanding with astounding speed. In a relatively short time the pharmaceutical firm of A. H. Robins Company was doing business all over the world and was one of the nation's leaders in its field. The Robins fortune today is in the hundreds of millions. Claiborne Robins has been extremely generous in using his wealth for the public good. He and his family contributed approximately $66,000,000 to various worthy causes between 1963 and 1974, including the $50,000,000 to the University of Richmond already mentioned, $8,000,000 more to the university for the Coliseum there, a pledge of $3,000,000 to VCU's Medical College of Virginia, nearly $200,000 to Virginia Union University, numerous smaller amounts to other educational institutions, and the Richmond Public Library's bookmobile.

Richmond has been blessed with other generous philanthropists in recent years. Adolph D. Williams, tobacconist and son of T. C. Williams, left $10,000,000 to various worthy causes on his death in 1952. The University of Richmond, Medical College of Virginia and Virginia Museum of Fine Arts each received about $2,500,000, and three other institutions $300,000 apiece.

Robert M. Jeffress died in 1967, leaving $7,500,000, to be devoted upon the death of his widow to research in chemical, medical and other scientific fields.

Sydney Lewis, founder in 1957 with his mother, Mrs. Dora Lewis, of Best Products Inc., a highly successful "catalogue-showroom merchandiser," has been generous in contributing to various causes. He and his wife have given $9,000,000 to the Washington & Lee Law School, $2,000,000 to Virginia Union University, a perhaps equal sum to the Jewish Welfare Fund, and over $600,000 to the Virginia Museum of Fine Arts.

A number of Richmond natives have had notable careers elsewhere. One of these is Langbourne M. Williams, president of Freeport Minerals for a quarter of a century and its chairman for another decade. He served in 1948 as first director of the industry division of the Marshall Plan for the rebuilding of Western Europe, with headquarters in Paris.

Ross R. Millhiser has risen rapidly to the top with Philip Morris, and has been successively president of Philip Morris U.S.A. and of Philip Morris Inc., which latter position he now holds.

Frederick E. Nolting, Jr., on the University of Virginia faculty since 1971, had a distinguished career in the diplomatic service. After serving in a number of positions, including that of alternate U.S. representative to the North Atlantic Council in Paris, he was appointed by President Kennedy in 1961 as U.S. ambassador to Vietnam. He was replaced in 1963 when U.S. policy toward the Diem regime began to change. Nolting consistently backed South Vietnam's elected government and strongly opposed the Kennedy administration's support of the *coup d'état* against President Diem. After Nolting was superseded, Diem was overthrown, with the connivance of Washington, and affairs in Vietnam went downhill from that time forward. Nolting resigned from the foreign service in 1964. He became vice-president for the European offices of Morgan

Guaranty Trust, Paris, France, and later assistant to the chairman in New York.[5]

Dr. Richard H. Meade, a native Richmonder, moved to Grand Rapids, Michigan, to practice his profession, and has achieved national eminence in the field of thoracic surgery. He was elected president of the American Association for Thoracic Surgery in 1955, and is the author of A History of Thoracic Surgery and An Introduction to the History of General Surgery. He also wrote an excellent biography of the famous eighteenth-century English physician Dr. Richard Mead (no relation).

A notable achievement in an entirely different field was that of William J. Barrow. Working in Richmond laboratories, this scholarly researcher made discoveries as to the durability of paper that greatly advanced our knowledge in this sphere and enabled paper manufacturers to produce a far more lasting product. For the past century, most books and periodicals have been published on rapidly deteriorating materials. It is now feasible, thanks largely to Barrow, for important books and magazines to be issued on papers lasting for hundreds, possibly thousands of years.

The Richmonder who won the most spectacular fame of all during this era is Lewis F. Powell, Jr., who was literally drafted for the United States Supreme Court in 1971. His ability, integrity and industry have made him one of the most admired members of the nation's highest tribunal, and prospects are excellent that he will be recognized as one of the truly great justices. Lewis Powell is the first Virginian named to the Supreme Court since Peter V. Daniel was appointed to that bench in 1841.

Various landmarks disappeared from the Richmond scene during the years that followed World War II. The city's streetcar system, which had pioneered for the whole country more than threescore years before, finally went out of existence and was replaced by buses in 1949. In the same year, the well-known Dunlop flour mill was wiped out by fire. This left only one of Richmond's famous nineteenth-century mills, the Gallego, which had long been inactive. It was demolished in 1970 to make way for a business development. Another landmark vanished in 1950 when the Westham Bridge over the James, built in 1911, was replaced by the much handsomer Huguenot Bridge. The Ninth-Street Bridge, a century-old landmark that had survived many vicissitudes and been condemned to oblivion several times, was replaced in 1973 with the four-lane Manchester Bridge, costing nearly $17,000,000.

Numerous important visitors came to Richmond in the postwar years. Most famous of all was Winston Churchill. He arrived in 1946, at the invitation of the General Assembly, and addressed that body at the Capitol. Britain's superlative wartime leader was in his best oratorical form, and was frequently interrupted by loud applause as he called for closer cooperation between Britain and the United States and paid tribute to "Richmond, the historic capital of world-famous Virginia." He was accompanied by Field Marshal Sir Henry Maitland ("Jumbo") Wilson and General Dwight D. Eisenhower. After Churchill sat down, there were insistent calls for "Ike!" "Ike!" The audience was determined that he should speak, and the former commander of the Allied armies in Europe responded gracefully. He began with the words, "It is one of the high honors of my life to return to a joint meeting of the legislature in the state in which my mother was born and reared." The applause he received when he concluded equaled the thunderous ovation accorded Churchill.

Much thought was given during these years to the problem of a memorial to the Richmonders who died in World War II. Dr. Henry W. Decker, chosen Virginia's "General Practitioner of the Year" in 1949, whose son had been lost in a Pacific typhoon, suggested a hospital as a memorial. The suggestion caught on, and D. Tennant Bryan and family donated their handsome home, Laburnum, with the fourteen surrounding acres. In 1957, Richmond Memorial Hospital opened there in a new building, with Dr. Decker as the first chief of staff.

Another significant development in the field of medicine and public health was the organization at Richmond in 1946 of the Virginia Council on Health and Medical Care. The concept originated with Miss Ellen Harvie Smith. National recognition has come to the Council under the leadership of its director, Edgar J. Fisher, Jr. The organization's most widely publicized activity has been the placement of doctors in rural areas of Virginia which have little or no medical service. By late 1975, no fewer than 834 of these physicians had been placed. A smaller number of dentists also had been steered to sections in need of them. The Council has been active, furthermore, in promoting improvements in dietetics and occupational therapy, and has sponsored numerous conferences on nutrition, crippled children and "health careers." Its program has served as a model for other states, and has been praised several times by the American Medical Association as probably the most effective and aggressive of its type in this country.

Richmond has been well-represented in Congress during the postwar years. J. Vaughan Gary succeeded Dave E. Satterfield, Jr., in 1945, and was reelected until he retired voluntarily two decades later. He had served four terms in the Virginia House of Delegates before going to Washington, and was never defeated at the polls. Conscientious and thorough, Vaughan Gary was patron of the appropriation bills that financed the Marshall Plan. He was also a recognized authority on postal affairs.

Dave E. Satterfield III succeeded Gary as congressman from the Richmond district, and has rendered excellent service. Like his predecessor, he has never been defeated for public office, having served in the City Council and state legislature before going to Congress, and he is respected as a man who "does his homework." Satterfield has been a leader in the fight against compulsory busing of school children to achieve integration, and is a strong believer in fiscal integrity. The esteem in which he is held by his colleagues is seen in his unanimous election as head of the Democratic Research Organization, a group of about sixty conservatives in the House.

A Richmonder so ultra-conservative that he almost makes Dave Satterfield appear to be a wild-eyed radical is T. Coleman Andrews, a founder of the John Birch Society. Andrews resigned from the society after eight years "for purely personal reasons," but his philosophy remains largely in tune with that of the John Birchers. His good record with the Richmond city administration in the late 1930s was discussed in Chapter Twenty. Andrews also served as State Auditor of Public Accounts, and found forty county treasurers "short" for an over-all total of $1,100,000.

President Eisenhower appointed him U. S. Commissioner of Internal Revenue in 1953, and he did much to clean up the bureau, which had fallen into serious disrepute during the Truman administration. However, while his restoration of public confidence in the agency was excellent, and he was thanked by the President for an "outstanding job," he seems to have been unnecessarily caustic and tactless. After serving for about two and a half years, he resigned to enter private business. Andrews ran for President in 1956 against Eisenhower on a States' rights ticket and got several hundred thousand votes. He was chairman of George C. Wallace's presidential campaign for the Richmond district in 1968, and his son, T. Coleman Andrews, Jr., a former member of the Virginia General Assembly, was chairman for Virginia. Four years later, Coleman Jr. was national and state chairman of Wallace's candidacy under the banner of the American party.

Richmond was visited by two natural calamities in the decades following World War II. The first was a tornado which ripped through part of the city in June 1951. Numerous houses were unroofed, and Monroe and Byrd parks lost many hundreds of trees, 1,500 of them in Dogwood Dell alone. Only one life was lost, that of a swan in Byrd Park.

More than twenty years later, in June 1972, Richmond seemed almost in danger of being swept downstream into the sea by the worst flood in the city's history, the aftermath of tropical storm Agnes. The river's crest at the city locks was 36.51 feet, said to be more than 6 feet above the previous record set in 1771. The volume of water was so enormous that Mayo's Bridge was completely submerged, while whole areas that escaped previous floods were inundated. The River Road Shopping Center at the northern end of the Huguenot Bridge was flooded. Damage to merchants in the lower Main Street area was unprecedented, since the water reached the second floors of some of the buildings for the first time in history. Thousands of sandbags were useless in protecting the pumping station at Seventeenth and Byrd streets, which had to shut down, with the result that water from the James pushed into the sewer system and bubbled up through manhole covers into the streets. The city's water filtration plant was closed by the raging flood, and drinking water was flown or trucked in. Heavily chlorinated water was available from the plant within two days. Three 25,000-gallon propane gas tanks broke from their moorings and the entire Fulton area was ordered evacuated. Police and 1,200 National Guardsmen were called out. The Richmond Boat Club on Mayo's Island, founded in 1876 as the Olympic Club, and the city's oldest surviving private club, had barely been able to function after it was hit by the serious flood of 1969; the much worse one of 1972 gave it the *coup de grâce*.

No Richmond lives were lost in the deluge of 1972, but there were seventeen deaths in other parts of Virginia, mostly from drowning. The city did not recover for months, but the mud and other debris were finally cleared away and the damage done in the river front areas was rectified. Richmond took this calamity in its stride as it had done with others over the years.

# TWENTY-TWO

# Richmond in the Mid-Seventies

RICHMOND in the mid-seventies is an intriguing blend of the old and the new, of Charleston and Savannah, on the one hand, and Atlanta and Dallas on the other. The former Confederate capital is showing *élan* and drive in business and industrial realms while clinging—a bit precariously at times—to its distinctive eighteenth- and nineteenth-century heritage.

The city's reputation for stodginess and stuffiness, often exaggerated, is fading steadily. Will Rogers, the cowboy humorist, said half a century ago: "The Prince of Wales was born in Richmond—Richmond, England, of course. He didn't have enough ancestors to be born in Richmond, Virginia." This amusing persiflage may have had some validity at the time, but no longer. Richmond today is far larger and more cosmopolitan, and ancestor worship is one of its distinctly minor concerns.

Various important municipal developments serve to illustrate the city's progressive thrust. At the same time, heroic efforts are being made to preserve and improve its surviving historic landmarks.

An exciting plan to upgrade 400 acres in the "Main-to-the-James" area for business and recreational purposes promises extensive development of the river's many attractions for the first time. Parks on both sides of the stream, a bicycle path, restored canal locks, wildlife refuges, apartments, hotels, motels and restaurants are in the prospectus for what was once a grimy, down-at-heel area, long graced by smoky railroad yards, dingy warehouses and weed-grown open spaces. Multibillion-dollar business developments are contemplated. The twenty-four-story First & Merchants National Bank Building is the first of these and the still more massive Federal Reserve Bank the second.

Portions of the antebellum James River & Kanawha Canal, near Twelfth and Byrd streets, have been tastefully restored by Reynolds Metals Company. Another important piece of rehabilitation recently completed on the canal is of the Tredegar Iron Works gun foundry, restored to its Civil War condition by the Ethyl Corporation. A small 1.3-acre park on the site of the canal's "Great Ship Lock" near Dock and Pearl streets is being created by the city. It includes a working demonstration of a canal lock system.

The downtown region north of Broad Street has been revitalized by the erection of the new city hall and the Coliseum, while extensive additional developments seem to be in prospect. A convention center, costing more than $11 million, and a complex of hotels, office buildings, parking facilities and retail shops calling for outlays of from $60 million to $90 million are planned.

The $200-million expressway brings with it hopes of ameliorating the traffic jams that everywhere are a curse of urban life. Some experts doubt that it represents the best approach to Richmond's problem, but the overwhelming consensus of the local business community is that it will go far to meet the need. Linked to highways I-95 and I-64, the expressway is a limited-access toll facility designed to cope with the flow of vehicles between the suburbs and downtown as well as to serve travelers from elsewhere who are desirous of bypassing the city's center.

Reorganization of the Chamber of Commerce as the Metropolitan Chamber of Commerce, with a doubled budget and expanded staff, has given that agency much greater momentum. Most of this was made possible during the presidency of Attorney Robert P. Buford, who had the imagination to see that the organization required new money and new blood. One result has been the good-looking, highly readable monthly magazine *Richmond*. The chamber also has added badly needed tours of the city for the benefit of visitors, who are thronging Virginia's capital in ever larger numbers.

There is an inevitable "fallout" of tourists from the two enormous and successful entertainment complexes—King's Dominion, 23 miles north of the city on I-95, and Busch Gardens, 55 miles to the southeast on I-64 or Route 60. Richmond also attracts thousands of visitors by virtue of its position in the fast-growing Urban Corridor, stretching from Washington to Hampton Roads. This corridor is an extension of the heavily populated region along the eastern seaboard, reaching from Boston to Washington and given the name "Megalopolis."

Much of Megalopolis suffered far more than Richmond in the recession of the seventies. Richmond's well-balanced economy withstood the slump's stresses and strains with relatively little dislocation, and its unemployment rate was almost the nation's lowest. U. S. Department of Commerce figures for 1973 gave Richmond's metropolitan area a per capita income of $5,691, highest in the Southeast, with the exception of three small Florida municipalities inhabited mainly by well-to-do retired persons. The metropolitan area previously included Henrico, Chesterfield and

Hanover counties, but in 1973 was expanded to take in Goochland, Powhatan and Charles City. Its population is in the vicinity of 600,000, of whom about 233,000 live within the 62.5 square miles of Richmond proper.

Twenty-three of those square miles, with nearly 50,000 inhabitants today, mostly white, were annexed by the city in 1970, but the award was contested, and the case has been passing through the courts. The only condition on which the city will be allowed to retain the annexed territory is through reinstitution of the ward system for the election of councilmen. This step backward into an outmoded and long-discarded municipal polity is deemed necessary by the federal courts in order that there may be no excessive "dilution of the black vote." It is to be hoped that return to the ward system will not be conducive to municipal corruption, from which the city has been almost entirely free for many years. This whole situation presents a new challenge to the Team of Progress (TOP), a group of prominent nonpartisan citizens, which replaced Richmond Forward in 1970.

Merger of Richmond with the counties of Henrico and Chesterfield is the city's greatest single need. Unfortunately, the idea received a body blow when Henrico's voters rejected merger in 1961. Antagonism between the city and the counties was greatly intensified when the Richmond School Board sought unsuccessfully to obtain a court order directing the busing of pupils from the heavily black city schools into the preponderantly white schools of the counties.

The desirability of merger is highlighted by the fact that an astonishingly large number of county residents make their livings in Richmond. In 1973 the city actually had the nation's highest percentage of commuters in its work force, namely 44 per cent. Roanoke was second, with 43.7, and Petersburg fourth, with 42.4. Washington, D.C., was third and New York City fifth.[1] The extraordinary number of persons commuting to various Virginia municipalities is accounted for, in part, by the fact that cities and counties in the Old Dominion are separate political entities, a condition to be found nowhere else on a statewide basis, although some other American cities are separate from the counties surrounding them. In 1970, according to the City Department of Planning and Community Development, no fewer than 51 per cent of all jobs in Richmond were filled by noncity residents. In view of the remarkable number of commuters in Richmond, it seems inevitable that the municipality and the surrounding counties will combine someday to their mutual advantage. They have too much in common to continue indefinitely with the present overlapping, duplication, hostility and needless expense.

Reluctance of nearby areas to merge with Richmond seems wholly unrelated to the notion, still prevalent here and there, that Richmonders

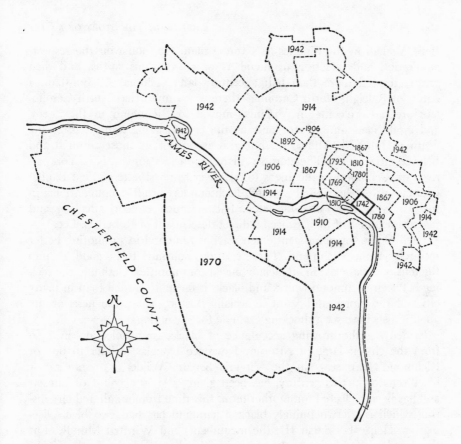

(4) The ten annexations that have occurred since Richmond was incorporated in 1742 are shown above. The large area of twenty-three square miles to the west and south, annexed in 1970 from Chesterfield County, is the latest territory to be brought into the city.

consider themselves somehow superior. Members of the General Assembly and others from various sections of the Commonwealth refer to Richmond occasionally as "the holy city." Whereas in years gone by there probably was some justification for regarding Richmonders as a bit supercilious, this is no longer true. Undoubtedly some of the criticism is traceable to the fact that there is covert jealousy of Richmond by virtue of its greater wealth and prestige, its numerous historic shrines and other attractions and its position as capital of both Virginia and the Confederacy.

Tending to refute any still prevailing notions that Richmonders look down on lesser mortals is the fact that persons who might appear to be "rank outsiders" can move to the city and win completely the hearts of its inhabitants. At least three examples may be cited:

Rabbi Edward N. Calisch, a native of Toledo, Ohio, came to Temple

Beth Ahabah in the nineties as a young man. He soon won the respect, admiration and affection of members of all religious faiths, and died greatly revered more than half a century later. Thomas C. Boushall, a native of Raleigh, North Carolina—there was a myth that North Carolinians are not welcome in Virginia—moved to Richmond in the 1920s, and established himself not only as the city's leading banker, after the death of John M. Miller, Jr., but also as one of its most admired and beloved citizens. Dr. Theodore F. Adams, born in Palmyra, New York, arrived in Richmond in the 1930s to take over the pastorate of First Baptist Church. When he retired in 1968, Richmonders of all denominations, in the words of the *Times-Dispatch*, felt as much esteem, affection and regard for him as if he had been a direct descendant of Robert E. Lee.

Each of the foregoing gentlemen was instrumental in promoting better race relations in Richmond. Those relations continue to be good, despite the tensions that exist in all racially mixed communities. Certainly the feeling between Richmond whites and blacks is far more cordial than in many cities of the North and West, especially Boston, where the heirs of the abolitionists have set a shocking example for the nation.

Evidencing the growing acceptance of blacks is the election in 1969 from the city at large of Attorney Lawrence Douglas Wilder to one of Richmond's two seats in the Virginia Senate. Wilder, the state's first black senator in this century, has been giving a good account of himself and has been reelected for another term, this time from an altered city district which is overwhelmingly black. Richmond has had two black vice-mayors, Henry L. Marsh III, the incumbent, and Winfred Mundle. For the decade ended in 1975, the maximum number of blacks on the Council has been three out of nine; usually there have been two.

Three Negroes were chosen for judicial positions in Richmond in 1973 and 1974. Leonard W. Lambert was selected by the nine white judges of Richmond's courts of record to be substitute judge of the Juvenile and Domestic Relations Court. Willard H. Douglas, Jr., was elected by the General Assembly as a full-time district judge presiding over the Juvenile and Domestic Relations Court. And finally, James E. Sheffield was appointed by Governor Mills E. Godwin, Jr., as a judge of Richmond Circuit Court, the first black in Virginia named to the bench of a court of record.

Mrs. Benjamin J. Lambert, Jr., mother of Leonard W. Lambert, mentioned above, was chosen Virginia's Mother of the Year for 1974. She and her husband, well-known Richmond caterers, are the parents of seven children, all of whom have done well in business or professional life. Several have been conspicuously successful.

Dr. Richard C. Hunter was chosen City Superintendent of Richmond's public schools in 1975, and many other Richmond Negroes have risen to high position in business and the professions. Impressive black bank

and insurance company headquarters north of Broad near the inter-
sections of First and Second with Clay and Leigh streets testify to this.
The downtown shopping area of Broad Street has become predominantly
black, with most of the stores catering primarily to that element of the
population, although they are nearly all owned by whites. Evidencing the
prosperity of the black community is the fact that many Negroes are occupying handsome homes on the North Side and around Maymont, while
an extraordinary number are driving new and expensive automobiles.

Compulsory busing of school children continues to be a subject of vigorous debate. Nearly all whites and many blacks contend that it is worse
than useless, while others say that it is the only practicable way to get
black children out of slum areas and give them steady contact with the
white world. Because of busing, thousands of white children have been
taken out of the Richmond public schools in recent years and enrolled in
nearby county schools or in private academies. The black percentage in
the city system, which stood at 78 at the opening of the 1975–76 session, is
mounting steadily.

The Richmond system continues to show dismal results in tests for
reading ability. Standings released in the spring of 1975 gave pupils in the
city's schools scores between the 18th and the 34th percentile, whereas the
50th is average. However, an intensive effort by City Superintendent
Thomas C. Little to emphasize the teaching of reading throughout the
system appeared to check the downtrend and to bring marked improvement in some instances. Unfortunately, failure and suspension rates for
the Richmond schools were about twice as high for the session of 1974–75
as those for the state as a whole.

On the favorable side, the number of disorderly incidents reported to
the police by Richmond school officials declined between 1971 and 1975,
although serious incidents continued. Rapes, shootings, robberies and attacks on teachers kept occurring. This is hardly surprising when it is noted
that the U. S. Subcommittee on Juvenile Delinquency reported no fewer
than 70,000 teachers physically assaulted during 1973, 100 students killed
and $500,000,000 worth of damage caused by vandals.

Crime in Richmond has skyrocketed, as has happened over most of the
world. The city's crime rate in 1972, including major property-related and
violent crimes, was double the 1962 rate. Since then the situation has become much worse.

Drugs are a grave problem and a cause of much concern in the schools.
A city agency estimated in 1975 that nine thousand Richmond youngsters
use drugs at least on an experimental basis, and that more than three
thousand are "hard-core abusers."

Tobacco is considered a dangerous drug in certain quarters, but the
campaign against it seems to have had little effect on cigarette sales in
Virginia or the rest of the nation. Richmond is no longer preeminent in

cigarette manufacture, since Winston-Salem, North Carolina, is now in the lead, but the presence in the city of Universal Leaf Tobacco Company, largest leaf tobacco organization on the globe, gives Richmond the edge over all other communities in the manufacture and sale of tobacco, and entitles it to be called the "tobacco capital of the world."

The city has lost Liggett & Myers, Larus & Bro. and P. Lorillard in recent years, and long-famous "Tobacco Row" on East Cary Street is virtually nonexistent. Only the substantial plant of the American Tobacco Company remains there. United States Tobacco Company is on the Jefferson Davis Highway.

The slow decline of tobacco manufacture in the city was checked and given a spectacular turn-around when Philip Morris constructed its ultramodern plant on Commerce Road, biggest single cigarette factory in the world, costing more than $200,000,000. This industrial establishment not only embodies the latest mechanical innovations, but is also exceptionally handsome and includes novel amenities for the comfort of its thousands of employees. The buildings and grounds have been lavishly beautified with paintings and other works of art.

Philip Morris is one of two Richmond corporations that have been conspicuous supporters of the arts. The other is First & Merchants National Bank, which, under the leadership of Chairman C. Coleman McGehee, has gone beyond all others in this regard.

Like Philip Morris, the bank is spending more than $100,000 in acquiring works by Virginia artists. In addition, it is sending these on tour over the state, together with works by non-Virginia artists that it has also acquired. First & Merchants publishes attractive illustrated brochures describing the sculpture, paintings, banners and tapestries distributed throughout its handsome building.

Philip Morris, with about 4,500 employees as of April 1975, is, of course, the mainstay of tobacco manufacture in the city, which has about 9,300 workers in all. This is the biggest total for any Richmond industry; chemistry and drugs come next, with 8,400. Other major industries are printing and publishing, paper and allied products, food and kindred products, and fabricated metals.

But the truly astonishing fact is that government in Richmond has no fewer than 58,000 employees. Of these, 8,400 are federal, while the remaining 49,600 are on the payroll of the city or state.[2] This gigantic, ever-mounting bureaucracy, widely duplicated throughout the United States, is enough to give any citizen pause.

Richmond is in an extremely strong position industrially and commercially vis-à-vis the other cities of the South. Companies with headquarters in Richmond are second only to those in Atlanta in sales volume, and ahead of those in Miami, Birmingham, Memphis and New Orleans, according to The South Magazine of Tampa, Florida (July–Aug. 1975).

Of the two hundred leading companies headquartered in ten Southern states, twelve are in Richmond. In sales the twelve rank as follows: Reynolds Metals, Seaboard Coast Lines, Ethyl Corporation, Universal Leaf, A. H. Robins, Robertshaw Controls, Best Products, General Medical, Media General, Overnite Transportation, Thalhimers and Ward's. Philip Morris is not included, since its headquarters are in New York. Roanoke has two of the two hundred companies and Norfolk one.

In addition to the diversification of its industry, one of Richmond's great assets is the fact that it has not had a major labor stoppage for many years. Its wage level is about midway between that of the North and that of the Deep South.

Several decades ago, an apocryphal story went the rounds. Over the loudspeaker on planes approaching Richmond were supposed to have come the words: "You are landing in Richmond. Turn your watches back twenty years." The situation that gave rise to this amusing yarn exists no longer, if it ever did.

Analysts feel that Richmond is increasing its momentum as an industrial, commercial and cultural center, and that the next decade or two will witness exceptional advances in the metropolitan area. And it will be, it is believed, an orderly growth, unlike the rip-roaring boom that swept over Atlanta during the sixties. Richmond recovered from the devastation of the Civil War half a century ago, but it was far from being the dynamic city then that it is today.

The concentration of institutions of higher learning in Richmond is one of the principal reasons for its rapid advance. Virginia Commonwealth University, the University of Richmond, Virginia Union University, Union Theological Seminary and the Presbyterian School of Christian Education are four-year institutions which add greatly to the city's cultural environment while some of them also furnish opportunities for practical scientific and vocational training. Randolph-Macon College at nearby Ashland is another great asset. The two-year community colleges in the area, J. Sargeant Reynolds and John Tyler, offer instruction in occupational fields as well as the liberal arts. New construction at the University of Richmond and Virginia Union increases those institutions' usefulness.

Other significant construction in progress at this time, or recently completed, includes the follow:

A new wing at the Virginia Museum of Fine Arts, costing more than $6,000,000, and enabling the museum to play an increasing role with its comprehensive programs and exhibits.

The White House of the Confederacy's new, air-conditioned museum, in which to house its priceless relics, and the refurbishing and refurnishing of the mansion to resemble as closely as possible the White House of the Civil War, all at a cost of about $2,000,000.

Extensive new construction and remodeling at Virginia Commonwealth

University, including projects at the Medical College of Virginia to cost scores of millions, and completion of the James Branch Cabell Library and the School of Business building.

Last, but by no means least, Richmond finally has a public library large enough and sufficiently well-stocked and well-staffed to meet the needs of the city. It opened in 1972 and incorporates the Dooley Library.

Richmond was largely "on dead center" from the onset of the Great Depression in the early 1930s until the early 1960s. Then suddenly things began to happen. No high-rise office or apartment buildings had gone up in the preceding thirty-year period, but the Ross Building, the Fidelity Building, the 700 Building, the Seventh & Franklin Building and the Eighth & Main Building, plus extensive additions to the United Virginia Bank and the Bank of Virginia, rose in rapid succession. Simultaneously, the new city hall and the Coliseum were erected north of Broad, and the expressway was begun. Several handsome high-rise apartments went up in midtown.

Richmond's two great department stores, Thalhimers, founded in 1842, and Miller & Rhoads, in 1885, expanded their facilities in the years following World War II. Each of these stores would do credit to any city in the United States, and for Richmond to have them both is rare good fortune. Many persons come from distant points to shop at Thalhimers and Miller & Rhoads. The stores have numerous branches in Virginia and North Carolina.

Richmond's banks underwent great expansion during the sixties and seventies, as a result of a more liberal state banking law, enacted in 1962, permitting branch banking and holding companies. One consequence was that they were able to handle much larger loans to Virginia industry, loans that previously had been obtained beyond the borders of the Commonwealth.

A disappointment in recent years has been the failure of the city to obtain approval from the U. S. Army Corps of Engineers of the long-sought plan to deepen the James River channel by 10 feet to 35 feet, from Richmond Deepwater Terminal to the river's mouth. The engineers turned down the plan in 1972 on the ground that it was not "economically justifiable." Their approval and resultant federal funding can perhaps be obtained at some future time when the project seems more feasible from an economic point of view.

Richmond enjoys great potential as a cattle shipping port, since it was

(5) Map shows the boundaries of the enlarged Historic Richmond Neighborhood around St. John's Church. The Historic Richmond Foundation has not only extended greatly the scope of its activities on Church Hill, as shown here, but it has chosen to work for the upgrading and restoration of other areas, including old Jackson Ward.

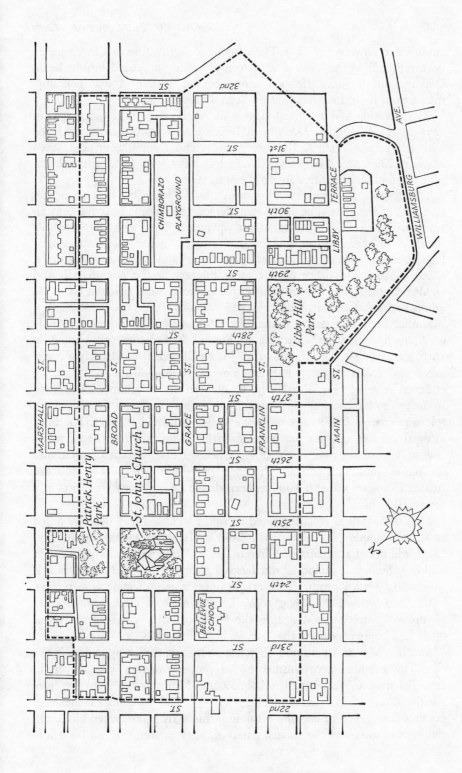

approved in 1970 by the U. S. Department of Agriculture as a livestock export terminal. At the same time, fifteen previously approved terminals, including Norfolk, were dropped. However, the volume of livestock shipments from Richmond has thus far been disappointing.

Revitalization and a general tidying up of the city's core was begun in 1975 by the Richmond Downtown Development Commission, equipped with a $900,000 budget. Improved streets and sidewalks on the seven blocks of Main Street between Fifth and Twelfth, with trees, sidewalk furniture and other amenities are on the agenda.

The upgrading of Shockoe Slip and its immediate vicinity is an important part of the plan. The area has undergone significant improvement already, with several good restaurants in operation. The quaint Slip, with its fountain for horses and its cobblestone paving, is one of Richmond's most historic spots, since it extends toward the canal and the river, and from it much tobacco and other produce was shipped in the seventeenth and eighteenth centuries. More recently, these streets were redolent with the aroma of wholesale fruit, vegetables and chickens.

Similar improvments are under way in other parts of the city, notably on Church Hill, where Historic Richmond Foundation, established in 1956, has saved the region around St. John's Church from steadily advancing decay, and transformed it into one of Richmond's most charming enclaves. The late Dr. Wyndham B. Blanton and a group of dedicated women were the moving spirits in this admirable enterprise. Dr. Blanton's role was crucial, but it was only one of his manifold services. His large medical practice did not prevent his writing definitive histories of medicine in Virginia as well as a history of Second Presbyterian Church, and serving as president of the Virginia Historical Society. The restored Adams House on Church Hill has been designated by the foundation as a memorial to him.

That organization recently raised its sights to encompass other blighted areas, and employed Michael W. Gold as full-time managing director. Large additional segments of Church Hill are now within its purview, as well as other areas, including old Jackson Ward, where the foundation is collaborating with prominent black business and professional men. The latter have formed the Maggie Walker Memorial Foundation, and are planning to preserve and restore the home of Mrs. Walker, as well as other handsome residences that survive in "the ward."

Another part of Richmond that has been beautifully upgraded is the Fan. This has been accomplished by the property owners who, in certain areas, have done over virtually whole blocks of houses, and in others have greatly improved individual homes. The roofs and columns of the large porches that served so useful a purpose in the early 1900s, when air conditioning was unknown, have been removed, brick or concrete has been substituted for the wooden porch flooring, while attractive ironwork has been added, with plantings of shrubs and flowers.

Whereas the exodus from Richmond to the suburbs continues, it is compensated for, in part, by a smaller number of persons who are moving from the suburbs into the Fan, and "doing over" houses there. Portions of the district are beset by parking and other problems, owing to the proximity of Virginia Commonwealth University.

Restoration or "recycling" of the four iron-front business structures extending from 1007 to 1013 East Main Street is an important service to those who desire the preservation of old Richmond. These buildings rose in 1866 from the ashes of the Civil War, and their striking iron fronts were made by Hayward, Bartlett of Baltimore. They have been reconditioned as desirable offices by Ironfront Associates, whose stockholders are several public-spirited local citizens.

The eighteenth-century Woodward house near Rocketts, where ships docked in early days, is being saved from destruction and restored. Probably the oldest frame house still standing in the city, the original core was built before 1782 by sea captain John Woodward.

Capitol Square has been rescued from irreparable damage at the hands of the General Assembly. That body proposed to abandon its chambers in the wings of the Capitol, and to place them underground in the square, at enormous cost in money and even greater cost in ruin to the lovely grass-covered enclosure with its quiet pastoral atmosphere. The scheme included structures looming out of the ground in front of the Capitol that resembled the hanging gardens of Babylon. An uprising of citizens, led by Lawrence Lewis, Jr., Richmond financier, effectively scotched the plan. The Assembly's manifest need for greater space will be met by providing offices and other facilities in the former home of the Life Insurance Company of Virginia, bordering Capitol Square and purchased by the state. Substitution of brick walks for those of concrete in the square is a recent improvement.

Hosannas should herald the fact that the Broad Street Station, one of the most spectacularly handsome railway stations in this country, has been saved from destruction. The state has bought it, along with the fifty-three-acre tract on which it stands, and is expected to use it for the projected State Science Museum, formerly planned for Byrd Park. It is contemplated that the museum will include a planetarium, a small auditorium with demonstration area for school or community groups, films, exhibits, reference materials and laboratory. The large tract of valuable land on which the station stands can also serve the Commonwealth in other important ways.

Further gratification is in order over the preservation of the Kent-Talbott-Valentine house at First and Franklin streets, purchased by the Garden Club of Virginia for headquarters. In addition, the John Marshall house has just undergone salutary renovation at the hands of the Association for the Preservation of Virginia Antiquities.

Monument Avenue, one of the truly splendid avenues in the United States, and Franklin Street, once Richmond's most aristocratic residential thoroughfare, have managed to retain a fair proportion of their pristine charm. John Kerr Branch's Tudor-style mansion, designed by John Russell Pope, also architect of the Broad Street Station, is the most sumptuous structure remaining on Monument, but it is no longer a residence. Frederic W. Scott's pillared town house in the beaux arts style, designed by Noland & Baskervill, is the most imposing mansion on Franklin Street. Part of it is being used by VCU.

Any achievements in renovating or restoring old buildings in Richmond should be put beside the almost incredible estimate of William B. O'Neal, chairman of the University of Virginia's Division of Architectural History, that more than 1,500 structures built in Richmond before 1850 were demolished between 1945 and 1968!

A small group of Richmonders deserves an accolade for preventing the demolitions from being even more extensive. Any list of such persons would have to recognize the superlative contributions of the Scott family. Miss Mary Wingfield Scott, author of the two definitive works on old Richmond houses, and purchaser and preserver of seven of the eight surviving houses on Linden Row, heads the list. Mrs. John H. (Elisabeth Scott) Bocock and Mrs. William T. (Mary Ross Scott) Reed, Jr., have been generous and indefatigable in the same cause. Mrs. Ralph T. Catterall also has been untiring, and available at all times for valuable counsel, stemming from her unparalleled knowledge of Richmond, past and present. S. Douglas Fleet, a prominent businessman with a sense of history, has given time, money and advice in various restorations. To such persons as these is due the fact that Richmond's antique charm has not been sacrificed completely to the all-consuming filling station, parking lot and bulldozer.

The trees that line the city's streets are particularly alluring. There are about 200,000 of them, many more than in the average municipality, and their cool shade offers soothing balm when the mercury mounts. Often their arching greenness above the street resembles a cathedral nave.

Flower vendors were a picturesque adornment in days gone by, but they are fading from the scene. Prices have escalated, and the vendors, mostly black, have to charge from $2 to $3 for a bouquet. This has come close to pricing their blooms out of the market. On the other hand, beautification of streets and squares in recent years with plantings of flowers has added greatly to the city's elegance.

Beautification also is going forward in another direction—at Maymont, the 100-acre parklike tract with its extraordinary mansion, left to Richmond by Major James H. Dooley. Maymont deteriorated as the years passed, and it has been taken over from the city by the privately run Maymont Foundation, successor to the Thalhimer Wildlife Foundation, which operated a wildlife exhibit there. Substantial funds have been raised, and the city still appropriates about $125,000 annually for operations. The vastly expensive residence, an elaborate "period piece" of the late nineteenth century, has been completely renovated, with its lavish furnishings. The gardens, the 126 varieties and subvarieties of trees, the nature center and the wildlife and domestic animal exhibits are all included in the program of renovation and renewal.

Richmond is a city of culture and refinement. Its educational institutions, libraries, art museum, symphony and numerous well-patronized bookstores all speak to this. It is also a leading medical center, with an extraordinary number of first-class hospitals.

The Medical College of Virginia is the central factor in Richmond's medical preeminence. Physicians of wide repute have practiced there and in other local hospitals over the years. Several have been mentioned already in these pages. A partial list of others whose pioneering contributions deserve to be recorded would include Drs. J. Shelton Horsley, William T. Graham, Beverley R. Tucker, Claude C. Coleman, M. Pierce Rucker, Austin I. Dodson, Frank S. Johns, Kinloch Nelson, DuPont Guerry, J. Morrison Hutcheson and David M. Hume.[3] There is also Dr. Harry M. Lyons, retired dean of the dental school at MCV, past president of three national dental organizations and easily the foremost figure Virginia has produced in the field of dentistry.

In addition to the foregoing, special mention should be made of Dr. Harry J. Warthen, Jr., scholarly editor of the *Virginia Medical Monthly* for twenty years, and organizer of the exceptionally fine Confederate Medical Exhibit shown throughout the Civil War Centennial. Dr. Charles M. Caravati deserves an accolade for his excellent *Medicine in Richmond, 1900–1975.*

The level of scholarship among Richmond's business and professional men is relatively high. During part of the fifties and all of the sixties four of the city's five leading bank presidents were Phi Beta Kappas.

One of these is J. Harvie Wilkinson, Jr., recently retired from the presidency of United Virginia Bank, which developed its present prestige under his leadership. Harvie Wilkinson is a businessman with a broad grasp of the cultural spectrum as well as of banking, and he has been active in many types of public service. He is chairman of the Virginia Council on Higher Education, and has served on the boards of the University of Virginia, Hollins College and the Brookings Institution. Other directorships include Philip Morris, Freeport Minerals and Media General. Wilkinson was a leader in persuading Virginia bankers and legislators to liberalize the banking laws to permit branches and holding companies.

Other Richmonders have been serving on the boards of New York corporations, the New York Stock Exchange and various nationally known institutions.

The late Samuel M. Bemiss was a successful businessman whose contributions in sharply contrasting fields were remarkable. His years as president of the Virginia Historical Society were especially fruitful, and he directed the society's removal from the Lee House to its new and modern headquarters in the annex adjoining Battle Abbey. As chairman of the Virginia State Library Board he was credited with launching the successful magazine *Virginia Cavalcade*. Sam Bemiss made a signal contribution in 1957 to Virginia's observance of the 350th anniversary of the Jamestown settlement. He was also a leader in founding the University Press of Virginia at Charlottesville, and after his death, his family contributed generously to the purchase of the organization's headquarters, which bears a bronze plaque in his memory.

Another extraordinary Richmonder is the brilliant George D. Gibson, an attorney with a national reputation in the field of corporate law, chairman of major committees of the American Bar Association, and an authority on Chinese, Japanese and Javanese art. Widely read in the histories of Great Britain, France, China and Japan, he is a master of the sparkling riposte and has been known to write a poem with alternate lines of French and Latin.

General Edwin Cox is a versatile and admired Richmond native who now lives a few miles away in his delightful early nineteenth-century residence, Holly Hill, at Aylett. He commanded the 176th Infantry in World War II, and retired as a much-decorated brigadier general. "Pete" Cox was awarded the Gold Medal of the American Institute of Chemists in 1965, the presentation being made by the internationally famous Dr. Vannevar Bush. He is astoundingly well-versed in history, and is past president of the Virginia Historical Society.

Richmond boasts of several national celebrities. In public affairs, U. S. Supreme Court Justice Lewis F. Powell, Jr., is preeminent, while Tom Wolfe is foremost in the realm of authorship. Their careers have been examined in earlier chapters. In sports, Arthur Ashe won the tennis singles championship at Wimbledon in 1975 and the World Championship in Tennis at Dallas the same year. He had previously starred on the U. S. Davis Cup team, and is regarded as both a superlative player and a credit to the game. Vinny Giles, now living in Richmond but a native of Lynchburg, won the British Amateur Golf Championship in 1975 by the overwhelming score of 8 and 7. Two Richmond-born motion-picture stars, Shirley MacLaine and Warren Beatty, are brother and sister, and were born in Richmond in the 1930s, when their father, Ira O. Beaty, was principal of Westhampton School. The U. S. Navy's first black admiral is Rear Admiral Samuel L. Gravely, Jr., who grew up in Fulton Bottom, and in 1975 was named commandant of the 11th Naval District in San Diego.

Life is more leisurely in Richmond than in many parts of the North and West, and the soft accents of the natives are not always comprehensible to visitors. True, hardly anybody in the city today says "cyah" or "gyah-den" for "car" and "garden," and the once prevalent broad "a" survives mainly in the pronunciation of "tomahto." But the authentic Richmond accent, like that of Virginia, is distinctive.

Richmonders are sometimes accused of dwelling in the past; yet a few years ago, on the birthday of Jefferson Davis, President of the Confederate States of America, twenty-seven persons were asked at random on Richmond streets to identify him, but only eight could do so.

The city's oldest and most prestigious country club, the Country Club of Virginia, is so "exclusive" that it has 5,600 members, counting men, women and children. Interest in tennis, golf, swimming or bridge, and fiscal solvency, have long since been regarded as more valid qualifications for membership than one's birthplace or one's forebears.

Of course, there is the Richmond German, which does stress family and background. But while those who belong come mainly from the city's old families, a good many members are without early Richmond connections. Dances at the German, complete with white tie and tails, are the ultimate in formality.

Conviviality of a less formal nature is growing in Richmond. A number of excellent restaurants have opened in recent years, and there are a few embryonic night clubs. Legalization of liquor by the drink has tended to elevate the level of dining as well as the number of patrons. It has also been helpful in bringing conventions to the city.

Richmond has always been conservative, politically and otherwise. It was a Federalist stronghold in the early 1800s, and then was dominated by the Whigs. During Reconstruction the suffering city was headquarters for the Conservative party, chief foe of the Radicals, and later it furnished most of the leading Funders, opponents of Mahone's Readjusters. More recently, much of the financial backing for the Byrd organization came from Richmond, and the city has gone Republican in four of the last five presidential elections.

Interfaith relations have been exceptionally good over the years. This was remarked upon long ago by Dr. Moses D. Hoge, and in late years Dr. Ariel Goldburg, rabbi emeritus of Temple Beth Ahabah, said that in Richmond "Jews and Christians are on a friendlier basis than in any other city in the country." Dr. Peter Mellete, the unusually competent Richmond head of the National Conference of Christians and Jews, is entitled to much credit for the fine relations that exist today.

Richmonders are no longer engaged in fighting the Civil War over again. True, a youngster at St. Christopher's School made a remark recently that might be taken as signifying the contrary. When one of his classmates mentioned that his father was "a Yankee," the boy replied, "It's impossible; all the Yankees were killed."

Yet members of the Ladies Hollywood Memorial Association, who have been decorating Confederate graves and statues of Southern leaders in the Civil War with Confederate flags on each Memorial Day since 1866, have had to abandon the time-honored rite. In 1974, the flags were stolen from the graves and statues at night by unknown persons, with the result that Mrs. James H. Donohue, Jr., president of the association, announced that it was futile to continue. This is nothing short of tragic. No Confederate sympathizer would think of robbing the graves of Union soldiers of their American flags on Memorial Day, but there are individuals in Richmond so intolerant as to deny those who wish to remember Southern heroes of more than a century ago.

Richmond has a special mystique, and is one of only about a half-dozen American cities of which this can be said. If there is a single explanation for this above all others, it is that Richmond was the capital of the Confederacy, the citadel defended for four years against invading armies. Once this mystique is gone, Richmond will be just another city.

John S. Wise wrote that before 1861, "nearly every distinguished foreigner felt that his view of America was incomplete" unless he visited Richmond. If the city of today is careful to guard its heritage and its culture, Richmond may once again be a mecca for visitors from beyond the seas.

This capital of the Commonwealth has known tragedy and defeat, but it has risen above the killing and maiming of its sons in the Civil War and the ruin of its business district, and has reentered the mainstream of American life. Yet as it moves forward into the new age, it must, above all, be zealous to guard and preserve those qualities that have set it apart, qualities that, once lost, can never be recovered.

# NOTES

## CHAPTER ONE – *The Cross at the Falls*

1. A *History of Richmond, 1607–1861*, Wirt Armistead Cate, unpublished manuscript at Valentine Museum, Richmond, p. 56 and note (hereafter cited as Cate). "Note on 'Belvidere,'" Edward L. Ryan, *Virginia Magazine of History and Biography* (hereafter *VMHB*), April 1931.

## CHAPTER TWO – *Byrd—The Reluctant Father*

1. Byrd Letter Book, Department of Research and Record, Colonial Williamsburg. Letter to Micajah Perry, May 25, 1727 (possibly May 21 or 23). Cited by Cate.
2. I am indebted to Mrs. William G. Leverty, who has made an intensive study of the Old Stone House, for much of the foregoing material.
3. *Jefferson the Virginian*, Dumas Malone, pp. 8, 9.
4. *Colonial Virginia*, Richard L. Morton, Vol. II, pp. 556–58. *Old Churches, Ministers and Families of Virginia*, Bishop William Meade, Vol. I, pp. 398, 400.
5. Cate, pp. 56–59. *Old Richmond Neighborhoods*, Mary Wingfield Scott, pp. 213–15.
6. *Virginia in Our Century*, Jean Gottmann, pp. 380–81.

## CHAPTER THREE – *Richmond in the Revolution*

1. *The Papers of Thomas Jefferson*, Julian P. Boyd, ed., Vol. IV, p. 507, note 508; p. 622, note 623.
2. I am indebted to James Gergat for material concerning James Lafayette gathered by him as a member of the Valentine Museum staff.

## CHAPTER FOUR – *Statesmen, Merchants, Fashions, Taverns and Hangings*

1. *Pennsylvania Gazette*, August 23, 1786.
2. Cate, pp. 138–40.
3. For a more detailed account of the convention, see *Edmund Pendleton*, David J. Mays, Vol. II, Chapters 13, 14, 15 and 16.

CHAPTER FIVE—*Gabriel's Insurrection—Greatest Slave Plot in U.S. History*

1. This chapter is based primarily on the following sources: James Monroe, Executive Papers, Sept. and Oct. 1800, and Executive Letter Books, Aug.–Oct. 1800, Virginia State Library. Condemned Slaves Executed, 1800–1801, Virginia State Library. Writings of James Monroe, Vol. III, Putnam, 1900. *Calendar of Virginia State Papers*, Vols. VI, IX and X. *Journal of the Virginia Senate, 1801–1802. Journal of the Virginia House, 1801.* T. W. Higginson, "Gabriel's Defeat," *Atlantic*, Sept. 1862. Herbert Aptheker, *American Slave Revolts*, New York, Columbia U., 1944. Gerald W. Mullin, *Flight and Rebellion: Slave Resistance in Eighteenth Century Virginia*, New York, Oxford, 1972, and R. H. Taylor, "Slave Conspiracies in North Carolina," *N. C. Historical Review*, Jan. 1928. William P. Palmer, M.D., articles in Richmond *Times*, Dec. 7, 21 and 28, 1890, Jan. 4 and 11, 1891, Nos. 100 to 105 in Palmer Scrapbook at Virginia Historical Society. William Joel Ernst, "Gabriel's Revolt: Black Freedom, White Fear," M.A. thesis, University of Virginia, 1968.

CHAPTER SIX – *Flour, Tobacco, Politics, Parsons, Quoits and Aaron Burr*

1. *Virginia: the New Dominion*, Virginius Dabney, p. 203.

CHAPTER SEVEN – *Schools, Artists, Mansions, Race Tracks and Theaters*

1. *The Seven-Thorned Queen: Postal History of Richmond, Virginia to 1865*, Daniel C. Warren, Vol. 37, American Philatelic Congress, pp. 54–55.
2. Cate, pp. 768–70. *Edgar Allan Poe: A Critical Biography*, Arthur Hobson Quinn, pp. 45–46 and Appendices, Sec. V, pp. 732–41.

CHAPTER EIGHT – *Fire, War and Depression*

1. *Old Richmond Neighborhoods*, Mary Wingfield Scott, p. 20.
2. "Prophet Without Honor," Edmund Berkeley, Jr., *VMHB*, April 1969.

CHAPTER NINE – *Lafayette, Pirates, Slave Traders and the Canal*

1. *Slave-Trading in the Old South*, Frederic Bancroft, pp. 94–104.

CHAPTER TEN – *Edgar Allan Poe in Richmond*

1. *Poe's Richmond*, Agnes M. Bondurant, p. 186.
   I wish to make special acknowledgment of my indebtedness to Arthur Hobson Quinn's biography *Edgar Allan Poe* for much of the material in this chapter. James

Southall Wilson's article "The Personality of Poe," VMHB, April 1959, also was extremely helpful.

## CHAPTER ELEVEN – *Richmond's Leadership Before the Civil War*

1. "Discontent, Disunity and Dissent in the Antebellum South," J. Stephen Knight, Jr., VMHB, Oct. 1973.
2. "Urban Imperialism in the Antebellum South, Richmond, 1850–1861," David R. Goldfield, *Journal of Southern History*, Feb. 1972.
3. Joseph C. Robert, *The Tobacco Kingdom*, p. 187.
4. John D. Imboden, *Report on Internal Commerce of the U.S., 1886*. p. 170, quoted by Goldfield, op. cit.
5. Robert, op. cit., p. 72.

## CHAPTER TWELVE – *On the Edge of the Precipice*

1. "Charles Dickens Sends His Sympathy," Randolph W. Church, *Virginia Cavalcade*, Summer 1971.
2. Cate, pp. 864–66, 875.
3. "The SS *Arctic* and Professor Johnson," Harry J. Warthen, Jr., M.D., in *Virginia Medical Monthly*, July 1974.
4. Jean Gottmann, *Virginia in Our Century*, p. 376. Francis Earle Lutz, *Chesterfield, An Old Virginia County*, p. 219.
5. Julia C. Pollard, *Richmond's Story*, p. 108.

## CHAPTER THIRTEEN – *Inside the Confederate Citadel*

1. Virginius Dabney, *Virginia: The New Dominion*, pp. 296–98. Margaret Sanborn, *Robert E. Lee*, Vol. II, p. 321.
2. Thomas C. DeLeon, *Four Years in Rebel Capitals*, pp. 224–25. Alfred Hoyt Bill, *The Beleaguered City*, pp. 124–25.
3. Clifford Dowdey, *Experiment in Rebellion*, p. 305. Wyndham B. Blanton, M.D., *Medicine in Virginia in the Nineteenth Century*, pp. 301–2.
4. James D. Horan, *Desperate Women*, p. 130.
5. Mary Wingfield Scott, *Houses of Old Richmond*, p. 70. "Crazy Bet, Union Spy," James H. Bailey, VC, Spring 1952. Horan, op. cit., p. 137.
6. DeLeon, op. cit., pp. 313–14, 316. Charles B. Dew, *Ironmaker to the Confederacy*, pp. 207–9. Bill, op. cit., pp. 156, 304.
7. Douglas S. Freeman, *The South to Posterity*, p. 14. Lenoir Chambers, *Stonewall Jackson*, Vol. II, pp. 458–59.

## CHAPTER FOURTEEN – *Rendezvous with Disaster*

1. Booker T. Washington, *Up from Slavery*, pp. 12–15. "Women of the Lost Cause," Bell I. Wiley, *American History Illustrated*, Dec. 1973.

2. Rembert W. Patrick, *"The Fall of Richmond,* p. 68. Alfred Hoyt Bill, *The Beleaguered City,* pp. 275–76.

## CHAPTER FIFTEEN – *Up from the Ruins*

1. Martha W. Owens, *The Development of Public Schools for Negroes in Richmond, Va., 1865–1900,* unpub. M.S. thesis, pp. 19–20.
2. Lenoir Chambers, *Salt Water and Printer's Ink,* p. 53.
3. Jack P. Maddex, Jr., *The Virginia Conservatives, 1867–1879,* p. 90. W. Asbury Christian, *Richmond, Her Past and Present,* p. 320.

## CHAPTER SIXTEEN – *Putting the War Behind*

1. "History of Monumental Church," J. Ambler Johnston, Medical College of Virginia *Bulletin,* Summer 1965. *Richmond, Her Past and Present,* W. Asbury Christian, p. 362.
2. Richmond *Enquirer,* April 19, 1874. Richmond *Dispatch,* April 22, 1874. *The Springs of Virginia,* Percival Reniers, p. 256.
3. *William Mahone of Virginia,* Nelson M. Blake, p. 113.
4. The entire sermon appears in *The Industrial History of the Negro Race of the U.S.,* Giles B. Jackson and D. Webster Davis, pp. 334–47.
5. "Industrial and Urban Progress in Virginia from 1880 to 1900," Allen W. Moger, *VMHB,* July 1958. Christian, op. cit., pp. 400–1.

## CHAPTER SEVENTEEN – *The Not Always Gay Nineties*

1. Leslie Winston Smith, *A Historical Study of the Role of the Industrialist in the Tobacco, Flour and Textile Industries of Virginia, 1866–1890,* pp. 41–45. See also Edith Lindeman's comprehensive article in the Richmond *Times-Dispatch,* Aug. 23, 1970, and S. J. Moore's booklet *The Jefferson Hotel.*
2. For a fuller account, see "The Richmond Academy of Medicine, 1820–1900," Harry J. Warthen, *Virginia Medical Monthly,* Oct. 1962.
3. Ruth Robertson McGuire, *Stuart McGuire,* p. 19.
4. J. Morrison Hutcheson, "George Ben Johnston, M.D., LL.D.," *Annals of Medical History,* Vol. 10, No. 1.
5. Thomas E. Walton, *The Negro in Richmond, 1880–1890,* p. 55.
6. "Virginia's Negro Regiment in the Spanish-American War," Willard B. Gatewood, Jr., *VMHB,* April 1972.

## CHAPTER EIGHTEEN – *Moving into the New Century*

1. Louis R. Harlan, *Booker T. Washington,* Preface, ix; pp. 297–98. Melvin Drimmer, ed., *Black History,* pp. 346–53, quoting August Meier's *Booker T. Washington.*

2. Ann B. Field, *Negro Protest in the New South: John Mitchell Jr.*, 1863–1902, p. 92.
3. Ann F. Alexander, *Black Protest in the New South: John Mitchell Jr.*, (1863–1929) and the Richmond Planet, p. 276, footnote.
4. Joan R. Sherman, "Daniel Webster Davis," *VMHB*, Oct. 1973.
5. Edgar E. MacDonald, "Glasgow, Cabell and Richmond," *Mississippi Quarterly*, Autumn 1974. Edgar E. MacDonald, "Cabell's Richmond Trial," *Southern Literary Journal*, Fall 1970. Ellen Glasgow, *The Woman Within*, pp. 129–36.

CHAPTER NINETEEN – *World War I, Cabell, Glasgow and the Roaring Twenties*

1. E. Stanly Godbold, Jr., *Ellen Glasgow and the Woman Within*, pp. 179–80.
2. Ibid., p. 131.
3. Ibid., pp. 122, 136.
4. John W. Daniel, *Speeches and Orations of John Warwick Daniel*, p. 411.

CHAPTER TWENTY – *The Great Depression and World War II*

1. J. Bryan III, "Richmond," *Saturday Evening Post*, Aug. 28, 1948.
2. F. Earle Lutz, *Richmond in World War II*, p. 34.

CHAPTER TWENTY-ONE – *The Postwar Years*

1. Robert A. Rankin, "The Richmond Crusade for Voters," *University of Va. News Letter*, Sept. 1974. Conversation with Dr. William S. Thornton.
2. Reuben E. Alley, *A History of Baptists in Virginia*, p. 321. Alley, *Frederic W. Boatwright*, pp. 92, 97–98, 110, 112, 113, 116–17.
3. Kilpatrick to Tom Waring, December 9, 1955; to Paul D. Hastings, December 28, 1955; to Hugh D. Grant, February 25, 1959; to Harry F. Byrd, January 18, 1960, cited by James W. Ely, Jr., in *The Crisis of Conservative Virginia*, unpub. Ph.D. diss. Kilpatrick to author, November 14, 1970.
4. James K. Sanford, *A Century of Commerce*, p. 187.
5. *U.S. News & World Report*, July 26, 1971, pp. 66–70.

CHAPTER TWENTY-TWO – *Richmond in the Mid-Seventies*

1. *Richmond News Leader*, May 18, 1973, from a study by Max Rogel's Washington, D.C., public relations firm for Continental Investment Corp. of Boston, Mass.
2. Report of Virginia Employment Commission.
3. I have compiled this list with the assistance of several veteran Richmond M.D.s.

# BIBLIOGRAPHY

## BOOKS

ABERNETHY, THOMAS P.: *The Burr Conspiracy*, New York, Oxford, 1954.

ADAIR, DOUGLASS: *Fame and the Founding Fathers*, New York, Norton, 1974.

ALLEN, HERVEY: *Israfel: The Life and Times of Edgar Allan Poe*, New York, Doran, 1926.

ALLEY, REUBEN E.: *Frederic W. Boatwright*, Richmond, U. of Richmond, 1973.

————: *A History of Baptists in Virginia*, Richmond, Virginia Baptist General Board, 1974.

AMBLER, CHARLES H.: *Thomas Ritchie: A Study in Virginia Politics*, Richmond, Bell Book, 1913.

AMMON, HARRY: *James Monroe: The Quest For National Identity*, New York, McGraw-Hill, 1971.

ANBUREY, THOMAS: *Travels Through the Interior Parts of America*, Vol. II, London, 1791.

ANDREWS, J. CUTLER: *The South Reports the Civil War*, Princeton, Princeton U. Press, 1970.

ANDREWS, MATTHEW PAGE: *The Soul of a Nation*, New York, Scribner's, 1943.

APTHEKER, HERBERT: *American Slave Revolts*, New York, Columbia U. Press, 1944.

ARBER, EDWIN A.: *Capt. John Smith of Willoughby*, Vol. I, Westminster, 1895.

BAGBY, GEORGE W.: *The Old Virginia Gentleman and Other Sketches*, New York, Scribner's, 1910.

BALLAGH, JAMES C.: *A History of Slavery in Virginia*, Baltimore, Johns Hopkins U. Press, 1902.

BANCROFT, FREDERIC: *Slave Trading in the Old South*, Baltimore, J. H. Furst, 1931.

BARBOUR, PHILIP L.: *The Three Worlds of Capt. John Smith*, Boston, Houghton Mifflin, 1964.

BASSETT, JOHN S., ed: *The Writings of Col. William Byrd of Westover*, Garden City, Doubleday, 1901.

BEIRNE, FRANCIS F.: *"Shout Treason": The Trial of Aaron Burr*, New York, Hastings, 1959.

BENTLEY, GEORGE R.: *A History of the Freedmen's Bureau*, Philadelphia, U. of Pennsylvania Press, 1955.

BEVERIDGE, ALBERT J.: *The Life of John Marshall*, 2 vols., Boston, Houghton Mifflin, n.d.

BEVERLEY, ROBERT: *The History and Present State of Virginia*, ed. with intro. by Louis B. Wright, Chapel Hill, U. of North Carolina Press, 1947.

BILL, ALFRED HOYT: *The Beleaguered City*, New York, Knopf, 1946.

BLAKE, NELSON M.: *William Mahone of Virginia*, Richmond, Garrett & Massie, 1935.

BLANTON, WYNDHAM B., M.D.: *Medicine in Virginia in the Seventeenth Century, Medicine in Virginia in the Eighteenth Century, Medicine in Virginia in the Nineteenth Century*, Richmond, William Byrd Press, 1930, Garrett & Massie, 1931, 1933.

BOLES, JOHN M., ed.: *America: the Middle Period*, Charlottesville, U. Press of Virginia, 1973.

BONDURANT, AGNES M.: *Poe's Richmond*, Garrett & Massie, 1942.

BOYD, JULIAN P.: *The Papers of Thomas Jefferson*, Vol. IX, Princeton, Princeton U. Press, 1951.

BRODIE, FAWN M.: *Thomas Jefferson: An Intimate Portrait*, New York, Norton, 1974.

BROOKS, VAN WYCK: *The World of Washington Irving*, New York, Dutton, 1944.

BROWN, ALEXANDER: *The Cabells and Their Kin*, Richmond, Garrett & Massie, 1939.

BRUCE, KATHLEEN: *Virginia Iron Manufacture in the Slave Era*, New York, Century, 1931.

BRUCE, WILLIAM CABELL: *John Randolph of Roanoke*, 2 vols., New York, Putnam, 1922.

BRYAN, JOHN STEWART: *Joseph Bryan, His Times, His Family and His Friends*, Richmond, Whittet & Shepperson, 1935.

BRYDON, G. MACLAREN: *Virginia's Mother Church*, Vol. I, Richmond, Virginia Historical Society, 1947; Vol. II, Philadelphia, Church History Society, 1952.

BUCKINGHAM, JAMES S.: *The Slave States of America*, Vol. II, London, Fisher & Son, 1842.

BUNI, ANDREW: *The Negro in Virginia Politics, 1902–1965*, Charlottesville, U. Press of Virginia, 1967.

BURNABY, REV. ANDREW: *Travels Through the Middle Settlements of North America in the Years 1759 and 1760*, second ed., London, 1775.

BYRD, WILLIAM: A *Journey to the Land of Eden*, New York, Macy-Masius, Vanguard, 1928.

————: *The Secret Diary of William Byrd of Westover, 1709–1712*, Louis B. Wright and Marion Tinling, eds., Richmond, Dietz, 1941.

————: *The London Diary, 1717–1721*, Louis B. Wright and Marion Tinling, eds., New York, Oxford, 1958.

CABELL, JAMES BRANCH: *Let Me Lie*, New York, Farrar, Straus, 1947.

————: *As I Remember It*, New York, McBride, 1955.

*Calendar of Virginia State Papers*, Vol. VI, ed. by Sherwin McRae, Richmond, 1886; Vol. IX, ed. by H. W. Flournoy, Richmond, 1890; Vol. X, 1892.

CALISCH, EDWARD N.: *Three Score and Twenty*, intro. by Edith Lindeman Calisch, Richmond, Old Dominion Press, 1945.

CAMPBELL, CHARLES: *History of the Colony and Ancient Dominion of Virginia*, Spartanburg, Reprint Co., 1965.

CARAVATI, CHARLES M., M.D., *Medicine in Richmond, 1900–1975*, Foreword by Virginius Dabney, Whittet & Shepperson, 1975.

CHAMBERS, LENOIR, and SHANK, JOSEPH E.: *Salt Water and Printers Ink*, Chapel Hill, U. of North Carolina Press, 1967.

CHANNING, WILLIAM H., ed.: *Memoir of William Ellery Channing*, Vol. I, Boston, Crosby & Nichols, 1934.

CHASTELLUX, MARQUIS DE: *Travels in North America in the Years 1780, 1781, 1782*, New York, White, Galleher & White, 1827.

CHESNUT, MARY BOYKIN: *A Diary From Dixie*, Ben Ames Williams, ed., Boston, Houghton Mifflin, 1949.

CHINARD, GILBERT, ed.: *Houdon in America*, Baltimore, Johns Hopkins U. Press, 1930.

————, ed.: *A Huguenot Exile in Virginia*, New York, Press of the Pioneers, 1934.

CHRISTIAN, GEORGE L.: *The Capitol Disaster*, Richmond, Richmond Press, 1915.

CHRISTIAN, W. ASBURY: *Richmond—Her Past and Present*, Richmond, L. H. Jenkins, 1912.

CLARK, EMILY: *Stuffed Peacocks*, New York, Knopf, 1927.

————: *Innocence Abroad*, New York, Knopf, 1931.

COLLIS, MAURICE: *Nancy Astor*, New York, Dutton, 1960.

COUPER, WILLIAM: *A Hundred Years at V.M.I.*, Richmond, Garrett & Massie, 1939.

CRESSON, W. P.: *James Monroe*, Chapel Hill, U. of North Carolina Press, 1940.

CROWE, EYRE: *With Thackeray in America*, New York, Scribner's, 1893.

CUTCHINS, JOHN A.: *A Famous Command: The Richmond Light Infantry Blues*, Richmond, Garrett & Massie, 1934.

————: *Memories of Old Richmond, 1881–1944*, Verona, Va., McClure Press, 1973.

DABNEY, VIRGINIUS: *Virginia: The New Dominion*, Garden City, Doubleday, 1971.

————: *Dry Messiah: The Life of Bishop Cannon*, New York, Knopf, 1949.

DABNEY, WENDELL P.: *Maggie L. Walker and the International Order of St. Luke*, Cincinnati, Dabney Pub. Co., 1927.

DANA, CHARLES A.: *Recollections of the Civil War*, New York, Appleton, 1898.

DANIEL, JOHN W.: *Speeches and Orations*, Lynchburg, J. P. Bell, 1911.

DANIELS, JONATHAN: *The Randolphs of Virginia*, Garden City, Doubleday, 1972.

DAVIS, RICHARD BEALE: *Intellectual Life in Jefferson's Virginia, 1790–1830*, Chapel Hill, U. of North Carolina Press, 1964.

————: *Francis Walker Gilmer, Life and Learning in Jefferson's Virginia*, Richmond, Dietz, 1939.

DECKER, FLORENCE B.: *Always of Good Courage: The Life of Henry Walker Decker, 1891–1971*, Aylett, Va., privately pub., 1974.

DE LA ROCHEFOUCAULT LIANCOURT, DUKES *Travels Through the U.S. of North America in the Years 1795, 1796 and 1797*, Vol. III, second ed., London, R. Phillips, 1800.

DELEON, T. C.: *Four Years in Rebel Capitals*, New York, Collier, 1962.

————: *Belles, Beaux and Brains of the Sixties*, New York, G. W. Dillingham, 1909.

DENNETT, JOHN R.: *The South As It Is, 1865–1866*, New York, Viking, 1965.

DEW, CHARLES: *Ironmaker to the Confederacy*, New Haven, Yale U. Press, 1966.

DOHERTY, JAMES L.: *Race and Education in Richmond*, Richmond, privately pub., 1972.

DOUBLEDAY, F. N.: *The Memoirs of a Publisher*, Garden City, Doubleday, 1972.

DOWDEY, CLIFFORD: *Experiment in Rebellion*, Garden City, Doubleday, 1946.

DRIMMER, MELVIN, ed.: *Black History, A Reappraisal*, Garden City, Doubleday, 1968.

DULANEY, PAUL S.: *The Architecture of Historic Richmond*, Charlottesville, U. Press of Virginia, 1968.

DUNAWAY, WAYLAND F.: *History of the James River & Kanawha Co.*, New York, AMS Press, 1969.

EATON, CLEMENT: *The Growth of Southern Civilization, 1790–1860*, New York, Harper, 1961.

————: *Freedom of Thought in the Old South*, Gloucester, Mass., Peter Smith, 1951.

ECKENRODE, H. J.: *The Revolution in Virginia*, Boston, Houghton Mifflin, 1916.

————: The Political History of Virginia During Reconstruction, Gloucester, Mass., Peter Smith, 1966.

EDMUNDS, POCAHONTAS W.: Virginians Out Front, Richmond, Whittet & Shepperson, 1972.

EWELL, GEN. R. S.: Evacuation of Richmond, Vol. 13, Southern Hist. Soc. Papers.

EZEKIEL, HERBERT T.: Recollections of a Virginia Newspaper Man, Richmond, Herbert T. Ezekiel pub., 1920.

———— and LICHTENSTEIN, GASTON: History of the Jews of Richmond, Richmond, Herbert T. Ezekiel pub., 1917.

FARRAR, EMMIE FERGUSON: Old Virginia Houses Along the James, New York, Hastings, 1957.

Fifty Years in Richmond, 1898–1948, Richmond, Valentine Museum, 1948.

Fifty Years of Collegiate: A History of the Collegiate Schools, 1915–1965, Richmond, Collegiate Historical Society, 1967.

FOSTER, SIR AUGUSTUS JOHN: Jeffersonian America, ed. with intro. by Richard Beale Davis, San Marino, Calif., Huntington Lib., 1954.

FRANKLIN, JOHN HOPE: The Militant South, 1800–1861, Cambridge, Harvard U. Press, 1956.

————: From Slavery to Freedom, New York, Knopf, 1967.

FREEMAN, DOUGLAS S.: R. E. Lee, 4 vols., New York, Scribner, 1934, 1935.

————: The South to Posterity, New York, Scribner, 1939.

————: Lee's Lieutenants, Vol. III, New York, Scribner, 1944.

GAY, THOMAS B.: The Hunton, Williams Firm and Its Predecessors, Vol. I, Richmond, Lewis Printing Co., 1971.

GODBOLD, E. STANLY, JR.: Ellen Glasgow and the Woman Within, Baton Rouge, Louisiana State U. Press, 1972.

GOTTMANN, JEAN: Virginia in Our Century, Charlottesville, U. Press of Virginia, 1969.

GRIGSBY, HUGH BLAIR: The Virginia Convention of 1829–30, New York, Da Capo Press, 1969.

GWATHMEY, JOHN H.: Justice John, Richmond, Dietz, 1934.

HANKINS, DEWITT: The First Fifty Years: A History of St. Christopher's School, Richmond, Whittet & Shepperson, 1961.

HARLAN, HOWARD H.: John Jasper: A Case History in Leadership, Charlottesville, U. of Virginia Press, 1936.

HARLAN, LOUIS R.: Booker T. Washington: The Making of a Black Leader, New York, Oxford, 1972.

HARLAND, MARION: Autobiography, New York, Harper, 1910.

HARRIS, ABRAM L.: The Negro as Capitalist: A Study of Banking and Business Among American Negroes, Amer. Acad. Polit. and Soc. Science, 1936.

HARRISON, MRS. BURTON: Recollections Grave and Gay, New York, Scribner, 1911.

HARRISON, FAIRFAX: *The Roanoke Stud, 1795–1833,* Richmond, Old Dominion Press, 1930.

———: *Landmarks of Old Prince William,* Berryville, Chesapeake Book Co., 1964.

HATCH, ALDEN: *The Byrds of Virginia,* New York, Holt, 1969.

HATCHER, WILLIAM E.: *John Jasper,* New York, Negro University Press, 1969.

HIBBS, HENRY H.: *A History of the Richmond Professional Institute,* Richmond, Whittet & Shepperson, 1973.

HOBSON, FRED C. JR.: *Serpent in Eden: H. L. Mencken and the South,* Chapel Hill, U. of North Carolina Press, 1974.

HORAN, JAMES D.: *Desperate Women,* New York, Putnam, 1952.

HUBBELL, JAY B.: *The South in American Literature,* Durham, Duke U. Press, 1954.

———: *South and Southwest,* Durham, Duke U. Press, 1965.

JACKSON, GILES B., and DAVIS, D. WEBSTER: *The Industrial History of the Negro Race in the U.S.,* Richmond, Virginia Press, 1908.

JACKSON, LUTHER P.: *Negro Officeholders in Virginia, 1865–1895,* Norfolk, Guide Quality Press, 1945.

JAMES, HENRY: *The American Scene,* Harper, 1907.

JANSON, CHARLES W.: *The Stranger in America,* London, Albion Press, 1807.

JONES, HUGH: *The Present State of Virginia,* ed. with intro. by Richard L. Morton, Chapel Hill, U. of North Carolina Press, 1956.

JONES, J. B.: *A Rebel War Clerk's Diary,* 2 vols., ed. by Howard Swiggett, New York, Old Hickory Bookshop, 1935.

JONES, VIRGIL CARRINGTON: *Eight Hours Before Richmond,* New York, Holt, 1957.

JORDAN, WINTHROP P.: *White over Black,* Chapel Hill, U. of North Carolina Press, 1968.

Journal of the Virginia Senate, 1801–2.

Journal of the Virginia House, 1801

KERN, M. ETHEL KELLEY: *The Trail of the Three Notched Road,* Richmond, William Byrd Press, 1928.

KING, EDWARD: *The Great South,* Vol. II, New York, Burt Franklin, 1869.

KUHLMANN, CHARLES B.: *The Development of the Flour Milling Industry in the U.S.,* Boston, Houghton Mifflin, 1929.

LATROBE, BENJAMIN H.: *The Journal of Latrobe,* New York, Appleton, 1905.

LITTLE, JOHN P.: *History of Richmond,* Richmond, Dietz, 1933.

LOCKE, MARY S.: *Anti-Slavery in America,* Boston, Ginn & Co., 1901.

LOSSING, BENSON J.: *Pictorial Field Book of the Revolution,* Vol. II, Freeport, N.Y., Books for Libraries Press, 1969.

LUTZ, F. EARLE: *Richmond in World War II,* Richmond, Dietz, 1951.

———: *Chesterfield, An Old Virginia County,* Richmond, Dietz, 1954.

MACRAE, DAVID: *The Americans at Home,* New York, Dutton, 1952.

MADDEX, JACK P. JR.: *The Virginia Conservatives, 1867–1879*, Chapel Hill, U. of North Carolina Press, 1970.

MALONE, DUMAS: *Jefferson the Virginian*, Vol. I, 1948; *Jefferson and the Ordeal of Liberty*, Vol. III, 1962; *Jefferson the President, First Term*, Vol. IV, 1970; *Jefferson the President, Second Term*, Vol. V, 1974, Boston, Little Brown.

MANARIN, LOUIS H., ed.: *Richmond at War: Minutes of the City Council, 1861–1865*, Chapel Hill, U. of North Carolina Press, 1966.

MARAMBAUD, PIERRE: *William Byrd of Westover*, Charlottesville, U. Press of Virginia, 1971.

MASON, FRANCES NORTON: *John Norton & Sons, Merchants of London and Virginia*, Richmond, Dietz, 1937.

———: *My Dearest Polly*, Richmond, Garrett & Massie, 1961.

MASSEY, MARY ELIZABETH: *Bonnet Brigades*, New York, Knopf, 1966.

MAYO, BERNARD: *Henry Clay, Statesman of the New West*, Hamden, Conn., Archon Books, 1966.

MAYS, DAVID J.: *Edmund Pendleton*, 2 vols., Cambridge, Harvard U. Press, 1952.

McCOLLEY, ROBERT: *Slavery and Jeffersonian Virginia*, Urbana, U. of Ill. Press, 1964.

McCONNELL, JOHN P.: *Negroes and Their Treatment in Virginia from 1865 to 1867*, Pulaski, Va., B. D. Smith & Bros., 1910.

McGUIRE, RUTH ROBERTSON: *Stuart McGuire*, Richmond, William Byrd Press, 1956.

McPHERSON, JAMES M.: *The Struggle for Equality*, Princeton, Princeton U. Press, 1964.

MEADE, ROBERT D.: *Patrick Henry, Practical Revolutionary*, Philadelphia, Lippincott, 1969.

———: *Judah P. Benjamin: Confederate Statesman*, New York, Oxford, 1943.

MEADE, BISHOP William: *Old Churches, Ministers, and Families of Virginia*, Philadelphia, Lippincott, 1857.

MEAGHER, MARGARET: *History of Education in Richmond*, Richmond, Works Progress Administration, 1939.

MENDELSOHN, JACK: *Channing, the Reluctant Radical*, Boston, Little Brown, 1972.

MORGAN, EDMUND S.: *Virginians at Home*, Williamsburg, Colonial Williamsburg, 1952.

MORTON, RICHARD L.: *Colonial Virginia*, 2 vols., Chapel Hill, U. of North Carolina Press, 1960.

———: *The Negro in Virginia Politics, 1865–1902*, Spartanburg, Reprint Co., 1973.

MULLIN, GERALD W.: *Flight and Rebellion: Slave Resistance in 18th Century Virginia*, New York, Oxford, 1972.

MUNFORD, GEORGE WYTHE: *The Two Parsons*, Richmond, J. K. K. Sleight, 1884.

NUCKOLS, R. R.: *A History of the Government of the City of Richmond*, Williams Printing Co., 1899.

*Of Two Virginia Gentlemen and Their McGuire's University School*, Richmond, Carmine Graphics, 1972.

OLMSTEAD, FREDERICK L.: *The Cotton Kingdom*, New York, Knopf, 1953.

O'NEAL, WILLIAM B.: *Architecture in Virginia*, New York, Walker & Co., 1968.

PATRICK, REMBERT W.: *The Fall of Richmond*, Baton Rouge, Louisiana State U. Press, 1960.

———: *The Reconstruction of the Nation*, New York, Oxford, 1967.

PATTERSON, A. W.: *Personal Recollections of Woodrow Wilson*, Richmond, Whittet & Shepperson, 1929.

PEARSON, CHARLES C.: *The Readjuster Movement in Virginia*, New Haven, Yale U. Press, 1917.

PELL, EDWARD L., ed.: *A Hundred Years of Richmond Methodism*, Idea Pub. Co., n.d.

PEMBER, PHOEBE Y.: *A Southern Woman's Story—Life in Confederate Richmond*, Bell I. Wiley, ed., Jackson, Tenn., McCavat-Mercer Press, 1959.

PHILLIPS, ULRICH B.: *American Negro Slavery*, Gloucester, Mass., Peter Smith, 1959.

PINCHBECK, RAYMOND P.: *The Virginia Negro Artisan and Tradesman*, Richmond, William Byrd Press, 1926.

POLLARD, JULIA C.: *Richmond's Story*, pub. by Richmond Public School Bd., 1954.

PORTER, ADMIRAL DAVID D.: *Incidents and Anecdotes of the Civil War*, New York, Appleton, 1885.

QUARLES, BENJAMIN: *The Negro in the Civil War*, Boston, Little Brown, 1953.

QUINN, ARTHUR HOBSON: *Edgar Allan Poe*, New York, Appleton, 1941.

RANDOLPH, EDMUND: *History of Virginia*, ed. with intro. by Arthur H. Shaffer, Charlottesville, U. Press of Virginia, 1970.

RENIERS, PERCIVAL: *The Springs of Virginia*, Chapel Hill, U. of North Carolina Press, 1941.

*Richmond, Capital of Virginia: Approaches to Its History*, by various hands, Richmond, Whittet & Shepperson, 1938.

*Richmond Portraits in an Exhibition of Makers of Richmond, 1737–1860*, Richmond, Valentine Museum, 1949.

ROBERT, JOSEPH C.: *The Tobacco Kingdom*, Durham, Duke U. Press, 1938.

ROSS, CAPT. FITZGERALD: *A Visit to the Cities and Camps of the Confederate States*, Edinburgh and London, Blackwood, 1865.

ROSS, ISHBEL: *First Lady of the South, The Life of Mrs. Jefferson Davis*, New York, Harper, 1958.

ROTBERG, ROBERT L., and CLAGUE, CHRISTOPHER K.: *Haiti: The Politics of Squalor*, Boston, Houghton Mifflin, 1971.

ROYALL, ANNE: *Sketches of History, Life and Manners in the U.S.*, pub. by author, 1826.

ROYALL, WILLIAM L.: *Some Reminiscences*, New York, Neale Pub. Co., 1909.

RYLAND, GARNETT: *The Baptists of Virginia*, Richmond, Whittet & Shepperson, 1955.

SANBORN, MARGARET: *Robert E. Lee*, 2 vols., Philadelphia, Lippincott, 1966, 1967.

SANFORD, JAMES K., ed. and compiler: *A Century of Commerce*, Richmond, Whittet & Shepperson, 1967.

SANGER, WILLIAM T.: *As I Remember*, Richmond, Dietz, 1972.

————: *Medical College of Virginia Before 1925 and University College of Medicine, 1893–1913*, Richmond, MCV Foundation, 1973.

SCHOEPF, JOHANN: *Travels in the Confederation, 1783–1784*, Vol. II, Cleveland, O., Arthur H. Clarke, 1911.

SCOTT, ANN F.: *The Southern Lady: From Pedestal to Politics, 1830–1930*, Chicago, U. of Chicago Press, 1970.

SCOTT, MARY WINGFIELD: *Houses of Old Richmond*, Valentine Museum, 1941.

————: *Old Richmond Neighborhoods*, Richmond, Whittet & Shepperson, 1950.

SIMCOE, LT. COL. J. G.: *Simcoe's Military Journal*, New York, Bartlett & Wellford, 1844.

SOMERS, ROBERT: *The Southern States Since the War*, New York, Macmillan, 1871.

SOUTHALL, J. P. C.: *In the Days of My Youth*, Chapel Hill, U. of North Carolina Press, 1947.

STANARD, MARY NEWTON: *Colonial Virginia, Its People and Its Customs*, Philadelphia, Lippincott, 1917.

————: *The Story of Virginia's First Century*, Philadelphia, Lippincott, 1928.

————: *Richmond, Its People and Its Story*, Philadelphia, Lippincott, 1923.

STAROBIN, ROBERT S.: *Industrial Slavery in the Old South*, New York, Oxford, 1970.

STERLING, ADA, ed.: *A Belle of the Fifties*, New York, Doubleday, 1904.

STITH, WILLIAM: *The History of the First Discovery and Settlement of Virginia*, Spartanburg, Reprint Co., 1965.

STRAUSS, LEWIS L.: *Men and Decisions*, Garden City, Doubleday, 1962.

STRODE, HUDSON: *Jefferson Davis*, Vols. II and III, New York, Harcourt, 1959, 1964.

STUART, M. S.: *An Economic Detour, A History of Insurance in the Lives of American Negroes*, New York, Wendell Malliet, 1940.

SYDNOR, BLANCHE WHITE: *First Baptist Church, 1780–1855*, Richmond, Whittet & Shepperson, 1955.

SYKES, CHRISTOPHER: *Nancy, The Life of Lady Astor*, New York, Harper, 1972.

TAYLOR, ALRUTHEUS A.: *The Negro in the Reconstruction of Virginia*, Washington, D.C., Assoc. for Study of Negro Life and Hist., 1926.

TAYLOR, WILLIAM H.: *The Book of Travels of a Doctor of Physic*, Philadelphia, Lippincott, 1871.

———: *De Quibus: Discourses and Essays*, Richmond, Bell Book, 1908.

THOMAS, EMORY M.: *The Confederate State of Richmond*, Austin, U. of Texas Press, 1971.

*The First 125 Years*, Bulletin, Med. Coll. of Virginia, Fall 1963.

*The Negro in Virginia*, Works Prog. Admin., New York, Hastings, 1940.

TREVELYAN, G. M.: *Illustrated English Social History*, Vol. II, London, Longman's, 1952.

TROWBRIDGE, JOHN T.: *The Desolate South, 1865–1866*, Gordon Carroll, ed., New York, Duell, Sloan, 1956.

TYLER, LYON G.: *Narratives of Early Virginia, 1606–1625*, New York, Barnes & Noble, 1959.

———: *The Letters and Times of the Tylers*, Vol. I, Richmond, Whittet & Shepperson, 1884.

VALENTINE, ELIZABETH GRAY: *Dawn to Twilight*, Richmond, William Byrd Press, 1929.

*Virginia, a Guide to the Old Dominion*, compiled by Works Prog. Admin., New York, Oxford, 1940.

WADDELL, JOSEPH A.: *Annals of Augusta County*, Richmond, William E. Jones, 1886.

WADE, RICHARD C.: *Slavery in the Cities*, New York, Oxford, 1964.

WALLACE, CHARLES M.: *The Boy Gangs of Richmond in the Dear Old Days*, Richmond, Richmond Press, 1938.

WASHINGTON, BOOKER T.: *Up from Slavery*, Garden City, Doubleday, n.d.

WEDDELL, ALEXANDER W.: *Richmond in Old Prints, 1737–1887*, Foreword by Douglas S. Freeman, Richmond, Johnson Pub. Co., 1932.

WEISS, SUSAN ARCHER: *The Home Life of Poe*, New York, Broadway Pub. Co., 1907.

WELD, ISAAC JR.: *Travels Through the States of America*, Vol. I, second ed., London, 1799.

WERTENBAKER, THOMAS J.: *Norfolk: Historic Southern Port*, second ed., Marvin W. Schlegel, ed., Durham, Duke U. Press, 1962.

———: *Torchbearer of the Revolution*, Princeton, Princeton U. Press, 1940.

WESSELLS, JOHN H. JR.: *The Bank of Virginia*, Foreword by Virginius Dabney, Charlottesville, U. Press of Virginia, 1973.

WILEY, BELL I.: *The Life of Johnny Reb*, Indianapolis, Bobbs-Merrill, 1943.

WILKINSON, J. HARVIE III: *Harry Byrd and the Changing Face of Virginia Politics*, Charlottesville, U. Press of Virginia, 1968.

WILLIAMS, FRANCES LEIGH: *Matthew Fontaine Maury, Scientist of the Sea*, New Brunswick, Rutgers U. Press, 1963.

————: *They Faced the Future*, Richmond, Whittet & Shepperson, 1951.

————: *A Century of Service*, Whittet & Shepperson, 1965.

WILLIAMS, J. K. B.: *Changed Views and Unforeseen Prosperity: Richmond of 1890 Gets a Monument to Lee*, Richmond, privately printed, 1969.

WIRT, WILLIAM: *The Letters of a British Spy*, New York, Harper, 1856, tenth ed.

WISE, JOHN S.: *The End of an Era*, ed. with intro by Curtis Carroll Davis, New York, Yoseloff, 1965.

WOLFE, TOM: *The New Journalism*, New York, Harper, 1973.

WRIGHT, LOUIS B., and TINLING, MARION: *Quebec to Carolina in 1785–1786*, San Marino, Huntington Lib., 1943.

WUST, KLAUS: *The Virginia Germans*, Charlottesville, U. Press of Virginia, 1969.

WYNES, CHARLES E.: *Race Relations in Virginia, 1870–1902*, Charlottesville, U. of Virginia Press, 1961.

## PAMPHLETS, MAGAZINES, TRACTS, ETC.

The following abbreviations are used:
*Virginia Magazine of History and Biography*, VMHB.
*Virginia Cavalcade*, VC.
*Journal of Southern History*, JSH.
Richmond *Times-Dispatch*, RTD.
Richmond *News Leader*, RNL.
*University of Virginia News Letter*, UVNL.
*Virginia Medical Monthly*, VMM.

"A Richmond Physician: George Ben Johnston, M.D., LL.D.," *Catholic Virginian*, July and Aug. 1931.

A Virginia Matron, "Richmond Fifty Years Ago," *The Land We Love*, July and Oct. 1867.

ALEXANDER, ROBERT L.: *Maximilian Godefroy in Virginia*," VMHB, Oct. 1961.

ALFRIEND, EDWIN M.: *Social Life in Richmond During the War*," *Cosmopolitan*, Dec. 1891.

"An Architect Looks at Richmond," VC, Winter 1867, unsigned.

AMMON, HARRY: "James Monroe and the Era of Good Feelings," VMHB, Oct. 1958.

ASHWORTH, MARY WELLS: "Douglas Southall Freeman," monograph pub. by Scribner, n.d.

Atkinson, Thomas P.: "Richmond and Her People As They Were in 1810, 1811 and 1812," Richmond *Whig & Advertiser*, Aug. 14, 18, 21, 25, 28, Sept. 5, 18, 22, 1868.

Bailey, James H.: "The Sullys, Searchers After Beauty," VC, Summer 1959.

————: "Crazy Bet, Union Spy," VC, Spring 1952.

Baker, Robert E.: "Richmond Quietly Leads Way in Race Relations," Washington *Post*, July 29, 1962.

Barbour, Philip, L.: "The First Reconnaissance of the James," VC, Autumn 1967.

————: "Captain Newport Meets Opechancanough," VC, Winter 1968.

Barrett, Philip: "Gilbert Hunt, the City Blacksmith," Richmond, James Woodhouse & Co., 1859.

Berkeley, Edmund Jr.: "Quoits, the Sport of Gentlemen," VC, Summer 1965.

————: "Prophet Without Honor: Christopher McPherson, Free Person of Color," VMHB, April 1969.

Berry, Thomas S.: "The Rise of Flour Milling in Richmond," VMHB, Oct. 1970.

*Black Swan, The*, pub. in Richmond at irreg. intervals, Dec. 1926 to Jan. 1931.

"The Negro in Richmond," Report of the Negro Welfare Survey Committee, pub. by Richmond Council of Social Agencies, 1929.

Blackford, Charles M.: "The Trials and Trial of Jefferson Davis," address to Va. State Bar Assn., 1900, Richmond, Whittet & Shepperson, 1960.

Blanton, Wyndham B., M.D.: "The Egyptian Building and Its Place in Medicine," VMM, March 1940.

Blanton, Natalie: Miss Jennie and Her Letters," Richmond, pub. by Ellett-St. Catherine's Alumnae Assoc., 1955.

Boney, F. N.: "Rivers of Ink and a Stream of Blood," VC, Summer 1968.

Boyd, Julian P.: "The Murder of George Wythe," Philadelphia, Philobiblon Club, 1949.

Bradley, Chester D.: "Was Jefferson Davis Disguised as a Woman When Captured?" *Journal of Miss. Hist.*, Aug. 1974.

Braun, Michael: "Plum Street Neighborhood," *Richmond*, June 1974.

Breeden, James O.: "Body Snatchers and Anatomy Professors," VMHB, July 1975.

Brewer, James H.: "The War Against Jim Crow in the Land of Goshen," *Negro History Bulletin*, Dec. 1960.

Brumbaugh, Thomas B., ed., "The Genesis of Crawford's Washington," VMHB, Oct. 1958.

————: "The Evolution of Crawford's Washington," VMHB, Jan. 1962.

Bryan, J. III: "Richmond," *Saturday Evening Post*, Aug. 28, 1948.

Buford, Rob: "The Life of James Branch Cabell," Richmond *Mercury*, Dec. 6, 1972.

*Cabellian, The*, pub. by Cabell Society, Autumn 1969 through Spring 1972.

CAMPBELL, JOHN A.: "Recollections of the Evacuation of Richmond," Baltimore, John Murphy & Co., 1880.

*Catalogue* of books in Richmond Public Library, 1855.

CHESTERMAN, EVAN R.: "Idle Reporter," series 1894–1911 in Richmond *Dispatch, Times-Dispatch* and *Evening Journal,* with series on duels in *Evening Journal,* 1907–09. Scrapbooks at Virginia Historical Society.

CHRISTIAN, GEORGE L.: "Reminiscences of Some of the Dead of the Bench and Bar of Richmond," *Virginia Law Register,* Jan. 1909.

CHRISTIAN, JUDGE JOSEPH: "The Capitol Disaster," VMHB, April 1960.

CHURCH, RANDOLPH W.: "Charles Dickens Sends His Sympathy," VC, Summer 1971.

CHYET, STANLEY F.: "Moses Jacob Ezekiel: A Childhood in Richmond," *American Jewish Historical Quarterly,* March 1973.

COLEMAN, ELIZABETH DABNEY: "The Captain Was a Lady," VC, Summer 1956.

———: "Penwomen of the Feminists," VC, Winter 1956.

———: "The Great Fresh of 1771," VC, Autumn 1951.

———: "Genteel Crusader," VC, Autumn 1954.

———: "Black Boanerges," VC, Winter 1954.

———: "Richmond's Flowering Second Market," VC, Spring 1955.

COSTEN, SYLVIA: "Aura from Eras of Elegance Clings to Anderson House," RNL, June 5, 1968.

COWARDIN, HENRY M.: Scrapbooks with clippings, mainly from Richmond *Dispatch* in the 1870s, 1880s and 1890s, lent by Mr. Cowardin.

CULLEN, JOSEPH P.: "Richmond Falls," *American History Illustrated,* Jan. 1974.

DABNEY, VIRGINIUS: "A Prophet of the New South," New York *Herald Tribune Magazine,* Aug. 25, 1929.

———: "Richmond Starts Its Third Century," New York *Herald Tribune Magazine,* Sept. 13, 1933.

———: "Reds in Dixie," *Sewanee Review,* Oct.-Dec. 1934.

———: "He Made the Court Supreme," *Saturday Evening Post,* Sept. 24, 1955.

———: "George Washington's Railroad," VC, Summer 1960.

———: "Henry St. George Tucker—Beloved Virginian," *Virginia and the Virginia Record,* April 1955.

DUKE, MAURICE: *John Wilfred Overall's Southern Punch,* unpublished paper.

EDWARDS, HORACE: "5000 Days in Richmond," privately pub., 1968.

ELLYSON, LOUISE: "Shy Grace Arents Left No Portraits, Only an Indelible Mark on Inner City," RTD, Aug. 30, 1970.

FISHER, EDGAR J. JR.: "The Virginia Council on Health and Medical Care, 1956–1971," UVNL, Feb. 15, 1972.

FREEMAN, ANNE HOBSON: "Mary Munford's Fight for a College for Women Coordinate with the U. of Virginia," VMHB, Oct. 1970.

————: "A Cool Head in a Warm Climate," VC, Winter 1962–63.

FULLER, CHARLES F. JR.: "Edwin and John Wilkes Booth, Actors at the Old Marshall Theatre in Richmond," VMHB, Oct. 1971.

GAINES, WILLIAM H. JR., "The Penitentiary 'House,'" VC, Summer 1956.

————: "The Evening of Their Glory," VC, Summer 1953.

————: "Guns, Silkworms and Pigs," VC, Autumn 1953.

————: "The Fires of Smithfield," VC, Winter 1954.

————: "Bench, Bar and Barbecue Club," VC, Autumn 1955.

————: "Warehouse and Roman Temple," VC, Winter 1951.

————: "Courthouses of Henrico and Chesterfield," Winter 1968.

GALE, ROBERT L.: "Thomas Crawford, Dear Lou and the Horse," VMHB, April 1960.

GATEWOOD, WILLARD B. JR.: "Virginia's Negro Regiment in the Spanish-American War," VMHB, April 1972.

GILLIAM, ALEXANDER G. JR.: "Our Own Virginia Artist," VC, Autumn 1961.

GOLDFIELD, DAVID R.: "Urban Imperialism in the Antebellum South, 1850–1861," JSH, Feb. 1972.

GRANT, WILLIAM A.: "The Virginians: A Thackeray Novel About the Old Dominion," VC, Autumn 1972.

HARLAN, LOUIS R.: "The Secret Life of Booker T. Washington," JSH, Aug. 1971.

HARRISON, CAROLINE RIVERS: "Historic Guide—Richmond and James River," Richmond, 1966, tenth ed., pub. by author.

HARRISON, M. CLIFFORD: "Soldier, Scholar, Gentleman," VC, Spring 1965.

HASSLER, WILLIAM W.: "Willie Pegram, Gen. Lee's Brilliant Young Artillerist," VC, Autumn 1973.

HEITE, EDWARD F.: "Judge Robert Ould," VC, Spring 1965.

————: "Yankees, Red Coats and Pie Plates," VC, Spring 1968.

————: "The Tunnels of Richmond," VC, Winter 1964.

————: "Richmond City Halls," VC, Autumn 1967.

————: "Virginia Twists the Lion's Tail," VC, Spring 1968.

HENLEY, BERNARD J.: Thirteen scrapbooks containing important material from Richmond newspapers from 1736 to 1892. Lent by Mr. Henley.

HENRIQUES, PETER R. "The Organization Challenged: John S. Battle, Francis P. Miller and Horace Edwards Run for Governor in 1949," VMHB, July 1974.

HIGGINSON, T. W.: "Gabriel's Defeat," Atlantic, Sept. 1862.

HOLT, MOLLY: "History of the Valentine Museum," Antiques, Jan. 1973.

HOUSTON, CHARLES: "Church Hill Revives," VC, Summer 1964.

HUTCHESON, J. MORRISON, M.D.: "George Ben Johnston, M.D., LL.D.," Annals of Medical History, New Series, Vol. 10, No. 1.

HUTCHESON, NAT G.: "What Do You Know About Horses?", Clarksville, Va., Clarksville Printing Co., n.d.

JACKSON, LUTHER P.: "Negro Religious Development From 1760 to 1860," *Journal of Negro History*, Vol. 31.

JARRETT, CALVIN: "Was George Wythe Murdered?", *VC*, Winter 1963–64.

JELLISON, CHARLES A.: "That Scoundrel Callender," *VMHB*, July 1959.

JOHNS, FRANK S.: "George Ben Johnston," *Southern Medicine & Surgery*, March 1944.

JOHNSTON, J. AMBLER: "History of Monumental Church," *Bulletin* of Med. Coll. of Virginia, Summer 1965.

JOHNSTON, JAMES HUGO: "The Participation of Negroes in the Government of Virginia from 1877 to 1888," *Journal of Negro Hist.*, July 1929.

JONES, JAMES P.: "The Annus Mirabilis and the Quakers That Rocked Virginia," *VC*, Summer 1973.

JONES, PAT: "The Versatile Dr. Taylor," *RTD*, Dec. 11, 1938.

*Journal of the Joint Assembly of the Commonwealth of Virginia*, March 8, 1946. Addresses of Winston S. Churchill and Dwight D. Eisenhower.

JOYNES, THOMAS R.: letter to Levin S. Joynes concerning the Richmond Theatre fire, *VMHB*, July 1943.

KIMBALL, WILLIAM J.: "Richmond Begins the Work of War," *VC*, Spring 1961.

———: "War-Time Richmond," *VC*, Spring 1962.

———: "Richmond, 1865: The Final Three Months," *VC*, Summer 1969.

KNIGHT, J. STEPHEN JR.: "Discontent, Disunity and Dissent in the Antebellum South: Virginia as a Test Case, 1844–1846," *VMHB*, Oct. 1973.

LEYBURN, JOHN: "The Fall of Richmond," *Harper's New Monthly*, June 1866.

LINDEMAN, EDITH, "When Richmond Had a Male Street and a Female One," *RTD*, July 29, 1973.

———: "Trolley Car Days," *RTD*, Sept. 2, 1973.

———: "When the Richmond Elite Came to Meet," *RTD*, May 24, 1970.

———: "When the Flicks Really Flickered," *RTD*, Feb. 11, 1971.

———: "Scholarly, Humorless Major Dooley," *RTD*, Aug. 16, 1970.

———: "Ginter, Pioneer of North Side," *RTD*, Aug. 23, 1970.

LOWE, RICHARD G.: "Virginia's Reconstruction Convention," *VMHB*, July 1972.

MACDONALD, EDGAR E.: "Glasgow, Cabell and Richmond, "*Mississippi Quarterly*, Autumn 1974.

———: "Cabell's Richmond Trial," *Southern Literary Journal*, Fall 1970.

MARTIN, PETE, "Century Plant," *Saturday Evening Post*, July 23, 1943.

MASSIE, DR. THOMAS: "Richmond During the War of 1812," *VMHB*, April 1900.

MAYO, ROBERT B.: "The Fine Arts Collection at the Valentine Museum," *Antiques*, Jan. 1973.

McCABE, W. GORDON: "George Ben Johnston, M.D.," extract from president's annual report to Virginia Historical Society, March 18, 1918.

MEAD, ERNEST: "The John Powell Collection of the Univ. of Virginia," *UVNL*, Nov. 15, 1972.

MEIER, AUGUST: "Toward a Reinterpretation of Booker T. Washington," *JSH*, May 1957.

—— and RUDWICK, ELLIOTT: "Negro Boycotts and Segregated Street Cars in Virginia," *VMHB*, Oct. 1973.

MITCHELL, ALICE BROADUS: "Columbia," *The Messenger*, U. of Richmond, April 1937.

MOGER, ALLEN W: "Industrial and Urban Progress in Virginia from 1880 to 1900," *VMHB*, July 1958.

MOORE, JOHN H.: "The Jefferson Davis Monument," *VC*, Spring 1961.

——: "Virginia's Football War of '97," *VC*, Winter 1962–63.

MOORE, S. J. JR.: "The Jefferson Hotel: A Southern Landmark," privately printed, 1940.

MORSE, NITA LIGON, and WILLIAMS, EDA CARTER: "The History of Sheltering Arms Hospital," privately pub., 1964.

NANCY, LADY ASTOR: Memoir dictated about 1953. Copy at Virginia Historical Society.

O'DONOVAN, PATRICK: "British Journalist Finds Richmond 'Saddest Place in America,'" *RNL*, April 23, 1958.

PALMER, WILLIAM PRICE, M.D.: series of more than one hundred historical articles pub. in Richmond *Times* in 1880s and 1890s, numbered but not dated. Scrapbook at Virginia Historical Society.

POLLARD EDWARD A.: "The Negro in the South," *Lippincott's Magazine*, April 1870.

POTEET, DAVID C.: "Arms for the Militia," *VC*, Winter 1966.

RANKIN, ROBERT A.: "The Richmond Crusade for Voters," *UVNL*, Sept. 1974.

*Report Accompanying the Proposed Charter of the City of Richmond*, 1947.

*Report of the Commission to Plan for the Establishment of a Proposed State University in the Richmond Metropolitan Area*, Richmond, 1967.

*Richmond*, magazine of Richmond Chamber of Commerce, July 1914–June 1933, incl., May 1974–Oct. 1975.

Richmond-First Club, "A 50-Year Participation in Local Government, 1919–1969," Richmond, 1970.

Richmond-First Club Report, "Why Richmond Needs a Unicameral Council," *RNL*, Dec. 10, 1936.

ROBERT, JOSEPH C.: "The Healing Arts and the American Way," MCV *Bulletin*, Vol. LIV, No. 2, 1956.

——: "William Wirt, Virginian," *VMHB*, Oct. 1972.

ROBERTS, JOHN G.: "Poet, Patriot and Pedagogue," *Arts in Virginia*, Winter 1966.

ROBERTSON, JUDGE JOHN: "Address on Opening the Richmond Atheneum," MacFarlane & Fergusson, 1852.

ROGERS, GEORGE: "Richmond's Seal Perpetuates 177-Year-Old Error," *RNL*, Sept. 17, 1959.

ROUSE, PARKE JR.: "Dr. Bennett Green and His Word-Book," *VMHB*, April 1974.

RYAN, EDWARD L.: "Note on 'Belvidere,'" *VMHB*, April 1931.

SALE, MARION MARSH: "Disaster at the Spotswood," *VC*, Autumn 1962.

SCOTT, MARY W., and CATTERALL, LOUISE F.: "Virginia's Capitol Square—Its Buildings and Its Monuments," Valentine Museum, 1957.

SCRIBNER, ROBERT L.: "The Baron of Renfrew," *VC*, Autumn 1956.

———: "The Code Duello in Virginia," *VC*, Summer 1953.

———: "Born of Battle," *VC*, Autumn 1953.

———: "General Practitioner of Letters," *VC*, Winter 1954.

———: "Touchdown!" *VC*, Autumn 1954.

———: "Belle Isle," *VC*, Winter 1955.

———: "Virginia House," *VC*, Winter 1955.

SEYMOUR, CHARLES JR.: "Early Republican Masterpiece," *Arts in Virginia*, Winter 1962.

SHERMAN, JOAN R.: "Daniel Webster Davis: A Black Virginia Poet in the Age of Accommodation," *VMHB*, Oct. 1973.

SHORT, JAMES R.: "Sir Moses Ezekiel: A Virginia Expatriate Sculptor," *VC*, Spring 1954.

———: "The Nation's Guest," *VC*, Autumn 1954.

SIMMS, L. MOODY JR.: "A Virginia Sculptor," *VC*, Summer 1970.

SIMPSON, JOSEPHUS: "The Best Negroes in the World," *Opportunity*, Sept. 1931.

SPENCER, FREDERICK J.: "The Great Idealist: Life and Times of Dr. Ennion G. Williams," *VMM*, Feb. 1968.

STANARD, WILLIAM G.: "The Homes of the Virginia Historical Society," *VMHB*, Jan. 1926.

STEWART, PETER C.: "Railroads and Urban Rivalries in Antebellum Eastern Virginia," *VMHB*, Jan. 1973.

STUART, MERIWETHER: "Col. Ulrich Dahlgren and Richmond's Underground," *VMHB*, April 1964.

TAYLOR, R. H.: "Slave Conspiracies in North Carolina," *N. C. Hist. Review*, Jan. 1928.

TAYLOR, WILLIAM H.: "Unremembered Men of Letters," *RNL*, Nov. 14–19, incl., and Nov. 21–22, 1938.

THOMAS, EMORY M.: "The Richmond Bread Riot of 1863," *VC*, Summer 1968.

TROUBETZKOY, ULRICH: "F. William Sievers, Sculptor," *VC*, Autumn 1962.

———: "The Governor's Mansion," *VC*, Summer 1961.

———: "W. L. Sheppard, Artist of Action," *VC*, Winter 1961–62.

———: "Fevret de St. Mémin's Gallery of Virginians," *VC*, Summer 1962.

———: "Col. Claudius Crozet," *VC*, Spring 1963.

———: "Fighting Words—The Story of Early Richmond Journalism," *Virginia Record*, July 1969.

TUCKER, EDWARD L.: "The Southern Literary Messenger and the Men Who Made It," *VC*, Summer 1971.

TYLER, MERLE: "Evenings of Song," VC, Autumn 1967.

WALLACE, LEE A. JR.: "The First Virginia Regiment of Virginia," VC, Autumn 1956.

WARREN, DANIEL C.: "The Seven-Thorned Queen: Postal History of Richmond to 1865," Vol. 37, American Philatelic Congress.

WARTHEN, HARRY J., M.D.: "Medicine and Shockoe Hill," Annals of Medical History, New Series, Jan. 1938.

————: "The S.S. Arctic and Professor Johnson," VMM, July 1974.

———— and WILLIAMS, CARRINGTON, M.D.: "History of the Richmond Academy of Medicine," VMM, Oct. 1962.

WEATHERS, WILLIE T.: "Judith W. McGuire, a Lady of Virginia," VMHB, Jan. 1974.

WEAVER, BETTIE WOODSON: "The Mines of Midlothian," VC, Winter 1961–62.

WEISS, SUSAN ARCHER: interview with Mrs. Carter, sister of Lieutenant James Gibbon, concerning theater fire of 1811, Dispatch, April 6, 1890.

WEITZEL, MAJ. GEN. GODFREY: "Richmond Occupied, April 3, 1865," ed. by Louis H. Manarin, pub. by Richmond Civil War Centennial Commission, 1965.

WICKHAM, ELIZABETH McC.: "Mr. Thackeray in Richmond," letter dated March 3, 1853, printed for Valentine Museum by Attic Press, 1955.

WILEY, BELL I.: "Women of the Lost Cause," American History Illustrated, Dec. 1973.

WILLIAMS, CARRINGTON: "The Family of Walter Armistead Williams and Alice Marshall Taylor Williams," privately printed, 1968.

WILLIAMS, EDA CARTER: "The Richmond German: 1866–1966," privately printed, 1966.

WILSON, JAMES SOUTHALL: "Poe's Mother," RTD, Dec. 10, 1961.

————: "The Personality of Poe," VMHB, April 1959.

WRIGHT, R. LEWIS: "James Warrell: Artist and Entrepreneur," VC, Winter 1973.

WYLLIE, JOHN COOK, ed.: "Observations Made During a Short Residence in Virginia," letter from Thomas H. Palmer, May 30, 1814, VMHB, Oct. 1968.

## UNPUBLISHED STUDIES AND DOCUMENTS

ALEXANDER, ANN F.: Black Protest in the New South: John Mitchell Jr. (1863–1929) and the Richmond Planet, Ph.D. diss., Duke U., 1972.

BEACH, REX: Judge Spencer Roane, a Champion of States Rights, M.A. thesis, U. of Virginia, 1941.

BERMAN, RABBI MYRON: Edward Nathan Calisch, An American Rabbi in the

*South—His Views on the "Promised Land,"* address to Amer. Jewish Hist. Soc., May 1972.

BROWN, EDWARD H.: *An Investigation of the Attitudes Expressed by Richmond's Press Toward Thomas Jefferson in the Presidential Elections of 1800, 1804 and 1808*, M.A. thesis, U. of Richmond, 1964.

CATE, WIRT ARMISTEAD: *A History of Richmond, 1607–1861*, 1505-page footnoted and indexed MS. at Valentine Museum.

CAUBLE, FRANK P.: *William Wirt and His Friends*, Ph.D. diss., U. of North Carolina, 1933.

COLEMAN, ANNIE C.: *The Negro in Virginia and South Carolina, 1861 to 1877*, M.A. thesis, Virginia State Coll., 1967.

*Condemned Slaves Executed, 1800–1801, Gabriel's Insurrection*, Auditor's Item 153, Box 2, Virginia State Lib. archives.

COOLEY, ROBERT G.: *James J. Kilpatrick: The Evolution of a Southern Conservative, 1955–1965*, M.A. thesis, U. of Virginia, 1971.

CUTLER, RONALD E.: *A History and Analysis of Negro Newspapers in Virginia*, M.A. thesis, U. of Richmond, 1965.

ELY, JAMES W. JR.: *The Crisis of Conservative Virginia: The Decline and Fall of Massive Resistance*, Ph.D. diss., U. of Virginia, 1971.

ERNST, WILLIAM JOEL: *Gabriel's Revolt: Black Freedom, White Fear*, M.A. thesis, U. of Virginia, 1968.

FIELD, ANN BARTON: *Negro Protest in the New South: John Mitchell Jr., 1863–1902*, M.A. thesis, Duke U., 1968.

GAINES, FRANCIS P. JR.: *The Virginia Constitutional Convention of 1850–51*, Ph.D. diss., U. of Virginia, 1950.

HAMMOCK, ALLAN S.: *The Leadership Factor in Black Politics: The Case of Richmond, Va.*, Ph.D. diss., U. of Virginia, 1972.

HEINEMANN, RONALD L.: *Depression and New Deal in Virginia*, Ph.D. diss., U. of Virginia, 1968.

JORDAN, GLADYS ELNORA WHITE: *The Negro in Richmond During the Civil War as Depicted by the Richmond Whig*, M.A. thesis, Va. State U., 1967.

LAND, ADA MAY: *The Migration into Richmond, 1775 to 1860*, M.A. thesis, U. of Richmond, 1949.

LASER, NORMAN J.: *Censorship of School Histories by the Confederate Veterans of Virginia, 1892–1932*, M.A. thesis, U. of Maryland, 1958.

*Minutes*, First African Baptist Church, 1841–1859, Va. State Lib.

MONROE, JAMES: Exec. Papers, Va. State Lib., Box 114, Sept.–Oct. 1800.

————: Exec. Letter Books, Va. State Lib., Folder 20, Aug. 10–Sept. 3, 1800; Folder 21, Sept. 3–17, 1800; Folder 22, Sept. 12–Oct. 5, 1800.

MYERS, GUSTAVUS A.: Memorandum of His Interview with Abraham Lincoln, April 5, 1865, Virginia Historical Society.

OURS, ROBERT M.: *Virginia's First Redeemer Legislature*, M.A. thesis, U. of Virginia, 1966.

OWENS, MARTHA W.: *The Development of Public Schools for Negroes in Richmond, Va., 1865–1900*, M.S. thesis, Va. State U., 1947.

POWELL, WILLIE HUGH: *The Negro in the Virginia Legislature During the Readjuster Period, 1879–1882*, M.A. thesis, Va. State U., 1966.

RAY, WILLIAM GRADY: *Thomas S. Martin's Campaign for the U. S. Senate, 1892–1893*, M.A. thesis, U. of Virginia, 1972.

READNOUR, HARRY WARREN: *Gen. Fitzhugh Lee: 1835–1905—A Biographical Study*, Ph.D. diss., U. of Virginia, 1971.

RICHARDSON, A. G.: *The Education of the Negro, 1831–1970* (*Virginia Style*). Lent by author, n.d.

ROGERS, ALBERT A.: *Family Life in 18th Century Virginia*, Ph.D. diss., U. of Virginia, 1939.

RUTHERFOORD, THOMAS: *Narrative of 1766–1852*. Original in Valentine Museum.

SHIBLEY, DONALD E.: *Election Laws and Electoral Practices in Virginia, 1867–1902*, Ph.D. diss., U. of Virginia, 1972.

SHOCKLEY, MARTIN S.: *A History of the Theatre in Richmond, 1819–1838*, Ph.D. diss., U. of North Carolina, 1938.

SMITH, BEATRICE M.: *Impressions of Virginia from Contemporary Accounts*, M.A. thesis, U. of Virginia, 1968.

SMITH, JAMES DOUGLAS: *The Virginia Constitutional Convention, 1867–1868*, M.A. thesis, U. of Virginia, 1956.

————: *Virginia During Reconstruction, 1865–1870*, Ph.D. diss., U. of Virginia, 1960.

SMITH, LESLIE W.: *Richmond During Presidential Reconstruction, 1865–1867*, Ph.D. diss., U. of Virginia, 1974.

SUTTON, ROBERT P.: *The Virginia Constitutional Convention of 1829–1830: A Profile Analysis of Late Jeffersonian Virginia*, Ph.D. diss., U. of Virginia, 1967.

WALLER, LINDEN B.: MS. of his recollections of antebellum Richmond, Valentine Museum.

WALTON, THOMAS S.: *The Negro in Richmond, 1880–1890*, M.A. thesis, Howard U., 1950.

WOLFE, JONATHAN J.: *Virginia in World War II*, Ph.D. diss., U. of Virginia, 1971.

# INDEX